European Privacy and Data Protection Law

European Privacy and Data Protection Law

Jos Dumortier
Pieter Gryffroy
Ruben Roex
Yung Shin Van Der Sype

This book was originally published as a monograph in the International Encyclopaedia of Laws/Privacy and Technology Law.

Founding Editor: Roger Blanpain
General Editor: Frank Hendrickx
Volume Editors: Jos Dumortier, Pieter Gryffroy, Ruben Roex & Yung Shin Van Der Sype

Wolters Kluwer

Published by:
Kluwer Law International B.V.
PO Box 316
2400 AH Alphen aan den Rijn
The Netherlands
E-mail: lrs-sales@wolterskluwer.com
Website: www.wolterskluwer.com/en/solutions/kluwerlawinternational

Sold and distributed by:
Wolters Kluwer Legal & Regulatory U.S.
7201 McKinney Circle
Frederick, MD 21704
United States of America
E-mail: customer.service@wolterskluwer.com

ISBN 978-94-035-0706-4

e-Book: ISBN 978-94-035-0836-8
web-PDF: ISBN 978-94-035-0846-7

The Authors

Prof. Dr Jos Dumortier studied Law at KU Leuven, Belgium (1973), Nancy (Centre Europeen Universitaire, France, 1974) and Heidelberg (DAAD, 1975), and Information Science (INFODOC) at the Université Libre de Bruxelles, Belgium. Between 1984 and 1992 he was part-time lecturer in Information Science at the University of Antwerp. In 1985 he became part-time lecturer and in 1993 full- time Professor in Law and ICT at KU Leuven. In 1990 he was the founder of the Interdisciplinary Centre for Law and Information Technology (currently 'CITIP') of which he acted as the first Director until 2014. Between 1987 and 2014 he was active in lecturing, research and consultancy in the area of Law & ICT and published several books and articles on this subject. From 1995 to 1998, Jos has been in charge, as a cabinet advisor of the Minister of Justice, of the legislative process regarding the Belgian personal data protection law. Today, Prof. Dumortier is a member of the Bar of Brussels as a founding partner of Timelex, a law firm specialised in information technology and data protection law (www.timelex.eu). Since the start of the law firm in 2007 his firm has conducted many policy support studies for the European Commission on various issues related to personal data protection and other legal issues relating to the digital single market. With his team at Timelex, Jos also provides legal guidance in many European research and innovation actions. Jos Dumortier participates in the boards of several national and international scientific and business societies, and he is a member of various editorial and programme committees.

The Authors

Pieter Gryffroy studied Law at KU Leuven (2014) and International and European Law at the Europa-Institut, University of Saarland (2015). While in Germany, Pieter was employed as an academic researcher at the Jean Monnet Chair for European Law and European Integration at Saarland University, Germany, focusing exclusively on data protection and privacy law. In 2016 Pieter joined the Bar of Brussels and started working for Timelex, a law firm specialised in information technology and data protection law. At Timelex, Pieter advises both private and public sector clients on a range of issues related to data protection and privacy, ICT law and cybersecurity. He also provides legal advice in European research and innovation actions, related to a variety of topics and sectors, but always involving new technologies and data-driven solutions. Pieter is an editor of the Cyber Law Series and the Privacy & Technology Law Series of the International Encyclopaedia of Laws.

Ruben Roex obtained his degree of Master in Economics, Law and Business Administration in 2009 and his Master's in Law degree in 2011, both at KU Leuven. Before Ruben joined Timelex in October 2014 he was a researcher at the Interdisciplinary Centre for Law and ICT (ICRI) at the Faculty of Law at KU Leuven. During three years (September 2011–September 2014) he participated in a number of research projects, including the Belgian Cybercrime Centre of Excellence for Training, Research and Education (B-CCENTRE). He also gave a number of guest lectures on a range of different topics in ICT law. Today Ruben Roex is an attorney and partner at Timelex, and advises private sector clients and public sector administrations on various matters within the IT law field, including e-commerce, privacy and data protection, consumer protection and cybersecurity. He is an academic assistant at the University of Ghent, guest lecturer at Vives Hogeschool in Kortrijk and Tilburg University and a frequent speaker in guest lectures on various ICT law topics. Recent work in the public sector has focused on cloud computing, data protection and electronic communications.

Dr Yung Shin Van Der Sype worked as an attorney at Timelex and Alston & Bird and recently (2022) joined Crowell & Moring LLP (Brussels). She focuses her practice on IT law and HR-related matters, including data protection, IT contracts and corporate security. Yung Shin has advised national and international clients in multiple industry sectors, ranging from healthcare to social media. She is an affiliated senior researcher at the Centre for IT & IP Law (University of Leuven) and co-editor of the Cyber Law Series and the Privacy & Technology Law Series of the International Encyclopaedia of Laws. She is a member of the editorial committee of the law journal *Privacy & Informatie* and the law journal *Sociaalrechtelijke Kronieken* (Social Law Chronicles). She is a board member of the Vereniging Sociaal Recht (Social Law Association) and the Belgian Esports Federation.

The Authors

Table of Contents

List of Abbreviations

AI	Artificial intelligence
AML	Anti-money laundering
APEC	Asia-Pacific Economic Cooperation
API	Application Program Interface
BCR	Binding Corporate Rules
CJEU	Court of Justice of the European Union
CNIL	Commission Nationale de l'informatique et des Libertés (France)
DPA	Data Protection Authority
DPIA	Data Protection Impact Assessment
DPO	Data Protection Officer
DSAR	Data Subject Access Request
DSR	Data Subject Request
ECHR	European Convention of Human Rights
ECtHR	European Court of Human Rights
EDPB	European Data Protection Board
EDPS	European Data Protection Supervisor
EEA	European Economic Area
HER	Electronic Health Records
ENISA	European Network and Information Security Agency
GDPR	General Data Protection Regulation (European Union)
HIPAA	Health Information Portability and Accountability Act (US)
IoT	Internet of Things
IP	Internet Protocol
ISO	International Organisation for Standardisation
ISP	Internet Service Provider
OECD	Organisation for Economic Co-operation and Development
OSS	One-Stop Shop
PIA	Privacy impact assessment
RFID	Radio-Frequency Identification

List of Abbreviations

RTBF	Right-to-be-forgotten
SaaS	Software as a Service
SAR	Subject Access Request
SCC	Standard contractual clauses
TCP	Transmission Control Protocol
TEU	Treaty of the European Union
TFEU	Treaty on the Functioning of the European Union
TLS	Transport layer security
UDHR	Universal Declaration of Human Rights
URL	Uniform resource locator
VOIP	Voice over IP
VPN	Virtual Private Network
WAN	Wide area network
WORM	Write once read many
XML	Extensible markup language

Preface

The explosion of the Internet, the digitalisation of all sectors of society and the generalised use of social media and other forms of electronic communications, have led to a broader focus on the protection of the privacy of individuals and the personal data processed about them. As a result, the field of privacy and data protection has de facto developed into a separate legal domain. It therefore no longer seems justified to continue treating privacy and data protection law as one of the chapters of the International Encyclopaedia of Cyber Law.

Consequently, the publisher and editors have decided to split Cyber Law into two fully fledged sections. The new International Encyclopaedia will have a new name; 'International Encyclopaedia of Privacy and Technology Law' to reflect this new vision. The titles of the two parts are 'Information and Technology Law' and 'Privacy and Data Protection Law' respectively.

Thus, below you will find the national monographs on 'Privacy and Data Protection Law'. Almost all countries in the world currently have provisions for the protection of citizens' private lives in their constitutions. Many countries have also introduced regulations that protect privacy in specific sectors, for example in the workplace or when using electronic communication media.

In addition to the protection of privacy, more and more countries have separate regulations for data protection. The European Union has set the tone for this, initially in the form of a Directive adopted in 1995 and, since 2016, with the entry into force of the General Data Protection Regulation, abbreviated as the GDPR.

The GDPR has direct effect in the Member States of the European Union and these countries, as members of the Council of Europe, are also subject to the European Convention and to the case law of the European Court of Human Rights. As a consequence, the basic rules on privacy and data protection are essentially the same in all EU countries. This does, however, not prevent Member States to enact national legislation in this domain, on top of this European legal framework. To get a grip on the multilayered mix of European and national rules, a reader must consider both European and national data protection and privacy law.

To avoid repeating the explanation of these basic European rules in each monograph, the national monographs of the EU Member States differ in both structure and content from the monographs on privacy and data protection in countries outside the EU. For the EU Member States, the basic rules, which apply in all these countries, are explained in the monograph on privacy and data protection law in the

EU. The national monographs of these Member States refer for the basic rules to the European monograph and deal only with the rules that are specific to the country concerned.

It is our ambition to publish and to regularly update not only this monograph relating to European privacy and data protection law, but also to do the same effort for the publication and regular updating of the national privacy and data protection legal framework in the twenty-seven European Union Member States. In parallel the Privacy and Data Protection part of the International Encyclopaedia of Privacy and Technology Law will publish and update national monographs dealing with the privacy and data protection laws of a large series of other countries worldwide.

General Introduction

1. This monograph is divided in two parts, respectively dedicated to ‘privacy protection’ and ‘data protection’. Although the concepts of ‘privacy’ and ‘data protection’ are closely related to each other, it is generally accepted nowadays, at least in Europe, that they must be clearly distinguished from each other.[1] The European Data Protection Directive of 1995, abrogated by the GDPR since 25 May 2018, still had as one of its objectives ‘the protection of the right to privacy with respect to the processing of personal data’.[2] In the General Data Protection Regulation (‘the GDPR’), the term ‘privacy’ no longer appears.[3]

2. Privacy law and data protection law have a different historical background. In the following pages we will briefly explain how the protection of privacy obtained a constitutional status after the Second World War, starting with the Universal Declaration of Human Rights adopted by the United Nations in 1949 and how it was subsequently included in the European Convention of Human Rights in 1950. Data protection laws, on the contrary, emerged for the first time almost twenty years later, when people started worrying about the consequences of processing personal information by means of computers.[4]

3. While the US Constitution does not explicitly mention privacy or data protection, protection of both the right to privacy protection and the right to data protection are today explicitly established at the constitutional level in Europe. The right to the protection of private life entered the European legal order with the adoption of the European Convention of Human Rights in 1949. It is also enshrined in

1. Juliane Kokott & Christoph Sobotta, The distinction between privacy and data protection in the jurisprudence of the CJEU and the ECtHR, *International Data Privacy Law,* Volume 3, Issue 4, November 2013, p. 222–228, https://doi.org/10.1093/idpl/ipt017.
2. Art. 1 of Directive 95/46/EC of the European Parliament and of the Council of 24 October 1995 on the protection of individuals with regard to the processing of personal data and on the free movement of such data, *OJ L 281, 23.11.1995, p. 31–50.*
3. Regulation (EU) 2016/679 of the European Parliament and of the Council of 27 April 2016 on the protection of natural persons with regard to the processing of personal data and on the free movement of such data, and repealing Directive 95/46/EC (General Data Protection Regulation) (Text with EEA relevance), *OJ L 119, 4.5.2016, p. 1–88.*
4. Corte, Lorenzo Dalla ‘A Right to a Rule: On the Substance and Essence of the Fundamental Right to Personal Data Protection.’ *Data Protection and Privacy: Data Protection and Democracy*.Ed. Dara Hallinan, Ronald Leenes, Serge Gutwirth and Paul De Hert. Oxford: Hart Publishing, 2020. 27–58; Gloria Gonzàlez Fuster, *Th e Emergence of Personal Data Protection as a Fundamental Right of the EU,* Springer Law, Governance and Technology Series 2014) 28.

Article 7 of the EU Charter.[5] The CJEU refers in numerous judgments to Articles 7 and 8 of the Charter, mentioning almost always both rights together.[6]

4. In earlier judgments, the Court of Justice of the European Union ('CJEU') regularly stated that compared to the right to privacy, the EU rules on data protection create a specific and reinforced system of protection.[7] The 'right to data protection' appeared with the Lisbon Treaty of 2009 in Article 16 of the Treaty on the Functioning of the European Union (TFEU) which mirrored the right to data protection established in Article 8 of the Charter of Fundamental Rights of the European Union.

5. The notion of 'private life', subject of legal protection, does not necessarily include all information on identified or identifiable persons. Registering one's name in a register, for example, will not always be considered as an intrusion into this person's privacy. On the contrary, data protection covers exactly this kind of activities. Every activity in which any kind of personal data is used, is under the scope of legal data protection provisions.

6. The term 'data protection' was derived from the German term 'Datenschutz'.[8] Outside Germany, what we call 'data protection' today was at the start primarily linked to 'privacy'.[9] While the nomenclature is problematic in several respects – not least because it fails to indicate the central interests served by the norms to which it is meant to apply – it has gained broad popularity in Europe and, to a lesser extent, elsewhere. Its use, though, is sometimes supplemented by the term 'data privacy' of 'information privacy'.[10] The latter nomenclature is arguably more appropriate than 'data protection' as it better communicates the central interest(s) at stake.[11]

7. Generally, the right to data protection is distinguished from the right to privacy by the fact that EU data protection rules look beyond consent only, which is a constitutive element of privacy – the concept of informational self-determination

---

5. Raphaël Gellert, Serge Gutwirth, The legal construction of privacy and data protection, Computer Law and Security Report, 29 (2013), pp. 522–530.
6. For example: CJEU,Case C-746/18, Judgment of 2 March 2021, Prokuratur, ECLI:EU:C:2021:15, https://eur-lex.europa.eu/legal-content/en/TXT/?uri=CELEX:62018CJ0746
7. CJEU, Case C-28/08, Judgment of 29 June 2010, *Bavarian Lager*, ECLI:EU:C:2010:378, https://eur-lex.europa.eu/legal-content/EN/TXT/?uri=CELEX%3A62008CJ0028.
8. *See*, e.g., the 1970 proposal by the (West) German Interparliamentary Working Committee for a 'Gesetz zum Schutz der Privatsphäre gegen Missbrauch von Datenbankinformationen': described in Bull, H.P., Datenschutz oder Die Angst vor dem Computer, Piper, Munich 1984, p. 85.
9. Council of Europe Resolution (73)22 on the Protection of the Privacy of Individuals vis-à-vis Electronic Data Banks in the Private Sector (adopted 26 Sept. 1973); Council of Europe Resolution (74)29 on the Protection of the Privacy of Individuals vis-à-vis Electronic Data Banks in the Public Sector (adopted 24th Sept. 1974).
10. 'Information Privacy Law' is the title of the handbook authored by Daniel Solove and Paul Schwartz, Aspen, Wolters Kluwer, Third edition, 2008, 1128 pages.
11. Lee Bygrave, Privacy and data protection in an international perspective, Scandinavian Studies in Law, Vol.56, p 168, https://www.scandinavianlaw.se/pdf/56-8.pdf.

– and 'create a system of checks and balances which ensures lawful processing also without asking the consent of the person involved'.[12]

8. The private sphere is a necessary condition for the individual to freely develop her or his personality. Only in the protection of privacy can people develop, learn and then exercise autonomy. The insecurity about what others know about you limits people's autonomy. For self-understanding as an autonomous person, it is therefore of essential importance for individuals to have control over how they represent themselves. Democracy relies on autonomous citizens. No wonder, that the secret ballot is an important tool of democratic elections – and the symbol of democracy. It makes sure people can vote freely and autonomously without being observed, coerced or intimidated. Totalitarian states purposely give their citizens as little privacy as possible in order to prevent them from developing an individual, autonomous personality. A uniform society without privacy is the goal of a dictatorship.[13]

9. Even though, everybody has some intuitive understanding of what privacy is, it is very difficult to articulate this understanding in a comprehensible and especially unambiguous way. Besides this fundamental problem it has to be acknowledged that privacy concerns many different aspects of personal life.[14]

10. This latter statement is valid for the protection of personal data as well but here, the legal rules are much more detailed and embedded in complex legal provisions. As a consequence, judging whether or not the right to protection of private life has been violated, will in the first place necessitate an examination of relevant jurisprudence, rather than diving into legislative texts. Data protection became something in itself with its own laws and even its own legal institutions. Data protection is specifically related to the legal rules that regulate to which extent and under which conditions information related to individual physical persons may be used. As Peter Blume once wrote: 'The ideas that determine these rules derive from the privacy discourse, but they are made precise with respect to the specific regulatory purpose. Data protection law is in a sense a more technical, detailed and detached kind of law than privacy law.'[15]

---

12. de Vries, S. (2015). The EU Single Market as 'Normative Corridor' for the Protection of Fundamental Rights: The Example of Data Protection. In S. de Vries, U. Bernitz & S. Weatherill (Eds.). *The EU Charter of Fundamental Rights as a Binding Instrument: Five Years Old and Growing* (Studies of the Oxford Institute of European and Comparative Law, pp. 235–260). Oxford: Hart Publishing. Retrieved 3 August 2021, from http://dx.doi.org.kuleuven.e-bronnen.be/10.5040/9781782258261.ch-011.
13. Volker Boehme-Neßler Privacy: a matter of democracy. Why democracy needs privacy and data protection, International Data Privacy Law, 2016, Vol. 6, No. 3, pp. 222–229.
14. Peter Blume, Data Protection and Privacy – Basic Concepts in a Changing World, https://www.scandinavianlaw.se/pdf/56-7.pdf.
15. Peter Blume, Data Protection and Privacy, Scandinavian Studies in Law, Volume 56, 2010, p. 154 https://www.scandinavianlaw.se/pdf/56-7.pdf.

Part I. Protection of Privacy

11. Many books about the legal notion of 'privacy' start with a reference to the famous article published by Samuel Warren and Louis Brandeis in the Harvard Law Review more than 130 years ago, in the winter of 1890.[16] For these authors 'privacy' meant the *right to be let alone* with respect to prying newspapers and photographers. Many years later, in 1915, Roscoe Pound viewed privacy as an expression of one's *personality,* focusing upon the right of the individual to define his or her essence as a human being.[17] More recently, American scholars such as Louis Henkin have marked privacy within the boundaries of *autonomy*, or the moral freedom of the individual to engage in his or her own thoughts, actions and decisions.[18]

12. In his very in-depth analysis of 100 years case law and legal doctrine in the US, one of Ken Gormley's conclusions is that the various approaches of the privacy right are directly linked to transformations in our way of life and the technology. 'Changes in American society and technology which threaten to invade the status quo and rearrange the line of demarcation between citizen and state, and citizen versus citizen, are prime candidates to generate new privacy rights. They must simmer over time, percolate and create a sense of societal urgency that the coveted trademarks of American individuality or equality are threatened. Only if such a mood is sustained over a period of time, with existing law failing to plug the gaps, will a new species of privacy take form to supplement the old technology, which have created a societal mood powerful enough to incubate a new, legally protected right and decisions.'[19]

13. Although 'privacy' as a legal concept exists already since the late nineteenth century, it has never been included as an 'umbrella right' in national constitutions or international treaties before the adoption by the UN of the Universal Declaration of Human Rights. One of the bases for the drafting of the UDHR was a paper that contained an overview of the protection of the private sphere in Member States at

16. Samuel D. Warren & Louis D. Brandeis, The Right to Privacy, 4 Harvard Law Review 193 (1890).
17. Roscoe Pound, Interests in Personality, 28 Harvard Law Review. 343 (1915).
18. Louis Henkin, Privacy and Autonomy, 74 Columbia Law Review, 1410, 1425 (1974).
19. Ken Gormley, 'One Hundred Years of Privacy,' Wisconsin Law Review 1992, no. 5 (1992): 1335–1442.

the time. Astonishingly enough, it showed that there was not one constitution examined in this document that contained the term of privacy or private life. The document revealed that prior to the adoption of the UDHR, national constitutions only protected the privacy of the home and correspondence more or less comprehensively.[20]

14. The UDHR was drafted in the years 1946–48. Two years of discussion resulted in a consensus with regard to the nature of the instrument (a 'Declaration').[21] The final text of Article 12 was formulated as follows: '*No one shall be subjected to arbitrary interference with his privacy, family, home or correspondence, nor to attacks upon his honour and reputation. Everyone has the right to the protection of the law against such interference or attacks.*' It was adopted by the General Assembly of the United Nations on 10 December 1948.[22]

15. The provision on privacy in the International Covenant on Civil and Political Rights – adopted more than seventeen years after the UDHR – is worded almost identically to Article 12 of the UDHR.[23] The sole difference between the two norms is that Article 17 of the ICCPR not only prohibits 'arbitrary' interferences with one's privacy and with more specific aspects of the private sphere, but also 'unlawful' ones. Article 17 of the ICCPR is worded as follows: '*1. No one shall be subjected to arbitrary or unlawful interference with his privacy, family, home or correspondence, nor to unlawful attacks on his honour and reputation. (emphasis added) 2. Everyone has the right to the protection of the law against such interference or attacks.*'

16. The drafting of the European Convention of Human Rights within the framework of the Council of Europe started in August 1949, roughly half a year after the adoption of the UDHR by the UN General Assembly. The Legal Committee elaborated a draft resolution indicating the general lines of the desired convention. '*In this convention, the Member States shall undertake to ensure to all persons residing within their territories: (1) ...(4) freedom from arbitrary interference in private and family life, home and correspondence, in accordance with Article 12 of the United Nations Declaration.*'[24]

20. Oliver Diggelmann and Maria Nicole Cleis, How the Right to Privacy Became a Human Right, Human Rights Law Review, 2014, 14, 441–458.
21. Hurst Hannum, The Status of the Universal Declaration of Human Rights in National and International Law, Georgia Journal of International and Comparative Law, Vol. 25, pp. 287–397 (1995).
22. Gordon Brown, The Universal Declaration of Human Rights in the 21st Century, Open Book Publishers, 2016, https://www.openbookpublishers.com/reader/467#page/1/mode/2up.
23. The International Covenant on Civil and Political Rights is a multilateral treaty adopted by United Nations General Assembly Resolution 2200A (XXI) on 16 December 1966, and in force from 23 March 1976.
24. Oliver Diggelmann and Maria Nicole Cleis, How the Right to Privacy Became a Human Right, Human Rights Law Review, 2014, 14, 441–458.

§1. European Convention of Human Rights

I. Introduction

17. The Convention for the Protection of Human Rights and Fundamental Freedoms, better known as the European Convention on Human Rights (ECHR), was opened for signature in Rome on 4 November 1950 and came into force on 3 September 1953. It was the first instrument to give effect to certain of the rights stated in the Universal Declaration of Human Rights and make them binding.[25]

18. Under the original system, three institutions were responsible for enforcing the obligations undertaken by the Contracting States: the European Commission of Human Rights, the European Court of Human Rights and the Committee of Ministers of the Council of Europe. All applications lodged under the Convention by individual applicants and Contracting States were the subject of a preliminary examination by the Commission, which decided whether they were admissible. If a complaint was declared admissible, and where no friendly settlement was reached, the Commission drew up a report establishing the facts and expressing a non-binding opinion on the merits of the case. The Commission and/or the government of the State in question could then decide to refer the case to the Court for a final, binding adjudication. If the case was not brought before the Court, the Committee of Ministers would decide.[26]

19. Since its adoption in 1950 the Convention has been amended several times and supplemented with many rights in addition to those set forth in the original text. Some of the rights initially not included have subsequently been added in additional protocols to the ECHR and in other conventions, particularly the European Social Charter of 1961.[27] All forty-seven Council of Europe members, comprising all the countries of the European continent with the exception of Belarus, are party to the Convention.

20. Today, the text of the Convention contains the basic version as amended by Protocols 11 and 14, and seven other protocols: the additional protocol (also called 'Protocol No. 1') and Protocols Nos. 4, 6, 7, 12, 13 and 16.[28] With the entry into force of Protocol 11 in 1998, the Court now automatically has jurisdiction over individual as well as intra-State applications.[29] Protocol 11 also marked the end of the

25. E. Bates, The Evolution of the European Convention of Human Rights. From its Inception to the Creation of a European Court of Human Rights, Oxford University Press, 2010, 563 p.
26. Martyn Bond, The Council of Europe and human rights. An Introduction to the European Convention of Human Rights, Council of Europe Publishing, Strasbourg, 2010, 86 p.
27. Kiestra L.R. (2014) Introduction to the European Convention on Human Rights. In: The Impact of the European Convention on Human Rights on Private International Law. T.M.C. Asser Press, The Hague. https://doi-org.kuleuven.e-bronnen.be/10.1007/978-94-6265-032-9_3.
28. https://echr.coe.int/Documents/Library_Collection_ProtocolsTable_ENG.pdf.
29. Art. 33 ECHR (each State Party to the ECHR may refer to the Court any alleged breach of the provisions of the ECHR or the protocols thereto by another State Party to the Convention).

Commission. A new permanent Court was introduced, which replaced the European Commission of Human Rights (Commission) and the old European Court of Human Rights.[30]

21. Originally, the Strasbourg machinery consisted of three entities: the Commission, established in 1954; the European Court of Human Rights (the old Court), established in 1959; and the Committee of Ministers of the Council of Europe. The new Court emphasised in its first cases after the entry into force of Protocol 11 that it considered the existing case law of both the Commission and the old Court as its own.

22. Protocol No. 15 brings some major changes to the process of lodging an application with the European Court of Human Rights that sits in Strasbourg. First, the time limit for submitting application will be reduced from the current six months to four months after a final domestic decision. This curtailed time period is, however, subject to a transition rule under which the four-month application period will not be effective before 1 February 2022. The shorter application period will also not apply to cases where the final national decision was given prior to the entry into force of the protocol, i.e., before 1 August 2021. Another major change concerns the admissibility criteria of a human rights application as related to 'significant disadvantage'. Following this amendment, accepting an application implies that the applicant must have suffered a significant disadvantage, even if the alleged human rights violation had not been duly considered by a domestic tribunal. Consequently, the European Court of Human Rights will no longer process applications that can be characterised as insignificant. The protocol underlines the subsidiarity of the application mechanism under the Convention in relation to applying the Convention at national level. Alleged human rights violations should primarily be processed before national courts. Protocol No 15 entered into force on 1 August 2021, following ratification by Italy on 21 April 2021 as the last State Party.

II. The European Court of Human Rights

23. Since 1998, the European Court of Human Rights ('ECtHR') has operated as a full-time court and individuals can apply to it directly. The Court examined hundreds of thousands of applications since it was set up. Its judgments are binding on the countries concerned. The Court is based in Strasbourg.,

24. It follows from Article 34 ECHR that an application can be received 'from any person, non-governmental organisation or group of individuals', provided that such an applicant is a victim of the alleged violation. In this article the Contracting Parties also 'undertake not to hinder in any way the effective exercise of this right to bring an application'. Yet it should be noted that in order for such an application

30. Yvonne Klerk, Protocol No. 11 to the European Convention for Human Rights: A Drastic Revision of the Supervisory Mechanism under the ECHR, Netherlands Quarterly of Human Rights, Vol 14, Issue 1, 1996, https://doi.org/10.1177/092405199601400104.

to be admissible, a few criteria have to be met. The various conditions of admissibility can be found not only in Article 34 ECHR, but also in Article 35 ECHR. The Court has held frequently with regard to these criteria that they should be interpreted with some degree of flexibility and without excessive formalism.[31]

25. Article 35(1) ECHR provides that all domestic remedies must first have been exhausted and that the application must be brought within six months after the final decision has been taken. Pursuant to Article 35(2), anonymous applications are not admissible, as well as applications that are substantially the same as a matter that has already been examined by the Court or has already been submitted to another procedure of international investigation or settlement and contains no relevant new information.

26. A newly added criterion is that of the 'significant disadvantage', which has been added in light of the Court's ever-increasing workload, and entails that the Court may reject cases, where the applicant has not suffered any significant disadvantage. The new provision does contain two safeguard clauses: the Court may only reject an application on the basis of this criterion, if the application has been duly considered at the national level. Moreover, respect for the rights guaranteed in the ECHR may require the Court to examine the merits of the case after all. The precise interpretation of the new admissibility criterion and its two safeguard clauses will have to be further clarified by the Court.

27. Even if an application is completely compatible with the ECHR and fulfils all the other admissibility criteria, an application may still be found inadmissible on the merits. The most frequent reason for this is that an application is held to be 'manifestly ill-founded'.[32] This term is always used when it is decided that an application does not warrant a formal examination of the merits (and a likely resulting judgment on the merits) after a preliminary examination of the case has demonstrated no apparent violation of any of the rights guaranteed in the ECHR.[33]

28. Over the last decades, the number of individual applications to the Court has increased steadily and has been exceeding the Court's capacities to a considerable extent. As regards the overload of the Court, one category of cases is of particular relevance, namely applications alleging violations of the Convention which derive from the same structural human rights problem in a Contracting State. They usually do not raise any new substantial questions as for the interpretation of the Convention and the Court merely must repeat its established case law. This problem has led to the introduction of 'pilot judgments'.

---

31. Mentzen v. Latvia (dec), http://hudoc.echr.coe.int/eng?i=001-70407.
32. Art. 35(3) ECHR.
33. Janneke Gerards, Margin of Appreciation and Incrementalism in the Case Law of the European Court of Human Rights, *Human Rights Law Review*, Volume 18, Issue 3, September 2018, Pages 495–515, https://doi.org/10.1093/hrlr/ngy017.

29. The pilot-judgment procedure aims at coping most effectively with widespread human rights problems leading to many repetitive applications. As the Court argues, this aim may not be reached by continuing to focus exclusively on the individual complaint and the violation of the applicant's rights when deciding a case, but it may only be achieved by taking also the structural roots of repeated violations into account.

30. One of the first examples of a pilot judgment was the judgment of the Court in Xenides-Arestis v. Turkey (2005).[34] The case concerned a Greek-Cypriot woman who lived in Nicosia, the capital of Cyprus. She owned land, houses and a shop in Northern Cyprus but had been prevented from living in her home or using her property since August 1974 as a result of the continuing division of Cyprus. She therefore brought a claim pursuant to Article 8 of the ECHR against Turkey. The Court concluded that the deprivation of her rights to enjoy her property constituted a violation of Article 8 of the European Convention. The most significant aspect of the decision in this case, however, is the Court's opinion requiring Turkey to address this issue in a systematic way in relation to all similarly situated applicants. The Court decided: 'It is inherent in the Court's findings that the violation of the applicant's rights … originates in a widespread problem affecting large numbers of people…. Moreover, the Court cannot ignore the fact that there are already approximately 1,400 property cases pending before the Court brought primarily by Greek Cypriots against Turkey. The Court considers that the respondent State must introduce a remedy, which secures genuinely effective redress for the Convention violations identified in the instant judgment in relation to the present applicant as well as in respect of all similar applications pending before the Court, in accordance with the principles for the protection of the rights laid down in Articles 8…. Such a remedy should be available within three months from the date on which the present judgment will be delivered, and the redress should occur three months thereafter.'

31. The Court has been a victim of its own success: over 50,000 new applications are lodged every year. It is important to understand that most of the applications brought to Strasbourg actually end up being found inadmissible. In 2020, 37,289 applications were declared inadmissible or struck out of the list of cases by a single judge, a Committee or a Chamber. Judgments were delivered in respect of 1,901 applications (compared with 2,187 in 2019). On 31 December 2020, the number of pending applications amounted to 62.000 of which 13,650 (22%) against Russia, 11,750 (19%) against Turkey and (16.8%) 10,400 against Ukraine. The Court endeavours to deal with cases within three years after they are brought, but the examination of some cases can take longer, and some can be processed more rapidly.

32. The case law of the European Court consists of judgments and decisions. A decision is usually given by a single judge, a Committee or a Chamber of the Court.

34. Xenides-Arestis v. Turkey, http://hudoc.echr.coe.int/fre?i=001-71800.

It concerns only admissibility and not the merits of the case. Normally, a Chamber examines the admissibility and merits of an application at the same time; it will then deliver a judgment

33. An important aspect is how the ECHR is generally applied by the national courts of the respective Contracting Parties and the position of the ECHR in the respective national legal orders.[35] This varies from country to country but may be an important factor for the impact of the ECHR on any given area of law. From the point of view of the Court, Contracting Parties are not obliged to incorporate the ECHR into their respective laws and may satisfy their commitments as to Article 1 ECHR in any way they choose.[36] Nevertheless, all Contracting Parties have now incorporated the ECHR into their domestic laws in one way or another. This does not mean that the position of the ECHR is identical in every Contracting Party; quite the contrary – the position of the ECHR may differ considerably.[37]

34. Within the context of the European Convention on Human Rights, Protocol 11 has created a quasi-appeal mechanism, which empowers the Grand Chamber of the Court to rehear cases already decided by a Chamber. According to Article 43 of the Convention, parties to a case can request its referral to the Grand Chamber. A panel of five judges of the Grand Chamber will then consider the request and accept the referral where the case involves a serious question of interpretation or application of the Convention or its protocols, or 'a serious issue of general importance'. If the panel accepts the request, the seventeen judges of the Grand Chamber rehear the case and deliver a judgment replacing the one delivered by the Chamber.[38]

35. Article 1 ECHR obliges the Contracting Parties to 'secure' the rights and freedoms contained in the Convention. This obligation, taken together with the text of the several following articles, has been interpreted as imposing both negative and positive obligations. Classic civil and political rights guarantee traditionally entailed negative obligations for the State, such as the requirement to abstain from torture, which can, for example, be found in Article 3 ECHR. In addition to the various negative obligations, there are also some positive obligations expressly stated in the ECHR, or they necessarily follow from the ECHR.

---

35. Brems, Eva., and Gerards, J. H. *Shaping Rights in the ECHR: the Role of the European Court of Human Rights in Determining the Scope of Human Rights*. Cambridge University Press, 2013.
36. Swedish Engine Drivers' Union, 6 February 1976, https://hudoc.echr.coe.int/eng?i=001-57527; *see also* Ireland v. the United Kingdom, 18 January 1978, para. 239, https://hudoc.echr.coe.int/eng?i=001-57506.
37. Georg Ress, The Effect of Decisions and Judgments of the European Court of Human Rights in the Domestic Legal Order, 40 Tex. Int'l L.J. 359 (2004–2005), pp. 359–385.
38. Bağlayan, B., Fahner, J.H., One Can Always Do Better': The Referral Procedure before the Grand Chamber of the European Court of Human Rights, Human rights law review, 2017-06, Vol.17 (2), p. 339-36.

III. The Committee of Ministers of the Council of Europe

36. The Statute of the Council of Europe, entered into force on 3 August 1949, defines in its Chapter IV the roles and functions of the Committee of Ministers. The Committee is the Council of Europe's statutory decision-making body. It is made up of the Ministers for Foreign Affairs of Member States. The Committee meets at ministerial level once a year. For example, the 131st Session of the Committee of Ministers was held by videoconference from Hamburg (Germany), on 21 May 2021, chaired by German Foreign Minister Heiko Maas. During the Session, Germany handed over the Chairmanship of the Committee of Ministers to Hungary and at deputies' level (Permanent Representatives to the Council of Europe) weekly.

37. The Committee of Ministers is the body where decisions of the Council of Europe are adopted. The most important of these decisions are the 'conventions', of which the ECHR is an example. Other types of decisions are the 'recommendations' and the 'resolutions'.

38. In accordance with Article 46 of the ECHR as amended by Protocol No. 11, the Committee of Ministers supervises the execution of judgments of the European Court of Human Rights. This work is carried out mainly at four regular meetings (DH meetings) every year. The Committee of Ministers' essential function is to ensure that Member States comply with the judgments and certain decisions of the European Court of Human Rights. The Committee completes each case by adopting a final resolution. In some cases, interim resolutions may prove appropriate. Both kinds of resolutions are public.

§2. Article 8 of the ECHR

I. Analysis of Article 8

39. Article 8 ECHR encompasses the right to respect for private and family life, home and correspondence. It reads as follows: '1.Everyone has the right to respect for his private and family life, his home and his correspondence. 2.There shall be no interference by a public authority with the exercise of this right except such as is in accordance with the law and is necessary in a democratic society in the interests of national security, public safety or the economic well-being of the country, for the prevention of disorder or crime, for the protection of health or morals, or for the protection of the rights and freedoms of others.'[39]

---

39. Andrew Drzemczewski, The right to respect for private and family life, home and correspondence as guaranteed by Article 8 of the European convention on human rights, Strasbourg: Council of Europe; 1984; Pablo Santolaya, The Right to a Private and Family Life (Notably Extended Right to Privacy) (Art. 8 ECHR), in: Roca, J. G., & Santolaya, P. (Eds.). (20 Mar. 2012). Europe of Rights: A Compendium on the European Convention of Human Rights. Leiden, The Netherlands: Brill | Nijhoff. doi: https://doi-org.kuleuven.e-bronnen.be/10.1163/9789004219915, p. 337–351.

A. Article 8(1)

40. Article 8 protects the right of 'everyone' to respect his private and family life, his home and his correspondence. The right is not restricted to a State's own citizens, but it is a right of every human being. It is not restricted to adults: children have a right to respect of private and family life, home and correspondence as well.[40]

41. The right encompassed by Article 8 is a right 'to respect' private and family life, home and correspondence. Respect in this context means not only 'refrain from interfering' but also includes, as will be clear from the following pages, 'active protection'.

42. The scope of each of the four rights protected by Article 8 is very broad. The right to private life embraces personal autonomy, the right to make choices regarding one's own life without interference by the state, to develop one's own personality and to establish relationships with others and to communicate. The notion of family life not only extends to the legally acknowledged ties between persons related by blood or marriage. Ties which are legally not recognised may also attract the protection afforded by the right to family life. 'Home' is the physically defined place where private life and family life develops. It does not matter whether this space is the property of the affected person or even legally inhabited. The notion also may also encompass business premises, and temporarily inhabited spaces. Finally, the right to respect for correspondence under Article 8 ECHR enshrines the right to uncensored and uninterrupted communication. Although the notion 'correspondence' might be understood as referring to letters only, it is acknowledged that Article 8 also affords protection to communication via all kinds of channels, including phone, internet, social media, etc.[41]

B. Article 8(2)

1. Interference by a Public Authority

43. Although the object of Article 8 is essentially that of protecting the individual against arbitrary interference by the public authorities, it does not merely compel the State to abstain from such interference. In addition to this primarily negative undertaking, the State may also have positive obligations to insure an

40. Hughes, K. (2012-03-08). The Child's Right to Privacy and Article 8 European Convention on Human Rights. In Law and Childhood Studies: Current Legal Issues Volume 14. : Oxford University Press. Retrieved 3 Aug. 2021, from https://oxford-universitypressscholarship-com.kuleuven.e-bronnen.be/view/10.1093/acprof:oso/9780199652501.001.0001/acprof-9780199652501-chapter-26; also Smyth, Ciara. 'The Best Interests of the Child in the Expulsion and First-Entry Jurisprudence of the European Court of Human Rights: How Principled Is the Court's Use of the Principle?' *European Journal of Migration and Law*, vol. 17, no. 1, 2015, pp. 70–103.

41. Witzleb, Normann. Emerging Challenges in Privacy Law: Comparative Perspectives. Cambridge University Press, 2014.

effective respect for private life. Where a case submitted to a judge relates to a negative obligation, an assessment must be undertaken whether the interference was in accordance with the law, in pursuit of a legitimate aim, and necessary in a democratic society. In the case of a positive obligation, the issue will be whether the importance of the interest at stake requires the imposition of the positive obligation sought by the individual. Both in the case of negative obligations and in implementing their positive obligations, the State enjoys a certain margin of appreciation.

44. The State's positive obligations under Article 8 implies that the authorities have a duty to apply criminal-law mechanisms of effective investigation and prosecution in case of allegations of serious acts of violence by private parties.[42] The ECtHR confirmed this principle, for example, in cases relating to the sexual abuse of a mentally handicapped individual, beating of a thirteen-year-old by an adult man or serious instances of domestic violence.[43] Although the object of Article 8 is essentially that of protecting the individual against arbitrary interference by the public authorities, there may be positive obligations inherent in effective respect for private or family life. These obligations may necessitate the adoption of measures designed to secure respect for private life even in the sphere of the relations of individuals between themselves. (The responsibility of the State may thus be engaged if the facts complained of stemmed from a failure on its part to secure to those concerned the enjoyment of a right enshrined in Article 8 of the Convention.[44]

2. In Accordance with the Law

45. Any interference by a public authority with an individual's right to respect for private life and correspondence must be with in accordance with the law.[45] The national law must be clear, foreseeable and adequately accessible. For example, with regard to surveillance activities by public authorities, the law must be sufficiently clear in its terms to give citizens an adequate indication of the conditions and circumstances in which the authorities are empowered to resort to any measures of secret surveillance and collection of data.[46]

---

42. Mowbray, Alastair R. *The Development of Positive Obligations under the European Convention on Human Rights by the European Court of Human Rights*. Hart Publishing, 2004.
43. For exemple: B.V. and others v. Croatia (dec), http://hudoc.echr.coe.int/eng?i=001-160248.
44. López Ribalda and Others v. Spain [GC], http://hudoc.echr.coe.int/eng?i=001-197098 (video surveillance using hidden cameras installed by the employer to discover fraud by cashiers in a supermarket).
45. Cinar, Ozgur Heval. 'The Current Case Law of the European Court of Human Rights on Privacy: Challenges in the Digital Age.' *The International Journal of Human Rights*, vol. 25, no. 1, 2021, pp. 26–51.
46. Shimolovos v. Russia, https://hudoc.echr.coe.int/fre?i=001-105217.

3. Necessary in a Democratic Society

46. Article 8 §2 enumerates the legitimate aims which may justify an infringement upon the rights protected in Article 8: 'in the interests of national security, public safety or the economic well-being of the country, for the prevention of disorder or crime, for the protection of health or morals, or for the protection of the rights and freedoms of others'.[47] It is for the State to demonstrate that the interference in an individual's private life pursued a legitimate aim. The European Court has found, for example, that immigration measures may be justified by the preservation of the country's economic well-being within the meaning of paragraph 2 of Article 8. The Court also found that a ban on full-face veils in public places served a legitimate aim taking into account the respondent State's point that the face plays an important role in social interaction. It was therefore able to accept that the barrier raised against others by a veil concealing the face was perceived by the respondent State as breaching the right of others to live in a space of socialisation which makes living together easier. On the contrary, however, the Court found that the government had provided no legitimate justification for allowing journalists to publish images of a person detained before trial, when there was no public safety reason to do so.

47. In order to determine whether a particular infringement upon Article 8 is 'necessary in a democratic society' the interests of the State must be balanced against the right of the individual. The notion of 'necessity' for the purposes of Article 8 means that the interference must correspond to a pressing social need, and, in particular, must remain proportionate to the legitimate aim pursued. When determining whether an interference was 'necessary', the margin of appreciation left to the State authorities must be considered, but it is a duty of the State to demonstrate the existence of a pressing social need behind the interference.[48]

C. Balance with Other Rights

48. The right to respect for private life must sometimes be balanced against other fundamental rights guaranteed by the ECHR. A relevant example regards the right to freedom of expression granted by Article 10. Relevant criteria for establishing the balance between this right and the respect for private life are: contribution to a debate of public interest, the degree of notoriety of the person affected, the subject of the news report, the prior conduct of the person concerned, the content, form and consequences of the publication, and, where appropriate, the circumstances in which the photographs were taken. Furthermore, in the context of an application lodged under Article 10, the Court examines the way in which the information was obtained and its veracity. With regard to the way in which the information was

47. Milenković, Jelena. 'The Right to Privacy under Article 8 of the European Convention of Human Rights and Legality of Epidemiological Monitoring Measures to Combat the Covid-19 Virus Pandemic.' *Zbornik Radova Pravnog Fakulteta u Nišu*, vol. 59, no. 89, 2020, pp. 303–320.
48. Roberts, Andy. 'Covert Video Identification: European Convention on Human Rights, Article 8.' *Journal of Criminal Law (Hertford)*, vol. 67, no. 6, 2003, pp. 480–485.

obtained, the Court has held that the press should normally be entitled to rely on the content of official reports without further verification of the facts presented in the document.[49]

II. Sphere of Private Life

A. Concept

49. Private life is a broad concept incapable of exhaustive definition.[50] It covers the physical and psychological integrity of a person and may 'embrace multiple aspects of the person's physical and social identity'.[51] However, through its case law, the Court has provided guidance as to the meaning and scope of private life for the purposes of Article 8.[52]

50. The notion of private life is not limited to an 'inner circle' in which the individual may live his own personal life as he chooses and excludes the outside world. There is a zone of interaction of a person with others, even in a public context, which may fall within the scope of 'private life'. As an example, one can refer to the case of a police investigator who had been found guilty of a serious breach of his professional duties for having solicited and accepted bribes in return for discontinuing criminal proceedings. The man had wished to practise as a trainee advocate after serving his sentence but was refused to register as a member of the Bar. The ECtHR found that restrictions on registration as a member of certain professions which could to a certain degree affect that person's ability to develop relationships with the outside world fell within the sphere of his or her private life.[53]

51. Restrictions imposed on access to a profession have been found to affect 'private life' within the meaning of Article 8 ECHR. For example, the European Court has found a violation of Article 8 where the applicant was transferred to a more minor role in a city which was less important in administrative terms, following a report that he had particular religious beliefs and that his wife wore an Islamic veil.[54]

52. Protection of private life evidently includes aspects such as gender identification, name and sexual orientation and sexual life. For example, legislation criminalising sexual acts between consenting homosexuals was found to breach Article 8

49. Mityanin and Leonov v. Russia, https://hudoc.echr.coe.int/fre?i=001-158638.
50. Niemietz v. Germany, https://hudoc.echr.coe.int/eng?i=001-57887, §29; Pretty v. the United Kingdom, https://hudoc.echr.coe.int/fre?i=001-60448, §61; Peck v. the United Kingdom, https://hudoc.echr.coe.int/fre?i=001-60898, §57.
51. Denisov v. Ukraine[GC], http://hudoc.echr.coe.int/eng?i=001-170359,§ 9. and Marper v. the United Kingdom[GC], http://hudoc.echr.coe.int/eng?i=001-90051, § 66.
52. Paradiso and Campanelli v. Italy[GC], http://hudoc.echr.coe.int/eng?i=001-170359, §159 http://hudoc.echr.coe.int/eng?i=001-90051.
53. Jankauskas v. Lithuania (no. 2), §§ 57–58, http://hudoc.echr.coe.int/eng?i=001-174617.
54. Sodan v. Turkey, §§ 57–60, http://hudoc.echr.coe.int/eng?i=001-160260.

ECHR.[55] However, Article 8 does not prohibit criminalisation of all private sexual activity.[56] In a series of cases, the ECtHR held that any ban on the employment of homosexuals in the military constituted a breach of the right to respect for private life.[57]

53. The Court has on several occasions examined whether individuals had a reasonable expectation that their privacy would be respected and protected. In that context, it has stated that a reasonable expectation of privacy is a significant though not necessarily conclusive factor. On the contrary, the Court decided to leave open the question of whether the applicant had a reasonable expectation of privacy because, in any event, 'an employer's instructions cannot reduce private social life in the workplace to zero. Respect for private life and for the privacy of correspondence continues to exist, even if these may be restricted insofar as necessary'.[58]

B. Workplace

54. Whether or not an individual had a reasonable expectation of privacy, communications in the workplace are covered by the concepts of private life and correspondence anyway.[59] In Bărbulescu v. Romania [GC], the ECtHR decided to leave open the question of whether the applicant had a reasonable expectation of privacy because, in any event, '*an employer's instructions cannot reduce private social life in the workplace to zero. Respect for private life and for the privacy of correspondence continues to exist, even if these may be restricted insofar as necessary*'. In this case, the Court also set down a detailed list of factors regarding States' positive obligation under Article 8.

55. Concerning the opening by a public employer of personal data on a work computer without the employee's knowledge and in his absence, the ECtHR, in the case of Libert v. France, did not accept that there had been no 'interference' with the right to respect for the applicant's private life because he had not properly labelled as private the files opened by his superiors. The Court, however, estimated that the interference could be justified since 'having noted that the applicant had used a substantial amount of the storage space on his work computer to store the files in question (1,562 files representing a volume of 787 megabytes), the SNCF and the domestic courts deemed it necessary to examine his case thoroughly'.[60]

55. Dudgeon v. the United Kingdom, http://hudoc.echr.coe.int/eng?i=001-57473; A.D.T. v. the United Kingdom, http://hudoc.echr.coe.int/eng?i=001-58922.
56. Laskey, Jaggard and Brown v. the United Kingdom, http://hudoc.echr.coe.int/eng?i=001-58021.
57. For example, in Lustig-Prean and Beckett v. the United Kingdom, http://hudoc.echr.coe.int/eng?i=001-58407.
58. Bărbulescu v. Romania[GC], http://hudoc.echr.coe.int/eng?i=001-177083.
59. *Ibid.*,
60. Libert v. France, http://hudoc.echr.coe.int/eng?i=001-181074 (the Court found that the domestic authorities had not overstepped their margin of appreciation and relied notably on the clear guidelines contained in the employer's computer charter).

56. In Antović and Mirković v. Montenegro, the case submitted to the ECtHR related to the installation of video surveillance cameras in university auditoria. The data protection agency had found this installation justified because, among other reasons 'there had been cases of destruction of university property, the bringing in of animals, drink and tobacco, and the presence of people who were not students'. The Court reiterated 'that 'private life' is a broad term not susceptible to exhaustive definition and that it would be too restrictive to limit the notion of 'private life' to an 'inner circle' in which the individual may live his own personal life as he chooses and to exclude therefrom entirely the outside world not encompassed within that circle'.[61] The Court, confirming its former jurisprudence, further held that that the notion of 'private life' may include professional activities or activities taking place in a public context and that, 'it is, after all, in the course of their working lives that the majority of people have a significant, if not the greatest, opportunity to develop relationships with the outside world, and it is not always possible to distinguish clearly which of an individual's activities form part of his professional or business life and which do not'.[62] Noting that university amphitheatres are the workplaces of teachers, the Court emphasised that video surveillance of employees at their workplace, whether covert or not, constitutes a considerable intrusion into their private life.[63]

57. In another case concerning covert video surveillance of employees, the ECtHR reiterated that 'the State, in the context of its positive obligations under Article 8, has struck a fair balance between the applicant's right to respect for her private life and both her employer's interest in protection of its property rights, guaranteed by Article 1 of Protocol no. 1 to the Convention, and the public interest in the proper administration of justice'.[64] In establishing this balance, the Court agreed with the German labour courts' finding 'that the employer's interest in the protection of its property rights could only be effectively safeguarded if it could collect evidence in order to prove the applicant's criminal conduct in proceedings before the domestic courts and if it could keep the data collected until the final determination of the Court proceedings brought by the applicant'. The Court observed, however, 'that the competing interests concerned might well be given a different weight in the future, having regard to the extent to which intrusions into private life are made possible by new, more and more sophisticated technologies'.

III. Physical and Moral Integrity

58. The concept of private life covers the physical and moral integrity of the person. This was e.g., confirmed by the ECtHR in the already cited case about the

61. Antović and Mirković v. Montenegro, http://hudoc.echr.coe.int/eng?i=001-178904, § 41.
62. *See* e.g., Niemietz v. Germany, https://hudoc.echr.coe.int/eng?i=001-57887; Halford v. the United Kingdom, https://hudoc.echr.coe.int/tur?i=001-58039; Bărbulescu v. Romania [GC], 5 September 2017, http://hudoc.echr.coe.int/eng?i=001-177083.
63. Antović and Mirković v. Montenegro, § 44 (in the particular case the ECtHR concluded that the interference in question was not in accordance with the law).
64. Köpke v. Germany (dec.); 5 October 2010, http://hudoc.echr.coe.int/eng?i=001-101536.

sexual assault of a mentally disabled 16-year old girl and the absence of criminal law provisions to provide her with effective and practical protection.[65] The authorities' positive obligations may include a duty to maintain and apply in practice an adequate legal framework affording protection against acts of violence by private individuals. This obligation may involve the adoption of specific measures, including the provision of an effective and accessible means of protecting the right to respect for private life.

A. Vulnerable Persons

59. In the case of Hadzhieva v. Bulgaria, the authorities had arrested the applicant's parents in her presence when she was 14 years old, leaving her alone without appropriate custody. Even though the applicable domestic law provided for the adoption of protective measures in such situations, the Court noted that the authorities had failed in their positive obligation to ensure that the applicant was protected and cared for in the absence of her parents, having regard to the risks to her well-being.[66]

60. In respect of children, the measures applied by the State to protect them against acts of violence falling within the scope of Article 8 should include reasonable steps to prevent ill-treatment of which the authorities have or ought to have, knowledge and effective deterrence against serious breaches of personal integrity.[67] Regarding serious acts such as rape and sexual abuse of children, where fundamental values and essential aspects of private life are at stake, it falls to the Member States to ensure that efficient criminal law provisions are in place.[68]

61. States should also provide adequate protection for dangerous situations, such as for a woman attacked in her home or for a woman who had acid thrown on her face.[69] This is particularly true when the State should have known of a particular danger. For example, the Court found a violation when a woman was attacked by stray dogs in an area where such animals were a common problem.[70] However, the Court does require a connection between the State and the injury suffered. If there is no clear link between State action (or inaction) and the alleged harm, such as fighting between school children, then the Court may declare the case inadmissible.[71]

65. X and Y v. the Netherlands, http://hudoc.echr.coe.int/eng?i=001-57603.
66. Hadzhieva v. Bulgaria, http://hudoc.echr.coe.int/eng?i=001-180486.
67. Z and Others v. the United Kingdom [GC], http://hudoc.echr.coe.int/eng?i=001-59455.
68. Wetjen and Others v. Germany, http://hudoc.echr.coe.int/eng?i=001-181583.
69. Sandra Janković v. Croatia, http://hudoc.echr.coe.int/eng?i=001-91608.
70. Georgel and Georeta Stoicescu v. Romania, http://hudoc.echr.coe.int/eng?i=001-105820.
71. Đurđević v. Croatia, http://hudoc.echr.coe.int/eng?i=001-105691.

B. Health and Well-Being

62. The ECtHR judged that the prohibition of abortion for reasons of health or well-being falls within the scope of the right to respect for one's private life and accordingly within Article 8. In particular, the Court held in this context that the State's obligations include both the provision of a regulatory framework of adjudication and enforcement machinery protecting individuals' rights, and the implementation, where appropriate, of specific measure.[72]

63. The Court has further determined that States have a positive obligation to ensure effective legal safeguards to protect women from non-consensual sterilisation, with a particular emphasis on the protection of reproductive health for women of Roma origin. In several cases, the Court has found that Roma women required protection against sterilisation because of a history of non-consensual sterilisation against this vulnerable ethnic minority.[73] This positive obligation of the State also applies to inadvertent sterilisation, when the doctor fails to perform adequate checks or obtain informed consent during an abortion procedure.[74]

64. An individual's right to refuse medical treatment falls within the scope of Article 8. This includes the rights of mentally ill patients to refuse psychiatric medication. A medical intervention in defiance of the subject's wishes will give rise to an interference with his or her private life and in particular his or her right to physical integrity.[75] In some circumstances forced medication of a mentally ill patient may be justified, in order to protect the patient and/or others. However, such decisions must be made against the background of clear legal guidelines and with the possibility of judicial review.[76]

65. The State has a positive obligation under Article 8, first, to have in place regulations compelling both public and private hospitals to adopt appropriate measures for the protection of their patients' physical integrity and, second, to provide victims of medical negligence access to proceedings in which they could, in appropriate cases, obtain compensation for damage.[77] This positive obligation is limited to the duty to establish an effective regulatory framework obliging hospitals and health professionals to adopt appropriate measures to protect the integrity of patients. Consequently, even where medical negligence has been established, the Court will not normally find a violation of Article 8. However, in very exceptional circumstances State responsibility may be engaged because of the actions and omissions of healthcare providers. Such exceptional circumstances may arise where a

72. A, B and C v. Ireland[GC], http://hudoc.echr.coe.int/eng?i=001-102332.
73. I.G. and Others v. Slovakia, http://hudoc.echr.coe.int/eng?i=001-114514.
74. Csoma v. Romania, http://hudoc.echr.coe.int/eng?i=001-115862.
75. X. v. Finland, http://hudoc.echr.coe.int/eng?i=001-111938.
76. Storck v. Germany, http://hudoc.echr.coe.int/eng?i=001-69374.
77. Mehmet Ulusoy and Others v. Turkey, http://hudoc.echr.coe.int/eng?i=001-194060.

patient's life is knowingly endangered by the denial of access to life-saving treatment; and where a patient did not have access to such treatment because of systemic or structural dysfunction in hospital services, and where the authorities knew or ought to have known of this risk and did not take the necessary measures to prevent it from being realised.[78]

66. In the case of Pretty v. the United Kingdom, the ECtHR decided that the right to decide the manner of one's death falls under the scope of Article 8 ECHR.[79] In later cases, the Court articulated that an individual's right to decide the way in which and at which point his or her life should end, provided that he or she is in a position to freely form his or her own judgment and to act accordingly, is one of the aspects of the right to respect for private life within the meaning of Article 8.[80] The Court has found that Member States have a wide margin of appreciation in respect of questions of assisted suicide. Permissible laws include the requirement that life ending drugs be provided only by prescription by a physician.[81]

67. Article 8 rights pertain, predominantly, to relationships between living human beings. However, the way in which the body of a deceased relative is treated, as well as issues regarding the ability to attend the burial and pay respects at the grave of a relative, come within the scope of the right to respect for family or private life.[82] Family members have, for example, challenged the length of time between death and burial and the treatment of the deceased's body before its return to the family. For example, the Court found that an extended delay in returning samples taken from the applicants' daughter's body by police, which prevented them from burying her in a timely manner, violated their right to private and family life.[83] The ECtHR also found that a hospital's removal of a deceased person's organs without informing his mother and without seeking her consent was not done in accordance with law and violated her right to private life under Article 8.[84]

C. Living Conditions

68. The right to respect of private life also includes the right to live in a healthy and safe environment. However, an issue under Article 8 only arises if individuals are directly and seriously affected by the nuisance in question and able to prove the direct impact on their quality of life.[85] The ECtHR stated that a certain minimum level of adverse effects of pollution on the individual's health or quality of life must be demonstrated. Article8 may apply in environmental cases whether the pollution is directly caused by the State or whether State responsibility arises from the failure

78. Lopes de Sousa Fernandes v. Portugal, http://hudoc.echr.coe.int/eng?i=001-166676.
79. Pretty v. United Kingdom, http://hudoc.echr.coe.int/eng?i=001-60448.
80. Haas v. Switzerland, http://hudoc.echr.coe.int/eng?i=001-102940.
81. *Ibid.*
82. Solska and Rybicka v. Poland, http://hudoc.echr.coe.int/eng?i=001-186135.
83. Girard v. France, http://hudoc.echr.coe.int/eng?i=001-105471.
84. Petrova v. Latvia, http://hudoc.echr.coe.int/eng?i=001-144997.
85. Fadeyeva v. Russia, http://hudoc.echr.coe.int/eng?i=001-69315.

to regulate private sector activities properly. In several cases, the failure to provide information about environmental risks or hazards was found to constitute a violation of Article 8.[86]

IV. Information Privacy

A. Basic Principles

69. The concept of 'private life' is not susceptible to exhaustive definition. It covers the physical and psychological integrity of a person and can therefore embrace multiple aspects of a person's identity.[87] Article 8 of the Convention is primarily intended to ensure the development, without outside interference, of the personality of each individual in his relations with other human beings. There is thus a zone of interaction of a person with others, even in a public context, which may fall within the scope of private life.

70. A person's reasonable expectations as to privacy may be a significant, although not necessarily conclusive, factor. For example, in the case of Benedik v. Slovenia, the applicant alleged that his right under Article 8 of the Convention had been breached because the police had unlawfully obtained information leading to his identification from his Internet service provider. The Court accepted that the applicant, when exchanging files with pornographic material through the Razorback network, expected, from his subjective angle, that such activity would remain private and that his identity would not be disclosed. However, the Court considered that the fact that he did not hide his dynamic IP address, assuming that it is possible to do so, cannot be decisive in the assessment of whether his expectation of privacy was reasonable from an objective standpoint. In this connection, it notes that the question is clearly not whether the applicant could have reasonably expected to keep his dynamic IP address private but whether he could have reasonably expected privacy in relation to his identity.[88]

71. The authorities' continued retention of fingerprints, cellular samples and DNA profiles after criminal proceedings had ended, constitutes a violation of Article 8 ECHR.[89] The ECtHR considers that particular attention should be paid to the protection of juveniles from any detriment that may result from the retention by the authorities of their private data following acquittals of a criminal offence.[90]

86. For example in Tătar v. Romania, http://hudoc.echr.coe.int/eng?i=001-90909.
87. Axel Springer AG v. Germany, http://hudoc.echr.coe.int/eng?i=001-109034.
88. Benedik v. Slovenia, http://hudoc.echr.coe.int/eng?i=001-182455 (in this case, the Court finally decided that the collection of information by the police did not have an adequate legal basis).
89. S. and Marper v. the United Kingdom [GC], http://hudoc.echr.coe.int/eng?i=001-90051.
90. *Ibid.*, §124.

B. Protection of a Person's Image

72. Regarding photographs, the ECtHR has stated that a person's image constitutes one of the chief attributes of his/her personality. Although freedom of expression includes the publication of photographs, the Court has nonetheless found that the protection of the rights and reputation of others takes on particular importance in this area, as photographs may contain very personal or even intimate information about an individual or his or her family.[91] Even a neutral photograph accompanying a story portraying an individual in a negative light constitutes a serious intrusion into the private life of a person who does not seek publicity.[92] Individuals have, furthermore, the right to control the use of their image, including the right to refuse publication thereof.[93]

73. When balancing the right to protection of private life under Article 8 and freedom of expression under Article 10 ECHR, the Court takes into consideration factors such as whether or not the publication constitutes a contribution to a debate of general interest; the public character of the person concerned and the subject of the report. Also relevant are the prior conduct of the person concerned; the content, form and consequences of the publication, the circumstances in which the photos were taken; and the severity of the sanction imposed.[94]

74. The State has positive obligations to ensure that efficient criminal or civil law provisions are in place to prohibit filming without consent. The Court has found, for example, video surveillance of public places where the images are recorded, stored and disclosed to the public to fall under Article 8.[95] Other cases related to video surveillance in a supermarket by an employer and in a university amphitheatre.[96]

75. The ECtHR has held on various occasions that the recording of a video in the law enforcement context or the release of photographs by police authorities to the media constituted an interference with their right to respect for private life. How long images are kept by the police, is also relevant. In Gaughran v. the UK, the

91. Von Hannover v. Germany, http://hudoc.echr.coe.int/eng?i=001-109029.
92. Rodina v. Latvia, http://hudoc.echr.coe.int/eng?i=001-202437.
93. Reklos and Davourlis v. Greece, http://hudoc.echr.coe.int/eng?i=001-90617 (photographs of a newly born baby were taken in a private clinic without the parents' prior consent).
94. Couderc and Hachette Filipacchi Associés v. France [GC], http://hudoc.echr.coe.int/eng?i=001-158861; Dupate v. Latvia, http://hudoc.echr.coe.int/eng?i=001-153893 (a magazine had published covertly taken photographs of the applicant, who was the partner of a public figure, when she was leaving hospital following the birth of their child).
95. Peck v. the United Kingdom http://hudoc.echr.coe.int/eng?i=001-60898 (disclosure to the media for broadcast use of video footage of an applicant whose suicide attempt was caught on surveillance television cameras).
96. López Ribalda and Others v. Spain, http://hudoc.echr.coe.int/eng?i=001-197098; Antović and Mirković v. Montenegro, http://hudoc.echr.coe.int/eng?i=001-178904 (violation since the relevant legislation explicitly provided for certain conditions to be met before camera surveillance is resorted to, and in the present case those conditions had not been met).

applicant's custody photograph was taken on his arrest; it was to be held indefinitely on a local database for use by the police and the police were able to apply facial recognition and facial mapping techniques to it. Therefore, the Court found that the taking and retention of the applicant's photograph amounted to an interference with the right to one's image.[97] Long-time storage can, however, be judged as necessary in a democratic society. This has been illustrated in a case where the Court found that the taking and retention of a photograph of a suspected terrorist without her consent was not disproportionate to the legitimate terrorist-prevention aims of a democratic society.[98]

C. Protection of Individual Reputation

76. In order for Article 8 to come into play, an attack on a person's reputation must attain a certain level of seriousness and be made in a manner causing prejudice to personal enjoyment of the right to respect for private life. This requirement pertains to both social and professional reputation. There must also be a sufficient link between the applicant and the alleged attack on his or her reputation.[99]

77. The extent of acceptable criticism in respect of a public figure is wider than in respect of ordinary citizens.[100] However, individuals who are not public figures may nevertheless expose themselves to journalistic criticism by publicly expressing ideas or beliefs likely to give rise to considerable controversy.[101]

78. An attack on personal honour and reputation must attain a certain level of seriousness and must have been carried out in a manner causing prejudice to the personal enjoyment of the right to respect for private life. The ECtHR has held that the reality of today is that millions of Internet users post comments online every day and many of these users express themselves in ways that might be regarded as offensive or even defamatory. However, the majority of comments are likely to be too trivial in character, and/or the extent of their publication is likely to be too limited, for them to cause any significant damage to another person's reputation.[102]

---

97. Gaughran v. the UK, http://hudoc.echr.coe.int/eng?i=001-200817.
98. Murray v. the United Kingdom, http://hudoc.echr.coe.int/eng?i=001-57895.
99. Denisov v. Ukraine [GC], http://hudoc.echr.coe.int/eng?i=001-186216 (dismissal from the position of President of a Court of Appeal; the Court decided in this particular case that neither the reasons for the applicant's dismissal were linked to nor that the consequences of that measure affected his 'private life').
100. Kaboğlu and Oran v. Turkey, http://hudoc.echr.coe.int/eng?i=001-187565.
101. Balaskas v. Greece, http://hudoc.echr.coe.int/eng?i=001-205545 (conviction for insult through the press of a journalist who had an article published in a local newspaper attributing the characteristics 'neo-Nazi' and 'theoretician of the entity 'Golden Dawn'' to the headmaster of a local high school).
102. Tamiz v. the United Kingdom (dec.), http://hudoc.echr.coe.int/eng?i=001-178106. (In this case, the Court also noted that this was not a case in which no measures were in place to enable the applicant to protect his Art. 8 rights.)

79. A relevant criterion taken into account refers to the concept of 'the reasonable reader' when approaching issues relating to satirical material. A wide margin of appreciation should be given to parody in the context of freedom of expression. Also the fact that the individual has made public particular details relating to his or her private life, for example making suggestions on his/her sexual orientation in a television show, must be considered.[103]

80. The ECtHR has, to date, left open the question of whether the private life aspect of Article 8 protects the reputation of a company. The Court emphasised, however, that there is a difference between the reputation of a legal entity and the reputation of an individual as a member of society. Whereas the latter may have repercussions on one's dignity, the former is devoid of that moral dimension. This difference is even more salient when it is a public authority that invokes its right to reputation.[104]

81. The reputation of a deceased member of a person's family may, in certain circumstances, affect that person's private life and identity, and thus come within the scope of Article 8.[105]

D. Right to Access Personal Information

82. Obtaining information necessary to discover the truth concerning important aspects of one's personal identity, such as the identity of one's parents, one's origins and aspects of one's childhood and early development, is particularly relevant for an individual's personal development. Birth, and in particular the circumstances in which a child is born, forms part of a child's, and subsequently the adult's, private life guaranteed by Article 8 of the Convention. The issue of access to information about one's origins and the identity of one's natural parents, must be judged with consideration of the interests of other parties. In a case of a mother who abandoned her child and explicitly requested anonymity, the ECtHR estimated the problem of anonymous births cannot be dealt with in isolation from the issue of the protection of third parties, essentially the adoptive parents, the father and the other members of the natural family. The Court noted in that connection that the applicant was 38 years old, having been adopted at the age of 4, and that non-consensual disclosure could entail substantial risks, not only for the mother herself, but also for

103. Sousa Goucha v. Portugal, http://hudoc.echr.coe.int/eng?i=001-161527 (a well-known celebrity alleged that he had been defamed during a television show shortly after making a public announcement concerning his sexual orientation).
104. Margulev v. Russia, http://hudoc.echr.coe.int/eng?i=001-196480 (a newspaper article had reported in a critical tone on the restoration works at the Tsaritsyno museum complex that they were being funded by Moscow City Council).
105. Jakovljević v. Serbia (dec.), http://hudoc.echr.coe.int/eng?i=001-206079 (The Court considered the complaint under Art. 8 that the military officials and military investigating authorities had disseminated offensive and inaccurate information about the personal and family life of that applicant's late son, but rejected it as inadmissible for the non-exhaustion of domestic remedies).

the adoptive family which brought up the applicant, and her natural father and siblings, each of whom also has a right to respect for his or her private and family life.[106]

83. With regard to accessing personal information held by security services, the Court has held that obstacles to access may constitute violations of Article 8. However, in cases concerning suspected terrorists, the Court has also held that the interests of national security and the fight against terrorism prevail over the applicants' interest in having access to information about them in the Security Police files.[107]

84. While the Court has recognised that, particularly in proceedings related to the operations of state security agencies, there may be legitimate grounds to limit access to certain documents and other materials, it has found this consideration loses much of its validity with respect to lustration proceedings. In the first place, lustration proceedings are, by their very nature, oriented towards the establishment of facts dating back to the communist era and are not directly linked to the current functions and operations of the security services. Thus, unless the contrary is shown on the facts of a specific case, it cannot be assumed that there remains a continuing and actual public interest in imposing limitations on access to materials classified as confidential under former regimes. Second, lustration proceedings inevitably depend on the examination of documents relating to the operations of the former communist security agencies. If the party to whom the classified materials relate is denied access to all or most of the materials in question, his or her possibilities to contradict the security agency's version of the facts would be severely curtailed. Finally, under the relevant laws, it is typically the security agency itself that has the power to decide what materials should remain classified and for how long. Since, it is the legality of the agency's actions which is in question in lustration proceedings, the existence of this power is not consistent with the fairness of the proceedings, including the principle of equality of arms. Thus, if a State is to adopt lustration measures, it must ensure that the persons affected thereby enjoy all procedural guarantees under the Convention in respect of any proceedings relating to the application of such measures.[108]

85. Respecting the confidentiality of health data is a vital principle, not only from the perspective of the individual but also to protect the society. It is crucial not only to respect the privacy of a patient, but also to preserve his or her confidence in the medical profession and in the health services in general. Without such protection, those in need of medical assistance may be deterred from revealing such information of a personal and intimate nature as may be necessary in order to receive appropriate treatment and, even, from seeking such assistance. They may thereby endanger their own health and, in the case of communicable diseases, that of the

106. Odièvre v. France [GC], http://hudoc.echr.coe.int/eng?i=001-60935.
107. Segerstedt-Wiberg and Others v. Sweden, http://hudoc.echr.coe.int/eng?i=001-75591.
108. Turek v. Slovakia, http://hudoc.echr.coe.int/eng?i=001-72354.

community. The domestic law must therefore afford appropriate safeguards to prevent any such communication or disclosure of personal health data as may be inconsistent with the guarantees in Article 8 of the Convention. The interest in protecting the confidentiality of health data will therefore weigh heavily in determining whether the interference was proportionate to the legitimate aim pursued. Such interference cannot be compatible with Article 8 unless it is justified by an overriding requirement in the public interest.[109]

86. There may be positive obligations inherent in effective respect for private or family life which require the State to provide essential information about risks to one's health in a timely manner. In particular, where a State engages in hazardous activities, which might have hidden adverse consequences on the health of those involved in such activities, respect for private and family life under Article 8 requires that an effective and accessible procedure be established which enables such persons to seek all relevant and appropriate information.[110]

V. Identity and Autonomy

A. Ethnic Identity

87. The right of members of a national minority to maintain their identity and to lead a private and family life in accordance with their tradition, is part of the Article 8 right to private and family life, with a consequent obligation placed upon States to facilitate, and not obstruct disproportionately, the traditional lifestyles of minorities.[111]

88. In the specific context of demonstrations motivated by hostility towards an ethnic group, mostly involving intimidation rather than physical violence, the Court drew inspiration from the principles established in cases concerning the freedom of

109. Z v. Finland, http://hudoc.echr.coe.int/eng?i=001-58033. (Following a complaint of a sexual offence, the police opened an investigation into attempted manslaughter, suspecting X of having deliberately subjected M. to a risk of infection with HIV. The police carried out a search at the hospital where the applicant and X had occasionally been treated. The police seized all the records concerning the applicant and appended copies of these to the record of the investigation concerning the charges against X of attempted manslaughter. These measures had been ordered by the prosecution. The ECrtHR considered that the seizure of the applicant's medical records and their inclusion in the investigation file were supported by relevant and sufficient reasons, the weight of which was such as to override the applicant's interest in the information in question not being communicated.)

110. Guerra and Others v. Italy, http://hudoc.echr.coe.int/eng?i=001-58135; McGinley and Egan v. the United Kingdom, http://hudoc.echr.coe.int/eng?i=001-58175; Roche v. the United Kingdom [GC], http://hudoc.echr.coe.int/eng?i=001-70662 (The applicant alleged that he was suffering from the effects of his exposure to toxic chemicals during tests carried out on him to conduct research into chemical weapons with a view to advancing the protection of the United Kingdom's armed forces against such weapons. The research included tests of gases on humans as well as on animals. Servicemen who participated in the tests were paid extra wages. The applicant complained, that he had had inadequate access to information about the tests).

111. Tasev v. North Macedonia, http://hudoc.echr.coe.int/eng?i=001-192985.

expression. Thus, the key factors to determine are whether the offending statements were made against a tense political and social background, whether they amounted to a direct or indirect call for violence, hatred or intolerance and their capacity to lead to harmful consequences. A legal framework should be in place for criminalising anti-minority demonstrations and should afford effective protection against harassment, threats and verbal abuse; otherwise, there may be a perception that the authorities tolerate such verbal intimidation and disturbances.[112]

89. The ECtHR established that there had been a violation of Article 8 in a case where the authorities had failed to protect the applicants, who belonged to a minority group, from an attack on their homes, had a certain role in the attack, where there was no effective domestic investigation, and taking into account the general background of prejudice against the particular minority community in the country.[113]

B. Gender Identity

90. Article 8 is applicable to the question of the legal recognition of the gender identity of transgender people who have undergone gender reassignment surgery, the conditions for access to such surgery and the legal recognition of the gender identity of transgender people who have not undergone, or do not wish to undergo, gender reassignment treatment.[114]

91. The European Court found a violation of Article 8 notably on the basis that a European and International consensus existed favouring the legal recognition of a transgender person's acquired gender. The Goodwin case raised the issue of whether or not the UK had failed to comply with a positive obligation to ensure the right of the applicant, a post-operative male to female transgender, to respect for her private life, in particular through the lack of legal recognition given to her gender reassignment. The Court held that there has been a failure to respect the applicant's right to private life since there were no significant factors of public interest to weigh against the interest of the applicant in obtaining legal recognition of her gender reassignment. The Court has recognised that, in the twenty-first century, the right of transgender people to personal development and to physical and moral security in the full sense enjoyed by others in society could not be regarded as a matter of controversy requiring the lapse of time to cast clearer light on the issues involved.[115]

92. The Court also held that making recognition of a transgender person's acquired gender conditional on sterilisation surgery or treatment, which they did not wish to undergo, amounted to making the full exercise of their right to respect for their private life conditional on their relinquishing the full exercise of their right to

112. Király and Dömötör v. Hungary, http://hudoc.echr.coe.int/eng?i=001-170391.
113. Burlya and Others v. Ukraine, http://hudoc.echr.coe.int/eng?i=001-187508.
114. Hämäläinen v. Finland, [GC], http://hudoc.echr.coe.int/eng?i=001-145768; Schlumpf v. Switzerland, http://hudoc.echr.coe.int/eng?i=001-90498.
115. CGoodwin v. the United Kingdom [GC], https://hudoc.echr.coe.int/fre?i=002-9155.

respect for their physical integrity as protected not only by Article 8 but also by Article 3 of the Convention (§ 131), this being in breach of their right to respect for their private life). In fact, the State enjoyed only a narrow margin of appreciation on the sterility requirement for two reasons: first, the condition that the change in one's appearance be irreversible touches an essential aspects of an individual's intimate identity, and even of his or her existence; second, a trend had emerged in Europe in recent years with regard to abandoning this criterion of sterility.[116]

93. The refusal to allow a transsexual to have his change of sex recorded in the civil-status register, although his physical appearance and social and family identity had been altered for a long time, constitutes a violation of his right to private life. The State has a positive obligation to put in place an effective and accessible procedure, which clearly defines conditions securing the applicant's rights.[117]

C. Appearance

94. The European Court has established that personal choices as to an individual's desired appearance, whether in public or in private, relate to the expression of his or her personality and thus fall within the notion of private life.[118]

95. In recent years a number of European countries have prohibited women from publicly wearing veils that cover their faces. The ECtHR found that Belgium's veil ban did not violate Article 8 ECHR. It estimated that, 'while it is true that the scope of the ban is broad, because all places accessible to the public are concerned, the contested provisions do not affect the freedom to wear in public any garment or item of clothing – with or without a religious connotation – which does not have the effect of concealing the face'. It concluded therefore: 'Consequently, having regard in particular to the breadth of the margin of appreciation enjoyed by the respondent State in the present case, the Court concludes that the ban imposed by the consolidated by-laws of the Vesdre police district can be regarded as proportionate to the aim pursued, namely the preservation of the conditions of 'living together' as an element of the 'protection of the rights and freedoms of others'.[119]

D. Origin

96. The right to obtain information in order to discover one's origins and the identity of one's parents as an integral part of identity protected under the right to private and family life. It is not compulsory for States to DNA test alleged fathers,

116. A.P., Garçon and Nicot v. France, http://hudoc.echr.coe.int/eng?i=001-172913.
117. Y.T. v. Bulgaria, http://hudoc.echr.coe.int/eng?i=001-203898.
118. Popa v. Romania (dec.), http://hudoc.echr.coe.int/eng?i=001-122439 (haircut); Tığ v. Turkey (dec.), http://hudoc.echr.coe.int/eng?i=001-69258 (denial of access to a university for wearing a beard).
119. Dakir v. Belgium, http://hudoc.echr.coe.int/eng/?i=001-175139; also S.A.S. v. France [GC], http://hudoc.echr.coe.int/eng?i=001-145466; Marshall, Jill. 'S.A.S. v. France: Burqa Bans and the Control or Empowerment of Identities.' *Human Rights Law Review*, vol. 15, no. 2, 2015, pp. 377–389.

but the legal system must provide alternative means enabling an independent authority to speedily determine a paternity claim. For example in the case of Mikulić v. Croatia, the applicant was born out of an extramarital relationship and complained that the Croatian judicial system had been inefficient in determining the issue of paternity, leaving her uncertain as to her personal identity. In that case the European Court held that the inefficiency of the domestic courts had left the applicant in a state of prolonged uncertainty as to her personal identity. The Croatian authorities had therefore failed to secure to the applicant the 'respect' for her private life to which she was entitled under the Convention.[120]

97. In Jäggi v. Switzerland, the ECtHR found the refusal by the authorities to authorise a DNA test on a deceased person, requested by the putative son wishing to establish his parentage with certainty, to violate Article 8. In that case, the applicant's interest in ascertaining the identity of his biological father prevailed over that of the remaining family of the deceased which opposed the taking of DNA samples.[121]

E. Name

98. Issues concerning an individual's first name and surname fall under the right to private life The European Court has ruled that the tradition of demonstrating family unity by obliging married women to adopt the surname of their husbands is no longer compatible with the Convention.[122]

99. As concerns the seizure of documents needed to prove one's identity, the Court has found an interference with private life as a result of a domestic court's withholding of identity papers following the applicant's release from custody, as papers were needed often in everyday life in order to prove one's identity.[123]

F. Citizenship

100. Article 8 cannot be interpreted as guaranteeing, as such, the right to a residence permit. This permit is in principle a matter for the domestic authorities alone.[124] In order to determine whether the interference is necessary in a democratic society, States are entitled to control the entry of aliens into their territory and their residence there. The Convention does not guarantee the right of an alien to enter or to reside in a particular country and, in pursuance of their task of maintaining public order, States have the power to expel an alien convicted of criminal

120. Mikulić v. Croatia, http://hudoc.echr.coe.int/eng?i=001-60035.
121. Jäggi v. Switzerland, http://hudoc.echr.coe.int/eng?i=001-76412.
122. Ünal Tekeli v. Turkey, http://hudoc.echr.coe.int/eng?i=001-67482.
123. Smirnova v. Russia, http://hudoc.echr.coe.int/eng?i=001-61262.
124. Kaftailova v. Latvia (striking out) [GC], http://hudoc.echr.coe.int/eng?i=001-83770.

offences.[125] However, the solution proposed must enable the individual in question to exercise unhindered his right to private and/or family life. Measures restricting the right to reside in a country may, in certain cases, entail a violation of Article 8 if they create disproportionate repercussions on the private or family life, or both, of the individuals concerned.[126]

101. On the contrary, Article 8 may involve a positive obligation in this context, to ensure effective enjoyment of the individual's private and/or family life. For example, national authorities infringe a stateless immigrant's right to private life by failing, for years, to regularise his resident's status and leaving him in a situation of insecurity. The State does not comply with its positive obligation to provide an effective and accessible procedure or combination of procedures enabling the immigrant to have the issues of his further stay and status in Croatia determined with due regard to his private-life interests under Article 8.[127]

102. Where there is an arguable claim that expulsion threatens to interfere with a non-citizen's right to respect for his private and family life, Article 13 in conjunction with Article 8 of the Convention requires that States must make available to the individual concerned the effective possibility of challenging the deportation or refusal of residence order and of having the relevant issues examined with sufficient procedural safeguards and thoroughness by an appropriate domestic forum offering adequate guarantees of independence and impartiality.[128]

103. Very serious reasons are required to justify the expulsion of a settled migrant who has lawfully spent all or the major part of his or her childhood and youth in a host country. In the specific case of a foreigner, who had arrived in the host country as a child with a tourist visa, which expired shortly after his arrival, and who had not known about his unlawful stay until he was 17 years old, the Court did not consider the applicant a 'settled migrant' because his residence in the host country had not been lawful. In such a case, it could neither be said that the refusal of a residence permit would require very serious reasons to be justified under Article 8 nor that it would violate that provision only in very exceptional circumstances. Instead, the assessment has to be carried out from a neutral starting point, taking into account the specific circumstances of the applicant's case.[129]

---

125. Üner v. the Netherlands [GC], http://hudoc.echr.coe.int/eng?i=001-77542.
126. Hoti v. Croatia, http://hudoc.echr.coe.int/eng?i=001-182448.
127. Sudita Keita v. Hungary, http://hudoc.echr.coe.int/eng?i=001-202433 (the applicant in this case had had protracted difficulties in regularising his legal situation for fifteen years, with adverse repercussions on his access to healthcare and employment and his right to get married).
128. De Souza Ribeiro v. France [GC], http://hudoc.echr.coe.int/eng?i=001-115498, § 83; M. and Others v. Bulgaria, http://hudoc.echr.coe.int/eng?i=001-105788, §§ 122–132; Al-Nashif v. Bulgaria, http://hudoc.echr.coe.int/eng?i=001-60522, § 133). Bettinson, Vanessa. 'Deportation of Migrant Following Criminal Conviction: European Convention on Human Rights, Article 8.' *Journal of Criminal Law (Hertford)*, vol. 74, no. 2, 2010, pp. 113–117.
129. Pormes v. the Netherlands*, http://hudoc.echr.coe.int/eng?i=001-203836.

VI. Family Life

A. *The Notion of 'Family'*

104. The notion of family life is an autonomous concept.[130] Whether or not 'family life' exists is essentially a question of fact depending upon the real existence in practice of close personal ties.[131] The notion of 'family' under Article 8 of the Convention is not confined solely to marriage-based relationships and may encompass other de facto 'family ties' where the parties are living together outside marriage.[132] Even in the absence of cohabitation there may still be sufficient ties for family life.[133] A same-sex couple living in a stable relationship falls within the notion of family life, in the same way as a heterosexual couple.

B. *Protection of Family Life*

105. The Court noted that within the Council of Europe, twenty-four of the forty-seven Member States had already enacted legislation recognising same-sex couples and affording them legal protection. It observed that in Italy there was a conflict between the social reality of the applicants, who lived openly as a couple, and their inability to secure any official recognition of their relationship. Noting that guaranteeing the recognition and protection of same-sex unions would not amount to any particular burden on the Italian State, it held that in the absence of marriage, same-sex couples like the applicants had a particular interest in obtaining the option of entering into a form of civil union or registered partnership, since this would be the most appropriate way in which they could have their relationship legally recognised and be guaranteed the relevant protection – in the form of core rights relevant to a couple in a stable and committed relationship – without unnecessary hindrance.

106. Moral considerations or on social acceptability must be taken seriously in a sensitive domain like artificial procreation. However, they are not in themselves sufficient reasons for a complete ban on a specific artificial procreation techniques such as ovum donation. Notwithstanding the wide margin of appreciation of the State, the legal framework for this purpose must be shaped in a coherent manner which allows the different legitimate interests involved to be adequately taken into account.[134]

130. Marckx v. Belgium, http://hudoc.echr.coe.int/eng?i=001-57534, § 31.
131. Paradiso and Campanelli v. Italy [GC], http://hudoc.echr.coe.int/eng?i=001-170359.
132. Van der Heijden v. the Netherlands [GC], http://hudoc.echr.coe.int/eng?i=001-110188.
133. Kroon and Others v. the Netherlands, http://hudoc.echr.coe.int/eng?i=001-57904, § 30.
134. S. H. and Others v. Austria, http://hudoc.echr.coe.int/eng?i=001-107325.

107. The notion of family life in Article 8 is not confined solely to marriage-based relationships and may encompass other de facto 'family' ties where the parties are living together outside marriage. The term extends equally to the relationship between natural fathers and their children born out of wedlock.[135]

108. Where the authorities have decided to replace the foster home arrangement with a more far-reaching type of measure, namely deprivation of parental responsibilities and authorisation of adoption, 'such measures should only be applied in exceptional circumstances and could only be justified if they were motivated by an overriding requirement pertaining to the child's best interests'.[136] A mother's financial situation cannot, without regard for changed circumstances, justify the removal of a child from her mother's care. Further, the absence of skills and experience in rearing children could hardly in itself be regarded as a legitimate ground for restricting parental authority or keeping a child in public care.

109. Family life includes at least the ties between near relatives, for instance those between grandparents and grandchildren, since such relatives may play a considerable part in family life.[137] The right to respect for family life of grandparents in relation to their grandchildren primarily entails the right to maintain a normal grandparent-grandchild relationship through contact between them.[138] However, the Court considers that contact between grandparents and grandchildren normally take place with the agreement of the person who has parental responsibility, which means that access of a grandparent to his or her grandchild is normally at the discretion of the child's parents.[139]

110. A refusal to allow a prisoner to attend the funerals of close relatives was held to amount to an interference with the respect for private and family life.[140] On the contrary, in an antiterrorism context, the Court found no violation of Article 8 as the judicial authorities had carried out a balancing exercise between the interests at stake, namely the applicant's right to respect for her family life on the one hand and public safety and the prevention of disorder and crime on the other.[141]

111. The States' interest in foiling attempts to circumvent immigration rules must not deprive foreign minors, especially if unaccompanied, of the protection their status warrants.[142] Where the risk to evade the supervision of the authorities is

135. Shavdarov v. Bulgaria, https://hudoc.echr.coe.int/eng?i=001-102414.
136. Aune v. Norway, https://hudoc.echr.coe.int/eng?i=001-101458.
137. Marckx v. Belgium, https://hudoc.echr.coe.int/eng?i=001-57534, § 45; Bronda v. Italy, https://hudoc.echr.coe.int/eng?i=001-58194, § 51; T.S. and J.J. v. Norway, https://hudoc.echr.coe.int/eng?i=001-168637, § 23.
138. Kruškić v. Croatia (dec.), https://hudoc.echr.coe.int/eng?i=001-149164, § 111; Mitovi v. the Former Yugoslav Republic of Macedonia, https://hudoc.echr.coe.int/eng?i=001-153812, § 58.
139. Kruškić v. Croatia (dec.), https://hudoc.echr.coe.int/eng?i=001-149164, § 112.
140. Płoski v. Poland https://hudoc.echr.coe.int/eng?i=001-60733, § 39; Vetsev v. Bulgaria, https://hudoc.echr.coe.int/eng?i=001-192997, § 59 (in French).
141. Guimon v. France, https://hudoc.echr.coe.int/eng?i=001-192616.
142. Mubilanzila Mayeka and Kaniki Mitunga v. Belgium, https://hudoc.echr.coe.int/eng?i=001-77447, § 81.

minimal, her detention in a closed centre for adults was found unnecessary. In another case, the domestic authorities placed two young children alone in administrative detention, refusing to entrust them to their father or even to come into contact with him. The Court held that the fact of placing certain members of the same family in a detention centre while other members of that family were free could be construed as interference with the exercise of their right to family life, regardless of the duration of the measure in question.[143]

112. Where immigration is concerned, Article 8, taken alone, cannot be considered to impose on a State a general obligation to respect a married couple's choice of country for their matrimonial residence or to authorise family reunification on its territory.[144] Nevertheless, in a case which concerns family life as well as immigration, the extent of a State's obligations to admit to its territory relatives of persons residing there will vary according to the particular circumstances of the persons involved and the general interest.[145] Factors to be taken into account in this context are the extent to which family life is effectively ruptured, the extent of the ties, whether there are insurmountable obstacles in the way of the family living in the country of origin of one or more of them and whether there are factors of immigration control (for example, a history of breaches of immigration law) or considerations of public order weighing in favour of exclusion.[146]

VII. Home

A. *Notion of 'Home'*

113. The answer to the question whether a habitation constitutes a 'home' under the protection of Article 8 §1 depends on the factual circumstances, namely the existence of sufficient and continuous links with a specific place. The term is not limited to property of which the applicant is the owner or tenant. It further extends to an individual's business premises or to a registered office, and to the branches or other business premises of a company.[147]

114. On the contrary, it neither applies to property on which it is intended to build a house, or to the fact of having roots in a particular area); nor does it extend to an artist's dressing room or to industrial buildings and facilities, such as a mill,

143. Moustahi v. France, https://hudoc.echr.coe.int/eng?i=002-12877.
144. Jeunesse v. the Netherlands [GC], https://hudoc.echr.coe.int/eng?i=001-147117, § 107; Biao v. Denmark [GC], https://hudoc.echr.coe.int/eng?i=001-163115, § 117.
145. Abdulaziz, Cabales and Balkandali v. the United Kingdom, https://hudoc.echr.coe.int/eng?i=001-57416, §§ 6768; Gül v. Switzerland, https://hudoc.echr.coe.int/eng?i=001-57975, § 38; Ahmut v. the Netherlands, https://hudoc.echr.coe.int/eng?i=001-58002, § 63; Osman v. Denmark, https://hudoc.echr.coe.int/eng?i=001-10512, § 54; Berisha v. Switzerland, https://hudoc.echr.coe.int/eng?i=001-122978, § 60.
146. Rodrigues da Silva and Hoogkamer v. the Netherlands, https://hudoc.echr.coe.int/eng?i=001-72205, § 38.
147. Niemietz v. Germany, http://hudoc.echr.coe.int/eng?i=001-57887; Société Colas Est and Others v. France, http://hudoc.echr.coe.int/eng?i=001-60431.

bakery or storage facility used exclusively for professional purposes or for housing farm animals. Similarly, a building that is not inhabited, empty or under construction may not be qualified as a 'home'.[148]

B. Housing Right

115. Article 8 cannot be construed as recognising a right to be provided with a home (or as conferring a right to live in a particular location.[149] Moreover, the scope of any positive obligation for the authorities to house the homeless is limited. For example, in a case relating to the Roma community in Slovenia, the ECtHR estimated that the respective municipal authorities undertook measures that provided the applicants with the opportunity to access drinking water, notwithstanding the irregular status of their settlements and the nature of the land the applicants' respective buildings had been built on. The Court further considered it reasonable that the State, or its local authorities, assume the responsibility for the provision of this service, while it is left to the owners to instal individual house connections at their own expense.[150]

116. It will sometimes be necessary for a Member State to attach and sell an individual's home in order to secure the payment of taxes due to the State. However, these measures must be enforced in a manner which ensures that the individual's right to his or her home is respected. In a case concerning the conditions of an enforced sale at auction of a house, to repay a tax debt, the Court found a violation because the owner's interests had not been adequately protected.[151] The Court also takes into account an occupant's vulnerability, with case law protecting minorities' lifestyles.[152]

C. Entering Private Homes

117. In order to collect evidence on certain offences, the authorities may consider it necessary to implement measures which entail entering a private home. The actions of the police when entering homes must be 'lawful' and proportionate to the

148. Halabi v. France, http://hudoc.echr.coe.int/eng?i=001-192 987.
149. Garib v. the Netherlands, [GC], http://hudoc.echr.coe.int/eng?i=001-177406 ('The information submitted therefore does not allow the Court to find that the consequences for the applicant of the refusal to her of a housing permit that would have allowed her to move to the B. Street dwelling amounted to such disproportionate hardship that her interest should outweigh the general interest served by the consistent application of the measure in issue.', §165).
150. Hudorovič and Others v. Slovenia, http://hudoc.echr.coe.int/eng?i=001-201646.
151. Rousk v. Sweden, http://hudoc.echr.coe.int/eng?i=001-123422.
152. *See*, for example, the EcrtHR case law relating to members of the Roma community: (Moldovan and Others v. Romania, http://hudoc.echr.coe.int/eng?i=001-69670; Remiche, Adélaïde. 'Yordanova and Others v. Bulgaria: The Influence of the Social Right t Adequate Housing on the Interpretation of the Civil Right to Respect for One's Home.' *Human Rights Law Review*, vol. 12, no. 4, 2012, pp. 787–800.

aim pursued. For example, in a case concerning the obligation imposed on high-level athletes falling within a 'target group' to give advance notification of their whereabouts so that unannounced anti-doping tests could be carried out, the ECtHR emphasised that home visits for the purposes of such testing were very different from those carried out under Court supervision, which were geared to investigating offences or seizing items of property. Such searches, by definition, struck at the heart of respect for the home and could not be treated as equivalent to the visits to the athletes' homes. The Court considered that reducing or cancelling the obligations of which the applicant had complained could increase the dangers of doping to their health and to that of the whole sporting community, and would run counter to the European and international consensus on the need to carry out unannounced tests. Consequently, the Court concluded that this was not a violation of Article 8 of the Convention.[153]

118. The Court found a violation of Article 8 where members of a special intervention unit wearing balaclavas and armed with machine guns had entered a private home at daybreak in order to serve charges on the applicant and escort him to the police station. The Court pointed out that safeguards should be in place in order to avoid any possible abuse and protect human dignity in such circumstance.[154]

119. The ECtHR is particularly vigilant where domestic law authorises house searches without a judicial warrant. It accepts such searches where the lack of a warrant is offset by effective subsequent judicial scrutiny of the lawfulness and necessity of the measure. Moreover, the warrant should be sufficiently precise. In the case of Sher and Others v. the United Kingdom, the authorities had suspected an imminent terrorist attack and initiated extremely complex investigations in order to foil the attack. The Court agreed that the search warrant had been couched in fairly broad terms. However, it considered that the fight against terrorism and the urgency of the situation could justify a search based on terms that were wider than would otherwise have been permissible. In cases of this nature, the police should be permitted some flexibility in assessing, on the basis of what is encountered during the search, which items might be linked to terrorist activities, and in seizing them for further examination.[155]

120. Searches of press premises aimed at obtaining information on journalists' sources can raise an issue under Article 8. In Ernst and Others v. Belgium, the Court considered disproportionate a series of searches conducted of journalists' professional and private premises. The journalists had not been charged with any offences, and the search warrants had been couched in broad terms and had not included any information on the investigation in question, the premises to be inspected and the items to be seized. Consequently, those warrants conferred too many powers on the

153. National Federation of Sportspersons' Associations and Unions (FNASS) and Others v. France, http://hudoc.echr.coe.int/eng?i=001-180276.
154. Kučera v. Slovakia, http://hudoc.echr.coe.int/eng?i=001-81731.
155. Sher and Others v. the United Kingdom, http://hudoc.echr.coe.int/eng?i=001-158032.

investigators, who had been able to copy and seize extensive data. Moreover, the journalists had not been informed of the reasons for the searches.[156]

D. Living Environment

121. Environmental pollution can raise an issue under Article 8 if the pollution has direct and immediate consequences for the right to respect for the home.[157] Moreover, the consequences of the environmental pollution must reach a certain 'threshold of severity', without necessarily seriously endangering the person's health. Assessment of this threshold depends on the circumstances of the case, such as the intensity and duration of the nuisance and its physical or mental effects on the individual's health or quality of life.[158]

122. When dealing with an allegation of environmental pollution affecting the right to the 'home', the Court adopts a two-stage approach. First of all, it considers the substantive merits of the domestic authorities' decisions, and second, it scrutinises the decision-making process. The violation may involve an arbitrary interference by the public authorities or a failure to honour their positive obligations. The Court reiterates that in both contexts regard must be had to the fair balance that has to be struck between the competing interests of the individual and of the community as a whole.[159]

123. The Court has, in particular, found violations of Article 8 owing to shortcomings attributable to the authorities in cases involving the use of dangerous toxic emissions as well as the flooding of housing located downstream of a reservoir, attributable to negligence on the part of the authorities.[160]

124. Nuisances caused by neighbours may affect peaceful enjoyment of one's home, whether they be caused by private individuals, business activities or public agencies. If the requisite threshold of severity is reached, the domestic authorities, having been duly informed about the nuisances, have an obligation to take effective measures to ensure respect for the right to peaceful enjoyment of the home.[161]

---

156. Ernst and Others v. Belgium, http://hudoc.echr.coe.int/eng?i=001-61214.
157. Fitzmaurice, Malgosia. 'The European Court of Human Rights, Environmental Damage and the Applicability of Article 8 of the European Convention on Human Rights and Fundamental Freedoms.' *Environmental Law Review*, vol. 13, no. 2, 2011, pp. 107–114.
158. López Ostra v. Spain, http://hudoc.echr.coe.int/eng?i=001-57905; Fadeyeva v. Russia, http://hudoc.echr.coe.int/eng?i=001-69315; Zammit Maempel v. Malta, http://hudoc.echr.coe.int/eng?i=001-107514.
159. Moreno Gómez v. Spain, http://hudoc.echr.coe.int/eng?i=001-67478; Hatton and Others v. the United Kingdom [GC], http://hudoc.echr.coe.int/eng?i=001-61188.
160. Giacomelli v. Italy, http://hudoc.echr.coe.int/eng?i=001-77785; (Kolyadenko and Others v. Russia, http://hudoc.echr.coe.int/eng?i=001-109283.
161. Mileva and Others v. Bulgaria, https://hudoc.echr.coe.int/Eng?i=001-101815, § 97, violation owing to a failure to prevent the unlawful operation of a computer club causing a nuisance in a block of flats).

VIII. Correspondence

A. Concept of 'Correspondence'

125. The notion of 'correspondence' covers a wide range of communications means, such as letters of a private or professional nature, but also, for example, packages seized by customs officers. It includes telephone conversations between family members but also calls from private or business premises and from a prison. It relates not only to interceptions of the content but also to other information relating to the conversation, such as the time, the duration, numbers dialled, etc. It is, moreover, evident that the concept covers modern communication technologies, such as data stored on smartphones, e-mail, navigation on Internet websites, social media, data stored on computer equipment, etc.[162]

126. The content and form of the correspondence is irrelevant. For instance, opening and reading a folded piece of paper on which a lawyer had written a message and handed it to his clients is considered as an interference in the correspondence.[163]

127. The State has a positive obligation to protect the privacy of the correspondence; this includes, for example, an obligation to investigate the violation of the confidentiality of the correspondence in the context of domestic violence.[164]

B. Protection of Correspondence in Prisons

128. The ECtHR has acknowledged that some measure of control over prisoners' correspondence is called for and is not of itself incompatible with the Convention. For example, some measure of control – as opposed to automatic, routine interference – aimed at preventing disorder or crime may be justified, for example in the case of correspondence with dangerous individuals or concerning non-legal matters.[165]

129. While it may be necessary to monitor detainees' contact with the outside world, including telephone contact, the rules applied must afford the prisoner appropriate protection against arbitrary interference by the national authorities.[166]

162. Saber v. Norway, http://hudoc.echr.coe.int/eng?i=001-206519; Wieser and Bicos Beteiligungen GmbH v. Austria, http://hudoc.echr.coe.int/eng?i=001-82711; Petri Sallinen and Others v. Finland, http://hudoc.echr.coe.int/eng?i=001-70283; Copland v. the United Kingdom, http://hudoc.echr.coe.int/eng?i=001-79996; Bărbulescu v. Romania [GC], http://hudoc.echr.coe.int/eng?i=001-177082.
163. Laurent v. France, http://hudoc.echr.coe.int/eng?i=001-183129.
164. Mileva and Others v. Bulgaria, http://hudoc.echr.coe.int/eng?i=001-101815 (violation owing to a failure to prevent the unlawful operation of a computer club causing a nuisance in a block of flats).
165. Jankauskas v. Lithuania, http://hudoc.echr.coe.int/eng?i=001-68394.
166. Doerga v. the Netherlands, http://hudoc.echr.coe.int/eng?i=001-61747.

130. Where domestic law allows interference, it must include safeguards to prevent abuses of power by the prison authorities. A law that simply identifies the category of persons whose correspondence 'may be censored' and the competent court, without saying anything about the length of the measure or the reasons that may warrant it, is not sufficient.[167] The Court also found a violation where the domestic provisions concerning the monitoring of prisoners' correspondence leave the national authorities too much latitude and give prison governors the power to keep any correspondence 'unsuited to the process of rehabilitating a prisoner', with the result that 'monitoring of correspondence therefore seems to be automatic, independent of any decision by a judicial authority and unappealable'.[168]

131. In a high-security prison, the storage of the numbers that a prisoner wished to call – a measure of which he had been notified – was considered necessary for security reasons and to avoid the commission of further offences (the prisoner had other ways of remaining in contact with his relatives, such as letters and visits).[169]

132. The reading of a prisoner's mail to and from a lawyer should only be permitted in exceptional circumstances when the authorities have reasonable cause to believe that the 'privilege is being abused' in that the contents of the letter endanger prison security or the safety of others or are otherwise of a criminal nature. What may be regarded as 'reasonable cause' will depend on all the circumstances but it presupposes the existence of facts or information which would convince an objective observer that the privileged channel of communication is being abused.[170]

C. Protection of Correspondence with Lawyers

133. Interferences in the correspondence between a lawyer and her/his client does not always represent a violation of Article 8 ECHR. For example, the ECtHR examined whether the obligation for lawyers to report their suspicions of unlawful money laundering activities by their clients, where such suspicions came to light outside the context of their defence role, amounted to disproportionate interference with the legal professional privilege. The Court concluded in this case that there was no such violation.[171]

134. On the contrary, since telephone tapping constitutes a serious interference with the right to respect for a lawyer's correspondence, it must be based on a 'law' that is particularly precise, especially as the technology available for use is continually becoming more sophisticated. In the Kopp v. Switzerland case, for example, the Court found a violation of Article 8, first because the law did not state clearly how

167. Calogero Diana v. Italy, http://hudoc.echr.coe.int/eng?i=001-58072.
168. Petra v. Romania, http://hudoc.echr.coe.int/eng?i=001-58244.
169. Coşcodar v. Romania (dec.), http://hudoc.echr.coe.int/eng?i=001-97942 (only in French).
170. Campbell v. the United Kingdom, http://hudoc.echr.coe.int/eng?i=001-57771; Boris Popov v. Russia, http://hudoc.echr.coe.int/eng?i=001-101323.
171. Michaud v. France, http://hudoc.echr.coe.int/eng?i=001-115377; also Versini-Campinchi and Crasnianski v. France, http://hudoc.echr.coe.int/eng?i=001-164228.

the distinction was to be drawn between matters specifically connected with a lawyer's work and those relating to activity other than that of counsel, and second, the telephone tapping had been carried out by the authorities without any supervision by an independent judge.[172]

D. Surveillance of Correspondence for Law Enforcement

135. Measures such as interception of telephone conversations represent a serious interference with the right to respect for correspondence and must be based on a 'law' that is particularly precise.[173] The rules must form part of a legislative framework affording sufficient legal certainty. They must be clear and detailed (the technology available for use is continually becoming more sophisticated), as well as being both accessible and foreseeable, so that anyone can foresee the consequences for themselves.[174] This requirement of sufficiently clear rules concerns both the circumstances in which and the conditions on which the surveillance is authorised and carried out. Since the implementation of measures of secret surveillance of communications is not open to scrutiny by the individuals concerned or the public at large, the 'law' would run counter to the rule of law if there were no limits to the legal discretion granted to the executive, or to a judge.[175]

136. Review and supervision of surveillance measures by law enforcement bodies may come into play at three stages: when the surveillance is first ordered, while it is being carried out, or after it has been terminated. As regards the first two stages, the very nature and logic of secret surveillance dictate that not only the surveillance itself but also the accompanying review should be effected without the individual's knowledge. Consequently, since the individual will necessarily be prevented from seeking an effective remedy of his or her own accord or from taking a direct part in any review proceedings, it is essential that the procedures established should themselves provide adequate and equivalent guarantees safeguarding his or her rights.[176]

137. Surveillance measures, such as phone-tapping operations can only be ordered on the basis of suspicions that can be regarded as objectively reasonable.[177] The Court has also underlined the importance of an authority empowered to authorise the use of secret surveillance being capable of verifying 'the existence of a reasonable suspicion against the person concerned, in particular, whether there are factual indications for suspecting that person of planning, committing or having

172. Kopp v. Switzerland, http://hudoc.echr.coe.int/eng?i=001-58144; *see also* Petri Sallinen and Others v. Finland, http://hudoc.echr.coe.int/eng?i=001-70283.
173. Kruslin v. France, http://hudoc.echr.coe.int/eng?i=001-57626; Huvig v. France, http://hudoc.echr.coe.int/eng?i=001-57627.
174. Valenzuela Contreras v. Spain, http://hudoc.echr.coe.int/eng?i=001-58208.
175. Karabeyoğlu v. Turkey, http://hudoc.echr.coe.int/eng?i=001-163455.
176. Roman Zakharov v. Russia [GC], http://hudoc.echr.coe.int/eng?i=001-159324.
177. *Ibid.*

committed criminal acts or other acts that may give rise to secret surveillance measures' and 'whether the requested interception meets the requirement of 'necessity in a democratic society' ... for example, whether it is possible to achieve the aims by less restrictive means'.[178]

138. The State must ensure effective protection of the data obtained from a surveillance operation and of the right of persons whose purely private conversations have been intercepted by the law enforcement agency. The ECtHR found a violation on account of leaks to the media and the broadcasting of a private conversation recorded, with the authorities' approval, on a telephone line belonging to a politician who was under investigation by the prosecuting authorities.[179]

E. Surveillance by State Intelligence Services

139. In its judgment of 1978 in Klass and Others v. Germany, the ECtHR stated, in particular: 'Democratic societies nowadays find themselves threatened by highly sophisticated forms of espionage and by terrorism, with the result that the State must be able, in order effectively to counter such threats, to undertake the secret surveillance of subversive elements operating within its jurisdiction. The Court has therefore to accept that the existence of some legislation granting powers of secret surveillance over the mail, post and telecommunications is, under exceptional conditions, necessary in a democratic society in the interests of national security and/or for the prevention of disorder or crime.'[180]

140. Alternately, a surveillance operation must, in general, be strictly necessary for the safeguarding of democratic institutions and, in particular, for the obtaining of vital intelligence in an individual operation.[181]

141. In addition, surveillance by state security services must have some basis in domestic law and be compatible with the rule of law. The law must be accessible to the person concerned and foreseeable as to its effects. Foreseeability in the special context of secret measures of surveillance cannot mean that individuals should be able to foresee when the authorities are likely to intercept their communications so that they can adapt their conduct accordingly. To avoid arbitrary interference, it is essential to have clear, detailed rules on the interception of telephone conversations. The law must be sufficiently clear to give citizens an adequate indication as to the

178. *Ibid.*; also Dragojević v. Croatia, http://hudoc.echr.coe.int/eng?i=001-150298.
179. Drakšas v. Lithuania, http://hudoc.echr.coe.int/eng?i=001-112588.
180. Klass and Others v. Germany, § 48, http://hudoc.echr.coe.int/eng?i=001-57510.
181. Szabó and Vissy v. Hungary, http://hudoc.echr.coe.int/eng?i=001-160020; *see also* the judgment in Roman Zakharov v. Russia [GC] which contains a thorough overview of the Court's case law under Art. 8 concerning the 'lawfulness' ('quality of law') and 'necessity' (adequacy and effectiveness of guarantees against arbitrariness and the risk of abuse) of a system of secret surveillance: http://hudoc.echr.coe.int/eng?i=001-159324.

circumstances in which and the conditions on which public authorities are empowered to resort to such kind of secret measures.[182]

142. To justify a secret surveillance measure, it is important to set out clearly the nature of the offences which may give rise to an interception order and a definition of the categories of people liable to have their telephones tapped. As regards the nature of the offences, the condition of foreseeability does not require States to set out exhaustively, by name, the specific offences which may give rise to interception. However, sufficient detail should be provided as to the nature of the offences in question. Interception measures in respect of a person who has not been suspected of an offence but might possess information about such an offence may be justified.[183]

143. There should be procedures to be followed for storing, accessing, examining, using, communicating and destroying intercepted data. For example, the case of Liberty and Others v. the United Kingdom concerned the interception by the Ministry of Defence, on the basis of a warrant, of the external communications of civil-liberties organisations. The Court found a violation, holding in particular that no indication of the procedure to be followed for selecting for examination, sharing, storing and destroying intercepted material had been accessible to the public.[184]

144. It is in principle desirable to entrust supervisory control to a judge, supervision by non-judicial bodies may be deemed compatible with the Convention, provided that the supervisory body is independent of the authorities carrying out the surveillance, and is vested with sufficient powers and competence to perform effective and continuous supervision.[185]

§3. Privacy Protection in the EU Charter

I. Background

145. The Treaty of Lisbon made a decisive step towards the creation of a common constitutional law for the EU and put the protection of fundamental rights in the European Union on a new footing. A new article on fundamental rights – Article 6 TEU – subjects the actions of the EU institutions and the Member States, insofar as they apply and implement Union law, to the Charter of Fundamental Rights of the European Union, which is made legally binding at EU level by a reference in that article. A draft of this Charter was solemnly proclaimed by the Presidents of the European Parliament, the Council and the European Commission at the beginning of the Nice European Council on 7 December 2000.

---

182. Weber and Saravia v. Germany, http://hudoc.echr.coe.int/eng?i=001-76586; Kennedy v. the United Kingdom, http://hudoc.echr.coe.int/eng?i=001-98473.
183. Roman Zakharov v. Russia [GC], http://hudoc.echr.coe.int/eng?i=001-159324; Greuter v. the Netherlands, http://hudoc.echr.coe.int/eng?i=001-22288.
184. Liberty and Others v. the United Kingdom, http://hudoc.echr.coe.int/eng?i=001-87207.
185. Roman Zakharov v. Russia [GC], http://hudoc.echr.coe.int/eng?i=001-159324.

146. During the negotiations on an EU constitution, the Charter of Fundamental Rights was revised and made an integral part of the Treaty establishing a Constitution for Europe of 29 October 2004. Following the failure of the treaty, the Charter of Fundamental Rights was again solemnly proclaimed as the 'European Union's Charter of Fundamental Rights', this time as a separate instrument, by the Presidents of the European Parliament, the Council and the European Commission on 12 December 2007 in Strasbourg. The EU Treaty refers to this version of the Charter in binding form. This makes the Charter of Fundamental Rights legally binding and also establishes the applicability of fundamental rights in Union law. However, this does not apply to Poland and the United Kingdom. These two Member States were unable, or did not wish, to adopt the system of fundamental rights of the Charter, as they were concerned that they would be obliged to surrender or at least change certain national positions concerning, for example, religious issues or the treatment of minorities. They remain, however, bound by the case law of the CJEU relating to the protection of fundamental rights and freedoms in the European Union.

147. The purpose of the Charter is to promote human rights within the territory of the EU. It is divided into six chapters: Dignity, Freedoms, Equality, Solidarity, Citizen's rights and Justice. Under the 'Freedoms' chapter, Article 7 reads as follows: '*Everyone has the right to respect for his or her private and family life, home and communications.*' Article 8 states: '*1. Everyone has the right to the protection of personal data concerning him or her. 2. Such data must be processed fairly for specified purposes and on the basis of the consent of the person concerned or some other legitimate basis laid down by law. Everyone has the right of access to data which has been collected concerning him or her, and the right to have it rectified. 3.Compliance with these rules shall be subject to control by an independent authority.*'

148. Title VII of the Charter contains 'general provisions governing the interpretation and application of the Charter'. Article 52(1) stipulates: ' *Any limitation on the exercise of the rights and freedoms recognised by this Charter must be provided for by law and respect the essence of those rights and freedoms. Subject to the principle of proportionality, limitations may be made only if they are necessary and genuinely meet objectives of general interest recognised by the Union or the need to protect the rights and freedoms of others.*'

149. Relevant for the interpretation of the provisions of the Charter is Article 52(3): 'In so far as this Charter contains rights which correspond to rights guaranteed by the Convention for the Protection of Human Rights and Fundamental Freedoms, the meaning and scope of those rights shall be the same as those laid down by the said Convention. This provision shall not prevent Union law from providing more extensive protection.' This provision confirms former case law of the CJEU. For example, in the famous judgment of 6 November 2003, C-101/01 (Bodil Lindqvist) the Court stated that 'The provisions of Directive 95/46 do not, in themselves, bring about a restriction which conflicts with the general principles of freedom of expression or other freedoms and rights, which are applicable within the

European Union and are enshrined inter alia in Article 10 of the European Convention for the Protection of Human Rights and Fundamental Freedoms signed at Rome on 4 November 1950.'

150. It follows from Article 52(3) that the level of protection guaranteed by the Charter may not disregard the level guaranteed by the ECHR. This does not prevent EU law from providing more extensive protection. It follows also that the Charter allows room for autonomous developments in the field of fundamental rights protection.[186] The Court of Justice recalled that the ECHR '*does not constitute, as long as the [EU] has not acceded to it, a legal instrument which has been formally incorporated into EU law ', and that normative consistency between the Charter and the ECHR may not adversely affect the autonomy of EU law*.[187] The European legislator is free to decide whether to impose a uniform level of protection that is higher than that guaranteed by the Charter. That uniform level of protection rules out diversity as it precludes the application of higher levels of protection provided for by national law. By contrast, where the EU legislature has not provided for a uniform level of protection, there is room for national diversity. However, that diversity is not absolute as it must, first, comply with the level of protection guaranteed by the Charter; and, second, respect the primacy, unity and effectiveness of EU law.

II. Role of the Charter in the European Legal Order

151. The Charter of the European Union is governed by the principle of conferral.[188] Article 51(1) states that: the provisions of this Charter are addressed to the institutions, bodies, offices and agencies of the Union with due regard for the principle of subsidiarity and to the Member States only when they are implementing Union law. They shall therefore respect the rights, observe the principles and promote the application thereof in accordance with their respective powers and respecting the limits of the powers of the Union as conferred on it in the treaties.[189] The Court of Justice held that in assessing national measures implementing EU law within the meaning of Article 51(1) of the Charter, 'it must be ascertained among

186. Lenaerts, Koen. 'The Role of the EU Charter in the Member States.' *The EU Charter of Fundamental Rights in the Member States*. Ed. Michal Bobek and Jeremias Adams-Prassl. Oxford: Hart Publishing, 2020. 19–36. EU Law in the Member States. *Bloomsbury Collections*,.http://dx.doi.org/10.5040/9781509940943.ch-001.
187. CJEU, Case C-492/18, judgment of 12 February 2019, ECLI:EU:C:2019:108, § 57, https://curia.europa.eu/juris/liste.jsf?language=en&td=ALL&num=C-492/18%20PPU; *see also* CJEU, Case C-524/15, judgment of 20 March 2018, Menci, ECLI:EU:C:2018:19, https://curia.europa.eu/juris/liste.jsf?language=en&num=C-524/15.
188. Art. 5(2) TEU: '2. Under the principle of conferral, the Union shall act only within the limits of the competences conferred upon it by the Member States in the treaties to attain the objectives set out therein. Competences not conferred upon the Union in the treaties remain with the Member States.'
189. CJEU, Case C-617/10, judgment of 26 February 2013, Akerberg Fransson, ECLI: EU:C:2013:105, § 21, https://curia.europa.eu/juris/documents.jsf?language=EN&critereEcli=ECLI:EU:C:2013:105.

other things whether the national legislation at issue is intended to implement a provision of (Union) law, what the character of that legislation is, and whether it pursues objectives other than those covered by (Union) law, even if it is capable of indirectly affecting that law, and also whether there are specific rules of Union law on the matter or capable of affecting it'.[190]

152. The Court of Justice recognised, albeit implicitly, that some provisions of the Charter may produce horizontal direct effect. The Court stated that no conclusion may be drawn from the fact that Article 51(1) of the Charter does not mention individuals among its addressees.[191] The fact that certain provisions of primary law are addressed principally to the Member States does not preclude their application to relations between individuals. The EU system of fundamental rights protection is an internal component of the rule of law within the EU. As such, that system benefits from the special features of EU law that include the principle of primacy and the principle of direct effect.[192]

III. Articles 7 and 8 CFR in the Case Law of the Court of Justice of the EU

153. Secondary legislation enacted by the Commission, the Council and the European Parliament can be annulled by the CJEU if it is not in line with the European Charter.[193] This has happened to Directive 2006/24/EC ('the Data Retention Directive') which required communications providers to retain large amounts of metadata – including information sufficient to trace and identify the source and destination of a communication, and regarding the date, time and type of communications –though not the actual content of communications. The Directive was found to constitute an unjustified interference with Articles 7 and 8 of the Charter. The Court considered that the Directive 'entails a wide-ranging and particularly serious interference with the fundamental rights to the respect for private life and to the protection of personal data, without that interference being limited to what is strictly necessary'.[194]

190. *Ibid.*, § 79.
191. CJEU, Case C-570/16, judgment of 6 November 2018, Bauer and Willmeroth, ECLI:EU:C:2018:871, §88, https://curia.europa.eu/juris/liste.jsf?num=C-569/16&language=en; also CJEU, Case C-684/16, judgment of 6 November 2018, Max-Planck-Gesellschaft zur Förderung der Wissenschaften, ECLI: EU:C:2018:874, https://eur-lex.europa.eu/legal-content/en/TXT/?uri=CELEX:62016CJ0684.
192. Koen Lenaerts, *supra*; pp. 32–35.
193. CJEU, Joined Cases C-446/12 to C-449/12, Judgment of 16 April 2015, Willems and Others, ECLI:EU:C:2015:238, para. 49, https://eur-lex.europa.eu/legal-content/EN/TXT/?uri=CELEX%3A62012CJ0446: 'Next, as regards Articles 7 and 8 of the Charter, it is clear from the case law of the Court that the fundamental rights guaranteed by the Charter must be respected where national legislation falls within the scope of EU law. In other words, the applicability of EU law entails the applicability of the fundamental rights guaranteed by the Charter'.
194. CJEU, Case C-293/12, judgment of 8 April 2014, Digital Rights Ireland, ECLI:EU:C:2014:238, https://eur-lex.europa.eu/legal-content/EN/TXT/?uri=CELEX%3A62012CJ0293.

154. Two preliminary references were made to the CJEU as a result of the annulment of the Data Retention Directive. The first, *Tele2 Sverige,* concerned a refusal by a Swedish communications provider to fulfil its obligations under the Swedish legislation that implemented the Data Retention Directive. When that refusal was challenged by the Swedish authorities, Tele2 brought proceedings in the administrative court. The referring Court asked the CJEU whether indiscriminate retention of electronic communications data is 'per se incompatible' with the Charter.[195] The CJEU observed that the Directive 2002/58/EC ('the e-Privacy Directive') 'to ensure full respect for the rights set out in Articles 7 and 8 of the Charter' and decided that the Directive, read in the light of Articles 7 and 8 of the Charter of Fundamental Rights must be interpreted as precluding national legislation which, for the purpose of fighting crime, provides for general and indiscriminate retention of all traffic and location data of all subscribers and registered users relating to all means of electronic communication. The Court also judged that the same provisions must be interpreted as precluding national legislation governing the protection and security of traffic and location data and, in particular, access of the competent national authorities to the retained data, where the objective pursued by that access, in the context of fighting crime, is not restricted solely to fighting serious crime, where access is not subject to prior review by a Court or an independent administrative authority, and where there is no requirement that the data concerned should be retained within the European Union.[196]

155. The second reference concerned the UK's Data Retention and Investigatory Powers Act 2014 ('DRIPA'). Under Section 1 of the DRIPA, the Secretary of State had power to require communication providers to retain unlimited metadata for one of a number of specified public policy purposes. The Court of Appeal referred two questions to the CJEU. The first asked whether the decision in *Digital Rights Ireland* laid down mandatory requirements of EU law; the second asked whether the CFR provided any greater level of rights protection in this regard than the European Convention on Human Rights. The CJEU held that national legislation providing for general and indiscriminate data retention is incompatible with Directive 2002/, as read in light of the CFR. The Court also took the opportunity provided by the English Court of Appeal to compare the CFR with the ECHR. The CJEU observed that Article 7 of the CFR 'has no equivalent in the ECHR' and that Union law is not precluded from 'providing protection that is more extensive than the ECHR'. It thereby reaffirmed the autonomy of EU fundamental rights law. The EUCJ agreed with the UK High Court that domestic law for data retention had to be implemented within the scope of the Union Law.[197]

156. The CJEU issued an opinion on the draft agreement between Canada and the European Union regarding the transfer of Passenger Name Record data from the

195. CJEU, Joined Cases C-203/15 and C-698/15, judgment of 21 December 2016, Tele2 Sverige AB, ECLI:EU:C:2016:970, https://eur-lex.europa.eu/legal-content/en/ALL/?uri=CELEX:62015CJ0203.
196. *Ibid.*, § 134.
197. CJEU, Case C-203/15, judgment of 21 December 2016, Tele2 Sverige, ECLI:EU:C:2016:970, https://eur-lex.europa.eu/legal-content/en/ALL/?uri=CELEX:62015CJ0203.

European Union to Canada. The CJEU considered the EU's draft passenger name records agreement with Canada to inadequately protect the rights laid down in arts 7 and 8 CFR. Reiterating the requirement under EU law that '*the high level of protection of fundamental rights and freedoms conferred by EU law continues where personal data is transferred from the European Union to a non-member country*', the CJEU stipulated a number of requirements relating to the processing, storage and use of personal data by the non-Member State. The Court emphasised that, as regards Article 7 of the Charter, it has held that the fundamental right to respect for private life, enshrined in that article, means that the person concerned may be certain that his personal data are processed in a correct and lawful manner. In order to carry out the necessary checks, that person must have a right of access to the data relating to him which is being processed.[198]

157. In the Google v. Spain case, the CJEU extended Articles 7 and 8 of the Charter to include a 'right to be forgotten'. The Court by considering Internet search engines to be data processors under Directive 95/46,45 the CJEU enabled individuals to invoke Charter rights against a private operator. The Court ruled that: '*the operator of a search engine is obliged to remove from the list of results displayed following a search made on the basis of a person's name links to web pages, published by third parties and containing information relating to that person, also in a case where that name or information is not erased beforehand or simultaneously from those web pages, and even, as the case may be, when its publication in itself on those pages is lawful*'. This duty exists where a data subject requests the removal of a link from the list of results following a balancing exercise 'having regard to all the circumstances of the case … the information and links concerned in the list of results must be erased'.[199]

158. In the (first) Schrems case, the CJEU invalidated Commission Decision 2000/520/EC the 'Safe Harbour arrangement'), which governed data transfers between the EU and the US. The Court estimated that '(the US) legislation permitting the public authorities to have access on a generalised basis to the content of electronic communications must be regarded as compromising the essence of the fundamental right to respect for private life, as guaranteed by Article 7 of the Charter.' The Court also judged that 'legislation not providing for any possibility for an individual to pursue legal remedies in order to have access to personal data relating to him, or to obtain the rectification or erasure of such data, does not respect the essence of the fundamental right to effective judicial protection, as enshrined in Article 47 of the Charter'. The first paragraph of Article 47 of the Charter requires everyone whose rights and freedoms guaranteed by the law of the European Union are violated of the right to an effective remedy before a tribunal in compliance with

---

198. CJEU, Opinion of the Court (Grand Chamber) of 26 July 2017, § 219, with reference to CJEU, Case C-553/07, judgment of 7 May 2009, Rijkeboer, ECLI:EU:C:2009:293, § 49, https://curia.europa.eu/juris/liste.jsf?num=C-553/07&language=en.

199. CJEU, Case C-131/12, judgment of 13 May 2014, *Google Spain SL v. Agencia Espanola de Proteccion de Datos (AEPD)),* ECLI:EU:C:2014:317, https://eur-lex.europa.eu/legal-content/EN/TXT/?uri=CELEX%3A62012CJ0131.

the conditions laid down in that article. The very existence of effective judicial review designed to ensure compliance with provisions of EU law is inherent in the existence of the rule of law.[200]

159. In the 'Schrems II' case, the Court of Justice examined Commission Decision 2016/1250 the objective of which was to replace the invalidated 'Safe Harbour' decision. The Court held that the requirements laid down by the GDPR concerning appropriate safeguards, enforceable rights and effective legal remedies must be interpreted as meaning that data subjects whose personal data are transferred to a third country pursuant to standard data protection clauses must be afforded a level of protection essentially equivalent to that guaranteed within the EU by the GDPR, read in the light of the Charter. The Court considered that the validity of that decision is not called into question by the mere fact that the standard data protection clauses in that decision do not, given that they are contractual in nature, bind the authorities of the third country to which data may be transferred. However, that validity, the Court adds, depends on whether the decision includes effective mechanisms that make it possible, in practice, to ensure compliance with the level of protection required by EU law and that transfers of personal data pursuant to such clauses are suspended or prohibited in the event of the breach of such clauses or it being impossible to honour them. The Court finds that Decision 2010/87 establishes such mechanisms. In that regard, the Court points out, in particular, that the decision imposes an obligation on a data exporter and the recipient of the data to verify, prior to any transfer, whether that level of protection is respected in the third country concerned and that the decision requires the recipient to inform the data exporter of any inability to comply with the standard data protection clauses, the latter then being, in turn, obliged to suspend the transfer of data and/or to terminate the contract with the former.[201]

§4. Electronic Communications Privacy

I. Background

160. Directive 2002/58/EC –'the e-Privacy Directive' – replaced Directive 97/66/EC – the Telecommunications Data Protection Directive,[202] which was part

---

200. CJEU (Grand Chamber), Case C-362/14, Judgment of 6 October 2015, Maximillian Schrems v. Data Protection Commissioner (Request for a preliminary ruling from the High Court, Ireland), ECLI:EU:C:2015:650, https://eur-lex.europa.eu/legal-content/EN/TXT/?uri=CELEX%3A62014CJ 0362.
201. CJEU, Case C-311/18, Judgment of 16 July 2020, Data Protection Commissioner v. Facebook Ireland and Maximillian Schrems. (Request for a preliminary ruling from the High Court, Ireland), ECLI:EU:C:2020:559, https://eur-lex.europa.eu/legal-content/EN/TXT/?uri=CELEX%3A62018CJ 0311.
202. Directive 97/66/EC of the European Parliament and the Council of 15 December 1997 concerning the processing of personal data and the protection of privacy in the telecommunications sector ('Telecommunications Data Protection Directive') [1997] OJ L24/01 (30.01.1998).

of the 1998 telecommunications regulatory package.[203] The latter Directive focused on 'the protection of personal data and privacy in the telecommunications networks, in particular with regard to the introduction of the Integrated Services Digital Network (ISDN)'.[204] Soon after its adoption, it became obvious that the European telecommunications regulatory framework would rapidly become obsolete given the wide range of 'new services which [had] become available and affordable for a large audience'.[205] It was therefore repealed and replaced in 2002 by the e-Privacy Directive, which wished to adapt the provision of the Telecommunications Data Protection Directive 'to developments in the markets and technologies for electronic communications services in order to provide an equal level of protection of personal data and privacy for users of publicly available electronic communications services, regardless of the technologies used'.[206]

161. The EU Regulatory Framework on electronic communications services and networks adopted in 2002 was amended in 2009 by two new directives, the Citizens' Rights Directive[207] and the Better Regulation Directive.[208] These directives aimed at the attainment of better regulation for competitive electronic communications in the European Union, the completion of the single market in electronic communications and a better connection with European citizens.[209] With regard to the notification of personal data breaches, Commission Regulation (EU) No 611/2013 of 24 June 2013 issued technical implementing measures setting forth the circumstances, formats and procedures applicable to the information and notification requirements referred to in Article 4(3) of the revised e-Privacy Directive. These measures entered into force on 25 August 2013.

---

203. For a more comprehensive analysis of the developments in the telecommunications sector that led to its full liberalisation in 1998 *see*: LAROUCHE, P., The Bases of EC Telecommunications Law after Liberalization, Hart Publishing, Oxford 2000.
204. Recital 6 of Directive 97/66/EC.
205. Communication from the Commission to the Council, the European Parliament, the Economic and Social Committee and the Committee of the Regions: Towards a new framework for Electronic Communications infrastructure and associated services – The 1999 Communications Review' COM(1999) 539 final, 10 November 1999, p. 45.
206. Recital 4 of the e-Privacy Directive.
207. Directive 2009/136/EC amending Directive 2002/22/EC on universal service and users' rights relating to electronic communications networks and services, Directive 2002/58/EC concerning the processing of personal data and the protection of privacy in the electronic communications sector and Regulation (EC) No 2006/2004 on cooperation between national authorities responsible for the enforcement of consumer protection laws ('Citizens' Rights Directive') [2009] OJ L337/11 (18.12.2009).
208. Directive 2009/140/EC amending Directives 2002/21/EC on a common regulatory framework for electronic communications networks and services, 2002/19/EC on access to, and interconnection of, electronic communications networks and associated facilities, and 2002/20/EC on the authorisation of electronic communications networks and services ('Better Regulation Directive') [2009] OJ L337/37 (18.12.2009).
209. Communication from the Commission to the European Parliament, the Council, the European Economic and Social Committee and the Committee of the Regions – Report on the outcome of the Review of the EU regulatory framework for electronic communications networks and services in accordance with Directive 2002/21/EC and Summary of the 2007 Reform Proposals' (2007) COM(2007) 696 final, 13(1)1.2007, pp. 3–4.

II. Relation to the GDPR

162. As stated in Article 1(2), the e-Privacy Directive *particularises* and *complements* the European legal framework on the processing and free movement of personal data in the Union. In other words, for privacy and data protection aspects that have not explicitly been dealt with in the e-Privacy Directive, remains fully applicable.[210] Article 95 of the GDPR on its side states that 'this regulation shall not impose additional obligations on natural or legal persons in relation to processing in connection with the provision of publicly available electronic communications services in public communication networks in the Union in relation to matters for which they are subject to specific obligations with the same objective set out in Directive 2002/58/EC'

163. The collection and processing of personal data in an electronic communications environment will, consequently, always have to correspond to the principles set forth under the GDPR. For instance, the GDPR provides that the collected data shall be processed fairly and lawfully, shall only be collected for specified, explicit and legitimate purposes and may not be further processed in a way that is incompatible with those purposes. The personal data shall furthermore be adequate, relevant and not excessive in relation to the purposes for which they are collected and/or further processed. The data shall be accurate and, where necessary, kept up to date. The personal data shall be kept in a form which permits identification of data subjects for no longer than is necessary for the purposes for which the data were collected or for which they are further processed (Article 5 GDPR), and so on. These overall principles maintain their entire significance in an electronic communications environment.

164. In 2019 the European Data Protection Board published an opinion on the interplay between the e-Privacy Directive and the GDPR, in particular regarding the competence, tasks and powers of data protection authorities.[211] The EDPB stated that, when the processing of personal data triggers the material scope of both the GDPR and the e-Privacy Directive, data protection authorities are competent to scrutinise the data processing operations which are governed by national e-Privacy rules only if national law confers this competence on them, and such scrutiny must happen within the supervisory powers assigned to the authority by the national law transposing the e-Privacy Directive.

---

210. Recital 10 e-Privacy Directive clarifies exactly this point: 'In the electronic communications sector, Directive 95/46/EC applies in particular to all matters concerning protection of fundamental rights and freedoms, which are not specifically covered by the provisions of this Directive, including the obligations on the controller and the rights of individuals. Directive 95/46/EC applies to non-public communications services.'

211. EDPB, Opinion 5/2019 of 12 March 2019 on the interplay between the e-Privacy Directive and the GDPR, in particular regarding the competence, tasks and powers of data protection authorities, https://edpb.europa.eu/our-work-tools/our-documents/opinion-board-art-64/opinion-52019-interplay-between-eprivacy_en.

165. An infringement of the GDPR might also constitute an infringement of national e-Privacy rules. The data protection authority may take this factual finding as to an infringement of e-Privacy rules into consideration when applying the GDPR (e.g., when assessing compliance with the lawfulness or fairness principle under article 5(1)a GDPR). However, any enforcement decision must be justified on the basis of the GDPR, unless the data protection authority has been granted additional competences by Member State law.[212]

166. The cooperation and consistency mechanisms available to data protection authorities under Chapter VII of the GDPR, concern the monitoring of the application of GDPR provisions do not apply to the enforcement of the national implementation of the e-Privacy Directive. The cooperation and consistency mechanism remains fully applicable, however, insofar as the processing is subject to the general provisions of the GDPR (and not to a 'special rule' contained in the e-Privacy Directive).[213]

III. The Proposal for an e-Privacy Regulation

167. The Commission announced already in the Communication accompanying the GDPR proposal of 2012 that the substantive legal consequences of the new Regulation for the e-Privacy Directive would be the object, in due course, of a review by the Commission, taking into account the result of the negotiations on the current proposals with the European Parliament and the Council.[214] A proposal for a regulation on the respect for private life and the protection of personal data in electronic communications (proposal for e-Privacy Regulation) was published on 10 January 2017.[215] The report of the Civil Liberties Committee (LIBE) of the European Parliament was adopted it in October 2017. The EDPB published a critical statement on the proposal[216]

168. In the Council, the discussions on the proposed e-Privacy Regulation were stalled for approximately four years. The Council published several redrafts of the proposal since September 2017 but the Austrian, Romanian, Finnish and Croatian presidencies were unable to reach a compromise. In July 2020, the German Presidency published its first discussion paper. National delegations rejected a revised version of the paper and on 23 November 2020 the German Presidency presented

212. *Ibid.*, p. 24.
213. *Ibid.*, p. 25.
214. http://eur-lex.europa.eu/LexUriServ/LexUriServ.do?uri=COM:2012:0009:FIN:EN:PDF, p. 4, footnote 15.
215. Proposal for a Regulation of the European Parliament and the Council concerning the respect for private life and the protection of personal data in electronic communications and repealing Directive 2002/58/EC (Regulation on Privacy and Electronic Communications), COM/2017/010 final.
216. EDPB in Statement on the revision of the e-Privacy Regulation, adopted on 25 May 2018, available at: https://edpb.europa.eu/system/files/2021-03/edpb_statement_032021_eprivacy_regulation_en_0.pdf.

its progress report, stating it would 'closely [work] with the forthcoming Portuguese Presidency to facilitate further discussions and to ensure smooth progress on the file'. The initiative was given utmost priority in the Joint Declaration of the European Parliament, the Council and the European Commission from 17 December 2020. On 5 January 2021, the Portuguese Presidency released a new draft version of the proposed e-Privacy Regulation. On 10 February 2021, the Member States agreed on a mandate for negotiations with the European Parliament.[217]

169. The main changes proposed by the Commission include the following:

– Privacy rules will also apply to market players providing electronic communications services such as WhatsApp, Facebook Messenger and Skype. This will ensure that these services guarantee the same level of confidentiality of communications as traditional operators.
– Contrary to a directive, a regulation is directly applicable and will provide to all people and businesses in the EU the same level of protection of their electronic communications..
– Protection will be guaranteed not only for communications content but also for metadata. Metadata — data that describes other data, such as author, date created and location— must be anonymised or deleted if users did not give their consent, unless the data is needed for billing.
– Once consent is given for communications data to be processed, traditional telecoms operators will have more opportunities to provide additional services. For example, they could produce heat maps indicating the presence of individuals.
– The cookie provision, which has resulted in an overload of consent requests for internet users, will be streamlined. The new rule would be more user-friendly as browser settings will provide an easy way to accept or refuse tracking cookies and other identifiers. The proposal also clarifies that no consent is needed for non-privacy intrusive cookies that improve internet experience, such as cookies to remember shopping-cart history or to count the number of website visitors.
– The European Commission's proposal bans unsolicited electronic communications by e-mail, SMS and automated calling machines. Depending on national law people will either be protected by default or be able to use a do-not-call list to stop marketing phone calls. Marketing callers will need to display their phone number or use a special prefix that indicates a marketing call.
– The enforcement of the confidentiality rules in the draft regulation is the responsibility of data protection authorities, already in charge of supervision and enforcement under the GDPR.

IV. Scope of the Current e-Privacy Directive

170. The e-Privacy Directive applies, according to the wording of its Article 3, 'to the processing of personal data in connection with the provision of publicly

217. EDPB, Statement 03/2021 on the e-Privacy Regulation, adopted on 9 March 2021, available at https://edpb.europa.eu/sites/edpb/files/files/file1/edpb_statement_on_eprivacy_en.pdf.

available electronic communications services in public communications networks in the Community, including public communications networks supporting data collection and identification devices'.[218] Therefore, in order to decide on the applicability of the e-Privacy Directive the following four questions must be answered in the affirmative:

(i) whether there is an electronic communications service?
(ii) whether this service is offered in an electronic communications network?
(iii) whether the aforementioned service and network are public? and
(iv) whether the network or service is provided in the Community?

171. The e-Privacy Directive defines the term '*communication*' in Article 2(d):'Communication' means any information exchanged or conveyed between a finite number of parties by means of a publicly available electronic communications service. This does not include any information conveyed as part of a broadcasting service to the public over an electronic communications network except to the extent that the information can be related to the identifiable subscriber or user receiving the information. The definition of communication clarifies that there needs to be information exchanged or conveyed between a *finite* number of parties. Information, which is part of a broadcasting service for the public and is provided over a public communications network is intended for a potentially unlimited audience, and therefore does not constitute a communication in the sense of the e-Privacy Directive.[219]

172. Consequently linear radio and television services offered via analogue terrestrial networks are not covered by the e-Privacy Directive, as they are broadcasting services, which are intended for a potentially unlimited audience. It is however clarified that when the individual subscriber or user who is receiving information that is part of a broadcasting service, as described above, can be identified, the information conveyed is covered by the e-Privacy Directive[220]. Thus, the concept of broadcasting which is intended for a potentially unlimited audience covers point to multipoint transmissions, such as near- video-on-demand services,[221] which are

---

218. Art. 3 e-Privacy Directive. This provision, on the services that are covered by the e-Privacy Directive, was amended during the 2009 review of the electronic communications legal framework via the Citizens' Rights Directive. The new Art. 3 of the e-Privacy Directive clarified that 'public communications networks supporting data collection and identification devices' are included under the scope of the e-Privacy Directive. Devices for data collection and identification can be contactless devices using radio frequencies, such as Radio Frequency Identification ('RFID') devices, which use radio frequencies to capture data from uniquely identified tags, which can then be transferred over existing communications networks. When such devices are connected to publicly available electronic communications networks or make use of electronic communications services as a basic infrastructure, the relevant provisions of the e-Privacy Directive apply, including those on data security, traffic and location data and on confidentiality.
219. Recital 16 of the 2002 e-Privacy Directive.
220. Recital 16 of the 2002 e-Privacy Directive.
221. For an analysis of the concept of broadcasting and the difference between video-on-demand and near-video-on-demand *see*: the CJEU Case C-89/04, Judgment of 2 June 2005, Mediakabel, ECLI: EU:C:2005:348, https://curia.europa.eu/juris/liste.jsf?language=en&num=C-89/04.

excluded from the scope of application of the e-Privacy Directive. Only when broadcasting is offered under a point-to-point scheme, such as in the case of video-on-demand services, does the Directive apply.[222]

173. In order for the e-Privacy Directive to apply, the processing of personal data has further to take place in connection with an **electronic communications service**. The term 'electronic communications service' is defined in Article 2(c) of the Framework Directive[223] as:

> […] a service normally provided for remuneration which consists wholly or mainly in the conveyance of signals on electronic communications networks, including telecommunications services and transmission services in networks used for broadcasting, but exclude services providing, or exercising editorial control over, content transmitted using electronic communications networks and services; it does not include information society services, as defined in Article 1 of Directive 98/34/EC, which do not consist wholly or mainly in the conveyance of signals on electronic communications networks.

174. An electronic communications service is a service within the meaning of Article 56 TFEU),[224] which guarantees the free movement of services. According to Article 57 TFEU in order for a service to be considered as one under the meaning of the treaties it should be normally provided for remuneration and it should, among others, be of a commercial nature.[225]

175. An electronic communications service is thus normally **provided for remuneration**, which should be interpreted with a broad meaning. The Court of Justice of the European Union has dealt with the concept of remuneration in the context of services offered within the European Union in various cases. In *Belgium v. Humbel* the Court considered that 'the essential characteristic of remuneration

---

222. Recital 16 of the 2002 e-Privacy Directive. *See also*: Asscher, L. F. and Hoogcarspel, S.A., *Regulating Spam: A European perspective after the adoption of the E-Privacy Directive* (Information Technology & Law Series, TMC Asser Press, The Hague 2006), p. 34.
223. European Parliament and the Council of the European Union, Directive 2002/21/EC of 7 March 2002 on a common regulatory framework for electronic communications networks and services ('Framework Directive') [2002] OJ L108/33 (24.04.2002). The Framework Directive contains the basic rules for the establishment of a harmonised framework for the regulation of electronic communications services and electronic communications networks. It also contains many of the definitions that need to be taken into account for the implementation of the e-Privacy Directive, such as the fundamental definitions of 'electronic communications service', 'electronic communications network', 'public communications network' or 'provision of an electronic communications network'.
224. Treaty on the functioning of the European Union, modified by the Treaty of Lisbon: Treaty of Lisbon amending the Treaty on European Union and the Treaty establishing the European Community, signed at Lisbon, 13 December 2007 [2007] OJ C306/1 (17.12.2007).
225. Art. 57 TFEU: '[…] 'Services' within the meaning of the treaties shall in particular include (a) activities of an industrial character; (b) activities of a commercial character; (c) activities of craftsmen; (d) activities of the professions'.

[…] lies in the fact that it constitutes consideration for the service in question'.[226] It is not the recipient who necessarily gives the remuneration; the critical element is that the remuneration is given to the provider of the service. In *Bond van Adverteerders v. Netherlands*, the Court of Justice confirmed that the remuneration does not need to come from the recipient of the service, i.e., the viewer; it suffices that the remuneration comes from another party, such as an advertiser.[227] The Court has ruled in various cases that a service can be considered as provided for remuneration even in cases when the provider is a non-profit organisation, when there is an 'element of chance' inherent in the return or when the service is of recreational or sporting nature, within this interpretation.[228] Therefore, an activity that gets profit via advertising can also be considered as provided for remuneration, even if remuneration does not come directly from the user.[229]

176. Not considered as 'electronic communications services' according to Article 2(c) of the Framework Directive are 'services providing, or exercising editorial control over, content transmitted using electronic communications networks and services; **it does not include information society services**, as defined in Article 1 of Directive 98/34/EC, which do not consist wholly or mainly in the conveyance of signals on electronic communications networks'.

177. The e-Privacy Directive presupposes the existence of an **electronic communications network**. The term 'electronic communications network' is defined in Article 2(a) of the Framework Directive as a set of systems, equipment, as well as active and passive elements permitting the transmission of signals, regardless of the content that these signals carry.[230] The definition of an electronic communications network, as amended by the Better Regulation Directive (2009/140/EC) reads as follows:

> 'Electronic communications network' means transmission systems and, where applicable, switching or routing equipment and other resources, including network elements which are not active, which permit the conveyance of signals by wire, radio, optical or other electromagnetic means, including satellite networks, fixed (circuit- and packet-switched, including Internet) and mobile terrestrial networks, electricity cable systems, to the extent that they are used for

226. CJEU, Case C-263/86, Judgment of 27 September 1988, *Belgium v. Humbel*, ECLI:EU:C:1988:451, 17, https://curia.europa.eu/juris/liste.jsf?language=en&jur=C,T,F&num=C-263/86&td=ALL.

227. CJEU, Case C-352/85, Judgment of 26 April 1988, *Bond van Adverteerders v. Netherlands*, ECLI:EU:C:1988:196, https://curia.europa.eu/juris/liste.jsf?language=en&num=C-352/85.

228. *See* for instance: CJEU, Case C-70/95 Judgment of 17 June 1997, *Sodemare*, ECLI:EU:C:1997:301, https://curia.europa.eu/juris/liste.jsf?language=en&num=C-70/95.

229. Queck, R. et al., 'The EU Regulatory Framework Applicable to Electronic Communications' in Garzaniti, L. and O'Regan, M. (eds), *Telecommunications, Broadcasting and the Internet - EU Competition Law & Regulation* (3rd edn, Sweet & Maxwell, London, 2010), para. 1-047.

230. Queck, Robert et al., 'The EU Regulatory Framework Applicable to Electronic Communications' in Garzaniti, Laurent and O'Regan, Matthew (eds), *Telecommunications, Broadcasting and the Internet - EU Competition Law & Regulation* (3rd edn, Sweet & Maxwell, London, 2010), para. 1-045.

the purpose of transmitting signals, networks used for radio and television broadcasting, and cable television networks, irrespective of the type of information conveyed.[231]

178. The Framework Directive defines also the term 'provision of an electronic communications network' under Article 2(m). The definition clarifies that the term 'provision of a network' shall be perceived in a broad way. 'Provision of an electronic communications network' means the establishment, operation, control or making available of such a network.[232]

179. The-e-Privacy Directive applies to **publicly available electronic communications services in public communications networks**. In order to apply the e-Privacy Directive, it is neither sufficient to have an electronic communications service, nor an electronic communications network involved. Both the relevant service and the network need to be public (or publicly available as is the term usually used in connection with electronic communications services). The Citizens Rights' Directive introduced a new recital, which clarified that the e-Privacy Directive does **not apply to closed user groups and corporate networks**:

> In line with the objectives of the regulatory framework for electronic communications networks and services and with the principles of proportionality and subsidiarity, and for the purposes of legal certainty and efficiency for European businesses and national regulatory authorities alike, Directive 2002/58/EC (Directive on privacy and electronic communications) focuses on public electronic communications networks and services, and does not apply to closed user groups and corporate networks.[233]

The Framework Directive provides a definition of the term 'public communications network'[234] – a definition also amended during the review of the regulatory framework on electronic communications.[235] 'Public communications network' means 'an electronic communications network used wholly or mainly for the provision of electronic communications services available to the public which support the transfer of information between network termination points'.

V. Territorial Application

180. Article 3 of the Directive states that the network or service needs to be provided 'in the Community' but in contrast to the Data Protection Directive, the

231. Art. 2(a) Framework Directive.
232. Art. 2(m) Framework Directive.
233. Recital 55 Citizens' Rights Directive.
234. Art. 2(d) Framework Directive.
235. The old definition of public communications network (Art. 2(d) 2002 Framework Directive) did not make any reference to Network Termination Points: 'Public communications network' means an electronic communications network used wholly or mainly for the provision of publicly available electronic communications services.

e-Privacy Directive does not contain an explicit provision with regard to the applicable national law. Article 4 of the Data Protection Directive states, for example, that 'each Member State shall apply the national provisions it adopts pursuant to this Directive to the processing of personal data where the processing is carried out in the context of the activities of an establishment of the controller on the territory of the Member State'.

181. In the absence of such an explicit provision with regard to the question of the applicable national law, the e-Privacy Directive follows the same logic as the other directives belonging to the European regulatory framework for electronic communications.[236] According to that logic, each National Regulatory Authority (NRA) is in charge of the regulation of the market players active on its national territory. General authorisations granted for those market players according to Directive 2002/20/EC (the Authorisation Directive) may be made subject to personal data and privacy protection specific to the electronic communications sector in conformity with Directive 2002/58/EC.[237] If Member States are competent to control the application of the provisions of the e-Privacy Directive before granting authorisations to network and service providers providing services on their territory, these provisions are evidently applicable to all providers operating on that territory. We therefore conclude that the rules of Article 4 of Directive 95/46/EC with regard to the geographical scope of the general data protection legal framework, are not applicable to the provisions of the e-Privacy Directive.

182. Consequently national provisions of a Member State transposing the e-Privacy Directive will be applicable to network and service providers operating on the territory of that Member State. As a result, the e-Privacy Directive is also applicable to network and service providers not established in the European Union, as long as they are providing networks and/or services on the territory of the Union.

VI. Security Breach Notification

183. Pursuant to Article 4.1 of the e-Privacy Directive, the provider of a publicly available electronic communications service must take appropriate technical and organisational measures to safeguard security of its services, if necessary in conjunction with the provider of the public communications network with respect to network security. Having regard to the state of the art and the cost of their implementation, these measures shall ensure a level of security appropriate to the risk presented.

184. In case of a particular risk of a breach of the security of the network, the provider of a publicly available electronic communications service must inform the subscribers concerning such risk and, where the risk lies outside the scope of the

236. According to the Authorisation Directive, this is the place where the services are provided.
237. *See* the Annex to the Authorisation Directive, A, nrs 7 and 16.

measures to be taken by the service provider, of any possible remedies, including an indication of the likely costs involved.[238]

185. ENISA, the European Network and Security Agency, issued proposals for the technical implementation of a security breach notification in the context of the e-Privacy Directive,[239] as well as a methodology for the assessment of the severity level of such breaches.[240]

VII. Confidentiality of Communications

186. Article 5.1 of the e-Privacy Directive relates to interception or surveillance of communications and related traffic data when they involve a public communications network and publicly available electronic communications services and is formulated as follows:

> 1. Member States shall ensure the confidentiality of communications and the related traffic data by means of a public communications network and publicly available electronic communications services, through national legislation. In particular, they shall prohibit listening, tapping, storage or other kinds of interception or surveillance of communications and the related traffic data by persons other than users, without the consent of the users concerned, except when legally authorised to do so in accordance with Article 15.1. This paragraph shall not prevent technical storage which is necessary for the conveyance of a communication without prejudice to the principle of confidentiality.[241]

187. The scope of this provision is clearly limited to communications and related traffic data 'by means of a public communications network'. However, as emphasised in Recital (10) 'in the electronic communications sector, the GDPR applies in particular to all matters concerning protection of fundamental rights and freedoms, which are not specifically covered by the provisions of this Directive, including the obligations on the controller and the rights of individuals. The GDPR applies, in other words, to non-public communications services'.

---

238. Barcelo R., Traung P. (2010) The Emerging European Union Security Breach Legal Framework: The 2002/58 e-Privacy Directive and Beyond. In: Gutwirth S., Poullet Y., De Hert P. (eds) *Data Protection in a Profiled World*. Springer, Dordrecht. https://doi.org/10.1007/978-90-481-8865-9_5; *see also*: Samson Esayas, Breach Notification Requirements under the European Union Legal Framework: Convergence, Conflicts, and Complexity in Compliance, 31 J. *Marshall J. Info. Tech. & Privacy L.* [i] (2014–2015).
239. ENISA, Recommendations for technical implementation of Art. 4, https://www.enisa.europa.eu/publications/art4_tech.
240. ENISA, Recommendations for a methodology of the assessment of severity of personal data breaches, https://www.enisa.europa.eu/publications/dbn-severity.
241. Art. 5.1 e-Privacy Directive.

188. Actions that enable the interception or surveillance of communications are thus allowed when the users concerned have given their consent.[242] Recital 17 of the e-Privacy Directive specifies that, 'for the purposes of this Directive, consent of a user or subscriber, regardless of whether the latter is a natural or a legal person, should have the same meaning as the data subject's consent as defined and further specified in Directive 95/46/EC. Consent may be given by any appropriate method enabling a freely given specific and informed indication of the user's wishes, including by ticking a box when visiting an Internet website'.

189. In the Privacy International judgment, the CJEU estimated that 'the prohibition on the interception of communications and data relating thereto laid down in Article 5(1) of Directive 2002/58 therefore encompasses any instance of providers of electronic communications services making traffic data and location data available to public authorities, such as the security and intelligence agencies, as well as the retention of that data by those authorities, regardless of how that data is subsequently used'. It finally concluded that Article 5(1) 'must be interpreted as precluding national legislation enabling a State authority to require providers of electronic communications services to carry out the general and indiscriminate transmission of traffic data and location data to the security and intelligence agencies for the purpose of safeguarding national security'.[243]

190. According to Article 5.2 of the Directive, communications may also be recorded, when legally authorised, if this is carried out in the course of a lawful business practice for the purpose of providing evidence of a commercial transaction or any other business communication.[244] This would, for example, cover the recording of a call made to a business call centre, provided that the user is made aware of the recording and its purpose and has a right to refuse the recording. Recital (23) specifies that 'confidentiality of communications should also be ensured in the course of lawful business practice. Where necessary and legally authorised, communications can be recorded for the purpose of providing evidence of a commercial transaction. Directive 95/46/EC applies to such processing. Parties to the communications should be informed prior to the recording about the recording, its purpose and the duration of its storage. The recorded communication should be erased as soon as possible and in any case at the latest by the end of the period during which the transaction can be lawfully challenged'.

191. Article 5.2 thus provides for an exception to the confidentiality of communications and the related traffic data in the context of lawful business practice. The provision allows for the recording of communications, if and when such recording is necessary and legally authorised (Recital 23), in order to provide evidence of a

242. CJEU, Joined Cases C-511/18, C-512/18 and C-520/18, Judgment of 6 October 2020, La Quadrature du Net and Others, ECLI:EU:C:2020:791, https://eur-lex.europa.eu/legal-content/en/TXT/?uri=CELEX:62018CJ0511.

243. CJEU, Case C-623/17, Judgment of 6 October 2020, Privacy International, ECLI:EU:C:2020:790, 82, https://eur-lex.europa.eu/legal-content/en/TXT/?uri=CELEX:62017CJ0623.

244. Art. 5.2 e-Privacy Directive.

commercial transaction or of any other business transaction. The issue with this particular provision is directly related with the scope ascribed to it in the national transpositions. In principle, the provisions of the e-Privacy Directive are meant to regulate the processing of personal data in a specific sector, i.e., the electronic communications sector. This follows directly from the scope-setting provision in Article 3 of the e-Privacy Directive, as well as the scope of the whole regulatory framework for electronic communications of which the e-Privacy Directive is an important part.

192. Exceptions to the prohibition of breaching confidentiality of communications may be included in national legislation for safeguarding national security, defence or public security and for the prevention, investigation, detection and prosecution of criminal offences or of unauthorised use of the telecommunications system. In these circumstances, data may be retained for a limited period.[245] Last but not least, there is a general exception for 'technical storage which is necessary for the conveyance of a communication without prejudice to the principle of confidentiality'.[246]

VIII. Cookies and Similar Techniques

193. Article 5.3 of the e-Privacy Directive reads as follows: 'Member States shall ensure that the storing of information, or the gaining of access to information already stored, in the terminal equipment of a subscriber or user is only allowed on condition that the subscriber or user concerned has given his or her consent, having been provided with clear and comprehensive information, in accordance with Directive 95/46/EC, inter alia, about the purposes of the processing. This shall not prevent any technical storage or access for the sole purpose of carrying out the transmission of a communication over an electronic communications network, or as strictly necessary in order for the provider of an information society service explicitly requested by the subscriber or user to provide the service.'[247]

A. *Scope of Application*

194. Recital 24 of the e-Privacy Directive, which refers to Article 5.3, clarifies that the '[t]erminal equipment of users of electronic communications networks and any information stored on such equipment are part of the private sphere of the users requiring protection under the European Convention for the Protection of Human Rights and Fundamental Freedoms'.[248] The recital refers to *any information* that is stored on the terminal equipment of a user and not only to information that qualifies as personal data, stressing that any such information is part of the private sphere of

245. Art. 15.1 e-Privacy Directive.
246. Art. 5.1 e-Privacy Directive.
247. Art. 5.3 e-Privacy Directive.
248. Recital 24 e-Privacy Directive.

the user and deserves protection. This supports the argument that the reference to information in Article 5.3 is intentional and aims at extending the scope of this provision not only to cases when the storing of information or the gaining of access to information entails personal data, but in all cases when any kind of information is involved.[249] The Article 29 Working Party confirmed this approach and took the position that as Article 5.3 of the e-Privacy Directive does not qualify the types of information, it 'is not a prerequisite for the application of this provision [i.e., Article 5.3] that this information is personal data within the meaning of Directive 95/46/EC'.[250]

195. The Article 29 Working Party in its opinion on online behavioural advertising dealt with the interpretation of the new Article 5.3 of the e-Privacy Directive and took the position that the changes introduced in this provision 'clarify and reinforce the need for users' informed prior consent', reaching a different conclusion to the position of the aforementioned thirteen Member States. The Article 29 Working Party broke down the new requirement in Article 5.3 to two clear conditions, which, when fulfilled, can legitimate the storing of information or the gaining of access to information that is already stored in the terminal equipment of the subscriber: on the one hand, the subscriber or the user has to be provided with clear and comprehensive information in accordance with the Data Protection Directive about, inter alia, the purposes of the processing; on the other hand, the subscriber or the user has to give his consent to the storage of or the access to information that is stored in his terminal equipment, after having been provided with the aforementioned information. These two conditions apply cumulatively. The Article 29 Working Party paid special attention to the latter condition, relating to the consent of the user or the subscriber, and derived the following two requirements from the wording of Article 5.3: i) consent must be obtained *before* the cookie is placed and/or information stored in the user's terminal equipment is collected, which is usually referred to as prior consent and ii) informed consent can only be obtained if prior information about the sending and purposes of the cookie *has been given to the user.*[251]

196. In the Planet49 judgment of 1 October 2019, the CJEU held that Art. 5.3 of the e-Privacy Directive is not to be interpreted differently according to whether or not the information stored or accessed on a website user's terminal equipment is personal data.[252]

249. DEBUSSERÉ, Frederic, 'The EU E-Privacy Directive: A monstrous attempt to starve the cookie monster?' (2005) 13 International Journal of Law and Information Technology, pp. 84–85.
250. Art. 29 Working Party, 'Opinion 2/2010 on online behavioural advertising, WP171' (2010), p. 9.
251. Art. 29 Working Party, 'Opinion 2/2010 on online behavioural advertising, WP 171' (2010), p. 13.
252. CJEU, Case C-673/17, Judgment of 1 October 2019, Planet49 GmbH, ECLI:EU:C:2019:801, https://eur-lex.europa.eu/legal-content/EN/TXT/?uri=CELEX%3A62017CJ0673.

B. Exceptions from the Consent Requirement

197. The storing of information or the gaining of access to information that is already stored in the terminal equipment of the subscriber or the user is allowed in two exceptional cases: (1) for the technical storage of or access to information for the sole purpose of carrying out the transmission of a communication over an electronic communications network and (2) for the provision of an information society service that is explicitly requested by the subscriber or the user, when the storing of or the access to information is strictly necessary for the provider.[253]

198. Neither the recitals of the 2002 e-Privacy Directive, nor those of the Citizens' Rights Directive provide any specificity in relation to these exceptions. The former exception can be seen as allowing the use of mere session cookies.[254] The latter relates to the provision of information society services that are explicitly requested by the subscriber or the user and when the storage of or the access to information is *strictly necessary* in order for the provider of the service to provide it.

It may seem strange that Article 5.3 of the e-Privacy Directive contains a specific information requirement, which would at first seem to overlap with the information requirement of the data controller, as specified by the GDPR. However, the scope of Article 5.3 covers not only personal data, but any kind of information and therefore the inclusion of the information requirement in Article 5.3 renders it obligatory, even when no processing of personal data is taking place.[255] The Article 29 Working Party has specified the information that should be provided to the users with regard to the installation and use of cookies:

> the user should be informed when a cookie is intended to be received, stored or sent […]. The message should specify, in generally understandable language, which information is intended to be stored in the cookie, for what purpose as well as the period of validity of the cookie.[256]

199. The information that has to be provided to the user or the subscriber before obtaining their consent should comply with Article 10 of the Data Protection Directive. More specifically, the user or the subscriber should be informed about the identity of the entity that wishes to store information or gain access to information that is already stored in his terminal equipment and about the purposes of the processing. Moreover, he should be provided with any information relating to the recipients or categories of recipients of the data, whether replies to the questions are obligatory or voluntary, as well as the possible consequences of failure to reply, and

253. Art. 5.3 e-Privacy Directive, last sentence.
254. Debusseré, Frederic, 'The EU E-Privacy Directive: A monstrous attempt to starve the cookie monster?' (2005) 13 International Journal of Law and Information Technology, p. 92.
255. Debusseré, Frederic, 'The EU E-Privacy Directive: A monstrous attempt to starve the cookie monster?' (2005) 13 International Journal of Law and Information Technology, p. 88.
256. Art. 29 Working Party, 'Recommendation 1/99 on Invisible and Automatic Processing of Personal Data on the Internet Performed by Software and Hardware, WP17' (1999), p. 3.

the existence of their right of access, the right to rectify the data concerning him and the right to refuse the storing of or the access to their information.

200. In the context of cookies and similar devices, the information on whether replies to the questions are obligatory or voluntary and on the possible consequences of failure to reply can be interpreted as information 'about whether allowing a cookie to be placed is required or not to visit the website or make use of its service and about the consequences of not allowing a cookie to be placed'.[257] Recital 25 of the 2002 e-Privacy Directive specified that the access to specific website content may be made conditional on the acceptance of a cookie or similar device after the user is provided with clear and comprehensive information, if the cookie is used for a legitimate purpose.[258] This means that a website or service provider can restrict access to the users, if they do not agree to accept cookies. The Article 29 Working Party criticised such an approach, finding that it can be contradictory to the position that the users should have the possibility to refuse the storage of a cookie on their personal computers. It therefore noted that this provision may need to be clarified or revised.[259] However, the Citizens' Rights Directive, which amended the e-Privacy Directive in 2009, did not provide any additional clarification on this point.

201. Given the modalities of the Internet and the lack of personal communication between the entity that wishes to instal and use cookies or similar devices and the user, the concept of giving this information 'in a clear and comprehensive way' is problematic. Does the provision of the information in the general terms and conditions or in the privacy policy of a service suffice for it to be considered as given 'in a clear and comprehensive way'? Recital 66 of the Citizens' Rights Directive, requires that the 'methods of providing information […] should be as user-friendly as possible'.[260]

202. Usually, the information requested by Article 5.3 is provided in the general terms and conditions or in the privacy policy of the providers' websites. However, the Article 29 Working Party considers information provided in this manner to be 'hidden' to the user and proposes that certain key information should be presented on the screen of the user in an interactive way, so that it is clearly spotted by the

---

257. DEBUSSERÉ, Frederic, 'The EU E-Privacy Directive: A monstrous attempt to starve the cookie monster?' (2005) 13 International Journal of Law and Information Technology, p. 87.
258. Recital 25 2002 e-Privacy Directive.
259. Art. 29 Working Party, 'Opinion 8/2006 on the review of the regulatory Framework for Electronic Communications and Services, with focus on the e-Privacy Directive, WP126' (2006), p. 3.
260. Recital 66 Citizens' Rights Directive. This Recital in fact repeats Recital 25 of the 2002 e-Privacy Directive, which stated that 'The methods for giving information, offering a right to refuse or requesting consent should be made as user-friendly as possible.' It is worth noting that Recital 25 of the 2002 e-Privacy Directive refers to the methods for offering a right to refuse or requesting consent, although Art. 5.3 of the 2002 e-Privacy Directive referred only to the right to refuse, while Recital 66 of the Citizens' Rights Directive refers only to the methods offering a right to refuse, although the amended Art. 5.3 of the e-Privacy Directive refers to the obtaining of the consent of the user or the subscriber.

user; the rest in layers. To this end, the Article 29 Working Party welcomes creativity in new ways of presenting the information to the user that would go beyond the current practices of pop-up windows.[261]

203. In the Planet49 case, the CJEU decided that Article 5(3) of Directive 2002/58, as amended by Directive 2009/136, must be interpreted as meaning 1) 'that the consent referred to in those provisions is not validly constituted if, in the form of cookies, the storage of information or access to information already stored in a website user's terminal equipment is permitted by way of a pre-checked checkbox which the user must deselect to refuse his or her consent', and 2) 'that the information that the service provider must give to a website user includes the duration of the operation of cookies and whether or not third parties may have access to those cookies'.[262]

IX. Processing of Traffic and Location Data

A. *Traffic Data*

204. Traffic data are 'any data processed for the purpose of the conveyance of a communication on an electronic communications network or for the billing thereof'.[263] They may include any translation of naming, numbering or addressing information by the network over which it is transmitted for the purpose of carrying out the transmission. The 2002 e-Privacy Directive specified that:

> [t]raffic data may, inter alia, consist of data referring to the routing, duration, time or volume of a communication, to the protocol used, to the location of the terminal equipment of the sender or recipient, to the network on which the communication originates or terminates, to the beginning, end or duration of a connection. They may also consist of the format in which the communication is conveyed by the network.[264]

205. Traffic data relating to subscribers and users that are processed and stored by a provider of a public communications network or service must, subject to certain exceptions, be erased or made anonymous when they are no longer needed for the purpose of the transmission of a communication.[265] However, certain data collected for the billing of subscribers and for interconnection payments may be processed up to the end of the period during which the bill may lawfully be challenged or payment may be pursued.[266] The processing of stored traffic data must respect

261. Art. 29 Working Party, 'Opinion 2/2010 on online behavioural advertising, WP171' (2010), p. 18.
262. CJEU, Case C-673/17, Judgment of 1 October 2019, Planet49 GmbH, ECLI:EU:C:2019:801, https://eur-lex.europa.eu/legal-content/EN/TXT/?uri=CELEX%3A62017CJ0673.
263. Art. 2(b) e-Privacy Directive.
264. Recital 15 2002 e-Privacy Directive.
265. Art. 6(1) e-Privacy Directive.
266. Art. 6.2 e-Privacy Directive. *See also* CJEU, Case C-119/12, Judgment of 22 November 2012, Josef Probst, ECLI:EU:C:2012:748, https://eur-lex.europa.eu/legal-content/en/TXT/?uri=CELEX:62012

the principle of proportionality in relation to the processed data. Therefore, the processing of data must be limited to processing the necessary data and must be adequate, relevant and not excessive in relation to the purposes of billing and making interconnection payments.[267] Although the e-Privacy Directive does not specify any time period in which traffic data may be lawfully stored, the Article 29 Working Party has indicated that a reasonable interpretation is that data may be stored for billing purposes for a maximum of three to six months, except if there is a dispute, in which case the data may be processed for a longer period.[268]

206. In derogation from Article 6 of the e-Privacy Directive, traffic data can be exceptionally retained for a limited period based on a specific legislative measure taken by the Member States. Such retention is only allowed when it *constitutes a necessary, appropriate and proportionate measure within a democratic society to safeguard national security (i.e., State security), defence, public security, and the prevention, investigation, detection and prosecution of criminal offences or of unauthorised use of the electronic communications.*[269]

207. Providers of publicly available electronic communications services may also process traffic data for the purpose of marketing electronic communications services, as well as for the provision of value-added services,[270] to the extent and for the duration that this is necessary for such services. This is allowed, provided that the subscriber or the user to whom the data relate has given his prior consent, which may be withdrawn at any time.[271] Compared to the Data Protection Directive, the specific provision of Article 6.3 of the e-Privacy Directive, by referring only to the prior consent of the subscriber or the user, imposes stricter rules for the processing of traffic data for the purpose of marketing electronic communications services, or for the provision of value-added services in the electronic communications sector.

CJ0119: 'Article 6(2) and (5) of Directive 2002/58/EC must be interpreted as authorizing a provider of public communications networks and of publicly accessible electronic communications services to pass traffic data to the assignee of its claims for payment in respect of the supply of telecommunications services for the purpose of recovery of those claims, and as authorising that assignee to process those data on condition, first, that the latter acts under the authority of the service provider as regards the processing of those data and, second, that that assignee confines itself to processing the traffic data necessary for the purposes of recovering the claims assigned. Irrespective of the classification of the contract of assignment, the assignee is deemed to act under the authority of the service provider, within the meaning of Article 6(5) of Directive 2002/58, where, for the processing of traffic data, it acts exclusively on the instructions and under the control of that provider. In particular, the contract concluded between them must contain provisions capable of guaranteeing the lawful processing, by the assignee, of the traffic data and of enabling the service provider to ensure, at all times, that that assignee is complying with those provisions.'

267. Art. 29 Working Party, 'Opinion 1/2003 on the storage of traffic data for billing purposes, WP69' (2003), p. 6.
268. Art. 29 Working Party, 'Opinion 1/2003 on the storage of traffic data for billing purposes, WP69' (2003), p. 7.
269. Art. 15.1 e-Privacy Directive.
270. Art. 2(g) e-Privacy Directive defines 'value-added service' as 'any service which requires the processing of traffic data or location data other than traffic data beyond what is necessary for the transmission of a communication or the billing thereof'.
271. Art. 6.3 e-Privacy Directive.

In practice it means that traffic data, unlike other categories of personal data, cannot be processed for direct marketing purposes on the basis of Article 6(1)(f) of the GDPR.

208. Whenever processing of traffic data takes place for the purposes of subscriber billing and interconnection payments, the service provider must inform the subscriber or thevalue-a user of both the types of traffic data that are being processed and the duration of the processing. When the processing of traffic data takes place for the marketing of electronic communications services of the provider or for the provision of value-added services, then the service provider has to provide the aforementioned information prior to obtaining the consent. The processing of traffic data must be restricted to persons acting under the authority of the public electronic communications network and service providers and be limited to what is necessary for the purposes of billing or traffic management, customer inquiries, fraud detection, marketing electronic communications services or providing value-added services.[272]

B. Location Data

1. Definition

209. 'Location data' means 'any data processed in an electronic communications network or by an electronic communications service, indicating the geographic position of the terminal equipment of a user of a publicly available electronic communications service'.[273] The term covers not only data that are processed in an electronic communications network, but also data processed by an electronic communications service.[274] Location data may, thus, refer to the geographic coordinates of the terminal equipment of a user, i.e., its latitude, longitude and altitude, to the identification of the network cell in which the terminal equipment is located at a given time, to the level of accuracy of the information that is related to the location of the user, as well as to the time this information was recorded.[275]

210. The concept of location data is closely related to the one of traffic data, which is defined as 'any data processed for the purpose of the conveyance of a communication on an electronic communications network or for the billing thereof'.[276] Traffic data refer, among others, to the location of the terminal equipment at the

---

272. Art. 6.5 e-Privacy Directive.
273. Art. 2(c) e-Privacy Directive.
274. Common Position (EC) No 16/2009 adopted by the Council on 16 February 2009 with a view to the adoption of a Directive 2009/ … /EC of the European Parliament and of the Council of … amending Directive 2002/22/EC on universal service and users' rights relating to electronic communications networks, Directive 2002/58/EC concerning the processing of personal data and the protection of privacy in the electronic communications sector and Regulation (EC) No 2006/2004 on consumer protection cooperation protection laws [2009] OJ (05.05.2009), C103 E/40.
275. Recital 14 2002 e-Privacy Directive.
276. Art. 2(b) e-Privacy Directive.

beginning and at the end of a communication[277] and therefore some traffic data are also location data. Similarly, location data that are processed for the purpose of the conveyance of an electronic communications network are also traffic data and should be processed in accordance with Article 6 of the e-Privacy Directive.

2. Location Data Other Than Traffic Data

211. Besides the location data that qualify also as traffic data and have to be processed in accordance with Article 6 of the e-Privacy Directive, there are location data that are 'not processed for the purpose of the conveyance of a communication on an electronic communications network or for the billing thereof'.[278] These data are referred to in the e-Privacy Directive as 'location data other than traffic data' and are processed for the provision of value-added services[279] that are based on the location of the user. Such value-added services are commonly known as location-based services and cover for instance services that provide the users with traffic information or offer guidance to drivers,[280] direct marketing services based on the location data of users and tracking services for children or for elderly people.

212. Within the protective ambit of Article 9 of the e-Privacy Directive, location data other than traffic data relating to users or subscribers of public communications networks or publicly available electronic communications services that are used for the provision of a location-based service, may be processed only when they are made *anonymous*, or when the users or subscribers have given their *consent* to the provision of such a location based service.[281] In any case, the location data may only be used to the extent and for the duration necessary for the provision of the value-added service.[282] The users and the subscribers should be given the opportunity to withdraw their consent for the processing of the location data at any time.[283] The withdrawal will be valid for the future.

213. The e-Privacy Directive explicitly requires that the service provider must, before obtaining the consent, provide the individual with specific information regarding the type of location data that will be processed, of the purposes and the duration of the processing and whether the data will be transmitted to a third party

277. Recital 15.
278. Art. 2(b) e-Privacy Directive.
279. Value-added services are defined in Art. 2(g) of the e-Privacy Directive as 'any service which requires the processing of traffic data or location data other than traffic data beyond what is necessary for the transmission of a communication or the billing thereof'.
280. Recital 35 2002 e-Privacy Directive.
281. Art. 9(1) e-Privacy Directive. A high-level description of the European framework on location-based services can be found at Hladik, Jorg, 'Location Based Services: European data protection rules for mobile commerce' (2009) 8 Privacy and Security Law Report, p. 24 ff.
282. Art. 9(1) e-Privacy Directive.
283. Art. 9(1) e-Privacy Directive.

for the purpose of providing the location based service.[284] To the extent that location data are also personal data, the general information obligations that are foreseen in the Data Protection Directive are also applicable.

214. A location-based service, falling under the scope of Article 9 of the e-Privacy Directive, can either be provided directly by the electronic communications operator, or there may be third parties, besides the electronic communications operator, involved, who provide the service based on location information that they obtain from the operator. However, only one of the parties involved in the provision of the location-based service should be responsible for offering the information relating to the processing of location data to the user or the subscriber: the one that determines the means and the purposes for the processing of the data and qualifies as data controller. In practice, this will be the party that is collecting the location data for processing, which in principle will be the provider of the location-based service. When this party does not have a direct contact with the user or the subscriber, the information should be provided by the electronic communications operator.

215. The information can be provided in various ways. It can for instance be provided every time the service is used, or in the general terms and conditions for the location-based service. In the latter case the service provider should make the information available so that the individuals concerned can consult it at any time and easily, such as via visiting a dedicated website or while using the service, by dialling, for instance, a toll-free number. It is debatable whether the information can be given in the general contract terms of the contract that is concluded between the subscriber and the operator, if it is clearly highlighted as relating to the provision of the location-based service.

216. The e-Privacy Directive requires the consent of the users or the subscribers for the processing of these data. Recital 35 of the Directive states that '[t]he processing of [location data other than traffic] data for value-added services should only be allowed where subscribers have given their consent'.[285] In many cases the subscriber to the service is also the user of the terminal equipment, for instance of the mobile device. In these cases no real practical difficulty arises, as the two roles, those of the user and the subscriber, coincide in one natural person. When both a user and a subscriber are involved in the processing of location data and these two attributes are allocated to different persons, questions arise as to whose consent needs to be obtained. The decision:

> [w]hether the consent to be obtained for the processing of personal data with a view to providing a particular value added service should be that of the user or of the subscriber, will depend on the data to be processed and on the type of

284. Art. 9(1) e-Privacy Directive.
285. Recital 35 2002 e-Privacy Directive.

service to be provided and on whether it is technically, procedurally and contractually possible to distinguish the individual using an electronic communications service from the legal or natural person having subscribed to it.[286]

217. In an attempt to shed light on the issue of whether it should be the user or the subscriber to offer his consent, the Article 29 Working Party has taken the position that when a location-based service is offered to 'private individuals, consent must be obtained from the person to whom the data refer, i.e., the user of the terminal equipment'.[287] Although this suggestion can be used as a general rule, when applying Article 9 of the e-Privacy Directive,[288] there are cases when the simple application of the aforementioned rule may be inefficient. The examples of localisation of minors and of employees for the provision of a value-added service are representative of situations when the user and the subscriber can be different natural persons and will therefore be discussed below.

218. The consent can be given in the general terms and conditions for the location-based service, in order to avoid the nuisance of consenting to each transmission of data for the purpose of providing the same value-added service.[289] However, the Article 29 Working Party has taken the position that the consent for the processing of the location data other than traffic data for the provision of the location-based service cannot be given as part of accepting the general terms and conditions for the electronic communications service that is offered.[290]

219. When the automatic localisation of the individual is required for the provision of a location-based service, the initiation of the process by the individual would amount to consenting to being located, provided that he is fully provided with the aforementioned information relating to the processing of his location data.[291] For instance when an individual can dial a specific number or send an SMS to a dedicated number in order to get information on the weather conditions at his location, then the dialling of the number or the sending of the SMS should be considered as consent to the processing of his location data.[292]

220. The users and the subscribers should also be offered the choice to temporarily refuse the processing of their location data for each connection to the network

---

286. Recital 31 2002 e-Privacy Directive.
287. Art. 29 Working Party, 'Opinion on the use of location data with a view to providing value-added services, WP115' (2005), p. 7.
288. The same is valid for Art. 6 of the e-Privacy Directive.
289. ECKHARDT, Jens, 'Zehnter Teil. Telekommunikationsgesetz (TKG)' in SPINDLER, Gerald and SCHUSTER, Fabian (eds), *Recht der elektronischen Medien* (Verlag C.H. Beck, München 2008), §98, para. 12; OHLENBURG, Anna, 'Der neue Telekommunikationsdatenschutz – Eine Darstellung von Teil 7 Abschnitt 2 TKG' [2004] Multimedia und Recht (MMR), p. 436.
290. Art. 29 Working Party, 'Opinion on the use of location data with a view to providing value-added services, WP115' (2005), p. 5.
291. Art. 29 Working Party, 'Opinion on the use of location data with a view to providing value-added services, WP115' (2005), p. 6.
292. Art. 29 Working Party, 'Opinion on the use of location data with a view to providing value-added services, WP115' (2005), p. 6.

or for each transmission of a communication, using simple means and free of charge.[293] This can for instance be done via a switch on/off option of the terminal equipment. The processing of location data may be undertaken only by persons acting under the authority of the network operator, the service provider or the third party providing the value-added service and only for the purposes of providing the value-added service.[294] When the location-based service requires the localisation of the user on an ongoing basis, it suffices when the consent is provided once before the localisation takes place and after the individual concerned is duly informed about the details relating to it. In addition, the provider should send regularly reminders to the terminal equipment of the individual about the localisation.[295] However, the danger lurks that the use of the location-based service may become cumbersome in case the users are sent notifications too frequently.[296]

221. An exception to the general rule of obtaining the consent of the subscriber or the user for the processing of location data (other than traffic data) exists in relation to emergency calls. National organisations handling emergency calls that are recognised as such are entitled to override the temporary denial or absence of consent of a subscriber or a user on a per-line basis for the purpose of responding to such calls.[297] This provision reflects the Universal Service Directive[298], which requires public telephone network operators to make caller location information available to authorities handling emergencies, to the extent technically feasible, for all calls made to the single European emergency call number '112'.[299]

222. It has been pointed out by the Article 29 Working Party that, while the obligations relating to the processing of location data for the provision of value-added services covers only mobile operators (or electronic communications operators in general), the third parties that are involved in the provision of a value-added service on the basis of location data that they receive from the mobile operators are bound by the obligations arising from the Data Protection Directive.[300]

---

293. Art. 9.2 e-Privacy Directive.
294. Art. 9.3 e-Privacy Directive.
295. Art. 29 Working Party, 'Opinion on the use of location data with a view to providing value-added services, WP115' (2005), p. 7.
296. GADZHEVA, Maya, 'Privacy concerns pertaining to location-based services' [2007] International Journal of Intercultural Information Management (IJIIM), p. 53.
297. Art. 10(b) e-Privacy Directive. Specifying further the provision of Art. 10 of the e-Privacy Directive, the Commission adopted a recommendation on the handling of location information of the caller for the purpose of location-enhanced emergency call services; Commission Recommendation of 25 July 2003 on the processing of caller location information in electronic communication networks for the purpose of location-enhanced emergency call services (2003/558/EC) [2003] OJ L108/49 (29.07.2003).
298. Directive 2002/22/EC of 7 March 2002 on universal service and users' rights relating to electronic communications networks and services ('Universal Service Directive') [2002] OJ L108/51 (24.04.2002).
299. Art. 26 Universal Service Directive.
300. Art. 29 Working Party, 'Opinion on the use of location data with a view to providing value-added services, WP115' (2005), p. 4.

223. Although location data other than traffic data can be processed only for the duration necessary for the provision of the value-added service, they can exceptionally be retained for a limited period based on a specific legislative measure taken by the Member States. Such retention is only allowed when it 'constitutes a necessary, appropriate and proportionate measure within a democratic society to safeguard national security (i.e., State security), defence, public security, and the prevention, investigation, detection and prosecution of criminal offences or of unauthorised use of the electronic communications'.[301]

224. The provisions in Articles 6.1 and 9.1 of the e-Privacy Directive stipulate what the provider must do to be allowed to process traffic data or location data, especially in the event that the purpose of the legitimate processing no longer requires it. For traffic data the provider must erase the data or must make it anonymous when it is no longer needed for the purpose of transmission, unless he can invoke exceptions (e.g., billing, interconnection payments, or retention obligations) which in turn will have specific erasure/anonymisation requirements. Location data should only be processed anonymously, unless the user or subscriber consents to the processing. Processing should only be allowed for the legitimate purpose of service provision, after which the data need to be deleted. Again there are exceptions, such as the one in Article 15.1 e-Privacy Directive regarding their retention in national law.

X. Directories of Subscribers

225. Subscribers must be informed, free of charge and before they are included in the directory, about the purpose(s) of a printed or electronic directory of subscribers available to the public or obtainable through directory enquiry services, in which their personal data can be included and of any further usage possibilities based on search functions embedded in electronic versions of the directory.[302] They should, in addition, be given the opportunity to determine whether their personal data are included in a public directory, and if so, which, to the extent that such data are relevant for the purpose of the directory as determined by the provider of the directory, and to verify, correct or withdraw such data. Not being included in a public subscriber directory, verifying, correcting or withdrawing personal data from it shall be free of charge.[303]

301. Art. 15.1 e-Privacy Directive.
302. Art. 14.1 e-Privacy Directive ; *see also* Mark Crichard, Privacy and electronic communications, Computer Law & Security Review, Volume 19, Issue 4, July 2003, pp. 299–303.
303. Art. 14.2 e-Privacy Directive; The CJEU ruled that the concept of 'requests' in this context, covers also requests made by an undertaking, established in a Member State other than that in which the undertakings which assign telephone numbers to subscribers are established, which requests the relevant information possessed by those undertakings in order to provide publicly available telephone directory enquiry services and directories in that Member State and/or in other Member States. See CJEU, Case C-536/15, Judgment of 15 March 2017, Tele2 (Netherlands), ECLI:EU:C:2017:214, https://eur-lex.europa.eu/legal-content/en/TXT/?uri=CELEX:62015CJ0536.

226. The CJEU held that Article 12 must be interpreted as not precluding national legislation under which an undertaking publishing public directories must pass personal data in its possession relating to subscribers of other telephone service providers to a third-party undertaking whose activity consists in publishing a printed or electronic public directory or making such directories obtainable through directory enquiry services, and under which the passing on of those data is not conditional on renewed consent from the subscribers, provided, however, that those subscribers have been informed, before the first inclusion of their data in a public directory, of the purpose of that directory and of the fact that those data could be communicated to another telephone service provider and that it is guaranteed that those data will not, once passed on, be used for purposes other than those for which they were collected with a view to their first publication.[304]

227. The above-mentioned principles apply to subscribers who are natural persons. Member States must, however, also ensure that the legitimate interests of subscribers other than natural persons with regard to their entry in public directories are sufficiently protected.[305]

228. Member States may require that for any purpose of a public directory other than the search of contact details of persons on the basis of their name and, where necessary, a minimum of other identifiers, additional consent be asked of the subscribers.[306]

XI. Unsolicited Direct Marketing Communications

A. *The Baseline of Article 13(1)*

229. Article 13(1) of the e-Privacy Directive regulates the use of specific electronic means for direct marketing purposes, as follows:

> The use of automated calling and communication systems without human intervention (automatic calling machines), facsimile machines (fax) or electronic mail for the purposes of direct marketing may be allowed only in respect of subscribers or users who have given their prior consent.[307]

230. Similar to many other provisions of the e-Privacy Directive, confusion exists as to whether or not this provision is applicable to messages sent by means of information society services, in particular via so-called webmail or via social media platforms such as Facebook, Twitter, etc. One of the reasons for this confusion is the fact that neither the Article 29 Working Party nor the EDPS have ever issued a

304. CJEU, Case C-543/09, Judgment of 5 May 2011, Deutsche Telekom, ECLI:EU:C:2011:279, https://eur-lex.europa.eu/legal-content/en/TXT/?uri=CELEX:62009CJ0543.
305. Articlle 14.4 e-Privacy Directive.
306. Art. 14.3 e-Privacy Directive.
307. Art. 13(1) e-Privacy Directive.

clear opinion on this topic. Because the scope of application of the e-Privacy Directive specifies that its provisions apply to electronic communications services, the Article 29 Working Party concluded in an Opinion of 2004 that Article 13(1) applies exclusively to 'messages by electronic communications'.[308]

231. Following this interpretation the provision is not applicable to messages exchanged via information society services. This viewpoint is in line with the viewpoint of the Article 29 Working Party with regard to the scope of Article 9 of the Directive. In its Opinion 13/2011 dealing with geolocation services on smart mobile devices the Article 29 Working Party, referring to the definition of 'electronic communications service' in Article 2, c) of the Framework Directive, clearly stated that 'the e-Privacy Directive does not apply to the processing of location data by information society services, even when such processing is performed via a public electronic communication network' (p. 9). Also in more recent opinions the Article 29 Working Party seemed to confirm that Article 13(1), like all other provisions of the Directive, covers only these techniques which can be considered as electronic communications, with the exclusion of information society services.[309]

232. Alternately, there seems to be a consensus about the fact that Article 13(1) is applicable to *any entity* that sends unsolicited communications via electronic communications. Article 13(1) does not prohibit only unsolicited direct marketing messages sent by providers of electronic communications services but is applicable to anyone who sends unsolicited direct marketing messages via electronic communications.[310] Not only the Article 29 Working Party but also the EDPS have confirmed this viewpoint.[311] The fact that not only electronic communications service providers are submitted to the prohibition to use e-mail for direct marketing purposes without prior consent, but virtually anyone using electronic communications, does not however mean that Article 13(1) is applicable to messages exchanged via information society services.[312]

233. The above interpretation with regard to the scope of Article 13(1) should normally lead to the conclusion that prior consent of the user is not required for

308. Art. 29 Working Party, Opinion 5/2004 on unsolicited communications for marketing purposes under Art. 13 of Directive 2002/58/EC, p. 4.
309. Art. 29 Working Party, Opinion 1/2008 on data protection issues related to search engines, WP148' (2008), p. 12.
310. Opinion 1/2008, oc., p. 12: 'Search engines therefore fall outside of the scope of the definition of electronic communication services. A search engine provider can however offer an additional service that falls under the scope of an electronic communications service such as a publicly accessible e-mail service which would be subject to e-Privacy Directive 2002/58/EC and Data Retention Directive 2006/24/EC.'
311. EDPS, Second opinion on the review of Directive 2002/58/EC concerning the processing of personal data and the protection of privacy in the electronic communications sector (Directive on privacy and electronic communications), adopted on 9 January 2009 [2009] OJ C128/28 (06.06.2009), para. 27.
312. This confusion has led to a note of the Ombudsmen of Sweden, Denmark and Norway sent to the Commission in 2012 about individual Facebook messages. *See* http://www.pcworld.com/article/2016581/scandinavia-cracks-down-on-facebooks-unsolicitedads.html (last viewed on 7 August 2021).

direct marketing messages sent via a webmail platform or via social media. In practice, however, as we will further describe, the provision of Article 13(1) has received sometimes a broader interpretation including also 'webmail' exchanged via the websites of information society service providers. One can therefore only conclude that the interpretation on this aspect of the scope of Article 13(1) is currently very ambiguous.

234. Fortunately there is less uncertainty with regard other aspects related to the scope of this provision. Based on Recital 30 of the Data Protection Directive, the Article 29 Working Party came to the conclusion that the concept of direct marketing should cover 'any form of sales promotion, including direct marketing by charities and political organisations (e.g., fund raising, etc.)'.[313]

235. The e-Privacy Directive further refers to the 'use of automated calling and communication systems without human intervention (automatic calling machines), facsimile machines (fax) or electronic mail'.[314] The common characteristic of these methods is that they are relatively easy and cheap to send, while they may impose a burden or even a cost to the recipient. Besides the nuisance caused to the recipients, in cases when such unsolicited commercial communication is sent in bulk, it can also cause problems for both the electronic communications networks and the terminal equipment of the recipients.

B. Definition of 'Electronic Mail'

236. 'Electronic mail' is defined in the e-Privacy Directive as 'any text, voice, sound or image message sent over a public communications network which can be stored in the network or in the recipient's terminal equipment until it is collected by the recipient'.[315] The definition of electronic mail refers to a public communications network and therefore excludes any text, voice, sound or image that is sent over a private communications network or in any case over a network that is not public. Under the concept of electronic mail one should include also SMS, MMS and other similar applications.[316] Moreover it requires that the 'message' can be stored in the network or in the recipient's terminal equipment until it is collected by

---

313. Art. 29 Working Party, Opinion 5/2004 on unsolicited communications for marketing purposes under Article 13 of Directive 2002/58/EC, WP90' (2004), p. 7.
314. Recital 40 2002 e-Privacy Directive. The reference to automatic calling and communications systems clearly leaves direct marketing methods that involve in-person communication out of the scope of this provision, such as in the case of telemarketing.
315. Art. 2(h) e-Privacy Directive.
316. Recital 40 e-Privacy Directive and Recital 67 Citizens' Rights Directive. Increasing technological progress and the decreasing cost of transmitting messages enabled the spread of unsolicited communications in new ways, such as via fax, SMS or MMS. These developments were taken into account by European legislator during the drafting of the e-Privacy Directive (referring to fax and SMS) and were further expanded to cover MMS and 'any other kinds of similar applications' via the Citizens' Rights Directive.

the recipient. For instance, the definition covers messages left on answering machines, voice mail service systems and newsletters sent by e-mail.[317]

237. The definition of electronic mail excludes any message that requires the simultaneous participation of the sender and the recipient.[318] Moreover, if a message cannot be stored in the network or in the terminal equipment of the recipient, until it is collected by him, then this message does not fall under the scope of application of Article 13(1) of the e-Privacy Directive.

238. It may be questioned whether the scope of Article 13(1) is restricted to e-mail messages accessed by means of a dedicated e-mail client software program or includes also e-mail accessed via a webmail service.[217] One could argue that in both cases the messages are transmitted via an electronic communications network (the Internet) and an electronic communications service (provided by the ISP). On top of this the information society service provider puts a web application to facilitate the e-mail management for the end user.[319]

239. In the case of StWL (Städtische Werke Lauf) the Court of Justice dealt with the question whether the criteria governing the concept of 'electronic mail' are met when an advertising message is displayed at random between the listed e-mail messages at the moment a webmail user opens his/her inbox page. The advertising message, automatically sent from a server, is displayed in the user's e-mail inbox, namely in a space normally reserved for private e-mails. The user is only able to free that space in order to obtain a view of all of his or her exclusively private e-mails after having checked the content of that advertising message, and only after having actively deleted it. If the user clicks on an advertising message, he or she is redirected to an Internet site containing the advertising in question, rather than continuing with the reading of his or her private emails. The Court estimated that, if advertising entries of any kind are displayed in the inbox of an Internet e-mail account, namely in the section in which all of the e-mails addressed to the user are displayed, that e-mail inbox must be regarded as constituting a means by which the advertising messages concerned are communicated to that user, which involves the use of his or her e-mail for the purposes of direct marketing, within the meaning of Article 13(1) of Directive 2002/58. Proceeding in that manner constitutes a use of electronic mail, within the meaning of Article 13(1) of Directive 2002/58, likely to

317. Art. 29 Working Party, Opinion 5/2004 on unsolicited communications for marketing purposes under Article 13 of Directive 2002/58/EC, WP90' (2004), p. 4.

318. Art. 29 Working Party, Opinion 5/2004 on unsolicited communications for marketing purposes under Article 13 of Directive 2002/58/EC, WP90' (2004), p. 4.

319. The Art. 29 Working Party stated: 'A search engine provider can however offer an additional service that falls under the scope of an electronic communications service.

Therefore one could disagree with the opinion that Art. 13 does not apply as soon as the recipient makes use of an information society service to access her or his mailbox. Messages are nowadays exchanged via all kinds of online platforms, such as LinkedIn, Facebook or Twitter. Because they are sent over a public communications network and stored on the server of the platform provider – which is 'in the network' – one could argue that such messages have to be considered as e-mail following the definition of Art. 2(h) of the Directive.

breach the objective, pursued by that provision, of protecting users from any intrusion into their private life by unsolicited communications for the purposes of direct marketing.[320]

240. Article 13(1) is only applicable if e-mail is 'used for the purpose of direct marketing'. It is irrelevant whether the direct marketing message is part of the message body or attached in a separate document. However direct marketing should be the primary purpose. This is the reason why, for example, a newsletter or a magazine, sent as an attachment to a conventional e-mail will not fall under the scope of Article 13(1), as long as the newsletter or magazine is primarily sent for a different purpose, other than merely direct marketing.

C. Recipients of Unsolicited Communications

241. The Citizens' Rights Directive broadened the protective ambit of Article 13(1) of the e-Privacy Directive in order to cover not only subscribers, but also users. It should be reminded that the e-Privacy Directive defines users as 'any natural person using a publicly available electronic communications service, for private or business purposes, without necessarily having subscribed to this service'.

242. In contrast, the term subscriber is not defined in the e-Privacy Directive. Instead, the definition of subscriber contained in the Framework Directive is applicable, according to which a subscriber is 'any natural person or legal entity who or which is party to a contract with the provider of publicly available electronic communications services for the supply of such services'.[321] According to this definition, the basic prerequisite for somebody to be classified as a subscriber is that the person has a contract with a provider of a publicly available electronic communications service, who will then actually offer the service. It is specified that the subscribers under this provision are natural persons, while Member States can broaden its scope in order to cover legal persons as well, if this is required for the latter's legitimate interests to be sufficiently protected.

D. Consent

243. The use of the systems and techniques mentioned in Article 13(1) for direct marketing purposes is allowed only after the prior consent of the users and subscribers involved. The requirement for prior consent lays down a general 'opt-in' rule for the sending out of direct marketing messages via automatic calling systems,

320. CJEU, Case C-102/20, Judgment of 25 November 2021, StWL Städtische Werke Lauf, ECLI: EU:C:2021:954, https://eur-lex.europa.eu/legal-content/EN/TXT/?uri=CELEX%3A62020CJ0102.
321. Art. 2(k) Framework Directive.

fax, e-mail, SMS, MMS or any similar methods. Consent can be given by any appropriate method, as long as it corresponds to the definition of consent in the GDPR.[322]

244. A valid consent cannot be obtained via a general e-mail sent to prospective recipients of unsolicited communications for direct marketing, requesting their consent to receive such communications.[323] It goes without saying that arbitrary collection of e-mail addresses or other information that falls under the scope of Article 13(1) with automatic means that do not involve the consent of the person concerned, such as the automatic harvesting of personal data from public Internet places via software programs, and their use for unsolicited communications for direct marketing is not permitted.[324]

E. Exception for Existing Customer Relationship

245. The e-Privacy Directive provides for derogation from the consent requirement covering situations when there is an existing customer relation for the sending of unsolicited communications for direct marketing purposes:

> where a natural or legal person obtains from its customers their electronic contact details for electronic mail, in the context of the sale of a product or a service, in accordance with Directive 95/46/EC, the same natural or legal person may use these electronic contact details for direct marketing of its own similar products or services provided that customers clearly and distinctly are given the opportunity to object, free of charge and in an easy manner, to such use of electronic contact details at the time of their collection and on the occasion of each message in case the customer has not initially refused such use.[325]

246. If a person or a company receives electronic mail contact details from its own customers (whether they be natural or legal persons) in the context of the sale of a product or a service, then direct marketing for its own similar products or services is allowed unless the customer explicitly opts out. This exception is also

322. Art. 2(f) e-Privacy Directive specifies that the consent of the user or the subscriber in the frame of the e-Privacy Directive corresponds to the consent of the data subject, as defined in the Data protection Directive.
323. Art. 29 Working Party, Opinion 5/2004 on unsolicited communications for marketing purposes under Article 13 of Directive 2002/58/EC, WP90' (2004), p. 5.
324. ASSCHER, Lodewijk F. and HOOGCARSPEL, Sjo Anne, *Regulating Spam: A European perspective after the adoption of the E-Privacy Directive* (Information Technology & Law Series, TMC Asser Press, The Hague 2006, p. 69 ff. CHENG, Tania, 'Recent international attempts to can spam' (2004) 20 Computer Law and Security Report, p. 477, implies that address harvesting should not be allowed under the U.K. legislation. In any case, such harvesting of personal data is not allowed under the Data Protection Directive, as it does not respect the finality principle and it does not provide the individuals concerned with the information that is required under that Directive: Article 29 WP, Opinion 5/2004 on unsolicited communications for marketing purposes under Article 13 of Directive 2002/58/EC, WP90'(2004), p. 6.
325. Art. 13(2) e-Privacy Directive.

known as 'soft opt-in'.[326] The use of the term 'soft opt-in' is used due to the fact that the customer has already given his electronic mail contact details to the sender in the context of a customer relation. However the term can be criticised, as the customers are given the opportunity to object to receiving direct marketing communications and they do not express in any way their agreement to receive such communications.

247. The exception is applicable when the sender, who can be either a natural or a legal person, obtains from its customers their electronic contact details for electronic mail in the context of the sale of a product or a service. However, even when the aforementioned conditions are fulfilled, the sender who has obtained electronic contact details for electronic mail from its customers cannot use it as he wishes, but only within the clearly defined frame provided for in Article 13(2) of the e-Privacy Directive. The sender can use electronic contact details for electronic mail only for direct marketing of its own similar products and services and on the condition that the customer has already been provided with the option to object to such use at the time of the collection of his details, free of charge and in an easy way.

248. In case the customer has not initially refused such use at the time of collection of his electronic contact details, although he is given the right to object, he should be given this opportunity each time he receives a message. This provision establishes a right to object to the use of the electronic contact details of a customer, instead of the stricter requirement for prior consent, which is applicable when there is no existing customer relationship between the sender and the recipient of the message. Given that Article 13(2) requires a right to object and lays down an exception from the requirement for prior consent stipulated in the first paragraph, it should be carefully examined, as it lowers the standards for user protection.

249. The collection of the e-mail address or the mobile phone number of the customer has to be obtained in the context of a sale of a product or a service. How broad is the scope of this exception for existing customers? Does it only cover customers who have purchased a product or a service? Could somebody who expressed interest in a product be contacted based on this exception, without having given his prior consent, although he did not complete the transaction? The term 'sale' replaced the term 'purchase' that was included in an early draft version of Article 13(2) in the 2002 e-Privacy Directive.[327] The European Parliament considered that the use of the term 'sale' instead of 'purchase' would provide additional safeguards

326. *See* among others: DONOVAN, Colleen, 'Implementation of the e-Privacy Directive in the UK.Understanding the new rules' (2004) 20 Computer Law and Security Report, p. 128; 6.
327. The term 'purchase' was replaced by the term 'sale' during the Second Reading of the European Parliament: European Parliament, European Parliament legislative resolution on the Council common position for adopting a European Parliament and Council Directive concerning the processing of personal data and the protection of privacy in the electronic communications sector (15396/2/2001 – C5-0035/2002 2000/0189(COD)) [P5_TA(2002)0261] – Second reading [2003] OJ C187E/103 (07.08.2003), Art. 13(2).

to the protection of citizens. The new wording would prevent senders from claiming that 'although no sale took place, a consumer could be included under the 'opt-out' regime as they had expressed an interest in purchasing a product'.[328] Therefore, the exception should only cover customers who have completed a sale, while potential customers should be contacted after they have provided their prior consent, in accordance with Article 13(1).[329]

250. The limitation to send direct marketing messages only for their own similar products or services is challenging to interpret. On the one hand the Directive refers to the sender's 'own' similar products or services, while on the other it restricts the existing customer exception to 'similar' products or services. With regard to the reference to the sender's 'own' similar products or services, subsidiaries or mother companies should not be understood as the same company.[330] The term 'similar products or services' is difficult to specify and the relevant products or services should be examined on a case-by-case basis. In general, the issue whether the products or services are similar with the ones that established the customer relationship between the sender and the recipient, should be approached in an objective way, examining the reasonable expectations of the recipients and not focus on the perspective of the sender.

251. The customer should be given the opportunity to object at the time of collection of his e-mail address. In case he does not refuse the use of his contact details, he should be given this opportunity on the occasion of every message he is receiving. He should be offered the means to express his objection free of charge and in an easy manner, at least by using the same communication method. In the context of emails or Internet websites, the opportunity to object can be provided via an 'unsubscribe' option.[331] With regard to direct marketing sent via SMS, it has been rendered that it is sufficient for the recipient to send an SMS to a dedicated number in order to indicate his objection to receiving an SMS with direct marketing content.[237] Although the UK ICO initially required a postal or e-mail address to be provided for the exercise of the right to object, they accepted the use of short codes

328. MAGEE, John, 'The law regulating unsolicited commercial e-mail: an international perspective' (2003) 19 Santa Clara Computer & High Technology Law Journal, p. 372.

329. ASSCHER, Lodewijk F. and HOOGCARSPEL, Sjo Anne, *Regulating Spam: A European perspective after the adoption of the E-Privacy Directive* (Information Technology & Law Series, TMC Asser Press, The Hague 2006, p. 48.

330. 'Article 29 Working Party, Opinion 5/2004 on unsolicited communications for marketing purposes under Article 13 of Directive 2002/58/EC, WP90' (2004), p. 9; Federation of European Direct and Interactive Marketing (FEDMA), 'European Code of Practice for the use of personal data in direct marketing – Electronic Communications Annex' (2010).

331. JAY, Rosemary, *Data Protection Law and Practice* (3rd edn Sweet & Maxwell London 2007, paras 22–47. 237.

Art. 29 Working Party, 'Opinion 5/2004 on unsolicited communications for marketing purposes under Art. 13 of Directive 2002/58/EC, WP90' (2004), p. 6; UK INFORMATION COMMISSIONER'S OFFICE (ICO), 'Guidance for marketers on the Privacy and Electronic Communications (EC Directive) Regulations 2003, Part 1: Marketing by electronic means (v3.1/08.10.2007)', pp. 18–19; JAY, Rosemary, *Data Protection Law and Practice* (3rd edn Sweet & Maxwell London 2007, paras 22–47.

under the conditions that the sender is clearly identified in the message, that the use of the short code does not incur a premium rate charge and that the provided short code is valid.[332]

F. Unsolicited Communications Via Other Means

252. Unsolicited communications for direct marketing can of course be sent using other means than those mentioned in paragraph 1 of Article 13; telemarketing, for instance[333], which involves in-person communication and is therefore left outside the scope of Article 13(1). Such telemarketing calls can be made either to a fixed line or to a mobile phone number. The e-Privacy Directive does not leave these cases completely unregulated. It rather requires that such unsolicited communications for direct marketing are not allowed either (a) without the consent of the subscribers or users concerned or (b) in respect of subscribers or users who do not wish to receive these communications.[334] This rule applies to natural persons, but the Member States can expand its protection to also cover legal persons, so that their legitimate interests are sufficiently protected.[335]

253. The advancements of technology create new ways for delivering advertising messages, such as pop-up windows with advertising content. Soon after the adoption of the 2002 e-Privacy Directive, the Commission was confronted with the question whether direct marketing via pop-up windows has to rely on prior consent of the recipient. The Commission found that 'messages that depend on the addressee being online and that disappear when this is not the case, are not covered by the definition of electronic mail'.[336] Therefore they should be treated under Article 13(3) that leaves the choice for their regulation to the Member States.

254. The e-Privacy Directive leaves it up to the Member States to choose between either requiring the prior consent of the subscribers or the users on the one hand, or giving the opportunity to subscribers or users to express their wish not to receive such communications. In the example of telemarketing, besides the explicit objection of a user to a telemarketing call, the latter choice offered by the Directive can be realised via the establishment of preference lists and have to be consulted by the senders of unsolicited communications for direct marketing before they send it.

332. UK INFORMATION COMMISSIONER'S OFFICE (ICO), 'Guidance for marketers on the Privacy and Electronic Communications (EC Directive) Regulations 2003, Part 1: Marketing by electronic means (v3.1/08.10.2007)', pp. 18–19.
333. Recital 42 of the 2002 e-Privacy Directive refers to 'person-to-person voice telephony calls'.
334. Art. 13.3 e-Privacy Directive.
335. Art. 13.5 e-Privacy Directive.
336. EUROPEAN PARLIAMENT, Written questions with answers: E-3392/02 by Astrid THORS to the Commission / Subject: Unsolicited advertising in Windows, protection of personal data in telecommunications networks [2003] OJ C155E/148 (03.07.2003).

XII. Disguising or Concealing the Identity of the Sender

255. The practice of sending electronic mail for the purposes of direct marketing, which disguise or conceal the identity of the sender on whose behalf the communication is made, which do not fulfil the information requirements that are laid down in the e-Commerce Directive for information society services, which do not have a valid address to which the recipient may send a request that such communications cease, or finally which encourage recipients to visit malicious websites, is prohibited.[337]

256. The amendments introduced to the e-Privacy Directive during the 2009 review expanded the protection offered to consumers in the 2002 e-Privacy Directive, by ensuring protection not only against unsolicited commercial communications, but also against scam emails and links to phishing websites sent via e-mail. Crucial for the legitimacy of the electronic mail that is sent for direct marketing is that it complies with the informational requirements that are established in Article 6 of the e-Commerce Directive and that it does not encourage the recipients to visit websites that contravene these requirements. Article 6 specifies the information as follows:

> (a) the commercial communication shall be clearly identifiable as such; (b) the natural or legal person on whose behalf the commercial communication is made shall be clearly identifiable; (c) promotional offers, such as discounts, premiums and gifts, where permitted in the Member State where the service provider is established, shall be clearly identifiable as such, and the conditions which are to be met to qualify for them shall be easily accessible and be presented clearly and unambiguously; (d) promotional competitions or games, where permitted in the Member State where the service provider is established, shall be clearly identifiable as such, and the conditions for participation shall be easily accessible and be presented clearly and unambiguously'.

XIII. Article 13(6) of the Directive

257. Besides the expansion of Article 13 to scam emails and links to phishing websites, the 2009 review of the e-Privacy Directive introduced a right for any individual or legal person, affected by spam, as well as e-mail service providers and other service providers, to initiate legal action against spammers.[338]

258. The economic impact of unsolicited communications, especially the vast amount of messages sent via e-mail, is potentially immense. Therefore, the e-Privacy Directive, via Article 4, implicitly creates an obligation for electronic communications service providers to make investments in order to protect users against spam. Member States may also take specific measures against or impose

337. Art. 13.4 e-Privacy Directive.
338. Recital 68, Citizens' Rights Directive.

penalties on providers of electronic communications services, who by their negligence contribute to infringements of national legislation regulating unsolicited marketing communications.[339]

XIV. Restrictions

259. Pursuant to Article 15.1 of the e-Privacy Directive, Member States may adopt legislative measures to restrict the scope of the rights and obligations provided for in Article 5, Article 6, Article 8(1), (2), (3) and (4), and Article 9 of the e-Privacy Directive when such restriction constitutes a necessary, appropriate and proportionate measure within a democratic society to safeguard national security (i.e., State security), defence, public security, and the prevention, investigation, detection and prosecution of criminal offences or of unauthorised use of the electronic communication system.

A. Serious Crime or Serious Threats

260. The Court of justice held that Article 15.1 'must be interpreted as precluding national legislation that permits public authorities to have access to a set of traffic or location data, that are liable to provide information regarding the communications made by a user of a means of electronic communication or regarding the location of the terminal equipment which he or she uses and to allow precise conclusions to be drawn concerning his or her private life, for the purposes of the prevention, investigation, detection and prosecution of criminal offences, without such access being confined to procedures and proceedings to combat serious crime or prevent serious threats to public security, and that is so regardless of the length of the period in respect of which access to those data is sought and the quantity or nature of the data available in respect of such a period.'[340]

261. The Court further decided that Article 15.1, read in the light of Articles 7 and 8 of the Charter of Fundamental Rights of the European Union, must be interpreted as meaning that the access of public authorities to data for the purpose of identifying the owners of SIM cards activated with a stolen mobile telephone, such as the surnames, forenames and, if need be, addresses of the owners, entails interference with their fundamental rights, enshrined in those articles of the Charter of Fundamental Rights, which is not sufficiently serious to entail that access being limited, in the area of prevention, investigation, detection and prosecution of criminal offences, to the objective of fighting serious crime.[341]

---

339. Art. 13(6) e-Privacy Directive.
340. CJEU, Case C-746/18, Judgment of 2 March 2021, Prokuratuur, ECLI:EU:C:2021:152, https://eur-lex.europa.eu/legal-content/en/TXT/?uri=CELEX:62018CJ0746.
341. CJEU, Case C-207/16, Judgment of 2 October 2018, Ministerio Fiscal, ECLI:EU:C:2018:788, https://curia.europa.eu/juris/document/document.jsf?docid=206332&mode=req&pageIndex=1&dir=&occ=first&part=1&text=&doclang=EN&cid=1159753.

B. Effective Review

262. By contrast, the CJEU also decided that Article 15.1 of the e-Privacy Directive does not preclude legislative measures that: allow, for the purposes of safeguarding national security, recourse to an instruction requiring providers of electronic communications services to retain, generally and indiscriminately, traffic and location data in situations where the Member State concerned is confronted with a serious threat to national security that is shown to be genuine and present or foreseeable, where the decision imposing such an instruction is subject to effective review, either by a Court or by an independent administrative body whose decision is binding, the aim of that review being to verify that one of those situations exists and that the conditions and safeguards which must be laid down are observed, and where that instruction may be given only for a period that is limited in time to what is strictly necessary, but which may be extended if that threat persists.[342]

263. It is, according to the CJEU, also justified for Member States, for the same reasons, to have recourse to an instruction requiring providers of electronic communications services, by means of a decision of the competent authority that is subject to effective judicial review, or to undertake, for a specified period of time, the expedited retention of traffic and location data in the possession of those service providers, provided that those measures ensure, by means of clear and precise rules, that the retention of data at issue is subject to compliance with the applicable substantive and procedural conditions and that the persons concerned have effective safeguards against the risks of abuse.

264. In the case of *Commissioner of the Garda Síochána and Others,* the CJEU held that Article 15(1) of Directive 2002/58, read in the light of Articles 7, 8 and 11 and Article 52(1) of the Charter, must be interpreted as precluding national legislation which assigns to a police officer, whose rank is not below that of chief superintendent, the power to carry out the prior review of requests for access to data issued by the police investigation services and to request the providers of electronic communications services to transmit the data that they retain to those services. To the extent that that officer does not have the status of a third party in relation to those services, he or she does not fulfil the requirements for independence and impartiality recalled in paragraph 108 of this judgment, notwithstanding the fact that he or she is assisted in that duty by a police unit, which benefits from a certain degree of autonomy in the exercise of its duties.[343]

342. CJEU, Joined Cases C-511/18, C-512/18 and C-520/18, Judgment of 6 October 2020, La Quadrature du Net and Others, ECLI:EU:C:2020:791, https://eur-lex.europa.eu/legal-content/en/TXT/?uri=CELEX:62018CJ0511.

343. CJEU, Case C-140/20, Judgment of 5 April 2022, Commissioner of the Garda Síochána and Others, ECLI:EU:C:2022:258, paras 102–114, https://eur-lex.europa.eu/legal-content/EN/TXT/?uri=CELEX%3A62020CJ0140.

C. Limited in Time

265. In the same judgment the Court held that Member States may provide, for the purposes of safeguarding national security, combating serious crime and preventing serious threats to public security, for the targeted retention of traffic and location data which is limited, on the basis of objective and non-discriminatory factors, according to the categories of persons concerned or using a geographical criterion, for a period that is limited in time to what is strictly necessary, but which may be extended. They are also allowed to provide for the general and indiscriminate retention of IP addresses assigned to the source of an Internet connection for a period that is limited in time to what is strictly necessary or for the general and indiscriminate retention of data relating to the civil identity of users of electronic communications systems.

D. Reason to Suspect

266. Article 15(1) must, pursuant to the jurisprudence of the CJEU, further be interpreted as not precluding national rules which requires providers of electronic communications services to have recourse, first, to the automated analysis and real-time collection, inter alia, of traffic and location data and, second, to the real-time collection of technical data concerning the location of the terminal equipment used, where – recourse to the real-time collection of traffic and location data is limited to persons in respect of whom there is a valid reason to suspect that they are involved in one way or another in terrorist activities and is subject to a prior review carried out either by a Court or by an independent administrative body whose decision is binding in order to ensure that such real-time collection is authorised only within the limits of what is strictly necessary. In cases of duly justified urgency, the review must take place within a short time.

E. Refusal of Illegal Evidence

267. According to the CJE, Article 15.1 of the e-Privacy Directive, interpreted in the light of the principle of effectiveness, requires national criminal courts to disregard information and evidence obtained by means of the general and indiscriminate retention of traffic and location data in breach of EU law, in the context of criminal proceedings against persons suspected of having committed criminal offences, where those persons are not in a position to comment effectively on that information and that evidence and they pertain to a field of which the judges have no knowledge and are likely to have a preponderant influence on the findings of fact.

F. Application to State Intelligence Services

268. In the Privacy International judgment, the CJEU decided that Article 15.1 of the e-Privacy Directive read in the light of Article 4(2) TEU, must be interpreted as meaning that national legislation enabling a State authority to require providers of electronic communications services to forward traffic data and location data to the security and intelligence agencies for the purpose of safeguarding national security falls within the scope of the Directive. The provision must be interpreted as precluding national legislation enabling a State authority to require providers of electronic communications services to carry out the general and indiscriminate transmission of traffic data and location data to the security and intelligence agencies for the purpose of safeguarding national security.[344]

344. CJEU, Case C-623/17, Judgment of 6 October 2020, Privacy International, ECLI:EU:C:2020:790, https://eur-lex.europa.eu/legal-content/en/TXT/?uri=CELEX:62017CJ0623.

Part II. Personal Data Protection

§1. Background

269. Legislation regarding the protection of individuals of whom personal data are being processed by means of computers, emerged at regional and national levels in Europe around 1970. In 1970, the German federal state of Hesse passed the first regional data protection law, which was also the first data protection law in the world. The Swedish Data Act was the world's first national data protection law and was enacted on 11 May 1973. It required licences by the Swedish Data Protection Authority for information systems handling personal data. During the 1970s other European countries, such as Germany, France, Italy and the United Kingdom adopted legislation on this topic as well. Meanwhile discussions started in the framework of the Council of Europe in view of a first international treaty in this domain.

I. Council of Europe Convention 108

270. On 28 January 1981 a 'Convention for the Protection of Individuals with regard to Automatic Processing of Personal Data' ('Convention No.108) was signed in the framework of the Council of Europe.[345] This Convention is the first binding international instrument protecting the individual against abuses which may accompany the collection and processing of personal data and regulating at the same time the international flow of personal data. In addition to providing guarantees in relation to the collection and processing of personal data, it prohibits the processing of 'sensitive' data on a person's race, politics, health, religion, sexual life, criminal record, etc., in the absence of proper legal safeguards. The Convention also enshrines the individual's right to know that information is stored on him or her and, if necessary, to have it corrected. Restriction on the rights laid down in the Convention are only possible when overriding interests (e.g., State security, defence, etc.) are at stake. The Convention also includes restrictions for transborder flows of personal data to States where legal regulation does not provide equivalent protection.[346]

---

345. https://www.coe.int/en/web/data-protection/home.
346. C. De Terwagne, Council of Europe convention 108+: A modernised international treaty for the protection of personal data, The computer law and security report, 2021-04, Vol.40.

271. Convention No. 108 entered into force, after five ratifications, on 1 October 1985. It is on 'open' treaty, which means that any country in the world with a complying data protection legislation can request invitation to accede. Today, the Convention counts fifty-five parties, including nine non-European countries such as Argentina, Burkina Faso, Mexico, Morocco, Senegal, Tunisia and Uruguay.[347] In addition, eight countries have received a status as observers, among which are the USA, Canada, Australia, Indonesia Japan, South Korea and the Philippines.

272. Since 2012, work has been undertaken aiming at a 'modernisation' of Convention No. 108, in order to adapt the protection of individuals to the technological evolution since the 1970s[348]. On 10 October 2018 a 'Protocol amending the Convention for the Protection of Individuals with regard to Automatic Processing of Personal Data' (ETS No. 223) has been opened for signature by the parties to Convention No. 108.[349] The amended 'Convention 108+' will enter into force on 11 October 2023 if there are thirty-eight parties to the Protocol at this date.[350]

II. Directive 1995/46/EC

273. Already back in April 1976 and subsequently in May 1979 the European Parliament asked the Commission to propose measures in the field of data protection. In July 1981, the Commission passed a Recommendation encouraging the Member States of the European Community, to sign and ratify Convention No. 108.[351] The idea was that if European countries had diverging laws in this field, this could create both barriers to the free flow of information and distortions of fair competition. Towards the end of the 1980s, the European Commission started to realise the urgency of the problem and, more in particular, became convinced that the Council of Europe Convention still allowed a too large room for divergencies to solve the issue. Moreover, Convention 108 neither provided anything concerning the question which national law should be applicable in transnational cases, nor did it include a control mechanism in the form of an independent supervisory body.[352] On 18 July 1990, the Commission finally launched its 'Proposal for a Council

347. https://www.coe.int/en/web/conventions/full-list/-/conventions/treaty/108/signatures?module=signatures-by-treaty&treatynum=108.
348. Sylvia Kierkegaard, Nigel Waters, Graham Greenleaf, Lee A. Bygrave Ian Lloyd, Steve Saxby, 30 years on. The review of the Council of Europe Convention 108, The computer law and security report, 2011, Vol.27 (3), pp. 223–231.
C. de Terwangne, The work of revision of the Council of Europe Convention 108 for the protection of individuals as regards the automatic processing of personal data, International review of law, computers & technology, 2014-05-04, Vol.28 (2), p.118-130; G. Greenleaf, 'Modernising' data protection Convention 108:A safe basis for a global privacy treaty?, The computer law and security report, 2013-08, Vol.29 (4), pp. 430–436.
349. https://www.coe.int/en/web/data-protection/convention108/modernised.
350. https://www.coe.int/en/web/conventions/full-list/-/conventions/treaty/223/signatures.
351. 81/679/EEC: Commission Recommendation of 29 July 1981 relating to the Council of Europe Convention for the protection of individuals with regard to automatic processing of personal data, *OJ L 246*, 29.8.1981, pp. 31–31. http://data.europa.eu/eli/reco/1981/679/oj.
352. G. Papapavlou, Latest developments concerning the EC draft data protection directives, in: J. Dumortier, Recent developments in data privacy law, Leuven University Press, 1992, pp. 29–42.C.

Directive concerning the protection of individuals in relation to the processing of personal data'.[353] More than five years later, on 24 October 1995, 'Directive 95/46/EC of the European Parliament and of the Council of 24 October 1995 on the protection of individuals with regard to the processing of personal data and on the free movement of such data' ('the Data Protection Directive) was finally adopted.[354]

274. The Data Protection Directive aimed at harmonising the existing national data protection laws adopted by the Member States between 1970 and 1990. It combined elements from these national laws while avoiding overlapping and other encumbrances. The main tendency of the Directive is to create legal clarity. Every data subject within a Member State could from now on be sure that data transfers to another Member State would cause no problems if these transfers were legally permissible in the own country. On the basis of the Directive, data protection became virtually equivalent in every single Member State. Moreover, no Member State could restrict data communication with another Member State on the basis that data protection in that Member State did not correspond to the common standard.

275. Directive 95/46/EC required Member States to create a national legal framework including prerequisites under which personal data processing was permitted and for the purposes of such processing. National legislators were requested to enshrine rights of information, access, correction, objection and erasure, in favour of data subjects, and to define obligations for notification and for supervision by independent bodies. They further had to set up rules regarding judicial remedies, liability as well as sanctions and to regulate data transfers to third countries.

276. The Data Protection Directive provided for a legal basis to establish a Working Party for cooperation among the supervisory authorities of the Member States. Article 29 of Directive 95/46/EC dealt with the composition of this Working Party and with the basic rules of procedure. Article 30 defined its tasks and competences. The so-called Article 29 Working Party was composed of one representative from each of the Member States' national supervisory authorities and included also the European Data Protection Supervisor (the 'EDPS') and a representative of the European Commission. One of the main tasks of the Working Party was to contribute to a uniform application of the Data Protection Directive in the Member States. In this context, it issued a large number of opinions, guidelines and recommendations, mostly related to the interpretation and application of particular concepts and provisions of Directive 95/46.[355] A list of sixteen working documents, recommendations and guidelines of the Article 29 Working Party have been endorsed by the European Data Protection Board, which succeeded the Working

353. https://eur-lex.europa.eu/procedure/EN/1990_287.
354. Official Journal L 281, 23/11/1995 P. 0031 – 0050.
355. At the time of writing, the archives of the Art. 29 Working Party documents are still accessible on the website of the European Commission at https://ec.europa.eu/newsroom/article29/items/itemType/1358.

Party at the entry into force of the GDPR in 2018.[356] As a consequence these documents remain valid guidance material for the interpretation of concepts and provisions of the GDPR.

277. The Data Protection Directive and the Member States' laws transposing this Directive have been the subject of interesting case law, in particular by the European Court of Justice. One of the most famous judgments of the ECJ in this field, in the Bodil Lindqvist case, related to the scope of application of the Directive.[357] In its ruling the Court declined the view according to which the Data Protection Directive was solely applicable to internal market issues. The Court decided that, on the contrary, the Directive was to be applied as a rule, while its non-application formed a mere exception to this rule. In the same judgment, the Court issued its interpretation of core concepts such as 'personal data', 'data relating to health' and 'transfer of personal data to third countries', which remain entirely valid under the GDPR.

278. Article 33 of the Data Protection Directive stated that the Commission should report to the Council and the European Parliament at regular intervals on the implementation of the Directive. The Commission presented its first report on 15 May 2003.[358] The Commission did not deny the fact that the transposition of the Directive by the Member States progressed rather slow and that the Directive did not create uniformity. Despite substantial divergencies between the implementation by the Member States, the Commission considered, however, that results of the review on balance militated against proposing modifications to the Directive at that stage. The European Parliament, in its answer to the Commission's report, shared the view, since experience with the Data Protection Directive was still very limited, it should not be amended for the time being. Current shortcomings in its implementation should be overcome by actions taken at the European and national level by Member States and by supervisory authorities.[359] Following the request of the European Parliament, the Commission proposed a Work Programme for better implementation of the Data Protection Directive. In a Communication of 7 March 2007 in which it examined the work conducted under this programme, the Commission stated that the actions undertaken had been positive. The Commission noticed that

356. https://edpb.europa.eu/sites/default/files/files/news/endorsement_of_wp29_documents_en_0.pdf.
357. CJEU, Case C-101/01, Judgment of 6 November 2003, Bodil Lindqvist, ECLI:EU:C:2003:596, https://eur-lex.europa.eu/legal-content/EN/TXT/?uri=CELEX%3A62001CJ0101.
358. First report on the implementation of the Data Protection Directive (95/46/EC), COM(2003) 265 final, Brussels, 15 May 2003, https://eur-lex.europa.eu/LexUriServ/LexUriServ.do?uri=COM:2003:0265:FIN:EN:PDF.
359. European Parliament, 14 February 2004, Report on the First Report of the Commission on the implementation of the Data Protection Directive (95/46/EC), https://www.europarl.europa.eu/sides/getDoc.do?pubRef=-//EP//TEXT+REPORT+A5-2004-0104+0+DOC+XML+V0//EN&language=en.

some Member States had not yet properly implemented the Directive and that substantial divergencies continued to exist. Submission of any legislative proposal to amend the Data Protection Directive was, however, not yet envisaged.[360]

III. The Lisbon Treaty of 2009

279. The European Council, which met in Lisbon on 18 and 19 October 2007 approved the so-called Lisbon Treaty, which replaced the draft Treaty establishing a Constitution for Europe. This new treaty introduced modifications both to the Treaty on European Union (Maastricht Treaty) and the Treaty establishing the European Community (Rome Treaty known in updated form as the Treaty on the Functioning of the European Union).[361] Article 6(2) of the TFEU introduced the right to data protection and a specific legal basis for data protection legislation in Article 16 TFEU. Moreover, the Lisbon Treaty eliminated most aspects of the so-called pillar structure introduced by the Maastricht Treaty with the consequence that the same basic legal protections should apply to all types of personal data processing. As already mentioned before, following the entry into force of the Lisbon Treaty in 2009, the fundamental rights charter of the European Union obtained the same legal value as the European Union treaties. The Charter referred to in the Treaty is an amended version of the 2000 document which was solemnly declared by the same three institutions a day before the signing of the Lisbon Treaty itself.

IV. The 2012 GDPR Proposal

280. With a view on the new possibilities for Union legislation introduced by the Lisbon Treaty, the European Commission published a Communication on 4 November 2010 in which it stated for the first time that, while the core principles of the Data Protection Directive remained valid, it could no longer meet the challenges of rapid technological and economic developments since 1995.[362] After an extensive consultation, both public and private, the Commission finally released a proposal for a General Data Protection Regulation on 25 January 2012.

281. On 27 April 2016, after more than four years of drafting and negotiations, the EU General Data Protection Regulation ('GDPR') was finally adopted at the EU level. The legislative package also included a directive, setting minimum standards

360. Communication from the Commission to the European Parliament and the Council on the follow-up of the Work Programme for better implementation of the Data Protection Directive, COM/2007/0087 final, 7 March 2007, https://eur-lex.europa.eu/legal-content/EN/ALL/?uri=CELEX:52007DC0087.
361. Consolidated version of the Treaty on the Functioning of the European Union, http://data.europa.eu/eli/treaty/tfeu_2012/oj.
362. Communication of the European Commission, 'A comprehensive approach on personal data protection in the European Union', COM(2010) 609 final, Brussels, 4 November 2010, https://eur-lex.europa.eu/LexUriServ/LexUriServ.do?uri=COM:2010:0609:FIN:EN:PDF.

for data processing for policing purposes.[363] The GDPR entered into force on 25 May 2016, twenty days after its publication in the EU Official Journal. Its provisions became directly applicable in all Member States two years after that date, on 25 May 2018.

V. The Law Enforcement Directive

282. The Law Enforcement Directive provides rules on the protection of natural persons with regard to the processing of personal data by competent authorities for the purposes of the prevention, investigation, detection or prosecution of criminal offences or the execution of criminal penalties, including the protection against threats to public security and its prevention.[364] It is intended to set minimum rules. The Directive does not preclude Member States from providing higher safeguards than those established in the Directive for the protection of the rights and freedoms of the data subject with regard to the processing of personal data by the envisaged competent law enforcement authorities.[365]

283. To fall within the scope of the Law Enforcement Directive, a data processing must meet two cumulative conditions. First, it must pursue one of the purposes mentioned in Article 1. The Directive is, in other words, primarily intended to apply to 'criminal matters' and, in particular, to activities carried out by the police, for instance in the context of preventing and recording certain offences during passenger travel or to processing operations set up for the management of enforcement actions linked to sentences ordered by judicial authorities. The provisions of the Directive may also be intended to govern processing carried out in the context of activities that do not specifically fall within the criminal sphere but which relate to police activities carried out prior to the commission of a criminal offence. The purposes covered by the Directive may thus include preventive police activities for the purpose of protecting against threats to public security that could lead to a criminal charge (police activities at demonstrations, sporting events, maintaining public order, etc.) and processing operations carried out for these purposes.

284. Second, the processing whatever its purpose, only falls within the scope of the Directive if it is carried out by a 'competent authority'. This term refers to: a) any public authority competent for the prevention and detection of criminal offences, the investigation and prosecution of criminal offences or the execution of criminal penalties (judicial authorities, the police, any other law enforcement

---

363. Directive (EU) 2016/680 of the European Parliament and of the Council of 27 April 2016 on the protection of natural persons with regard to the processing of personal data by competent authorities for the purposes of the prevention, investigation, detection or prosecution of criminal offences or the execution of criminal penalties, and on the free movement of such data, and repealing Council Framework Decision 2008/977/JHA, *OJ L 119, 4.5.2016, p. 89–131..*

364. Art. 1(1) of the Directive.

365. Hudobnik, M.M. Data protection and the law enforcement directive: a procrustean bed across Europe?. *ERA Forum* **21,** 485–500 (2020); Leiser, M; Custers, B, The Law Enforcement Directive, European data protection law review (Internet), 2019, Vol.5 (3), pp. 367–378.

authorities, etc.) and b) any other body or entity to which the law of a Member State entrusts the exercise of public authority and prerogatives of public power for the purpose of implementing processing covered by this Directive (for example, the internal security services of the public transport networks, sports federations approved for the purpose of providing security at sporting events, etc.).

285. As will be explained in following sections, the GDPR does not apply to processing carried out in the exercise of activities that do not fall within the scope of European Union law, such as state security or national defence activities.[366] Since these activities are outside the scope of Union law, the Directive is not applicable either and remains governed by Member States law.[367] Outside of the scope of the GDPR are also processing activities 'by competent authorities for the purposes of the prevention, investigation, detection or prosecution of criminal offences or the execution of criminal penalties, including the safeguarding against and the prevention of threats to public security'.[368]

286. The terminology used in the Law Enforcement Directive and many obligations under the Directive are identical to those under the GDPR:[369]

- implement appropriate technical and organisational measures to ensure and to be able to demonstrate that processing is performed in accordance with this Directive (Article 19);
- implement data protection by design and by default (Article 20);
- use processors that provide sufficient guarantees and act only on instructions from the controller (Article 22);
- maintain a record of processing activities (Article 24);
- implement logging measures (Article 25);
- cooperate with the supervisory authority in the performance of its tasks on request (Article 26);
- carry out a data protection impact assessment when the processing is likely to result in a high risk to the rights and freedoms of natural persons (Article 27);
- consult the supervisory authority in advance in the cases listed in Article 28 of the Directive;
- implement appropriate measures to ensure a level of security appropriate to the risk, in particular as regards the processing of special categories of personal data referred to in Article 10 (Article 29);

366. Art. 2(2)(a) of the GDPR.
367. These activities must, however, sometimes take into consideration specific provisions of Union law which are applicable to electronic communications providers. *See* Part I: D.12.6.
368. Art. 2(2)(d) of the GDPR.
369. Marquenie, Thomas. 'The Police and Criminal Justice Authorities Directive: Data Protection Standards and Impact on the Legal Framework.' *Computer Law & Security Review*, vol. 33, no. 3, 2017, pp. 324–340; Laura Drechsler, 'Comparing LED and GDPR Adequacy: One Standard Two Systems', (2020), 1, Global Privacy Law Review, Issue 2, pp. 93–103.

- notify the supervisory authority of a personal data breach without undue delay, and, where feasible, not later than 72 hours after having become aware of it, when the breach is likely to result in a risk to the rights and freedoms of natural persons (Article 30);
- communicate the personal data breach to the data subject without undue delay where the personal data breach is likely to result in a high risk to his/her rights and freedoms (Article 31);
- designate a data protection officer under the conditions set out in Article 32 of the Directive;
- respect the conditions defined for the transfer of personal data to third countries or to international organisations (Article 35 and following).[370]

287. Other obligations are specific to the Directive:

- where applicable and as far as possible, to make a clear distinction between personal data of different categories of data subjects, such as persons convicted of a criminal offence, victims of a criminal offence, other parties to a criminal offence, etc. (Article 6);
- distinguish between personal data (personal data based on facts/personal data based on personal assessments) and ensure the quality of personal data (Article 7);
- processing must be lawful, i.e., necessary for the performance of a task carried out by a competent authority, for the purposes of this Directive, and based on Union law or Member State law (Article 8);
- processing of special categories of data is allowed only where strictly necessary (Article 10).

288. Some rights included in the GDPR are absent in the Law Enforcement Directive (e.g., the right to portability) or may be subject to limitations. The rights of natural persons recognised in the Directive are:

- information to be made available to the data subject, subject to possible limitations (Article 13);
- the right of access (Article 14), subject to limitations in whole or in part, in particular in order not to obstruct investigations, or to avoid prejudicing the prevention or detection of criminal offences, etc. (Article 15). In practice, the limitation

370. Regarding the application of the provisions regarding data transfers to third countries, *see also* EDPB, Recommendations 01/2021 on the adequacy referential under the Law Enforcement Directive, adopted on 2 February 2021, also EDPB, Opinion 15/2021 regarding the European Commission Draft Implementing Decision pursuant to Directive (EU) 2016/680 on the adequate protection of personal data in the United Kingdom, adopted on 13 April 2021, https://edpb.europa.eu/our-work-tools/our-documents/opinion-led/opinion-152021-regarding-european-commission-draft_en.

of the right of access may lead to the implementation of an 'indirect right of access', i.e., exercised through the intermediary of the competent supervisory authority (Article 17);[371]
– the right to rectification or erasure of personal data (Article 16).

289. Article 62(6) of the Law Enforcement Directive requires the Commission to review, by 6 May 2019, other EU legal acts that regulate competent authorities' personal data processing for law enforcement purposes, in order to assess the need to align them with the Directive and, where appropriate, to make proposals for amending them to ensure consistency in the protection of personal data within the scope of the Law Enforcement Directive. In this perspective, the Commission has set out the results of its review in a Communication which specifies ten legal acts that should be aligned with the Law Enforcement Directive and a timetable for doing so.[372] A first proposal to amend Directive 2014/41/EU of the European Parliament and of the Council regarding the European Investigation Order in criminal matters has been published by the European Commission on 20 January 2021.[373]

§2. Structure of the GDPR

290. The GDPR contains 173 Recitals and 99 Articles. The ninety-nine Articles structured in eleven Chapters.

(1) Chapter I – General Provisions: Subject matter and objectives (Article 1), Material scope (Article 2), Territorial scope (Article 3) and Definitions (Article 4);
(2) Chapter II – Principles: General principles related to personal data processing (Article 5), Lawfulness of processing (Article 6), Conditions for consent (Article 7), Conditions applicable to child's consent in relation to information society services (Article 8), Processing of special categories of personal data (Article 9); Processing of personal data relating to criminal convictions and offences (Article 10), Processing which does not require identification (Article 11);
(3) Chapter III – Rights of Data Subjects, divided in 5 sections: 1) Transparency and modalities (Article 12), 2) Information and access to personal data (Articles 12–15), 3) Rectification and Erasure (Articles 16–20, including also the right to data portability)), 4) Right to object and automated individual decision-making (Articles 21–22) and 5) Restrictions (Article 23);

371. Vogiatzoglou, Plixavra; Quezada Tavárez, Katherine; Fantin, Stefano; Dewitte, Pierre, From Theory To Practice: Exercising The Right Of Access Under The Law Enforcement And PNR Directives, Journal of Intellectual Property, Information Technology and E-Commerce Law; 2020; Vol. 11; issue 3; pp. 274 – 302.
372. Communication from the Commission to the European Parliament and the Council, Way forward on aligning the former third pillar acquis with data protection rules, 24 June 2020, COM(2020) 262 final.
373. European Commission, Proposal for a Directive amending Directive 2014/41/EU, as regards its alignment with EU rules on the protection of personal data, COM(2021) 21 final.

(4) Chapter IV – Controller and Processor, also divided in 5 Sections: 1) General obligations (Articles 24–31), 2) Security of personal data (Articles 32–34), 3) Data protection impact assessment and prior consultation (Articles 35–36), 4) Data protection officer (Articles 37–39), and 5) Codes of conduct and certification (Articles 40–43);
(5) Chapter V – Transfers of personal data to third countries or international organisations (Articles 44–50);
(6) Chapter VI – Independent Supervisory Authorities, divided in 2 sections: 1) Independent status (Articles 51–54) and 2) Competence, tasks and powers (Articles 55–59);
(7) Chapter VII – Cooperation and Consistency, divided in 3 sections: 1) Cooperation (Articles 60–62), 2) Consistency (Articles 63–67) and 3) European Data Protection Board (Articles 68–76);
(8) Chapter VIII – Remedies, Liability and Penalties (Articles 77–84);
(9) Chapter IX – Provisions relating to specific processing situations: Processing and freedom of expression and information (Article 85), Processing and public access to official documents (Article 86), Processing of the national identification number (Article 87), Processing in the context of employment (Article 88), Safeguards and derogations relating to processing for archiving purposes in the public interest, scientific or historical research purposes or statistical purposes (Article 89) Obligations of secrecy (Article 90) and Existing data protection rules of churches and religious associations (Article 91);
(10) Chapter X – Delegated Acts and Implementing Acts (Articles 92–93);
(11) Chapter XI – Final Provisions (Articles 94–99).

§3. Subject Matter and Objectives of the GDPR (Article 1)

291. Article 1(1) of the GDPR states: 'This Regulation lays down rules relating to the protection of natural persons with regard to the processing of personal data and rules relating to the free movement of personal data.' This provision expresses the double purpose of the Regulation and transposes the mandate given to the Union in Article 16(2) TFEU: 'The European Parliament and the Council, acting in accordance with the ordinary legislative procedure, shall lay down the rules relating to the protection of individuals with regard to the processing of personal data by Union institutions, bodies, offices and agencies, and by the Member States when carrying out activities which fall within the scope of Union law, and the rules relating to the free movement of such data. Compliance with these rules shall be subject to the control of independent authorities.' This mandate is mandatory: the rules in this domain are laid down by Union law. Member States are only entitled to adopt or maintain national law on the processing of personal data or on the free movement of personal data insofar as this is explicitly provided for in the GDPR. The main restrictions related to this mandate given to the Union legislator are listed in Article 23 of the Regulation.

292. Article 1(2) determines: 'This Regulation protects fundamental rights and freedoms of natural persons and in particular their right to the protection of personal data'. This provision refers, on the one hand to Article 16(1) TFEU: 'Everyone has the right to the protection of personal data concerning them.' On the other hand, it establishes a link with the 'fundamental rights and freedoms of natural persons' and makes clear that the protection of personal data is just one of these fundamental rights. This is clarified in Recital (4) which reads: 'The right to the protection of personal data is not an absolute right; it must be considered in relation to its function in society and be balanced against other fundamental rights, in accordance with the principle of proportionality. This Regulation respects all fundamental rights and observes the freedoms and principles recognised in the Charter as enshrined in the treaties, in particular the respect for private and family life, home and communications, the protection of personal data, freedom of thought, conscience and religion, freedom of expression and information, freedom to conduct a business, the right to an effective remedy and to a fair trial, and cultural, religious and linguistic diversity.'

293. Article 1(3) is primarily addressed to the Member States, stating: 'The free movement of personal data within the Union shall be neither restricted nor prohibited for reasons connected with the protection of natural persons with regard to the processing of personal data'. This provision is relevant in situations where the GDPR explicitly allows Member States to adopt different rules. In such situations, one Member State that adopted a higher level of protection, can neither restrict nor prohibit the free flow of personal data to other Member States having chosen for a lower protection level. The application of this principle must, however, consider the possibility of Member States to restrict the free flow of personal data for reasons listed in Article 23 of the GDPR, for example if such restrictions are justified for reasons of national security, defence, etc.

§4. SCOPE

I. Material Scope (Article 2 GDPR)

294. The Regulation applies to 'the processing of personal data wholly or partly by automated means, and to the processing other than by automated means of personal data which form part of a filing system or are intended to form part of a filing system'.[374] This material scope is identical to the one defined in the 1995 Directive.[375]

---

374. Art. 2.1.
375. Voigt, Paul, and Von dem Bussche, Axel. 'Scope of Application of the GDPR.' *The EU General Data Protection Regulation (GDPR)*, Springer International Publishing, Cham, 2017, pp. 9–30.

A. *Personal Data*

295. Article 4(1) defines 'personal data' as 'any information relating to an identified or identifiable natural person 'data subject'; an identifiable person is one who can be identified, directly or indirectly, in particular by reference to an identifier such as a name, an identification number, location data, online identifier or to one or more factors specific to the physical, physiological, genetic, mental, economic, cultural or social identity of that person'. The definition is, consequently, very broad.[376]

1. Any Information

296. The concept of 'personal data' includes 'any information', irrelevant of its nature or of the medium used for its transmission.[377] With regard to its nature, the concept refers not only to 'private' information but covers publicly known information as well.[378] It can be objective information, such as a name, date or place of birth, profession, etc. but also subjective information, such as an opinion expressed by someone or an evaluation or assessment relating to a person. For example, in the Nowak case, the CJEU ruled that 'the expression 'any information' [...] reflects the aim of the EU legislature to assign a wide scope to [the concept of personal data], which is not restricted to information that is sensitive or private, but potentially encompasses all kinds of information, not only objective but also subjective, in the form of opinions and assessments'.[379]

297. Any kind of information is included in the concept of 'personal data', irrelevant of its form, be it alphabetical, numerical, graphical or acoustic. It can consequently be textual information, structured in the form of records in a database but also unstructured, for example in a report or an e-mail. But it can also consist in a picture, a drawing, a voice mail or a video.

298. Biometric information, such as fingerprints or facial image characteristics, is also covered by the concept of 'personal data'. Article 4(14) of the Regulation defines 'biometric data' as '*personal data resulting from specific technical processing relating to the physical, physiological or behavioural characteristics of a natural person, which allow or confirm the unique identification of that natural person,*

376. Purtova, Nadezhda. 'The Law of Everything.: Broad Concept of Personal Data and Future of EU Data Protection Law.' *Law, Innovation and Technology*, vol. 10, no. 1, 2018, pp. 40–81; Paul Schwartz and Daniel Solove 'Reconciling Personal Information in the United States and European Union' (2014) 102 *California Law Review* 877.
377. Art. 29 Working Party, Opinion 4/2007 on the concept of personal data, 20 June 2007, pp. 6–9.
378. Judgment of the European Court of Justice C-101/2001of 6.11.2003 (Lindqvist), §24: '*The term undoubtedly covers the name of a person in conjunction with his telephone coordinates or information about his working conditions or hobbies*'.
379. CJEU, Case C-434/16, Judgment of 20 December 2017, *Peter Nowak v. Data Protection Commissioner*, ECLI:EU:C:2017:994, https://eur-lex.europa.eu/legal-content/en/TXT/?uri=CELEX:62016CJ0434.

such as facial images or dactyloscopy data'. 'Biometrical' is consequently narrower than 'biological' since the former term refers to uniquely identifying information.[380]

299. Body tissue samples, for example stored in biobanks, cannot be considered as 'information' as such but the annotations added to these samples usually refer to the individual from whom the sample has been extracted.[381] These annotations have to be qualified as personal data. The collection, storage and use of tissue samples themselves is subject to separate sets of rules in the European Union.[382]

2. Relating To

300. In order to qualify as 'personal data' the information should 'relate to' an individual natural person. Information items such as a name, an e-mail address, a facial photograph on a passport, etc. are evidently covered by the definition. These items do directly relate to the individual. Other information may relate indirectly to an individual such as a photograph of a house, a car registration plate, a dynamic IP-address.[383]

301. Recital 30 of the GDPR states that 'Individuals may be associated with online identifiers provided by their devices, applications, tools and protocols, such as Internet Protocol addresses, cookie identifiers or other identifiers such as Radio Frequency Identification tags. This may leave traces which, in particular when combined with unique identifiers and other information received by the servers, may be used to create profiles of the individuals and identify them.'

---

380. Kindt. Els, *Privacy and Data Protection Issues of Biometric Applications: A Comparative Legal Analysis*. 1st ed. 2013. ed., Springer Netherlands: Imprint: Springer, 2013.
381. Bygrave, Lee A. The Body as Data – Biobank Regulation via the Back Door of Data Protection Law, Law, Innovation and Technology 2 Law Innovation & Tech. (2010), pp. 1–26; L Bygrave, 'Information Concepts in Law: Generic Dreams and Definitional Daylight' (2015) 35(1) *Oxford Journal of Legal Studies* 91–120); WG Urgessa, 'The Feasibility of Applying EU Data Protection Law to Biological Materials: Challenging 'Data' as Exclusively Informational' (2016) 7 *JIPITEC, p. 96.*.
382. *See* e.g., Commission Directive 2006/86/EC of 24 October 2006 implementing Directive 2004/23/EC of the European Parliament and of the Council as regards traceability requirements, notification of serious adverse reactions and events and certain technical requirements for the coding, processing, preservation, storage and distribution of human tissues and cells (Text with EEA relevance), Official Journal L 294, 25/10/2006, pp. 32–50.
383. Regarding a dynamic IP-address: CJEU, Case C-582/14, Judgment of 19 October 2016, Breyer, ECLI:EU:C:2016:779, https://eur-lex.europa.eu/legal-content/en/TXT/?uri=CELEX:62014CJ0582: 'a dynamic IP address registered by an online media services provider when a person accesses a website that the provider makes accessible to the public constitutes personal data within the meaning of that provision, in relation to that provider, where the latter has the legal means which enable it to identify the data subject with additional data which the internet service provider has about that person'. *See also* FJ Zuiderveen Borgesius, 'Breyer Case of the Court of Justice of the European Union: IP Addresses and the Personal Data Definition' (2017) 3(1) *European Data Protection Law Review* 130Ib.

302. In a Working Paper of 2007, the Article 29 WP gave the following example: 'The value of a particular house is information about an object. Data protection rules will clearly not apply when this information will be used solely to illustrate the level of real estate prices in a certain district. However, under certain circumstances such information should also be considered as personal data. Indeed, the house is the asset of an owner, which will hence be used to determine the extent of this person's obligation to pay some taxes, for instance. In this context, it will be indisputable that such information should be considered as personal data.'[384]

303. In the same Working Paper, the Article 29 WP estimated that information must not necessarily be 'about' a person. Besides this 'content element', information may also qualify as 'personal data' when a 'purpose element' or a 'result element' is present. A 'purpose element' can be considered to exist when the data are used or are likely to be used, taking into account all the circumstances surrounding the precise case, with the purpose to evaluate, treat in a certain way or influence the status or behaviour of an individual.[385] Finally, data can be considered to 'relate' to an individual because their use is likely to have an impact on a certain person's rights and interest.[386] It is worthwhile to mention that, in the Nowak case, the above-mentioned criteria are also used by the CJEU.[387]

304. In the *Worten* judgment, the CJEU held that a record of working time, which indicates, in relation to each worker, the times when working hours begin and end, as well as the corresponding breaks and intervals, is included within the concept of 'personal data', within the meaning of that provision.[388]

305. The CJEU ruled, in the case of *YS and Others*, that the concept of 'personal data' must be interpreted as meaning that the data relating to an applicant for a residence permit contained in an administrative document, such as the 'minute' at issue in the main proceedings, setting out the grounds that the case officer puts forward in support of the draft decision which he is responsible for drawing up in the context of the procedure prior to the adoption of a decision concerning the application for such a permit and, where relevant, the data in the legal analysis contained in that document, are 'personal data' within the meaning of that provision, whereas, by contrast, that analysis cannot in itself be so classified.[389]

---

384. Art. 29 Working Party, Opinion 4/2007 on the concept of personal data, 20 June 2007, p. 9.
385. *Ibid.*, p. 10. The example mentioned in this WP136 is the call log of a telephone inside a company office (which can be used for several purposes).
386. *Ibid.*, p. 11. The example mentioned relates to a system of satellite location is set up by a taxi company which makes it possible to determine the position of available taxis in real time.
387. CJEU, Case C-434/16, Judgment of 20 December 2017, Peter Nowak v. Data Protection Commissioner, ECLI:EU:C:2017:994, para. 35, https://eur-lex.europa.eu/legal-content/en/TXT/?uri=CELEX:62016CJ0434.
388. CJEU, Case C-342/12, Judgment of 30 May 2013, Worten, ECLI:EU:C:2013:355, https://eur-lex.europa.eu/legal-content/en/TXT/?uri=CELEX:62012CJ0342.
389. CJEU, Case C-141/12, Judgment of 17 Jul 2014, YS and Others, ECLI:EU:C:2014:2081, https://eur-lex.europa.eu/legal-content/en/TXT/?uri=CELEX:62012CJ0141: 'Legal analysis 'is not in itself liable to be the subject of a check of its accuracy by that applicant and a rectification'.

306. On the contrary, the CJEU decided, in the Nowak judgment, that the term 'personal data' must be interpreted as meaning that the written answers submitted by a candidate at a professional examination and any comments made by an examiner with respect to those answers constitute personal data, within the meaning of that provision'.[390]

3. Identified or Identifiable

307. To be characterised as 'personal data' the information should concern an identified or identifiable person. Recital 26 specifies this condition as follows: 'To determine whether a person is identifiable, account should be taken of all the means reasonably likely to be used, such as singling out, either by the controller or by any other person to identify the individual directly or indirectly. To ascertain whether means are reasonably likely to be used to identify the individual, account should be taken of all objective factors, such as the costs of and the amount of time required for identification, taking into consideration both available technology at the time of the processing and technological development.'

308. In the Breyer case the CJEU examined the situation in which an online media services provider, namely the Federal Republic of Germany, registers IP addresses of the users of a website that it makes accessible to the public, without having the additional data necessary in order to identify those users.[391] The IP addresses were 'dynamic', in other words assigned for each Internet connection and replaced when subsequent connections are made, and not 'static' IP addresses, which are invariable and allow continuous identification of the device connected to the network. The data consisting in a dynamic IP address and the date and time that a website was accessed from that IP address registered by an online media services provider do not, without more, give this media service provider the possibility to identify the user who consulted that website during that period of use. In order to identify the connected device, one needs the assistance of the Internet services provider who has additional data which, if combined with the IP address would enable the device to be identified.

309. The CJEU first observed that an identifiable person is one who can be identified, directly or indirectly. The use of the word 'indirectly' suggests that, in order to treat information as personal data, it is not necessary that that information alone allows the data subject to be identified. Furthermore, Recital 26 of the GDPR states that, to determine whether a person is identifiable, 'account should be taken of all the means reasonably likely to be used, such as singling out, either by the controller or by another person to identify the natural person directly or indirectly'. The CJEU

390. CJEU, Case C-434/16, Judgment of 20 December 2017, Peter Nowak v. Data Protection Commissioner, ECLI:EU:C:2017:994, https://eur-lex.europa.eu/legal-content/en/TXT/?uri=CELEX:62016CJ0434.

391. CJEU, Case C-582/14, Judgment of 19 Oct 2016, Breyer, ECLI:EU:C:2016:779, https://eur-lex.europa.eu/legal-content/en/TXT/?uri=CELEX:62014CJ0582.

found that these wordings 'suggests that, for information to be treated as 'personal data' within the meaning of Article 2(a) of that directive, it is not required that all the information enabling the identification of the data subject must be in the hands of one person'.[392]

310. Recital 26 of the GDPR also states: 'To ascertain whether means are reasonably likely to be used to identify the natural person, account should be taken of all objective factors, such as the costs of and the amount of time required for identification, taking into consideration the available technology at the time of the processing and technological developments.' On the question when means are not reasonably likely to be used to identify the natural person, the CJEU took the viewpoint that this 'would not be the case if the identification of the data subject was prohibited by law or practically impossible on account of the fact that it requires a disproportionate effort in terms of time, cost and manpower, so that the risk of identification appears in reality to be insignificant'.

311. Regarding the specific circumstances of the Breyer case, the CJEU finally decided that 'Although the referring Court states in its order for reference that German law does not allow the Internet service provider to transmit directly to the online media services provider the additional data necessary for the identification of the data subject, it seems however, subject to verifications to be made in that regard by the referring Court that, in particular, in the event of cyberattacks legal channels exist so that the online media services provider is able to contact the competent authority, so that the latter can take the steps necessary to obtain that information from the Internet service provider and to bring criminal proceedings'.[393] The Court concluded, therefore, that 'it appears that the online media services provider has the means which may likely reasonably be used in order to identify the data subject, with the assistance of other persons, namely the competent authority and the Internet service provider, on the basis of the IP addresses stored'.[394]

312. Recital 26 of the GDPR also states that 'the principles of data protection should therefore not apply to anonymous information, that is information which does not relate to an identified or identifiable natural person or to data rendered anonymous in such a way that the data subject is not or no longer identifiable. This Regulation does therefore not concern the processing of such anonymous information, including for statistical and research purposes'.

313. Alternately 'data which has undergone pseudonymisation, which could be attributed to a natural person by the use of additional information, should be considered as information on an identifiable natural person'. According to Article 4(5) of the GDPR, 'pseudonymisation' means 'the processing of personal data in such a manner that the personal data can no longer be attributed to a specific data subject without the use of additional information, provided that such additional information

392. *Ibid.*, § 46.
393. *Ibid.*, § 47.
394. *Ibid.*, § 48.

is kept separately and is subject to technical and organisational measures to ensure that the personal data are not attributed to an identified or identifiable natural person'.

314. The application of pseudonymisation to personal data can reduce the risks for the data subjects concerned and help controllers and processors meet their data protection obligations. The explicit introduction of 'pseudonymisation' through the articles of this Regulation is thus not intended to preclude any other measures of data protection.[395]

315. In order to create incentives for applying pseudonymisation when processing personal data, measures of pseudonymisation whilst allowing general analysis should be possible within the same controller when the controller has taken technical and organisational measures necessary to ensure, for the respective processing, that the provisions of this Regulation are implemented, and ensuring that additional information for attributing the personal data to a specific data subject is kept separately. The controller processing the data shall also refer to authorised persons within the same controller.[396]

316. The GDPR does not apply to data of deceased persons. Member States may provide for rules regarding the processing of data of deceased persons.

4. 'Natural Person'

317. The GDPR does only apply to processing of personal data relating to natural persons. The protection afforded by the Regulation concerns natural persons, whatever their nationality or place of residence, in relation to the processing of personal data. Recital 20 states that 'With regard to the processing of data which concern legal persons and in particular undertakings established as legal persons, including the name and the form of the legal person and the contact details of the legal person, the protection of this Regulation should not be claimed by any person.'

B. Processing

318. Article 4 (3) 'processing' means any operation or set of operations which is performed upon personal data or sets of personal data, whether or not by automated means, such as collection, recording, organisation, structuring, storage, adaptation or alteration, retrieval, consultation, use, disclosure by transmission, dissemination or otherwise making available, alignment or combination, restriction, erasure or destruction.

---

395. Recital 28 of the GDPR.
396. Recital 30 of the GDPR.

319. 'Filing system' means any structured set of personal data which are accessible according to specific criteria, whether centralised, decentralised or dispersed on a functional or geographical basis Recital 13 specifies: 'The protection of individuals should apply to processing of personal data by automated means as well as to manual processing, if the data are contained or are intended to be contained in a filing system. Files or sets of files as well as their cover pages, which are not structured according to specific criteria, should not fall within the scope of this Regulation.'

320. In the Jehovah Witnesses case, the CJEU found that that the concept of a 'filing system', 'covers a set of personal data collected in the course of door-to-door preaching, consisting of the names and addresses and other information concerning the persons contacted, if those data are structured according to specific criteria which, in practice, enable them to be easily retrieved for subsequent use. In order for such a set of data to fall within that concept, it is not necessary that they include data sheets, specific lists or other search methods'.[397] However, the Court also confirmed that 'the content of a filing system must be structured in order to allow easy access to personal data' and that although the legislature did not set out the criteria according to which that filing system must be structured, 'it is clear from those recitals that those criteria must be 'relat[ed] to individuals'.[398]

321. As a consequence, the provisions of the GDPR are not applicable to any paper document which contains a name of an individual natural person or other information making this individual identifiable. For example, if written notes of a recruitment interview are filed, together with many other documents related to the job applicant, in a folder relating to the latter person, the information mentioned about third persons (for example name of a supervisor in a previous job) in the interview report included in those folders, is not 'structured according to specific criteria related to those third persons'. Therefore, although the notes relating to the job applicant, if structured according to criteria relating to this applicant (for example, the family name) in order to allow easy access to these personal data, these notes do not qualify as personal data processing relating to any other third person mentioned in these notes.

C. Controllers and Processors

1. Definition of Controller

322. A controller is defined by Article 4(7) GDPR as 'the natural or legal person, public authority, agency or other body which, alone or jointly with others, determines the purposes and means of the processing of personal data; where the

397. CJEU, Case C-25/17, Judgment of 10 July 2018, Jehovan todistajat, ECLI:EU:C:2018:551, https://eur-lex.europa.eu/legal-content/en/TXT/?uri=CELEX:62017CJ0025.
398. *Ibid.*, para. 57.

purposes and means of such processing are determined by Union or Member State law, the controller or the specific criteria for its nomination may be provided for by Union or Member State law'.

323. Under the GDPR, a controller can be '*a natural or legal person, public authority, agency or other body*'. This means that, in principle, there is no limitation as to the type of entity that may assume the role of a controller. It might be an organisation, but it might also be an individual or a group of individuals.[399] In practice, it is usually a legal person or a public authority that acts as a controller within the meaning of the GDPR. However, in the Jehovah Witnesses case, the CJEU qualified the individual members of a religious community as (joint) controllers, together with the religious community itself. The Court considered 'that members of the Jehovah's Witnesses Community who engage in preaching determine in which specific circumstances they collect personal data relating to persons visited, which specific data are collected and how those data are subsequently processed'. The CJEU did not accept the position of the Jehovah Witnesses which consisted in qualifying exclusively the individual members as the controllers, and not the religious community as such. In the opinion of the Court, the definition of controller '*must be interpreted as meaning that it supports the finding that a religious community is a controller, jointly with its members who engage in preaching, of the processing of personal data carried out by the latter in the context of door-to-door preaching organised, coordinated and encouraged by that community, without it being necessary that the community has access to those data, or to establish that that community has given its members written guidelines or instructions in relation to the data processing'*.[400]

324. Processing of personal data by employees performed in the context of activities of a legal person or public authority may be presumed to take place under that organisation's control.[401] In exceptional circumstances, however, it may occur that an employee is authorised to processes personal data for his or her own purposes.[402]

325. Recital 31 of the GDPR states that 'public authorities to which personal data are disclosed in accordance with a legal obligation for the exercise of their official mission, such as tax and customs authorities, financial investigation units, independent administrative authorities, or financial market authorities responsible for

---

399. For example, in CJEU, Case C-25/17, Judgment of 10 July 2018, Jehovan todistajat, ECLI:EU:C:2018:551, para. 75, https://eur-lex.europa.eu/legal-content/en/TXT/?uri=CELEX:62017CJ0025, the CJEU considered that a religious community of Jehovah's witnesses acted as a controller, jointly with its individual members. Judgment in *Jehovah's witnesses*, C-25/17, ECLI:EU:C:2018:551, para. 75.

400. CJEU, Case C-25/17, Judgment of 10 July 2018, Jehovan todistajat, ECLI:EU:C:2018:551, para. 75, https://eur-lex.europa.eu/legal-content/en/TXT/?uri=CELEX:62017CJ0025.

401. Employees who have access to personal data within an organisation are generally not considered as 'controllers' or 'processors', but rather as 'persons acting under the authority of the controller or of the processor' within the meaning of Art. 29 GDPR.

402. Art. 29 Working Party, Opinion 1/2010 on the concepts of 'controller' and 'processor', 16.02.2010, 00264/10/EN WP 169.

the regulation and supervision of securities markets should not be regarded as recipients if they receive personal data which are necessary to carry out a particular inquiry in the general interest, in accordance with Union or Member State law. The processing of personal data by those public authorities should comply with the applicable data protection rules according to the purposes of the processing'.[403]

326. In the Land Hessen case, a citizen, after his submission of a petition to the Petitions Committee of the Parliament of *Land* Hessen, applied to that committee, on the basis of Article 15 of the GDPR, for access to the personal data concerning him, recorded by that committee when dealing with his petition. The CJEU estimated that Article 4(7) 'must be interpreted as meaning that, insofar as a Petitions Committee of the parliament of a Federated State of a Member State determines, alone or with others, the purposes and means of the processing of personal data, that committee must be categorised as a 'controller,' within the meaning of that provision, and consequently the processing of personal data carried out by that committee falls within the scope of that regulation and, in particular, of Article 15 thereof'.[404]

327. A controller is a body that *decides* certain key elements about the processing. This controllership may be defined by law or may stem from an analysis of the factual elements or circumstances of the case. In the opinion of the EDPB, one should look at the specific processing operations in question and understand who determines them, by first considering the following questions: '*why is this processing taking place*?' and '*who decided that the processing should take place for a particular purpose?*'[405]

328. The concept of controller is a functional concept and it is therefore based on a factual rather than a formal analysis. In order to facilitate the analysis, certain rules of thumb and practical presumptions may be used to guide and simplify the process. In most situations, the 'determining body' can be easily and clearly identified by reference to certain legal and/or factual circumstances from which 'influence' normally can be inferred, unless other elements indicate the contrary. Two categories of situations can be distinguished: (1) control stemming from *legal provisions*; and (2) control stemming from *factual influence*.[406]

329. Where the controller has been specifically identified by law this will be decisive for establishing who is acting as controller. However, more commonly, rather than directly appointing the controller or setting out the criteria for its

---

403. Recital 31 also states: 'The requests for disclosure sent by the public authorities should always be in writing, reasoned and occasional and should not concern the entirety of a filing system or lead to the interconnection of filing systems.'

404. CJEU, Case C-272/19, Judgment of 9 July 2020, *Land Hessen*, ECLI:EU:C:2020:535, https://eur-lex.europa.eu/legal-content/EN/TXT/?uri=CELEX%3A62019CJ0272.

405. EDPB, Guidelines 07/2020 on the concepts of controller and processor in the GDPR, para. 19, https://edpb.europa.eu/our-work-tools/our-documents/guidelines/guidelines-072020-concepts-controller-and-processor-gdpr_en.

406. *Ibid.*, § 20.

appointment, the law will establish a task or impose a duty on someone to collect and process certain data. In those cases, the purpose of the processing is often determined by the law. The controller will normally be the one designated by law for the realisation of this purpose, this public task. For example, this would be the case where an entity which is entrusted with certain public tasks (e.g., social security) which cannot be fulfilled without collecting at least some personal data, sets up a database or register in order to fulfil those public tasks. In that case, the law, albeit indirectly, sets out who is the controller. More generally, the law may also impose an obligation on either public or private entities to retain or provide certain data. These entities would then normally be considered as controllers with respect to the processing that is necessary to execute this obligation.[407]

330. With regard to personal data processing by public authorities, it is not always easy to determine at which level of the administrative hierarchy the controller must be designated. Is the controller 'the State', 'the government', 'the minister in charge of the specific domain', 'the agency acting under the responsibility of the minister'? When answering such questions, it is important to keep in mind at which level the data subject can, in an optimal way, exercise his or her data subject rights. This principle has also been applied in the Regulation (EU) 2018/1725 on the protection of natural persons with regard to the processing of personal data by the EU institutions, bodies, offices and agencies and on the free movement of such data. Article 3(8) of this Regulation defines 'controller' as 'the Union institution or body or the directorate-general or any other organisational entity which, alone or jointly with others, determines the purposes and means of the processing of personal data'.[408] It is also worth to note that the term 'public authority' does not mean that only authorities belonging to the executive power can act as a controller. In the Land of Hessen case, the CJEU qualified the 'petition committee' of a regional parliament as the controller to which the data subject could address his access request.[409]

331. The need for factual assessment also means that the role of a controller does not stem from the nature of an entity that is processing data but from its concrete activities in a specific context. In other words, the same entity may act at the same time as controller for certain processing operations and as processor for others, and the qualification as controller or processor has to be assessed with regard to each specific data processing activity. For example, in a group of undertakings, the

407. *Ibid.*, paras 21–22.
408. Regulation (EU) 2018/1725 of the European Parliament and of the Council of 23 October 2018 on the protection of natural persons with regard to the processing of personal data by the Union institutions, bodies, offices and agencies and on the free movement of such data, and repealing Regulation (EC) No 45/2001 and Decision No 1247/2002/EC (Text with EEA relevance., PE/31/2018/REV/1, *OJ L 295, 21.11.2018, p. 39–98; see also* European Data Protection Supervisor (EDPS), EDPS Guidelines on the concepts of controller, processor and joint controllership under Regulation (EU) 2018/1725, 7.11.2019; Cimina, Veronique. 'The Data Protection Concepts of 'Controller', 'Processor' and 'Joint Controllership' under Regulation (EU) 2018/1725.', *ERA Forum* **21,** 639–654 (2021).
409. CJEU, Case C-272/19, Judgment of 9 July 2020, Land Hessen, ECLI:EU:C:2020:535, https://eur-lex.europa.eu/legal-content/EN/TXT/?uri=CELEX%3A62019CJ0272.

subsidiaries of the head office may be qualified as processors for the data processing activities in the context of a centralised client information system, but as far as they are employing local personnel, they will in principle be qualified as controllers by the local employment, social security or tax laws.

332. In many cases, an assessment of the contractual terms between the different parties involved can facilitate the determination of which party (or parties) is acting as controller. Even if a contract is silent as to who the controller is, it may contain sufficient elements to infer who exercises a decision-making role with respect to the purposes and means of the processing. It may also be that the contract contains an explicit statement as to the identity of the controller. The EDPB estimates that '*if there is no reason to doubt that this accurately reflects the reality, there is nothing against following the terms of the contract. However, the terms of a contract are not decisive in all circumstances, as this would simply allow parties to allocate responsibility as they see fit. It is not possible either to become a controller or to escape controller obligations simply by shaping the contract in a certain way where the factual circumstances say something else*'.[410]

333. Article 4(7) recognizes that the 'purposes and means' of the processing might be determined by more than one actor. It states that the controller is the actor who 'alone or jointly with others' determines the purposes and means of the processing. This means that several different entities may act as controllers for the same processing, with each of them then being subject to the applicable data protection provisions. The GDPR regulates this situation explicitly in its Article 26, which provides that '*[w]here two or more controllers jointly determine the purposes and means of processing, they shall be joint controllers*'.

334. The controller must decide on both purpose *and* means of the processing. As a result, if one legal person or public authority determines only the purpose, leaving the decisions about the means entirely to another legal person or public authority, both will qualify as controllers. Determining who is the controller is primarily important with regard to the exercise of the data subject rights. This has been highlighted by the CJEU in the Google Spain case, in which it held that '*controllers must ensure, within the framework of their responsibilities, powers and capabilities, that the data processing in question meets the requirements of Directive 95/46 in order that the guarantees laid down by the Directive may have full effect and that effective and complete protection of data subjects, in particular of their right to privacy, may actually be achieved*'.[411] In the opinion of the EDPB, the controller is the

410. *Ibid.*, § 25.
411. CJEU, Case C-131/12, Judgment of 13 May 2014, *Google Spain SL v. Agencia Espanola de Proteccion de Datos (AEPD)*, ECLI:EU:C:2014:317, paras 38 and 83, https://eur-lex.europa.eu/legal-content/EN/TXT/?uri=CELEX%3A62012CJ0131.

actor who has determined *why* the processing is taking place (i.e., 'to what end'; or 'what for') and *how* this objective shall be reached (i.e., which means shall be employed to attain the objective).[412]

335. In practice, if a controller engages a processor to carry out the processing on its behalf, it often means that the processor shall be able to make certain decisions of its own on how to carry out the processing. The EDPB recognizes that some margin of manoeuvre may exist for the processor also to be able to make some decisions in relation to the processing. In this perspective, there is a need to provide guidance about which level of influence on the 'why' and the 'how' should entail the qualification of an entity as a controller and to what extent a processor may make decisions of its own. When one entity clearly determines purposes and means, entrusting another entity with processing activities that amount to the execution of its detailed instructions, the situation is straightforward, and there is no doubt that the second entity should be regarded as a processor, whereas the first entity is the controller.[413]

336. Regarding the determination of means, a distinction can be made between essential and non-essential means. 'Essential means' are traditionally and inherently reserved to the controller. While non-essential means can also be determined by the processor, essential means are to be determined by the controller. According to the EDPB, 'essential means' are means that are closely linked to the purpose and the scope of the processing, such as the type of personal data which are processed ('*which data shall be processed*?'), the duration of the processing ('*for how long shall they be processed?*'), the categories of recipients ('*who shall have access to them?*') and the categories of data subjects ('*whose personal data are being processed?*'). Together with the purpose of processing, the essential means are also closely linked to the question of whether the processing is lawful, necessary and proportionate. 'Non-essential means' concern more practical aspects of implementation, such as the choice for a particular type of hard- or software or the detailed security measures which may be left to the processor to decide on.[414]

337. As a consequence, it is not necessary that the controller actually has access to the data that is being processed. It suffices that the controller has a determinative influence on the purpose and (essential) means of the processing. Access to the personal data should ideally be granted on 'need-to-know' basis. If there is no specific reason why, in a group of undertakings, the head office should have access to data relating, for example, to employees or job applicants, such access should be avoided. In his comprehensive and critical analysis of the concepts of 'controller' and 'processor', B.Van Alsenoy writes: '*Traditionally, the legal status of controller*

412. EDPB, Guidelines 07/2020 on the concepts of controller and processor in the GDPR, para. 33, https://edpb.europa.eu/our-work-tools/our-documents/guidelines/guidelines-072020-concepts-controller-and-processor-gdpr_en.
413. *Ibid.*, § 35.
414. *Ibid.*, para. 38.

has been attached to a party's authority to decide about the processing, rather than its involvement in the processing itself.'[415]

2. Joint Controllers

338. As already mentioned, Article 26 of the GDPR provides that *'[w]here two or more controllers jointly determine the purposes and means of processing, they shall be joint controllers'*. Joint controllership thus exists with regard to a specific processing activity when different parties determine *jointly* the purpose and means of this processing activity. 'Jointly' must be interpreted as meaning 'together with' or 'not alone', in different forms and combinations.[416]

339. Not all processing involving several entities give rise to joint controllership. The overarching criterion for joint controllership to exist is the joint participation of two or more entities in the determination of the purposes and means of a processing. More specifically, joint participation needs to include the determination of purposes on the one hand and the determination of means on the other hand. If each of these elements are determined by all entities concerned, they should be considered as joint controllers of the processing at issue.[417]

340. Joint participation in the determination of purposes and means implies that more than one entity have a decisive influence over whether and how the processing takes place. In practice, joint participation can take several different forms. For example, joint participation can take the form of a common decision taken by two or more entities or result from 'converging decisions' by two or more entities regarding the purposes and essential means. Joint participation through a *common decision* means deciding together and involves a common intention in accordance with the most common understanding of the term 'jointly' referred to in Article 26 of the GDPR.

341. As such, an important criterion to identify converging decisions in this context is whether the processing would not be possible without both parties' participation in the purposes and means in the sense that the processing by each party is inextricably linked. In the Wirtschaftsakademie judgment, the CJEU applied this criterion on the case of educational services by means of a fan page hosted on Facebook. Fan pages are user accounts that can be set up on Facebook by individuals or businesses. To do so, the author of the fan page, after registering with Facebook, can use the platform designed by Facebook to introduce himself to the users of that

415. Van Alsenoy, B. Data Protection Law in the EU: Roles, Intersentia, Mortsel, 2019, § 1180; *see also* Van Alsenoy, Brendan. 'Allocating Responsibility among Controllers, Processors, and 'Everything in between': the Definition of Actors and Roles in Directive 95/46/EC.' *The Computer Law and Security Report*, vol. 28, no. 1, 2012, pp. 25–43.

416. EDPB, Guidelines 07/2020 on the concepts of controller and processor in the GDPR, § 47, https://edpb.europa.eu/our-work-tools/our-documents/guidelines/guidelines-072020-concepts-controller-and-processor-gdpr_en.

417. *Ibid.*, para. 50.

social network and to persons visiting the fan page, and to post any kind of communication in the media and opinion market. Administrators of fan pages can obtain anonymous statistical information on visitors to the fan pages via a function called 'Facebook Insights' which Facebook makes available to them free of charge under non-negotiable conditions of use. That information is collected by means of evidence files ('cookies'), each containing a unique user code, which are active for two years and are stored by Facebook on the hard disk of the computer or on other media of visitors to fan pages. The user code, which can be matched with the connection data of users registered on Facebook, is collected and processed when the fan pages are opened.

342. The CJEU observed, first, that Facebook Inc. and, for the European Union, Facebook Ireland must be regarded as primarily determining the purposes and means of processing the personal data of users of Facebook and persons visiting the fan pages hosted on Facebook. The Court stated, on the contrary, that the administrator of a fan page hosted on Facebook, by creating such a page, gives Facebook the opportunity to place cookies on the computer or other device of a person visiting its fan page, whether or not that person has a Facebook account. It also noted that the administrator of the fan page, with the help of filters made available by Facebook, defines the criteria in accordance with which the statistics are to be drawn up and even designate the categories of persons whose personal data is to be made use of by Facebook. In particular, the administrator of the fan page can ask for — and thereby request the processing of — demographic data relating to its target audience, including trends in terms of age, sex, relationship and occupation, information on the lifestyles and centres of interest of the target audience and information on the purchases and online purchasing habits of visitors to its page, the categories of goods and services that appeal the most, and geographical data which tell the fan page administrator where to make special offers and where to organise events, and more generally enable it to target best the information it offers. The Court concluded, therefore that, '*In those circumstances, the administrator of a fan page hosted on Facebook, such as Wirtschaftsakademie, must be regarded as taking part, by its definition of parameters depending in particular on its target audience and the objectives of managing and promoting its activities, in the determination of the purposes and means of processing the personal data of the visitors to its fan page. The administrator must therefore be categorised, in the present case, as a controller responsible for that processing within the European Union, jointly with Facebook Ireland.*'[418]

343. It is interesting to mention that the CJEU in its *Wirtschaftsakademie* judgment, again emphasised the link between the controllership of personal data processing and the protection of the data subjects. The Court held that 'the recognition of joint responsibility of the operator of the social network and the administrator of a fan page hosted on that network in relation to the processing of the personal data

418. CJEU, Case C-210/16, Judgment of 5 June 2018, Wirtschaftsakademie Schleswig-Holstein, ECLI-:EU:C:2018:388, para. 39, https://eur-lex.europa.eu/legal-content/EN/TXT/?uri=CELEX%3A62016CJ0210.

of visitors to that page contributes to ensuring more complete protection of the rights of persons visiting a fan page'. In other words, when deciding who among the parties involved in a data processing, should be recognised as the controller, one must also consider the position of the data subject.[419]

344. The Court, in the same judgment, also confirmed that the responsibilities of joint controllers are not necessarily equal. 'The existence of joint responsibility does not necessarily imply equal responsibility of the various operators involved in the processing of personal data. On the contrary, those operators may be involved at different stages of that processing of personal data and to different degrees, so that the level of responsibility of each of them must be assessed with regard to all the relevant circumstances of the particular case.'[420]

345. As already mentioned before, the CJEU held, in the *Jehovah Witnesses* case, that a religious community is a controller, jointly with its members who engage in preaching, for the processing of personal data carried out by the latter in the context of door-to-door preaching organised, coordinated and encouraged by that community, without it being necessary that the community has access to those data, or to establish that that community has given its members written guidelines or instructions in relation to the data processing.[421] The Court considered, on the one hand, that the individual members of the community who engage in preaching 'determine in which specific circumstances they collect personal data relating to persons visited, which specific data are collected and how those data are subsequently processed' but that, on the other hand, the community 'organised, coordinated and encouraged' the door-to-door preaching.[422]

346. In *Fashion ID*, the CJEU dealt with joint controllership in the context of an online clothing retailer who embedded on its website the 'Like' social plugin from the social network Facebook ('the Facebook 'Like' button'). When a visitor consults the website of Fashion ID, that visitor's personal data are transmitted to Facebook Ireland as a result of that website including that button. This transmission occurs without that visitor being aware of it regardless of whether or not he or she is a member of the social network Facebook or has clicked on the Facebook 'Like' button. The referring court, in its request for a preliminary ruling, essentially asked, whether the operator of a website, such as Fashion ID, that embeds on that website a social plugin causing the browser of a visitor to that website to request content

419. *Ibid.*, para. 42.
420. *Ibid.*, para. 43.
421. CJEU, Case C-25/17, Judgment of 10 July 2018, Jehovan todistajat, ECLI:EU:C:2018:551, para. 75, https://eur-lex.europa.eu/legal-content/en/TXT/?uri=CELEX:62017CJ0025.
422. Regarding the question if the Jehovah religious community not only determined the purpose but also the means, the Court noted that 'the congregations of the Jehovah's Witnesses Community keep lists of persons who no longer wish to receive a visit, from those data which are transmitted to them by members who engage in preaching' and further that the community 'organises and coordinates the preaching activities of its members, in particular, by allocating areas of activity between the various members who engage in preaching'. *Ibid.*, § 70–71.

from the provider of that plugin and, to that end, to transmit to that provider the personal data of the visitor can be considered to be a controller, despite that operator being unable to influence the processing of the data transmitted to that provider as a result.

347. The Court held in this case that the objective of the broad definition of the concept of 'controller' is to ensure the effective and comprehensive protection of the persons concerned and that the existence of joint liability does not necessarily imply equal responsibility of the various operators engaged in the processing of personal data. On the contrary, those operators may be involved at different stages of that processing of personal data and to different degrees, with the result that the level of liability of each of them must be assessed with regard to all the relevant circumstances of the particular case. In other words, the CJEU repeated that one should primarily consider the position of the data subject.

348. The CJEU noted, in this particular case, that, by embedding on its website the Facebook 'Like' button, Fashion ID appears to have made it possible for Facebook Ireland to obtain personal data of visitors to its website and that such a possibility is triggered as soon as the visitor consults that website, regardless of whether or not the visitor is a member of the social network Facebook, has clicked on the Facebook 'Like' button or is aware of such an operation.[423] It further pointed out ' *that the operations involving the processing of personal data in respect of which Fashion ID is capable of determining, jointly with Facebook Ireland, the purposes and means are, for the purposes of the definition of the concept of 'processing of personal data' the collection and disclosure by transmission of the personal data of visitors to its website. By contrast, in the light of that information, it seems, at the outset, impossible that Fashion ID determines the purposes and means of subsequent operations involving the processing of personal data carried out by Facebook Ireland after their transmission to the latter, meaning that Fashion ID cannot be considered to be a controller in respect of those operations*'.

349. The Court, subsequently, examined who determines the 'collection and disclosure by transmission' of the data. With regard to the means, the Court held that Fashion ID appears to have embedded on its website the Facebook 'Like' button made available to website operators by Facebook Ireland while fully aware of the fact that it serves as a tool for the collection and disclosure by transmission of the personal data of visitors to that website. As to the purposes of those operations involving the processing of personal data, it observed that Fashion ID's embedding of the Facebook 'Like' button on its website allows it to optimise the publicity of its goods by making them more visible on the social network Facebook when a visitor to its website clicks on that button.[424] The CJEU, therefore, concluded that '*the*

423. CJEU, Case C-40/17, Judgment of 29 Jul 2019, Fashion ID, ECLI:EU:C:2019:629, para. 75, https://eur-lex.europa.eu/legal-content/en/TXT/?uri=CELEX:62017CJ0040.
424. *Ibid.*, para. 80.

operator of a website, such as Fashion ID, that embeds on that website a social plugin causing the browser of a visitor to that website to request content from the provider of that plugin and, to that end, to transmit to that provider the personal data of the visitor can be considered to be a controller' but it added '*That liability is, however, limited to the operation or set of operations involving the processing of personal data in respect of which it actually determines the purposes and means, that is to say, the collection and disclosure by transmission of the data at issue.*'[425]

350. The *Fashion ID* decision of the CJEU learns that joint controllership requires that two or more entities have exerted influence over the means of the processing but that this does not mean that, for joint controllership to exist, each entity involved needs in all cases to determine all of the means. Different entities may be involved at different stages of that processing and to different degrees. Different joint controllers may therefore define the means of the processing to a different extent, depending on who is effectively in a position to do so.[426] It may also be the case that one of the entities involved provides the means of the processing and makes it available for personal data processing activities by other entities. The entity who decides to make use of those means so that personal data can be processed for a particular purpose also participates in the determination of the means of the processing. This scenario can notably arise in case of platforms, standardised tools, or other infrastructure allowing the parties to process the same personal data and which have been set up in a certain way by one of the parties to be used by others that can also decide how to set it up.[427]

351. The fact that several actors are involved in the same processing does not mean that they are necessarily acting as joint controllers of such processing. Not all kind of partnerships, cooperation or collaboration imply qualification of joint controllers as such qualification requires a case-by-case analysis of each processing at stake and the precise role of each entity with respect to each processing. In its guidelines, the EDPB mentions the example of a situation where several entities use a shared database or a common infrastructure but where each entity independently determines its own purposes. Also, there can be situations where various actors successively process the same personal data in a chain of operations, each of these actors having an independent purpose and independent means in their part of the chain. In the absence of joint participation in the determination of the purposes and

425. *Ibid.*, para. 86.
426. Van Alsenoy, Brendan, et al. 'Social Networks and Web 2.0: Are Users Also Bound by Data Protection Regulations?' *Identity in the Information Society*, vol. 2, no. 1, 2009, pp. 65–79. Also Van Alsenoy, Brendan. 'Allocating Responsibility among Controllers, Processors, and 'Everything in between': the Definition of Actors and Roles in Directive 95/46/EC.' *The Computer Law and Security Report*, vol. 28, no. 1, 2012, pp. 25–43.
427. EDPB, Guidelines 07/2020 on the concepts of controller and processor in the GDPR, para. 63, https://edpb.europa.eu/our-work-tools/our-documents/guidelines/guidelines-072020-concepts-controller-and-processor-gdpr_en.

means of the same processing operation or set of operations, joint controllership has to be excluded and the various actors must be regarded as successive independent controllers.[428]

3. Definition of Processor

352. A processor is defined in Article 4 (8) of the GDPR as a natural or legal person, public authority, agency or another body, which processes personal data on behalf of the controller. Similar to the definition of controller, the definition of processor envisages a broad range of actors – it can be '*a natural or legal person, public authority, agency or other body*'. This means that there is in principle no limitation as to which type of actor might assume the role of a processor. It might be an organisation, but it might also be an individual. The two basic conditions for qualifying as processor are: being *a separate entity* in relation to the controller and processing personal data *on the controller's behalf.*

353. A separate entity means that the controller decides to delegate all or part of the processing activities to an external organisation. Within a group of companies, one company can be a processor to another company acting as controller, as both companies are separate entities. Alternately, a department within a company cannot be a processor to another department within the same entity. If the controller decides to process data itself, using its own resources within its organisation, for example through its own staff, this is not a processor situation. Employees and other persons that are acting under the direct authority of the controller, such as temporarily employed staff, are not to be seen as processors since they will process personal data as a part of the controller's entity. In accordance with Article 29, they are also bound by the controller's instructions.

354. Processing personal data on the controller's behalf first requires that the separate entity processes personal data for the benefit of the controller. In Article 4(2), processing is defined as a concept including a wide array of operations ranging from collection, storage and consultation to use, dissemination or otherwise making available and destruction. Second, the processing must be done on behalf of a controller but otherwise than under its direct authority or control. Acting 'on behalf of' means serving someone else's interest and recalls the legal concept of 'delegation'. In the case of data protection law, a processor is called to implement the instructions given by the controller at least with regard to the purpose of the processing and the essential elements of the means. The lawfulness of the processing according to Article 6, and if relevant Article 9, of the Regulation will be derived from the controller's activity and the processor must not process the data otherwise than according to the controller's instructions. Even so, as described above, the controller's instructions may still leave a certain degree of discretion about how to best serve the controller's interests, allowing the processor to choose the most suitable technical and organisational means.

---

428. *Ibid.*, paras 67–70.

355. Acting 'on behalf of' also means that the processor may not carry out processing for its own purpose(s). As provided in Article 28(10), a processor infringes the GDPR by going beyond the controller's instructions and starting to determine its own purposes and means of processing. The processor will be considered a controller in respect of that processing and may be subject to sanctions for going beyond the controller's instructions.[429]

D. Exceptions

1. Outside the Scope of Union Law

356. Article 2 of the GDPR states that it does not apply to the processing of personal data: (a) in the course of an activity which falls outside the scope of Union law; (b) … ; (c) by the Member States when carrying out activities which fall within the scope of Chapter 2 of Title V of the Treaty on European Union; (Chapter 2 Specific provisions on the common foreign and security policy).

357. Recital 14 explains: 'This Regulation does not address issues of protection of fundamental rights and freedoms or the free flow of data related to activities which fall outside the scope of Union law, such as activities concerning national security, nor does it cover the processing of personal data by the Member States when carrying out activities in relation to the common foreign and security policy of the Union.'

358. First, Article 2(2)(a) of the GDPR provides that that regulation does not apply to the processing of personal data 'in the course of an activity which falls outside the scope of Union law'. The CJEU has held that this exception to the applicability of the GDPR must, like the other exceptions laid down in Article 2(2), be interpreted strictly.[430]

359. The Court has repeatedly held that only the processing of personal data in the course of an activity of the State or of State authorities which was previously expressly listed in Article 3(2) of Directive 95/46 or in the course of an activity which could be classified in the same category was excluded from the scope of that directive.[431] It follows that Article 2(2)(a) of the GDPR, read in the light of Recital

429. B. Van Alsenoy, 'Allocating responsibility among controllers, processors, and 'everything in between': the definition of actors and roles in Directive 95/46/EC', op. cit. *supra* note 5, 34 and T. Olsen and T. Mahler, 'Identity management and data protection law: Risk, responsibility and compliance in 'Circles of Trust' –Part II', (2007) *Computer, Law & Security Review*, p. 419.

430. CJEU, Case C-272/19, Judgment of 9 July 2020, Land Hessen, ECLI:EU:C:2020:535, para. 68, https://eur-lex.europa.eu/legal-content/EN/TXT/?uri=CELEX%3A62019CJ0272, and CJEU, Case C-311/18, Judgment of 16 July 2020, Data Protection Commissioner v. Facebook Ireland and Maximillian Schrems. (Request for a preliminary ruling from the High Court, Ireland), ECLI:EU:C:2020:559, para. 84, https://eur-lex.europa.eu/legal-content/EN/TXT/?uri=CELEX%3A62018CJ0311.

431. CJEU, Case C-101/01, Judgment of 6 November 2003, Bodil Lindqvist, ECLI:EU:C:2003:596, paras 42 to 44, https://eur-lex.europa.eu/legal-content/EN/TXT/?uri=CELEX%3A62001CJ0101;

16, must be regarded as being designed solely to exclude from the scope of that regulation the processing of personal data carried out by State authorities in the course of an activity which is intended to safeguard national security or of an activity which can be classified in the same category, with the result that the mere fact that an activity is an activity characteristic of the State or of a public authority is not sufficient ground for that exception to be automatically applicable to such an activity.[432]

360. The activities having the aim of safeguarding national security that are envisaged in Article 2(2)(a) of the GDPR encompass, in particular, those that are intended to protect essential State functions and the fundamental interests of society. The CJEU found, in the *Latvijas Republikas Saeima* case, that activities relating to road safety do not pursue such an objective and consequently cannot be classified in the category of activities having the aim of safeguarding national security, which are envisaged in Article 2(2)(a) of the GDPR.[433]

2. Household Exception

361. The GDPR does further not apply to processing of personal data by a natural person in the course of a purely personal or household activity and thus without a connection with a professional or commercial activity. Personal and household activities could include correspondence and the holding of addresses, or social networking and online activity undertaken within the context of such personal and household activities. However, this Regulation should apply to controllers or processors which provide the means for processing personal data for such personal or household activities.[434]

362. In the *Lindqvis*t judgment, the CJEU held that the 'household exception' must be interpreted as relating only to activities which are carried out in the course of private or family life of individuals, which is clearly not the case with the processing of personal data consisting in publication on the Internet so that those data

---

CJEU, Case C-73/16, Judgment of 27 September 2017, Peter Puškár, ECLI:EU:C:2017:725, paras 36 and 37, https://eur-lex.europa.eu/legal-content/en/TXT/?uri=CELEX:62016CJ0073; CJEU, Case C-25/17, Judgment of 10 July 2018, Jehovan todistajat, ECLI:EU:C:2018:551, para. 38, https://eur-lex.europa.eu/legal-content/en/TXT/?uri=CELEX:62017CJ0025.

432. CJEU, Case C-272/19, Judgment of 9 July 2020, Land Hessen, ECLI:EU:C:2020:535, para. 70, https://eur-lex.europa.eu/legal-content/EN/TXT/?uri=CELEX%3A62019CJ0272.

433. CJEU, Case C-439/19, Judgment of 22 June 2021, Latvijas Republikas Saeima, ECLI:EU:C:2021:504, para. 68, https://curia.europa.eu/juris/liste.jsf?lgrec=fr&td=%3BALL&language=en&num=C-439/19&jur=C.

434. Chen, Jiahong, et al. 'Who Is Responsible for Data Processing in Smart Homes? Reconsidering Joint Controllership and the Household Exemption.' *International Data Privacy Law*, vol. 10, no. 4, 2020, pp. 279–293.

are made accessible to an indefinite number of people.[435] With regard to the processing of data regarding personal tax information which had already been published in a Finnish newspaper, the CJEU decided that activities involving the processing of personal data relating to such personal data files which contain solely, and in unaltered form, material that has already been published in the media, fall within the scope of application of the Data Protection Directive.[436]

363. In the *Jehovah Witnesses* case, the referring Court asked the CJEU what significance was to be given to the fact that the preaching activity in the course of which the data is collected concerns the personal religious practice of the members of a religious community. The Court estimated that door-to-door preaching, in the course of which personal data are collected by members of the Jehovah's Witnesses Community, is, by its very nature, intended to spread the faith of the Jehovah's Witnesses Community among people who do not belong to the faith of the members who engage in preaching. Therefore, that activity is directed outwards from the private setting of the members who engage in preaching. Furthermore some of the data collected by the members of that community who engage in preaching are sent by them to the congregations of that community which compile lists from that data of persons who no longer wish to receive visits from those members. Thus, in the course of their preaching, those members make at least some of the data collected accessible to a potentially unlimited number of persons. The Court decided, therefore, that the collection of personal data by members of a religious community in the course of door-to-door preaching and the subsequent processing of those data does not constitute processing of personal data carried out by a natural person in the course of a purely personal or household activity.'[437]

364. The CJEU dealt more extensively with the household exemption in the *Ryneš* case. Mr Ryneš installed and used a camera system located under the eaves of his family home. The camera was installed in a fixed position and could not turn; it recorded the entrance to his home, the public footpath and the entrance to the house opposite. The system allowed only a visual recording, which was stored on recording equipment in the form of a continuous loop on a hard disk drive. As soon as it reached full capacity, the device would record over the existing recording, erasing old material. No monitor was installed on the recording equipment, so the images could not be studied in real time. Only Mr Ryneš had direct access to the system and the data. Mr Ryneš's only reason for operating the camera was to protect the property, health and life of his family and himself. Indeed, both Mr Ryneš and his family had for several years been subjected to attacks by persons unknown whom it had not been possible to identify. One night, a further attack took place. One of the windows of Mr Ryneš's home was broken by a shot from a catapult. The

---

435. CJEU, Case C-101/01, Judgment of 6 November 2003, Bodil Lindqvist, ECLI:EU:C:2003:596, para. 47, https://eur-lex.europa.eu/legal-content/EN/TXT/?uri=CELEX%3A62001CJ0101.
436. CJEU, Case C-73/07, Judgment of 16 Dec 2008, Satakunnan Markkinapörssi and Satamedia, ECLI:EU:C:2008:727, para. 49, https://eur-lex.europa.eu/legal-content/en/TXT/?uri=CELEX:62007CJ0073.
437. CJEU, Case C-25/17, Judgment of 10 July 2018, Jehovan todistajat, ECLI:EU:C:2018:551, para. 51, https://eur-lex.europa.eu/legal-content/en/TXT/?uri=CELEX:62017CJ0025.

video surveillance system at issue made it possible to identify two suspects. The recording was handed over to the police and relied on in the course of the subsequent criminal proceedings. However, following a request from one of the suspects for confirmation that Mr Ryneš's surveillance system was lawful, the data protection supervisory authority found that Mr Ryneš had infringed the data protection law.

365. The Court, on the one hand, found that, to the extent that video surveillance covers, even partially, a public space and is accordingly directed outwards from the private setting of the person processing the data in that manner, it cannot be regarded as an activity which is a purely 'personal or household' activity. On the other hand, the CJEU held that one must also take into account the legitimate interests pursued by the controller, such as the protection of the property, health and life of his family and himself. The Court concluded, curiously enough, that '*the operation of a camera system, as a result of which a video recording of people is stored on a continuous recording device such as a hard disk drive, installed by an individual on his family home for the purposes of protecting the property, health and life of the home owners, but which also monitors a public space, does not amount to the processing of data in the course of a purely personal or household activity*'.[438]

366. In its *Buivids*-judgment of 14 February 2019, the CJEU also dealt with the question under which conditions video recording by a private person falls under the household exemption. The case relates to Mr Buivids, who made a video recording in a station of the Latvian national police while he was making a statement in the context of administrative proceedings which had been brought against him. Mr Buivids published the recorded video which showed police officers going about their duties in the police station, on 'YouTube'. After that video had been published, the National Data Protection Agency found that Mr Buivids had infringed the Personal Data Protection Law because he had not informed the police officers, as data subjects, of the intended purpose of the processing of personal data concerning them. The National Data Protection Agency therefore requested Mr Buivids to remove that video from the internet.

367. The Court found that, 'since Mr Buivids published the video in question on a video website on which users can send, watch and share videos, without restricting access to that video, thereby permitting access to personal data to an indefinite number of people, the processing of personal data at issue in the main proceedings does not come within the context of purely personal or household activities'.[439]

---

438. CJEU, Case C-212/13, Judgment of 11 December 2014, Ryneš, ECLI:EU:C:2014:2428, https://eur-lex.europa.eu/legal-content/EN/TXT/?uri=CELEX%3A62013CJ0212, in fine. *See also* EDPB, Guidelines 3/2019 on processing of personal data through video devices, paras 11–13.
439. CJEU, Case C-345/17, Judgment of 14 February 2019, Buivids, ECLI:EU:C:2019:122, https://eur-lex.europa.eu/legal-content/EN/TXT/?uri=CELEX%3A62017CJ0345. The CJEU, however, finally decided in this case that video recording, such as in the particular case of Mr Buivids, 'may constitute a processing of personal data solely for journalistic purposes, within the meaning of that

3. Law Enforcement

368. Pursuant to Article 2(e) of the GDPR, its provisions do not apply to personal data processing by competent authorities for the purposes of prevention, investigation, detection or prosecution of criminal offences, the execution of criminal penalties, including the safeguarding against and the prevention of threats to public security. Data processed by public authorities under this Regulation when used for the purposes of prevention, investigation, detection or prosecution of criminal offences or the execution of criminal penalties should be governed by the Law Enforcement Directive.[440]

369. Member States may entrust competent authorities within the meaning of the Law Enforcement Directive with other tasks which are not necessarily carried out for the purposes of the prevention, investigation, detection or prosecution of criminal offences or the execution of criminal penalties, including the safeguarding against and prevention of threats to public security, so that the processing of personal data for those other purposes, insofar as it is within the scope of Union law, fall within the scope of the GDPR.[441]

370. With regard to the processing of personal data by those competent authorities for purposes falling within the scope of the GDPR, Member States may maintain or introduce more specific provisions to adapt the application of the rules of the GDPR. These provisions may determine more precisely specific requirements for processing of personal data by those competent authorities for those other purposes, taking into account the constitutional, organisational and administrative structure of the respective Member State.[442]

371. When processing of personal data by private bodies falls within the scope of the GDPR, Member States have the possibility under specific conditions to restrict by law certain obligations and rights when such a restriction constitutes a necessary and proportionate measure in a democratic society to safeguard specific important interests including public security and the prevention, investigation, detection or prosecution of criminal offences or the execution of criminal penalties, including the safeguarding against and the prevention of threats to public security. This is relevant for instance in the framework of anti-money laundering or the activities of forensic laboratories.[443]

372. The GDPR applies also to the activities of courts and other judicial authorities. Union or Member State law could specify the processing operations and processing procedures in relation to the processing of personal data by courts and other

---

provision, insofar as it is apparent from that video that the sole object of that recording and publication thereof is the disclosure of information, opinions or ideas to the public'.

440. *See* above, paras 283–290.

441. Recital 19 of the GDPR.

442. *Ibid.*

443. *Ibid.*, in fine.

judicial authorities. The competence of the supervisory authorities should not cover the processing of personal data when courts are acting in their judicial capacity, in order to safeguard the independence of the judiciary in the performance of its judicial tasks, including its decision-making. Supervision of such data processing operations may be entrusted to specific bodies within the judicial system of the Member State, which should in particular control compliance with the rules of the GDPR, promote the awareness of the judiciary of their obligations and deal with complaints in relation to such processing.[444]

373. The concept of 'competent authority' must be understood in relation to the protection of personal data in the fields of judicial cooperation in criminal matters and police cooperation, in view of the arrangements which may prove necessary, in that regard, because of the specific nature of those fields. In addition, Recital 11 of the Law Enforcement Directive explains that the GDPR applies to processing of personal data that is carried out by a 'competent authority', within the meaning of Article 3(7) of the directive, but for purposes other than those of the Directive.

4. Union Institutions

374. The GDPR does not apply to the processing of personal data by Union institutions.[445] However, already before the Lisbon Treaty, Article 286 of the Treaty establishing the European Community required the application to the Community institutions and bodies of the Community acts on the protection of individuals with regard to the processing of personal data and the free movement of such data. Since data protection in Europe, before the entry into force of the GDPR, was regulated by a European directive, which is by definition only addressed to Member States, this topic had to be dealt with in a separate legislative instrument. This was done in the Regulation (EC) No 45/2001 of the European Parliament and of the Council, which applied to the processing of personal data by the Union institutions, bodies, offices and agencies.[446] The aim was to ensure both effective compliance with the rules governing the protection of individuals' fundamental rights and freedoms and the free flow of personal data between Member States and the Community institutions and bodies or between the Community institutions and bodies for purposes connected with the exercise of their respective competences.[447]

375. Recital 17 of the GDPR states that 'in order to provide a strong and coherent data protection framework in the Union, the necessary adaptations of Regulation (EC) No 45/2001 should follow after the adoption of this Regulation, in order to allow application at the same time as this Regulation'. These adaptations have

444. Recital 20 of the GDPR.
445. Art. 2(3) of the GDPR.
446. Regulation (EC) No 45/2001 of the European Parliament and of the Council of 18 December 2000 on the protection of individuals with regard to the processing of personal data by the Community institutions and bodies and on the free movement of such data, *OJ L 8, 12.1.2001, p. 1–22.*.
447. Recital 13 of Regulation(EC) No. 45/2001.

been done in Regulation (EU) 2018/1725 which repealed Regulation (EC) 45/2001 and brings it into line with the GDPR. This Regulation lays down the rules for data protection in the EU institutions – as well as the duties of the European Data Protection Supervisor.[448]

376. Regulation (EU) 2018/1725 ensures that EU institutions and bodies provide transparent and easily accessible information on how personal data is used, as well as foresee clear mechanisms for individuals to exercise their rights; it also reconfirms, clarifies and enhances the role of data protection officers within each EU institution and of the EDPS. The guidelines of the EDPS are addressed to the Union institutions but they provide at the same time useful guidance and tools for the application of the GDPR.[449]

5. Intermediary Service Providers

377. Pursuant to Article 2(4) of the GDPR, its provisions shall be without prejudice to the application of Directive 2000/31/EC, in particular of the liability rules of intermediary service providers in Articles 12 to 15 of that Directive.

378. Articles 12 to 15 of the e-Commerce Directive[450] establish the liability of intermediary service providers when they merely transmit, in a communication network, information provided by a recipient of the service, or when they provide access to a communication network (Article 12), for the automatic, intermediate and temporary storage of that information, performed for the sole purpose of making more efficient the information's onward transmission (Article 13) or for hosting information provided by the recipient of a service (Article 14). Pursuant to Article 15 of the e-Commerce Directive, Member States shall neither impose a general obligation on providers, when providing the services covered by Articles 12, 13 and 14, to monitor the information which they transmit or store, nor a general obligation actively to seek facts or circumstances indicating illegal activity. As a consequence of Article 2(4) of the GDPR the limited liability of intermediary 'information society' service providers is also applicable on damage caused by violations of the GDPR.

448. Regulation (EU) 2018/1725 of the European Parliament and of the Council of 23 October 2018 on the protection of natural persons with regard to the processing of personal data by the Union institutions, bodies, offices and agencies and on the free movement of such data, and repealing Regulation (EC) No 45/2001 and Decision No 1247/2002/EC (Text with EEA relevance.)PE/31/2018/REV/1, *OJ L 295, 21.11.2018, p. 39–98.*.

449. All guidelines are available at https://edps.europa.eu/data-protection/our-work/subjects/regulation-20181725_en.

450. Directive 2000/31/EC of the European Parliament and of the Council of 8 June 2000 on certain legal aspects of information society services, in particular electronic commerce, in the Internal Market ('Directive on electronic commerce') *OJ* L 178, 17 July 2000, http://data.europa.eu/eli/dir/2000/31/oj.

E. Delegation to Member States' Law

379. Although it is a Regulation, contrary to a Directive directly applicable to natural and legal persons and other entities in the whole of the European Union, the GDPR still gives leeway to Member States legislators to regulate a series of matters on which it has not been possible to find a compromise at the Union level. Notable examples are:

- Article 6(2), allowing Member States to maintain or introduce more specific provisions to adapt the application of the rules of the GDPR with regard to processing for compliance with a legal obligation to which the controller is subject or to processing which is necessary for the performance of a task carried out in the public interest or in the exercise of official authority vested in the controller;
- Article 8(1) in fine, stating that Member States may provide by law for a lower age for the direct provision of information society services to a child, provided that such lower age is not below 13;
- Article 9(4) enabling Member States to maintain or introduce further conditions, including limitations, with regard to the processing of genetic data, biometric data or data concerning health;
- Article 43 leaving it to the Member States to ensure that certification bodies are accredited by their data protection supervisory authorities or by their national accreditation bodies.

380. In addition to these delegations to the national legislators of the Member States, the GDPR has left it to the Member States to take action in a series of specific situations. It concerns in particular:

- the right to freedom of expression and to information when processing personal data for journalistic purposes and for purposes of academic, artistic or literary expression;
- ensuring public access to official documents;
- protection of the national identification number;
- protection of the rights of employees and employers in the employment context;
- allowing processing of personal data for archiving purposes in the public interest, for scientific or historical research purposes or statistical purposes;
- the exercise of powers by the supervisory authority in relation to a controller or processor subject to an obligation to professional secrecy under national law;
- the processing of personal data by churches and religious associations.

For these particular situations, the European legislator has left it to an extent up to the Member States to decide how the differing rights and obligations should be weighed against one another.

381. Considering that Member States must adopt national laws to reconcile these obligations and rights with the right to data protection, it is to be expected that there are, and will continue to be, differences in the emphases that national legislators place when they implement these provisions. To nonetheless have some limited form of control, Member States are required to report on their national implementing laws to the European Commission, at least with regard to laws relating to:

- exemptions and derogations to the provisions of the GDPR foreseen in Article 85.2 GDPR;
- the protection of the rights and freedoms in respect of the processing of employee's data in the employment context;
- the exercise of powers by the supervisory authority in relation to a controller or processor subject to an obligation to professional secrecy under national law.

Moreover, since national law is key here, one must once more make the analysis as to which national law applies. For each of the provisions in Chapter IX GDPR, the European legislator has clarified which national law to apply. Sometimes such clarification is found in the recitals, rather than the substantive provisions themselves.

1. Protection of Personal Data and the Right to Freedom of Expression and to Information

382. Article 85(1) GDPR gives Member States the task to reconcile the right to freedom of expression and to information with the right to data protection. To do that, Article 85(2) GDPR clarifies for which provisions of the GDPR Member States should, by law, introduce exemptions or derogations whenever personal data are processed for journalistic purposes and the purposes of academic, artistic or literary expression.[451] The derogations and exemptions concern the provisions related to:

- the general principles of processing;
- the rights of the data subject;
- controllers and processors;
- transfers of personal data to third countries or international organisations;
- the independent supervisory authorities;
- cooperation and consistency;
- specific data processing situations.

For a controller to determine which national law to apply and therefore to assess which exemptions and derogations he can rely on, Recital 153 GDPR clarifies that it is the national law to which the controller is subject.

451. Erdos, David. 'From the Scylla of Restriction to the Charybdis of Licence? Exploring the Scope of the 'Special Purposes' Freedom of Expression Shield in European Data Protection.' *Common Market Law Review*, vol. 52, no. 1, 2015, pp. 119–153.

383. Article 9 of Directive 95/46/EC imposed a similar task on Member States but limited the scope of the exemptions and derogations to those circumstances where the processing of personal data was carried out 'solely' for journalistic purposes or the purpose of artistic or literary expression and then '*only if they are necessary to reconcile the right to privacy with the rules governing freedom of expression*'. Hence, compared with Article 9 Directive 95/46/EC, Article 85.1 GDPR is significantly more open-ended. Under the GDPR, it is the Member States' task to reconcile the right to freedom of expression and to information with the right to data protection, which may include the processing of personal data for journalistic purposes and purposes of academic, artistic or literary expression, but it is no longer limited to those purposes.[452]

384. That said, Recital 153 GDPR confusingly repeats the wording of Article 9 Directive 95/46/EC, stating that there should be derogations or exemptions from certain provisions of the GDPR for the processing of personal data 'solely' for journalistic purposes, or for the purposes of academic, artistic or literary expression. This once again seems to limit the scope of Article 85.1 GDPR. The final sentence of that Recital luckily emphasizes the broadened scope by stating that it is necessary to interpret notions relating to the freedom of expression, including journalism, broadly. This leads to the necessary conclusion that Article 85.1 GDPR's scope has indeed been broadened, irrespective of the repetition of the word 'solely' in Recital 153 GDPR.

385. Although Article 85 GDPR refers to more purposes for processing personal data than 'just' journalism, most case law regarding this provision concerns the area of tension between the right to data protection and processing personal data for journalistic purposes.[453] As REVENTLOW notes, personal data are very often the raw material for journalism and unsatisfactory implementation of Article 85 GDPR by Member States allows the GDPR to be weaponised to the detriment of the right to freedom of expression and to information.[454]

386. As explained above, the last sentence of Recital 153 GDPR emphasizes that the importance of the right to freedom of expression in every democratic society warrants a broad interpretation of notions relating to that freedom, including journalism. That raises the question: when does one speak about journalism? Is it required to be a professional journalist? Should only media companies or members

452. N.J. Reventlow, 'Can the GDPR and Freedom of Expression Coexist?', *AJIL* 6 January 2020, 114, p. 32; Jozwiak, Magdalena. 'Balancing the Rights to Data Protection and Freedom of Expression and Information by the Court of Justice of the European Union.' *Maastricht Journal of European and Comparative Law*, vol. 23, no. 3, 2016, pp. 404–420.

453. M. Jozwiak, 'The Scale Matters: The ECtHR Grand Chamber Finds That Prohibition of Mass Publication of 'Raw' Taxation Data Does Not Infringe Right to Freedom of Expression.' *European Data Protection Law Review (Internet)*, vol. 4, no. 1, 2018, pp. 127–134.

454. N.J. Reventlow, 'Can the GDPR and Freedom of Expression Coexist?', *AJIL* 6 January 2020, 114, p. 31.

of the press who have registered as journalists or who are bound by a deontological code of journalists be allowed to rely on the exemptions and derogations offered in Article 85.2 GDPR?

387. Authors have noted that the case law of the CJEU on the relationship between the right to freedom of expression and the right to data protection has been somewhat vague, with the Court refusing to take a firm position.[455] With regard to the notion of journalism, however, the CJEU's position is quite clear: as Recital 153 now explicitly explains, the notion should be interpreted broadly. In its *Buivids*-judgment, the CJEU referred to its earlier judgment in the *Satamedia*-case and observed that the exemptions and derogations for the processing of personal data for journalistic purposes are not only reserved for media undertakings but apply to every person engaged in journalism.[456] Journalism, according to the CJEU, is any activity that has as its purpose the disclosure to the public of information, opinions or ideas, irrespective of the medium which is used to transmit them.[457] Whether a person is or is not a professional journalist, does not in itself determine whether the derogations and exemptions under Article 85 apply.[458]

388. In the *Buivids*-case the CJEU had to decide whether a person who made a YouTube video of his encounter with law enforcement agents, could be considered a journalist. That person, Mr *Buivids*, was not a professional journalist, but the CJEU nonetheless noted that '*the fact that Mr Buivids uploaded the recorded video online on such an Internet site, in this case www.youtube.com, cannot in itself preclude the classification of that processing of personal data as having been carried out 'solely for journalistic purposes*', [...]'. Hence, the scope of Article 85 GDPR is not limited to traditional news outlets, such as television news channels and official newspapers, but can in theory include any sort of medium or format used to share information, opinions or ideas with the public.[459]

389. It goes without saying, however, that this should not mean that any publication of information on the Internet automatically falls under the exemptions and derogations of Article 85 GDPR, since this would in essence render the GDPR moot

455. H. Kranenborg, 'Article 85. Processing and freedom of expression and information' in C. Kuner, L.A. Bygrave and C. Docksey, *The EU General Data Protection Regulation (GDPR) A commentary*, Oxford, Oxford University Press, 2020, p. 1202.
456. CJEU, Case C-345/17, Judgment of 14 February 2019, Buivids, ECLI:EU:C:2019:122, paras 50–52, https://eur-lex.europa.eu/legal-content/EN/TXT/?uri=CELEX%3A62017CJ0345.
457. CJEU, Case C-73/07, Judgment of 16 Dec 2008, Satakunnan Markkinapörssi and Satamedia, ECLI:EU:C:2008:727, para, 61, https://eur-lex.europa.eu/legal-content/en/TXT/?uri=CELEX:62007CJ0073.
458. *Ibid.*, para. 55.
459. Erdos, David. 'Special, Personal and Broad Expression: Exploring Freedom of Expression Norms under the General Data Protection Regulation.' *Yearbook of European Law*, vol. 40, 2021, pp. 398–430.

in the majority of processing activities online. The CJEU noted that for the exemptions and derogations to apply, the sole purpose of the publication should be to disclose information, opinions or ideas to the public.[460] To determine whether this is the case, the CJEU referred to criteria that have been developed by the European Court of Human Rights, which include '*contribution to a debate of public interest, the degree of notoriety of the person affected, the subject of the news report, the prior conduct of the person concerned, the content, form and consequences of the publication and the manner and circumstances in which the information was obtained and its veracity*'.[461] Although it will always be up to the Member States to implement Article 85 GDPR and for the national courts to determine when a particular processing activity can be considered as journalism, it is clear that the notion of journalism should never be interpreted restrictively.

2. Protection of Personal Data and Access to Public Access to Official Documents

390. Article 86 GDPR enshrines the European Union's and the Member States' obligation to reconcile the right to public access to official documents with the right to the protection of personal data by including in Union or Member State law the circumstances in which a public body or a private body for the performance of a task carried out in the public interest may grant access to personal data included in official documents.[462] Or in other words, EU and Member State law should outline when a public sector body, or a private sector body performing a task in the public interest, should be allowed to grant access to documents they hold which contain personal data.[463]

391. Recital 154 GDPR clarifies that public access to official documents may be considered to be in the public interest. This leads KRANENBORG to the conclusion that Article 86 GDPR does nothing more than declaring that public access to official documents is a legitimate objective pursued by a legal obligation or a necessary processing activity for the performance of a task in the public interest in the sense of Articles 6.1.c and 6.1.e GDPR.[464] Recital 154 GDPR equally confirms the GDPR's prevalence over Directive 2003/98/EC, which has been replaced in the

---

460. CJEU, Case C-73/07, Judgment of 16 Dec 2008, Satakunnan Markkinapörssi and Satamedia, ECLI:EU:C:2008:727, para. 69, https://eur-lex.europa.eu/legal-content/en/TXT/?uri=CELEX:62007CJ0073.
461. *Ibid.*, 66.
462. Kajcsa, Andrea. 'Access to official document in the light of the General Data Protection Regulation', *Perspectives of Law and Public Administration*, vol. 7, no. 2, 2018, pp. 193–198.
463. The need for a balance between these two rights is not new. *See* e.g., Kranenborg, Herke. 'Access to Documents and Data Protection in the European Union: On the Public Nature of Personal Data.' *Common Market Law Review*, vol. 45, no. 4, 2008, pp. 1079–1114.
464. H. KRANENBORG, 'Article 86. Processing and public access to official documents' in C. KUNER, L.A. BYGRAVE and C. DOCKSEY, *The EU General Data Protection Regulation (GDPR) A commentary*, Oxford, Oxford University Press, 2020,

meantime by Directive (EU) 2019/1024, and that protection of personal data in public sector information cannot be diminished by applying the rules on the reuse of public sector information.[465]

3. Protection of Personal Data and the National Identification Number

392. National identification numbers and other identifiers of general application (e.g., ID card numbers or tax identification numbers) are often subject to specific national laws that set forth the circumstances in, and conditions under, which these numbers can be processed. Article 87 GDPR allows Member States to continue to determine such national laws on the processing of national identification numbers and other identifiers. Article 87 GDPR nonetheless requires that, where such laws exist, the number or identifier can only be processed under appropriate safeguards as provided for under the GDPR. In other words, these numbers and identifiers cannot be subject to a level of protection that is lower than the one provided for personal data in the GDPR.

4. Protection of Personal Data and the Employment Context

393. Member States can tailor the application of the general rules imposed by the GDPR to the specificities of the national employment context. According to Article 88.1 GDPR, such tailoring can be done through national law or through collective agreements, in particular in the following areas:

- recruitment;
- performance of the employment contract, which in turn includes:
- discharge of obligations laid down by law or by collective agreements;
- management;
- planning and organisation of work;
- equality and diversity in the workplace;
- health and safety at work;
- protection of employer's or customer's property;
- enjoyment of rights and benefits related to employment;
- termination of the employment relationship.

Recital 155 GDPR gives an example of what can constitute a tailoring of the GDPR's provisions to the national employment context and refers to the circumstances where an employee would be able to give valid consent for the processing of his personal data.

The Member States can tailor the application of the GDPR to the needs of their employment context but cannot diminish the basic level of protection offered by the

465. Directive (EU) 2019/1024 of the European Parliament and of the Council of 20 June 2019 on open data and the reuse of public sector information, *O.J.L.* 172, 26 June 2019, pp. 56–83.

GDPR. Article 88.2 GDPR states that the rules Member States introduce must include measures to safeguard the data subject's human dignity, legitimate interests and fundamental rights.

5. Processing Personal Data for Research or Archiving Purposes

394. Articles 5.1.b, 5.1.e and 9.2.j GDPR create a special, somewhat more flexible, data protection regime for processing activities which are carried out 'for archiving purposes in the public interest, for scientific or historical research purposes or for statistical purposes'. To benefit from this more flexible regime, the processing activities must comply with Article 89 and specifically Article 89.1 GDPR.

Article 89 GDPR further shapes this flexible regime for the aforementioned processing activities, thereby highlighting the importance ascribed by the European legislator to research, statistical and archiving purposes. Evidence can be found in several recitals of just how important the European legislator considers these processing purposes, thereby warranting a more flexible regime.[466]

It is against this backdrop that one must interpret the flexible regime created by Articles 5.1.b, 5.1.e, 9.2.j and 89 GDPR. It is by no means meant to disable in its entirety the application of the GDPR to processing of personal data in the context of the aforementioned activities, but rather meant to allow processing of personal data to happen in a way that allows personal data to be protected without robbing these activities from their intended outcomes.

395. The regime set forth in Article 89 GDPR relies on requiring:

- those engaging in research or archiving activities to take appropriate safeguards when processing personal data;
- Member States or the European Union to take the necessary legislative actions to allow derogations from certain rights of the data subject.

396. Article 89 GDPR has a specific scope of application, applying only where the processing of personal data happens for the purposes of historical or scientific research, for statistical purposes or for the purposes of archiving in the public interest. A thorough understanding of this article thus requires a good understanding of what is construed as historical or scientific research, as statistics or as archiving in the public interest.

---

466. E.g.,: Recital 157 GDPR, which refers to the coupling of registries for the benefit of research, stresses the possibilities for obtaining new knowledge in important medical and social science fields.

Recital 158 GDPR, which refers to archiving purposes in the public interest, stresses the importance of archiving for instance to provide information related to political behaviour under a totalitarian state or related to genocide, war crimes, the Holocaust, etc.

Recital 159 GDPR, which refers to scientific research, stresses that 'scientific research' should be interpreted broadly and refers to the creation of the European Research Area.

a. The Notions of 'Scientific or Historical Research'

397. As noted earlier, Recital 159 GDPR requires the notion of scientific research to be interpreted broadly. While there is no legal definition of what constitutes 'scientific research', the European Data Protection Supervisor ('EDPS') noted that scientific research applies the scientific method of observing phenomena, formulating and testing a hypothesis for those phenomena, and concluding as to the validity of the hypothesis.[467] The EDPS further noted that the role of research is to provide knowledge that in turn can improve the quality of life for a number of people and improve the efficiency of social services.[468] Research can include technological development, can be fundamental or applied, can be publicly or privately funded and can therefore be of an academic as well as a commercial nature.[469] The key characteristic of scientific research is that it is beneficial to society as a whole and that scientific knowledge is a public good.

398. The notion of historical research has not been defined in the GDPR either, but one can build upon what was observed for scientific research above, meaning that fundamental or applied or commercial or publicly funded historical research is in scope. Recital 160 GDPR refers specifically to genealogical research, but the notion of historical research should not be limited to solely genealogical research. Any research which focuses on events or facts that have come to pass, would be in scope.

b. The Concept of 'Archiving in the Public Interest'

399. Although a formal definition of 'archiving in the public interest' is not included in the GDPR, a description can be found in Recital 158 GDPR:

> Public authorities or public or private bodies that hold records of public interest should be services which, pursuant to Union or Member State law, have a legal obligation to acquire, preserve, appraise, arrange, describe, communicate, promote, disseminate and provide access to records of enduring value for general public interest.

The European Archives Group, an expert group composed by the European Commission, notes that to consider something an archive in the public interest, one must not look at the nature of the archive itself but to the mission of the institution that holds them.[470] This European Archives Group also observes that in order for something to be considered archiving in the public interest, all the aforementioned activities must be present: acquiring, preserving, appraising, arranging, describing, communicating, promoting, disseminating and providing access to records. If not all

467. European Data Protection Supervisor, A Preliminary Opinion on data protection and scientific research, 6 January 2020, p. 10, https://edps.europa.eu/sites/edp/files/publication/20-01-06_opinion_research_en.pdf.
468. *Ibid.*, p. 11.
469. *Ibid.*.
470. European Archives Group, Guidance on data protection for archive services, October 2018, p. 10, https://ec.europa.eu/info/sites/default/files/eag_draft_guidelines_1_11_0.pdf.

of them are present, the European Archives Group is of the opinion that one should consider whether the activity can be construed as historical research rather than archiving in the public interest.

400. Recital 162 GDPR provides a definition of what should be construed as processing for statistical purposes:

> Statistical purposes mean any operation of collection and the processing of personal data necessary for statistical surveys or for the production of statistical results. Those statistical results may further be used for different purposes, including a scientific research purpose.

That same recital further clarifies that the result of the processing for statistical purposes shall not be personal data, but shall be aggregate data, and that neither the result nor the underlying personal data can be used in support of measures or decisions regarding any particular person. The emphasis therefore lies on the fact that results of statistical analysis should not relate to one or only a few individuals, because the results are in that case not aggregated.

c. Taking Appropriate Safeguards

401. The flexibility offered to controllers processing personal data for historical and scientific research purposes, archiving purposes and statistical purposes is of course not meant to be a free pass on the warranties and protections provided by the GDPR. It is a regime that is heavily reliant on the accountability of those controllers, complemented with the obligation of the Member States to implement national legislation that fosters or even requires such adequate safeguards.[471]

402. Article 89.1 GDPR neither enumerates an exhaustive list of safeguards, nor does it impose specific safeguards to be taken by the controller. It does, however, prescribe that as part of those safeguards, the controller should take technical and organisational measures which should particularly ensure that the principle of data minimisation is respected. This provision complements Article 5.1.j GDPR, which requires the controller to take technical and organisational measures to safeguard the rights of the data subject in relation to the longer data retention periods allowed for personal data processed for the aforementioned purposes. This means that the primary focus of the technical and organisation measures should be on data minimisation, taking into account the fact that the controller is allowed to retain personal data longer.

The GDPR contains several examples of what technical and organisational measures can be.[472] Article 89.1 GDPR refers to pseudonymisation and anonymisation where such measures are not inherently incompatible with the purposes for processing. Member States can impose more specific measures, but it should be borne in mind that the European legislator has clearly endeavoured to foster an environment

---

471. Art. 9.2.j GDPR, Art. 89.2 and 89.3 GDPR as well as Recital 156 GDPR.
472. *See* particularly Art. 32 GDPR.

that facilitates scientific research, archiving in the public interest and statistics. Hence, measures imposed by national law should not work prohibitively to process personal data for these purposes, even where those personal data are health data or other special categories of data or where research requires the combination of different data sets.[473]

d. Derogations from Data Subject Rights

403. The processing purposes covered in Article 89 GDPR are typically processing purposes which are reliant on vast data sets, obtained from a range of different sources which may or may not have been initially collected for completely different purposes than those cited in Article 89 GDPR. It is therefore not unlikely that it is very difficult or even downright impossible to comply with one or more of the processing purposes set forth in Article 89 GDPR or that compliance with those rights would make it impossible to process personal data for those purposes.

404. Articles 89.2 and 89.3 GDPR allow the European and national legislators to provide for derogations to (some of) the data subject rights. Which rights can be derogated from depends on the processing purpose under consideration. Where it concerns personal data processed for scientific or historical research purposes or for statistical purpose, the European Union or its Member States can derogate from the right to access (Article 15 GDPR), the right to rectification (Article 16 GDPR), the right to restriction of processing (Article 18 GDPR) and the right to object to processing (Article 21 GDPR). Where the processing is done for archiving purposes in the public interest, derogations are possible from all of the aforementioned rights, as well as the right to receive notification of rectification of personal data or restriction of processing (Article 19 GDPR) and the right to data portability (Article 20 GDPR). A derogation from one or more of these rights requires adequate safeguards for the (other) rights and freedoms of the data subjects and they only apply to the extent that the granting of such right would render the achievement of the purpose impossible or would seriously impair it. Hence, the derogation must be necessary.[474] When personal data are processed for multiple purposes, the derogations shall only apply for the purposes mentioned in Article 89 GDPR.[475]

405. As a final note, it should be mentioned that Recital 161 GDPR clarifies that, where consent is required to participate in research activities in the context of clinical trials, the Clinical Trials Regulation will apply.[476] In other words, the consent requirements set forth in the Clinical Trials Regulation continue to apply notwithstanding the provisions of Article 89 GDPR.

---

473. Recital 157 and 159 GDPR.
474. Art. 89.2 and 89.3 GDPR.
475. Art. 89.4 GDPR.
476. Regulation (EU) 536/2014 of the European Parliament and of the Council of 16 April 2014 on clinical trials on medicinal products for human use, and repealing Directive 2001/20/EC, *OJ.L.* 158, 27 May 2014, p. 1.

f. Exercise of Powers by the Supervisory Authority and Obligations of Secrecy

406. In many Member States certain categories of controllers or processors are subject to national rules on professional secrecy, which ensure the confidentiality of information in an almost absolute way. Healthcare professionals and lawyers are typical examples of categories of controllers who need to maintain the confidentiality of the information received from, or about, their patients and clients respectively, even in front of a judge.

407. Article 90 GDPR gives the Member States the possibility to ensure that such obligations to professional secrecy or equivalent obligations of secrecy under national law can be reconciled through Member State law with the right to protection of personal data in relation to supervisory authorities when they exercise the powers set forth in Article 58.1.e and f GDPR. Member States can only adopt such rules where it is necessary and proportionate and they should be limited to personal data that has been received or obtained as part of an activity subject to the secrecy obligations.

g. The Processing of Personal Data by Churches and Religious Associations

408. Article 91 GDPR allows Member States, which had specific legislation in place related to the processing of personal data by churches and religious associations or communities at the time of the introduction of the GDPR, to keep such specific legislation. Germany, Italy, France and Poland are examples of Member States that have such specific legislation.[477] These Member States are required, however, to bring the existing legislation in line with the GDPR. Churches and religious associations and communities in principle do not get a more lenient regime than other controllers and processors.

409. The background of Article 91 is the autonomy of the church vis-à-vis the State.[478] According to church authorities, the fundamental right to data protection would be limited by the fundamental right to religious freedom in the institutional sense, which gives the Church autonomy to establish its own forms of organisation and operation.[479]

II. Territorial Scope (Article 3 GDPR)

410. Article 3 of the GDPR outlines the territorial scope of its provisions. Whether or not these provisions are applicable from a territorial viewpoint,

---

477. Regarding Germany, *see* Ziekow, Arne. *Datenschutz und Evangelisches Kirchenrecht: Eigenständigkeit und Eigengearttheit des Datenschutzgesetzes der EKD*. Mohr Siebeck, 2002.
478. Robbers, Gerhard. 'Church Autonomy in the European Court of Human Rights—Recent Developments in Germany.' *The Journal of Law and Religion*, vol. 26, no. 1, 2010, pp. 281–320.
479. Montserrat Gas-Aixendri. 'Protection of Personal Data and Apostasy: Comparative Law Considerations.' *A Journal of Church and State*, vol. 57, no. 1, 2015, pp. 72–89.

essentially depends on the answer to two questions: i) is the controller or the processor established in the Union, or, if not, ii) is the processing targeting data subjects in the Union?[480]

A. *Controller or Processor Established in the Union*

411. Article 3(1) of the GDPR states that the Regulation 'applies to the processing of personal data in the context of the activities of an establishment of a controller or a processor in the Union, regardless of whether the processing takes place in the Union or not'.

412. Recital 19 further explains: 'Any processing of personal data in the context of the activities of an establishment of a controller or a processor in the Union should be carried out in accordance with this Regulation, regardless of whether the processing itself takes place within the Union or not. Establishment implies the effective and real exercise of activity through stable arrangements. The legal form of such arrangements, whether through a branch or a subsidiary with a legal personality, is not the determining factor in this respect.'

413. Article 3(1) GDPR makes reference not only to an establishment of a controller, but also to an establishment of a processor. As a result, the processing of personal data by a processor may also be subject to EU law by virtue of the processor having an establishment located within the EU. Article 3(1) ensures that the GDPR applies to the processing by a controller or processor carried out in the context of the activities of an establishment of that controller or processor in the Union, regardless of the actual place of the processing.[481]

414. The EDPB recommends a threefold approach in determining whether or not the processing of personal data falls within the scope of the GDPR pursuant to Article 3(1). First one has to consider the definition of an 'establishment' in the EU within the meaning of EU data protection law.[482] The second step consists in looking at what is meant by 'processing in the context of the activities of an establishment in the Union. In a third step one should examine how the GDPR applies regardless of whether the processing carried out in the context of the activities of this establishment takes place in the Union or not.[483]

480. Andreas T Kaltsounis. 'Re-Examining the GDPR's Territorial Scope.' *Computer and Internet Lawyer*, vol. 37, no. 5, 2020, pp. 10–1.
481. About this extension to processors, *see* Els J. Kindt, 'Why research may no longer be the same: About the territorial scope of the New Data Protection Regulation', (2016) 32 CLS Rev 729, 741.
482. *See also* CJEU, Case C-131/12, Judgment of 13 May 2014, *Google Spain SL v. Agencia Espanola de Proteccion de Datos (AEPD)*, ECLI:EU:C:2014:317, para. 50, https://eur-lex.europa.eu/legal-content/EN/TXT/?uri=CELEX%3A62012CJ0131.
483. EDPB, Guidelines 3/2018 on the territorial scope of the GDPR (Art. 3), adopted on 12 November 2019, p. 5, https://edpb.europa.eu/our-work-tools/documents/public-consultations/2018/guidelines-32018-territorial-scope-gdpr-article_en.

1. Establishment in the Union

415. An establishment in this context 'implies the effective and real exercise of activity through stable arrangements.[484] The legal form of such arrangements, whether through a branch or a subsidiary with a legal personality, is not the determining factor in that respect'. This wording is identical to that found in Recital 19 of Directive 95/46/EC, to which reference has been made in several CJEU rulings broadening the interpretation of the term 'establishment', departing from a formalistic approach whereby undertakings are established solely in the place where they are registered.[485]

416. The CJEU ruled that the notion of establishment extends to any real and effective activity – even a minimal one – exercised through stable arrangements. In order to determine whether an entity based outside the Union has an establishment in a Member State, both the degree of stability of the arrangements and the effective exercise of activities in that Member State must be considered in the light of the specific nature of the economic activities and the provision of services concerned. This is particularly true for undertakings offering services exclusively over the Internet.[486] The threshold for 'stable arrangement' can actually be quite low when the centre of activities of a controller concerns the provision of services online. As a result, in some circumstances, the presence of one single employee or agent of a non-EU entity in the Union may be sufficient to constitute a stable arrangement (amounting to an 'establishment' for the purposes of Art 3(1)) if that employee or agent acts with a sufficient degree of stability.[487]

417. When an employee is based in the EU but the processing is not being carried out in the context of the activities of the EU-based employee in the Union (i.e., the processing relates to activities of the controller outside the EU), the mere presence of an employee in the EU will not result in that processing falling within the scope of the GDPR. In other words, the mere presence of an employee in the EU is not as such sufficient to trigger the application of the GDPR, since for the processing in question to fall within the scope of the GDPR, it must also be carried out in the context of the activities of the EU-based employee. The fact that the non-EU entity responsible for the data processing does not have a branch or subsidiary in a Member State does not preclude it from having an establishment there within the meaning of EU data protection law. Although the notion of establishment is broad,

484. Recital 22 of the GDPR.
485. Miadzvetskaya, Yuliya, and Van Calster, Geert. 'Google at the Kirchberg Dock. On Delisting Requests, and on the Territorial Reach of the Eu's Gdpr.' *European Data Protection Law Review (Internet)*, vol. 6, no. 1, 2020, pp. 143–151.
486. CJEU, Case C-230/14, Judgment of 1 Oct 2015, Weltimmo, ECLI:EU:C:2015:639, para. 18, https://eur-lex.europa.eu/legal-content/EN/TXT/?uri=CELEX%3A62014CJ0230.
487. *Ibid.*, para. 29; Art. 29 Data Protection Working Party, Update of Opinion 8/2010 on applicable law in light of the CJEU Judgment in Google Spain, WP 179 (16 December 2015).

it is not without limits. It is not possible to conclude that the non-EU entity has an establishment in the Union merely because the undertaking's website is accessible in the Union.[488]

2. Processing in the Context of an Establishment in the Union

418. If a controller or processor established outside the Union exercises a real and effective activity – even a minimal one – through 'stable arrangements', regardless of its legal form (e.g., subsidiary, branch, office), in the territory of a Member State, this controller or processor can be considered to have an establishment in that Member State. Once this has been established, it is, in the second place, important to consider whether the processing of personal data takes place 'in the context of the activities of' such an establishment.

419. Article 3(1) confirms that it is not necessary that the processing in question is carried out 'by' the relevant EU establishment itself; the controller or processor will be subject to obligations under the GDPR whenever the processing is carried out 'in the context of the activities' of its relevant establishment in the Union.[489] The EDPB recommends that determining whether processing is being carried out in the context of an establishment of the controller or processor in the Union for the purposes of Article 3(1) should be carried out on a case-by-case basis. Each scenario must be assessed on its own merits, taking into account the specific facts of the case. The EDPB considers that, for the purpose of Article 3(1), the meaning of 'processing in the context of the activities of an establishment of a controller or a processor' is to be understood in light of the relevant case law.[490] On the one hand, with a view to fulfilling the objective of ensuring effective and complete protection, the meaning of 'in the context of the activities of an establishment' cannot be interpreted restrictively.[491]

420. On the other hand, the existence of an establishment within the meaning of the GDPR should not be interpreted too broadly to conclude that the existence of any presence in the EU with even the remotest links to the data processing activities of a non-EU entity will be sufficient to bring this processing within the scope of EU

488. EDPB, Guidelines 3/2018 on the territorial scope of the GDPR, p. 6, https://edpb.europa.eu/our-work-tools/documents/public-consultations/2018/guidelines-32018-territorial-scope-gdpr-article_en.
489. CJEU, Case C-191/15, Judgment of 28 July 2016, Verein für Konsumenteninformation, ECLI:EU:C:2016:612, https://eur-lex.europa.eu/legal-content/EN/TXT/?uri=CELEX%3A62015CJ019 1.
490. In the *Google Spain* case, the CJEU held that the processing of personal data is carried out in the context of the activities of an establishment of the controller on the territory of a Member State when the operator of a search engine sets up in a Member State a branch or subsidiary which is intended to promote and sell advertising space offered by that search engine and which orientates its activity towards the inhabitants of that Member State.
491. EDPB, Guidelines 3/2018 on the territorial scope of the GDPR, p. 6, https://edpb.europa.eu/our-work-tools/documents/public-consultations/2018/guidelines-32018-territorial-scope-gdpr-article_en.

data protection law. Some commercial activity carried out by a non-EU entity within a Member State may indeed be so far removed from the processing of personal data by this entity that the existence of the commercial activity in the EU would not be sufficient to bring the data processing by the non-EU entity within the scope of EU data protection law.[492]

421. The data processing activities of a data controller or processor established outside the EU may be inextricably linked to the activities of a local establishment in a Member State, and thereby may trigger the applicability of EU law, even if that local establishment is not actually taking any role in the data processing itself.[493]

422. If a case-by-case analysis on the facts shows that there is an inextricable link between the processing of personal data carried out by a non-EU controller or processor and the activities of an EU establishment, EU law will apply to that processing by the non-EU entity, whether or not the EU establishment plays a role in that processing of data. In *Verein für Konsumenteninformation*, the CJEU was asked to clarify whether or not the processing of personal data by *Amazon EU* must comply with the data protection rules of each Member State to which its commercial activities are directed. While indicating that mere accessibility of a website does not suffice to constitute a relevant 'establishment', the Court suggested that there may be an establishment other than *Amazons EU*'s Luxembourg headquarters in the context of which the processing of personal data is being carriedout. If the referring Court found that to be the case, the processing of personal data by *Amazon EU* would be governed by the law of the Member State to which it directs its activities. The CJEU left it to the referring court, however, to determine whether there is indeed an establishment on the territory of a Member State other than Luxembourg in the context of which the processing of personal data is taking place.[494]

3. Processing In or Outside the Union

423. Article 3(1) of the GDPR further specifies that the Regulation applies to processing in the context of the activities of an establishment in the EU 'regardless

492. Art 29 Working Party, WP 179 update – Update of Opinion 8/2010 on applicable law in light of the CJEU judgment in Google Spain, 16 December 2015, and also EDPB, Guidelines 3/2018 on the territorial scope of the GDPR, p. 8, https://edpb.europa.eu/our-work-tools/documents/public-consultations/2018/guidelines-32018-territorial-scope-gdpr-article_en.

493. CJEU, Case C-507/17, Judgment of 24 September 2019, *Google v. CNIL*, ECLI:EU:C:2019:772, para. 50, https://eur-lex.europa.eu/legal-content/en/TXT/?uri=CELEX:62017CJ0507: '(…)*the activities of the operator of the search engine and those of its establishment situated in the Union are inextricably linked since the activities relating to the advertising space constitute the means of rendering the search engine at issue economically profitable and that search engine is, at the same time, the means enabling those activities to be performed, the display of the list of results being accompanied, on the same page, by the display of advertising linked to the search terms (see, to that effect*'.

494. CJEU, Case C-191/15, Judgment of 28 July 2016, Verein für Konsumenteninformation, ECLI: EU:C:2016:612, para. 81, https://eur-lex.europa.eu/legal-content/EN/TXT/?uri=CELEX%3A62015CJ0191.

of whether the processing takes place in the Union or not'. It is the presence, through an establishment, of a data controller or processor in the EU and the fact that a processing takes place in the context of the activities of this establishment that trigger the application of the GDPR to its processing activities. The place of processing is therefore not relevant in determining whether or not the processing, carried out in the context of the activities of an EU establishment, falls within the scope of the GDPR.[495]

424. The text of Article 3(1) does not restrict the application of the GDPR to the processing of personal data of individuals who are in the Union. The EDPB therefore considers that any personal data processing in the context of the activities of an establishment of a controller or processor in the Union would fall under the scope of the GDPR, regardless of the location or the nationality of the data subject whose personal data are being processed.[496] This approach is supported by Recital 14 of the GDPR which states that '[t]he protection afforded by this Regulation should apply to natural persons, whatever their nationality or place of residence, in relation to the processing of their personal data'.[497]

425. A processor in the EU should not be considered to be an establishment of a data controller within the meaning of Article 3(1) merely by virtue of its status as processor on behalf of a controller. By instructing a processor in the Union, the controller not subject to GDPR is not carrying out processing 'in the context of the activities of the processor in the Union'. The processing is carried out in the context of the controller's own activities; the processor is merely providing a processing service which is not 'inextricably linked' to the activities of the controller. The EDPB considers that the processing activities of the data controller would not be deemed as falling under the territorial scope of the GDPR merely because it is processed on its behalf by a processor established in the Union. However, even though the data controller is not established in the Union and is not subject to the provisions of the

495. The CJEU has stated this in several judgments, e.g., in CJEU, Case C-210/16, Judgment of 5 June 2018, Wirtschaftsakademie Schleswig-Holstein, ECLI:EU:C:2018:388, para. 57, https://eur-lex.europa.eu/legal-content/EN/TXT/?uri=CELEX%3A62016CJ0210.

496. EDPB, Guidelines 3/2018 on the territorial scope of the GDPR, p. 10, https://edpb.europa.eu/our-work-tools/documents/public-consultations/2018/guidelines-32018-territorial-scope-gdpr-article_en.

497. For comments on this 'extraterritorial' application of the GDPR, *see* e.g., Ryngaert, Cedric, and Taylor, Mistale. 'The GDPR as Global Data Protection Regulation?' *AJIL Unbound*, vol. 114, 2020, pp. 5–9; *see also* Paul de Hert and Michal Czerniawski, 'Expanding the European data protection scope beyond territory: Art. 3 of the General Data Protection Regulation in its wider context' (2016) 6 IDPL 230, 237; Merlin Gömann, 'The new territorial scope of EU data protection law: deconstructing a revolutionary achievement' (2017) 54 CM L Rev 567, 575; Greze, B. (2019). The extra-territorial enforcement of the GDPR: A genuine issue and the quest for alternatives. *International Data Privacy Law*, 9(2), 109–128; Van Alsenoy, Brendan. 'Reconciling the (Extra)Territorial Reach of the GDPR with Public International Law.' *Data Protection and Privacy Under Pressure. Transatlantic Tensions, EU Surveillance and Big Data*, Maklu, 2017, pp. 77–100.

GDPR as per Article 3(2), the data processor, as it is established in the Union, will be subject to the relevant provisions of the GDPR as per Article 3(1).[498]

B. Controller or Processor Not Established in the Union

426. Article 3(2) of the GDPR states that the Regulation 'applies to the processing of personal data of data subjects who are in the Union by a controller or processor not established in the Union, where the processing activities are related to: (a) the offering of goods or services, irrespective of whether a payment of the data subject is required, to such data subjects in the Union; or (b) the monitoring of their behaviour as far as their behaviour takes place within the European Union'.

1. Data Subjects in the Union

427. The wording of Article 3(2) refers to 'personal data of data subjects who are in the Union'. The application of the targeting criterion is therefore not limited by the citizenship, residence or other type of legal status of the data subject whose personal data are being processed. Recital 14 confirms this interpretation and states that '[t]he protection afforded by this Regulation should apply to natural persons, whatever their nationality or place of residence, in relation to the processing of their personal data'.

428. The requirement that the data subject be located in the Union must be assessed at the moment when the relevant processing activity takes place, i.e., at the moment of offering of goods or services or the moment when the behaviour is being monitored, regardless of the duration of the offer made or monitoring undertaken. The EDPB considers however that, in relation to processing activities related to the offer of services, the provision is aimed at activities that intentionally, rather than inadvertently or incidentally, target individuals in the EU. Consequently, if the processing relates to a service that is only offered to individuals outside the EU but the service is not withdrawn when such individuals enter the EU, the related processing will not be subject to the GDPR. In this case the processing is not related to the intentional targeting of individuals in the EU but relates to the targeting of individuals outside the EU which will continue whether they remain outside the EU or whether they visit the Union.[499]

---

498. EDPB, Guidelines 3/2018 on the territorial scope of the GDPR, p. 12, https://edpb.europa.eu/our-work-tools/documents/public-consultations/2018/guidelines-32018-territorial-scope-gdpr-article_en.

499. EDPB, Guidelines 3/2018 on the territorial scope of the GDPR, p. 15, https://edpb.europa.eu/our-work-tools/documents/public-consultations/2018/guidelines-32018-territorial-scope-gdpr-article_en.

2. Offering of Goods or Services

429. Recital 23 of the GDPR specifies that 'In order to ensure that individuals are not deprived of the protection to which they are entitled under this Regulation, the processing of personal data of data subjects who are in the Union by a controller or a processor not established in the Union should be subject to this Regulation where the processing activities are related to the offering of goods or services to such data subjects irrespective of whether connected to a payment or not. In order to determine whether such a controller or processor is offering goods or services to data subjects who are in the Union, it should be ascertained whether it is apparent that the controller is envisaging the offering of services to data subjects in one or more Member States in the Union. Whereas the mere accessibility of the controller's or an intermediary's website in the Union or of an e-mail address and of other contact details or the use of a language generally used in the third country where the controller is established, is insufficient to ascertain such intention, factors such as the use of a language or a currency generally used in one or more Member States with the possibility of ordering goods and services in that other language, and/or the mentioning of customers or users who are in the Union, may make it apparent that the controller envisages offering goods or services to such data subjects in the Union. '

430. The elements listed in the recital are quite similar to the ones used by the CJEU in its case law based on Council Regulation 44/200125 on jurisdiction and the recognition and enforcement of judgments in civil and commercial matters, and in particular its Article 15(1)(c).[500] The CJEU held that, in order to determine whether a trader can be considered to be 'directing' its activity to the Member State of the consumer's domicile, within the meaning of Article 15(1)(c), the trader must have manifested its intention to establish commercial relations with such consumers. In this context, the CJEU considered evidence able to demonstrate that the trader was envisaging doing business with consumers domiciled in a Member State.[501]

431. While the notion of 'directing an activity' differs from the 'offering of goods or services', the EDPB estimates that this case law can be of assistance when considering whether goods or services are offered to a data subject in the Union. When taking into account the specific facts of the case, the following factors could therefore inter alia be taken into consideration, possibly in combination with one another: the EU or at least one Member State is designated by name with reference to the good or service offered; the data controller or processor pays a search engine operator for an Internet referencing service in order to facilitate access to its site by consumers in the Union; or the controller or processor has launched marketing and

500. Regulation No 593/2008 on the law applicable to contractual obligations (Rome I),[2008] OJ L-177/6-16.
501. CJEU, Joined cases C-585/08 and C-144/09, Judgment of 7 December 2010, Pammer v. Reederei Karl Schlüter GmbH & Co and Hotel Alpenhof v. Heller, ECLI:EU:C:2010:740, https://eur-lex.europa.eu/legal-content/en/TXT/?uri=CELEX:62008CJ0585,.

advertisement campaigns directed at an EU country audience.; the international nature of the activity at issue, such as certain tourist activities; the mention of dedicated addresses or phone numbers to be reached from an EU country; the use of a top-level domain name other than that of the third country in which the controller or processor is established, for example '.de', or the use of neutral top-level domain names such as '.eu'; the description of travel instructions from one or more other EU Member States to the place where the service is provided; the mention of an international clientele composed of customers domiciled in various EU Member States, in particular by presentation of accounts written by such customers; the use of a language or a currency other than that generally used in the trader's country, especially a language or currency of one or more EU Member states; the data controller offers the delivery of goods in EU Member States.[502]

432. Several of the elements listed above, if taken alone may not amount to a clear indication of the intention of a data controller to offer goods or services to data subjects in the Union, however, they should each be taken into account in order to determine whether the combination of factors relating to the data controller's commercial activities can together be considered as an offer of goods or services directed at data subjects in the Union. It is however important to recall that Recital 23 confirms that the mere accessibility of the controller's, processor's or an intermediary's website in the Union, the mention on the website of its e-mail or geographical address, or of its telephone number without an international code, does not, of itself, provide sufficient evidence to demonstrate the controller or processor's intention to offer goods or a services to a data subject located in the Union. In this context, the EDPB recalls that when goods or services are inadvertently or incidentally provided to a person on the territory of the Union, the related processing of personal data would not fall within the territorial scope of the GDPR.

3. Monitoring of Behaviour

433. The processing of personal data of data subjects who are in the Union by a controller or processor not established in the Union should also be subject to the GDPR when it is related to the monitoring of the behaviour of such data subjects as far as their behaviour takes places within the European Union. Recital 24 specifies that '*In order to determine whether a processing activity can be considered to monitor the behaviour of data subjects, it should, be ascertained whether individuals are tracked on the Internet including potential subsequent use of data processing techniques which consist of profiling an individual, particularly in order to take decisions concerning her or him or for analysing or predicting her or his personal preferences, behaviours and attitudes*'.

434. For Article 3(2)(b) to trigger the application of the GDPR, the behaviour monitored must first relate to a data subject in the Union and, as a cumulative criterion, the monitored behaviour must take place within the territory of the Union.

502. EDPB, Guidelines 3/2018 on the territorial scope of the GDPR, p.18.

The nature of the processing activity which can be considered as behavioural monitoring is further specified in Recital 24 which states that 'in order to determine whether a processing activity can be considered to monitor the behaviour of data subjects, it should be ascertained whether natural persons are tracked on the Internet including potential subsequent use of personal data processing techniques which consist of profiling a natural person, particularly in order to take decisions concerning her or him or for analysing or predicting her or his personal preferences, behaviours and attitudes'. The EDPB considers that tracking through other types of network or technology involving personal data processing should also be taken into account in determining whether a processing activity amounts to a behavioural monitoring, for example through wearable and other smart devices.

435. As opposed to the provision of Article 3(2)(a), neither Article 3(2)(b) nor Recital 24 expressly introduce a necessary degree of 'intention to target' on the part of the data controller or processor to determine whether the monitoring activity would trigger the application of the GDPR to the processing activities. However, the use of the word 'monitoring' implies that the controller has a specific purpose in mind for the collection and subsequent reuse of the relevant data about an individual's behaviour within the EU. The EDPB does not consider that any online collection or analysis of personal data of individuals in the EU would automatically count as 'monitoring'. It will be necessary to consider the controller's purpose for processing the data and, in particular, any subsequent behavioural analysis or profiling techniques involving that data.

436. The EDPB takes into account the wording of Recital 24, which indicates that to determine whether processing involves monitoring of a data subject behaviour, the tracking of natural persons on the Internet, including the potential subsequent use of profiling techniques, is a key consideration. The application of Article 3(2)(b) where a data controller or processor monitors the behaviour of data subjects who are in the Union could therefore encompass a broad range of monitoring activities. In a critical analysis of Article 3 of the GDPR, B. Van Alsenoy concluded: 'Where the monitoring of data subjects in the EU is concerned (…) no specific safety valves are provided for. In my opinion, applicability of the GDPR can be readily justified once the monitoring activity reaches a certain level of intrusiveness. In the absence of further clarification, however, considerable uncertainty remains as to when exactly article 3(2)(b) will be triggered'.[503]

---

503. Van Alsenoy, Brendan. 'Reconciling the (Extra)Territorial Reach of the GDPR with Public International Law.' *Data Protection and Privacy Under Pressure. Transatlantic Tensions, EU Surveillance and Big Data*, Maklu, 2017, p. 97.

C. Application of the GDPR in Other Places under Member State Law

437. The GDPR applies to the processing of personal data by a controller not established in the Union, but in a place where the national law of a Member State applies by virtue of public international law.[504]

438. The EDPB therefore considers that the GDPR applies to personal data processing carried out by EU Member States' embassies and consulates located outside the EU as such processing falls within the scope of the GDPR by virtue of Article 3(3). A Member State's diplomatic or consular post, as a data controller or processor, would then be subject to all relevant provisions of the GDPR, including when it comes to the rights of the data subject, the general obligations related to controller and processor and the transfers of personal data to third countries or international organisations.

439. Though not related to the application of Article3(3), a different situation is the one where, by virtue of international law, certain entities, bodies or organisations established in the Union benefit from privileges and immunities such as those laid down in the Vienna Convention on Diplomatic Relations of 196127, the Vienna Convention on Consular Relations of 1963 or headquarter agreements concluded between international organisations and their host countries in the Union. In this regard, the EDPB recalls that the application of the GDPR is without prejudice to the provisions of international law, such as the ones governing the privileges and immunities of non-EU diplomatic missions and consular posts, as well as international organisations. At the same time, it is important to recall that any controller or processor that falls within the scope of the GDPR for a given processing activity and that exchanges personal data with such entities, bodies and organisations have to comply with the GDPR, including where applicable its rules on transfers to third countries or international organisations.

D. Duty to Have a Representative in the Union

440. The GDPR imposes an obligation to designate a representative in the Union to any controller or processor falling under the scope of Article 3(2), unless they meet the exemption criteria as per Article 27(2). In order to facilitate the application of this specific provision, the EDPB deems it necessary to provide further guidance on the designation process, establishment obligations and responsibilities of the representative in the Union as per Article 27

---

504. Christopher Kuner, International Organizations and the EU General Data Protection Regulation, 19 Int'l Orgs. L. Rev. 158 (2019); Kuner, Christopher. 'The GDPR and International Organizations.' *AJIL Unbound*, vol. 114, 2020, pp. 15–19.

§5. Principles Relating to the Processing of Personal Data (Article 5 GDPR)

441. This section covers the general principles relating to the processing of personal data contained in Article 5 GDPR, also sometimes referred to as the 'data quality principles' or 'principles relating to data quality' in reference to their designation under the Data Protection Directive.[505] These principles set out general requirements that must be complied with in relation to any processing of personal data under the GDPR. The general requirements of the principles are reflected throughout the GDPR in specific articles and obligations, but are nonetheless enforceable obligations in themselves, meaning that a failure to comply with these principles can result in liability and/or fines.

442. The principles contain basic requirements for the processing of personal data, that relate to the data itself, as well as the context of the processing operation. While the text of the principles has been slightly updated, the main idea is still the same as under the Directive, and is in fact based on guidelines of the Organisation for Economic Co-operation and Development (OECD) dating back as far as 1980.[506]

443. The principles, as they are reflected in the current text of the GDPR are the following:

- personal data must be processed lawfully, fairly and in a transparent manner in relation to the data subject (**'lawfulness, fairness and transparency'**);[507]
- personal data must be collected for specified, explicit and legitimate purposes and not further processed in a manner that is incompatible with those purposes (**'purpose limitation'**);[508]
- personal data must be adequate, relevant and limited to what is necessary in relation to the purposes for which they are processed (**'data minimisation'**);[509]
- personal data must be accurate and, where necessary, kept up to date (**'accuracy'**);[510]
- personal data must be kept in a form which permits identification of data subjects for no longer than is necessary for the purposes for which the personal data are processed (**'storage limitation'**);[511]

505. Directive 95/46/EC of the European Parliament and of the Council of 24 October 1995 on the protection of individuals with regard to the processing of personal data and on the free movement of such data, OJ L 281, 23.11.1995, pp. 31–50. This is the legislation preceding the GDPR.
506. OECD Guidelines on the Protection of Privacy and Transborder Flows of Personal Data (1980, updated 2013).
507. Art. 5(1), a) GDPR..
508. Art. 5 (1), b) GDPR..
509. Art. 5(1), c) GDPR.
510. Art. 5(1), d) GDPR.
511. Art. 5(1), e) GDPR.

– personal data must be processed in a manner that ensures appropriate security of the personal data, including protection against unauthorised or unlawful processing and against accidental loss, destruction or damage, using appropriate technical or organisational measures **('integrity and confidentiality')**.[512]

It is the controller (i.e., the entity determining the purpose and means of the processing) who shall be responsible for, and be able to demonstrate compliance with the foregoing principles. This responsibility to both comply with the rules and be able to prove such compliance, is also a principle in itself **('accountability')**.[513]

444. Failure to comply with the principles, or to be able to demonstrate such compliance,[514] can lead to fines up to EUR 20,000,000 or 4% of the worldwide annual turnover of the infringer[515] and other sanctions by a supervisory authority,[516] as well as liability in relation to the affected data subjects.[517] The fines that can be imposed are the maximum sanctions under the GDPR, which illustrates the fundamental importance of the principles. Hence, it is of considerable importance for any controller (and by extension for its processor(s)) to ensure compliance with these principles throughout the lifecycle of the intended data processing activities. All seven principles are discussed in more detail below.

I. Lawfulness, Fairness and Transparency

445. The first principle relating to the processing of personal data is that data must be processed lawfully, fairly and in a transparent manner in relation to the data subject. In order to grasp the meaning of this first principle, the constituting parts must be analysed in more detail.

A. Lawfulness

446. The first requirement of the first principle is that personal data must be processed lawfully. This requirement of lawfulness first of all refers to the requirement for every processing activity to have a legal ground under Article 6 GDPR. Thus, for a processing operation to be lawful, it needs to be:

– validly consented to by the data subject (Article 6 (a) GDPR); or
– necessary for the performance of a contract (Article 6 (b) GDPR); or
– necessary for compliance with a legal obligation (Article 6 (c) GDPR); or

512. Art. 5(1), f) GDPR.
513. Art. 5(2) GDPR.
514. This is because the principle of accountability not only requires compliance but also the ability to demonstrate compliance.
515. Art.83 (5) GDPR.
516. *See* Art. 58(2) GDPR for other powers of the supervisory authority.
517. Art.82 GDPR.

- necessary to protect the vital interests of the data subject or another natural person (Article 6 (d) GDPR); or
- necessary for performing a task in the public interest or in the exercise of official authority vested in the controller (Article 6(e) GDPR); or
- necessary for the legitimate interests pursued by the controller or by a third party, provided those interests are not overridden by the interests or fundamental rights and freedoms of the data subject.

The applicability of these legal grounds is explained in detail in part F below.

447. However, the principle of lawfulness has a broader application than Article 6 GDPR and demands more generally that all applicable legal rules are complied with in any processing situation, as was already the case under the DPD.[518] Thus, if an employer is processing personal data of its employees, it will have to comply with applicable labour law, social law or fiscal law as well. Another example would be a doctor processing personal data of its patients. If the doctor does not respect his/her legal obligations with regards to professional secrecy when processing this information, he/she would be in breach of the principle of lawfulness, even if all other rules of the GDPR were respected.

B. Fairness

448. The second element of the first principle relates to the relationship between the controller and the data subject, requiring that the personal data is processed fairly in relation to the data subject. This means that the data subject must be aware of the processing operations and its goals, as well as the potential risks involved.[519]

449. In other words, the principle of fairness requires a respect for the reasonable expectations of the data subject in relation to the processing operation, based on the information given to him or her by the controller.[520] For example, the principle of fairness forbids hidden or not communicated processing operations or processing operations which are said to be for one reason (e.g., security), but in reality have another goal (e.g., commercial), especially where this could not be reasonably expected by the data subject based on the information given to him or her by the controller.

---

518. Cécile De Terwangne,'Article 5. Principles relating to processing of personal data', in Christopher Kuner, Lee A. Bygrave, Christopher Docksey (eds.), *The EU General Data Protection Regulation (GDPR) – A commentary*, 2020, p. 314.
519. *See* European Union Agency for Fundamental Rights and Council of Europe, Handbook on European data protection law, 117 (Publications Office of the European Union 2018) and recital 39 GDPR: 'Natural persons should be made aware of risks, rules, safeguards and rights in relation to the processing of personal data and how to exercise their rights in relation to such processing.'
520. Art. 29 Working Party, Guidelines on transparency under Regulation 2016/679 (WP260), para. 30. These guidelines were endorsed by the European Data Protection Board in its Endorsement 1/2018, https://ec.europa.eu/newsroom/article29/items/622227/en.

450. Note that the fairness principle adds a specific element to the information obligation of the controller that is not contained in the specific obligations of Articles 13 and 14 GDPR,[521] namely, that the data subject must also be made aware of the potential risks involved in the processing.

451. Another effect of the principle of fairness is that it could force a controller to gather information with a data subject directly, although it was possible to get the same information from a third party, or to obtain consent (again) for the reuse for different purposes of data it already holds on a data subject, if the reuse is not in line with the reasonable expectations of the data subject, even if all other requirements of the GDPR are fulfilled.[522]

C. Transparency

452. The third aspect of the first principle is that the processing activity carried out by the controller must be transparent in relation to the data subject. This means that whenever a controller is processing personal data on data subjects, it should be transparent to those data subjects that:

- 'personal data concerning them **are** collected, used, consulted or otherwise processed'; and
- **'to what extent** the personal data are or will be processed'.[523]

453. In particular, Recital 39 mentions that the following essential elements must be clarified:[524]

- the identity of the controller;
- the purposes of the processing, these should be explicit and legitimate, and determined at the time of collection (in other words, controllers cannot define or change purposes later on for the same processing);
- which information is being processed; and
- the risks, rules, safeguards and rights relating to the processing.

---

521. These articles deal with the right of the data subject to be informed in two mutually exclusive scenarios: when the data has been gathered with the data subject directly (Art. 13 GDPR) and when the data has been gathered by the controller with a third party (Art. 14 GDPR).
522. This could for example be the case when reusing data for research purposes. Say that a university has gathered data for one research project and wishes to reuse it for another, totally different research project. In such a case the GDPR normally would consider the new research as compatible with the original purpose (even though it may be subject to certain conditions under national law), and the university may not need direct interaction with the data subject in order to have a legal ground for the processing (it could under certain conditions rely on its legitimate interest). Nonetheless, when such processing could not be expected by the data subject, the principle of fairness would forbid the university to go ahead. In that case, the most logical solution would be to provide information to the data subject on this new research project, and to ask for the data subject's consent in reusing the same information.
523. Recital 39 GDPR.
524. These general requirements are also present in Art. 12 GDPR, which is discussed in s. H below.

454. These elements are significantly expanded upon in Article 13 and 14 GDPR, which define what information must be provided to the data subject in two mutually exclusive scenarios: when the data has been gathered with the data subject directly (Article 13 GDPR) and when the data has been gathered by the controller with a third party (Article 14 GDPR). These articles define the *content* of the information that is to be given to the data subject, i.e., what categories of information must be provided. The requirements of these articles are discussed in detail below. Transparency under the GDPR however, as clarified by the Article 29 Working Party[525] in its guidelines on transparency,[526] relates not only to *what* is being communicated, but also, and more importantly to *how* that information is provided to the data subject.

455. Importantly, transparency does not only apply to the information obligations under Article 13 and 14 GDPR, but to any information meant for the data subject or communication with a data subject. This includes the exercise of data subject rights, as well as the case where the controller must communicate to the data subject about a data breach.[527]

456. The guidelines on transparency define the following elements of transparency, namely that any information or communication towards the data subject:

- must be concise, transparent, intelligible and easily accessible;
- must be in clear and plain language;
- must be in writing or by other means (including orally, when so requested and the data subject is identified);
- must generally be provided free of charge; and
- when providing information to children and other vulnerable people, must consider their particularities and tailor the information to their needs.[528]

These elements are all reflected in Article 12 GDPR, which sets out the general conditions for the exercise of data subject rights. Thus, like lawfulness, transparency is in large part made operational through other specific obligations in the GDPR. Article 12 will be discussed in more detail in §8, section I below.

525. The Art. 29 Working Party is a body that was set up under Arts 29 and 30 of the Data Protection Directive (Directive 95/46/EC of the European Parliament and of the Council of 24 October 1995 on the protection of individuals with regard to the processing of personal data and on the free movement of such data, OJ L 281, 23.11.1995, pp. 31–50). It issues authoritative guidelines and opinions on matters of data protection law under the Directive. Since the entry into force of the GDPR on 25 May 2018, the European Data Protection Board, has taken over this role (*see* Art. 68 and further GDPR). The European Data Protection board has specifically endorsed several of the guidelines of the Art. 29 Working Party, namely those already taking into account the GDPR. Those guidelines retain their authoritative value and are still relevant.
526. Art. 29 Working Party, Guidelines on transparency under Regulation 2016/679 (WP260).
527. Art. 34 GDPR; clarified in Art. 29 Working Party, Guidelines on transparency under Regulation 2016/679 (WP260), para. 70.
528. Art. 29 Working Party, Guidelines on transparency under Regulation 2016/679 (WP260), paras 7–22.

457. However, despite the reflection of the principle of transparency in Article 12 GDPR, and with regards to the content in Articles 13 and 14 GDPR, the principle is still enforceable in its own right. Thus, it is in theory possible for a controller to adhere to Article 12 GDPR, and, depending on the situation Article 13 or 14 GDPR, and still be in breach of the principle of transparency, e.g., by failing to inform the data subject on the risks of the processing, where those risks are sizeable and relevant. Moreover, as already outlined above, transparency is intrinsically linked to the aspect of fairness, given that, in order to determine whether a processing activity is fair, the information already given to the data subject by the controller must be taken into account.

II. Purpose Limitation

458. The second principle relating to the processing of personal data is the principle of purpose limitation. Purpose limitation is a key concept in EU data protection law,[529] which requires that any processing of personal data may only be done for a specific, explicit and legitimate purpose. This purpose must be communicated to the data subject in advance. For this to be possible, the purpose of the processing operation must be very clearly defined by the controller in advance of the processing. Consequently, purposes that are vague or very broadly described, will not be compliant with the GDPR.

459. This principle of purpose limitation protects the data subject against a mentality on the controller's side of gathering and storing data, just because it could be useful in the future, for yet undefined purposes. In that sense, the principle of purpose limitation is strongly connected with the principles of transparency and fairness, since having a clearly defined purpose in advance of the processing enables the data subject to know what to expect.[530]

460. In order to accommodate for the reality that even a diligent controller cannot always foresee every purpose for which the data will be needed, the GDPR allows the controller to process the same data for additional purposes, when these are compatible with the original purpose. Unless *prima facie* obvious, the lawfulness of such use depends on a balancing test, which takes into account several elements. The elements are discussed in more detail below.

461. Taking into account the foregoing points, the principle of purpose limitation has two building blocks which are discussed in more detail in Sections A and B below:

---

529. For a brief history on the concept, please refer to Art. 29 Working Party, Opinion 03/2013 on purpose limitation, pp. 6–11.
530. That predictability is part of this principle is recognised in Recital 50 of the GDPR, in relation to what additional purposes are compatible with the original purpose, and more generally in Art. 29 Working Party, Opinion 03/2013 on purpose limitation, p.13.

1 data may only be collected and used for specified, explicit and legitimate purposes (Section A); and
2 data may not be further processed in a way incompatible with those purposes (Section B).

462. There are however two limited exceptions to the rule that only compatible further use is allowed with the same data. First, Article 6(4) GDPR, clarifies that there are two other scenarios where, although the purpose of the newly intended processing activity is not compatible with the original purpose for which the data were collected, the controller can still reuse the data:

- the data subject consents to this use; or
- there is a provision in EU law or in Member State law that specifically provides for this further processing.

This exception is discussed in more detail in section C below.

463. Second, there is a general exception for further processing for archiving purposes in the public interest, scientific or historical research purposes or statistical purposes. Irrespective of the specific intentions of the intended processing activities or these purposes, they are considered to always be compatible with the original purpose. To balance this exception, additional safeguards may be imposed on such processing activities. This exception is discussed in more detail in section D below.

A. *Specified, Explicit and Legitimate Purposes*

464. The first building block of the principle of purpose limitation is that the purpose of the processing activity must be:

- specified;
- explicit; and
- legitimate.

In the following sections, these three elements are discussed in more detail. For some practical examples, please refer to the Article 29 Working Party's Opinion 03/2013 on purpose limitation, Annex 3.[531]

1. Specified

465. The specification of the purpose is a basic building block of purpose limitation and requires the controller to define the purpose of the processing, prior, and in any event at the latest at the time of collection of the personal data needed for that processing. In other words, the controller must consider prior to the processing

531. Art. 29 Working Party, Opinion 03/2013 on purpose limitation, p. 51.

what the personal data it intends to collect will be used for, and whether all data is necessary, adequate and relevant to the identified purpose. Moreover, the purpose must be sufficiently detailed. Vague or general purposes such as 'improving the users experience', 'security purposes', 'our legitimate interests', 'to conduct our business', etc. are not sufficiently specific.

466. The exact level of detail required will depend on the controller and the intended processing.[532] The more complicated the context of the processing activity, the more detail will be required to ensure the purpose of the processing is still specific. To this extent, layered information notices/privacy policies may be used by the controller to explain the different purposes to the data subject, where main purposes are further split up in sub-purposes and information is provided on different levels, so the data subject can easily access the information according to his or her desired level of detail and taking into account his or her specific situation (where perhaps not all information is equally relevant). An example of a layered information notice is a privacy policy on a website where the data subject can show/hide certain information and click through to the relevant sections by way of hyperlinks attached to titles or keywords.

467. The fact that the purpose of the processing activity for which personal data is being gathered must be specified does not prevent that data is collected and used for more than one purpose. However, such purposes must be clearly distinguished from one another, as well as the potentially separate legal grounds that may support the different processing activities.[533]

468. Moreover, every processing activity may only use the data that is necessary, adequate and relevant for that specific activity, which in turn depends on the specified purpose of the processing activity. In that way, the principle of purpose limitation is also linked to the principle of data minimisation, which is discussed in more detail under section III below, and in essence requires that personal data should only be processed if the purpose of the processing could not reasonably be fulfilled by other means, i.e., by using less personal data.

469. In the case of *„SS' SIA v. Valsts ieņēmumu dienests*, the Court of Justice held that that the collection by the tax authorities of a Member State from an economic operator of information involving a significant amount of personal data is subject to the requirements of that regulation, in particular those set out in Article 5(1) thereof. Tax authorities of a Member State may not derogate from the provisions of Article 5(1) where such a right has not been granted to them by a legislative measure within the meaning of Article 23(1) of the GDPR. This does not preclude the tax authorities of a Member State from requiring a provider of Internet advertisement services to disclose to them information relating to taxpayers who

532. Art. 29 Working Party, Opinion 03/2013 on purpose limitation, p.16 at fn. 34 and examples at pp. 51–55.
533. This is because every processing activity has one and only one purpose.

have published advertisements in one of the sections of their Internet portal, provided, in particular, that those data are necessary in the light of the specific purposes for which they are collected and that the period to which the data collection relates does not exceed the period strictly necessary to achieve the objective of general interest sought.[534]

2. Explicit

470. Not only must the purpose of the processing activity be specified at the side of the controller, the controller must also make this purpose explicit, i.e., clearly reveal, explain or express it in some intelligible form.[535] This is done as part of providing information to the data subject under Article 13 or 14 GDPR.

471. The objective of this requirement is that the purposes are specified without ambiguity or vagueness, so that they are understood by all potential stakeholders[536] without doubt as to their meaning. It also serves to ensure that no purpose is kept secret by the controller. The meaning of the indicated purpose should be sufficiently clear, irrespective of the different backgrounds (cultural, linguistic, education) of the stakeholders, their level of understanding, or special needs.[537]

3. Legitimate

472. The third element of purpose specification is that the purpose must be legitimate. Like the principle of lawfulness discussed above, the requirement of legitimacy of the purpose is broader than having a legal ground under Article 6 GDPR. In fact, legitimacy refers to compliance with all legal rules applicable in the given context (e.g., labour law, consumer law, contract law) and thus depends on the relationship between the controller and the data subject. Legitimacy does not only refer to compliance with formal laws, but to compliance with law in the broadest sense, including legal principles, constitutional principles, judicial precedents and jurisprudence, etc.[538]

473. According to the Article 29 Working Party, legitimacy even includes, within the confines of the law, other elements such as customs, codes of conduct and other forms of self-regulation, codes of ethics, contractual arrangements. Moreover, even the general context and the facts of the case, and specifically the relationship between the controller and the data subject may be considered in determining whether an intended processing activity has a legitimate purpose or

534. CJEU, Case C-175/20, Judgment of 24 February 2022, *'SS' SIA v. Valsts ieņēmumu dienests*, ECLI: EU:C:2022:124, https://eur-lex.europa.eu/legal-content/EN/TXT/?uri=CELEX:62020CJ0175.
535. Art. 29 Working Party, Opinion 03/2013 on purpose limitation, p. 17.
536. This includes not only the data subject but also the controller's staff, any involved processors and even the data protection authority.
537. Art. 29 Working Party, Opinion 03/2013 on purpose limitation, p. 17.
538. Art. 29 Working Party, Opinion 03/2013 on purpose limitation, p. 20.

not.[539] Given that legitimacy must be understood in such a broad sense, the evaluation of the legitimacy of a given purpose may change over time, in response, not only to changing legislation, but also to broader changes in society and culture, as well as scientific and technological developments.

474. In one of the earliest judgments relating to European data protection law, the CJEU held that the then applicable Directive 1995/46/EC did not preclude national legislation requesting disclosure to the Austrian '*Rechnunghof*' of detailed personal data regarding the remuneration earned by staff members of public bodies, provided that it is shown that the wide disclosure not only merely of the amounts of the annual income above a certain threshold of persons employed by the bodies subject to control by the Rechnungshof but also of the names of the recipients of that income is necessary for and appropriate to the objective of proper management of public funds pursued by the legislature.[540]

B. Compatible Use

475. Article 5(1) (b) GDPR, which contains the purpose limitation principle, specifies that 'Personal data shall be collected for specified, explicit and legitimate purposes and not further processed in a manner that is incompatible with those purposes.' Hence, in principle, only further processing that is compatible is allowed.

476. The Article 29 Working Party clarified in its guidelines on purpose limitation that the Data Protection Directive (DPD) did not differ between processing for originally specified purposes and processing for compatible purposes which were defined subsequently, but rather between the data processing operation of collection of the data and any subsequent 'further processing'. Hence, 'further processing' encompasses all processing beyond the collection of the data. This means that the controller should not only show that processing operations for new purposes are 'not incompatible' (i.e., compatible) with the purposes for which the data were collected, but should also do this for the processing necessary for the original purposes, which were initially communicated to the data subject. Although perhaps somewhat confusing, this simply means that any processing operation after the processing activity that is the collection of the data, should be in line with the purposes communicated to the data subject at the time of collection and should not exceed the reasonable expectations of the data subject based on that communication.[541]

539. Art. 29 Working Party, Opinion 03/2013 on purpose limitation, p. 20.
540. CJEU, Joined cases C-465/00, C-138/01 and C-139/01, Judgment of 20 May 2003, *Österreichischer Rundfunk*, ECLI:EU:C:2003:294, https://eur-lex.europa.eu/legal-content/en/TXT/?uri=CELEX:62000CJ0465.
541. *See* Recital 50 GDPR: 'In order to ascertain whether a purpose of further processing is compatible with the purpose for which the personal data are initially collected, the controller, after having met all the requirements for the lawfulness of the original processing, should take into account[…] in particular the reasonable expectations of data subjects based on their relationship with the controller as to their further use.' This also complies with the principles of transparency and fairness.

477. The Article 29 Working Party however still makes a distinction between original purposes, communicated to the data subject, and 'new purposes', which were not communicated at the time of collection of the data. For original purposes, the Article 29 Working Party states that the compatibility of the processing would be *prima facie* obvious if the controller limits itself to processing data specifically for those clearly defined original purposes in a way which is customary to achieve the purposes in question. Only if the processing were to go beyond this, it should be submitted to a compatibility assessment, just like subsequently defined (new) purposes. For newly defined purposes, the Article 29 WP identifies two scenarios as well: either the incompatibility of the proposed reuse is obvious, or the proposed reuse warrants a compatibility assessment.

478. In both cases where a compatibility assessment is necessary, such an assessment must not be purely formal, i.e., based on the text of the information provided to the data subject, but must be substantive and take into account not only the text, but also the context and other relevant factors.[542] The following key factors are relevant considerations in determining whether further processing is compatible with the purposes for which the data were collected, and which were communicated to the data subject:[543]

- **'The relationship between the purposes for which the data have been collected and the purposes of the further processing'**:[544] in order to assess the relationship, all relevant factors must be taken into account, including how the purpose communicated to the data subject is commonly understood by relevant stakeholders. If a further processing operation was already implied in the initial purpose or is a logical next step, it would not be problematic. Situations where there is only a partial link or no link at all may still be compatible, but the greater the distance of the intended processing operation from the purposes communicated at collection, the more problematic for compatibility;
- **'The context in which the data have been collected and the reasonable expectations of the data subject as to their further use'**:[545] this aspect mostly focuses on the broader context of the data collection, as well as the reasonable expectations of the data subject. Note that the data subject is not a concrete person, but is defined as a reasonable person in the data subject's situation. In practice then, a controller will have to look at the type(s)/group(s) of data subject involved and specifically the nature of its relationship with the data subjects involved and the broader context in which the data was gathered. This includes not only the reasonable expectations of the data subjects based on the information given to them by the controller, but also what is customary or expected in practice, given the context and the specific relationship (commercial, governmental, etc.). Of course, the information given is still a very (and typically still the most) relevant point in

542. Art. 29 Working Party, Opinion 03/2013 on purpose limitation, p. 21.
543. Art. 29 Working Party, Opinion 03/2013 on purpose limitation, pp. 23–27.
544. Art. 29 Working Party, Opinion 03/2013 on purpose limitation, pp. 23–24.
545. Art. 29 Working Party, Opinion 03/2013 on purpose limitation, pp. 24–25.

making this assessment and the level of transparency here is important to determine what further use is acceptable. With regards to the relationship, it is important to take into account the balance of power between the data subject and the controller. If the data subject was for example legally obliged to provide the information (e.g., when applying for governmental services), then the compatibility assessment must be more stringent. In general, the more **specific** and **restrictive** the context of the collection, the more limitations will be imposed on further use. This is because such a context limits the reasonable expectation of the data subject. In general then, the more surprising, unexpected or unusual the further use, the more likely it is to fail the compatibility test;

- **'The nature of the data and the impact of the further processing on the data subjects'**:[546] this aspect highlights that data protection law essentially aims to protect individuals against the impact of an excessive, unexpected, unreasonable or improper use of their data. Hence, the impact on the data subject is the central point of focus. The nature of the data is relevant because it directly influences the potential negative impact on the data subject. After all, some categories of data are inherently more sensitive than others. A further processing of an e-mail address for new purposes is intrinsically less risky than further processing of health data, financial information or biometric information for purposes the data subject was never informed about. In general, the more sensitive the personal data under consideration for further processing, the more narrow the scope for compatible use. In assessing the impact on the data subject, the controller must take into account, both positive and negative effects, as well as the emotional impact on the data subject. Moreover, the controller must not only consider its own actions, but the potential for future decision or actions by third parties in relation to this further processing, especially taking into account whether this may lead to the exclusion or discrimination of the data subjects. Hence, the manner in which the further processing is intended to be carried out is also very relevant. If the controller of the further processing is a third party rather than the original controller which collected the data, the data being publicly disclosed to a large number of persons, the processing concerns a large amount of personal data or is it being combined with other data, this may be problematic for the compatibility finding, given that there is a potential negative impact on the data subject. In general, the more **negative** or **uncertain** the potential consequences, the more unrealistic it is that further processing will be compatible with the original purposes for which the data was collected;
- **'The safeguards applied by the controller to ensure fair processing and to prevent any undue impact on the data subjects':**[547] the last element in assessing compatibility, is the safeguards applied by the controller to make the processing more fair and to minimise impact on the data subject. Such safeguards may come in different forms. Article 29 mentions as an example that the functional separation/isolation of the data used for the new purposes from the original data,

546. Art. 29 Working Party, Opinion 03/2013 on purpose limitation, pp. 25–26.
547. Art. 29 Working Party, Opinion 03/2013 on purpose limitation, pp. 26–27.

e.g., by (partially) anonymising the data,[548] pseudonymising it or aggregating the data, which might require technical and operational measures. Another safeguard mentioned is the provision of additional information or the respecification of the purposes so as to increase the transparency towards the data subject. Last the Article 29 Working Party also mentions that the (renewed) consent of the data subject can be an appropriate safeguard. This idea has been retained in the GDPR and is discussed in section C below.

These key factors have been explicitly included in the text of the GDPR, reading together Article 6(4) GDPR and Recital 50 of the GDPR.

479. An important remark with regards to this compatibility assessment is that, next to being a substantive assessment rather than purely formal, it must be approached as a balanced multi-criteria evaluation. This means that neither are the above key factors necessarily exhaustive, nor is their weight in this balancing exercise predefined. It is up to the controller to justify all elements of its assessment, the weight given to different factors, and to defend its findings. For some practical examples to further illustrate this assessment, please see Annex 4 of the Article 29 Working Party's Opinion on purpose limitation.[549]

480. If the controller finds that the intended further processing is compatible, it may go ahead with the processing, and, following Recital 50 of the GDPR, it does not need a separate legal basis, but rather can in principle rely on the legal basis on which the data were collected, and which was communicated to the data subject. Nonetheless, the controller must still, prior to the further processing, inform the data subject about that further processing (Article 13(3)GDPR).

481. If, on the contrary, the controller comes to the conclusion that the intended further processing is incompatible, it must in principle not carry out the processing activity. There are however, two scenarios mentioned in Article 6(4) GDPR, that would still allow for the further processing to take place. These are discussed in the following section.

---

548. Note that anonymisation is a difficult concept. If data is fully and truly anonymised (and it is often debatable whether that is possible), then the data would no longer be personal data under the GDPR. However, the operation of anonymising the dataset would still be further processing. Also, it would often be arguable that data sets that have been anonymised are, depending on the techniques used either still personal data because of the ever-increasing capacity for reidentification or could become personal data again in the future and must, therefore, be treated as such in order to prevent non-compliant activities with that data.
549. Art. 29 Working Party, Opinion 03/2013 on purpose limitation, pp. 56–70.

C. Acceptable Incompatible Use

482. Article 6(4) GDPR clarifies that certain further processing activities are allowed, even though they may not hold up under the compatibility test,[550] in two hypotheses:

(1) if the data subject consents to this processing; or
(2) where EU law or Member State law foresees such processing.

483. In the first hypothesis, the data subject is contacted in order to ask whether they allow the intended further processing that is not (or not clearly enough) compatible with the initial purposes which were communicated to the data subject upon first collecting the data. Because consent has to be a 'freely given, specific, informed and unambiguous indication of the data subject's agreement to the processing of personal data',[551] the data subject is put in a position of control, where he or she must be clearly informed about the purpose of the new processing activity, and can freely refuse his or her consent, blocking the intended new processing.

484. In the original draft of the GDPR, not only consent, but also the other legal grounds were considered to be able to 'cover' an intended incompatible use. In the author's opinion, the EU legislator was correct in not retaining other legal grounds than consent, because of one pertinent difference between consent and the other legal grounds: in order for consent to be valid, the data subject must be free to refuse the processing operation, without having to give reasons. Consent must also specifically be 'informed', i.e., based on understandable information about the intended processing. This helps make the further processing that was unforeseeable and incompatible fair. The other legal grounds do not provide the same safeguards, and are consequently not equally appropriate to make an incompatible use acceptable.

485. The second hypothesis in Article 6(4) GDPR relates to the situation where either EU law or Member State law clearly allows for (or obliges the controller to undertakes) a processing activity that would otherwise be incompatible with the original purposes. This is only accepted by the GDPR when the law in question 'constitutes a necessary and proportionate measure in a democratic society to safeguard' the vital objectives contained in Article 23(1) GDPR, such as national security, defence, public security, or the prevention, investigation, detection or prosecution of criminal offences or the execution of criminal penalties. This hypothesis is logically limited in scope and for example encompasses the situation where a company receives a request for a competent authority to transmit information

550. Recital 50 of the GDPR specifies: 'Where the data subject has given consent or the processing is based on Union or Member State law which constitutes a necessary and proportionate measure in a democratic society to safeguard, in particular, important objectives of general public interest, the controller should be allowed to further process the personal data **irrespective of the compatibility of the purpose.'**
551. Recital 32 GDPR, linked to the validity of consent under Art. 7 GDPR.

relating to one of its customers who is suspected of having committed a crime, and is required to comply with this request by applicable national law.

D. Further Processing for Research or Archiving Purposes

486. Another specific situation in relation to the topic of purpose limitation is the situation in which the intended further processing is for archiving purposes in the public interest, scientific or historical research purposes or statistical purposes. Such forms of further processing are deemed to be compatible with the original purposes for which the data have been collected.[552] This rule is meant to add legal certainty to certain activities which are considered important for society (e.g., scientific research).The data subject will in principle need to be informed about the further processing, although there are some specific exceptions when the controller is a third party (see §8, section II, part Ebelow).[553]

487. The assumed compatibility of further processing for archiving in the public interest, scientific or historical research or statistical analysis, does not in any way affect the other GDPR rules and principles. All relevant factors and circumstances of the intended further processing must still be taken into account, and specifically, the controller must take appropriate safeguards to prevent, or at least minimise, the impact of the further processing on the data subject.[554] Relevant here is the idea of functional separation, i.e., for the controller to implement measure to ensure that the data used for further processing for statistical, archiving or research purposes are not used also to take decision or perform other actions with respect to individuals. Measures may include pseudonymisation[555] or anonymisation[556] (where appropriate and possible while still fulfilling the purpose of the further processing), and the controller must take technical and organisation measures to ensure that only the strictly

552. Art. 5(1), b) GDPR; Recital 50 GDPR; Art. 89 GDPR.
553. *See* Arts 13 and 14 GDPR respectively.
554. Art. 89 GDPR; Art. 29 Working Party, Opinion 03/2013 on purpose limitation, p. 28.
555. Pseudonymisation is a technique or procedure that aims to de-identify sets of personal data by replacing personally identifiable information fields within a data record with artificial identifiers, or pseudonyms. In order to accomplish this, the controller may require a third party to do the pseudonymisation or may do so itself. In the latter case however, the controller must ensure functional separation through technical and organisational measures within its own organisation. *See* Recital 29 GDPR.
556. Anonymisation is a procedure by which personal data is de-identified with the purpose of making any reidentification of data subjects in the future impossible. Recital 26 GDPR specifies that 'To ascertain whether means are reasonably likely to be used to identify the natural person, account should be taken of all objective factors, such as the costs of and the amount of time required for identification, taking into consideration the available technology at the time of the processing and technological developments.' Hence, whether data is to be considered truly anonymous under the GDPR, depends on a number of objective circumstances. Modern technology, however, makes true and lasting anonymisation difficult, as there is ever more information available as well as tools to process this information, making it increasingly more likely that a motivated third party, with access to enough data sources, could cross-reference data in order to reidentify specific individuals. There is a separate opinion on anonymisation techniques, *see* Art. 29 Working Party, Opinion 05/2014 on Anonymisation Techniques.

necessary data is used (data minimisation, see section III below).[557] The specific goals of the intended archiving or research activity will determine what data must be used and, therefore, what measures must be taken in order to achieve functional separation, i.e., to ensure that further processing does not impact the data subject.

488. The Article 29 Working Party identified three scenarios in this regard:

(1) In the first scenario the further processing can be carried out with unidentifiable data, i.e., data which has been anonymised with certain techniques or has been aggregated in such a way that it is no longer (reasonably) possible to identify the data subjects.[558]
(2) In the second scenario, the further processing is carried out with indirectly identifiable data, i.e., data that has been aggregated to a lower level, only partially anonymised, has been key-coded or pseudonymised, the result of which is that the risk of the data subject being reidentified has been strongly reduced.[559]
(3) In the third scenario, the further processing is carried out with directly identifiable personal data, because the nature of the research demands this.

489. Depending on what scenario the further processing corresponds with, additional measures such as increased security and access restriction may be required.[560] In general, the easier it is to identify the data subject, the more additional safeguards will be needed. Taking scientific research as an example, this means that research that can be done with (arguably) complete anonymisation[561] will tend to need fewer additional safeguards than research that needs to process personal data without any form of pseudonymisation or anonymisation.

490. In addition to these general requirements provided by the GDPR, the GDPR clarifies that Member States should impose specific measures in relation to safeguards. Recital 156 GDPR states: 'Member States should provide for appropriate safeguards for the processing of personal data for archiving purposes in the public interest, scientific or historical research purposes or statistical purposes', indicating that Member States are allowed and expected to introduce their own rules, which may be general or context/sector-specific, where they can more precisely determine the balance and the necessary safeguards for further processing for

557. Art. 89(1) GDPR; Art. 29 Working Party, Opinion 03/2013 on purpose limitation, pp. 30–32.
558. Here, if true anonymisation is reached, the GDPR would in principle not apply (*see* recital 26 GDPR). However, it is a risky position for a controller to take this stance and not apply the GDPR, as a Court or a data protection authority might disagree on this point, especially when, despite the controller's best efforts and application of best practice measures, data subjects are reidentified at some point.
559. The GDPR recognises that such a situation can reduce the risks for the data subject and can help controllers to meet their diverse data protection obligations. *See* Recital 28 GDPR.
560. For more examples of additional safeguards, *see* Art. 29 Working Party, Opinion 03/2013 on purpose limitation, p.32.
561. For more information about the requirements for 'full' anonymisation, *see* Art. 29 Working Party, Opinion 05/2014 on Anonymisation Techniques.

archiving purposes, research purposes or statistical purposes. Such legal rules may then be further supplemented by (professional) ethics codes, specific guidance and forms of self-regulation.

491. Moreover, as Article 89 (2) and (3) GDPR clarifies, such Member State law (as well as EU law), may provide for derogations to certain data subject rights, depending on the specific purpose, when the exercise of these rights (e.g., right to access, right to object to the processing) would be likely to render impossible or seriously impair the achievement of the specific purposes of the intended further processing. Such derogations must be accompanied by conditions and safeguards laid down by law.

The following subsections will provide some more detail on the three categories of further processing of Article 89 GPDR:

(1) Further processing for archiving purpose in the public interest (section 1).
(2) Further processing for scientific or historical research purposes (section.2).
(3) Further processing for statistical purposes (section 3).

1. Archiving Purposes in the Public Interest

492. Under the GDPR, further processing for archiving purposes in the public interest is applicable to further processing by public authorities or private bodies, which are under a legal obligation to 'acquire, preserve, appraise, arrange, describe, communicate, promote, disseminate and provide access to records of enduring value for general public interest'.[562] For such activities, and in relation to this specific type of controller (as identified by law), Member States may foresee in derogations from the following data subject rights:

- right to access (Article 15 GDPR);
- right to rectification (Article 16 GDPR);
- right to restriction of processing (Article 18 GDPR);
- right to objection (Article 21 GDPR).

493. Derogations may be necessary, for example in order to ensure that specific information relating to horrendous political behaviour, war crimes, crimes against humanity, or genocide remains available to the general public, in its original form. Note that the GDPR does not apply to the data of deceased persons. Hence, such data can in principle be processed without restriction.[563]

494. Importantly, derogations to the above data subject rights can only be imposed when the exercise of these rights would be 'likely to render impossible or seriously impair the achievement of the specific purposes, and such derogations are

562. Recital 158 GDPR.
563. Albeit that Member States may provide for rules on this point (*see* recital 27 GDPR).

necessary for the fulfilment of those purposes'. Moreover, such derogations must be accompanied by conditions and safeguards laid down by law.

2. Scientific or Historical Research Purposes

495. The second category of further processing is the further processing for historical or scientific research purposes, bearing in mind that the GDPR does not apply to deceased persons. Such data can, therefore, in principle be processed without restriction for research purposes.[564] However, it is not always practical to distinguish the data relating to the deceased from the data relating to data subjects who are alive. As a consequence, the controller must often treat the whole dataset as personal data within the scope of the GDPR.

496. Research is a broad category, with historical research including genealogical purposes, and includes for technological development and demonstration, fundamental research, applied research and privately funded research.[565] It also specifically includes medical research, which because of the sensitive nature of the data may require further safeguards.[566]

497. Note that in order to benefit from this exception, the controller must not have a specific quality, such as is required for the further processing for archiving in the public interest. Hence, it applies to private companies and for-profit organisations, as well as to universities and research institutes.

498. It is up to the Member States to define specific rules in relation to scientific research, including possible derogations to the following data subject rights:

- right to access (Article 15 GDPR);
- right to rectification (Article 16 GDPR);
- right to restriction of processing (Article 18 GDPR);
- the notification obligation of the controller to inform each recipient to whom the personal data of the data subject have been disclosed after rectification or erasure of data (Article19);
- right to data portability (Article 20 GDPR);
- right to objection (Article 21 GDPR).

499. Derogations can only be imposed when the exercise of these rights 'are likely to render impossible or seriously impair the achievement of the specific purposes, and such derogations are necessary for the fulfilment of those purposes'. Moreover, such derogations must be accompanied by conditions and safeguards laid down by law.

---

564. Albeit that Member States may provide for rules on this point (*see* recital 27 GDPR).
565. Recital 159 GDPR.
566. Recital 157 and 159 GDPR.

500. In general, Member State law will impose safeguards for research activities, which should take into account the three different types of scenarios described above (not identifiable anonymised data, indirectly identifiable data or identifiable data), to define the additional safeguards. It should be noted that, where identifiable data is not needed, a typical safeguard will be to pseudonymise it or anonymise it, depending on whether the resulting data set is still sufficient to reach the research's purposes. Moreover, where research relates to special categories of data (Article 9 GDPR, see §7 below) such as health data, the necessary additional safeguards should be stricter.

501. The controller must not only comply with the national law on this point, as well as other (sectoral) rules, guidelines or codes of conduct, but must always make its own determination under the general rules of the GDPR as well with regards to any additional safeguards that may be needed.

502. A recent opinion of the European Data Protection Supervisor[567] illustrates that finding a balance in research remains a difficult exercise throughout Europe, with certain parties complaining that the GDPR provides too much leeway, while other parties consider it too restrictive.

3. Statistical Purposes

503. The third category of further processing is processing for statistical purposes, which Recital 162 GDPR clarifies as meaning 'any operation of collection and the processing of personal data necessary for statistical surveys or for the production of statistical results', which clearly is a broad definition. Like further processing for research purposes, further processing for statistical purposes may in principle apply to any controller, and includes statistical activities for commercial purposes as well as statistics for the public interest.

504. The statistical results produced by this type of processing is rarely an end in itself, and may be used for different purposes, including scientific research or commercial insight. However, the concept of further processing for statistical purposes does imply that 'that the result of processing for statistical purposes is not personal data, but aggregate data, and that this result or the personal data are not used in support of measures or decisions regarding any particular natural person.'[568] Hence, activities such as profiling for direct marketing, brokering of personal data

567. The European Data Protection Supervisor (EDPS) is an independent supervisory authority, whose duties and powers have been laid down in Regulation (EU) 2018/1725 (the 'GDPR for EU institutions'). Its primary objective is to ensure that European institutions and bodies respect the data protection regulation, as well as the right to privacy, when they process personal data and develop new policies. The reference is to its opinion on data protection and scientific research, first published 6 January 2020. *See* European Data Protection Supervisor, Opinion on data protection and scientific research (2020).
568. Recital 162 GDPR.

or advertising based on location are not processing activities for statistical purposes, since they focus on the level of the individual. On the contrary, statistics meant to bring insight into general trends and preferences are allowed, also when they are created for purely commercial purposes. Next to general statistics by public or private organisations, the exception for the further processing for statistical purposes also covers the (confidential) statistics made by national statistical offices.

505. As with the previous exceptions, EU or Member State law may provide for derogations from data subject rights, if the exercise of those rights is 'likely to render impossible or seriously impair the achievement of the specific purposes, and such derogations are necessary for the fulfilment of those purposes'.

506. Recital 162 GDPR clarifies that EU or Member State law should also 'determine statistical content, control of access, specifications for the processing of personal data for statistical purposes and appropriate measures to safeguard the rights and freedoms of the data subject and for ensuring statistical confidentiality'. Member State may implement this freely, either in general terms and/or with sector or context specific legislation.

E. Conclusion

507. The foregoing sections show the importance of the principle of purpose limitation and hence, the importance of clearly defining the purposes as exhaustively and precisely as possible at the outset of the processing activity. Equally, it is important to communicate these purposes, and possible different legal grounds relied upon beforehand. This will be further be elaborated on below in §8, section II, relating to the right of the data subject to be informed.

508. A proper definition of the purpose will make the further processing more likely to be allowed as compatible. Even if not compatible, the controller may still go ahead if the data subject consents or if so required by law. Moreover, in some circumstances (archiving, research, statistics), the compatibility is assumed, although the controller must still provide appropriate safeguards, in accordance with applicable law and other applicable rules.

509. It should be pointed out that the controller may always choose to start a new processing operation altogether, rather than relying on compatible use. The controller may then also potentially rely on another legal ground in comparison to the first processing operation. In that case, the controller may not further use the data collected for the initial purposes, but must collect it again from the data subject or a third party (if that third party is allowed to share the data under its relationships with the data subject) and comply with both the requirements of that legal ground, as well as other GDPR requirements.

III. Data Minimisation

510. The third general principle of data processing under the GDPR is that the data processed must be 'adequate, relevant and limited to what is necessary in relation to the purposes for which they are processed',[569] otherwise referred to as the data minimisation principle.

511. The data minimisation principle is in essence an expression of proportionality, meaning no more data must be processed than is strictly speaking required to attain the purpose. Recital 39 of the GDPR clarifies: 'Personal data should be processed only if the purpose of the processing could not reasonably be fulfilled by other means.' This means that the controller must question whether it can reach its goals through the use of other, less invasive or intrusive means, especially with regards to the amount and type of data used, including the sensitivity of the data. Not only the amount of data categories and elements must be limited to what the controller strictly needs, but the controller must also question whether all data is needed in a fully identifiable form in order to reach the legitimate purpose it has set out. If for example, the processing operation could reasonably be carried out successfully while pseudonymising or even anonymising (part of) the data set, the controller must do so.

512. A specific implementation of this principle can be found in Article 11 GDPR, which states that, 'If the purposes for which a controller processes personal data do not or do no longer require the identification of a data subject by the controller, the controller shall not be obliged to maintain, acquire or process additional information in order to identify the data subject for the sole purpose of complying with [the GDPR]'.[570] An example of such a situation would be the case where the controller has cameras around the entrance of its buildings for security purposes. While the footage of the camera certainly is personal data in relation to the persons entering and leaving the building, the controller cannot, in principle identify them on that basis alone. Article 11(1) GDPR specifies that the controller is in that case not be obliged to process additional information, purely for GDPR compliance, e.g., to make sure that if a data subject should want to exercise his or her rights, the controller is already able to identify him or her.[571] Moreover, as Recital 39 explicitly states, the principle of data minimisation also requires that 'the period for which the personal data are stored is limited to a strict minimum'. In that sense, data minimisation is directly linked to the principle of storage limitation, which is discussed in section V below.

569. Art. 5(1), c) GDPR.
570. Art. 11(2) GDPR.
571. However, as Art. 11(2) GDPR clarifies, if the data subject then provides additional information enabling the identification, then the controller will have to allow the data subject to exercise his or her rights, under the conditions applicable to those rights. *See* for more information s. H below.

IV. Accuracy

513. The fourth principle of data processing is that personal data must be 'accurate and, where necessary, kept up to date; **every reasonable step** must be taken to ensure that personal data that are inaccurate, having regard to the purposes for which they are processed, are erased or rectified without delay'.[572]

514. It is clear from the wording of the GDPR that this is an obligation of means, and the reasonability of the efforts that are required by the controller will depend on the situation at hand, and must be assessed in the light of the purposes for which the data was collected.[573] If, for example, the processing at issue is sending advertisement by e-mail to the e-mail addresses in a database, the reasonable steps that the controller will have to take to keep the data up to date will be limited. This has to do with the fact that the impact on the data subject is limited if the data subject receives e-mail on an outdated e-mail account, or does not receive the e-mail at all. Even if the e-mail address has been reassigned to another person, the impact on that data subject is not very serious either. The situation would be different if the controller is an organisation providing credit scores on the data subject. In such cases, outdated information might lead the data subject to miss out on a loan, and application or something similar. In such a context, the requirement for the controller to keep the database(s) it works with up to date would be much more stringent. It is up to the controller to actively monitor the need for updating or correcting, and this must be carried out without delay.

515. In addition to the active duty of the controller to monitor accuracy, the principle of accuracy is also reflected in several data subject rights, namely the right of access, the right to rectification and the right to erasure. These rights, which are discussed in more detail in §8, aim to enable the data subject to know what data the controller processes on him or her, and to ask for either rectification or erasure, depending on the circumstances.[574] Thus, the data subject may actively prompt the controller to take action on this point. Moreover, Article 16 GDPR clarifies that the data subject also has the right to have incomplete personal data complemented, should this be of relevance in the light of the purposes for which the data are being processed.[575]

---

572. Art. 5(1), d) GDPR.
573. CJEU, Case C-434/16, Judgment of 20 December 2017, *Nowak*, ECLI:EU:C:2017:994, https://eur-lex.europa.eu/legal-content/en/TXT/?uri=CELEX:62016CJ0434.
574. As will be explained in §8, s. I below, this does not automatically mean the controller has to grant such a request. Certain general conditions apply to the data subject's exercise of its rights, as well as specific conditions depending on the right that is being invoked.
575. This was previously included in the accuracy principle under the Data Protection Directive (Directive 95/46/EC of the European Parliament and of the Council of 24 October 1995 on the protection of individuals with regard to the processing of personal data and on the free movement of such data, OJ L 281, 23.11.1995, pp. 31–50), but was not explicitly retained in the GDPR. However, by its inclusion in Art. 16, it clarifies that the data subject still has this guarantee.

516. Despite this, it is not necessarily so that information relating to a data subject, which is factually incorrect, is also inaccurate in the sense of the GDPR.[576] An exam, for example, may contain personal data and opinions of the examinee and thus be personal data, but incorrect answers in that context would not necessarily be inaccurate data in the sense of the GDPR, although such data may be inaccurate if it is linked to the wrong data subject or is (accidentally) used in a different context that the context in which it was collected.[577] Another example is changing the findings of a doctor in a medical record, purely because the findings turned out to be wrong. In such a case, an annotation or remark would be better, as the findings in itself (even though they were wrong), are not inaccurate in the sense that they represented the reality of the doctor's assessment at that time, which may still be relevant for future diagnoses. Similar examples can be thought of in a number of sectors, where information revealing personal data, such as opinions, decisions or advice, may be accurate information, even though they are (or have turned out to be) factually incorrect or no longer represent the opinion of the person who initially expressed them. Accuracy or inaccuracy under the GDPR will depend on the specific context at hand.

V. Storage Limitation

517. The fifth principle of data processing requires that personal data is 'kept in a form which permits identification of data subjects for no longer than is necessary for the purposes for which the personal data are processed'.[578] Recital 39 GDPR clarifies that the storage period must be limited to a **strict minimum**. In order to make this operational, the controller must establish time limits for erasure, or at least for a periodic review of whether the data is still needed for the purposes for which it has been collected and is being processed.

518. Moreover, the controller must think about storage duration in advance and on a case-by-case basis, as Articles 13 and 14 GDPR require[579] the controller to either tell the data subject the intended duration or, if not possible, the criteria that

576. *See* on the difficult question of when incorrect or imprecise data is inaccurate under the GDPR: Frederik Zuiderveen Borgesius, Dara Hallinan, 'Opinions can be incorrect (in our opinion)! On data protection law's accuracy principle', *International Data Privacy Law* 2020, Vol 10(1), 1–10; Jiahong Chen, 'The Dangers of Accuracy: Exploring the Other Side of the Data Quality Principle', *European Data Protection Law Review* 2018, Vol. 4(1), 36–52.

577. *See* CJEU, Case C-434/16, Judgment of 20 December 2017, *Nowak*, ECLI:EU:C:2017:994, para. 54, https://eur-lex.europa.eu/legal-content/en/TXT/?uri=CELEX:62016CJ0434.

578. Art. 5(1), e) GDPR.

579. When reading these articles, one might notice that in fact this part of the information of the second paragraph of those articles, which must only be provided when 'necessary to ensure fair and transparent processing in respect of the data subject'. However, the Art. 29 Working Party in its opinion on transparency, has clarified, that there should be no distinction between these paragraphs, and that this information is always necessary to ensure fair and transparent processing (Art. 29 Working Party, Guidelines on transparency under Regulation 2016/679, para. 19). Even though this is a strong statement, and arguably goes against the wording of the law, these guidelines have been endorsed by the European Data Protection Board (the entity replacing the Art. 29 Working Party as the body providing EU-wide authoritative guidance) in its Endorsement 1/2018 (https://

will be used by the controller to determine that period. Hence, undefined periods are no longer acceptable under the GDPR. As will be explained further in more detail, the requirement of transparency in the context of Article 13 and 14 GDPR requires the controller to differentiate between different data and purposes and to specify what the intended storage duration is for each of them or, if not possible, the criteria that will be used to determine the different periods.

519. The principle of storage limitation does not imply that storage periods must always be very short. If suitable justification exists, long periods are permissible. A good example is the situation in which the controller has a legal obligation to retain the data for a number of years. In such cases, it cannot be disputed that this storage period in compliance with the law is a strict minimum. Equally, the GDPR does not strictly speaking prevent life-long processing activities. Personal data collected by a public authority in the context of the civil register for example, may last for as long as the data subject lives.

520. Article 5 (1), e) clarifies that when personal data is being processed solely for archiving purposes in the public interest, scientific or historical research purposes or statistical purposes, storage periods may be longer than this strict minimum in principle required by the GDPR. However, as discussed above, appropriate safeguards, including technical and organisation measures to safeguard the rights and freedoms of the data subject, must be put in place, in accordance with Article 89 GDPR. Such measures may include pseudonymisation, access control, increased security, etc.; and where possible within the context of the further processing, data may be anonymised.

521. In fact, anonymisation is a recourse also outside the scenario of further processing solely for archiving purposes in the public interest, scientific or historical research purposes or statistical purposes, and may be used by any controller who has identified that the strict minimum storage period for a certain set of data is about to lapse. If the controller wants to keep this data, but does not have a justification for doing so, it could proceed to fully anonymise the data (i.e., ensure that the data subject is no longer in any way identifiable), in which case the GDPR does no longer apply to the processing of this information.[580] There are however, two problems with this approach. First, the data may no longer be (as) useful after anonymisation. Second, anonymisation is not something that is easy to achieve or to rely on,

edpb.europa.eu/sites/default/files/files/news/endorsement_of_wp29_documents.pdf), and thus this guideline is considered authoritative and is considered best practice.

580. Recital 26 of the GDPR specifies: 'The principles of data protection should therefore not apply to anonymous information, namely information which does not relate to an identified or identifiable natural person or to personal data rendered anonymous in such a manner that the data subject is not or no longer identifiable.' It also specifies that 'To ascertain whether means are reasonably likely to be used to identify the natural person, account should be taken of all objective factors, such as the costs of and the amount of time required for identification, taking into consideration the available technology at the time of the processing and technological developments.' Hence, whether data is to be considered truly anonymous under the GDPR, depends on a number of objective circumstances.

as there are no agreed standard procedures on how to do this, and the risk that the data subject will be reidentified is very real in the current reality of rapid technological development and ever-increasing access to data. Even in situations where the controller is in good faith convinced that it has anonymised a certain data set and has used state-of-the-art techniques, a motivated third party with the necessary resources may still be able to reidentify the data subject soon thereafter. Thus, depending on the situation, anonymisation may not be tenable, forcing the controller to continuously consider the result as personal data, to which the storage limitation principle applies. Whether data can be considered as truly anonymous (and consequently, free for use irrespective of the GDPR's requirements), will depend on the specific situation at hand,[581] the techniques that have been used to anonymise,[582] and the controller's risk-appetite.[583]

522. It should be noted that the principle of storage limitation is also linked to the right to erasure, also commonly known as the 'right to be forgotten', provided for in Article 17 GDPR (see §8, section V below). This right gives the data subject the possibility to request of the controller the deletion of data that is no longer necessary for the purposes for which the data was collected or otherwise processed. Hence, here as well the data subject can prompt the controller to take action on this point.

VI. Integrity and Confidentiality

523. The sixth principle contained in Article 5(1) GDPR, titled the principle of 'integrity and confidentiality', demands that personal data is 'processed in a manner that ensures **appropriate security** of the personal data, including protection against unauthorised or unlawful processing and against accidental loss, destruction or damage, **using appropriate technical or organisational measures**'.[584] This principle reflects the need in a digitised and interconnected world for personal data to be protected against third parties with unlawful intentions. In order to do so the controller must take all appropriate organisational measures (e.g., access control rules, regular password changes, physical security measures) as well as technical measures (login requirements, advanced authentication, firewalls, etc.) to ensure an appropriate level of security.

524. The GDPR does not require absolute security of the processing operation, i.e., measures of security which would prevent any security incident or data

581. For example, processing operations that are purely internal, are typically less risky than where this date is used to produce a report, study or other results which will be made public.
582. *See* for more details on this: Art. 29 Working Party, Opinion 05/2014 on Anonymisation Techniques (WP216).
583. After all, if the data considered by the controller to be anonymous and then further processed for other purposes which would not have been allowed by the GDPR is again linked to an identified or identifiable data subject, it becomes personal data once more and the controller will virtually undeniably be in breach of the GDPR, possibly leading to fines and liability.
584. Art. 5(1), f) GDPR.

breach[585] (which would also be impossible to comply with), but a measured approach, based on the specific situation at hand. Hence, the use of the word 'appropriate' in Article 5(1), f) GDPR for determining both the measures to be taken as well as the resulting level of security.

525. The GDPR specifically mentions the following measures, to be implemented 'as appropriate':[586]

- 'the pseudonymisation[587] and encryption of personal data;
- the ability to ensure the ongoing confidentiality, integrity, availability and resilience of processing systems and services;
- the ability to restore the availability and access to personal data in a timely manner in the event of a physical or technical incident;
- a process for regularly testing, assessing and evaluating the effectiveness of technical and organisational measures for ensuring the security of the processing'.[588]

526. In order to determine what measures are appropriate, the controller should consider all of the following aspects:[589]

- the state of the art;
- the costs of implementation;
- the nature, scope, context and purpose of processing;
- the potential risks for the data subjects if something were to go wrong, taking into account the varying likelihood and severity of such scenarios.

527. In essence, the more sensitive the data is (e.g., health data, data relating to criminal convictions), or the more risks the intended processing operation presents (e.g., processing that may give rise to discrimination, identity theft, financial loss, physical damage in case of unauthorised use or loss of the data), the more advanced measures the controller will have to take in order to ensure security.[590]

528. The controller must carry out the risk assessment in relation to the impact on the data subject on the basis of objective factors[591] and must, if the intended processing activity is likely to result in a high risk, carry out a data protection impact

585. For more details on data breaches and the obligations of the controller in that event, *see* §9, s. VI, subss B and C below.
586. Art. 32 (1) GDPR.
587. As recognised in Recital 28 of the GDPR, pseudonymisation can help reduce the risk to the data subjects and can help the controller to meet its obligations under the GDPR. Pseudonymisation is also a security measure in the sense that it prevents a third party who unlawfully obtains the data to identify individuals, since the direct identifying information (name, address, etc.) has been kept functionally separate from the pseudonymised data, assuming that data is not also unlawfully accessed by the same third party.
588. Art. 32 GDPR.
589. *Ibid.*
590. *See* Recital 75 GDPR for further guidance for some scenarios in which extra care will be necessary.
591. Recital 76 GDPR.

assessment (see further, under §9 section VII).[592] Based on this assessment, taken together with the findings on the other three aspects mentioned above, the controller should be able to determine the appropriate security measures. The requirement of integrity and confidentiality and the accompanying risk assessment is specified in more detail in the obligations of Article 24 GDPR (responsibility and accountability of the controller), Article 25 GDPR (Data protection by design and default) and Article 32 GDPR (security of processing).

VII. Accountability

529. The last principle relating to data processing contained in Article 5 GDPR is the principle of accountability, on which Article 5(2) GDPR states the following: 'The controller shall be responsible for, and be able to demonstrate compliance with [the other six principles discussed above].' As explained by the Article 29 Working Party's opinion on accountability,[593] the principle of accountability of the controller, principally requires two things:

(1) for the controller to put into place appropriate and effective measures to implement the principles relating to data processing, i.e., measures that, taking into account the nature, scope, context and purposes of the processing and the risk to data subjects involved, would – under normal circumstances – guarantee that all other data processing principles are adhered to;[594] and
(2) be able to demonstrate that such measures have been taken, upon request. This means that the controller must have documentation ready to show both data subjects and supervisory authorities the measures that have been taken to achieve compliance with the principles of data processing.

530. In its opinion, the Article 29 Working Party clarifies that accountability and responsibility go hand in hand and are both elements of good data protection governance.[595] Hence, the principle of accountability under the GDPR aims to oblige the controller to take its responsibly, as well as make the actions that have been taken verifiable. This includes the proof that the measures taken to comply with the other principles discussed in the preceding sections are reasonably effective, considering the specific circumstances.[596]

531. The controller remains accountable through the processing lifecycle and must review, and where necessary, update the measures taken.[597] Regular updates

592. Art. 35 GDPR.
593. Art. 29 Working Party, Opinion 3/2010 on the principle of accountability (WP173).
594. *See* Art. 29 Working Party, Opinion 3/2010 on the principle of accountability (WP173), para. 28 and Recital 74 GDPR.
595. *See* Art. 29 Working Party, Opinion 3/2010 on the principle of accountability (WP173), para. 21.
596. Recital 74 GDPR: 'In particular, the controller should be obliged to implement appropriate and effective measures and be able to demonstrate the compliance of processing activities with [the GDPR], including the effectiveness of the measures.'
597. Art. 24(1) GDPR.

are advisable, in addition to any reviews when there is a security incident, or when there are significant changes in external factors, such as the state-of-the-art or the cost of implementation of such measures.

532. The principle of accountability is reflected in many other obligations under the GDPR. Specifically, it is implemented in a general sense in Article 24 GDPR 'responsibility of the controller', which extends the accountability idea of ensuring compliance and being able to prove compliance at all times to the whole of the GDPR's obligations. Other expressions of the idea of accountability can be found for example in Article 25 GDPR (data protection by design and default), Article 30 GDPR (requirement to keep a record of processing activities), Article 32 GDPR (security of processing), Article 35 and 36 GDPR (Data impact assessments and prior notification) and Article 37 GDPR (designation of a Data Protection Officer).[598]

§6. Legal Grounds for the Processing of Personal Data (Article 6 GDPR)

533. This section addresses the essential requirement that every processing of personal data must be based on a legal ground, of which the GDPR defines six, without any hierarchy.[599] Having a legal ground is a *conditio sine qua non* for the processing of personal data, meaning any given processing operation must have one legal ground (and only one) to rely on.[600] Article 6(1) of the GDPR, that defines the legal grounds reads: 'Processing shall be lawful only if and to the extent that at least one of the following [legal grounds] applies.' This means that there can be no lawful processing without a valid legal ground. Finding a justifiable legal ground for an intended processing is, therefore, a task of paramount importance, and a failure to do so will entail the impossibility to carry out the intended processing activity. However, this must not be interpreted as meaning that the mere presence of a legal ground is sufficient in and by itself. On the contrary, for the controller to be compliant with the GDPR, it also has to respect all the principles relating to the processing of data discussed in §5 above, as well as all other specific obligations of the GDPR. Finding a legal ground is therefore merely a starting point, albeit an important one.

598. Moreover, accountability is also, albeit to a more limited extent, applicable to processors, through specific processor obligations in the GDPR, such as can be found for example in Art. 28(3), h) GDPR and Art. 30(2) GDPR.

599. Art. 6 GDPR.

600. This follows from the fact that the controller must inform the data subject on the legal ground it relies on for every processing operation (Arts 13 and 14 GDPR). This has also been explicitly confirmed in the Art. 29 Working Party's guidelines on consent under the GDPR. *See* Art. 29 Working Party, Guidelines on consent under regulation 2016/679 (WP259), s. 6. These guidelines were explicitly confirmed by the European Data Protection Board in its Endorsement 1/2018.

534. In practice, finding a justifiable legal ground is often not the difficult part, but rather the correct choice of a legal ground when several options present themselves. As will be explained in more detail further, the controller must choose one legal ground (and only one) for every processing activity and the choice of legal ground implies certain consequences down the line, which the controller must take into account at the outset.[601] Consequently, if the legal ground chosen and relied on by the controller is not accepted by the competent data protection authority in case of infringement proceedings, this effectively means the controller will be in breach of essential obligations under the GDPR, which may lead to fines and/or liability. Hence, it is worth the effort to examine all six legal grounds in more detail to highlight their specific scopes. The following sections deal with the legal grounds one by one.

I. Consent (Article 6(1), a) GDPR)

535. Consent is the first legal ground mentioned in Article 6 GDPR, and without a doubt the most well known. The GDPR defines consent as 'any freely given, specific, informed and unambiguous indication of the data subject's wishes by which he or she, by a statement or by a clear affirmative action, signifies agreement to the processing of personal data relating to him or her'.[602]

536. The concept of consent in essence is quite simple; it means that a processing is getting its initial justification in the unambiguous permission of the data subject to go ahead with the intended processing, based on clear and accessible information about what the controller intends to do. Consent is considered an important tool in European Data protection law, as it enables the data subject to have a measure of control over the data protection activities surrounding his or her person.[603] Hence the obligatory use of consent as the only permissible legal ground for the processing of cookie information and, in principle, for direct marketing communications.[604] Another example relates to the use of consent as the only legal ground that in and by itself may 'cover' (i.e., justify) an incompatible further processing activity.[605]

601. Choice of legal ground notably has an effect on applicability of certain data subject rights. Controllers must take this into account when identifying the appropriate legal basis in order to respect the principle of fairness, i.e., they must not unduly try to limit data subject's rights and control over the processing. (European Data Protection Board, Guidelines 2/2019 on the processing of personal data under Art. 6(1)(b) GDPR in the context of the provision of online services to data subjects, para. 1, https://edpb.europa.eu/sites/default/files/files/file1/edpb_guidelines-art_6-1-b-adopted_after_public_consultation_en.pdf).
602. Art. 4(11) GDPR.
603. *See* the report of the European Parliament (the LIBE committee) of 21 November 2013 on the proposal for a regulation of the European Parliament and of the Council on the protection of individuals with regard to the processing of personal data and on the free movement of such data (General Data Protection Regulation) (COM(2012)0011 – C7-0025/2012 – 2012/0011(COD)), p. 200 *in fine*.
604. This is regulated by Directive 2002/58/EC of the European Parliament and of the Council of 12 July 2002 concerning the processing of personal data and the protection of privacy in the electronic

537. However, despite the use of consent as a legal ground having some potential to empower data subjects in their control over processing activities relating to their person, consent also holds the potential to be abused by controllers to justify processing activities for which they otherwise cannot find a justification.[606] To keep the balance, the GDPR defines four **conditions** for consent to be valid, in order to protect the data subject; namely that consent must be:

(1) freely given; and
(2) specific; and
(3) informed; and
(4) an unambiguous indication of the data subject's wishes, through a clear affirmative action.

All of these conditions have a number of implications and are discussed in more detail in section A below. It is up to the controller to **demonstrate** that the data subject has consented in a valid manner.

538. Another balancing measure provided by the GDPR is the data subject's right to withdraw his or her consent at all times. The data subject can withdraw consent at any time and without having to give a reason. Moreover, the controller must inform the data subject about this possibility before the processing activity takes place, and it must be as easy to withdraw consent as it was to give consent.[607] In principle, the withdrawal of consent does not affect the validity of the consent and the lawfulness processing up until that point.[608]

539. A specific situation in relation to consent is where the data subject involved is a child or another type of vulnerable data subject. Section B below discusses this in more detail. Other special situations can be found in certain articles of the GDPR requiring consent to be explicit (section C below), the use of 'old' consent given under the Data Protection Directive (section D below) and in the use of consent in scientific research (section E below). Moreover, the use of consent as a legal ground has other implications, namely linked to data subject rights (section G below).

---

communications sector (Directive on privacy and electronic communications), Official Journal L 201, 31/07/2002 P. 0037 – 0047; often referred to as the e-Privacy Directive. *See* Art. 5(3) (cookies) and Art. 13 (direct marketing) thereof. There is however an exception for direct marketing for similar products (Art. 13(2).

605. The 'in and by itself' is relevant here. After all, Art. 6(4) GDPR also allows incompatible further use based on explicit provision of EU or Member State law, which may very well be an obligation for the controller. In such a scenario, the controller may in such cases rely on Art. 6(1), c) (compliance with a legal obligation), to justify the processing.

606. The Art. 29 Working Party already indicated this in its opinion 2011 opinion on consent (Art. 29 Working Party Opinion 15/2011 on the definition of consent (WP187)), and then built on this in its guidelines on consent under the GDPR (Art. 29 Working Party, Guidelines on consent under regulation 2016/679 (WP259)).

607. Art. 7(3) GDPR.

608. *Ibid.* This is different in case the withdrawal of consent has negative consequences for the data subject. In that case, the consent will have been invalid from the start.

A. *Conditions for Valid Consent (Article 7 GDPR)*

1. Freely Given

540. The first condition for consent to be valid under the GDPR, is that it is free, i.e., that the data subject can freely decide whether or not to give consent. There must be a genuine choice. Hence, in general terms, if the data subject is in any way deceived, intimidated, coerced, or otherwise compelled to give consent, e.g., because they will endure significant negative consequences (e.g., substantial costs) if they do not consent, the consent will be invalid.[609] There are four main scenarios that could affect the data subject's true freedom to grant consent or not, and they are discussed below.

a. Imbalance of Power

541. The first scenario in which consent would be invalid because of a lack of free choice by the data subject, is in cases where there is a clear imbalance in power between the data subject and the controller. Two examples can illustrate:

(1) A public authority requests information from a data subject in the exercise of its official functions, e.g., providing a certain public service. The data subject must give its consent to receive the service and has no realistic alternative to saying 'yes'. In such a situation, consent cannot be deemed to be truly freely given and is consequently invalid.[610] This would be different if the processing at hand is e.g., a public consultation which is absolutely optional, and opting out of which entails no negative consequences for the data subject.[611]

(2) An employer processes personal data on its employees, e.g., for HR purposes. Given the dependency of the employer on his or her employee for his/her livelihood, it is a real worry that a data subject employee would be predisposed to agree to the processing, out of fear for negative consequences if they were to refuse. Whether such repercussions are imagined or real in any specific workplace does not change this assessment. Hence, it is very challenging for an employer to establish valid consent in relation to its employees. Limited exceptions may be possible, however, if the controller can demonstrate genuine choice in that situation. An example could be the processing of contact details of employees who are going to attend the office party in order to prepare for the event (send the invitation, order enough food

609. EDPB, Guidelines 05/2020 on consent under Regulation 2016/679, paras 13–15, https://edpb.europa.eu/sites/default/files/files/file1/edpb_guidelines_202005_consent_en.pdf; Art. 29 Working Party, Guidelines on consent under regulation 2016/679 (WP259), p. 5; Art. 29 Working Party Opinion 15/2011 on the definition of consent (WP187), p. 12.

610. In such cases, the public authority should rely on another legal ground, Art. 6(1), e) (performance of a task in the public interest or exercise of official authority) or Art. 6(1), c) (legal obligation of the controller), as the case may be.

611. EDPB, Guidelines 05/2020 on consent under Regulation 2016/679, paras 16–20; Art. 29 Working Party, Guidelines on consent under regulation 2016/679 (WP259), p. 6.

and drinks, communicate the venue), unless refusing the processing (e.g., by refusing to attend the event) could negatively impact the employees who do so in a significant manner (e.g., not being considered for promotion, being intentionally excluded from events or meetings by management, etc.).[612]

542. The above examples are not exhaustive. Imbalance of power may exist in other situations as well. Consent can only be valid if there is no risk of 'deception, intimidation, coercion or significant negative consequences'[613] for the data subject who does not grant consent. In case of doubt, the controller who is in a situation of power towards the data subject should likely assume consent to be invalid in that situation.

b. Detriment

543. The second scenario in which consent would be invalid is the situation in which, despite there being no clear (initial) imbalance of power, the data subject is in any way restricted in their freedom to **refuse or later withdraw** consent. Detriment in refusing or withdrawing consent would exist where the data subject incurs costs in withdrawing (or not granting) consent, or is subject to any form of deception, intimidation or coercion to obtain his or her consent or to avoid its withdrawal, or is subject to other forms of significant negative consequences when refusing or withdrawing consent.[614]

544. An example can illustrate this situation: a data subject downloads a popular app on its smartphone, which asks the user access to the phone's accelerometer (step counter). This data is not necessary for the app to function, although useful for the controller who can learn about activity levels and provide services in the app with that information. The user is asked consent to access this data, but can freely refuse. However, when the user consents and later wants to revoke consent, the app blocks several functions. In this case there is no real or formal imbalance of power, hence consent could be valid. There is also seemingly nothing wrong with the data subject's initial consent. However, when the data subject wishes to withdraw consent, he or she is no longer fully free to do this, as the app (which, perhaps, the data subject has come to rely on) will no longer function. At the very least, the data subject had been deceived about this. In such a case, detriment exists and the consent

612. EDPB, Guidelines 05/2020 on consent under Regulation 2016/679, paras 21–23; Art. 29 Working Party, Guidelines on consent under regulation 2016/679 (WP259), p. 7.

613. EDPB, Guidelines 05/2020 on consent under Regulation 2016/679, para. 24; Art. 29 Working Party, Guidelines on consent under regulation 2016/679 (WP259), p. 7; Art. 29 Working Party Opinion 15/2011 on the definition of consent (WP187), p. 12.

614. Recital 42 GDPR:' Consent should not be regarded as freely given if the data subject has no genuine or free choice or is unable to refuse or withdraw consent without detriment; *see also* EDPB, Guidelines 05/2020 on consent under Regulation 2016/679, paras 46–54; Art. 29 Working Party, Guidelines on consent under regulation 2016/679 (WP259), pp. 10–11.

given for the processing of the data from the phone's accelerometer will have been invalid and must no longer be used by the controller (i.e., erased).[615]

c. Conditionality/Obligatory Consent

545. The third scenario in which consent cannot be deemed to be freely given, is the situation where consent to a processing activity is presented as a condition to a contract or service, i.e., made obligatory if the data subject wants to enter into the contract or use the service. This issue typically presents itself in the context of online services, including social media, where the data subject has to consent to a number of processing activities to register and enjoy the services. Another example is where a cookie wall blocks access to services and functionalities until the user has consented to have information stored in the terminal equipment used, or to grant access to information already stored there.

546. The GDPR, in Article 7(4) GDPR and Recital 43 GDPR clarifies that consent is not valid if the processing is not necessary to perform the contract, yet made obligatory.[616] On the contrary, if the processing is necessary for the performance of the contract, it can be made obligatory. However, in such cases, consent is not the appropriate legal ground, Article 6(1) b) GDPR (performance of a contract) is.[617]

547. In order to fully assess the scope of this rule, one needs to understand when a processing is truly 'necessary to perform the contract'. It is clear from official guidance from the Article 29 Working Party[618] as well as the more recent guidance of the European Data Protection Board,[619] that this must be interpreted strictly, meaning that the collecting and processing of personal data is only allowed if it objectively is needed to carry out the specific contract with the data subject, e.g., the processing of the data subject's address in order to deliver the goods that were ordered, the processing of the data subject's credit card details for the processing of the payment to pay for the goods, etc. Other processing operations that might be useful for the controller, or even necessary to maintain its business model (but not to perform the contract, strictly speaking), are not covered by this concept.[620]

615. EDPB, Guidelines 05/2020 on consent under Regulation 2016/679, paras 46–54; Art. 29 Working Party, Guidelines on consent under regulation 2016/679 (WP259), p.11, recital 42 GDPR.
616. This does not necessarily mean that such processing is not possible. It can in theory still be justified by another legal ground of Art. 6(1) GDPR.
617. EDPB, Guidelines 05/2020 on consent under Regulation 2016/679, paras 31–33; Art. 29 Working Party, Guidelines on consent under regulation 2016/679 (WP259), p. 8 *in fine*.
618. Art. 29 Working Party, Opinion 06/2014 on the notion of legitimate interest of the data controller under Art. 7 of Directive 95/46/EC, pp. 16–17.
619. European Data Protection Board, Guidelines 2/2019 on the processing of personal data under Art. 6(1) (b) GDPR in the context of the provision of online services to data subject, ss 2.4–2.5, https://edpb.europa.eu/sites/default/files/files/file1/edpb_guidelines-art_6-1-b-adopted_after_public_consultation_en.pdf.
620. European Data Protection Board, Guidelines 2/2019 on the processing of personal data under Art. 6(1) (b) GDPR in the context of the provision of online services to data subject, para. 25, para. 53.

548. Hence, in typical situations of access to online services, the controller will have to rely on another legal ground than Article 6(1) b) GDPR for those processing activities that are not strictly needed to perform the contract, but are typically in its commercial interest and may be necessary for its business model to function. Since other legal grounds will not likely be applicable in such scenarios, the controller will have to rely on consent and consequently must organise matters in such a way that the data subject can refuse the processing operations that are not strictly needed to perform the contract.

549. An example can illustrate this: just like in the preceding example, a data subject downloads a popular app on its smartphone, which asks the user access to the phone's accelerometer (step counter). However, rather than giving the option to the user to freely accept or refuse this, this time the app does not allow the user to register if the consent is not given. The app, however, does not strictly need this data to function, although it is interesting for the owner of the app and the commercial use of this data is an essential part of their business model. Under such circumstances, the consent provided by the data subject would not be valid. For the same reason the aforementioned cookie walls preventing access to services or functionalities are not compliant with the GDPR, since they do not present the data subject with a genuine choice to refuse consent.[621]

550. Because consent cannot be made obligatory, it cannot be demanded as the counter-performance (i.e., 'payment') of the contract by the service provider. Voluntary consent to processing activities in the commercial benefit of the service provider are of course possible, but the service must be available also if the user decides to not consent to such use.[622]

551. It should be pointed out that, despite the foregoing points, the wording of the GDPR leaves some (albeit minimal) room for obligatory consent to be valid. Recital 43 GDPR states that in cases of consent being made mandatory despite not being necessary for the performance of a contract or service, consent is '**presumed**' to be invalid. Presumed seems to imply that the controller could prove the opposite. However, such exceptions will, if possible, be very limited and the controller will have to be able to demonstrate that it can actually rely on valid consent,[623] assuming all the risk of a data protection authority or a Court finding such a reasoning unconvincing.[624] In its guidelines, the Article 29 Working Party already highlighted that the possibility for the data subject to find another contract provider/service provider in the market, who offers a similar service but without the data processing that

---

621. EDPB, Guidelines 05/2020 on consent under Regulation 2016/679, paras 39–41.
622. Hence, this does not touch upon the debate on whether data subjects can pay with their data for 'free' online services, such as the typical social media services. It must however not be demanded, e.g., by refusing the registration of an account if the data subject does not agree to this type of processing.
623. This is based on the controller's obligation of accountability.
624. EDPB, Guidelines 05/2020 on consent under Regulation 2016/679, paras 35–36; Art. 29 Working Party, Guidelines on consent under regulation 2016/679 (WP259), p. 9; *see also* Arts 82 and 83 GDPR.

is being made obligatory by the controller, is not a sufficient argument to make such obligatory consent valid, which was explicitly confirmed by the EDPB as well.[625]

d. Granularity

552. The last scenario in which consent can at times not be deemed to be freely given is when the consent is bundled for multiple processing operations for more than one purpose, and does not enable the data subjects to freely choose which processing operations to allow (or not) despite this being appropriate in the given context, but rather forces an 'accept all' or 'decline all' approach, the latter sometimes being combined with a denial of access to the service or the content in question. In such cases, the consent is not sufficiently granular, because it does not allow the data subject to make a sufficiently nuanced choice. Recitals 32 and 43 GDPR clarify that consent may be bundled for all processing operations needed for the same purpose,[626] but that separate consent is required where appropriate, i.e., for each separate purpose for which the controller intends to process the data.[627]

553. An example can illustrate: if a retailer asks consent to use an e-mail address for direct marketing and to share these details with other companies in their group, there are two purposes. Consent needs to be asked on the level of each separate purpose. In other words, customers must be able to decide whether they want either direct marketing or their details to be shared in the group, neither, or both. If however different processing operations are needed for a specific purpose, e.g., the direct marketing purpose (registering the e-mail in a file, consulting the file, forwarding the addresses to the responsible person, sending out the e-mail, etc.), there is no need to ask consent for each specific step.

625. EDPB, Guidelines 05/2020 on consent under Regulation 2016/679, paras 37–38; Art. 29 Working Party, Guidelines on consent under regulation 2016/679 (WP259), pp. 9–10.

626. For example, if a controller, relying on consent aims to gather a data subject's e-mail address for the purposes of sending a newsletter and to send commercial offers, the data subject should be able to choose whether it wants both those types of communication, only one, or neither. The GDPR requires this level of granularity. However, one could also further differentiate those activities, in which case the processing that has as its purpose to send a newsletter includes the following underlying processing operations/activities: collecting the data, storing the data, using the data to send the emails. It is not required by the GDPR to offer the data subject the option to refuse these underlying processing operations, as they are necessary for and implied by the purpose, to which the data subject can give its consent or not. Hence, the underlying processing operations are covered by consent to the purpose (Recital 32 GDPR). Underlying processing operations must also not be communicated to the data subject under Art. 13 or 14 GDPR. However, the controller must analyse whether all its activities are covered by the identified purposes which were communicated to the data subject, as part of its accountability and other obligations under the GDPR. In as far as some underlying processing operations would not be necessary for or implied by the purpose(s) communicated to the data subject, then this will mean that those processing operations are in fact serving another purpose, which the controller must make explicit, and for which the consent of the data subject must be asked specifically and separately.

627. EDPB, Guidelines 05/2020 on consent under Regulation 2016/679, paras 42–45; Art. 29 Working Party, Guidelines on consent under regulation 2016/679 (WP259), p. 10.

554. The aim of the requirement for consent to be granular is again to enable genuine and detailed choice for the data subject. It is closely linked to the requirement that consent must be specific, which is discussed in the next section.

2. Specific

555. Consent must not only be freely given, but, as Article 6(1), a) GDPR specifies, can only be given for **'one or more specific purposes'**. In order to comply with this, the controller must do three things:[628]

(1) it must, before the processing activity **define specific purposes,** as well as the data needed in order to fulfil those purposes. As described under §5, section II above, purposes must be sufficiently clear, and not vague to avoid function creep, i.e., the phenomenon where the controller forces ever more activities under the umbrella of the initial vague purpose (e.g., 'we will use your data for our business'); and
(2) the controller must foresee **sufficient granularity in its consent requests**, as explained in the preceding section, where the data subject is given the freedom to give or refuse consent for every separate purpose; and
(3) the controller must **provide clear information with each separate consent request** (i.e., per purpose) and clearly separate the information about consent from other information it may be giving (and may be required to give) the data subject, so that the data subject can easily distinguish the relevant information. Information must be accessible, clear and easy to understand. See for more on this, the requirement for consent to be informed in the next section.

    If a controller wants to engage in further processing for other purposes than the specific purposes indicated in the initial consent, a renewed consent for those specific purposes will be needed.[629]

3. Informed

556. The third requirement for valid consent is that consent must be informed. After all, if consent is not accompanied by clear, easy-to-understand and accessible information about the purposes of the processing for which the controller is asking that consent, user/data subject control over the processing relating to his or her person becomes illusory. The requirement for consent to be informed is closely related to the fundamental principles discussed above, namely the principles of lawfulness, fairness and transparency.

---

628. EDPB, Guidelines 05/2020 on consent under Regulation 2016/679, paras 55–61; Art. 29 Working Party, Guidelines on consent under regulation 2016/679 (WP259), pp. 11–12.
629. Art. 6(4) GDPR; this is an example of incompatible further processing which is covered by the consent of the data subject to such processing, *see* §5, s. II.C above.

557. Hence, to be valid, consent must be accompanied by sufficient information, in 'an intelligible and easily accessible form,[630] using clear and plain language' that is clearly distinguishable from other matters (in case of written declaration, such as a privacy policy, which also concerns other matters).[631] Moreover, the controller must tailor its information to its audience. It is up to the controller to demonstrate that it has provided this information to the data subject.[632] For more information on the manner in which information must be provided to the data subject, see §8, section I on transparent information and communication below. For more information on the concept of transparency, see §5, section I.C above.

558. In any case, the very minimum that is required for informed consent is the following:[633]

- the controller's identity;
- the purpose of each of the processing operations for which consent is sought;
- what (type of) data will be collected and used;
- the existence of the right to withdraw consent;
- information about the use of the data for automated decision-making in accordance with Article 22 (2)(c) GDPR where relevant; and
- the possible risks of data transfers outside the EEA.

However, the Article 29 Working Party and EDPB indicate in their opinions on consent[634] that more information may be needed to allow the data subject to truly understand the context of the proposed processing.

559. In addition, the controller will likely have to provide additional information in any case because of its positive obligations under Article 13 and 14 GDPR.[635] Article 13 (1) and 14 (1) GDPR may be fulfilled by the above list, depending on the situation, but may also require more information to be provided

630. The GDPR does not define the form. Hence this could in principle be text, video or audio, or even oral information; *see* EDPB, Guidelines 05/2020 on consent under Regulation 2016/679, paras 66–73; Art. 29 Working Party, Guidelines on consent under regulation 2016/679 (WP259), p. 13 *in fine*.
631. Art. 7(2) GDPR; This also applies in other situations, e.g., consent requested as part of another document/other information, e.g., a contract (*see* EDPB, Guidelines 05/2020 on consent under Regulation 2016/679, para. 71).
632. Recital 42 GDPR. This also follows from the principle of accountability.
633. EDPB, Guidelines 05/2020 on consent under Regulation 2016/679, paras 64–65; Art. 29 Working Party, Guidelines on consent under regulation 2016/679 (WP259), p. 13.
634. EDPB, Guidelines 05/2020 on consent under Regulation 2016/679, para. 65; Art. 29 Working Party, Guidelines on consent under regulation 2016/679 (WP259), p. 13.
635. The Art. 29 Working Party and EDPB acknowledge this, as well as the benefits of an integrated approach, i.e., providing all information at the same time in a single document. *See* EDPB, Guidelines 05/2020 on consent under Regulation 2016/679, para. 72; Art. 29 Working Party, Guidelines on consent under regulation 2016/679 (WP259), p. 15.

to the data subject. Moreover, Article 13(2) and 14(2) require additional information to be provided when this is necessary to ensure a fair and transparent processing. Since the Article 29 Working Party has, in its opinion on transparency,[636] taken the position that this information of Article 13(2) and 14(2) GDPR must always be provided, the above list will have to be further elaborated with the relevant elements of Article 13(2) or 14(2) GDPR respectively. For more details on the requirements of Articles 13 and 14, see §8, section II below.

4. Unambiguous

560. The last requirement for consent to be valid, is that it is an unambiguous indication that the data subject agrees to the proposed processing. Recital 32 GDPR clarifies that consent should be established by a 'clear affirmative act', which could be a written statement, including by electronic means, or even an oral statement. The GDPR is not prescriptive in terms of the form of the consent. Consent can therefore be given in a number of ways, as long as the act is clear and affirmative and it is 'obvious' that the data subject has consented to the particular processing.[637] Examples include writing a statement, ticking a box online, choosing settings of an information society service (e.g., Facebook, Google) and providing a signature or an e-signature.

561. Notwithstanding the principal lack of formal requirements, consent has to be affirmative, which means that consent by silence or lack of action is not valid. Hence, the 'pre-ticked' tick boxes for newsletters, etc., which were omnipresent in the online context prior to the GDPR, are no longer valid, nor are opt-out constructions, where the data subject is assumed to have consented and merely offered an option to opt out of the data processing in some way.[638] Moreover, consent has to be separate from the agreement of a user to a contract or general terms and conditions and cannot be obtained in the same motion.[639]

562. In the case of Orange Romania, the CJEU ruled that a contract for the provision of telecommunications services which contains a clause stating that the data subject has been informed of, and has consented to, the collection and storage of a copy of his or her identity document for identification purposes is not such as to demonstrate that that person has validly given his or her consent, as provided for in those provisions, to that collection and storage, where a) the box referring to that

636. Art. 29 Working Party, Guidelines on transparency under Regulation 2016/679 (WP260), para. 23.
637. EDPB, Guidelines 05/2020 on consent under Regulation 2016/679, para. 75; Art. 29 Working Party, Guidelines on consent under regulation 2016/679 (WP259), p. 15.
638. EDPB, Guidelines 05/2020 on consent under Regulation 2016/679, paras 79–81; Art. 29 Working Party, Guidelines on consent under regulation 2016/679 (WP259), pp. 15–16; *see* CJEU, Case C-673/17, *Bundesverband der Verbraucherzentralen und Verbraucherverbände - Verbraucherzentrale Bundesverband e.V. v. Planet49 GmbH*, ECLI:EU:C:2019:801, https://eur-lex.europa.eu/legal-content/EN/TXT/?uri=CELEX%3A62017CJ0673.
639. EDPB, Guidelines 05/2020 on consent under Regulation 2016/679, para. 81; Art. 29 Working Party, Guidelines on consent under regulation 2016/679 (WP259), p. 16.

clause has been ticked by the data controller before the contract was signed, or b) where the terms of that contract are capable of misleading the data subject as to the possibility of concluding the contract in question even if he or she refuses to consent to the processing of his or her data, or c) where the freedom to choose to object to that collection and storage is unduly affected by that controller, in requiring that the data subject, in order to refuse consent, must complete an additional form setting out that refusal.[640]

563. If the consent is provided in by electronic means, Recital 32 GPDR also specifies that the request for consent must be 'clear, concise and not *unnecessarily* disruptive to the use of the service for which it is provided'. However, this does not mean that consent may not be disruptive to the flow of the service at all. If there is no disruption whatsoever, this may lead to the situation where the action required of the data subject to consent to the intended processing becomes arguably ambiguous. For example, scrolling down or swiping through a website, would not satisfy the requirement of a clear and affirmative action, because an alert that to continue to scroll indicates consent would be difficult to distinguish and may be missed by the data subject. Consequently, this would not be sufficiently unambiguous and a more disruptive action is warranted in this context. Moreover, if consent is so easily established, it may be difficult to offer an opt-out mechanism that is as easy as granting consent, which is required by the GDPR (see section 5, b) below).[641]

5. Other Conditions

564. As already discussed above, Article 7 GDPR requires two more things for valid consent:

(1) the controller must be able to demonstrate consent; and
(2) the controller must inform the data subject of his/her right to withdraw consent prior to the processing, and it must be as easy to withdraw consent as it was to give consent.

a. Controller Must Be Able to Demonstrate Consent

565. The requirement for the controller to demonstrate consent flows from its accountability obligation, but is explicitly repeated in Article 7(1) GDPR. The GDPR leaves the controller free in its means on how to organise this evidence, as long as the retained evidence can demonstrate all aspects of consent. If, for example,

640. CJEU, Case C-61/19, Judgment of 11 November 2020, Orange Romania, ECLI:EU:C:2020:901, https://eur-lex.europa.eu/legal-content/en/TXT/?uri=CELEX:62019CJ0061.
641. *See* on this EDPB, Guidelines 05/2020 on consent under Regulation 2016/679, paras 82–86; Art. 29 Working Party, Guidelines on consent under Regulation 2016/679 (WP259), pp. 16–17.

the controller's workflow does not sufficiently retain proof of the data subject's affirmative action, the controller may run into trouble proving that there was indeed valid consent, and may expose itself to fines and liability.[642]

566. One specific aspect of this is need to demonstrate consent is that, in order to have undisputable proof of consent, the controller may need to refresh the consent given by the data subject at regular intervals. Since the GDPR does not define a duration for consent in general, the duration of consent will depend on the context and scope of the consent given, and on the reasonable expectations of the data subject,[643] taking into account the information originally given to the data subject.[644] Refreshing consent (i.e., asking for consent again), which includes given the data subject updated information, would ensure that the controller is in full compliance and is for that reason best practice. If the processing operations however have changed or evolved considerably in the meantime, the original consent would in any case no longer be valid, and the controller would in this case be obliged to obtain new consent.[645]

b. Data Subject Must Be Able to Withdraw Consent

567. Article 7 also requires that the data subject is informed about its right to withdraw consent, and that consent is as easy to withdraw as it was to give consent. The controller must make sure to enable this in an appropriate manner. If consent was for example given electronically, withdrawing consent should be possible through the same system/platform and should not require undue effort on the part of the data subject.[646] As discussed above, the data subject should be able to withdraw consent without detriment and free of charge.[647]

568. In principle, when consent has been withdrawn, the controller will have to cease all processing operations based on that consent. This will typically include the deletion of the data, unless the controller is also processing the same data on the basis of another legal ground.[648] Note that a withdrawal of consent cannot be 'covered' by another legal ground. The controller must choose a legal ground when determining purposes and must communicate this to the data subject. It cannot later

642. Under Arts 82 and 83 GDPR.
643. EDPB, Guidelines 05/2020 on consent under Regulation 2016/679, paras 104–111; Art. 29 Working Party, Guidelines on consent under regulation 2016/679 (WP259), p. 21.
644. This also flows from the principles of fairness and transparency.
645. EDPB, Guidelines 05/2020 on consent under Regulation 2016/679, paras 104–111; Art. 29 Working Party, Guidelines on consent under regulation 2016/679 (WP259), p. 21.
646. EDPB, Guidelines 05/2020 on consent under Regulation 2016/679, paras 112–116; Art. 29 Working Party, Guidelines on consent under regulation 2016/679 (WP259), p. 21.
647. EDPB, Guidelines 05/2020 on consent under Regulation 2016/679, paras 114; Art. 29 Working Party, Guidelines on consent under regulation 2016/679 (WP259), p. 21.
648. EDPB, Guidelines 05/2020 on consent under Regulation 2016/679, paras 116–117; Art. 29 Working Party, Guidelines on consent under regulation 2016/679 (WP259), p. 22.

decide to change the legal ground.[649] The aforementioned hypothesis where the controller is also processing the data on another legal ground therefore presupposes that this was decided separately before the consent was withdrawn and that this took place for another specified purpose, which was previously communicated to the data subject. The data subject's withdrawal however does not affect the legitimacy of the controller's processing of the data prior to the withdrawal, i.e., during the period where there was valid consent, if the controller can indeed demonstrate that the consent was valid.

B. *Consent of Children*

1. General Consent of Children

569. In order to obtain valid consent in relation to children specific rules apply. Recital 38 GDPR clarifies that 'children merit specific protection with regard to their personal data, as they may be less aware of the risks, consequences and safeguards concerned and their rights in relation to the processing of personal data'. This is especially true if the controller is profiling children or targeting them specifically. In such cases, the controller should use clear and plain language, which the child can understand.[650]

570. Whether or not parental consent is needed in relation to children, will depend on the situation at hand. There are two scenarios. First, if the situation at hand involves an information society service[651] (e.g., Facebook, YouTube) offered directly to a child (e.g., the registration and use of social media accounts by and for a child), Article 8 GDPR will apply. This article imposes in principle that consent of the child in this context can only be lawful where the child is at least 16 years old, although the Member States can reduce this age to 13. This is called the age of digital consent. If the child is younger than this, parental authorisation (i.e., by a parent/ a legal guardian) will always be needed for the use of such services.

571. Second, in any other situation than the offering of information society services directly to a child, the need for parental consent will be determined by the age of the minor and the relevant applicable national law.[652] If a minor for example wants to subscribe to a loyalty card of a clothing store, national law will determine

649. EDPB, Guidelines 05/2020 on consent under Regulation 2016/679, paras 118–120; Art. 29 Working Party, Guidelines on consent under regulation 2016/679 (WP259), p. 23.
650. Recital 58 GDPR, Art. 12 (1) GPDR.
651. Information society services are defined in Art. 4(25) GDPR, by reference to Directive 2015/1535, which defines information society services as 'services, normally provided for a remuneration, at a distance, by electronic means and at the individual request of a recipient of services'. For instance, Google was held to fall within this definition in CJEU, Joined Cases C-236/08 to C-238/08, Judgment of 23 March 2010, *Google France and Google*, ECLI:EU:C:2010:159, https://curia.europa.eu/juris/liste.jsf?num=C-236/08.
652. EDPB, Guidelines 05/2020 on consent under Regulation 2016/679, para. 151; Art. 29 Working Party, Guidelines on consent under regulation 2016/679 (WP259), p. 27.

at what age the minor is able to validly enter into this type of contract. In any case, whether or not the child itself can enter into the contract, or whether there is a need for parental authorisation or not, the controller who is targeting children or who's products or services are especially used by children must adapt its information so that children can understand.[653] This holds true even in the specific case of Article 8 GDPR. While that article transfers the consent for children below the age of digital consent to the holders of the parental responsibility, it does not detract from the child's right to be informed in a way that he or she can understand.[654]

572. In a similar vein, vulnerable people other than children deserve additional protection too. When a controller is for example targeting its goods or services at people with a disability or people who may have difficulties accessing information, the controller will need to target its information to this audience.[655]

2. Consent in Relation to the Offering of Information Society Services Directly to a Child (Article 8 GDPR)

573. As explained above, Article 8 applies in relation to the offering of information society services directly[656] to a child.[657] Information society services are defined in Article 4(25) GDPR, by reference to Directive 2015/1535,[658] which defines information society services as 'services, normally provided for a remuneration, at a distance, by electronic means and at the individual request of a recipient of services'.[659] Most online services for communication or for online delivery of other services would fall within this category, including all forms of social media services, e.g., Facebook, Instagram, Twitter, etc.[660] The fact that these services are

653. Art. 29 Working Party, Guidelines on transparency under Regulation 2016/679 (WP260), paras 14–15. There is an exception for the situation where the children addressed or targeted are very young and/or pre-literate, in which case transparency measures may also be aimed primarily at the holders of the parental responsibility over a child, given that children of this age would be likely incapable of understanding even to most basic written or non-written information.
654. Art. 29 Working Party, Guidelines on transparency under Regulation 2016/679 (WP260), para. 15.
655. Art. 29 Working Party, Guidelines on transparency under Regulation 2016/679 (WP260), para. 16.
656. 'Directly' does not mean 'exclusively'. Hence, it does not only include service specifically made for children (e.g., Youtube Kids), but also all types of services that are also accessible to children (e.g., the regular version of Youtube). *See* Eva Lievens, Valerie Verdoodt, 'Looking for Needles in a Haystack: Key Issues Affecting Children's Rights in the General Data Protection Regulation', *Computer Law & Security Review* 2018, Vol. 34 (2), 269–278, p. 272.
657. A child is defined as any person below the age of 18; *see* Art. 29 Working Party, Guidelines on consent under Regulation 2016/679 (WP259), at fn. 61.
658. Directive (EU) 2015/1535 of the European Parliament and of the Council of 9 September 2015 laying down a procedure for the provision of information in the field of technical regulations and of rules on Information Society services, OJ L 241, 17.9.2015, pp. 1–15.
659. Directive (EU) 2015/1535, Art. 1(b).
660. Another example that falls within this category is Google, as held by the Court of Justice in CJEU, Joined Cases C-236/08 to C-238/08, Judgment of 23 March 2010, *Google France and Google*, ECLI:EU:C:2010:159, https://curia.europa.eu/juris/liste.jsf?num=C-236/08.

in practice not remunerated by the user, does not detract from their qualification as such, since their provision nonetheless constitutes an economic activity (e.g., through advertising income).[661]

574. If such services are offered directly to a child, and the intended processing is based on consent,[662] then Article 8 GDPR applies. In order to assess whether services are offered directly to a child, all relevant evidence will be taken into account, but it is up to the service provider as controller to demonstrate that this is not the case to escape the application of Article 8 GDPR.

575. As mentioned before, if Article 8 GDPR applies, then the child's consent is only valid if the child in question has reached 16 years of age, although Member States are left the freedom to reduce this threshold, as long as the lower age chosen by the Member State in question is not lower than 13 years.[663] In such cases, where the child has reached the age of digital consent, the controller can obtain valid consent from the child directly, provided that it ensures that all its communications are also tailored to the level of understanding of a child.[664] Where the controller is providing its service cross-border, it is up to the controller to deal with the challenge of diverse age thresholds in the different Member States.[665]

576. If however, the child is below the age of digital consent as defined by the applicable Member State law (or laws), then the controller will have to obtain consent or authorisation by the holder of the parental responsibility over the child.[666] This requirement does not affect general contract law of the Member States, but applies irrespective of whether national contract law would allow a child of the given ago to enter into a contract of the type of the information society service in question.[667] Hence, even if it would be permissible under Member State contract law for the child e.g., to register a Facebook account (i.e., accept Facebook's terms and conditions and enter into a contract), Facebook would still have to ensure consent or authorisation of the holders of parental responsibility over the child to make

661. This follows from Recital 18 of Directive 2001/31/EC (Directive 2000/31/EC of the European Parliament and of the Council of 8 June 2000 on certain legal aspects of information society services, in particular electronic commerce, in the Internal Market ('Directive on electronic commerce'), OJ L 178, 17.7.2000, pp. 1–16); *see also* European Data Protection Board, Guidelines 2/2019 on the processing of personal data under Art. 6(1)(b) GDPR in the context of the provision of online services to data subjects, para. 3.
662. If the intended processing is based on another legal ground, Art. 8 GDPR does not apply. In such cases however, other restrictions will apply. If the controller relies on the performance of a contract as a legal ground (Art. 6(1), b) GDPR), the child will have to be capable to enter into the contract and the processing will need to be strictly necessary. If the controller were to rely on its legitimate interests, it will have to stand the balance test of Art. 6(1), f) GDPR, which is very challenging when minors are involved. More on this in the sections below on these legal grounds.
663. Art. 8 (1) GDPR.
664. Recital 58 GDPR, Art. 12 (1) GPDR; *see also* Art. 29 Working Party, Guidelines on transparency under Regulation 2016/679 (WP260), paras 14–15.
665. EDPB, Guidelines 05/2020 on consent under Regulation 2016/679, para. 131; Art. 29 Working Party, Guidelines on consent under regulation 2016/679 (WP259), p. 25.
666. Art. 8(1) GDPR.
667. Art. 8(3) GDPR.

the processing lawful, if the child is under the age of digital consent as defined by Member State law implementing the GDPR. There is however an exception to this rule in the context of the provision of preventative or counselling services offered directly to a child.[668] An example of such a service would be the provision of online child protection services (e.g., an online 'hotline' for minors that are the victim of parental abuse). In those cases, no consent of the holder of parental responsibility is needed.

577. Article 8(2) GDPR obliges the controller 'to make **reasonable efforts** to verify in such cases that consent is given or authorised by the holder of parental responsibility over the child**, taking into consideration available technology**'. Although the GDPR does not specify this explicitly, the same can be assumed to be true in case of the controller trying to prove that the child in question already reached the age of digital consent, and therefore did not need parental consent/ authorisation.[669] This follows from the controller's accountability obligation, and if the controller fails to be able to demonstrate that it undertook reasonable efforts to verify the child's age, the processing would be unlawful.

578. The GDPR neither defines in what manner the controller must verify the age of the child in question, nor in what way the authenticity of parental consent/ authorisation must be verified (i.e., verification that the authorisation was indeed given by the holder of parental consent over the child). In its opinions on consent, the Article 29 Working Party and the EDPB clarify that such checks must not lead to excessive data processing but must be proportionate to the risks present in the proposed processing activities.[670] For low-risk situations, it could suffice for a new subscriber or user of a service to fill out their year of birth in a form or to fill out a form (or check a box), stating that they are not a minor (or that they are, then leading to parental consent being asked) in order to verify the age of the new user. If however, there is a higher risk, more invasive procedure may be envisioned (e.g., proof of identity and date of birth). In the same vein, verification of parental responsibility can be done by e-mail or other simple means in low-risk cases, but high-risk cases may require further proof, e.g., through the use of a third-party verification service.[671] The precise measures to be taken are also defined taking into account that controllers should only make 'reasonable efforts […] taking into consideration available technology', not guarantee a result.[672] Hence, there is some leeway for controllers to argue for specific methods that may be easier or more affordable to

---

668. Recital 38 GDPR.
669. EDPB, Guidelines 05/2020 on consent under Regulation 2016/679, para. 133; Art. 29 Working Party, Guidelines on consent under regulation 2016/679 (WP259), p. 25.
670. EDPB, Guidelines 05/2020 on consent under Regulation 2016/679, paras 135–136; Art. 29 Working Party, Guidelines on consent under regulation 2016/679 (WP259), pp. 25–26.
671. EDPB, Guidelines 05/2020 on consent under Regulation 2016/679, para. 137; Art. 29 Working Party, Guidelines on consent under regulation 2016/679 (WP259), pp. 25–26.
672. *See* on this also *See* Eva Lievens, Valerie Verdoodt, 'Looking for Needles in a Haystack: Key Issues Affecting Children's Rights in the General Data Protection Regulation', *Computer Law & Security Review* 2018, Vol. 34 (2), 269–278, p. 274.

implement but offer less certainty. Controllers should, however, under their accountability obligation in general be able to demonstrate the process they have chosen to implement and the results of these checks for every data subject and should prove they avoid excessive processing.

579. As noted above, the fact that the controller cannot obtain consent directly from the child which has not reached the age of digital consent, does not mean that the child loses its right to be informed. This is maintained throughout the relationship with the controller.[673] This includes the fact that the controller must inform the data subject about its options when it reaches the age of digital consent.

580. When the child reaches the age of digital consent, he or she can decide to confirm, modify or withdraw the consent given by the holder of parental responsibility. In practice, if there is no action by the child reaching the age of digital consent, the parental consent remains a valid ground for processing.[674] This is acceptable given the fact that the child will always have the option to withdraw consent at any time afterwards, and without having to give a reason, as is the general rule with consent.[675]

C. *Explicit Consent*

581. Section I, A above discussed the conditions of consent as a legal ground under the GDPR. One of the conditions for valid consent is that it must be given through a clear, affirmative action, so that the indication of the data subject's wishes to give consent is unambiguous. In that sense, valid consent under the GDPR is always explicit to an extent, but a literal reading of the text of the GDPR does not reveal this as a general requirement.

582. However, in some specific cases where serious data protection risks (may) emerge, the text of the GDPR does specifically require for the consent to be **explicit**. One example is Article 9 GDPR (discussed below), which in principle forbids the processing of special categories of sensitive data (e.g., health data), unless a justification ground applies. The first justification ground is that 'the data subject has given *explicit consent* to the processing of those personal data for one or more specified purposes. Other examples include automated individual decision-making (Article 22 GDPR) and transfers of personal data to third countries or international organisations in the absence of adequate safeguards implemented by the controller (Article 49 GDPR). In those cases, the GDPR, by adding the word 'explicit', clearly imposes a stricter duty on the controller in relation to how the consent is expressed by the data subject than in cases of 'regular' consent.

---

673. Art. 29 Working Party, Guidelines on transparency under Regulation 2016/679 (WP260), para. 15.
674. EDPB, Guidelines 05/2020 on consent under Regulation 2016/679, paras 147–149; Art. 29 Working Party, Guidelines on consent under regulation 2016/679 (WP259), p. 27.
675. Art. 7(3) GDPR.

583. It is up to the controller to define how to implement explicit consent. One safe way to do this would be to have the data subject give an express (written) statement of consent, which refers to the intended processing activities. However, as with 'regular' consent, the GDPR does not impose any form requirements. Hence, explicit consent could also be established in different ways, including online or over the telephone (e.g., with the data subject pushing buttons or providing oral confirmation). In these cases, the controller may be additionally incentivised to use a best practice measure, namely two-stage verification of consent, where an initial consent (e.g., an online signature) is verified by a second action (e.g., a follow-up e-mail where the data subject is asked to confirm its initial consent). In the end, it is up to the controller to be able to demonstrate valid consent, as well as the fact that this consent, given the specific circumstances was 'explicit'.[676]

D. Consent Given Before the Entry into Force of the GDPR

584. Another specific situation concerns the status of consent that was given by data subjects under the regime of the Data Protection Directive, i.e., before the entry into force of the GDPR. The rule here is rather simple: if the consent given before the entry into force of the GDPR would have been valid under the new rules of the GDPR, then the consent remains in principle valid also under the GDPR.[677] It is up to the controller to see whether the consent gathered before the entry into force of the GDPR was indeed valid under the new rules. Often, this will not be the case, as the practice in many Member States allowed forms of consent that would no longer be valid under the GDPR (e.g., pre-ticked boxes, opt-out systems, consents without sufficient information, insufficiently granular consents, consents without a sufficient clear affirmative action such as scroll-through consents, etc.).[678]

585. As always, it is up to the controller to prove that consent was validly given. If the controller did not gather evidence of this at the time, this will effectively mean that the controller will have to seek consent again and document this. In addition, there may be general concerns over the lasting validity of old consent. While the GDPR does not as such define a time limit or validity date for consent, principles such as fairness will require the controller to remain reasonable in how long it considers consent to be valid.

---

676. For more details on this *see* EDPB, Guidelines 05/2020 on consent under Regulation 2016/679, paras 91–102; Art. 29 Working Party, Guidelines on consent under regulation 2016/679 (WP259), pp. 18–20.
677. Recital 171 GDPR; Art. 29 Working Party, Guidelines on consent under regulation 2016/679 (WP259), p. 30.
678. Art. 29 Working Party, Guidelines on consent under regulation 2016/679 (WP259), pp. 30–31.

E. Consent in Scientific Research

586. In scientific research there is often a need for humans as research participants, e.g., to test a product or medicine, to obtain opinions, etc. If the controller bases such research on consent as a legal ground,[679] the controller must make sure to do its best to fulfil the conditions of consent set out in section I.A above. However, as Recital 33 GDPR acknowledges: 'It is often not possible to fully identify the purpose of personal data processing for scientific research purposes at the time of data collection. Therefore, data subjects should be allowed to give their consent to certain areas of scientific research when in keeping with recognised ethical standards for scientific research.' Scientific research is not defined in the GDPR but must be interpreted in a broad manner, however without stretching the concept beyond its common meaning.[680]

587. Hence, Recital 33 GDPR brings into play a degree of flexibility for the controller, with regards to the degree of specification and granularity required for valid consent in the context of scientific research, although Recital 33 GDPR does not disapply the conditions for valid consent. Hence, scientific research projects still need a well-described purpose, but Recital 33 GDPR allows that, where it is not possible to determine these purposes in enough detail at the outset, it would be permissible to describe these purposes in more general terms.[681]

588. This means that it would for example be permissible to allow data subjects to consent to processing for more generally described research purposes. The controller must however try to respect the essence of the consent requirements to the best of its abilities, e.g., by defining the specific stages of the research project that are already known at the outset, so the data subjects are given the opportunity to consent only to certain areas of research or parts of the research project, to the extent that this is allowed by the intended purpose of the research.[682] Moreover, if the research, as it advances, requires subsequent steps and processing activities that were not envisioned, consent should be obtained before this next stage in the research.[683] Hence, the GDPR allows for some leeway in specificity of the consent,

679. This is however by no means obligatory. Other legal grounds, such as legitimate interest may be available.
680. Recital 159 GDPR; the Art. 29 Working Party and the EDPB 'considers the notion may not be stretched beyond its common meaning and understands that 'scientific research' in this context means a research project set up in accordance with relevant sector-related methodological and ethical standards, in conformity with good practice'. (Art. 29 Working Party, Guidelines on consent under regulation 2016/679 (WP259), p. 28); *see also* EDPB, Guidelines 05/2020 on consent under Regulation 2016/679, para. 153.
681. EDPB, Guidelines 05/2020 on consent under Regulation 2016/679, paras 155–156; Art. 29 Working Party, Guidelines on consent under regulation 2016/679 (WP259), p. 28.
682. Recital 33 GDPR.
683. EDPB, Guidelines 05/2020 on consent under Regulation 2016/679, para. 159; Art. 29 Working Party, Guidelines on consent under regulation 2016/679 (WP259), p. 29.

as long as there is sufficient transparency (e.g., through a comprehensive research plan made available to data subjects) to cover for this.[684]

589. In addition, the controller may want to put into place other appropriate safeguards (such as anonymisation, additional security measures and data minimisation measures) are in place, to comply with applicable law and to meet its other GDPR obligations.[685] Where the data involved in the research belong to a special category mentioned under Article 9 GDPR (e.g., health data), the leeway provided by Recital 33 GDPR will need to be interpreted more strictly, and additional safeguards may be necessary.[686]

590. Moreover, in research settings, the controller must always apply the applicable ethical rules and procedures,[687] and must ensure that, where there are several different 'consents' involved, this is clear to the data subject.[688] Typically, participants will have to consent to participate in research projects as part of applicable ethical rules and/or procedures.[689] If the controller also relies on consent as a legal ground under the GDPR, this means there are two separate consents. This should be sufficiently distinguished, so this distinction and its consequences are clear to the data subject. Sometimes there may even be more than two consents. This would for example be the cases in clinical trials with human participants, to which the clinical trials regulation applies.[690] This regulation requires another consent still.[691]

591. An important remark is that when research relies on consent as a legal ground, there must be an option for the consent to be withdrawn. There is no exemption to this rule for scientific research. If the controller relies on consent, it must be able to grant this right.[692]

684. EDPB, Guidelines 05/2020 on consent under Regulation 2016/679, paras 161–162; Art. 29 Working Party, Guidelines on consent under regulation 2016/679 (WP259), p. 29.
685. EDPB, Guidelines 05/2020 on consent under Regulation 2016/679, para. 160; Art. 29 Working Party, Guidelines on consent under regulation 2016/679 (WP259), p. 29; *see also* Art. 89 GDPR.
686. EDPB, Guidelines 05/2020 on consent under Regulation 2016/679, para. 157; Art. 29 Working Party, Guidelines on consent under regulation 2016/679 (WP259), p. 28.
687. Art. 29 Working Party, Guidelines on consent under regulation 2016/679 (WP259), p. 28.
688. EDPB, Guidelines 05/2020 on consent under Regulation 2016/679, para. 154; Art. 29 Working Party, Guidelines on consent under regulation 2016/679 (WP259), p. 28.
689. Note that if this is not so, the research may not qualify as scientific research under the GDPR and may not benefit from Recital 33 GDPR; the Art. 29 Working Party and the EDPB 'considers the notion [of scientific research] may not be stretched beyond its common meaning and understands that 'scientific research' in this context means a research project set up in accordance with relevant sector-related methodological and ethical standards, in conformity with good practice'. (EDPB, Guidelines 05/2020 on consent under Regulation 2016/679, para. 153; Art. 29 Working Party, Guidelines on consent under regulation 2016/679 (WP259), p. 28).
690. Regulation (EU) No 536/2014 of the European Parliament and of the Council of 16 April 2014 on clinical trials on medicinal products for human use, and repealing Directive 2001/20/EC, OJ L 158, 27.5.2014, pp. 1–76.
691. Art. 28 of Regulation 535/2014 (EU).
692. EDPB, Guidelines 05/2020 on consent under Regulation 2016/679, para. 163; Art. 29 Working Party, Guidelines on consent under regulation 2016/679 (WP259), pp. 29–30.

F. Relation to Other Legal Grounds

592. Consent is the primary legal ground to give control back to the data subject, as the data subject is free to either grant consent or not, and must at all times be able to withdraw consent in an easy manner. Importantly, consent cannot be replaced by another legal ground, for example legitimate interests (Article 6(1), f) GDPR), when an individual withdraws consent, as this would be fundamentally unfair to the data subject.[693] When consent is withdrawn, no further processing can take place on that basis, even though the same data can at times continue to be processed if this is happening on another legal ground and for other purposes.

593. This means that a controller relying on consent must understand that the legal ground for processing may at any time disappear if the data subject decides to withdraw consent and must be able to accommodate this, typically including also the erasure of the data. Therefore, consent is not always the appropriate ground and controllers looking for continuity in processing may want to explore if other legal grounds can be relied on, such as contract (Article 6(1), b) GDPR), legal obligation (Article 6(1), c) GDPR), necessity to perform a public task (Article 6(1), e) GDPR) or legitimate interests (Article 6(1), f) GDPR), as these legal grounds offer more stability and may therefore be more appropriate. Consent may in fact be most appropriate as a legal ground when processing cannot reasonably be based on any other legal ground, given the specific circumstances.

594. While consent cannot be replaced by another legal ground, the opposite is in fact possible, looking at Article 6(4) GDPR. This article allows a controller to go ahead with incompatible further processing when the data subject consents to this incompatible processing, having been duly informed. This means that an intended incompatible further processing of data, initially gathered and processed based on legitimate interest (Article 6(1), f) GDPR), can be covered by consent of the data subject. The same is true for incompatible further processing where the original processing was based on any other legal ground, including consent itself.

G. Consent and Data Subject Rights

595. The choice of a legal ground by a controller is attached to some consequences in terms of data subject rights that the controller needs to grant (or not). An important consequence of using the legal ground of consent, as mentioned above is that Article 7(3) GDPR requires that the data subject can at any time withdraw consent. This moreover needs to be facilitated as the data subject must be informed about this right of withdrawal and it should be as easy to withdraw consent as it was to grant consent in the first place.

693. EDPB, Guidelines 05/2020 on consent under Regulation 2016/679, paras 121–123; Art. 29 Working Party, Guidelines on consent under regulation 2016/679 (WP259), p. 23.

596. When a data subject withdraws consent, Article 17 GDPR specifies that data subjects in principle[694] have the right to erasure of their data. Moreover, in the case data were collected in the offer of information society services under Article 8 GDPR, the data subject will also have a right to erasure, even if he/she is no longer a child.[695]

597. In addition, the legal ground of consent will trigger the applicability of a right to data portability when the processing is carried out by automated means (Article 20 GDPR). The controller must be able to accommodate this. Conversely, the right to object (Article 21 GDPR) does not apply when relying on consent, although this is sufficiently balanced by the fact that the data subject can simply withdraw consent at any time, thereby effectively objecting to the continued processing.

598. Articles 13/14 (right to information), 15 (right to access), 16 (right to rectification) and 18 (right to restriction of processing) GDPR also apply. Moreover, data subjects have the right not to be subjected to automated individual decision-making, including profiling, under Article 22 GDPR, unless one of the exceptions of Article 22(2) GDPR applies. See §8 below for more details on the different data subject rights.

II. Performance of a contract (Article 6(1), b) GDPR)

599. The second legal ground defined in Article 6 GDPR, allows processing which 'is necessary for the *performance of a contract to which the* ***data subject is party*** or in order to take steps at the request of the data subject prior to entering into a contract'.[696] Hence, this processing ground covers two distinct situations:

(1) when the processing is necessary for the performance of a contract with the data subject;
(2) when the processing prior to the contract is necessary to conclude the contract, and is done at the request of the data subject.

Both situations are discussed separately below in section A and B. Section C discusses the relationship between this legal ground and the other legal grounds. Moreover, as explained above the choice of this legal ground has implications on data subject rights. Section D below covers this topic.

694. Art. 17 also contains some exceptions, which are discussed in §8, s. V below.
695. Recital 65 GDPR.
696. Art. 6(1), b) GDPR.

A. *Processing Necessary for the Performance of a Contract with the Data Subject*

600. Article 6(1), b) GDPR allows the processing of personal data that is necessary to perform a contract to which the data subject is party. Hence, there are three conditions:

(1) there must be a valid contract;[697] and
(2) the data subject must be party to that contract; and
(3) the intended processing by the controller must be **necessary** for the **performance** of that contract.

601. Consequently, in order for Article 6(1) b) to apply, the data subject must be able to validly enter into the contract. Contracts with minors or specifically vulnerable groups of people, whose capacity to enter into a contract may be restricted, will be subject to national law and jurisprudence on the matter. This also means that a controller cannot rely on Article 6(1) b) to perform a contract to which the data subject is not formally a party, even though the contract may have an impact on the data subject.

602. However, it is mostly the third condition that justifies further explanation. In order to determine what kind of processing is necessary for the performance of a valid contract, to which the data subject is a party, it must be kept in mind that the concept of necessity effectively has an independent meaning under EU law, and, as the Court of Justice clarified,[698] must be interpreted in the light of the objectives of data protection law, notably also in the light of the principle of fairness.[699]

603. This means that 'necessity' must be interpreted strictly, and that the collecting and processing of personal data is allowed under Article 6(1), b) GDPR only if it objectively is needed to carry out the specific contract with the data subject. Examples include the processing of the data subject's address in order to deliver the goods that were ordered and the processing of the data subject's credit card details for the processing of the data subject's payment.[700] Other processing operations,

697. European Data Protection Board, Guidelines 2/2019 on the processing of personal data under Art. 6(1) (b) GDPR in the context of the provision of online services to data subject, para. 26.
698. CJEU, C-524/06, Judgment of 16 December 2008, *Heinz Huber v. Bundesrepublik Deutschland*, ECLI:EU:C:2008:724, para. 52, https://curia.europa.eu/juris/liste.jsf?language=en&jur=C,T,F&num=c-524/06.
699. European Data Protection Board, Guidelines 2/2019 on the processing of personal data under Art. 6(1) (b) GDPR in the context of the provision of online services to data subject, para. 23.
700. Art. 29 Working Party, Opinion 06/2014 on the notion of legitimate interest of the data controller under Article 7 of Directive 95/46/EC, p. 16; European Data Protection Board, Guidelines 2/2019 on the processing of personal data under Art. 6(1) (b) GDPR in the context of the provision of online services to data subject, s. 2.5.

which could be useful for the controller, (and even necessary to maintain its business model), but not to perform the contract, are not covered by this legal ground.[701] Neither are obligations that are unilaterally imposed by the controller.[702]

604. Moreover, it is not because the language of the contract covers a certain processing activity, that it is therefore necessary to perform that contract.[703] An example could be the case where a data subject buys goods online and is obliged to register a profile to finish the checkout. In that profile, the user's purchase history is maintained, as well as other information, preferences, user tastes and lifestyle elements. In that case, the data subject will need to accept the terms and conditions of both the sale and the registered user platform in order to continue, but this does not make the processing of the data subject's user tastes, and buying behaviour necessary to perform the contract, even if the terms and conditions of the platform specify this.

605. Rather than the text, the exact purpose of the contract, i.e., its fundamental objectives must be used as a measure to assess whether a processing activity is necessary for the performance of the contract or not.[704] This means that there is a clear connection between the assessment of necessity and the purpose limitation principle discussed above. If the purposes of the processing activities overlap with what is strictly speaking necessary to perform the contract, then Article 6(1), b) GDPR would be available as a legal ground to justify that processing. Moreover, the controller will in this situation also need to respect the principles of purpose limitation and data minimisation discussed in §5, sections II and III above.[705]

606. In effect, the controller must be able to demonstrate that it cannot, as a matter of fact, perform the contract with the data subject without processing the personal data in question in the proposed manner. If other realistic alternatives would exist, the controller cannot rely on Article 6(1), b) GDPR.[706] Hence, processing for 'service improvement', 'fraud prevention' or for advertising purposes are all examples of processing activities that, while useful to the controller and perhaps very much requested by the data subject, are not strictly speaking required to perform the contract in question.[707] Moreover, the controller must also be able to prove that, in order to determine the necessary processing activities, it is relying on the

701. European Data Protection Board, Guidelines 2/2019 on the processing of personal data under Art. 6(1) (b) GDPR in the context of the provision of online services to data subject, para. 25, para. 53.
702. Art. 29 Working Party, Opinion 06/2014 on the notion of legitimate interest of the data controller under Article 7 of Directive 95/46/EC, p. 16, *in fine*.
703. Art. 29 Working Party, Opinion 06/2014 on the notion of legitimate interest of the data controller under Art. 7 of Directive 95/46/EC, pp. 16–17.
704. Art. 29 Working Party, Opinion 06/2014 on the notion of legitimate interest of the data controller under Article 7 of Directive 95/46/EC, p. 17.
705. European Data Protection Board, Guidelines 2/2019 on the processing of personal data under Art. 6(1) (b) GDPR in the context of the provision of online services to data subject, paras 14–15.
706. European Data Protection Board, Guidelines 2/2019 on the processing of personal data under Art. 6(1) (b) GDPR in the context of the provision of online services to data subject, para. 25, para. 30.
707. European Data Protection Board, Guidelines 2/2019 on the processing of personal data under Art. 6(1) (b) GDPR in the context of the provision of online services to data subject, paras 48–56.

mutually understood purpose(s) of the contract, and not purely on its own perspective. For this reason, the controller needs to take into account the perspective of an average data subject so as to ensure genuine mutual understanding on the contractual purpose.[708]

607. There are some borderline situations, where it may be arguable whether or not Article 6(1), b) GDPR can apply as a legal ground. In those cases, the controller may need to gather further information and prepare a detailed reasoning for why it considers a given processing activity to be strictly necessary to perform the contract. An example is the situation of an employer who wants to establish a company-wide internal database for employees, in which the names, and contact details of all employees are recorded. In some businesses, it may be arguable that this processing is necessary to perform the employment contract. However, in other situations, the specific circumstances may show that this is more of a nice thing to have rather than an indispensable tool. However, in those cases other legal grounds, such as the legitimate interest of the employer to establish this for efficiency and safety purposes may be available to allow the controller to still carry out such processing.[709]

608. In addition to the fact that the processing has to be **necessary** for the performance of the contract, Article 6(1), b) GDPR also only covers the actual normal **performance** of the contract, and does not include further processing in the context of actions or incidents triggered by non-compliance (e.g., Court proceedings), although sending formal reminders (about payments, correcting errors or delays in performance) is included in the normal performance of a contract, as this can be reasonably expected.[710] Equally, storing information in relation to a contractual warranty can be covered by Article 6(1), b) GDPR.[711]

609. In case of termination of the contract, the controller may perform some final processing, if necessary to terminate the contract, e.g., in order to return goods or payment or to finalise administration. Other further processing, such as processing of the same data under a new legal basis, is not permissible.[712] In principle, at the time of termination, the data subject will have the right to ask for erasure of the data that is now no longer needed under Article 17(1), a) GDPR. There are however some exceptions for the controller, e.g., when this data is needed to defend itself in future legal proceedings. This may for example be relevant for the information in

708. European Data Protection Board, Guidelines 2/2019 on the processing of personal data under Art. 6(1) (b) GDPR in the context of the provision of online services to data subject, para. 32.
709. Art. 29 Working Party, Opinion 06/2014 on the notion of legitimate interest of the data controller under Article 7 of Directive 95/46/EC, p. 17.
710. Art. 29 Working Party, Opinion 06/2014 on the notion of legitimate interest of the data controller under Article 7 of Directive 95/46/EC, pp. 17–18; European Data Protection Board, Guidelines 2/2019 on the processing of personal data under Art. 6(1) (b) GDPR in the context of the provision of online services to data subject, para. 38.
711. European Data Protection Board, Guidelines 2/2019 on the processing of personal data under Art. 6(1) (b) GDPR in the context of the provision of online services to data subject, para. 39.
712. European Data Protection Board, Guidelines 2/2019 on the processing of personal data under Art. 6(1) (b) GDPR in the context of the provision of online services to data subject, paras 41–42.

the context of an employment contract that has been terminated. For more information, see §8, section V below on the right to erasure.

B. Processing Prior to the Contract

610. Article 6(1), b) GDPR also applies to processing situations which are **necessary** in order to enter into a contract, if this processing is done on request of the data subject, rather than at the initiative of the controller or a third party. For that reason, sending the data subject an offer or quote on the data subject's request will be allowed, if other GDPR principles are respected (e.g., not more data asked than strictly needed), whereas direct marketing on the initiative of the controller or a third party will not be covered by Article 6(1), b) GDPR.[713]

611. In some situations, although the initiative to conclude the contract may come from the data subject, certain pre-contractual processing activities will not be covered by Article 6(1), b) GDPR because they in reality result from either a legal obligation on the controller (e.g., a legally required credit identity verification by a bank) or are carried out to safeguard the controller's legitimate interest (e.g., a medical check-up before being able to conclude an insurance contract, a credit check by a bank before being granted a loan).[714] In such cases, the controller should choose Article 6(1), c) or f), respectively, because they are more appropriate.[715]

C. Relation to Other Legal Grounds

612. As already touched upon above, Article 6(1), b) GDPR is a legal ground with a restrictive scope. However, processing activities intended by the controller in relation to a contract, which are not included in the scope of Article 6(1), b) GDPR may still be permissible, if the controller can rely on another legal ground.

613. Typical candidates are consent of the data subject (Article 6(1), a) GDPR), or the legitimate interests of the controller (Article 6(1), f) GDPR). For more information on these legal grounds, see section I above and section VI below. Such processing will however need to meet the stringent conditions of those legal grounds and will need to comply with all other requirements of the GDPR. For example, if

713. Art. 29 Working Party, Opinion 06/2014 on the notion of legitimate interest of the data controller under Article 7 of Directive 95/46/EC, p. 18.
714. Art. 29 Working Party, Opinion 06/2014 on the notion of legitimate interest of the data controller under Article 7 of Directive 95/46/EC, p. 18.
715. The European Data Protection Board adds that, when identifying the appropriate legal ground, controllers must exercise due care, and take into account the impact on the data subject's rights, in order to comply with the principle of fairness (European Data Protection Board, Guidelines 2/2019 on the processing of personal data under Art. 6(1) (b) GDPR in the context of the provision of online services to data subject, para. 1).

a service provider wants to carry out activities of behavioural advertising, this can be permissible if it can obtain the data subject's consent or if its legitimate interests can justify it (Article 6(1), f) GDPR).

614. It should be pointed out in this regard that Article 6(1), a) and Article 6(1), b) GDPR are mutually exclusive: if the processing is necessary for the performance of the contract, it should be based on Article 6(1), b) GDPR and not on consent. Conversely, if the processing is not necessary for the performance of the contract, it is not appropriate to base it on Article 6(1), b) GDPR nonetheless and it must be based on another legal ground, of which consent is one (and typically a good candidate, for that matter).[716] Hence, a processing can never be suited for both Article 6(1), a) and Article 6(1), b) GDPR, which however could be true for Article 6(1), a) and Article 6(1), f) GDPR.

615. Another important relation between legal grounds in the context of contracts relates to the choice of a legal ground for obligatory processing activities. Such activities cannot be based on consent, as consent would not be free. If the processing activities are necessary for the performance of the contract, they should be based on Article 6(1), b) GDPR. If not, then they should be based on the legitimate interest of the controller (Article 6(1), f) GDPR), in which case the controller will have to make a balancing test, proving that its interest is legitimate and not overridden by the rights and freedoms of the data subject (for more on this, see section VI below on Article 6(1), f) GDPR).

616. The controller must take these different aspects into account when determining the legal ground(s) for the different intended processing operations. The principles of fairness and purpose limitation demand that the controller be precise in defining its purposes as well as the appropriate legal basis to rely on.[717]

617. Moreover, in order to comply with the principle of transparency, the controller must clearly communicate these diverse legal grounds to the data subject prior to the processing, as well as the consequences for the data subject's rights, the exercise of which may depend on the applicable legal grounds. It must be avoided that the data subject is confused as to which purposes (and the processing operations and personal data connected to these purposes) are linked to which legal basis.[718] See §8, section II below on the information obligations of the controller, as contained in Article 13 and 14 GDPR.

---

716. European Data Protection Board, Guidelines 2/2019 on the processing of personal data under Art. 6(1) (b) GDPR in the context of the provision of online services to data subject, para. 19.
717. European Data Protection Board, Guidelines 2/2019 on the processing of personal data under Art. 6(1) (b) GDPR in the context of the provision of online services to data subject, para. 1, para. 18.
718. European Data Protection Board, Guidelines 2/2019 on the processing of personal data under Art. 6(1) (b) GDPR in the context of the provision of online services to data subject, para. 20.

D. Performance of a Contract and Data Subject Rights

618. As stated before, the legal ground determines the applicability of certain data subject rights. In principle, at the time of termination of the contract on which the processing under Article 6(1), b) GDPR is based, the data subject will have the right to ask for erasure of the data that is now no longer needed by the controller. This is defined in Article 17(1),a) GDPR. There are however some exceptions for the controller, e.g., when this data is needed to defend itself in future legal proceedings. This may for example be relevant for the information in the context of an employment contract that has been terminated.

619. Moreover, for processing activities on the basis of Article 6(1), b) GDPR, the right to data portability (Article 20 GDPR) also applies, when the processing is carried out by automated means. The data subject however, does not have the right to object under Article 21 GDPR in the context of processing which is based on Article 6(1), b) GDPR. This is the consequence of the narrow scope of this legal ground, which assumes that every processing activity is strictly necessary for the performance of a valid contract, to which the data subject has agreed. It would then also be useless to allow the data subject a right to object to such processing, thereby unduly hindering the contract's performance.

620. Articles 13/14 (right to information), 15 (right to access), 16 (right to rectification) and 18 (right to restriction of processing) also apply. Moreover, data subjects have the right not to be subjected to automated individual decision-making, including profiling, under Article 22 GDPR, unless one of the exceptions of Article 22(2) GDPR applies. See §8 below for more details on the different data subject rights.

III. Compliance with a Legal Obligation (Article 6(1), c) GDPR)

621. Article 6(1), c) GDPR provides for the third legal ground, i.e., when the processing is **necessary** for compliance to a legal obligation to which the controller is subject. Necessity, as clarified in section II.A above, has an independent meaning under EU law,[719] and must be interpreted in the light of the objectives of data protection law, notably including the principle of fairness. However, the specific circumstances and the context of the legal ground at hand must also be duly taken into account.

---

719. CJEU, C-524/06, Judgment of 16 December 2008, *Heinz Huber v. Bundesrepublik Deutschland*, ECLI:EU:C:2008:724, para. 52, https://curia.europa.eu/juris/liste.jsf?language=en&jur=C,T,F&num=c-524/06.

A. General

622. This legal ground applies to both public and private sector controllers, as long as they are directly subject to the legal obligation at issue. Examples include the checks a bank has to do in the context of anti-money laundering legislation, the employer's obligations to report salary data to social security and tax authorities or the mandatory sharing of information in the public sector between administrations who need data that another administration holds. All these processing activities are based on a specific legal obligation and allow for a limited processing as prescribed by law.

623. The legal obligation must be based in Member State law or European Union law, and must determine the purpose(s) of the intended processing. It must meet an objective of public interest and be proportionate to the legitimate aim pursued.[720] The GDPR does not require a specific law for each individual processing operation. Rather, a law can serve as the basis for several processing operations which are needed for the purposes of carrying out a legal obligation.[721]

624. Law and legal obligation must be interpreted in a broad manner here. The application of Article 6(1), c) GDPR does not necessarily require a legislative act adopted by parliament,[722] but covers a broader array of measures, as long as the controller is obliged to carry out the processing to fulfil its legal obligation and does not retain an undue degree of discretion.[723] It is permissible that legislation in some cases only sets out the general obligation, with secondary legislation or binding decisions and guidance of competent authorities setting out further obligations and implementation rules.[724]

625. In essence, the legal obligation, whatever the form, must be sufficiently clear and precise, so as to both give a clear instruction to the controller, as well as to be foreseeable to the persons subject to it.[725] Recital 41 GDPR specifies that case law of the Court of Justice and the Court of Human Rights must be taken into account in order to determine this foreseeability. Article 6(3) GDPR specifies that the legal basis (i.e., the law laying down the obligation), may adapt the application

720. Art. 6(3) GDPR. This of course entails it must duly respect the concerned persons' privacy and data protection rights, as laid down in Arts 7 and 8 of the Charter of fundamental rights of the European Union (OJ C 326, 26.10.2012, p. 391–407) and Art. 8 of the European Convention on Human Rights.
721. Recital 41 GDPR.
722. Recital 41 GDPR.
723. Art. 29 Working Party, Opinion 06/2014 on the notion of legitimate interest of the data controller under Article 7 of Directive 95/46/EC, p. 19.
724. Art. 29 Working Party, Opinion 06/2014 on the notion of legitimate interest of the data controller under Article 7 of Directive 95/46/EC, pp. 19–20.
725. Recital 41 GDPR and Art. 29 Working Party, Opinion 06/2014 on the notion of legitimate interest of the data controller under Article 7 of Directive 95/46/EC, pp. 19–20.

of the rules of the GDPR and lists some elements from case law[726] (as well as others) as non-limitative examples of specific provisions that may be included in the law to meet the requirements of foreseeability, as well as proportionality with the legitimate objective of public interest that is being pursued, and compliance with GDPR principles and rules:

- the general conditions governing the lawfulness of the processing by the controller in the context of the legal obligation;
- the type of data which are to be processed;
- the data subjects that are concerned by the legal obligation;[727]
- the entities to which the data may be disclosed;
- the purposes for which the data may be disclosed;
- details on purpose limitation;
- appropriate storage periods;
- specific indications of processing operations and processing procedures to be used/followed, including measures to be taken to ensure lawful and fair processing in the context of the legal obligation.

626. The fact that Article 6(3) GDPR allows Member States to adapt the application of the GDPR on this point should be understood in a limited sense. They cannot overturn GDPR principles, but can e.g., adapt the choice of data to be processed, which is normally for the controller to determine, by defining this by law. In the same sense, Member State law could define a storage period that is much longer than what a controller could usually defend, if there is a good reason for such a prolonged storage period (otherwise this might not be proportionate).

627. While the GDPR neither requires a specific law per processing operation, nor necessarily for a law detailing a legal processing obligation to cover all listed elements above, it does require a degree of specificity as to the processing operation to be undertaken by the controller who is subject to the legal obligation, even if this is done by way secondary legislation or other implementing measures. Very general and vague legal obligations, which leave the controller an undue degree of discretion on how to comply with the legal obligation (e.g., what data to process, who to disclose it to would not be covered by Article 6(1), c). GDPR.[728]

628. In addition to the foregoing, the GDPR leaves Member States the room to maintain or introduce more specific provisions to adapt the application of the rules of the GDPR by determining more specific additional requirements for the processing in the context of legal obligations in specific sectors or situations, including the

726. ECtHR, Judgment of 4 May 2000, *Rotaru v. Romania*, https://hudoc.echr.coe.int/eng#{%22itemid%22:[%22001-58586%22]}; ECtHR, Judgment of 4 December 2015, *Roman Zakharov v. Russia*, https://hudoc.echr.coe.int/eng#{%22itemid%22:[%22001-159324%22]}.
727. This may also in principle include children and vulnerable categories.
728. Art. 29 Working Party, Opinion 06/2014 on the notion of legitimate interest of the data controller under Article 7 of Directive 95/46/EC, pp. 19–20.

imposition of additional measures to ensure lawful and fair processing.[729] The elements listed above should be considered in this situation as well.

629. Hence, in relation to the legal ground of Article 6(1), c), the requirements may differ depending on the sector or situation and on the applicable Member State law. These kinds of carve-outs, where the Member States are granted significant leeway to adopt or maintain separate rules, detract from the objective of unification of data protection law across the EU which is inherent in the EU legislator's choice for a Regulation rather than a Directive.

B. Relation to Other Legal Grounds

630. The scope of Article 6(1), c) is limited. Where a controller would want to carry out additional processing outside what is strictly required to fulfil the purposes of the legal obligation or outside what is strictly required by law, then the controller will have to rely on another legal ground to justify this processing operation, most likely on consent (Article 6(1), a) GDPR) or legitimate interest (Article 6(1), f) GDPR).

631. The same reasoning must be made by a controller who is intending to carry out a processing operation in the broader context of regulatory obligations, but which are not covered by a legal obligation per se, such as intended processing operations based on general policy guidance by a regulatory authority, proposing some best practice measures which happen to entail some processing of personal data. In such cases, the controller must rely on another ground, such as its legitimate interest (Article 6(1), f) GDPR).[730]

C. Legal Obligations and Data Subject Rights

632. In relation to the processing of information by the controller on the legal ground of having a legal obligation to do so, there is neither a right to object, nor a right to data portability. A right to erasure in principle[731] applies when the data is no longer necessary, were unlawfully processed or must actually be erased pursuant to the legal obligation (e.g., after a certain time has lapsed).

633. Articles 13/14 (right to information), 15 (right to access), 16 (right to rectification) and 18 (right to restriction of processing) also apply. Moreover, data subjects have the right not to be subjected to automated individual decision-making, including profiling, under Article 22 GDPR, unless one of the exceptions of Article 22(2) GDPR applies. See §8below for more details on data subject rights.

---

729. Art. 6(2) GDPR.
730. Art. 29 Working Party, Opinion 06/2014 on the notion of legitimate interest of the data controller under Article 7 of Directive 95/46/EC, p. 20.
731. This is because Art. 17 also contains some exceptions, which are discussed in §8, s. V below.

IV. Protection of Vital Interests (Article 6(1), d) GDPR)

634. Article 6(1), d) GDPR provides that processing is also lawful when this is **necessary** to protect the **vital interests** of the data subject or another natural person. Necessity, as clarified in section II.A above, has an independent meaning under EU law,[732] and must be interpreted strictly and in the light of the objectives of data protection law, notably including the principle of fairness (i.e., based on the reasonable expectation of the data subject). However, the specific circumstances and the context of the legal ground at hand must also be duly taken into account.

A. General

635. 'Protecting vital interests' should be understood as situations where there is a threat that poses a risk of injury or other damage to the health, physical integrity or life of the data subject or another person,[733] including the worsening of their situation, which necessitates action that includes the processing of personal data on the data subject. An example situation covered by this legal ground is a medical emergency: e.g., where the data subject has lost consciousness and needs medical treatment or where the data subject is a (young) child incapable of giving consent and the holder of the parental responsibility cannot be identified or located. In such cases, the data subject cannot give consent, but certain information (e.g., data relating to its blood group, medical history, etc.) needs to be processed at once in order to ensure proper medical treatment. In cases where consent is possible, it must be preferred as a legal ground.[734]

636. Recital 46 GDPR provides an example of a situation where this ground can be relied upon in order to safeguard the interests of another person than the data subject, namely in the humanitarian emergencies, such as the spread of an epidemic or in case of a natural or man-made disaster. In such cases, it may be necessary for a doctor or other medical personnel to process personal data on infected persons or victims, in order to obtain the necessary information to take actions, especially in order to save or better treat other patients. As always the processing must be necessary, but in case this criterion is fulfilled, the processing can go ahead, even if the data subject is in no position to agree to the processing (taking blood, running tests, analysing injuries, etc.).

---

732. CJEU, C-524/06, Judgment of 16 December 2008, *Heinz Huber v. Bundesrepublik Deutschland*, ECLI:EU:C:2008:724, para. 52, https://curia.europa.eu/juris/liste.jsf?language=en&jur=C,T,F&num=c-524/06.
733. Art. 29 Working Party, Opinion 06/2014 on the notion of legitimate interest of the data controller under Article 7 of Directive 95/46/EC, p. 20; *see also* recitals 46 and 112 GDPR.
734. Art. 29 Working Party, Opinion 06/2014 on the notion of legitimate interest of the data controller under Article 7 of Directive 95/46/EC, p. 20.

B. Relation to Other Legal Grounds

637. Recital 46 GDPR specifies that, where processing data based on the vital interest of another natural person, this legal ground should only be relied on only where the processing 'cannot manifestly be based on another legal basis '[735] and must therefore be considered only as a last resort. Where medical emergency processing of personal data, e.g., in the context of an epidemic or disaster is done by public authorities in the public interest, likely Article 6(1), e) would provide a legal ground (performance of a task in the public interest, and some processing operations may also be covered by a legal obligation (Article 6(1), c) GDPR). In those cases, the controller should attempt to rely on any another appropriate legal basis (including consent, if the data subject is conscious), before turning to Article 6(1), d). Generally, where consent is possible in the context of medical emergencies, it will be preferable.[736]

C. Protection of Vital Interests and Data Subject Rights

638. In relation to the processing of information by the controller on the legal ground of protecting the vital interests of the data subject or another natural person, there is neither a right to object, nor a right to data portability. A right to erasure in principle[737] applies when the data is no longer necessary, where unlawfully processed or must actually be erased pursuant to the legal obligation (e.g., after a certain time has lapsed).

639. Articles 13/14 (right to information), 15 (right to access), 16 (right to rectification) and 18 (right to restriction of processing) also apply. Moreover, data subjects have the right not to be subjected to automated individual decision-making, including profiling, under Article 22 GDPR, unless one of the exceptions of Article 22(2) GDPR applies. See §8below for more details on data subject rights.

V. Performance of a Public Interest Task or Exercise of Official Authority (Article 6(1), e) GDPR)

640. Article 6(1), e) GDPR allows the processing of data which is 'necessary for the performance of a task carried out in the public interest or in the exercise of official authority vested in the controller'. Necessity, as clarified in section II.A above, has an independent meaning under EU law,[738] and must be interpreted strictly and in the light of the objectives of data protection law, notably including the principle

735. Recital 46 GDPR.
736. Art. 29 Working Party, Opinion 06/2014 on the notion of legitimate interest of the data controller under Article 7 of Directive 95/46/EC, p. 20.
737. This is because Art. 17 also contains some exceptions, which are discussed in §8, s. V below.
738. CJEU, C-524/06, Judgment of 16 December 2008, *Heinz Huber v. Bundesrepublik Deutschland*, ECLI:EU:C:2008:724, para. 52, https://curia.europa.eu/juris/liste.jsf?language=en&jur=C,T,F&num=c-524/06.

of fairness (i.e., based on the reasonable expectation of the data subject). However, the specific circumstances and the context of the legal ground at hand must also be duly taken into account. In the context of Article 6(1), e) GDPR, the CJEU's *Huber* case,[739] specifically indicates that processing may be considered necessary where it makes the performance of the public task more effective. Despite that, proportionality concerns still have to be applied strictly, i.e., if there is a less intrusive alternative available to reach the goal (as effectively), this alternative should be chosen.

A. General

641. Article 6(1), e) GDPR covers two situations:

(1) processing necessary for the performance of a task carried out in the public interest; and
(2) processing necessary for the performance of a task in the exercise of official authority vested in the controller.

642. The task, whether carried out in the public interest or in the exercise of official authority, must be based in Member State law or European Union law, which must determine the purpose(s) of the intended processing and must meet an objective of public interest and be proportionate to the legitimate aim pursued.[740]

643. Just like in the case of Article 6(1), c) GDPR discussed above, the GDPR does not require a specific law for each individual processing operation. A single law can serve as the basis for several processing operations which are needed for the purposes of carrying out the tasks at hand.[741] The application of Article 6(1) e) does also not require the law to be an act of parliament per se.[742] By analogy to the situation under Article 6(1),c) GDPR, it is permissible that legislation in some cases only sets out the general obligation, with secondary legislation or binding decisions and guidance of competent authorities setting out further obligations and implementation rules. As the Article 29 Working party notes, the scope of Article 6(1), e) may be very broad, 'which pleads for a strict interpretation and a clear identification, on a case-by-case basis, of the public interest at stake and[/or] the official authority justifying the processing'.[743]

---

739. CJEU, C-524/06, Judgment of 16 December 2008, *Heinz Huber v. Bundesrepublik Deutschland*, ECLI:EU:C:2008:724, paras 58–62, https://curia.europa.eu/juris/liste.jsf?language=en&jur=C,T,F&num=c-524/06.
740. Art. 6(3) GDPR. This of course entails it must duly respect the concerned persons' privacy and data protection rights, as laid down in Arts 7 and 8 of the Charter of fundamental rights of the European Union (OJ C 326, 26.10.2012, p. 391–407) and Art. 8 of the European Convention on Human Rights.
741. Recital 41 GDPR.
742. Recital 41 GDPR.
743. Art. 29 Working Party, Opinion 06/2014 on the notion of legitimate interest of the data controller under Article 7 of Directive 95/46/EC, p. 22.

644. Like in the case of Article 6(1),c) GDPR above, Member States may define a number of specific provisions (Article 6(3) GDPR) and may maintain or introduce more specific provisions in certain sectors or certain situations (Article 6(2) GDPR). Here as well, the law providing the legal basis for the task of public interest or the official authority, may in addition determine:

- the general conditions governing the lawfulness of the processing by the controller in the context of carrying out that task;
- the type of data which are to be processed;
- the data subjects that are concerned by the task;[744]
- the entities to which the data may be disclosed for the purpose of the tasks;
- the purposes for which the data may be disclosed;
- details on purpose limitation;
- appropriate storage periods;
- specific indications of processing operations and processing procedures to be used/followed, including measures to be taken to ensure lawful and fair processing in the context of the performance of the task.

645. Article 6(1), e) applies to both the public and private sector in principle, as long as the task is being carried out in the public interest or through official authority vested in the controller.[745] Recital 45 specifies: 'It should also be for Union or Member State law to determine whether the controller performing a task carried out in the public interest or in the exercise of official authority should be a public authority or another natural or legal person governed by public law, or, where it is in the public interest to do so, including for health purposes such as public health and social protection and the management of healthcare services, by private law, such as a professional association.' Hence, as long as it is in the public interest to do so, private partners may be given tasks of public interest or may be vested with official authority, in which case they will be able to rely on Article 6(1), e) GDPR for the processing that is necessary to perform those tasks. That being said, it should be pointed out that Article 6(1), e) will only apply to private entities in limited circumstances (e.g., a transportation company providing universal services, a company part of a public-private partnership which has been given specific tasks in the public interest, etc.). It is however, applicable to every public administration in the exercise of their powers.

646. Moreover, Article 6(1), e) GDPR will in fact be the default legal ground for public authorities, because consent will often not be able to be given freely by the citizens involved, and the GDPR excludes legitimate interest as a legal ground for any processing carried out by public authorities in the performance of their

744. This may in principle also include children and vulnerable groups of people.
745. Art. 29 Working Party, Opinion 06/2014 on the notion of legitimate interest of the data controller under Article 7 of Directive 95/46/EC, p. 21.

tasks.[746] Thus, as the Article 29 Working Party recognizes, 'Article 7(e) has similarities with Article 7(f), and in some contexts, especially for public authorities, Article 7(e) may replace Article 7(f).'[747]

647. This shows that Article 6(1), e) GDPR tends to be a broader ground than Article 6(1), c) GDPR, which leaves more leeway to the controller, especially when this is a public administration, to determine what processing activities are necessary to fulfil a certain mission in the public interest or in the exercise of official authority, although the GDPR foresees the same possibilities as under Article 6(1), c) GDPR for Member State law and EU law to regulate the processing in great detail.[748]

648. This is in fact a logical situation, as it is impossible to determine upfront what processing activities a public administration will need to perform its broader societal missions. Take a local public administration of a city as an example. Rather than defining every processing operation, the Member State's law will define broader 'goals' of the city, e.g., local law enforcement, road management, primary education, permits, city planning, traffic, housing, social tasks, cultural tasks, etc. There may be some implementing law and guidance, but in order to function the public administration will have to be given a significant amount of leeway, which clearly distinguished this from the legal obligation ground of Article 6(1), c) GDPR, where the lack of leeway/discretion is a defining factor.

649. However, and especially in cases where private entities are given tasks of public interest or official authority is being vested in them, there are good reasons for the legislator to be (much) more precise in defining the processing activities.

650. Under the Data Protection Directive,[749] this legal ground could also be relied upon by a controller who wished to disclose data to a third-party controller, in whom official authority had been vested. This language is no longer retained in the GDPR. Consequently, such a transfer would only be possible if there is a legal obligation to do so or the controller sending the information can rely on another legal ground to do so (e.g., because it is necessary for the performance of its own public task).

B. Relation to Other Legal Grounds

651. Whenever available, Article 6(1), e) will tend to be the preferred legal ground. There are several reasons for that:

---

746. Art. 6(1), *in fine* GDPR.
747. Art. 29 Working Party, Opinion 06/2014 on the notion of legitimate interest of the data controller under Article 7 of Directive 95/46/EC, p. 22.
748. *See* Art. 6(2) and (3) GDPR.
749. Directive 95/46/EC of the European Parliament and of the Council of 24 October 1995 on the protection of individuals with regard to the processing of personal data and on the free movement of such data, OJ L 281, 23.11.1995, pp. 31–50.

- contrary to consent, it cannot be withdrawn;
- it tends to be less restrictive than Article 6(1), c);
- it does not require a balancing exercise, like Article 6(1), f) (see further);
- it is broader in application than Article 6(1), b).

Moreover, in most situations where Article 6(1) applies, e.g., a city administration providing public services:

- consent will not be valid. For example, to receive a public service, certain data will have to be provided. If the citizen refuses, it will not receive the service. In such a situation free consent is impossible; and
- there will be no strict legal obligation defining the processing at hand; and
- Article 6(1), f) will be unavailable, as public administrations are precluded from using Article 6(1), f) for processing carried out in the performance of their tasks; and
- Article 6(1), b) will be inapplicable, inappropriate or too limited. This is because, even for those interactions with the citizen that could be considered as a contract, typically the public administration will want to carry out more processing activities to satisfy its mission than is strictly speaking necessary to carry out the contract (and only the contract at hand).

  Even if the controller is a private entity, Article 6(1), e) GDPR is the logical choice for carrying out the task in the public interest or in the exercise of official authority, which has been assigned to that controller.

C. *Performance of a Task in the Public Interest or in the Exercise of Official Authority and Data Subject Rights*

652. In relation to the processing of information by the controller in the performance of task in the public interests or in the exercise of official authority, there is a right to object. This right helps balance the fact that Article 6(1), e) GDPR can indeed by quite broad as a legal ground.

653. There is however no right to data portability. A right to erasure in principle[750] applies when the data is no longer necessary, when the data subject has successfully objected to the processing and there are no overriding legitimate grounds to maintain the processing, when the data were unlawfully processed to begin with, or when the data must be erased pursuant to a legal obligation (e.g., after a certain time has lapsed).

654. Articles 13/14 (right to information), 15 (right to access), 16 (right to rectification) and 18 (right to restriction of processing) also apply. Moreover, data subjects have the right not to be subjected to automated individual decision-making, including profiling, under Article 22 GDPR, unless one of the exceptions of Article 22(2) GDPR applies. See §8 below for more details on data subject rights.

750. This is because Art. 17 also contains some exceptions, which are discussed in §8, s. V below.

VI. Legitimate Interests (Article 6(1), f) GDPR)

655. Article 6(1), f) GDPR contains the last legal ground justifying the processing of personal data under the GDPR, namely when 'processing is **necessary** for the purposes of the **legitimate interests** pursued by the **controller or by a third party**, except where such interests are overridden by the interests or fundamental rights and freedoms of the data subject which require protection of personal data, in particular where the data subject is a child'.

656. Here as well, necessity, has an independent meaning under EU law,[751] and must be interpreted strictly and in the light of the objectives of data protection law, notably including the principle of fairness (i.e., based on the reasonable expectation of the data subject). Hence, processing must in any case be limited to what is necessary to attain the legitimate purposes identified by the controller.

657. Article 6(1), f) GDPR thus allows processing necessary for the purposes set out by the controller that are in its legitimate interests or, importantly, are in the legitimate interest of a third party. The existence of a legitimate interest must be carefully assessed in every specific case and must be proven by the controller. The GDPR names only a few examples of legitimate interests that may justify processing of personal data, including processing of personal data for direct marketing and fraud prevention purposes,[752] but provides no comprehensive enumeration of situations in which the legal ground could apply. Hence, in principle legitimate interest is a very broad legal ground. Section A below elaborates on what can constitute a legitimate interest pursued by the controller or a third party.

658. For this reason, the second part of Article 6(1), f) GDPR introduces a limitation on the broad scope of this legal ground, by excluding the situations where the interests or the fundamental rights of the data subject override the legitimate interests of the controller or the third party, which the controller is pursuing through the proposed processing. This is commonly referred to as the balancing test. It is up to the controller to carry out this test and to maintain evidence of this, as well as the outcomes to justify the processing under the accountability principle discussed in §5, section VII above. Moreover, the controller has to do this not only at the moment of the initial decision, but maintain this (and perhaps update this) as long as it relies on the legitimate interest to justify the processing.[753] In its *ASNEF and FECEMD* judgment, the Court of Justice clarified that national law of the Member States is

---

751. CJEU, C-524/06, Judgment of 16 December 2008, *Heinz Huber v. Bundesrepublik Deutschland*, ECLI:EU:C:2008:724, para. 52, https://curia.europa.eu/juris/liste.jsf?language=en&jur=C,T,F&num=c-524/06.
752. Recital 47 GDPR. The GDPR also provides some more specific examples in Recitals 48, 49 and 113.
753. Irene Kamara and Paul de Hert, 'Understanding the Balancing Act behind the Legitimate Interest of the Controller Ground: A Pragmatic Approach', in Evan Selinger, Jules Polonetsky, and Omer Tene, *Cambridge Handbook of Consumer Privacy*, 2018, 321–352, s. 5.1.

not allowed to add conditions to the use of Article 6(1), f) GDPR.[754] The balancing test is discussed in more detail in section B below.

659. Moreover, as Article 6(1), f) specifies, this balancing test must be applied even more strictly when the data subject is a child. By analogy, this would also be true if the data subject is not a child, but belongs to a vulnerable category. See section C below for more details.

A. Legitimate Interests Pursued by the Controller or a Third Party

660. In order to rely on Article 6(1), f) GDPR, the controller of the processing needs to be able to rely on a legitimate interest pursued by itself or a third party, for which the intended processing is necessary. This interest will then need to be balanced against the interests and rights of the data subject, in order for the controller to go ahead with the processing. Identifying a legitimate interest is, however, the first step and if the controller is not able to do so, it can *a priori* not rely on Article 6(1), f) GDPR as a legal ground.

661. In order to determine what is covered by a legitimate interest, it must first be identified what is understood under the GDPR as an 'interest'. The Article 29 Working Party has clarified that an interest is to be understood broadly, as the stake the controller may have in the processing or the benefit that it (or society) may derive from the processing at hand.[755] Companies, for example may have an interest in ensuring security of the premises, and health and safety of the staff, for which it could for example introduce a number of processing activities with specific purposes that help realise those interests, such as access control procedures, identity verification, camera surveillance, etc.[756] An interest must however be sufficiently clearly articulated and must be real and present, not purely hypothetical, vague or speculative.[757] Some interests may benefit society at large, as well as the controller or the third party involved. The only relevance of this is that it may have an influence during the balancing test, as is explained further.

662. Second, in order to define the scope of the concept of 'legitimate interest', it must be defined what makes an interest 'legitimate' or 'illegitimate'. The use of the word legitimate, as opposed to 'legal interests' or 'legally protected interests'

754. CJEU, Joined cases C-468/10 and C-469/10, Judgment of 24 November 2011, *Asociación Nacional de Establecimientos Financieros de Crédito (ASNEF) and Federación de Comercio Electrónico y Marketing Directo (FECEMD) v. Administración del Estado*, ECLI:EU:C:2011:777, para. 32, https://curia.europa.eu/juris/liste.jsf?num=C-468/10&language=en.

755. Art. 29 Working Party, Opinion 06/2014 on the notion of legitimate interest of the data controller under Article 7 of Directive 95/46/EC, p. 24.

756. Recital 47 GDPR also mentions this: 'Such legitimate interest could exist for example where there is a relevant and appropriate relationship between the data subject and the controller in situations such as where the data subject is a client or in the service of the controller.'

757. Art. 29 Working Party, Opinion 06/2014 on the notion of legitimate interest of the data controller under Article 7 of Directive 95/46/EC, p. 24.

seems to indicate that the concept of legitimacy should be interpreted broadly here.[758] This has been confirmed by the Article 29 Working Party, which has clarified that, in principle, all interests that are acceptable under the law are legitimate interests, whether trivial or compelling, straightforward and universally accepted or controversial. Whether or not the processing will be allowed will be determined during the balancing test, and it is there that a controller who is looking to justify a controversial processing will have to demonstrate that the processing is acceptable. Acceptable under the law simply refers to the fact that the interest must not be in breach of applicable (mandatory) law.[759]

663. Hence, to be considered as a relevant 'legitimate interest' under Article 6(1), f) GDPR, the interest must:

- be lawful; and
- be sufficiently clearly articulated to allow for the balancing test to be carried out; and
- represent a real and present interest.

664. Last, the interest must be either pursued by the controller or a third party. Hence, it is permissible for the controller to invoke a lawful, clearly articulated, real and present legitimate interest of a third party to justify its processing. However, Article 6(1), f) GDPR does not contain an obligation for the controller to process data in the interest of a third party, merely the possibility to do so.[760]

665. The text of the Data Protection Directive[761] seemed to limit this scenario to the disclosure of data to a third party or parties, who had a legitimate interest in processing that data.[762] Examples of such scenarios included:

- The disclosure of data in the public interest or a third party's interest, e.g., where the controller goes beyond its legal obligations to assist law enforcement or private stakeholders in order to combat illegal activities.
- The sharing of data for historic, or scientific research, e.g., by allowing access to the controller's existing databases, subject to appropriate safeguards.
- The publishing of data for transparency and accountability purposes, e.g., salaries of top management, which is done primarily for the interests of the third parties (general public, stakeholders, journalists, employees).

758. Irene Kamara and Paul de Hert, 'Understanding the Balancing Act behind the Legitimate Interest of the Controller Ground: A Pragmatic Approach', in Evan Selinger, Jules Polonetsky, and Omer Tene, *Cambridge Handbook of Consumer Privacy*, 2018, 321–352, s. 4.3.1.
759. Art. 29 Working Party, Opinion 06/2014 on the notion of legitimate interest of the data controller under Article 7 of Directive 95/46/EC, p. 24.
760. CJEU, Case C-13/16, Judgment of 4 May 2017, *Rīgas satiksme*, ECLI:EU:C:2017:336, para. 26, https://curia.europa.eu/juris/liste.jsf?num=C-13/16.
761. Directive 95/46/EC of the European Parliament and of the Council of 24 October 1995 on the protection of individuals with regard to the processing of personal data and on the free movement of such data, OJ L 281, 23.11.1995, pp. 31–50.
762. *See* Art. 7, f) of the Data Protection Directive.

The GDPR no longer makes that distinction. This means that a controller can also rely on the legitimate interests of a third party to justify a processing activity, even if the data is not necessarily disclosed to that third party. For example, a company may process certain personal data on is customers in order to guarantee the security of its systems, as well as those of its suppliers and related third parties. This activity can in principle be justified on Article 6(1), f) GDPR, even if the controller does not intend to disclose this data to the third party, save where legally or contractually obliged.

666. Of course, as already mentioned above, identifying a legitimate interest is just the starting point for the controller. In addition to having a legitimate interest to rely on, Article 6(1), f) GDPR also requires that this interest is not overridden by the interest and rights of the data subject, i.e., the controller must balance its own interests against the impact that the processing may have on the data subjects concerned. The following section explains the balancing test that the controller must carry out.

B. Balancing Test

667. The second part of the reasoning under Article 6(1), f), is that the legitimate interest identified by the controller, must be balanced against the rights and interests of the data subjects. On one side of the figurative scales are the interests of the controller, which may vary from insignificant to very compelling. In that context it is not only important what the legitimate interest of the controller is (and whether it is compelling or not), but also which purposes the controller has defined and what processing operations are proposed to be carried out in order to pursue the identified legitimate interest.

668. An example can illustrate: while it is generally accepted that companies as a controller have a compelling legitimate interest in learning about their customers' preferences in order to perform optimised (direct) marketing,[763] this does not automatically give the controller the permission to carry out any and every processing operation that may support that goal, such as the intensive online or offline monitoring of its customers or the combination of vast amounts of data from different sources (including purchased data), without the knowledge or consent of the customers. Such activities would likely be a significant intrusion and would not survive the balancing exercise. Moreover, they may not even be necessary to reach the purpose of the processing, and already fail the necessity test mentioned above. Hence, even if the legitimate interest in general is compelling, the controller must be reasonable in its implementation of this interest and limit the data collection and (further) processing to what is necessary. In general, the more extensive the proposed processing, the more challenging it will be to justify it and to balance it against the data subject's rights and interests.

763. Recital 47 GDPR even specifically mentions it.

669. On the other side of scales, the controller must take into account the potential impact on the data subject if the processing is indeed carried out as intended.[764] The controller must take into account not only the data subject's fundamental rights and freedoms (including to privacy and data protection), but also more broadly the data subject's interests. Note that the GDPR does not introduce legitimate as a requirement here, which indicates that even individuals engaged in illegal activities should not be subjected to a disproportionate interference with their rights and interests.[765] In order to carry out the balancing test, the controller must take into account the potential impact on the data subject, which may vary from trivial to very serious.[766]

670. In general, the Article 29 Working Party states the following on balancing both the sides:

> Legitimate interests of the controller, when minor and not very compelling may, in general, only override the interests and rights of data subjects in cases where the impact on these rights and interests are even more trivial. On the other hand, important and compelling legitimate interests may in some cases and subject to safeguards and measures justify even significant intrusion into privacy or other significant impact on the interests or rights of the data subjects.[767]

Hence, in principle there is no preference for either side and all will depend on the specifics of the case at hand. As the Article 29 Working Party also notes, implementing sufficient safeguards (e.g., encryption, pseudonymisation, a voluntary opt-out, various technical and organisational measures) may help tip the balance in the controller's favour and must be taken into account when determining the potential impact on data subjects.

671. Consequently, the following steps are necessary to determine whether Article 6(1), f) GDPR is applicable as a legal ground:

- assessing the controller's legitimate interest; and
- assessing the impact on data subjects; and
- determining the result of the provisional balance, i.e., without safeguards; and
- adding additional safeguards to come to the result of the final balance, i.e., with safeguards).

These steps are discussed in detail in what follows.

---

764. Art. 29 Working Party, Opinion 06/2014 on the notion of legitimate interest of the data controller under Article 7 of Directive 95/46/EC, pp. 37–38.
765. Art. 29 Working Party, Opinion 06/2014 on the notion of legitimate interest of the data controller under Article 7 of Directive 95/46/EC, p. 30.
766. Art. 29 Working Party, Opinion 06/2014 on the notion of legitimate interest of the data controller under Article 7 of Directive 95/46/EC, pp. 37–38.
767. Art. 29 Working Party, Opinion 06/2014 on the notion of legitimate interest of the data controller under Article 7 of Directive 95/46/EC, p. 30.

It should be noted that this kind of assessment is also required to comply with the principle of data protection by design and default (Article 25 GDPR) and, in some cases, a data protection impact assessment may be required (Article 35 GDPR).

1. Assessing the Controller's Legitimate Interest

672. The first side of the balance is the controller's legitimate interest, which can range from trivial to compelling, and which can be straightforward or more controversial. The following subsections summarise existing guidance on what the controller must take into account when assessing its own side of the balance.

673. In any case, the controller must not only identify its legitimate interest precisely, but must also identify what processing operations are necessary to pursue this interest, and must, in doing so, respect the principles relating to data protection, as discussed in §5 above, such as lawfulness, fairness, transparency, purpose limitation, data minimisation, etc.

a. Exercise of a Fundamental Right

674. The Article 29 Working Party recognizes that several fundamental rights and freedoms, exercised by the controller may come into conflict with the data subject's right to privacy and data protection.[768] A journalist publishing incriminating details on a high-ranking politician, for example, would be exercising the right of freedom of expression and informing the general public, which would speak for such a processing to be allowed, despite the significant effects it would have on the data subject at issue, i.e., the politician.[769]

675. However, the fact that the controller is exercising a fundamental right of its own, does not provide it with a blanket permission. In order for the processing to be covered under Article 6(1), f) GDPR, the processing must be limited to what is necessary and proportionate to exercise the fundamental right in question. To help guide that assessment, the controller should take into account any specific legislation, case law or jurisprudence or authoritative guidelines. In addition, (professional) codes of conduct and other more informal guidance may play a role as well.[770] Additional safeguards may also be necessary, depending on the circumstances.[771]

---

768. Art. 29 Working Party, Opinion 06/2014 on the notion of legitimate interest of the data controller under Article 7 of Directive 95/46/EC, p. 34.
769. Art. 29 Working Party, Opinion 06/2014 on the notion of legitimate interest of the data controller under Article 7 of Directive 95/46/EC, p. 34.
770. Art. 29 Working Party, Opinion 06/2014 on the notion of legitimate interest of the data controller under Article 7 of Directive 95/46/EC, pp. 34–35.
771. Art. 29 Working Party, Opinion 06/2014 on the notion of legitimate interest of the data controller under Article 7 of Directive 95/46/EC, p. 35.

b. Public Interest/Interests of the Wider Community

676. As mentioned above, a controller may sometimes want to invoke the fact that the legitimate interest it (or a third party) is pursuing is in fact beneficial to the public interest or the interests of the wider community/society. Examples include processing activities by charitable organisations or non-profit organisations for the fulfilment of their goals, but also the case where the private business interests of a company overlap with public interest (to some degree). An example is the interest of a private company in combating fraudulent use of its services, which coincides with the public's interest to have fraudulent activities detected, exposed and discouraged.[772]

677. The fact that the controller does not only act in its own interests, but also in the interests of the wider community, can add 'weight' to the controller's part of the scales, helping it to justify the intended processing activity. The more compelling the public interest, and the more acknowledged and expected this is in the wider community, the more weight it will have.[773] This should, however, not be read as a permission for private enforcement of the law or other intrusive practices.[774]

c. Other Legitimate Interests

678. This is the standard scenario, in which the controller is neither specifically exercising a fundamental right, nor acting in the public interest, but for purely private legitimate interests. This may be the case for example, where processing is useful but cannot be grounded on Article 6(1), b), c), or e) GDPR, because it was not strictly necessary in that context. In such cases, the processing may still be permittable under legitimate interests. For example, a company making a 'who is who' with pictures of all its employees may in certain cases not be able to justify this under Article 6(1), b) GDPR as strictly necessary for the execution of the employment contract, but this may be permissible under Article 6(1), f) GDPR if the company can rely on legitimate interests to do this (better communication, security, faster response times, etc.)[775]

679. Here as well, the more compelling the legitimate interest of the controller, and the more acknowledged and expected it is in the wider community that the controller may perform such processing, the more weight this interest will have.[776]

772. Art. 29 Working Party, Opinion 06/2014 on the notion of legitimate interest of the data controller under Article 7 of Directive 95/46/EC, p. 35.
773. Art. 29 Working Party, Opinion 06/2014 on the notion of legitimate interest of the data controller under Article 7 of Directive 95/46/EC, p. 35.
774. Art. 29 Working Party, Opinion 06/2014 on the notion of legitimate interest of the data controller under Article 7 of Directive 95/46/EC, p. 35.
775. Art. 29 Working Party, Opinion 06/2014 on the notion of legitimate interest of the data controller under Article 7 of Directive 95/46/EC, pp. 35–36.
776. Art. 29 Working Party, Opinion 06/2014 on the notion of legitimate interest of the data controller under Article 7 of Directive 95/46/EC, p. 36.

d. Legal and Cultural/Societal Recognition of the Legitimacy of the Interests

680. As already indicated above, legal and cultural or societal recognition of the legitimacy of the interests pursued by the controller will help to add weight to that interest. The more acknowledged and expected such processing is, the more easily the balance will tip in favour of the controller. Legal recognition can exist when the pursuit of the public or private interest pursued by the controller is specifically allowed or encouraged by law, even when this is not obligatory. This also includes any authoritative guidance, even if non-binding.[777] Societal recognition has an even broader scope and will include general cultural and societal expectations, even in a given community only and without any legal basis.[778]

681. However, as always, it is not because processing in a certain interest is acknowledged and expected, that the controller has complete freedom in organising this. Best practices will need to be followed, and all GDPR principles, including data minimisation, purpose limitation and storage limitation will have to be adhered to.

2. The Impact on Data Subjects

682. Having assessed the controller's own side of the balance, the controller will need to define the impact of the processing on interests and fundamental rights and freedoms of the data subject.

a. Assessment of the Impact

683. First, generally, in assessing the impact on the data subject, both positive and negative consequences must be taken into account. Such consequences include a broad scope of effects. Negative consequences, for example, are not limited to damage or harm that may come to the data subject (e.g., discrimination, defamation, reputation damage, damage to negotiation power or autonomy, damage to health or property), but encompasses also broader emotional impact, such as irritation, anger, fear or distress which may be the result of a processing activity by the controller that the data subject did not want, expect or realise was going to happen.[779]

684. In assessing the impact, the controller does not only have to take into account its own intended future actions, but also future decisions and actions by

777. Art. 29 Working Party, Opinion 06/2014 on the notion of legitimate interest of the data controller under Article 7 of Directive 95/46/EC, p. 36.
778. Art. 29 Working Party, Opinion 06/2014 on the notion of legitimate interest of the data controller under Article 7 of Directive 95/46/EC, p. 36.
779. Art. 29 Working Party, Opinion 06/2014 on the notion of legitimate interest of the data controller under Article 7 of Directive 95/46/EC, p. 37.

third parties, whether positive or negative. The controller must take due care in considering the cumulative effect of all the potential future impact of the processing, from all identified risk sources.[780]

685. In addition determining the **severity** of the potential consequences, which may range from low or trivial (e.g., occasional annoyance of the data subject) to very serious (loss of life, bodily harm, substantial damage to property), the controller also needs to determine the **likelihood** that the risk will materialize. Taken together, the severity of the risk and the likelihood of it materialising will determine the impact on the data subject.[781]

686. While the impact assessment draws on general principles of risk assessment, it is important to note that in this specific context, the assessment of risk cannot be a purely quantitative exercise. Even if there are only a small number of data subjects involved or the processing only has an impact on a minority of the data subjects concerned, the controller will still need to carefully consider whether the processing is permissible. If even a single individual is likely to be significantly and disproportionately impacted in a negative manner, the controller may need to consider the need for additional safeguards or may need to abandon the processing.[782]

b. Nature of the Data

687. When considering the impact on the data subject, the type of data used will be relevant. Generally, the more sensitive the data is, the larger the potential impact on data subjects will tend to be. The use of biometric data, health data, genetic information and other special categories under Article 9 GDPR (see §7, section I below) will definitely require a more restrictive approach, but also other categories of data can be sensitive, such as communication data, location data or financial data.[783] The GDPR does not forbid the use of this data in the context of the controller pursuing its legitimate interests, but the controller's interest will need additional 'weight' to justify this. Using a fingerprint or an iris scan to limit access to a high-security area such as a laboratory carrying out dangerous research, will for example be a permittable use of such sensitive data, whereas the use of biometrics in a more trivial situation of access control (e.g., for the staff of the local retailer to access their break room), will be unlikely to pass the balance test.[784]

---

780. Art. 29 Working Party, Opinion 06/2014 on the notion of legitimate interest of the data controller under Article 7 of Directive 95/46/EC, p. 37.
781. Art. 29 Working Party, Opinion 06/2014 on the notion of legitimate interest of the data controller under Article 7 of Directive 95/46/EC, p. 38.
782. Art. 29 Working Party, Opinion 06/2014 on the notion of legitimate interest of the data controller under Article 7 of Directive 95/46/EC, p. 38.
783. Art. 29 Working Party, Opinion 06/2014 on the notion of legitimate interest of the data controller under Article 7 of Directive 95/46/EC, p. 38.
784. Art. 29 Working Party, Opinion 06/2014 on the notion of legitimate interest of the data controller under Article 7 of Directive 95/46/EC, pp. 38–39.

688. Even data that is not sensitive in itself and may seem innocuous at first sight, can in given situations or when processed in larger quantities, have a potentially significant impact on the data subject. In such cases the controller will also need to carefully consider whether its interests justify such processing and whether additional safeguards need to be taken.[785] In this context it may be relevant to know whether the data are publicly known. While there is no blanket permission to use this data simply because it has been made public, this is a relevant factor in determining the potential impact of the processing on the data subject. The processing of publicly known data will tend to have a smaller impact, although in certain situation and depending on how and in what context this data is processed, it might still have a significant impact on the data subject nonetheless.[786]

c. The Way Data Are Being Processed

689. In addition to the type of data being processed, the manner in which this is happening is also relevant to determine the impact on the data subject. Relevant factors include:[787]

- whether the controller will disclose the data to a large number of persons or make it publicly available;
- whether there are large amounts of data being processed;
- whether the data is being combined with other data sets already available to the controller.

690. For the first factor, the main risk is that the impact is potential impact is multiplied by the disclosure to a large number of people or the general public. For the last two factors, the risk lies in the fact that this kind of processing may lead to advanced, unexpected findings, which are more sensitive than the original innocuous data, or may lead to inaccurate findings or predictions concerning the data subject, which may be highly intrusive to the individual's privacy and private life. To illustrate: certain common security solutions used in medium and large companies enable large-scale deep packet inspection. While the controller has a legitimate interest of ensuring security, it must duly take into account the intrusion this represents in the privacy of its employees.[788]

691. In addition to the above-mentioned factors, many other aspects of the manner in which data is being processed may be relevant to determine the impact on data subjects. In general however, the more **negative or uncertain** the potential

785. Art. 29 Working Party, Opinion 06/2014 on the notion of legitimate interest of the data controller under Article 7 of Directive 95/46/EC, p. 39.
786. Art. 29 Working Party, Opinion 06/2014 on the notion of legitimate interest of the data controller under Article 7 of Directive 95/46/EC, p. 39.
787. Art. 29 Working Party, Opinion 06/2014 on the notion of legitimate interest of the data controller under Article 7 of Directive 95/46/EC, p. 39.
788. Art. 29 Working Party, Opinion 06/2014 on the notion of legitimate interest of the data controller under Article 7 of Directive 95/46/EC, pp. 39–40.

impact of the processing is, the more unlikely that the processing will pass the balancing test.[789] Especially relevant is whether there are alternative methods available, which are less intrusive, uncertain or have less negative impact on the data subject. As will be discussed further, additional safeguards may help tip this balance in favour of the controller.

d. Reasonable Expectations of the Data Subject

692. A factor mentioned specifically by the GDPR in Recital 47 is the reasonable expectations of the data subject, taking into account the relationship between the data subject and the controller (e.g., data subject is a client or an employee of the controller) and what the data subject could reasonably expect at the time and in the context of the collection of the personal data.[790] In order to determine the reasonable expectations, the controller must take account of the whole factual context.[791]

693. Recital 47 mentions a lack of reasonable expectations as a prime example of a situation in which the interests and rights of the data subject would override the legitimate interest of the controller. This is especially relevant to further processing. As discussed in §5, section II on purpose limitation above, the more specific and restrictive the context of collection, the more limitations there will be on any further use. The same applies here.

694. The CJEU has, for example, ruled that hat Article 6(1)(c) and Article 7(f) of Directive 95/46, read in the light of Articles 7 and 8 of the Charter, must be interpreted as not precluding national provisions which authorise the installation of a video surveillance system, such as the system at issue in the main proceedings, installed in the common parts of a residential building, for the purposes of pursuing legitimate interests of ensuring the safety and protection of individuals and property, without the consent of the data subjects, if the processing of personal data carried out by means of the video surveillance system at issue fulfils the conditions laid down in Article 7(f).[792]

e. Status/Relationship of the Controller and the Data Subject

695. The last factor that is important in determining the impact on the data subject, is the relationship between the controller and the data subject, and/or the status of the data subject. The reasoning is that, where the controller is in a position of

---

789. Art. 29 Working Party, Opinion 06/2014 on the notion of legitimate interest of the data controller under Article 7 of Directive 95/46/EC, p. 40.
790. Art. 29 Working Party, Opinion 06/2014 on the notion of legitimate interest of the data controller under Article 7 of Directive 95/46/EC, p. 40.
791. Art. 29 Working Party, Opinion 06/2014 on the notion of legitimate interest of the data controller under Article 7 of Directive 95/46/EC, p. 40.
792. CJEU, Case C-708/18, Judgment of 11 December 2019, Asociatia de Proprietari bloc M5A-ScaraA, ECLI:EU:C:2019:1064, https://eur-lex.europa.eu/legal-content/GA/TXT/?uri=CELEX:62018CJ0708.

power, there should be due care to not abuse this power to impose processing activities on the data subject. Such a position of power may exist because the controller is a multinational company or a dominant market player, or because the data subject is inherently in a position of weakness. This may be the case when the data subject is a child or otherwise belongs to a vulnerable group of society, which demands special protection. Examples including, the mentally ill, asylum seekers, the elderly, handicapped people, etc. Moreover, even average data subjects may be in a weak position depending on the specific context: an employee, student or patient would for example be in a weak position when the controller is their employer, university or doctor.[793]

696. The controller must take into account any weaknesses in the status of the data subject or any power imbalance in the relationship and must give this sufficient weight in the balancing exercise. This does not mean that the processing is forbidden, or that there may not be any negative impact on the data subject. However, the controller must make sure that the legitimate interests it is pursuing justifies such an intrusion, that there were no less intrusive means available to reach the same goal and, where applicable, that all necessary safeguards have been implemented.[794]

3. Provisional Balance

697. Once the controller has clearly identified its own legitimate interest and the processing actions necessary to pursue this interest, as well as the potential impact on the data subjects to the best of its abilities, it must make a provisional balance of its interest vs. the potential impact of the processing on the interests, rights and freedoms of the data subject. In certain cases, this balance may be clear, e.g., where the controller has a very compelling interest and there is only a negligible potential impact on the data subjects. In other cases, the balance may be more difficult to find, or may indicate that the interests and rights of the data subject override the controller's legitimate interest. The provisional balance is only a first indication and not a final determination. This is because, in theory, the provisional balance does not yet take into account any safeguards the controller might implement. After this is done, the final balance and decision can be made.

698. The controller should never stop at the level of the provisional balance, unless it is abandoning the idea of pursuing its legitimate interest. This means that, even if the balance is clearly in favour of the controller, the controller must still consider whether additional safeguards may be appropriate to further reduce the risk of

793. Art. 29 Working Party, Opinion 06/2014 on the notion of legitimate interest of the data controller under Article 7 of Directive 95/46/EC, pp. 40–41.
794. Art. 29 Working Party, Opinion 06/2014 on the notion of legitimate interest of the data controller under Article 7 of Directive 95/46/EC, pp. 40–41.

negative impact on the data subject.[795] This obligation follows from several controller obligations under the GDPR, such as:

- the principle of fairness;
- the principle of purpose limitation;
- the principle of data minimisation;
- the principle of storage limitation;
- the principle of integrity and confidentiality;
- the obligations contained in Article 25 GDPR (data protection by design and default);
- the obligations contained in Article 32 (security measures).

699. If the balance is unclear or even tipped towards the data subjects' rights and interest overriding the legitimate interest of the controller, the controller will have to consider not only the safeguards necessary pursuant to its general obligations such as listed above, but also more significant safeguards, to further reduce the negative impact on the data subject, so it can to tip the scales in its favour.

4. Additional Safeguards Applied by the Controller

700. As explained above, the controller may need to consider additional safeguards in order to a) ensure compliance with its other obligations under the GDPR, and b) in order to tip the scales in its favour. Applying such safeguards may be part of a data protection by design approach of the controller (Article 25 GDPR), or may be part of (the preparation of) a data protection impact assessment (Article 35 GDPR). Examples of safeguards are:[796]

- technical and organisational measures to ensure that data cannot be used to take decisions or other actions with regards to the concerned data subjects ('functional separation');
- anonymisation (e.g., directly after collection of the data);
- pseudonymisation;
- encryption;
- very strict data collection (i.e., collecting the very minimum of data, interpreting the data minimisation principle as strictly as possible);
- immediate deletion of data after use;
- use of privacy-enhancing technologies;
- increased transparency (helps reduce the impact);
- provide a general and unconditional opt-out of the processing (mimicking the right to withdraw consent);

---

795. Art. 29 Working Party, Opinion 06/2014 on the notion of legitimate interest of the data controller under Article 7 of Directive 95/46/EC, p. 41.
796. Art. 29 Working Party, Opinion 06/2014 on the notion of legitimate interest of the data controller under Article 7 of Directive 95/46/EC, p. 42.

– provide data portability or implement other measures to empower data subjects to access, modify, delete, or otherwise further process (or let third parties process) their data.

701. It is up to the controller to determine the appropriate safeguards depending on the context and to make a final determination on the balancing test after all appropriate safeguards have been taken into consideration. It should be noted that measures like encryption or pseudonymisation, while they may reduce the risk of a negative impact on the data subject, do not automatically have the effect of legitimising a processing activity under Article 6(1), f) GDPR. They are merely a relevant factor in the balancing test.[797]

5. Conclusion on the Balancing Test: Accountability and Transparency

702. The foregoing sections have described the various elements of the balancing test. It is clear from this that the determination is a difficult one and that the final decision is up to the controller. To help controllers make this determination, Article 29 Working Party has created a quick guide on how to carry out a balancing test, also providing twenty-six examples to illustrate the process.[798]

703. At first sight it may seem like Article 6(1), f) GDPR is a loophole or may strongly hurt legal certainty. However, the principles of accountability and transparency, and their practical implementation help prevent such effects.

704. The principle of accountability means that the controller must document its reasoning in determining the balance, and will be held accountable by a data protection authority or a Court if it has failed to do so in sufficient detail, or has made (wilful) mistakes in striking the balance, unduly giving its own interests more weight than those of the data subjects. Given that the GDPR has a strong enforcement system with large fines being a possible consequence of such behaviour, as well as liability, the controller cannot simply use Article 6(1), f) GDPR as a loophole or last resort.

705. The principle of accountability is strongly linked to the principle of transparency, and it is transparency that helps address the concern of a lack of legal certainty for the data subject. Under the principle of transparency, read together with the information obligations of Articles 13 and 14 GDPR, the controller must inform the data subject in sufficient detail about the legitimate interests it relies on. It must

797. Art. 29 Working Party, Opinion 06/2014 on the notion of legitimate interest of the data controller under Article 7 of Directive 95/46/EC, p. 42; it should be noted that the same is true for anonymisation measures, unless the controller can prove that there's full anonymisation and the GDPR does no longer apply, which is difficult. *See* Art. 29 Working Party, Opinion 05/2014 on Anonymisation Techniques. Hence, anonymisation is typically used as a safeguard, rather than as a claim to escape the substantive application of the GDPR.

798. *See* Art. 29 Working Party, Opinion 06/2014 on the notion of legitimate interest of the data controller under Article 7 of Directive 95/46/EC, Annex I and II (pp. 55–68).

do so prior to the processing and in a clear and accessible manner. This enables the data subject to form reasonable expectations about the processing that will be linked to it. If the interest is not sufficiently detailed or changes, the controller will have to postpone processing until it has reassessed the balance and communicated its clarified interests to the data subject. It can be recommended that the controller also explains the reasons why it considers the data subject's rights and interests do not override its own interests, so as to invite public scrutiny by stakeholders and data subjects, and that the controller defines the processing operations that will be necessary to pursue the legitimate interest(s) it invokes.

C. Data Subject Is a Child or a Vulnerable Person

706. Article 6(1), f), GDPR mentions that the fact that a data subject is a child must be given particular weight in the balancing exercise. By analogy, this is also applicable to otherwise vulnerable data subjects.

707. In those cases, the controller must duly take into account the data subject's weaknesses and vulnerabilities, which significantly raises the bar for the balancing test to tip in favour of the controller. Hence, the controller will likely need to implement additional safeguards in an attempt to make the processing permissible. Generally, however, the controller will need to be much more restrictive in invoking Article 6(1), f), GDPR when children or vulnerable persons are involved.

708. In any case, the controller will have to devote additional effort to transparency, by adapting the information to the level of a child or the vulnerable category (e.g., by using videos, pictures, etc.). This is a general controller obligation,[799] but may be a factor in the balancing exercise as well.

D. Legitimate Interests for Public Administrations

709. Article 6(1), *in fine* GDPR, specifies that Article 6(1), f) GDPR 'shall not apply to processing carried out by public authorities in the performance of their tasks'. Recital 47 clarifies that this is because it is for the legislator to provide by law for the legal basis for public authorities to process personal data. This is logical to an extent. Indeed, given that Article 6(1), e) GDPR will typically be based on legal provisions stating a broader mission or goal, the public administrations will have a significant measure of leeway in defining how to implement the tasks that are necessary to reach these goals. To that extent they do not need to rely on legitimate interests and do not need to go through a difficult balancing exercise, since the legislator has given them a permission to carry out processing within a given scope, as long as such processing is necessary and proportionate.

799. Under the principle of transparency, and under Arts 13 and 14 GDPR.

710. However, the full exclusion of legitimate interests as a legal ground for public administrations may lead to absurd situations, where a public administration is not able to ensure its own proper management, functioning and security, simply because its public goals laid down by law do not provide for this. Hence, as confirmed by the Article 29 Working Party,[800] one way to overcome this impasse is to interpret the exclusion in Article 6(1), *in fine* GDPR narrowly, as only relating to performance of their tasks covered by Article 6(1), e) GDPR. Hence, if there is a legitimate interest for public administration to do this, depending on whether there is a legal mandate covering this action, Article 6(1) e) GDPR or Article 6(1), f) GDPR would apply.

711. As a result, Article 6(1), f) GDPR seems to have a limited application to public administrations as well. Article 6(1), f) GDPR should however not be used to circumvent legal limits or to expand a legal mandate. It should only be used by a public administration where there is no legal mandate covering the legitimate interests at issue.

E. Relation to Other Legal Grounds

712. As indicated by the Article 29 working Party: Article [6(1), f) GDPR] should neither be seen as a legal ground that can only be used sparingly to fill in gaps for rare and unforeseen situation as 'a last resort' – or as a last chance if no other grounds may apply nor should it be seen as a preferred option and its use unduly extended because it would be considered as less constraining than the other grounds. Rather, it is as valid a means as any of the other grounds for legitimising the processing of personal data.[801]

713. Indeed, Article 6(1), f) GDPR has its own justified field of application, where other grounds are not appropriate or are not sufficient for the intended processing, although it is legitimate. Some examples can illustrate:

- an employer wants to create an internal 'who is who' directory. In this case consent would be difficult to obtain because the data subject is an employee, and it is unlikely that such a processing is necessary for the performance of the contract with all employees. The controller however has a legitimate interest in doing so (security, better organisation, etc.) and may go ahead, provided the interests of its employees do not override its own. One way to help legitimise this processing is to add an opt-out in order to give the data subject a measure of control despite the inapplicability of consent as a legal ground;

800. *See* Art. 29 Working Party, Opinion 06/2014 on the notion of legitimate interest of the data controller under Article 7 of Directive 95/46/EC, p. 23.
801. *See* Art. 29 Working Party, Opinion 06/2014 on the notion of legitimate interest of the data controller under Article 7 of Directive 95/46/EC, p. 49.

- a retailer wants to send offers to existing customers for products that are similar to the ones the customers already bought. In such a case, the e-Privacy Directive[802] allows the controller to carry out this processing on the basis of legitimate interest, rather than obliging it to have consent, as is the case for all other situations of direct marketing. In such cases, customers must still be given the opportunity to object/opt out of such communications, both at the initial collection and in any subsequent communication, but their prior consent for such unsolicited communications is not required;
- in Case C-13/16,[803] the Court of Justice dealt with the following situation: a passenger opening the door of a taxi had damaged a trolleybus of Riga's public transport company. The company wanted to obtain the necessary personal details to sue the passenger from the police. The question in this case was whether the police is obliged under data protection law to provide the public company with those details so it can pursue its legitimate interest, to the extent that the police does not have a legal obligation to do so. The Court of Justice clarified that the police could in principle rely on the third party's legitimate interests to justify such a disclosure under Article 6(1), f) GDPR but was under no obligation to do so. Hence, Article 6(1), f) GDPR can be relied upon to provide information outside what an entity is legally obliged to, if the balancing test is passed;
- a city wants to carry out experimental research, testing new technological solutions in a monitored testing environment, e.g., an innovation zone, a living lab, etc., which are geographically determined zones in a city where innovation partners can pilot new technologies and solutions. However, as the outcomes of such research are unsure and may find very broad application, it is difficult for the city as a controller to cover this under one of their specific missions or public tasks, certainly given that this research is not strictly speaking necessary at the given time to perform the tasks vested in the city and to provide its services to the citizens. Hence, Article 6(1), e) GDPR cannot be relied on. Obtaining consent from every person who enters the zone will not be pragmatically feasible. Hence, the city can most appropriately rely on its legitimate interests to cover the processing that is implied in such research. As explained above, there is some leeway for public administrations to rely on legitimate interests. The city will of course have to justify this, making the balancing test and document this process for reasons of accountability. However, as designing better public services and assessing the potential of new technologies is in principle beneficial to the citizens, such a processing may very well be possible on the ground of Article 6(1), f) GDPR.

---

802. Directive 2002/58/EC of the European Parliament and of the Council of 12 July 2002 concerning the processing of personal data and the protection of privacy in the electronic communications sector (Directive on privacy and electronic communications), Official Journal L 201, pp. 37–47, Art. 13(2).
803. CJEU, Case C-13/16, Judgment of 4 May 2017, *Rīgas satiksme*, ECLI:EU:C:2017:336, https://curia.europa.eu/juris/liste.jsf?num=C-13/16.

F. Legitimate Interests and Data Subject Rights

714. An important consequence of the choice for legitimate interests as a legal ground is that Article 21 GDPR provides that a data subject can at all times object to the processing, on grounds relating to his or her particular situation. The controller will then have to stop the processing unless the controller can demonstrate that there are compelling legitimate grounds which override the data subject's interests. See §8, section VIII below on the right to object for more information.

715. Whenever Article 6(1), f) GDPR is relied upon for direct marketing purposes, the data subject can object to such processing at any time, without having to provide a reason, and without the option for the controller to demonstrate compelling grounds to continue the processing.

716. There is however no right to data portability. A right to erasure in principle[804] applies when the data is no longer necessary, when the data subject has successfully objected to the processing and there are no overriding legitimate grounds to maintain the processing (except for in the case of direct marketing, where erasure must always be granted) or when the data were unlawfully processed to begin with (e.g., after a certain time has lapsed).

717. Articles 13/14 (right to information), 15 (right to access), 16 (right to rectification) and 18 (right to restriction of processing) also apply. Moreover, data subjects have the right not to be subjected to automated individual decision-making, including profiling, under Article 22 GDPR, unless one of the exceptions of Article 22(2) GDPR applies. See §8 below for more details on data subject rights.

§7. Special Categories of Data (Articles 9 and 10 GDPR)

I. Special categories under Article 9 GDPR

A. The Principle: Processing Special Categories Is Forbidden (Article 9(1) GDPR)

718. Article 9 GDPR introduces an additional layer to the legality of the processing of personal data for certain special categories of data, namely for:

- personal data revealing racial or ethnic origin;
- personal data revealing political opinions;
- personal data revealing religious or philosophical beliefs;
- personal data revealing trade union membership;

804. This is because Art. 17 also contains some exceptions, which are discussed in §8, s. V below.

- genetic data;[805]
- biometric data, when processed for the purpose of uniquely identifying a person;[806]
- data concerning health;[807]
- data concerning a natural person's sex life or sexual orientation.

The principle is that all processing of such categories of personal data is **prohibited**.

719. However, Article 9(2), provides for a limited number of exceptions. Controllers who wish or need to process personal data that belongs to one of the above categories will therefore have to be able to rely on an exception under Article 9(2) GPDR, in addition to having a legal ground under Article 6 GDPR. These are cumulative conditions and the controller must be able to demonstrate that it has both a justifiable legal ground under Article 6 GDPR and can rely on an exception under Article 9(2) GDPR to justify the processing activity.[808] While several of the exceptions of Article 9(2) GDPR 'hint' at the most suitable legal ground, they are not legal grounds in themselves. In addition, all other rules of the GDPR have to be taken into account here as well, such as the principle of fairness, purpose limitation, data minimisation, etc.

720. The reasoning behind the structure of Article 9 GDPR is that the above-mentioned categories are by their very nature particularly sensitive, and their processing without specific protection would create significant risks to the fundamental

805. Art. 4(13) GDPR defines genetic data as 'personal data relating to the inherited or acquired genetic characteristics of a natural person which give unique information about the physiology or the health of that natural person and which result, in particular, from an analysis of a biological sample from the natural person in question'.
806. Art. 4(14) GDPR defines biometric data as: 'personal data resulting from specific technical processing relating to the physical, physiological or behavioural characteristics of a natural person, which allow or confirm the unique identification of that natural person, such as facial images or dactyloscopic data'; As Recital 51 GDPR clarifies, the processing of photographs does not necessarily imply the processing of biometric data, unless specific technical means are used (such as facial recognition software) allowing the unique identification or authentication of a natural person.
807. Art. 4(15) GDPR defines data concerning health as 'personal data related to the physical or mental health of a natural person, including the provision of healthcare services, which reveal information about his or her health status'. The Court of Justice has indicated that this is a broad category in CJEU, Case C-101/01, Judgment of 6 November 2003, *Lindqvist*, ECLI:EU:C:2003:596, para. 50, https://curia.europa.eu/juris/liste.jsf?num=C-101/01. The GDPR specifies that health data includes 'all data pertaining to the health status of a data subject which reveal information relating to the past, current or future physical or mental health status of the data subject', as well as information collected in the registration of healthcare services,' a number, symbol or particular assigned to a natural person to uniquely identify the natural person for health purposes' and 'information derived from the testing or examination of a body part or bodily substance, including from genetic data and biological samples; and any information on, for example, a disease, disability, disease risk, medical history, clinical treatment or the physiological or biomedical state of the data subject independent of its source, for example from a physician or other health professional, a hospital, a medical device or an in vitro diagnostic test.' (Recital 35 GDPR).
808. *See also* Recital 51 GDPR: 'In addition to the specific requirements for such processing, the general principles and other rules of this Regulation should apply, in particular as regards the conditions for lawful processing.'

rights and freedoms of the data subject,[809] as the illegitimate use of such data could lead to serious discrimination and could significantly hurt the data subject's interests. Infringement of Article 9 GDPR will expose the controller to the highest level of fines (Article 83(5), a) GDPR), as well to potential litigation and liability.

721. One side note here is the European legislator has chosen to work with a limited, albeit broad, list of categories of data that deserve specific protection because they are considered to be inherently sensitive. *A contrario* that means that any category of data not included in the list does not benefit from the specific protection of Article 9 GDPR. This however does not mean that such data cannot be 'sensitive' in the broader sense of the word. Also note that 'sensitive data' is not a legal concept under the GDPR and not part of the Article 9 GDPR terminology, although this is frequently overlooked in practice and especially in the media.[810] Therefore, certain types of data may be sensitive (e.g., financial information, data relating to a child), depending on the context (e.g., your financial information processed by your bank to deliver banking services vs. your financial information sold to a third party for marketing purposes), but are not protected under Article 9 GDPR. The GDPR does, however, provide protection for such categories of data too, both through the general principles of processing, such as purpose limitation, transparency, lawfulness and fairness and, in some cases through specific provision targeting such situations (e.g., processing data relating to a child on consent or legitimate interest is subject to specific rules as discussed above).

B. The Exceptions (Article 9(2) GDPR)

722. Article 9(2) GDPR provides a number of exceptions to the principle that the processing of special categories of data listed in Article 9(1) GDPR is prohibited. They are discussed separately in the following subsections. As a general rule, the exceptions must be interpreted restrictively.

1. The Data Subject Has Explicitly Consented to the Processing (Article 9(2), a) GDPR)

723. The first exception to the prohibition of Article 9(1) GDPR is when the data subject has **explicitly** consented to the processing of the personal data at issue for one or more specified purposes. As mentioned above in §6, section I.C on explicit consent, the word 'explicit' indicates that a greater level of care must be exercised by the controller in making sure the consent of the data subject is active and clear, and well informed. It should however be noted that the fact that a controller relies on the data subject's consent under Article 9(2), a) GDPR does not *ipso facto* mean it relies on consent under Article 6(1), a) GDPR, although this may be a logical choice. These consents are separate concepts and the controller needs both an

809. Recital 51 GDPR.
810. The GDPR only mentions 'sensitive data' in Recital 10.

exception ground under Article 9(2) GDPR and a legal basis under Article 6 GDPR to justify the processing of special categories of data.

724. The exception ground of Article 9(2), a) GDPR only applies for one or more specified purposes, and insofar that EU or Member State does not restrict the application of this exception. This is especially relevant in relation to the processing of genetic data, biometric data or data concerning health, because Article 9(4) GDPR allows Member States to maintain or introduce further conditions, including limitations, with regard to the processing of those types of data.

725. Explicit consent may be difficult in certain situations, by analogy to consent under Article 6(1), a) GDPR. An employer, for example, will not be able to rely on this exception to process any data belonging to the special categories about its employees. Explicit consent may also not be feasible for other, more practical reasons, e.g., in scientific research involving a great number of participants or where the data can no longer be clearly linked to one specific individual or doing so would require a disproportionate effort or the collection of a disproportionate amount of additional data.

2. The Processing Is Necessary to Carry Out Obligations or Exercise Rights of the Controller or the Data Subject in the Field of Employment, Social Security and Social Protection Law (Article 9(2), b) GDPR)

726. The second exception of Article 9(2) GDPR allows processing of special categories of data insofar as this is necessary to carry out obligations or exercise rights, of both the controller and the data subject in the fields of employment, social security and social protection law, if:

- this has a legal basis in EU law, Member State law, or a collective agreement pursuant to Member State law; and
- that legal basis provides for 'appropriate safeguards for the fundamental rights and the interests of the data subject'.

727. When relying on a legal justification in EU or Member State law (or in a collective agreement), the controller must restrict itself to those processing operations that are necessary and appropriate for reaching the legitimate goal specified in the legal basis, and respect all other GDPR requirements, including those of the legal ground under Article 6 it relies on to make its processing lawful. The legal basis may specify the processing activities that are necessary and could do so in varying detail. In doing so, the Member States must limit itself to what is necessary and appropriate for the legitimate objectives pursued.[811]

---

811. CJEU, Joined Cases C-465/00, C-138/01 and C-139/01, Judgment of 20 May 2003, *Österreichischer Rundfunk and Others*, ECLI:EU:C:2003:294, https://eur-lex.europa.eu/legal-content/en/TXT/?uri=CELEX:62000CJ0465.

728. Take as an example an employer who wants to use biometric data (e.g., fingerprint, face scan, iris scan) to monitor the working times of its employees. While it has a legal basis to monitoring of the working times (for payment purposes, for purposes of control), the question arises whether this would include the processing of biometric data. The controller will have to demonstrate that this is proportional in the given context, to comply with the principle of data minimisation. If a viable alternative (like a badge) is available, this will be difficult to justify. In addition, the controller will have to prove that the processing is either necessary for the performance of the employment contract (Article 6(1), b) GDPR) (which will be difficult), or, if relying on its legitimate interests, will have to demonstrate that its legitimate interests are not overridden by the interests of the data subject (Article 6(1), f) GDPR). In this balancing exercise it will also be relevant whether viable alternatives exist and whether the use of biometrics is optional or mandatory (i.e., whether there is an opt-out or not).

729. However, the legal basis in EU or national law may also contain explicit derogations from the principle of Article 9(1), specifically allowing the processing of categories of personal data covered under Article 9(1). This must be possible where this is in the public interest to do so.[812]

3. The Processing Is Necessary to Protect the Vital Interests of the Data Subject or of Another Natural Person and the Data Subject Is Physically or Legally Incapable of Giving Consent (Article 9(2), c) GDPR)

730. For the exception of Article 9(2), c) GDPR to apply, two conditions must be fulfilled:

(1) the vital interests of the data subject or a third person must be at stake; and
(2) the data subject must be physical or legally incapable to give consent.

731. By analogy to the legal ground of vital interests under Article 6(d) GDPR, this exception allows the processing of e.g., health data in cases where the vital interests (health, physical integrity, life)[813] of the data subject or a third person are in danger, e.g., in a medical emergency. Recital 46 GDPR indicates that processing may also be carried out when important grounds of public interest justify this. Hence, this exception could also arguably serve when this is 'necessary for humanitarian purposes, including for monitoring epidemics and their spread or in situations of humanitarian emergencies, in particular in situations of natural and man-made disasters'.

732. The exception of Article 9(2), c) GDPR only applies where the data subject is either physically (the data subject is very ill, or unconscious) or legally (e.g., a

812. Recital 52 GDPR.
813. Art. 29 Working Party, Opinion 06/2014 on the notion of legitimate interest of the data controller under Article 7 of Directive 95/46/EC, p. 20; recitals 46 and 112 GDPR.

minor in a medical emergency, when the holder of parental responsibility cannot be identified or located and the processing must go ahead to safeguard the vital interests) incapable to give (explicit) consent. In all other situations, consent under Article 9(2), a) GDPR is preferable.

4. The Processing Is Carried Out by a Foundation, Association or Any Other Not-for-Profit Body with a Political, Philosophical, Religious or Trade Union Aim in the Course of Its Legitimate Activities (Article 9(2), d) GDPR)

733. The exception of Article 9(2), d) GDPR permits the processing of special categories of data by a foundation, association or any other not-for-profit body, if it has a political, philosophical, religious or trade union aim and when their purpose is 'to permit the exercise of fundamental freedoms'.[814] Hence, the exception does not apply to any non-profit, but only to those aimed at exercising freedoms such as:

- churches and religious organisations;
- foundations for the protection of freedoms (e.g., anti-discrimination organisations);
- trade unions.

734. Moreover, the exception only applies to the processing these bodies do within the course of their legitimate activities and only in relation to members or former members or persons who have regular contact with the controller in connection with its purposes, i.e., for the internal functioning. Moreover, for the exception to apply, the personal data may not be disclosed outside that body without the consent of the data subjects.

735. Hence, a religious organisation may for example take notes of an organisational meeting in which the participants discuss how to best reach their public, even if this reveals the beliefs of the participants to this meeting, whether members or not. This information may however not be made public or transferred outside the organisation without the data subject's consent. In the same vein, this information may not be used for other purposes than those pursued by the organisation in question 'to permit the exercise of fundamental freedoms'.[815] Marketing by such an organisation for example, could not include the processing of special categories of data relying on the exception of Article 9(2), d) GDPR.

5. The Processing Relates to Personal Data That Have Been Manifestly Made Public by the Data Subject (Article 9(2), e) GDPR)

736. The exception of Article 9(2), e) GDPR applies to special categories of data, where the specific data at issues has **manifestly** been made public by the data

814. Recital 51 GDPR.
815. Recital 51 GDPR.

subject. The use of the word 'manifestly' implies not only an affirmative act by the data subject, but also that the data subject must have clearly known that the result of its actions would be that the information would become public. Moreover, the information must have been made public by the data subject itself. Information that has illegally been made public is not covered by this exception.[816]

737. Hence, information that has been posted on social media (in public mode), published in mass media or similar actions would be covered by this exception. The European Data Protection Board has clarified in the context of video surveillance by controllers that the mere fact that a data subject enters into the range of a camera does not imply that the data subject has made special categories of data relating to him/her public.[817]

738. It is important to note that, even if the data has been manifestly made public by the data subject, this does not imply a blanket permission for use. The controller must still have a legal ground under Article 6 GDPR and follow all other obligations of the GDPR (data minimisation, purpose limitation, etc.).

6. The Processing Is Necessary for the Establishment, Exercise or Defence of Legal Claims or for Courts Acting in Their Judicial Capacity (Article 9(2), f) GDPR)

739. This exception is meant to safeguard the right to a fair trial and an effective judicial remedy, both for plaintiffs and defendants. It allows them to process special categories of data where this is necessary to establish their claims or to prepare a defence.

740. The exception applies not only to the parties, both also to their lawyers, to courts and tribunals. It applies in Court proceedings, administrative procedures and out-of-court procedures, such as mediation, binding third-party decisions and arbitration,[818] and to both public and private law.[819]

741. However, since all exceptions under Article 9(2) GDPR must be interpreted restrictively, there must be a real and actual interest in the head of the controller. For the plaintiff and their legal counsel, this must mean there is either a claim pending or there is the concrete intention to bring a claim in the (near) future. For

816. Ludmila Georgieva, Christopher Kuner, 'Article 9. Processing of special categories of personal data', in Christopher Kuner, Lee A. Bygrave, Christopher Docksey (eds.), *The EU General Data Protection Regulation (GDPR) – A commentary*, 2020, p. 378 *in fine*.
817. European Data Protection Board, Guidelines 3/2019 on processing of personal data through video devices, para. 70, https://edpb.europa.eu/sites/default/files/files/file1/edpb_guidelines_201903_video_devices_en_0.pdf.
818. Recital 52 GDPR.
819. Ludmila Georgieva, Christopher Kuner, 'Article 9. Processing of special categories of personal data', in Christopher Kuner, Lee A. Bygrave, Christopher Docksey (eds.), *The EU General Data Protection Regulation (GDPR) – A commentary*, 2020, p. 379.

the defence and their counsel this means there must be an existing claim, judicial or extrajudicial procedure.[820] The same is true for the court, third-party decider(s) or arbitrator(s).

7. The Processing Is Necessary for Reasons of Substantial Public Interest (Article 9(2), g) GDPR)

742. Article 9(2), g) GDPR allows the processing of special categories of data for reasons of **substantial** public interest and where this has a basis in Union or Member State law, which:

- is proportionate to the aim pursued;
- respects the essence of the right to data protection;
- provides for suitable and specific measures to safeguard the fundamental rights and the interests of the data subject.

743. The GDPR does not clearly define what type of public interest can be qualified as 'substantial'.[821] Note that this is not a requirement for the legal ground of public interest provided in Article 6(1), e) GDPR. The standard here is clearly higher, as is also indicated by the examples the GDPR provides of general[822] public interest:

- Recital 46 GDPR acknowledges processing 'necessary for humanitarian purposes, including for monitoring epidemics and their spread or in situations of humanitarian emergencies, in particular in situations of natural and man-made disasters' may serve 'important grounds of public interest';
- Recital 55 allows 'the processing of personal data by official authorities for the purpose of achieving the aims, laid down by constitutional law or by international public law, of officially recognised religious associations' on the grounds of public interest;
- Recital 56 allows the processing of data on people's political opinions by political parties in the course of electoral activities, where this is necessary for the operation of the democratic system in a Member State.

744. Hence, it is clear that the scope of this exception is limited. Note that even in cases where the exception applies, the processing has to have a basis in law and must respect data protection, as well as provide appropriate safeguards.

---

820. *Ibid.*.
821. The Art. 29 Working Party already critiqued this in its 2011 advice paper on special categories of data. *See* Art. 29 Working party, Advice paper on special categories of data ('sensitive data'), p. 11.
822. As opposed to public interest in the area of health (Art. 9(2), i) GDPR) and archiving in the public interest, statistics and research (Art. 9(2), j) GDPR).

8. The Processing Is Necessary for the Purposes of Preventive or Occupational Medicine, for the Assessment of the Working Capacity of the Employee, Medical Diagnosis, the Provision of Health or Social Care or Treatment or the Management of Health or Social Care Systems and Services (Article 9(2), h) GDPR)

745. Article 9(2), h) GDPR provides a broad exception for the processing of special categories of data for the purposes of healthcare, specifically where the 'processing is necessary for the purposes of preventive or occupational medicine, for the assessment of the working capacity of the employee, medical diagnosis, the provision of health or social care or treatment or the management of health or social care systems and services'. This includes medical treatment and care, work-related medical checks and the processing activities necessary for running national healthcare systems and providing services. The term social should be understood broadly and includes all types of assistance granted by social security authorities.[823] Recital 53 GDPR clarifies that processing should be carried out 'only where necessary to achieve those purposes for the benefit of natural persons and society as a whole'.

746. In order to benefit from the exception the processing must:

- have a basis in Union or Member State law or must be done pursuant to a contract with a health professional; and
- must be carried out by or under the responsibility of a professional subject to the obligation of professional secrecy under Union or Member State law or rules established by national competent bodies or by another person also subject to an obligation of secrecy under Union or Member State law or rules established by national competent bodies.[824]

747. Hence, these types of processing activities can be carried out by professionals who are under an obligation of secrecy, such as doctors, dentists, psychologists, hospitals and insurance companies. A contract with a health professional may be used to justify the processing but is not necessary if there is a basis in law (e.g., for insurance companies). For the determination of which professionals are covered by this exception, Article 9(3) GDPR refers to national law and hence the scope may differ from Member State to Member State.

748. It is noteworthy that the right of erasure can be refused by the controller processing data under this exception (see §8, section V.D below).[825]

823. Ludmila Georgieva, Christopher Kuner, 'Article 9. Processing of special categories of personal data', in Christopher Kuner, Lee A. Bygrave, Christopher Docksey (eds.), *The EU General Data Protection Regulation (GDPR) – A commentary*, 2020, p. 380.
824. Art. 9(3) GDPR.
825. Art. 17(3), c) GDPR.

9. The Processing Is Necessary for Reasons of Public Interest in the Area of Public Health (Article 9(2), i) GDPR)

749. The exception of Article 9(2), i) GDPR covers the processing of special categories of data where this is necessary for reasons of public interest in the area of public health. Recital 54 GDPR specifies that 'public health' includes 'all elements related to health, namely health status, including morbidity and disability, the determinants having an effect on that health status, healthcare needs, resources allocated to healthcare, the provision of, and universal access to, healthcare as well as healthcare expenditure and financing and the causes of mortality.

750. Article 9(2), i) gives the following examples: 'protecting against serious cross-border threats to health or ensuring high standards of quality and safety of healthcare and of medicinal products or medical devices'. The exception may also be used for 'health security, monitoring and alert purposes, the prevention or control of communicable diseases and other serious threats to health'.[826]

751. In order to benefit from the exception:

- it must have a basis in Union or Member State law;
- that law must provide for suitable and specific measures to safeguard the rights and freedoms of the data subject, in particular professional secrecy.

752. Moreover, such processing must not result in processing 'for other purposes by third parties such as employers or insurance and banking companies'.[827] It is clear that this is a narrow exception which is intended for public health authorities and NGOs, or other bodies working in the field of public health, disaster relief and humanitarian aid.[828] Note that medical research within the boundaries of the scope of this exception is also covered.[829]

753. It is noteworthy that the right of erasure can be refused by the controller processing data under this exception (see §8, section V.D below).[830]

826. Recital 52 GDPR.
827. Recital 54 GDPR.
828. Ludmila Georgieva, Christopher Kuner, 'Article 9. Processing of special categories of personal data', in Christopher Kuner, Lee A. Bygrave, Christopher Docksey (eds.), *The EU General Data Protection Regulation (GDPR) – A commentary*, 2020, p. 380.
829. Ludmila Georgieva, Christopher Kuner, 'Article 9. Processing of special categories of personal data', in Christopher Kuner, Lee A. Bygrave, Christopher Docksey (eds.), *The EU General Data Protection Regulation (GDPR) – A commentary*, 2020, p. 379.
830. Art. 17(3), c) GDPR.

10. The Processing Is Necessary for Archiving Purposes in the Public Interest, Scientific or Historical Research Purposes or Statistical Purposes (Article 9(2), j) GDPR)

754. The last exception of Article 9(2) allows the processing of special categories of data when this 'is necessary for archiving purposes in the public interest, scientific or historical research purposes or statistical purposes in accordance with Article 89(1) GDPR' and must be based on EU or Member State law that is:

- proportionate to the aim pursued; and
- respects the essence of the right to data protection; and
- provides for suitable and specific measures to safeguard the fundamental rights and the interests of the data subject.

755. Appropriate safeguards are also required by Article 89(1) GDPR, which specifically mentions the principle of data minimisation, meaning that data may only be processed if strictly necessary. In addition other measures may be taken.

756. Note that only the archiving ground requires 'public interest'. While research may definitely be in the public interest, this is not per se required in order to process special categories of data under Article 9(2), j) GDPR. Note that whether the research is in the public interest may however be relevant in terms of the fairness of the processing, in the balancing exercise under Article 6(1), f) GDPR and may be relevant in terms of the national legislation implementing Article 89 and in particular Article 89(2).

C. Additional Conditions or Limitations in Member State Law

757. Article 9(4) GDPR allows Member States to 'maintain or introduce further conditions, including limitations, with regard to the processing of genetic data, biometric data or data concerning health'. Hence, for these three special categories of data, and only for these three categories, there may generally be divergent rules depending on the Member State. Taking health data as an example, it will be up to the Member States to define whether or not a data subject may explicitly consent to the use of his/her data, e.g., by an app that tracks health data, and whether there are additional conditions the app developer/operator as a controller must fulfil, e.g., to have the processing be done under the responsibility of a doctor or a health professional.

D. Appropriate Safeguards

758. Several of the exceptions in Article 9(2) GDPR refer to appropriate safeguards, as well as certain recitals and Article 89 GDPR. In addition, other exceptions of Article 9(2) GDPR refer to 'specific measures to safeguard the rights and freedoms of the data subject'. As pointed out by the Article 29 Working Party already in 2011, the law contains no definition or clarification on what this means.[831]

759. Whenever EU or Member State law clearly and exhaustively define the safeguards, the controller could arguably suffice to follow the law. If however the law leaves a significant leeway, is clearly insufficient, or in cases where the controller must itself decide on such safeguards (e.g., Article 9(2), d) or under Article 89(1), perhaps in addition to national legal requirements), the situation is much less self-evident.

760. Neither are the different formulations used in the GDPR clearly demarcated, nor is it immediately clear what the difference is between such additional safeguards and the safeguards that must be taken by a controller in application of general principles underlying the GDPR, such as data minimisation or data security and integrity. The only guidance that can be derived from the text of the GDPR is that the standard which is expected from the controller will be higher in certain cases, namely where special categories of data are processed, or where data is processed outside its original purpose for archiving purposes in the public interest, scientific or historical research purposes or statistical purposes, and especially when that data in addition belongs to a special category (e.g., health data).

E. Other Implications when Processing Special Categories of Personal Data

761. Under Article 9 GDPR, a controller has to be able to be able to justify its intended processing of special categories of personal data under one of the exceptions in Article 9(2) GDPR. In addition however, the fact that the processing concerns special categories of personal data also has the following main consequences:

- the controller must carry out a Data Protection Impact Assessment if the processing is 'on a large scale'[832] (Article 35 GDPR);
- the controller must appoint a Data Protection officer if its core activities consist of processing special categories of data on a large scale[833] (Article 37 GDPR);
- the controller must exercise extra care when considering if it can use the special categories for compatible purposes (Article 6(4), c) GDPR);
- when processing special categories of data, the controller may only use automated individual decision-making, including profiling unless 'point (a) or (g) of Article 9(2) applies and suitable measures to safeguard the data subject's rights and freedoms and legitimate interests are in place' (Article 22 (4) GDPR);

---

831. Art. 29 Working Party, Advice paper on special categories of data ('sensitive data'), p. 11.
832. For the meaning of large scale, *see* Recital 91 GDPR and Art. 29 Working Party, Guidelines on Data Protection Impact Assessment (DPIA) and determining whether processing is 'likely to result in a high risk' for the purposes of Regulation 2016/679, p. 10; Art. 29 Working Party, Guidelines on Data Protection Officers ('DPOs'), pp. 7–8. Both guidelines have been confirmed by the European Data Protection Board in its endorsement 1/2018.
833. *Ibid.*.

– the processing of special categories of personal data on a large scale or not is of relevance in other obligations as well, such as Article 27(2), a) GDPR (appointment of a representative in the EU).

These consequences will be discussed below under the relevant sections.

762. Another relevant implication is that, since Article 9(2) GDPR does not recognise 'necessary for the performance of a contract' as an exception to the general prohibition of Article 9(1) GDPR, controllers and Member States that deal with contracts that present the need for processing of special categories of data will have to rely on one of the specific exceptions of Article 9(2) sub-paragraphs b) to j). Consequently, if none of the specific situations of the exceptions b) to j) of Article 9(2) GDPR apply, they will have to obtain valid and explicit consent to justify the processing.'[834]

II. Data Relating to Criminal Convictions and Offences (Article 10 GDPR)

763. Article 10 GDPR provides a special rule relating to the processing on the basis of Article 6(1) GDPR of personal data 'relating to criminal convictions and offences or related security measures'. Such processing is only allowed:

– under the control of official authority; or
– when the processing is authorised by Union or Member State law providing for appropriate safeguards for the rights and freedoms of data subjects.

Article 10 GDPR also specifies that any comprehensive register of criminal convictions may only be kept under the control of official authority.

764. Article 10 GDPR applies to data relating to criminal convictions and offences. Whilst the European Parliament had proposed the express inclusion in that provision of the words 'administrative sanctions', that proposal was not adopted.[835] That fact is all the more noteworthy because the provision that preceded Article 10 of the GDPR, namely Article 8(5) of Directive 95/46, which referred, in its first sub-paragraph, to 'offences' and 'criminal convictions', enabled the Member States, in its second sub-paragraph, to 'provide that data relating to administrative sanctions ... also be processed under the control of official authority'. It is thus clear from reading Article 8(5) as a whole that the term 'offence' in the 1995 Directive referred only to criminal offences.

765. According to the jurisprudence of the CJEU, the concept of 'criminal conviction and offence', requires an autonomous and uniform interpretation throughout the European Union, having regard to the objective pursued by that provision and

834. EDPB, Guidelines 05/2020 on consent under Regulation 2016/679, para. 99; Art. 29 Working Party, Guidelines on consent under Regulation 2016/679, p. 19.
835. *See* OJ 2017 C 378, p. 430.

the context of which it forms part.[836] This means, on the one hand, that the classification given by the Member State concerned to those offences is not conclusive in that regard as the classification may vary from one country to another.[837]

766. On the other hand, national law will in fact to a certain extent determine the meaning of what constitutes a criminal offence, since the CJEU has determined three relevant factors to take into account to determine what constitutes criminal proceedings (i.e., proceedings relating to criminal offences):[838]

(1) the legal classification of the offence under the applicable Member State law;
(2) the nature of the offence; and
(3) the nature and degree of severity of the penalty that the person concerned is liable to incur.

767. These criteria will help determine whether a given offence is a 'criminal offence' and helps to distinguish between criminal offences and e.g., administrative offences to which Article 10 GDPR does not apply.[839] None of the three criteria alone will, however, be decisive. The CJEU clarified its position in this regard in the case of *Latvijas Republikas Saeima,*[840] where it dealt with the question whether Article 10 applies to the processing of personal data relating to penalty points imposed on drivers of vehicles for road traffic offences.

768. Latvian legislation provides for the imposition of penalty points on drivers of vehicles who have committed a road traffic offence and upon whom a financial or other penalty has been imposed. Those points are entered by a public body, the CSDD, in the national register of vehicles and their drivers on the day upon which the period for appealing against the decision imposing that penalty expires. Road traffic offences and the penalties for punishing them fall within administrative law in Latvia and the aim of imposing penalty points is not to inflict a further penalty but to heighten awareness of the drivers concerned, by encouraging them to adopt

---

836. CJEU, Case C-287/98, Judgment of 19 September 2000, *Linster*, ECLI:EU:C:2000:468, para. 43, https://curia.europa.eu/juris/liste.jsf?language=en&num=C-287/98; CJEU, Case C-673/17, Judgment of 1 October 2019, *Planet49*, ECLI:EU:C:2019:801, para. 47, https://eur-lex.europa.eu/legal-content/EN/TXT/?uri=CELEX%3A62017CJ0673.

837. CJEU, Case C-60/12, Judgment of 14 November 2013, *Baláž*, ECLI:EU:C:2013:733, para. 26 and 35, https://curia.europa.eu/juris/liste.jsf?num=C-60/12&language=EN.

838. CJEU, Case C-489/10, Judgment of 5 June 2012, *Bonda*, ECLI:EU:C:2012:319, para. 37, https://curia.europa.eu/juris/liste.jsf?num=C-489/10&language=EN; CJEU, Case C-537/16, Judgment of 20 March 2018, *Garlsson Real Estate and Others*, ECLI:EU:C:2018:193, para. 28, https://curia.europa.eu/juris/liste.jsf?language=en&num=C-537/16; CJEU, Case C-481/19, Judgment of 2 February 2021, *Consobà*, ECLI:EU:C:2021:84, para. 42.

839. Ludmila Georgieva, 'Article 10. Processing of personal data relating to criminal convictions and offences', in Christopher Kuner, Lee A. Bygrave, Christopher Docksey (eds.), *The EU General Data Protection Regulation (GDPR) – A commentary*, 2020, p. 388.

840. CJEU, Case-C-439/19, Judgment of 22 June 2021, *Latvijas Republikas Saeima*, ECLI:EU:C:2021:504, https://curia.europa.eu/juris/liste.jsf?lgrec=fr&td=%3BALL&language=en&num=C-439/19&jur=C.

safer driving behaviour. When a certain number of penalty points is reached, the person concerned may be banned from driving for a specified period. Referring to Recital 10 of the GDPR, the Court held that the Regulation is intended to contribute to the accomplishment of an area of freedom, security and justice by ensuring a consistent and high level of protection of natural persons with regard to the processing of personal data, which requires the level of protection to be equivalent and homogeneous in all the Member States. It would be contrary to such an objective if the enhanced protection provided for in Article 10 of the GDPR applied to the processing of personal data relating to road traffic offences only in some Member States, and not in others, solely because those offences are not classified as criminal in the latter Member States. Hence, Article 10 GDPR applies to this type of offences as well, and may apply to other offences that are classified as administrative sanctions in one or more Member States.

769. The reasoning underlying Article 10 GDPR is that data relating to criminal convictions and offences is of an extremely sensitive nature and may seriously prejudice data subjects. Hence such data can only be lawful where it is carried out under the control of an official authority,[841] or specifically provided for by law.

770. Notably, Article 10 GDPR does not apply to the processing of personal data 'by competent authorities for the purposes of the prevention, investigation, detection or prosecution of criminal offences or the execution of criminal penalties, including the safeguarding against and the prevention of threats to public security'.[842] In such cases, a special regime applies, which is provided by Directive 2016/680,[843] commonly known as the Law Enforcement Directive (LED). This Directive covers the processing of personal data by competent law enforcement authorities 'for the purposes of the prevention, investigation, detection or prosecution of criminal offences or the execution of criminal penalties'. The GDPR and the LED are mutually exclusive and hence either the one or the other applies.[844]

771. Hence, Article 10 GDPR applies only to processing operations other than those which are 'for the purposes of the prevention, investigation, detection or prosecution of criminal offences or the execution of criminal penalties'. It applies to

---

841. It should be pointed out that a generic right of supervision by an official authority is not sufficient. *See* Ludmila Georgieva, 'Article 10. Processing of personal data relating to criminal convictions and offences', in Christopher Kuner, Lee A. Bygrave, Christopher Docksey (eds.), *The EU General Data Protection Regulation (GDPR) – A commentary*, 2020, p. 389.
842. Art. 2(2), d) GDPR.
843. Directive (EU) 2016/680 of the European Parliament and of the Council of 27 April 2016 on the protection of natural persons with regard to the processing of personal data by competent authorities for the purposes of the prevention, investigation, detection or prosecution of criminal offences or the execution of criminal penalties, and on the free movement of such data and repealing Council Framework Decision 2008/977/JHA, OJ L 119, pp. 89–131.
844. Art. 2(2), d) GDPR, Art. 1(1) and 2(1) LED, Art. 9 LED.

competent authorities (law enforcement authorities) as well as to public bodies which are not competent authorities and to private bodies.[845]

772. For processing within the scope of the GDPR, which is carried out by or under the control[846] of competent authorities, Member States are allowed to maintain or introduce more specific provisions to adapt the application of the GDPR.[847] An example could be the processing of data relating to criminal convictions and offences for research purposes by Law Enforcement Authorities. Such provisions may determine more precisely specific requirements for the processing of personal data by competent authorities for such purposes other than those listed in the LED, taking into account the constitutional, organisational and administrative structure of the respective Member State.[848] Such measures will have to respect all principles of human rights law (i.e., will need to be necessary and proportionate), as they might likely contain a restriction of the right to privacy and/or data protection.

773. For private bodies (and by extension also for public entities other than competent authorities or under the control of competent authorities), processing of data relating to criminal convictions and offences will only be allowed if:

- this is specifically provided for by law; and
- the law provides for appropriate safeguards for the rights and freedoms of data subjects; and
- the provision is a necessary and proportionate measure in a democratic society to safeguard specific important interests including public security and the prevention, investigation, detection or prosecution of criminal offences or the execution of criminal penalties, including the safeguarding against and the prevention of threats to public security.[849]

As examples the GDPR mentions the processing of data relating to criminal convictions and offences by companies in the framework of anti-money laundering and the activities of private forensic laboratories.

§8. Data Subject Rights (Articles 12–23 GDPR)

774. As has already been mentioned in the previous sections, the data subjects have a number of rights in relation to the processing of their personal data. Each

845. Ludmila Georgieva, 'Article 10. Processing of personal data relating to criminal convictions and offences', in Christopher Kuner, Lee A. Bygrave, Christopher Docksey (eds.), *The EU General Data Protection Regulation (GDPR) – A commentary*, 2020, p. 386.
846. A generic right of supervision by an official authority is not sufficient to establish such control. *See* Ludmila Georgieva, 'Article 10. Processing of personal data relating to criminal convictions and offences', in Christopher Kuner, Lee A. Bygrave, Christopher Docksey (eds.), *The EU General Data Protection Regulation (GDPR) – A commentary*, 2020, p. 389.
847. Recital 19 GDPR.
848. Recital 19 GDPR.
849. Art. 10 GDPR and Recital 19 GDPR.

right has a specific scope and conditions for application, as well as certain exceptions. Each right is discussed separately in the sections below.

775. However, before discussing any specific rights, attention must be given to the general rules established by GDPR on how controllers must interact with data subjects. Therefore, section I below first addresses this topic.

776. In addition, Article 23 GDPR leaves the Member States some leeway to restrict data subject rights when this is necessary and proportionate to safeguard essential elements of a democratic society. This is discussed in section X below.

I. General Rules in Relation to Interaction with Data Subjects (Articles 11 and 12 GDPR)

777. The core of the general rules relating to the interaction with data subjects can be found in Article 12 GDPR on transparent information, communication and modalities for the exercise of the rights of the data subject, the elements of which are discussed in several subsections below. Although Article 12 is the first article of the chapter relating to the rights of the data subject (chapter III of the GDPR), the discussion of its elements must be preceded by a mention of Article 11 GPDR, which establishes an important principle of the relation between the controller and the data subject, namely that the controller is not in principle required to be able to identify the data subject, as is elaborated in subsection A below. Section B to D elaborate on the general rules of Article 12 GDPR.

A. No Obligation for the Controller to Be Able to Identify the Data Subject (Article 11 GDPR)

778. Article 11(1) GDPR specifies that in cases where the controller does not need to identify the data subject for its processing purposes, it cannot be obliged to maintain, acquire or process additional information in order to identify the data subject solely to comply with the GDPR.[850] The same is true when the processing of the controller may have needed to identify the data subject initially, but no longer requires this. In effect, this rule implements the idea of data minimisation, specifically allowing the controller to process personal data even if the controller cannot identify the data subject.

779. Given the broad definition of personal data as any information relating to an identified or (directly or indirectly) identifiable natural person, and taking into

850. *See* for a detailed discussion Mike Hintze, 'Viewing the GDPR through a de-identification lens: a tool for compliance, clarification, and consistency', *International Data Privacy Law* 2018, Vol. 8(1), 86–101.

account recent case law of the Court of Justice,[851] it is perfectly possible for a controller to process personal data without having identified the data subject. A website owner, for example, may collect IP-address-based statistics, without having identified the person behind the IP address. Following the aforementioned case law, IP addresses are nonetheless personal data, and so the GDPR applies in full, even if the controller only has a very hypothetical possibility to connect a name to the IP address. Controllers in that situation are not obliged to make efforts to identify data subjects if their own purposes do not require this. Another example that could help illustrate this rule is the processing by a controller consisting of camera surveillance. In this case as well, the controller will not simply on the basis of the camera images be able to identify all data subjects. Following Article 11 GPDR, the controller is under no obligation to identify (all) individuals that have been taped, if its own purposes do not require this.[852] Hence, the principle of Article 11(1) GDPR is important to deal with situations where the controller cannot identify the data subject,[853] yet is not dealing with anonymous information either, meaning the GDPR still applies.

780. The consequence of Article 11(1) GDPR, as defined in Article 11(2) GDPR, is that, if the controller can demonstrate that it is not in a position to identify the data subject, it is in principle not held to provide a number of data subject rights, namely those provided in Articles 15–20 GDPR. The controller does still need to inform the data subject (Article 13 GDPR-, and especially also about the fact that it is not able to identify the data subject and hence cannot provide rights such as the right of access, right of rectification, right to erasure or right to data portability. The right to object (Article 21 GDPR) and not to be subjected to automated individual decision-making, including profiling (Article 22 GDPR) still apply.

781. However, in such cases, the data subject, which should have been informed about this situation, may provide additional information to the controller to enable the controller to identify him or her. In that case, Articles 15–20 GDPR become applicable again. Nonetheless, this means that controllers may decide that, in certain situations, it will try to limit the interaction with the data subjects by not identifying them. For certain controllers, this principle is of essential importance. Take the activities of a Computer Security Incidents Response Team as an example.

851. *See* CJEU, Case C-582/14, Judgment of 19 October 2016, *Breyer*, ECLI:EU:C:2016:779, https://eur-lex.europa.eu/legal-content/en/TXT/?uri=CELEX:62014CJ0582 and references there.

852. *See* EDPB Guidelines 3/2019 on processing of personal data through video devices, paras 94–96.

853. This means that the controller is lacking certain information to identify the data subject, i.e., has no access to such information (any more). This goes beyond pseudonymisation measures where the controller has merely separated certain identifying information but can still obtain this information. *See* on this Mike Hintze, 'Viewing the GDPR through a de-identification lens: a tool for compliance, clarification, and consistency', *International Data Privacy Law* 2018, Vol. 8(1), 86–101, p. 91; Runshan Hu, Sophie Stalla-Bourdillon, Mu Yang, Valeria Schiavoand Vladimiro Sassone, 'Bridging policy, regulation and practice? A techno-legal analysis of three types of data in the GDPR', in Ronald Leenes, Rosamunde van Brakel, Serge Gutwirth, and Paul De Hert, *Data Protection and Privacy: the Age of Intelligent Machines* (Computers, Privacy and Data Protection; Vol. 10), 2017, 115–142.

Many of the activities of such a team, trying to monitor cyber threats, will be to process data that does not directly enable them to identify the data subject by name, such as IP addresses. Nonetheless, because this is personal data, the GDPR is applicable. Forcing such controllers to identify the data subject would effectively render their operation impossible.

B. Transparent Information and Communication

782. Article 12 GDPR lays down the basic principles of interaction with data subjects, as they are generally applicable to all controllers. These rules of transparency apply to:

- The information provided to data subjects before the processing when the information is being collected directly with the data subject (Article 13 GDPR).
- The information provided to data subjects before the processing when the information is obtained from a third party (Article 14 GDPR).
- Any communication with regards to data subject rights, and during the exercise of those rights by data subjects, including any answer, request for information or other communication (Articles 15–22 GDPR).
- Communications to data subjects in the context of a data breach (Article 34 GDPR).

Hence, whether the interaction at issue is the controller providing information to the data subject or the controller communicating with the data subject, e.g., in the context of a request for the exercise of a data subject right, does not change the general rules on transparency.

783. The first aspect to be discussed is the general **transparency requirements**. The GDPR stipulates that all information provided to a data subject, and every communication with a data subject, should:[854]

- be concise and transparent,[855] intelligible,[856] and easily accessible;[857]

854. Art. 12(1) GDPR.

855. Concise and transparent means that the controller must present information efficiently and succinctly to avoid information fatigue, including during communications with the data subject. The GDPR-related information must be clearly distinguished from other information such as contractual provisions. In addition, in an online context the controller must use ICT methods available to help present the information in a better way. A layered privacy policy/statement or information notice which can easily be navigated by the data subject deserves recommendation (Art. 29 Working Party, Guidelines on transparency under Regulation 2016/679 (WP260), para. 8). An example of a layered information notice is a privacy policy on a website where the data subject can show/hide certain information and click through to the relevant sections by manner of hyperlinks in the policy, attached to titles or keywords.

856. Intelligible means that the information or communication must be able to be understood by an average member of the intended audience. It should also focus on the consequences of the processing.

- use clear and plain language;[858]
- when addressing children and other vulnerable people, take these vulnerabilities in account.[859]

The controller must take appropriate measures to ensure this.

784. The GDPR does not generally regulate the **substantive content** of the communication/information, except for the information to be provided to the data subject in the context of the information obligation under Articles 13 and 14 GDPR (see section II below). Consequently, in other cases than under Article 13 and 14 GDPR, it will be up to the controller to determine what contents are necessary in the given context and what level of detail is required.

785. The second main aspect to be discussed is the **method of delivery of the information or to carry out the communication**. The GDPR does not mandate a specific delivery method in which the information or communication must be realised. Article 12(1) GDPR states that 'The information shall be provided in writing, or by other means, including, where appropriate, by electronic means. When requested by the data subject, the information may be provided orally, provided that the identity of the data subject is proven by other means.'

786. Hence, the default is for the information to be provided in writing, although the GDPR also allows other, unspecified, means, including electronic means where appropriate. Electronic means may be digital written documents, or may include

---

The controller must make sure that the information is intelligible for the groups of data subjects concerned (Art. 29 Working Party, Guidelines on transparency under Regulation 2016/679 (WP260), paras 9–10).

857. Easily accessible means that the data subject should not have to seek out the information, it should be immediately apparent where this can be found and how it can be accessed. Information may be provided to the data subject directly, by signposting it or providing a link to it, or in the form of answers to questions. The only requirement is that, whatever the practical implementation, it is easy to find and to access (Art. 29 Working Party, Guidelines on transparency under Regulation 2016/679 (WP260), para. 11).

858. The language used in the information should be plain and clear. This means that information should be provided in as simple a manner as possible, avoiding the use of complex sentences and grammatical structures. Moreover, the information should be concrete and definitive, not abstract, ambivalent or leaving room for different interpretations. Formulations such as 'may', 'might', 'could', 'some', 'possible', 'potential', etc. should be avoided and be replaced by precise indications of the controller's intentions, which helps to make the processing fair towards the data subject. The language should be easy to read, using the active tense rather than the passive tense. Language that is not commonly known, such as legalistic, technical or specialist terminology and formulations should be avoided. When the controller targets different language groups, it must provide accurate and easy-to-understand translations (Art. 29 Working Party, Guidelines on transparency under Regulation 2016/679 (WP260), paras 12–13).

859. In addition to the foregoing requirements, when addressing children or vulnerable people, the controller must ensure that the vocabulary, tone and style of the language used is appropriate to and resonates with children or the category of vulnerable people involved, so that they recognise that the message is directed at them. The controller must assess its audience's likely level of understanding, as is generally the case, i.e., based on an average member of the intended audience (Art. 29 Working Party, Guidelines on transparency under Regulation 2016/679 (WP260), paras 14–16).

other electronic means such as 'contextual pop-up notices, 3D touch or hover-over notices and privacy dashboards'.[860] When using digital/electronic written text, the use of layered privacy statements/notices are recommendable to help the data subject navigate the different topics.[861] When using contextual pop-ups, hover-over notices, etc. the controller must make sure that the entirety of the information provided through such means is also accessible in one single place, whether electronic or in paper format.[862]

787. Other electronic means, which can be used in addition to written content can include videos or voice alerts.[863] Examples of 'other means', whether electronic or not, are cartoons, infographics, flowcharts and other forms of visualisation, e.g., animations, pictograms, comics, etc.[864] The same reasoning goes for any communication where the context warrants the use of additional means in addition to written information.

788. The controller may even provide the information or conduct the communication orally[865] if so requested by the data subject, provided that the identity of the data subject is known and proven by other means, so as to make sure the data subject has indeed received the information or communication. In the context of providing information under Article 13 or 14 GDPR, this is not especially challenging, as this information is typically generally available, also to future customers/users, etc., i.e., data subjects the controller cannot identify yet.[866] The requirement to identify the data subject is more relevant in the context of the exercise by a data subject of one of its rights. The controller should require more than a mere assertion by the individual that they are a specific person.[867] The oral provision of information may also be used as an additional means of providing information, e.g., next to written information to help clarify the written contents. Whenever relying on oral information, the controller must make sure to gather evidence or produce a record so it can demonstrate (for the purpose of complying with its accountability requirement) that the data subject requested oral information, the method through which the data subject was identified and the fact that information was provided.[868]

860. Art. 29 Working Party, Guidelines on transparency under Regulation 2016/679 (WP260), para. 18.
861. An example of a layered information notice is a privacy policy on a website where the data subject can show/hide certain information and click through to the relevant sections by manner of hyperlinks in the policy, attached to titles or keywords.
862. Art. 29 Working Party, Guidelines on transparency under Regulation 2016/679 (WP260), para. 17.
863. Art. 29 Working Party, Guidelines on transparency under Regulation 2016/679 (WP260), para. 18; in theory these means could even be used by themselves, but this will be a tall order for the controller to demonstrate that this by itself has provided the data subject with sufficient detail.
864. Art. 29 Working Party, Guidelines on transparency under Regulation 2016/679 (WP260), para. 18.
865. This also includes pre-recorded audio or automated oral information (Art. 29 Working Party, Guidelines on transparency under Regulation 2016/679 (WP260), para. 21).
866. The Art. 29 Working Party states: 'information to be provided under Articles 13 and 14 may be provided by oral means without the controller requiring a data subject's identity to be proven.' (Art. 29 Working Party, Guidelines on transparency under Regulation 2016/679 (WP260), para. 20 *in fine*).
867. Art. 29 Working Party, Guidelines on transparency under Regulation 2016/679 (WP260), para. 20.
868. Art. 29 Working Party, Guidelines on transparency under Regulation 2016/679 (WP260), para. 21.

789. **The GDPR does not provide any hierarchy between the different methods of delivery**. It is up to the controller to select the appropriate method or methods depending on the particular circumstances, namely the usual method of interaction with the data subject and the context in which the data were collected. It is for example permissible to work with information on paper and some oral explanations at a trade fair, whereas this would not fit the collection of data through a website.

790. Importantly, all information and any communication must in principle be provided to the data subject **free of charge**.[869] This also means that the controller may not make information or communications condition upon e.g., the purchase of or payment for services or goods.[870] Hence, an online retailer providing its privacy policy only after the purchase has been made, would be in breach of the GDPR.

C. Facilitation of the Exercise of Data Subject's Rights

791. Article 12(2) GDPR contains a clear and general obligation for the controller to facilitate the data subject's exercise of his/her rights, meaning the controller not only has to react to a data subject's request, but must also make it easy for the request to be submitted and handled. Recital 59 clarifies that the controller should provide means for requests to be made electronically, especially where the personal data are being processed by electronic means. This means, for example, that a data subject who wants to exercise one of its rights against a website operator who has gathered data on him/her online, should not be forced to write a letter to exercise its rights. More generally, Article 12(2) GDPR means that the controller must take reasonable measures to make the exercise of data rights easy for the data subject in the given context. The general modalities imposed by the GDPR are discussed in the section below.

792. Even a controller who cannot identify the data subjects in application of Article 11 GDPR must in principle facilitate data subject rights, and must inform the data subject of the fact that it is not able to identify them and grant them rights, in principle. However, the data subject may choose to provide additional information allowing his/her identification, in which case the controller must act.[871]

---

869. Art. 12 (5) GDPR. The controller must also provide this information proactively under Arts 13/14 GDPR. The data subject may in principle also ask for additional information, free of charge, but there are two exceptions, namely where the information requests are manifestly unfounded or excessive, especially where there are multiple repetitive requests. In such cases the controller can charge a reasonable fee or even refuse to provide further answers, as all relevant information will at that point already have been provided.
870. Art. 29 Working Party, Guidelines on transparency under Regulation 2016/679 (WP260), para. 22.
871. Arts 11 and 12 GDPR.

D. Modalities for the Exercise of Data Subject Rights

793. In addition to Article 12(2) GDPR, which generally obliges the controller to facilitate the exercise of data subject rights, Article 12(3)- 12(6) GDPR defines more specific modalities for the exercise of data subject rights (Articles 15–22 GDPR), which includes the request of the data subject to exercise a right and any communication with the data subject in that context. Note that modalities are aimed at the controller's behaviour. With the exception of providing information to identify him-/herself, the data subject is not subject to additional requirements in order to submit a request, such as providing a motivation or a purpose for submitting the request. In addition to facilitating the submission of the request, the modalities the controller must respect are the following:

- The controller must **verify the identity** of the natural person making the request. This follows from the fact that allowing the exercise of a data subject's rights (e.g., rights of access, right to rectification, right to erasure) by another person would effectively constitute a data breach, where the data relating to that particular data subject is disclosed, altered or lost without this having been the intention of the data subject or the controller. Hence, the controller must be able to identify the data subject before being able to grant the request. Article 12(6) GDPR clarifies that where the controller has reasonable doubts concerning the identity of the person making the request, it may request additional information necessary to identify the data subject. A common example is requesting a copy of the national identity card of the natural person submitting the request.[872] If the data subject fails to provide the requested information (or equivalent information enabling his or her identification), the controller is justified in refusing to grant the request, at least for as long as the information needed for identification is not provided. Both in considering whether this is necessary, and in determining what additional information must be provided, the controller must take into account the principle of data minimisation and consider how it can reach its goal of identification without requesting more (or more sensitive) data than needed. This also means that where the controller already has identified the natural person making the request beyond reasonable doubt, requesting additional information will not be allowed.
- The controller must provide the data subject with information on the actions taken[873] **without undue delay** and, in any event within **one month** after receipt of the request. The controller may extend this period by two further months if the complexity of the request or the number of requests justifies this. In such a case, the controller still has to inform the data subject without undue delay and at the

872. However, it should be noted that in its draft 2022 guidelines on the right of access, the EDPB states that this should not generally be considered as an appropriate way of authentication. *See* for details European Data Protection Board, Draft Guidelines 01/2022 on data subject rights – Right of access, para. 69 and following (s. 3.3 of the guidelines) and in particular para. 74, https://edpb.europa.eu/system/files/2022-01/edpb_guidelines_012022_right-of-access_0.pdf.
873. This wording indicates that the right must not completely be granted within that period, even if the controller decides to do so. However, the controller must inform the data subject on its decision and the status.

latest within the first month following receipt of the request of the extension, its duration and the reasons for the delay.[874]

- Where the request is made by electronic means (which, as seen above, may be obligatory depending on the context of data collection), then in principle the answer should also be provided electronically, except where the data subject requests otherwise.[875] By extension, if the data subject must also provide further information, e.g., relating to its identity, this should in principle also be possible electronically.
- **The requirement to answer without undue delay does not mean the controller must always grant the request**, but rather that it must provide the data subject with information on its position and the actions it has taken. If the controller intends to refuse the request, it should provide the reasons for this decision.[876] Equally, the controller may decide immediately not to take action on the request, because it's prima facie invalid, or for other reasons. In such cases, the controller must also inform the data subject without undue delay and latest within one month. Such refusal must be accompanied by the reasons for not taking action and the possibility for the data subject to lodge a complaint with a supervisory authority or to seek judicial remedies if the data subject is dissatisfied.[877]
- Both the exercise of the rights, as well as any communications or provision of information by the controller must in principle be **free of charge**. There are **two exceptions** to this, namely where the requests from a given data subject are either manifestly unfounded or excessive (in particular when they are repetitive). In such cases, which effectively amount to abuse of rights by the data subject, the controller may decide to either refuse to act on the request, stating its reasons, or to charge a reasonable fee taking into account the administrative costs of the additional work needed to provide the information/communication or taking the requested action.[878] It is up to the controller to demonstrate the manifestly unfounded or excessive character of the data subject's request.[879]

II. Right to Be Informed (Articles 13 and 14 GDPR)

794. The first right to be discussed, is the data subject's right to be informed, the conditions for which are contained in:

- Articles 13 GDPR, when the data is collected from the data subject directly.

874. Art. 12(3) GDPR.
875. Art. 12(3) GDPR.
876. Recital 59 GDPR.
877. Art. 12(4) GDPR.
878. Art. 12(5) GDPR; In this regard, the Court of Justice has stated that a fee charged for the exercise of a data subject right, must not exceed the cost of communicating such data (CJEU, Case C-486/12, Judgment of 12 December 2013, *X*, ECLI:EU:C:2013:836, para. 31, https://curia.europa.eu/juris/liste.jsf?num=C-486/12&language=EN). The case in question related to Art. 12 of the Data Protection Directive, where fees for the right of access were generally allowed if not excessive. This can however *mutatis mutandis* be applied to the more limited situation of fee charging under the GDPR.
879. Art. 12(5) GDPR, *in fine*..

– Article 14 GDPR, when the data have not been obtained from the data subject, e.g., from a third-party controller, a publicly available source, a data broker or other data subjects.

The discussion below will highlight the differences between the two articles where relevant.

795. The right to be informed is slightly different than most other data subject rights under the GDPR, in the sense that it does not require the data subject to submit a request to the controller, but the controller must proactively provide this right. Information is moreover a basic right under the GDPR, and is important to determine the controllers' compliance with its transparency obligations, to determine the fairness of the processing and to determine the correct application of purpose limitation. It is also a party of a proper data protection by design and default strategy (Article 25 GDPR) and of a data protection impact assessment (Article 35 GDPR).

796. In what follows the following aspects of the right to information are discussed:

– the substantive content;
– the timing for the provision of information;
– the general transparency requirements;
– the delivery method;
– the exceptions to the information obligation.

The following sections will deal with each aspect separately. An additional section deals with some special situations.

A. *The Substantive Content of the Information to Be Provided to the Data Subject*

797. Articles 13 and 14 GDPR provide largely similar lists of required items of information that must be provided to the data subject. Articles 13(1) and 14(1) GDPR provide basic information that must always be provided, and Article 13(2) and 14(2) provide for additional items of information to be provided when this is necessary 'to ensure fair and transparent processing'. However, as already noted above, the Article 29 Working Party, herein confirmed by the European Data Protection Board has stated that there should be no difference between the status of the items of information contained in the first paragraph of Articles 13 and 14 GDPR and those contained in the second paragraph. Where applicable, all information is of equal importance and must be provided to the data subject.[880]

798. The following table provides an overview of the content that is required by Articles 13 and 14 GDPR.

880. Art. 29 Working Party, Guidelines on transparency under Regulation 2016/679 (WP260), para. 23.

Required item of information	Relevant article if the personal data is collected directly from the data subject	Relevant article if the personal data it not obtained from the data subject
The identity and contact details of the controller,[881] and, where applicable their representative.[882]	Article 13(1), a) GDPR	Article 14(1), a) GDPR
The contact details for the Data Protection Officer, where applicable.[883]	Article 13(1), b) GDPR	Article 14(1), b) GDPR
The purposes of the processing and the legal basis[884] for the processing, including information on the processing of data under Article 9 or 10 GDPR, where applicable.[885]	Article 13(1), c) GDPR	Article 14(1), c) GDPR
If the controller relies on legitimate interests (Article 6(1), f) GDPR), the legitimate interests pursued by the controller or a third party.[886]	Article 13(1), d) GDPR	Article 14(2), b) GDPR
The categories of personal data concerned.[887]	Not required/not relevant	Article 14(1), d) GDPR

881. This information should allow easy identification of the controller. It should preferably allow for different forms of communication, so the data subject can use a method of communication he/she has access to and is comfortable with.
882. Representatives are appointed by controllers under Art. 27 GDPR, where the controller is not established in the EU.
883. Data Protection Officers must only be appointed by certain controllers. *See* Art. 37 GDPR.
884. This means the ground under Art. 6 GDPR that is being relied on by the controller.
885. Where special categories under Art. 9 GDPR are being processed, the exception must be indicated. Where data is processed under Art. 10 GDPR, the Eu or Member State law relied upon must be mentioned, where applicable (*see* Art. 29 Working Party, Guidelines on transparency under Regulation 2016/679 (WP260), table in Annex).
886. The text of the GDPR requires as a minimum that the interests are communicated. However, as a matter of best practice, the controller should also share information with the data subject on the balancing test that was carried out. This can be done by providing such information in a layered statement or notice, e.g., in a privacy policy online where the data subject can show/hide this information or click through to the relevant section. Another option would be to give this information to the data subject on request only (*see* Art. 29 Working Party, Guidelines on transparency under Regulation 2016/679 (WP260), table in Annex).
887. This is required only in the scenario where the data have not been collected with the data subject, because in that case logically the data subject lacks awareness on what categories of personal data are being processed. Note that the controller must mention categories and not data items. However, in order to comply with its transparency obligation, it will have to be plain and clear in defining the categories. Counting data items, especially sensitive data under a certain category that does not

The recipients of the data (or the categories of recipients).[888]	Article 13(1), e) GDPR	Article 14(1), e) GDPR
Details on transfers of personal data outside the EEA:[889] – whether any transfers to a third country or an international organisation are intended; – what safeguards for transfers apply/ are applied (including the existence or absence an adequacy decision by the European Commission); – the means how to obtain a copy of those safeguards, where they have been made available.	Article 13(1), f) GDPR	Article 14(1), f) GDPR

typically include this data or does not evoke the thought of this data will be in breach of the transparency obligations. It should be reiterated here that, when providing information, the controller must take into account the level of understanding of an average member of the intended audience, i.e., the concerned data subjects (Art. 29 Working Party, Guidelines on transparency under Regulation 2016/679 (WP260), para. 9).

888. As indicated in Art. 4(9) GDPR, any natural or legal person, public authority, agency or another body can be a recipient, irrespective of whether they are a third party to the controller or not. Hence, a branch, subsidiary or parent company of the controller which has legal personality can be a recipient as well, even though it is not strictly speaking a third party to the controller. The same is true for joint controllers and processors, which can be recipients as well. The controller is not obliged to name the recipients but can provide the data subject with categories. The choice however, is not entirely free. The controller should opt for the information that is most meaningful for the data subjects, which will in practice typically be named recipients. If controllers opt to use categories, they should be specific in defining those categories, mentioning the activities, industry, sector and subsector and the location of the recipients (*see* Art. 29 Working Party, Guidelines on transparency under Regulation 2016/679 (WP260), table in Annex). Note also that Art. 4(9) GDPR excludes public authorities receiving personal data in the framework of a particular inquiry in accordance with Union or Member State law for its definition of recipients.

889. The GDPR provides for several options to justify the transfer of personal data outside the EEA, i.e., to a third country or an international organisation. Adequacy decisions are one such option, which provide for a blanket authorisation. In all other circumstances (binding corporate rules, standard data protection clauses, derogations for specific situations), this must be more specific. Information must be provided on this, and the data subject must be told what safeguards apply, and, where relevant, if they have been made public, how they can be accessed and how a copy can be obtained. To make the information meaningful, generally the affected third countries will have to be named (*see* Art. 29 Working Party, Guidelines on transparency under Regulation 2016/679 (WP260), table in Annex).

The storage period (or if not possible, criteria used to determine that period).[890]	Article 13(2), a) GDPR	Article 14(2), a) GDPR
The rights of the data subject to:[891] – access; – rectification; – erasure; – restriction on processing; – objection to processing; and – portability.	Article 13(2), b) GDPR	Article 14(2), c) GDPR
Where the processing is based on consent or explicit consent, the right for the data subject to withdraw consent at any time.[892]	Article 13(2), c) GDPR	Article 14(2), d) GDPR

890. This follows from the principle of storage limitation. Because it is not always possible to determine the exact number of years, reference may be made to the criteria which will be used to determine the period. Storage periods are often influenced by legal retention requirements. Hence, it is permissible for the controller to refer to a legal requirement and the current term imposed (e.g., ten years), as laws may change over time. However, while it is permissible for the controller to not name and exact number of years or only give a current indication, this does not mean it can suffice with vague references such as 'as long as needed for our purposes' or 'as long as necessary'. The data subject must be able to assess with a measure of certainty what the retention period will be for data relating to him/her. For purposes of transparency the controller should differentiate between different purposes and different categories of data involved, where this is appropriate. This also includes the archiving of certain data, beyond active processing (*see* Art. 29 Working Party, Guidelines on transparency under Regulation 2016/679 (WP260), table in Annex).

891. The information should describe the rights and adapt them to the context of the processing scenario(s). It should include a summary of what the data subject must do to exercise the right, and any limitations of the right. The right to object in particular, which applies when the controller is invoking legitimate interests or relying on a public task/mission, must be explicitly brought to the data subject's attention latest at the time of the first communication with/to the data subject, and must be clearly presented clearly and separately from any other information (Art. 21(4) GDPR and Art. 29 Working Party, Guidelines on transparency under Regulation 2016/679 (WP260), table in Annex).

892. This information should also include how consent can be withdrawn practically and should take into account the principle of Art. 7(3) GDPR that consent should be as easy to withdraw as it was to give it (Art. 29 Working Party, Guidelines on transparency under Regulation 2016/679 (WP260), table in Annex). Arts 13 and 14 GDPR specify that this withdrawal does not affect the lawfulness of the processing based on consent before the withdrawal. It deserves recommendation to add this to the information given to the data subject.

The fact that the data subject has a right to lodge a complaint with a supervisory authority.[893]	Article 13(2), d) GDPR	Article 14(2), e) GDPR
Information on whether the data:[894] – must be provided pursuant to a contractual or statutory requirement; – must be provided to enter into a contract; – must be provided obligatorily, and on the potential consequences of a failure to do so.	Article 13(2), e) GDPR	Not required/not relevant
The source from which the personal data originate and whether this came from a publicly available source.[895]	Not required/not relevant	Article 14(2), f) GDPR

893. The information given by the controller should indicate that, in accordance with Art. 77 GDPR, the data subject may lodge the complaint with the supervisory authority competent in the Member State where he/she has his/her habitual residence, and can hence not be forced to follow the (lead) supervisory authority of the controller. In addition the data subject can also lodge a complaint with the supervisory authority of the Member State where he/she has his/her place of work, or where the infringement of the GDPR occurred. This does not prevent the controller from inviting the data subject to first talk to the controller before lodging an official complaint.

894. This item of information is only relevant where the data is being gathered directly with the data subject and where it is up to the data subject to decide what information to provide. In the scenario of Art. 14 GDPR the controller has decided what information to gather. This requirement aims to clarify which fields of data are required by the controller and must be provided, as well as the ground for such obligation and the possible consequences of doing so. For example, an employee who has to provide certain data to its employer so the employer can fulfil his own obligations will have to be informed by the employer on the fact that this data must be provided, and the consequences the employee may suffer if he/she does not provide the data, whether they are based on the employment contract or directly flow from statutory law. Online forms, e.g., to register an account on a given website will need to inform the data subject on what fields are required to register a profile. Conversely, this means that the data subject will also know what fields are optional. Certain fields may also not be strictly required to enter into the contract with the website operator/service provider, but may be needed by that controller. In that case, it must indicate so and the consequences of failing to provide this information, namely the impossibility to register an account. This is without prejudice to what has been said on obligatory consent above, should the controller rely on consent as a legal ground.

895. The specific source should be provided unless this is not possible, e.g., because data from many sources has been combined and is available to the controller without the controller being able to determine which data came from which source, e.g., when the controller obtained the data set from a data broker who had already integrated different sources. In such cases, the controller should at least provide the nature of the sources, whether they are publicly/privately held, the type(s) of organisation(s) involved and the industry/sector (Art. 29 Working Party, Guidelines on transparency under Regulation 2016/679 (WP260), table in Annex and para. 60.

The existence of automated decision-making, including profiling. If this is applicable: meaningful information about the logic used, and the significance and envisaged consequences of the processing for the data subject.[896]	Article 13(2), f) GDPR	Article 14(2), g) GDPR

B. The Timing of the Provision of Information

799. As a general rule, information has to be provided to data subjects at the start of the processing activity. This is required to make the processing fair.[897] Depending on the scenario (data collected with data subject vs. data collected from other sources), slightly different rules apply. The following sections deal with Article 13 and 14 GDPR separately.

1. Article 13 GDPR

800. Article 13 GDPR applies when the data are gathered with the data subject directly. This includes situations where the data subject consciously provides the data (e.g., filling in an online form), but also includes data gathered by the controller by observation (e.g., cameras, sensors, etc.).

896. Arts 13 and 14 GDPR make the meaningful information on the logic involved, the significance and the envisaged consequences of such processing for the data subject obligatory only for cases covered by Art. 22(1) and (4) GDPR, i.e., where the decision-making procedures legal effects for the data subject or similarly significantly affects him or her. However, it is best practice to also add this information in other situations where automated decision-making or profiling is used, e.g., direct marketing (*see* Art. 29 Working Party, Guidelines on Automated individual decision-making and Profiling for the purposes of Regulation 2016/679 (WP251), in particular p. 16 *in fine*). A related discussion is whether this point of information in Art. 13 GDPR implies that there is a right to an explanation of an automated decision after the fact, rather than only information upfront (which is when the information in Art. 13 GDPR is in principle delivered). *See* on these topics: Sandra Wachter, Brent Mittelstadt, Luciano Floridi, 'Why a Right to Explanation of Automated Decision-Making Does Not Exist in the General Data Protection Regulation', *International Data Privacy Law* 2017, Vol. 7(2), 76–99; Andrew D. Selbst, Julia Powles, 'Meaningful information and the right to explanation', *International Data Privacy Law* 2017, Vol. 7(4), 233–242; Gianclaudio Malgieri, Giovanni Comandé, 'Why a Right to Legibility of Automated Decision-Making Exists in the General Data Protection Regulation', *International Data Privacy Law* 2017, Vol. 7(4), 243–265; Isak Mendoza, Lee A. Bygrave, 'The right Not to be Subject to Automated Decisions Based on Profiling, in Tatiana-Eleni Synodinou, Philippe Jougleux, Christiana Markou, Thalia Prastitou (eds.), *EU Internet Law*, 2017, 77–98.

897. Recital 60 GDPR states: 'The principles of fair and transparent processing require that the data subject be informed of the existence of the processing operation and its purposes.' *See also* Art. 29 Working Party, Guidelines on transparency under Regulation 2016/679 (WP260), para. 26.

801. In all such situations, the GDPR requires the information to be provided 'at the time when the personal data are obtained'.[898] This wording clearly indicates that the information cannot be provided *post factum* and hence, it must effectively be provided before or latest at the time that processing commences through collection of the data.

802. How this is done pragmatically speaking depends on the scenario. Filling out an online form, for example, should include a link to the privacy policy/ information notice and a check box to verify and demonstrate that the data subject declares to have read the information. In the case of data collected by observation, e.g., camera monitoring or sensor monitoring in a given area, the information should be provided at the point where the data subject enters that area, e.g., through a sign. For more details on how to provide information in this scenario, please refer to the section on delivery methods below.

2. Article 14 GDPR

803. In the scenario of Article 14 GDPR, where data has been obtained from another source than the data subject him-/herself,[899] different rules apply. This is because of the different setting in which the data are gathered. A controller buying a data set from a data broker, for example, will first need to access said data before it can inform the data subjects involved of any intended processing activities. Hence, it would be impossible to require the controller to inform data subject at the time of collection of the data by the controller.

804. Instead, the principle in this scenario is that the controller must inform the data subject within a **'reasonable period'** after obtaining the data, and **latest within one month**, 'having regard to the specific circumstances in which the personal data are processed'.[900] To determine this reasonable period, the controller has to take into account the reasonable expectations of the data subject, as well as the effects the processing may have on them and their ability to exercise their rights. Whenever possible, the information should be provided well in advance of the one-month time limit in order to make the processing fair and transparent.[901]

805. Hence, one month is an absolute limit, and the controller cannot simply wait until the last moment to provide the information if there is no good reason for doing so.[902] In addition, there are two specific scenarios that may further curtail the general rule:

---

898. Art. 13(1) GDPR.
899. Such as a third-party controller, publicly available sources, data brokers, other data subjects, etc.
900. Art. 14(3), a) GDPR.
901. Recitals 39 and 60 GDPR. *See also* Art. 29 Working Party, Guidelines on transparency under Regulation 2016/679 (WP260), para. 28.
902. Art. 29 Working Party, Guidelines on transparency under Regulation 2016/679 (WP260), para. 28.

(1) In case the data are being used to contact the data subject, the information must be provided latest at the time of the first communication with the data subject.[903] Hence, if a controller decides to contact the data subject the next data after obtaining the data, the reasonable period will be less than one day, and the information will need to be provided latest with that communication. This exception however does not allow to lengthen the one-month period. Hence, if the controller decides to first contact the data subject two months after obtaining the data, it must still provide the information beforehand, i.e., within a reasonable period and at latest within the first month after obtaining the data.

(2) In case the data are disclosed to another recipient,[904] whether a third party or not, the information must be provided to the data subject, latest at the time of first disclosure.[905] Again, this rule cannot be used to circumvent the general rule. Hence, if disclosure is intended only two months after obtaining the data (or is not intended at all), the general rule applies (i.e., within a reasonable period and latest within one month).

C. The General Transparency Requirements

806. As already explained above in regards to the general rules of transparency in communication with the data subject, the GDPR stipulates that all information provided to a data subject, and every communication with a data subject, should:[906]

– be concise and transparent,[907] intelligible,[908] and easily accessible;[909]

---

903. Art. 14(3), b) GDPR.

904. Recipient is a broad term defined in Art. 4(9) GDPR and includes any party that has legal personality, whether a third party or a party linked to the controller (e.g., subsidiary, parent company, joint controller, processor). Art. 29 Working Party, Guidelines on transparency under Regulation 2016/679 (WP260), at fn. 33. Note also that Art. 4(9) GDPR excludes public authorities receiving personal data in the framework of a particular inquiry in accordance with Union or Member State law for its definition of recipients.

905. Art. 29 Working Party, Guidelines on transparency under Regulation 2016/679 (WP260), para. 27.

906. Art. 12(1) GDPR.

907. Concise and transparent means that the controller must present information efficiently and succinctly to avoid information fatigue, including during communications with the data subject. The GDPR-related information must be clearly distinguished from other information such as contractual provisions. In addition, in an online context the controller must use ICT methods available to help present the information in a better way.

908. Intelligible means that the information or communication must be able to be understood by an average member of the intended audience. It should also focus on the consequences of the processing. The controller must make sure that the information is intelligible for the groups of data subjects concerned (Art. 29 Working Party, Guidelines on transparency under Regulation 2016/679 (WP260), paras 9–10).

909. Easily accessible means that the data subject should not have to seek out the information, it should be immediately apparent where this can be found and how it can be accessed. Information may be provided to the data subject directly, by signposting it or providing a link to it, or in the form of answers to questions. The only requirement is that, whatever the practical implementation, it is easy to find and to access (Art. 29 Working Party, Guidelines on transparency under Regulation 2016/679 (WP260), para. 11).

- use clear and plain language;[910]
- when addressing children and other vulnerable people, take these vulnerabilities in account.[911]

807. The same applies to the information provided in the context of Articles 13 and 14 GDPR. In order to make the processing fair towards the data subject, the data subject must be truly informed, and understand the intended processing and its possible consequences.[912] This is especially important where the processing is complex, because of the number of actors involved or the technological complexity.[913] The controller must take appropriate measures to ensure this and if necessary, trial different options before 'going live'.[914]

D. The Delivery Methods

808. Section I.B above already explained that the delivery method of information in the GDPR is not strictly prescribed by the GDPR. In principle, the method of delivery is written, including by electronic means, but may also be provided by other means (e.g., videos, infographics, illustrations), including orally if requested by the data subject and the data subject can be identified by other means. The same applies to information provided under Article 13 and 14 GDPR.

809. In addition, specifically for Articles 13 and 14 GDPR, the GDPR provides that information 'may be provided in combination with standardised icons in order

910. The language used in the information should be plain and clear. This means that information should be provided in as simple a manner as possible, avoiding the use of complex sentences and grammatical structures. Moreover, the information should be concrete and definitive, not abstract, ambivalent or leaving room for different interpretations. Formulations such as 'may', 'might', 'could', 'some', 'possible', 'potential' etc. should be avoided and be replaced by precise indications of the controller's intentions, which helps to make the processing fair towards the data subject. The language should be easy to read, using the active tense rather than the passive tense. Language that is not commonly known, such as legalistic, technical or specialist terminology and formulations should be avoided. When the controller targets different language groups, it must provide accurate and easy-to-understand translations (Art. 29 Working Party, Guidelines on transparency under Regulation 2016/679 (WP260), paras 12–13).
911. In addition to the foregoing requirements, when addressing children or vulnerable people, the controller must ensure that the vocabulary, tone and style of the language used is appropriate to and resonates with children or the category of vulnerable people involved, so that they recognize that the message is directed at them. The controller must assess its audience's likely level of understanding, as is generally the case, i.e., based on an average member of the intended audience (Art. 29 Working Party, Guidelines on transparency under Regulation 2016/679 (WP260), paras 14–16).
912. Recital 39 GDPR: 'Natural persons should be made aware of risks, rules, safeguards and rights in relation to the processing of personal data and how to exercise their rights in relation to such processing.'
913. Recital 58 GDPR.
914. Art. 29 Working Party, Guidelines on transparency under Regulation 2016/679 (WP260), para. 25.

to give an easily visible, intelligible and clearly legible manner a meaningful overview of the intended processing'.[915] Icons may indeed strongly facilitate the understanding of the data subject of the proposed processing and their use should be encouraged,[916] but the controller must take care to not oversimplify, thereby unduly shortening information or presenting it incorrectly.[917]

810. Generally, the most important factor in determining the appropriate delivery method is the idea of facilitating the data subject's ease of access to and comprehension of the information. Article 12(1) GDPR specifies that in relation to Article 13 and 14 GDPR, the controller 'shall take appropriate measures' to provide the information in 'a concise, transparent, intelligible and easily accessible form, using clear and plain language in particular for any information addressed specifically to a child'. Hence, the delivery method will be determined based on the needs of the specific situation to comply with the general transparency requirements, as discussed in section I above.

811. In most situations under Article 13 and 14 GDPR, the controller will want to use written information (whether or not electronically), to be able to demonstrate that it has complied with the information requirements of Article 13/14 GDPR.[918] If oral information is used as a stand-alone option, the controller will need to maintain evidence of this provision.

812. However, in order to accommodate the access of the data subject as well as his or her comprehension of the information, delivery methods may be combined. An example can illustrate: in the context of research, research participants may be informed orally and may be shown a video with information before participating. In addition, they are given written informed on a paper informed consent form, which they have to sign, but the same information is given to them also online, for the data subjects to consult at any time. In this manner, data subjects are given easy-to-understand oral information, but also have the written information to fall back on. Another example could be the use of pre-recorded messages in a telephonic environment, where the data subject is referred to a website with the information in written form should he/she want to consult the information again or can provide his/her e-mail address for the controller to e-mail the relevant information.

---

915. Art. 12(7) GPDR. This article also specifies that 'Where the icons are presented electronically they shall be machine-readable.' For an overview of current approaches and ideas on icons in data protection, *see* Arianna Rossi, Monica Palmirani, 'What's in an Icon? Promises and Pitfalls of Data Protection Iconography', in Ronald Leenes, Dara Hallinan, Serge Gutwirth, Paul de Hert, *Data Protection and Privacy: Data Protection and Democracy*, 2020, 59–92.

916. Some even argue that supervisory authorities should take the use of icons into account in determining fines regardless of whether standardisation exists; *see* Zohar Efroni, Jakob Metzger, Lena Mischau, Marie Schirmbeck, 'Privacy Icons: A Risk-Based Approach to Visualisation of Data Processing', *European Data Protection Law Review* 2019, Vol. 5(3), 352–366, p. 366.

917. *See* on this Christopher Mondschein, 'Some Iconoclastic Thoughts on the Effectiveness of Simplified Notices and Icons for Informing Individuals as Proposed in Article 12 (1) and (7) GDPR', *European Data Protection Law Review* 2016, Vol. 2(4), 507–520, p. 514 and following.

918. This is also part of the accountability obligation.

813. Another way to accommodate the data subject is to manage the amount of information given to the data subject at a given time, which should help the data subject to process this information. This is generally referred to as using a layered approach to the provision of information. Using a layered approach basically means that the data subject is initially provided with only basic information and can decide for himself/herself whether more information is wanted. This helps the controller to be complete, while preventing information fatigue for the data subject.[919]

814. Layers may exist either within a same delivery method, or separate delivery methods may be used in the layered approach:

- In an online context, a layered privacy policy/information notice on a website, exists in providing a complex privacy policy in another form than just plain text. It could for example exist of a text with only headings and summarised information, where the data subject can then show/hide additional information. Another example would be to provide headings in the beginning of the policy as a table of contents (or throughout the policy in a side bar), so the data subject can easily navigate to the sections that are relevant to him/her. Importantly, the information must be consistent and the (navigation of the) layers must not be confusing for the data subject.
- In the context of video surveillance for example, the controller can combine a sign at the entrance to the camera-surveyed zone with a link to information on a website. The information on the sign will be the first layer and rather basic, whereas the information on the website will be complete. The information on the website can then itself be layered as well.[920]
- Taking the research participants as an example again, the first layer of information may be provided orally, with the second layer being the written information being made available on paper and/or online. The written information may then in itself be layered as well. Even written information on paper may be layered, e.g., by providing a table of contents, summaries, etc. The use of pictograms, infographics, and visualisation tools may also constitute a 'layer' in the information.

815. A last method to facilitate the data subject's access to and comprehension of the information required under Article 13/14 GDPR, is to use 'push' and 'pull' notices to provide information in a digital context. Push notices refer to 'just-in-time' ad hoc information provision, e.g., through pop-ups during the process of data collection on a website.[921] Pull notices, on the contrary, refer to the facilitation of access to information by the use of methods such as permission management, privacy dashboards or tutorials, e.g., in the context of an online service for which the data subject has a registered profile. They may also be ad hoc added to the process

919. Art. 29 Working Party, Guidelines on transparency under Regulation 2016/679 (WP260), para. 25.
920. *See* EDPB, Guidelines 3/2019 on processing of personal data through video devices, s. 7, https://edpb.europa.eu/sites/default/files/files/file1/edpb_guidelines_201903_video_devices_en_0.pdf.
921. Art. 29 Working Party, Guidelines on transparency under Regulation 2016/679 (WP260), para. 39.

of the use of the service/website, to facilitate a more natural access to the information and even to provide the data subject with a measure of control over the processing.[922] Push and pull notices will often be a layer of the provision of information, with a full information notice being made available as well for oversight. In order to determine what means are necessary, the controller will need to consider the specific context of the processing and the intended audience of data subjects.

E. Exceptions

816. The GDPR also foresees some limited exceptions to the controller's obligation to provide information on the processing to the data subject. The following sections deal with the exception applicable, depending on the scenario (data collected with the data subject directly vs. data obtained from another source).[923]

1. Article 13 GDPR

817. Article 13 GDPR only foresees one limited exception, namely 'where and insofar as, the data subject already has the information'. The exception may find application in case the data subject signs up for other services with the same controller, e.g., adds/allows another functionality to an existing online service. In such cases the controller can suffice with providing the information the data subject does not already have, (e.g., the purposes and legal basis for the new processing, recipients, retention period) and does not have to provide information again that has remained unchanged (e.g., the identity and contact details of the controller and data protection officer). In practice, controllers will often refer to an existing (general) privacy policy/information notice that has previously been made available to and been accepted by the data subject and will only provide additional information in the privacy policy/information notice for the additional service. The exception is only applicable to the extent that the data subject already had all the other relevant information as prescribed by Article 13 GDPR.[924] It is up to the controller to demonstrate the applicability of this exception under its obligation of accountability.

922. Art. 29 Working Party, Guidelines on transparency under Regulation 2016/679 (WP260), para. 39.
923. Additional exceptions are possible pursuant to Art. 23 of the GDPR but must fulfil the conditions mentioned in that article. *See also* CJEU, Case C-201/14, Judgment of 1 October 2015, Smaranda Bara & Others, ECLI:EU:C:2015:638, https://eur-lex.europa.eu/legal-content/EN/TXT/?uri=CELEX%3A62014CJ0201. The Court held that Arts 10, 11 and 13 of Directive 95/46/EC (currently Arts 13–14 and 23 GDPR), must be interpreted as precluding national measures, such as those at issue in the main proceedings, which allow a public administrative body of a Member State to transfer personal data to another public administrative body and their subsequent processing, without the data subjects having been informed of that transfer or processing.
924. Art. 29 Working Party, Guidelines on transparency under Regulation 2016/679 (WP260), para. 56.

2. Article 14 GDPR

818. Article 14 GDPR provides for a set of exceptions rather than just one. Nonetheless, these exceptions deal only with specific situations and should be interpreted and applied narrowly.[925] The following exceptions may exempt the controller from having to provide information to the data subject, insofar as:[926]

- The data subject already has the information.[927]
- The provision of information **proves impossible**[928] **or would require disproportionate effort,**[929] especially in the context of archiving in the public interest, scientific or historical research or statistical purposes under Article 89 GDPR.[930] In such cases, the controller must take appropriate measures to protect the data subject's rights, freedoms and legitimate interests, such as making the information publicly available.[931]

---

925. Art. 29 Working Party, Guidelines on transparency under Regulation 2016/679 (WP260), para. 57.
926. Note that, like in Art. 13 above, the exceptions only apply insofar as it covers to all the information that must normally be provided. Hence, if it only partially covers the information, the controller will still be held to provide the missing information not covered by an exception.
927. Art. 14(5), a) GDPR.
928. Impossible means impossible. There are no degrees of impossibility, so a data controller relying on this exception must be able to demonstrate the factors that prevent it from informing the data subjects. Typically such factors originate directly from the fact that the data were not gathered with the data subject. If such factors were, over time, to disappear, the controller must immediately inform the data subjects at that point (Art. 29 Working Party, Guidelines on transparency under Regulation 2016/679 (WP260), para. 59 and 62). A specific situation exists where the source of the data cannot be traced. Again, there must be real impossibility, not a mere difficulty. In such cases, Recital 61 GDPR clarifies that general information on the source must be provided, to the extent possible, such as the nature of the sources, whether they are publicly/privately held, the type(s) of organisation(s) involved and the industry/sector (Art. 29 Working Party, Guidelines on transparency under Regulation 2016/679 (WP260), table in Annex and para. 60. All other elements of the information obligation under Art. 14 (1) and (2) GDPR that can be provided by the controller must still be provided as normal, as exceptions only exempt the controller 'insofar as' they apply to the situation at hand, i.e., insofar as they apply to the relevant items of information listed by Art. 14 (1) and (2) GDPR.
929. Disproportionate efforts may exist in situations where, because the data are not gathered with the data subject directly, it proves difficult, yet not impossible to provide the data subjects with information directly. Recital 62 GDPR indicates that this may be the case because of the number of data subjects involved (e.g., very large studies) or the age of the data (old data, hard to track the data subjects). Equally, it may be the case that data subjects are hard to identify, e.g., because data has been anonymised or pseudonymised and direct identifiers have been lost or are not available to the controller. It is relevant in this regard that Art. 11(1) GDPR states that the controller shall not be obliged to obtain additional data for the sole purpose of identifying the data subject for complying with the GDPR. Hence, the controller is not forced to go on a fishing expedition to try and identify data subjects. This exception is not very well defined, but it is clear it must be strictly interpreted and cannot be routinely relied upon (Art. 29 Working Party, Guidelines on transparency under Regulation 2016/679 (WP260), paras 61–62). It is up to the controller to demonstrate that informing the data subjects directly would require a disproportionate effort.
930. Art. 14(5), b) GDPR.
931. Art. 29 Working Party, Guidelines on transparency under Regulation 2016/679 (WP260), para. 64. One may wonder what the difference is what other information notices/privacy policies, which are generally publicly available. The relevant distinction here is that in other cases, the data subject is known and informed directly about this information and where it can be found (e.g., through the process on the website, by e-mail, etc.). In this exceptional case, the information is made available

- In addition, in the context of archiving in the public interest, scientific or historical research or statistical purposes under Article 89 GDPR, if the provision of information would be **likely to render impossible or seriously impair** the achievement of the objectives of the processing.[932] In such cases, the controller must take appropriate measures to protect the data subject's rights, freedoms and legitimate interests, such as making the information publicly available.[933]
- The controller is subject to national or EU law which requires the controller to obtain or disclose the personal data in question and that law provides appropriate protection for the data subject's legitimate interests.[934]
- The personal data must remain confidential under an obligation of professional secrecy regulated by EU or Member State law, including a statutory obligation of secrecy.[935]

F. Special Situations

819. In addition to Articles 13 and 14 GDPR, the data subject also has a right to be informed in the following situations:

- **When changes in the processing occur**: the information requirement does not only exist at the start of the processing but throughout its lifecycle. If the controller intends to change the processing and the information notice in any substantial manner, e.g., change the purpose, or change the identity of the controller, it must communicate this to the data subject, in a manner that the data subject will actually notice, e.g., through a dedicated e-mail on the subject. Such communication should as always be being concise, transparent, intelligible, easily accessible and use clear and plain language.[936]

---

online, but without the data subjects getting a specific pointer. Consequently, it can be expected that many data subjects will be unaware of the information.

932. Art. 14(5), b) GDPR. To rely on this exception the controller will have to demonstrate that the provision of information alone would (likely) nullify the objectives of the processing (Art. 29 Working Party, Guidelines on transparency under Regulation 2016/679 (WP260), para. 65).
933. Art. 29 Working Party, Guidelines on transparency under Regulation 2016/679 (WP260), para. 64.
934. Art. 14(5), c) GDPR. The legal basis relied upon must clearly apply to the controller and require it to obtain or disclose the data. It must also show that it complies with the measures to protect the data subject's legitimate interests laid down by that law. In addition, the controller must make it clear to data subjects that it obtains or discloses personal data in accordance with the law in question, unless it is legally prohibited from doing so. Logically, Art. 14(5), c) GDPR does not apply where the information is directly gathered with the data subject. In such cases Art. 13 GDPR applies (Art. 29 Working Party, Guidelines on transparency under Regulation 2016/679 (WP260), para. 66).
935. Art. 14(5), d) GDPR. The obligation must clearly apply to the controller and must have the consequence that it prohibits the controller from providing all the information that it would normally have to provide to the data subject. If the obligation of secrecy only covers certain elements, then only those elements may be withheld (Art. 29 Working Party, Guidelines on transparency under Regulation 2016/679 (WP260), para. 67).
936. Art. 29 Working Party, Guidelines on transparency under Regulation 2016/679 (WP260), para. 29. Conversely, correcting typos or grammar in the information notice would for example not be substantial enough to trigger the need for a communication to the data subject.

- **When the controller intends to carry out further processing**: both Article 13(3) and Article 14(4) GDPR foresee that the controller must inform the data subject about any further processing it intends to do. What is meant here is compatible further processing, as discussed in §5, section II.B above. In such cases the controller must communicate the new purpose, as well as additional information, as indicated by Articles 13(3) and 14(4) GDPR. This must be in a timely manner, so as to make the processing fair towards the data subject. When relying on another legal ground than consent (Article 6(1), a) GDPR) or an explicit provision of national or EU law (Article 6(1), c) GDPR), information should also be provided on the compatibility analysis.[937]
- **When the processing is carried out by joint controllers**: under Article 26 GDPR, the data subject has a right to be informed about the essence of the arrangement between the different controllers involved, in particular with regards to their respective duties and the modalities for the data subject to exercises his/her rights.
- **When a data breach has occurred that is likely to result in a high risk for the data subject**: Article 34 GDPR obliges the controller, which has undergone a personal data breach, to inform the data subjects without undue delay if such a breach is likely to result in a high risk for the data subjects involved. In such a case the controller has to describe in clear and plain language the nature of the personal data breach, the likely consequences, the measures already taken or proposed by the controller to address the breach (including measures to mitigate the possible adverse effects), and the name and contact details of the Data Protection Officer, or other contact point where the data subject can obtain more information.

III. Right of Access (Article 15 GDPR)

820. Article 15 GDPR provides for a right of access by the data subject. The right of access allows the data subject[938] to proactively contact the controller[939] in an attempt to verify the details and the lawfulness of any processing concerning

937. Art. 29 Working Party, Guidelines on transparency under Regulation 2016/679 (WP260), paras 45–48.
938. As a default, the idea is that the data subject must exercise this right him-/herself. However, since the GDPR does not provide any rules on the subject, general Member State law relating to representation applies in this context. In the same vein, nothing prevents a third party from supporting the data subject in submitting a request. In principle, children can submit their own requests. Requests by the holders of parental responsibility should be allowed where the child authorises this, where the child does not sufficiently understand how to exercise the right, or where it is clearly in the child's best interest to do so (*See also*: Gabriela Zanfir-Fortuna, 'Article 15. Right of access by the data subject', in Christopher Kuner, Lee A. Bygrave, Christopher Docksey (eds.), *The EU General Data Protection Regulation (GDPR) – A commentary*, 2020, pp. 460–461).
939. Art. 15 GDPR foresees the right of access against the controller, but under Art. 28(3), e) GDPR, the processor may also aid in this, depending on the contractual arrangements between them. This must be communicated to the data subject clearly, so he/she knows whom to address. When there are multiple controllers, Art. 26 GDPR requires them to communicate to the data subject who he/she must address to exercise his/her rights.

him/her. In the words of the Court of Justice, the data subject has the right to be 'certain that his personal data are processed in a correct and lawful manner'.[940] The exercise of the right of access should be easy and be able to be done at reasonable intervals, if the data subject so wishes.[941]

821. Under Article 15 GDPR, the data subject has a right to:

- **obtain confirmation** whether or not data on him/her is being processed[942] by the controller;
- **access** to **the data**[943][944] that is being processed;[945]
- if data is being processed, the following **information:**

---

940. CJEU, Case C-553/07, Judgment of 7 May 2009, *Rijkeboer*, ECLI:EU:C:2009:293, para. 49, https://curia.europa.eu/juris/liste.jsf?num=C-553/07&language=en.
941. Recital 63 GDPR.
942. Being processed means that the data is still in one way or another processed by the controller at the time of the data subject's request. It should be reiterated here that processing is a very broad concept under the GDPR, and simple storage of the data may suffice. If however, the data has been deleted (e.g., live video surveillance with footage being deleted every X hours), the controller can respond to an access request (at least for that data), by indicating that no data is still 'being processed' (European Data Protection Board, Guidelines 3/2019 on processing of personal data through video devices, para. 92).
943. Access to the data does not necessarily include access to the document in which the data is contained, and a summary may in certain cases be sufficient. The Court of Justice decided this in a case where applicants for a resident permit, whose application had been rejected and who wanted access to the minute, an internal document in which the reviser of their application explained the decision internally. The applicants only obtained access to the summary of the minute, as well as the accompanying information, as required by data protection law. The Court found that the minute indeed constituted personal data, but reasoned that providing the summary and accompanying information was sufficient, as extending the right of access to that internal document would not serve to protect the data subject's privacy or aid in the protection of his/her data, but would rather constitute a right of access to administrative documents not contained in the data protection legislation (CJEU, Joined Cases C-141/12 and C-372/12, Judgment of 17 July 2014, *YS*, ECLI:EU:C:2014:2081, https://eur-lex.europa.eu/legal-content/en/TXT/?uri=CELEX:62012CJ0141). This position was nuanced by the Court in another case. In Nowak (CJEU, Case C-434/16, Judgment of 20 December 2017, *Nowak*, ECLI:EU:C:2017:99, https://eur-lex.europa.eu/legal-content/en/TXT/?uri=CELEX:62016CJ0434) the Court was tasked with determining whether there is a right of access to exam papers containing not only the exam answers provided by the data subject, but also comments made by the examiner. The Court determined that both categories constituted personal data relating to the data subject taking the exam, and that the data subject has a right of access, 'insofar as' that data is liable to be checked for accuracy and the need for its retention by the controller, i.e., in as far as this is needed to enable the data subject to verify that the data being processed relating to him/her is processed in a correct and lawful manner, and to exercise other data subject rights like rectification and erasure (CJEU, Case C-434/16, *Nowak*, ECLI:EU:C:2017:99, paras 56–57). Hence, in this case the Court allowed full access to the document, but still curtailed it slightly. Notably, there is a case pending before the CJEU which will address this topic once again: CJEU, Case C-487/21, *Österreichische Datenschutzbehörde and CRIF*. The 2022 EDPB draft guidelines reflect this position: Art. 15 cannot be understood as granting the right to only a summary of the data, but at the same time cannot be widened to include all of the documentation in which data may be included. Art. 15 GDPR only grants a right of access to the data undergoing processing, not necessarily to a copy of the complete original documents. European Data Protection Board, Draft Guidelines 01/2022 on data subject rights – Right of access, para. 23, 150.
944. Data in this sense covers many types of data: structure and unstructured, observed and raw data, inferred and derived data, etc. Also explicitly covered is non-structured electronic data such as

- the purposes of the processing;
- the categories of personal data concerned;
- the recipients or categories of recipients;[946]
- the retention period, if possible, or otherwise the criteria used to determine that period;
- the existence of the rights of rectification, erasure, restriction and objection;
- the existence of the right to lodge a complaint with a supervisory authority;
- where the data was not collected with the data subject directly, any available information on their source;
- when the controller is using automated decision-making processes, including profiling, meaningful information about the logical used and the significance and envisioned consequences of such processing, at least in those cases where this produces legal effects for the data subject or similarly significantly affects him or her;[947]
- information on the appropriate safeguards taken to transfer data outside the EEA;

---

recordings of telephone conversations (*See* European Data Protection Board, Draft Guidelines 01/2022 on data subject rights – Right of access, para. 96, 104).

945. This covers data processed in both IT and non IT filing systems (European Data Protection Board, Draft Guidelines 01/2022 on data subject rights – Right of access, para. 123).

946. In *Rijkeboer*, the Court of Justice addressed the question of Mr Rijkeboer, who had requested the city of Rotterdam to notify him of all instances in which data relating to him had been disclosed to third parties in the two years preceding his request. Mr Rijkeboer wished to know the identity of those persons and the content of the data disclosed to them, and in particular, to whom his former address had been disclosed. National rules limited the retention of that information on recipients to one year, while the underlying data on Mr Rijkeboer was of course kept for a much longer period. The CJEU found that the right of access applies not only to the present but also to the past (i.e., the controller must not only list very recent or future recipients, but also past ones), stating that the one-year rule was not a fair balance between the data subject's interests in protecting its privacy and the controller's burden to store that information and leaving it up to the Member State to find a more reasonable balance (CJEU, Case C-553/07, Judgment of 7 May 2009, *Rijkeboer*, ECLI-:EU:C:2009:293, https://curia.europa.eu/juris/liste.jsf?num=C-553/07&language=en). Hence, the controller must also provide information on past recipients. This can be limited in time by national law, but must strike a fair balance. The meaning of 'recipient' here is the same as under Arts 13 and 14 GDPR above, namely as any legal person, public authority, agency or another body, to which the personal data are disclosed (Art. 4(9) GPDR). Note that Art. 4(9) GDPR excludes public authorities receiving personal data in the framework of a particular inquiry in accordance with Union or Member State law for its definition of recipients. Notably, there is a case pending before the Court of Justice, which will address the obligation to disclose the recipients of personal data once again: CJEU, C-154/21, *Österreichische Post AG.*.

947. In analogy to this point under Art. 13 GDPR above, there is a discussion whether this includes the right for an automated decision to be explained. *See* references under footnote 859 above. *See also*: Lee A. Bygrave, 'Article 22. Automated individual decision-making, including profiling', in Christopher Kuner, Lee A. Bygrave, Christopher Docksey (eds.), *The EU General Data Protection Regulation (GDPR) – A commentary*, 2020, p. 538 and references there. *See also* the following arguing for the existence of such a right: Jef Ausloos, Pierre Dewitte, 'Shattering one-way mirrors- data subject access rights in practice', *International Data Privacy Law* 2018, Vol. 8, 1–25, p. 24 and following; Maria Mitjans Serveto, 'Practitioner's corner – Exercising GDPR Data Subjects' Rights: Empirical Research on the Right to Explanation of News Recommender Systems, *European Data Protection Law Review* 2020, 593–601; Max van Drunen, Natali Helberger, Mariella Bastian, 'Know your algorithm: what media organisations need to explain to their users about news personalisation', *International Data Privacy Law* 2019, Vol. 9(4), 220–235. For arguments against the existence of such a right, *see* for example Sandra Wachter, Brent Mittelstadt, Luciano Floridi, 'Why

– obtain a free[948] **copy of the data**[949] undergoing processing, unless this adversely affects the rights and freedoms of others.[950]

822. **The general modalities discussed in section I above apply to the exercise of this right**. This includes that information must be specific, concise, transparent and intelligible and that the exercise of this right must generally be facilitated by the controller. This must in principle be done free of charge and, where data are processed by electronic means, the controller should also provide means for the requests to be made electronically. Requests must be processed without undue delay, within the specified time limits (one month, maximum three).[951] Where appropriate, the controller may even give the data subject direct access to the data in its systems. To this extent, Recital 63 GDPR states that 'Where possible, the controller should be able to provide remote access to a secure system which would provide the data subject with direct access to his or her personal data'. This is however not a strict obligation. If the controller does provide remote access, the security of such a system would be of paramount importance to prevent unauthorised access.[952]

---

a Right to Explanation of Automated Decision-Making Does Not Exist in the General Data Protection Regulation', *International Data Privacy Law* 2017, Vol. 7(2), 76–99; Merle Temme, 'Algorithms and Transparency in View of the New General Data Protection Regulation, *European Data Protection Law Review* 2017, 473–485, p. 481 and following.

948. Art. 12(5) GDPR. However, Art. 15(3) GDPR specifies that for any further copies the controller may charge a reasonable fee based on administrative costs. The rules for excessive requests of Art. 12(5) also apply here. When the data subject requests the copy by electronic means, the controller must provide this in a commonly used electronic form, unless otherwise requested by the data subject (Art. 15(3) GDPR).

949. Obtaining a copy of the data does not necessarily extend to taking a copy of the whole document or file in which the data are held. *See* comments at fn. 937 above. This may in practice impose a document by document extraction of relevant data or redaction of non-relevant data.

950. Recital 63 GDPR clarifies that this includes trade secrets or intellectual property and in particular the copyright protecting the software. However, other examples exist as well. In its guidelines on processing in the context of video devices, the European Data Protection Board indicated that sharing a copy of a video surveillance tape on which others can be identified, may fall under this exception, although the controller must not use this as an excuse, and where possible, implement technical measures to enable access and the right to a copy (European Data Protection Board, Guidelines 3/2019 on processing of personal data through video devices, para. 94). *See also* the guidance on this in European Data Protection Board, Draft Guidelines 01/2022 on data subject rights – Right of access, paras 166–172.

951. Notably, the EDPB highlights in its 2022 draft guidance relating to the right of access that an extension to three months should be the exception, not the rule, and only applies to complex requests. The mere fact that complying with the request requires a great effort does not automatically make the request complex. The EDPB however lists some factors that may justify the complexity of a request, which would justify an extension: the amount of data concerned, the difficulty in retrieving information because of how the data is stored or processed, the need to redact information and the situation in which the data requires further work in order to be intelligible for the data subject. In addition, the fact that the controller receives a large number of requests does not automatically trigger an extension either. This is only the case when an extraordinary event temporarily overwhelms the controller, not when the controller is structurally not capable to handle the amount of requests it receives. *See* European Data Protection Board, Draft Guidelines 01/2022 on data subject rights – Right of access, paras 160–162.

952. *See* on this Andrew Cormack, 'Is the Subject Access Right Now Too Great a Threat to Privacy?', *European Data Protection Law Review 2016*, 15–27, p. 26 and following.

823. Recently, the EDPB published draft guidelines on the right to access.[953] These guidelines are not yet final at the time of writing, but it is still useful to discuss some relevant elements here, as the guidelines will likely not be changed materially upon final adoption and they provide significant guidance affecting the exercise of the right of access. With regards to providing the information required by Article 15(1), a) to h) (the elements of which are described in detail above), the EDPB has clarified that controllers may need to provide tailored information to the requesting data subject to meet their information obligation, rather than simply referring to the same general information that can be found in the applicable privacy policies/information notices. Some pieces of information, e.g., the recipients of the data, may change depending on the data subject. Moreover, the controller must specify other elements, e.g., the specific purposes pursued with regards to the requesting data subject. A mere reference to the general purposes of the controller set out in the privacy policy is not sufficient.[954] General information may only be used if it overlaps with the tailored information that should be provided. In addition, in order to provide meaningful access in a concise, transparent, intelligible and easily accessible form using clear and plain language, the EDPB states that the controller may need to accompany access to certain data, such as log files or raw data, with additional information to make the data to which access is provided intelligible for the data subject.[955] This obligation seems to constitute a material extension of Article 15 GDPR, which in itself does not contain an explicit obligation to explain personal data.

824. In those same guidelines, the EDPB also reminds controllers that no formal requirements exist to submit an access request. This means controllers cannot refuse an access request because the data subject does not indicate the legal basis of its request or correctly references the right of access.[956] Equally, the data subject should not have to motivate why they want to exercise their right, meaning controllers should also not ask or assess why the data subject is submitting the request, but only what they are requesting.[957] However, despite there being no formalities, the EDPB also clarifies that a controller is not obliged to act on requests sent to a random or incorrect address or to any communication channel that is clearly not intended to receive requests regarding data subject's rights. This includes e-mails sent to the controller's employees where the employee in question may not be involved in the processing of requests coming from data subjects (e.g., drivers, cleaning staff). The controller can consider such requests ineffective, assuming the

953. European Data Protection Board, Draft Guidelines 01/2022 on data subject rights – Right of access, version for public consultation adopted on 18 January 2022, https://edpb.europa.eu/system/files/2022-01/edpb_guidelines_012022_right-of-access_0.pdf.
954. For more information *see* European Data Protection Board, Draft Guidelines 01/2022 on data subject rights – Right of access, para. 110 and further (s. 4.3 of the draft guidelines).
955. European Data Protection Board, Draft Guidelines 01/2022 on data subject rights – Right of access, para. 138 and further.
956. European Data Protection Board, Draft Guidelines 01/2022 on data subject rights – Right of access, para. 50, 52.
957. European Data Protection Board, Draft Guidelines 01/2022 on data subject rights – Right of access, para. 13.

controller has provided the data subject with and appropriate communication channel.[958] However, this does not detract from the controller's general obligation to deal with requests, which means that even if the data subject uses a different communication channel to the preferred channel indicated by the controller, the controller should in principle handle such a request.[959] The controller should generally undertake all reasonable efforts to make sure that the exercise of data subject rights is facilitated, i.e., that requests are dealt with appropriately, even if sent through another communication channel than the preferred one. This is especially the case where a request is sent to an employee who deals with the data subject's affairs on a daily basis.[960] Mechanisms to improve internal communications between employees for such matters should be implemented.[961]

825. In addition to what was already described above, the draft EDBP guidelines also provide ample details on the proportionality assessment of identification of the requesting person, in particular providing some nuance on when it is appropriate to ask for a copy of the person's ID card[962] and on requests made through third parties.[963] Finally, the EDPB clarifies that, where the data subject clarifies that the request is based on sectorial or national legislation providing specific access rights in addition to the GDPR, the controller may be required to provide separate replies. This would in no way override the obligations under the GDPR, at least in as far as there are no restrictions set out by the applicable law.[964]

826. Since Article 15 provides no express exceptions, the controller will therefore always have to grant access requests, unless it does not process personal data on the data subject,[965] or the request is manifestly unfounded or excessive. Even in those cases, whoever, the controller will have to provide the data subject with an answer to that extent.

827. In its 2022 draft guidelines, the EDPB has stressed that a request can only be considered as manifestly unfounded if the requirements of Article 15 GDPR are clearly and obviously not met when applying an objective approach. Since there are so few requirements the scope of this exception will be extremely limited. Even if

958. European Data Protection Board, Draft Guidelines 01/2022 on data subject rights – Right of access, para. 54.
959. European Data Protection Board, Draft Guidelines 01/2022 on data subject rights – Right of access, para. 53.
960. European Data Protection Board, Draft Guidelines 01/2022 on data subject rights – Right of access, para. 53, 55.
961. European Data Protection Board, Draft Guidelines 01/2022 on data subject rights – Right of access, para. 56.
962. European Data Protection Board, Draft Guidelines 01/2022 on data subject rights – Right of access, para. 69 and further (s. 3.3 of the guidelines).
963. European Data Protection Board, Draft Guidelines 01/2022 on data subject rights – Right of access, para. 79 and further (s. 3.4 of the guidelines).
964. Restrictions would have to comply with Art. 23 GDPR in order to modify the application of the GDPR. *See* §8, s. X below on the restriction of data subject rights allowed by Art. 23 GDPR and the conditions for such restrictions.
965. Or does not do so any more, e.g., because the data have been deleted. In that case the controller should inform the data subject thereof.

a request relates to data not covered by the GDPR, the EDPB would consider it not to be manifestly unfounded but simply not subject to the GDPR and therefore not an Article 15 GDPR request at all. In addition, a request regarding processing activities not carried out by the controller would also not be manifestly unfounded but would require the controller to confirm that these data are not processed by the controller.[966] Improper or unobjective language (e.g., emotional language, accusations, etc.) in any case neither suffice to render a request manifestly unfounded, nor does the fact that the data subject has in the past submitted manifestly unfounded or excessive requests.[967] This leaves little room, if any at all, for the application of the concept of manifestly unfounded.

828. For a request to be considered excessive, it must be assessed if the data subject is making repetitive requests at unreasonable intervals, depending on the specific circumstances of the request.[968] The mere fact that it would take the controller a vast amount of time and effort to provide the requested information will neither in itself render a request excessive, nor would it be considered excessive to request access to all data processed.[969] Notably, the guideline clearly states that the controller cannot rely on a proportionality argument to justify not complying with the right of access.[970] In that regard it is important to mention Recital 63, which states that, where the controller processes a large quantity of information concerning the data subject, the controller may, before granting access, request that the data subject specifies the information or processing activities to which the request relates. However, if the data subject then requests access to all data, the controller must in principle still grant this request.[971] The 2022 draft EDPB guidelines clarify that in fact an access request should always be understood as a request for all data, unless explicitly requested otherwise by the data subject. Only when the controller processes a lot of data on the data subject and there is a risk that the data subject would be confronted with an overflow of information in which they are not really interested, may the controller ask the data subject to specify the information or processing to which the request relates before the information is delivered. In any case the

966. European Data Protection Board, Draft Guidelines 01/2022 on data subject rights – Right of access, para. 173–178.
967. European Data Protection Board, Draft Guidelines 01/2022 on data subject rights – Right of access, para. 178.
968. European Data Protection Board, Draft Guidelines 01/2022 on data subject rights – Right of access, para. 179 and further.
969. In addition, the EDPB also states that the following does not render the request excessive: the fact that no reasons are given by the data subject or that the controller regards the request as meaningless, the use of improper or impolite language, or the fact that the data subject intends to use the data to file further claims against the controller (European Data Protection Board, Draft Guidelines 01/2022 on data subject rights – Right of access, para. 187).
970. European Data Protection Board, Draft Guidelines 01/2022 on data subject rights – Right of access, para. 164.
971. Gabriela Zanfir-Fortuna, ‘Article 15. Right of access by the data subject’, in Christopher Kuner, Lee A. Bygrave, Christopher Docksey (eds.), *The EU General Data Protection Regulation (GDPR) – A commentary*, 2020, pp. 465–466.

controller must try to facilitate the process in such circumstances by e.g., employing self-service online tools or other technical measures to support the data subject's access to the information that is relevant to them.[972] The principle still stands however that the data subject can insist on getting access to everything. Request that may be considered excessive are those made with malicious intent to harass the controller or cause disruption, or when the individual data subject offers to withdraw it in return for a benefit, or where the request is unreasonably repetitive taking into account the circumstances.[973] Controllers must be able to demonstrate that the request truly is excessive, which means they should document that decision.

829. Given the foregoing, there is quite little leeway for a controller to escape the application of the right of access. A last relevant consideration however, is that Recital 63 GDPR generally states that the exercise of the right to access 'should not adversely affect the rights or freedoms of others, including trade secrets or intellectual property and in particular the copyright protecting the software',[974] although these considerations must not lead to a full refusal to provide information to the data subject. In other words, there seems to be some limited leeway to be explored by a controller to restrict the information given to the data subject, as well as with regards to the provision of a copy.[975] For what concerns the provision of a copy, this is explicitly repeated in Article 15(4) GDPR. The EDPB agrees that this also covers access through other means.[976] However, the controller must not use this as an excuse and implement the necessary measures to try and avoid existing issues in an effort to facilitate the right of access.[977] In its 2022 draft guidance on the right to access, the EDBP provides some guidance on how to balance the competing interests in this case. As a principle, where a limitation applies, the controller should redact the protected information instead of rejecting to provide a copy of the personal data. However, where it is impossible to find a solution of reconciliation, the controller has to decide in a next step which of the conflicting rights and freedoms prevails and whether access should be given or not. If the controller decides to restrict access, or generally does not provide full access (i.e., provides access but with redaction of data), it has to provide information the data subject of the reasons

---

972. European Data Protection Board, Draft Guidelines 01/2022 on data subject rights – Right of access, para. 35.
973. European Data Protection Board, Draft Guidelines 01/2022 on data subject rights – Right of access, para. 179 and further. As relevant circumstances, the EDPB mentions: how often the data is altered, the nature of the data, the purposes of the processing and whether the subsequent requests concern the same type of information or processing activities or different ones (European Data Protection Board, Draft Guidelines 01/2022 on data subject rights – Right of access, para. 183).
974. As clarified by the EDPB, the economic interests of a company are not enough to justify this (European Data Protection Board, Draft Guidelines 01/2022 on data subject rights – Right of access, para. 168).
975. *See also* CJEU, Joined Cases C-141/12 and C-372/12, Judgment of 17 July 2014, *YS*, ECLI-:EU:C:2014:2081, https://eur-lex.europa.eu/legal-content/en/TXT/?uri=CELEX:62012CJ0141, and CJEU, Case C-434/16, Judgment of 20 December 2017, *Nowak*, ECLI:EU:C:2017:99, https://eur-lex.europa.eu/legal-content/en/TXT/?uri=CELEX:62016CJ0434, and comments at fn. 937 above.
976. European Data Protection Board, Draft Guidelines 01/2022 on data subject rights – Right of access, para. 167.
977. This follows from Art. 12(2) GDPR. *See also*: European Data Protection Board, Guidelines 3/2019 on processing of personal data through video devices, para. 94.

and do so without delay, i.e., within one month. The explanation has to clearly refer the concrete circumstances and reasons for restricting the access, so that the data subject can assess whether to accept this or take action against this refusal or limitation. In that explanation or answer, the controller has to mention the possibility for the data subject to lodge a complaint with a supervisory authority (Article 77 GDPR) or to seek a juridical remedy (Article 79 GDPR).[978]

IV. Right of Rectification (Article 16 GDPR)

830. Article 16 GDPR provides for the data subject's right to rectification. This right is inherently linked to the right of access. Once a data subject has accessed its data with a controller, he/she can not only verify the lawfulness of the processing, but also the completeness and accuracy of the data relating to him/her. This may be of considerable importance, because incorrect or incomplete information may have real consequences for the data subject, e.g., an incorrect shipping address will lead to good not being obtained, an incorrect bank account to money not being received, an incomplete profile to the data subject missing out on certain benefits, etc.[979] The exercise of the right of rectification is effectively the data subject's active counterpart of the controller's obligation under the principle of accuracy.

831. For this reason, Article 16 states that 'the data subject shall have the right to obtain from the controller without undue delay the rectification of inaccurate personal data concerning him or her'. Moreover, in the situation where the data is not inaccurate, but rather incomplete, 'the data subject shall have the right to have incomplete personal data completed, including by means of providing a supplementary statement'. When completing the data, the purposes of the processing must be taken into account, so as not to provide too much information.

832. It should be pointed out that the right of rectification is directly linked to the data processing principle of accuracy, as this right enables data subjects to ensure and verify that the controller respects this principle. As explained above in §5, section IV on accuracy, information revealing personal data, such as opinions, decisions or advice, may be accurate information, even though they are (or have turned out to be) factually incorrect or no longer represent the opinion of the person who initially expressed them.[980] An example mentioned in §5, section IV above as well is a medical report where the diagnosis has turned out to be incorrect. While

978. *See* European Data Protection Board, Draft Guidelines 01/2022 on data subject rights – Right of access, paras 166–172.
979. The Court of Justice has also consistently emphasised the importance of this right. *See* for example CJEU, Case C-434/16, Judgment of 20 December 2017, *Nowak*, ECLI:EU:C:2017:99, para. 49, https://eur-lex.europa.eu/legal-content/en/TXT/?uri=CELEX:62016CJ0434 and CJEU, Case C-362/14, Judgment of 6 October 2015, *Schrems*, ECLI:EU:C:2015:650, para. 95, https://eur-lex.europa.eu/legal-content/EN/TXT/?uri=CELEX%3A62014CJ0362.
980. *See* on the difficult question of when incorrect or imprecise data is inaccurate under the GDPR: Frederik Zuiderveen Borgesius, Dara Hallinan, 'Opinions can be incorrect (in our opinion)! On data

this makes the personal data at issue wrong, it does not necessarily make them inaccurate as that was the doctor's finding at the time and may even have been correct given the state of the art at that time. In any case the incorrect diagnosis and related findings could still be of medical value for follow-up treatment. Hence, rectification in the form of changing the data may not be appropriate in such cases. Where the original data nonetheless does not accurately represent the current situation however, e.g., because the diagnosis remains inaccurate and would not have been arrived at under the current state of the art, a right to rectification will still apply. In such cases, however, the data can be said to be incomplete rather than inaccurate, and hence it is more appropriate to supplement the report than to retroactively change the initial findings.

833. **The general modalities discussed in section I above apply to the exercise of this right.** This includes that the exercise of this right must be facilitated by the controller, in principle free of charge and, where data are processed by electronic means the controller should also provide means for the requests to be made electronically. Requests must be processed without undue delay, within the specified time limits (one month, maximum three). Where appropriate, the controller may even give the data subject direct access and allow him/her to make the rectifications directly.

834. Importantly, where the controller rectifies any data (or allows a data subject to directly rectify or supplement data), Article 19 GDPR requires the controller to communicate this to 'each recipient to whom the personal data have been disclosed, unless this proves impossible or requires disproportionate effort'.[981] Article 19 GDPR does not detail what information must be provided to the recipients, but at least the fact of the rectification should be communicated. Moreover, if the data subject so requests, the controller must inform the data subject about those recipients.[982] The idea of this provision is to enable the exercise of the right of rectification across different relevant controllers more easily. Forwarding the fact that

---

protection law's accuracy principle', *International Data Privacy Law* 2020, Vol 10(1), 1–10; Jiahong Chen, 'The Dangers of Accuracy: Exploring the Other Side of the Data Quality Principle', *European Data Protection Law Review* 2018, Vol. 4(1), 36–52.

981. In its Judgement *Breyer*, the Court of Justice clarified that disproportionate effort can be present 'in terms of time, cost and manpower' (CJEU, C-582/14, Judgment of 19 October 2016, *Breyer*, ECLI:EU:C:2016:779, para. 46, https://eur-lex.europa.eu/legal-content/en/TXT/?uri=CELEX:62014CJ0582).

982. As already indicated above, the Court of Justice considered it essential for a data subject to be informed about the recipients of its data to be able to effectively exercise his or her rights (CJEU, Case C-553/07, Judgment of 7 May 2009, *Rijkeboer*, ECLI:EU:C:2009:293, paras 53–54, https://curia.europa.eu/juris/liste.jsf?num=C-553/07&language=en). Hence, the data subject must be informed about recipients. Note that Arts 13/14 and 15 GDPR allow the controller in limited cases to limit itself to informing the data subject about the categories of recipients, rather than naming recipients. The controller may even suffice with this in its main documentation, i.e., the record of processing activities under Art. 30 GDPR. There is a clear tension between this and the text of Art. 19 GDPR to specify 'each recipient'. Hence, a situation could exist where a controller cannot notify a recipient because it does not have the means to identify all recipients. The question is then whether the controller must still inform the data subject about those recipients. It is this author's position that under its accountability obligation, the controller must keep track of all recipients by

information has been rectified might lead to the recipients also updating their information or taking contact with the data subject, if the rectification is also relevant in that context, so the data subject does not have to introduce multiple requests. At the same time, it also provides the data subject with a measure of control, as he/she can then reach out to those controllers-recipients, if he/she so wishes. In addition, Article 19 GDPR also enables the data subject to an extent to pick and choose from the right to rectification, erasure and restriction, depending on the circumstances. For example, where a data subject requests the rectification of old data with the controller to whom he/she initially provided the data, it may want all recipients of that old data to erase the data, where those recipients no longer need that data, or to restrict their processing of it, where those rights apply, depending on the circumstances. A proactive controller looking to facilitate the data subject's exercise of his/her rights, could decide to include such information in the notification to the recipients, so the data subject does not have to introduce erasure requests with all the recipients. For more information on the interdependencies between these rights, please consult the sections below on the right to erasure and the right to rectification and their respective scopes of application.

V. Right to Erasure ('Right to Be Rorgotten') (Article 17 GDPR)

A. *Introduction*

835. Article 17 of the GDPR contains probably the most (in)famous right of the GDPR, namely the right to erasure, referred to, both in literature and in the GDPR itself as the 'right to be forgotten'.[983] In this context, the Court of Justice's 2014 landmark case *Google Spain*[984] must be mentioned, which definitely fuelled the debate about a 'right to be forgotten' while the GDPR's text was not yet finalised.

836. In *Google Spain*, the question at issue was whether Google could be considered a data controller of its indexing activities, based on which the search results linked to a given query are displayed, and whether the data subject rights contained in the Data Protection Directive (right to object and right to erasure) could oblige Google to delete items from this list of results. In the proceedings leading to this case before the Court of Justice, a Spanish national, Mr Gonzalez, wanted the erasure of certain search results displayed when one would make a search on the basis of his name, namely the link to a newspaper article, wherein it was indicated that, years prior, he had undergone a procedure of forced recovery of social security debts. Because Mr Gonzalez had since become fully solvent, the information now

name, even if in some circumstances it can limit the disclosure of recipients to categories (Art. 13/14, Art. 15 GDPR). The controller must still have this information available and should be able to communicate all recipients to the data subject, also those who it could not notify, or notification of which would have required disproportionate effort.

983. For a detailed analysis of the right to erasure and its function, *see* Jef Ausloos, *The Right to Erasure in EU Data Protection Law*, 2020.

984. CJEU, Case C-131/12, Judgment of 13 May 2014, *Google Spain*, ECLI:EU:C:2014:317, https://eur-lex.europa.eu/legal-content/EN/TXT/?uri=CELEX%3A62012CJ0131.

seemed fully irrelevant and, while no longer having a value to the general public, continued to cause considerable damage in Mr Gonzalez's life.

837. The Court found that indeed, Mr Gonzalez should have a right to obtain from Google the delisting of the irrelevant search items, however, without touching upon the newspaper's right to keep the content online. Only the link to the content was cut. According to the Court, Google, as a controller of its indexing activities, plays an important role in the diffusion of information on the Internet. Hence, in relation to this processing activity the data subject may use a right to object in specific situations and may hence request erasure of results when these are no longer relevant. The Court also specified that, as a rule, the data subject's rights override not only the economic interest of Google, but also the interest of the general public in having access to that information when making a search with the data subject's name, although some exceptions to this principle were introduced as well (e.g., when the data subject is a public figure or when there is a specific public interest to know things such as in the case of serious criminal convictions, etc.).[985]

838. The *Google Spain* case is often referred to as a landmark case in relation to the 'right to be forgotten'. Strictly speaking, however, the case did not deal with the right to be forgotten, as it did not touch upon the question whether the newspaper had to delete the article in question, which was damaging the data subject years after it was relevant. Instead *Google Spain* only addressed the search engine's role in linking to this irrelevant content.[986] *Google Spain* was however undoubtedly a landmark case, both in relation to the territorial application of EU data protection law, and because it declared the existence of a right to obtain 'delisting'/dereferencing' of irrelevant search results from search engine operators as a specific application of existing data subject rights (right to object and right to erasure), where a query is carried out on the basis of the data subject's name. While the right to obtain 'delisting'/dereferencing' can be considered a part of the larger concept of a 'right to be forgotten', it is by no means synonymous with the broader concept.[987]

---

985. The application of this remains difficult in practice. *See* on this European Data Protection Board, Guidelines 5/2019 on the criteria of the Right to be Forgotten in the search engines cases under the GDPR (part 1), https://edpb.europa.eu/sites/default/files/files/file1/edpb_guidelines_201905_rtbfsearchengines_afterpublicconsultation_en.pdf. There was also a long-standing discussion about whether the delisting of a search result by name was to be applied by the search engine on all versions of its search engine, i.e., whether Google Inc. (now Google LLC) could be required to delist the result not only in the EU, but also globally, including the google.com domain. On this question, the CJEU ruled that the right to delist is limited to the EU, however provided that Google effectively prevents, or at least seriously discourages people in the EU to gain access to the results on the google.com domain or any other domain where the delisting has not been implemented (CJEU, Case C-507/17, Judgment of 24 September 2019, *Google*, ECLI:EU:C:2019:772, https://eur-lex.europa.eu/legal-content/en/TXT/?uri=CELEX:62017CJ0507).

986. Herke Kranenborg, 'Article 17. Right to erasure ('right to be forgotten')', in Christopher Kuner, Lee A. Bygrave, Christopher Docksey (eds.), *The EU General Data Protection Regulation (GDPR) – A commentary*, 2020, p. 479.

987. *See* for a pertinent discussion on the broader concept and on how to integrate the right to delist: Oskar Gstrein, The Cascade of Decaying Information: Putting the 'Right to be Forgotten' in Perspective, Computer and Telecommunications Law Review, Vol. 21, No. 2, 2015, pp. 40–48; *see* on

839. Hence, the findings of *Google Spain* should be primarily linked to the specific context of a request for 'delisting'/dereferencing' against a search engine. It should be noted, however, that within that context, the findings of *Google Spain* remain relevant, since Article 17 GDPR allows for the continued existence of a 'right to delist/dereference' after the entry into force of the GDPR. Hence, it remains possible under the GDPR to request erasure of search results from a search engine operator. In late 2019, the EDPB even issued guidance on the application of Article 17 GDPR in this specific context.[988]

840. It would be outside of the scope of this monograph to discuss the various aspects of a conceptual right to be forgotten, or to provide a detailed analysis of the legislative process leading to the current Article 17 GPDR. It suffices to indicate that some elements, including the right to delist, have been incorporated in the right to erasure of Article 17 GDPR. Hence, Article 17 GDPR is referred to in the GDPR as 'Right to erasure ('right to be forgotten')'. Recital 65 GDPR clarifies, however, that the data subject only has 'a "right to be forgotten" where the retention of such data infringes this Regulation or Union or Member State law to which the controller is subject'. This shows that the 'right to be forgotten' under the GDPR must be understood as limited to situations where retention of data infringes or would infringe specific EU or national (data protection) rules, or rules and principles (such as storage limitation or purpose limitation/specification) of the GDPR. Article 17 GDPR specifies which rules are within scope of the 'right to be forgotten' in EU law, the consequences of granting the right, and applicable exceptions.

841. Hence, to know what the 'right to be forgotten' effectively means under the GDPR, it suffices to focus on the substantive rules contained in Article 17 GDPR, which will further only be referred to as the right to erasure, to avoid terminological confusion. That is also the primary term used in Article 17 GPDR itself.

B. Scope of Application

842. The right to erasure applies in a limited number of scenarios, namely where:[989]

- the personal data are no longer necessary in relation to the purposes for which they were collected or otherwise processed;

---

the origins of the right to be forgotten: Alessandro Mantelero, 'The EU Proposal for a General Data Protection Regulation and the roots of the 'right to be forgotten'', *Computer Law & Security review* 2013, Vol. 29(3), 229–235.

988. European Data Protection Board, Guidelines 5/2019 on the criteria of the Right to be Forgotten in the search engines cases under the GDPR (part 1).

989. Art. 17(1) GDPR.

- the data subject withdraws consent on which the processing is based and there is no other legal ground for the processing';[990]
- the data subject successfully objects to the processing pursuant to Article 21(1) and there are no overriding legitimate grounds for the processing, or the data subject objects to the processing pursuant to Article 21(2);[991]
- the personal data have been unlawfully processed;
- the personal data have to be erased for compliance with a legal obligation in Union or Member State law to which the controller is subject;
- the personal data have been collected in relation to the offer of information society services referred to in Article 8(1).[992]

When exercising the right to erasure, the data subject should indicate which ground is applicable.

843. **The general modalities discussed in section I above apply to the exercise of this right.** This includes that the exercise of this right must be facilitated by the controller, in principle free of charge and, where data are processed by electronic means the controller should also provide means for the requests to be made electronically. Requests must be processed without undue delay, within the specified time limits (one month, maximum three).

C. *Consequences of Granting the Right*

844. If the controller finds that a right to erasure applies, the controller must carry out this erasure without undue delay.[993] While this may seem straightforward, the controller must ensure erasure of the data on all its systems used to process the data, which may at times pose problems, e.g., where technology makes erasure difficult or impossible (e.g., blockchain) or where data relating to a given data subject cannot be erased without also erasing other data (e.g., tapes).

845. In addition to internally deleting the data, Article 17(2) GDPR also requires the controller to take reasonable steps, including technical measures, 'to inform controllers which are processing personal data that the data subject has requested the

990. This could be the case when the controller is processing the same set of data for different purposes and on different legal grounds. This is possible and deletion of this data cannot be required if it is still needed for processing activities where the controller still has a legal ground to continue processing.
991. Art. 21(2) deals with the specific case of direct marketing on the basis of legitimate interests (Art. 6(1), f) GDPR) or for a public mission (Art. 6(1), e) GDPR), in which case the data subject can always object, without having to state reasons. Art. 21(1) GDPR deals with the general scenario, where the data subject objects to a processing on the basis of legitimate interests (Art. 6(1), f) GDPR) or for a public mission (Art. 6(1), e) GDPR), for grounds relating to his or her particular situation. In such cases, the controller can refuse the objection in a limited number of cases (*see* §8, s. VIII on the right to object below).
992. In this case the data have to be erased upon simple request. Recital 65 GDPR clarifies that the data subject can also exercise this right when he/she is no longer a child.
993. Art. 17(1) GDPR.

erasure by such controllers of any links to, or copy or replication of, those personal data'. The controller only has to do this if the data subject so requests and, in determining the reasonable steps, the controller may take into account the available technology and the cost of implementation. The fact that the data subject must request this notification shows that the GDPR has considered the situation where the data subject wants certain data deleted with one controller, but not with another. Depending on the situation, the data subject may exercise different rights with different controllers, with regards to the same items of personal data, such as rectification, erasure or restriction of processing. For this reason, Article 17(2) GDPR is not automatically launched.

846. In addition to Article 17(2) GDPR, Article 19 GDPR also applies when the controller grants a request for erasure. As discussed above, Article 19 GDPR requires the controller to communicate the fact of erasure to 'each recipient to whom the personal data have been disclosed, unless this proves impossible or requires disproportionate effort'.[994] Article 19 GDPR does not detail what information must be provided to the recipients, but at least the fact of the erasure should be communicated. Moreover, if the data subject so requests, the controller must inform the data subject about those recipients.[995] In the context of erasure, it will be important that the controller provides the data subject with the list of recipients before communicating the fact of erasure to the recipients themselves, so as to provide that some recipients proactively erase data that was actually still needed, leading to problems for the data subject. Of course, a proactive controller looking to facilitate the data subject's exercise of his/her rights, may adapt the communication to the recipients to indicate that the data subject does not want erasure with those recipients (but e.g., restriction of processing, see section VI below).

---

994. In its Judgement *Breyer*, the Court of Justice clarified that disproportionate effort can be present 'in terms of time, cost and manpower' (CJEU, C-582/14, Judgment of 19 October 2016, *Breyer*, ECLI-:EU:C:2016:779, para. 46, https://eur-lex.europa.eu/legal-content/en/TXT/?uri=CELEX:62014CJ0582).

995. As already indicated above, the Court of Justice considered it essential for a data subject to be informed about the recipients of its data to be able to effectively exercise his or her rights (CJEU, Case C-553/07, Judgment of 7 May 2009, *Rijkeboer*, ECLI:EU:C:2009:293, paras 53–54, https://curia.europa.eu/juris/liste.jsf?num=C-553/07&language=en). Hence, the data subject must be informed about recipients. Note that Arts 13/14 and 15 GDPR allow the controller in limited cases to limit itself to informing the data subject about the categories of recipients, rather than naming recipients. The controller may even suffice with this in its main documentation, i.e., the record of processing activities under Art. 30 GDPR. There is a clear tension between this and the text of Art. 19 GDPR to specify 'each recipient'. Hence, a situation could exist where a controller cannot notify a recipient because it does not have the means to identify all recipients. The question is then whether the controller must still inform the data subject about those recipients. It is this author's position that under its accountability obligation, the controller must keep track of all recipients by name, even if in some circumstances it can limit the disclosure of recipients to categories (Art. 13/14, Art. 15 GDPR). The controller must still have this information available and should be able to communicate all recipients to the data subject, also those who it could not notify, or notification of which would have required disproportionate effort.

D. Exceptions

847. In contrast with the foregoing data subject rights, Article 17 GDPR provides for an explicit list of exceptions, i.e., cases where the controller can, despite the applicability of a ground for erasure, still refuse to grant this erasure. Exceptions exist because deleting personal data is a very permanent action and in many cases such data cannot be gathered again. Hence, it may in some limited circumstances be warranted that the controller nonetheless maintains the data for as long as there is an overriding reason to do so.

848. The GDPR defines five overriding reasons to resist a valid erasure request, namely where the continued processing is necessary:[996]

(1) for exercising the right of freedom of expression and information;[997]
(2) for compliance with a legal obligation under Union or Member State law to which the controller is subject or for the performance of a task carried out in the public interest or in the exercise of official authority vested in the controller, which requires the continued processing;[998]
(3) for reasons of public interest in the area of public health in accordance with points (h) and (i) of Article 9(2) as well as Article 9(3) GDPR;[999]
(4) for archiving purposes in the public interest, scientific or historical research purposes or statistical purposes in accordance with Article 89(1) GDPR,

---

996. Art. 17(3) GDPR.

997. A data subject may for example request from a search engine that certain search results are deleted because they are no longer relevant. If the request is valid, the search engine, as a controller, must in principle erase the results. However, as indicated in *Google Spain*, particular reasons may exist to refuse a valid request, namely when the continued availability of those results is particularly relevant with regards to the public's right to be informed. A similar reasoning is applied by Art. 17 GDPR, also with regards to erasure requests which would have the effect of curtailing the freedom of expression. *See* on this also European Data Protection Board, Guidelines 5/2019 on the criteria of the Right to be Forgotten in the search engines cases under the GDPR (part 1), pp. 11–12.

998. An example of this was provided in the CJEU's *Manni* ruling (CJEU, Case C-398/15, Judgment of 9 March 2017, *Manni*, ECLI:EU:C:2017:197, https://curia.europa.eu/juris/liste.jsf?language=en&num=C-398/15). In this case, the Court of Justice had to answer the question whether a right of erasure could be invoked with regard to certain personal data contained in a public register, which related to a company that had been liquidated two years prior. The register was kept by a public authority, which was the controller of the data contained therein. This controller was under a legal obligation to maintain the register according to national rules. The CJEU found that the continued processing of such data, prescribed by national Member State law, is permissible, and explained that Member States could not be held to guarantee the erasure of data relating to a dissolved company in such circumstances (CJEU, Case C-398/15, *Manni*, ECLI:EU:C:2017:197, para. 56, https://curia.europa.eu/juris/liste.jsf?language=en&num=C-398/15). However, the CJEU acknowledged that it would be exceptionally justified to allow the limitation of access to such information, even with regards to third parties demonstrating a specific interest in consulting that data. Such a limitation could however only be granted on a case-by-case basis, when the affected data subject can present compelling legitimate grounds for the limitation and after a sufficiently long period has passed after the dissolution of the company concerned (CJEU, Case C-398/15, *Manni*, ECLI:EU:C:2017:197, para. 64, https://curia.europa.eu/juris/liste.jsf?language=en&num=C-398/15).

999. For example, in the context of the 2020 coronavirus crisis, personal data, including health data has been gathered by and shared among different controllers (hospitals, public health organisations, governments, companies) to react to the crisis as well as possible. It will be useful to keep certain

insofar as granting the erasure is likely to render impossible or seriously impair the achievement of the objectives of that processing;[1000]

(5) for the establishment, exercise or defence of legal claims.[1001]

849. It should also be pointed out that the GDPR also furnishes the data subject with another right, namely the right to obtain the restriction of the processing, which, depending on the circumstances may be more appropriate. This right is subject to fewer exceptions and may effectively reach a similar result for the data subject. The right to restriction is discussed in the next section.

VI. Right to Restriction of Processing (Article 18 GDPR)

A. *Introduction*

850. Article 18 GDPR provides for a right to restriction of processing. Restriction of processing in principle means that personal data shall, with the exception of storing the data, no longer be processed, although the GDPR provides for some exceptions.

B. *Scope of Application*

851. The data subject has the right to obtain a restriction of processing from the controller when:[1002]

data (or elements of data, even aggregated, pseudonymised or anonymised) in order to better prepare for future pandemics, even when the data are no longer necessary for reacting to the coronavirus crisis. To the extent that the data that needs to be retained still constitutes personal data (i.e., is not fully anonymised), certain controllers may refuse valid erasure requests by data subjects, when there are reasons of public health to do so. A controller may justify such action especially where it has been instructed by the government to do so.

1000. This exception may for example be applied by a research institute, which, in the course of carrying out research is confronted with erasure requests, which, if granted, would render the objectives of the research impossible to achieve or would seriously impair them.

1001. This exception is for example relevant in the context of the dismissal of an employee. After dismissal certain documents, e-mails and other materials containing personal data relating to the dismissed employee may in fact become superfluous and their retention no longer necessary in relation to the purposes for which they were collected or otherwise processed. However, if the employee then later on decides to dispute his/her dismissal, such documents, e-mails or other materials may become relevant evidence for the employer to defined itself against a claim of wrongful dismissal. Equally, if the employee was disgruntled and has caused damage upon leaving the company (e.g., stealing data, company secrets or equipment, etc.), then the employer may need certain documents, e-mails and other materials containing personal data to prove the damage. In all such cases, the employer will be entitled to keep and process such information for as long as it may be needed to establish a claim, exercise it, or defend itself. The period of retention here will depend on the term of limitation or the duration of the trial, because after that reasons cease to exist, erasure will principally be mandatory again (if the request is valid), save where another exception applies (e.g., the employer has a legal obligation to retain certain information).

1002. Art. 18(1) GDPR.

- The accuracy of the personal data is contested by the data subject. In that case, the restriction applies for a period enabling the controller to verify the accuracy of the personal data.
- The processing is unlawful and the data subject opposes the erasure of the personal data and requests the restriction of their use instead.
- The controller no longer needs the personal data for the purposes of the processing, but they are required by the data subject for the establishment, exercise or defence of legal claims.
- The data subject has objected to processing pursuant to Article 21(1). In such cases, the restriction applies pending the verification whether the legitimate grounds of the controller override those of the data subject.

852. If one of these grounds applies, then the restriction must be granted. As indicated by the above scenarios in which the data subject can obtain restriction, the right of restriction is most typically a part of the exercise of another data subject right, and is used as either a temporary measure pending the granting or refusal or such a right (objection, rectification) or as an alternative to erasure.

853. **The general modalities discussed in section I above apply to the exercise of this right.** This includes that the exercise of this right must be facilitated by the controller, in principle free of charge and, where data are processed by electronic means the controller should also provide means for the requests to be made electronically. Requests must be processed without undue delay, within the specified time limits (one month, maximum three).

C. Consequences of Granting the Right

854. As clarified by Article 18(2) GDPR, restriction means that the data controller must no longer process the data, with the exception of further storing the data. The controller must make this operational, e.g., by temporarily moving the data, restricting access by technical means, or clearly indicating the restriction in its internal systems.[1003] There are, however, some exceptions to this principle. The controller can continue processing despite the applicability of a restriction of processing when:

- the data subject consents to this continued processing;[1004]
- this is necessary for the establishment, exercise or defence of legal claims;
- this is necessary for the protection of the rights of another natural or legal person;
- this is required for reasons of important public interest of the EU or a Member State.

1003. Recital 67 GDPR.

1004. Note that such consent will have to comply with all conditions for free and informed consent. Hence, if the controller is using its dominant position to force such consent, this will not justify the continued processing.

855. Once a restriction has been obtained, irrespective of whether an exception for continued processing applies or not, the GDPR requires two additional things of the controller. First, in compliance with Article 19 GDPR, the controller must communicate that restriction of processing has been granted/obtained to 'each recipient to whom the personal data have been disclosed, unless this proves impossible or requires disproportionate effort'.[1005] Article 19 GDPR does not detail what information must be provided to the recipients, but at least the fact of the restriction should be communicated. Moreover, if the data subject so requests, the controller must inform the data subject about those recipients.[1006] As discussed in the preceding sections, the mechanism of Article 19 GDPR acknowledges that, depending on the specific circumstances, there may be situations where the exercise of the rights of rectification, erasure or restriction with one controller does not necessarily entail the wish of the data subject to exercise that same right with the recipients. For example, the data subject may wish that one controller restricts the processing of personal data that is no longer needed by the controller, but which the data subject needs or may need for establishing a legal claim, but may want recipients who have copies of the data to erase that data altogether.

856. Second, once the data subject has obtained restriction of processing, it must be informed by the controller before the restriction of processing can be lifted.[1007] Hence, in the data subject disputes the accuracy of data concerning him/her, and requests the controller to rectify that data and restrict processing in the meantime, the controller may lift the restriction once the data has been rectified or if it finds that the data was already accurate and complete, but it must inform the data subject prior to lifting the restriction. This gives the data subject time to decide on another possible course of action.

1005. In its Judgement in the *Breyer* case, the Court of Justice clarified that disproportionate effort can be present 'in terms of time, cost and manpower' (CJEU, C-582/14, Judgment of 19 October 2016, *Breyer*, ECLI:EU:C:2016:779, para. 46, https://eur-lex.europa.eu/legal-content/en/TXT/?uri=CELEX:62014CJ0582).

1006. As already indicated above, the Court of Justice considered it essential for a data subject to be informed about the recipients of its data to be able to effectively exercise his or her rights (CJEU, Case C-553/07, Judgment of 7 May 2009, *Rijkeboer*, ECLI:EU:C:2009:293, paras 53–54, https://curia.europa.eu/juris/liste.jsf?num=C-553/07&language=en). Hence, the data subject must be informed about recipients. Note that Arts 13/14 and 15 GDPR allow the controller in limited cases to limit itself to informing the data subject about the categories of recipients, rather than naming recipients. The controller may even suffice with this in its main documentation, i.e., the record of processing activities under Art. 30 GDPR. There is a clear tension between this and the text of Art. 19 GDPR to specify 'each recipient'. Hence, a situation could exist where a controller cannot notify a recipient because it does not have the means to identify all recipients. The question is then whether the controller must still inform the data subject about those recipients. It is this author's position that under its accountability obligation, the controller must keep track of all recipients by name, even if in some circumstances it can limit the disclosure of recipients to categories (Art. 13/14, Art. 15 GDPR). The controller must still have this information available and should be able to communicate all recipients to the data subject, also those who it could not notify, or notification of which would have required disproportionate effort.

1007. Art. 18(3) GPDR.

VII. Right to Data Portability (Article 20 GDPR)

A. *Introduction*

857. Article 20 GDPR contains an entirely new right under the GDPR, aimed at providing the data subject with an additional measure of control over his/her data, namely the right to data portability, i.e., the right to obtain the personal data relating to him/her, which he/she has previously provided to the controller and the right to transmit those data to another controller without hindrance of the first controller.

858. The right to data portability finds its main application in the situation where the data subject wants to change service providers and requires its data from the previous service provider to be used by the new service provider. The need for this could for example arise where a data subject is using a health app which tracks a number of statistics, and want to change to another app after a few years. In such a context the history data is still very relevant, and would ideally be transferred to the new app. The right to data portability makes this possible.

B. *Scope of Application*

859. The right to data portability applies only where:[1008]

- the processing is based on consent or on a contract (Article 6(1), a) or 6(1), b) and 9(2), a) GDPR);[1009] and
- the processing is carried out by automated means.

860. Notably, the right only applies to personal data concerning the data subject, which he or she 'has provided to' the controller. See section C below for more details on exactly what data is included in the scope.

1008. Art. 20(1) GDPR.

1009. Note that Art. 9(2), a) GDPR is not a legal ground in itself. However, with regards to special categories of data, the right to data portability only applies when the exception relied upon is consent, i.e., Art. 9(2), a) GDPR. In its opinion on the right to data portability, the Art. 29 Working Party has indicated that it would be best practice for controllers relying on other legal grounds, to provide a measure of portability as well, giving the example of a tax authority providing for an easy way for the citizen to download past personal income tax filings (Art. 29 Working Party, Guidelines on the right to data portability (WP242), p. 8 at fn. 16). This is not necessarily at odds with Art. 20(2) GDPR and Recital 68 GDPR, which clarify that the right, even with regards to special categories of data processed on the exception of consent under Art. 9(2), a) GDPR does not apply in the context of a controller carrying out a public mission/tasks and 'by its very nature, […]should not be exercised against controllers processing personal data in the exercise of their public duties'. Strictly speaking, the GDPR only clearly indicates that portability in that context is not a right of the data subject, which does not prevent the controller from offering it to some extent nonetheless. This may even be required by other applicable rules, law or principles (of good administration).

861. The general modalities discussed above apply to the exercise of this right. This includes that the exercise of this right must be facilitated by the controller, in principle free of charge and the controller should also provide means for the requests to be made electronically. Requests must be processed without undue delay, within the specified time limits (one month, maximum three). It should be repeated that, where the controller does not have sufficient information to identify the data subject, it should request this information before granting a request.

C. Consequences of Granting the Right

862. Where the right to data portability applies, the data subject shall have the right to '*receive the personal data concerning him or her, which he or she has provided to a controller*'.[1010] The specific wording of Article 20(1) GDPR determines the scope of the data, which the data subject can request from the controller, as explained in what follows.

863. First of all, the data has to be personal data. Other data is not covered by the right to data portability. Where the controller has pseudonymised the data, the right in principle still applies, although with the limitation of Article 11(2), GDPR, namely that the controller cannot be obliged to process additional data for the sole purposes of granting data subject rights. Hence, where the controller can carry out its processing activities without identifying the data subject, portability will not apply unless the data subject provides additional information allowing its identification.

864. Second, the right to data portability only applies to the personal data *provided by*[1011] the data subject to the controller. The choice for the words 'provided by' indicates a more narrow scope than for example the right to information, which applies to all personal data *collected from* the data subject. In its opinion on data portability, the Article 29 Working Party proposes a divide between data actively and knowingly provided by the data subject, which would be included, and data that was inferred and derived by the controller, which would be excluded.[1012] Hence, in the example of the health app above, the direct measurements (heart rate, steps counted, etc.) would be covered by the right to data portability, while insights, statistics and other observations produced by the app, would not be covered by the right to data portability. Such an approach does not only match the text of the GDPR, but also serves to protect the know-how and other intellectual property of

1010. Art. 20(1) GDPR.
1011. *See* for an analysis of this and the discussion that exists around this term Paul De Hert, Vagelis Papakonstantinou, Gianclaudio Malgieri, Laurent Beslay, Ignacio Sanchez, 'The right to data portability in the GDPR: Towards user-centric interoperability of digital services', *Computer Law & Security Review* 2018, Vol. 34(2), 193–203.
1012. Art. 29 Working Party, Guidelines on the right to data portability (WP242), p. 10.

the first controller.[1013] While the Article 29 Working party also shows a respect for intellectual property and trade secrets,[1014] it also clearly indicates that a potential business risk is not a basis for refusal of portability.[1015] It is up to the controller to take the applicable intellectual property into account when designing the process of granting portability.

865. Still, discussion exists on exactly what data is included in the right to data portability.[1016] Taking the health app as an example again, while the direct measurements seem to clearly be data that is provided by the data subject, since the data subject actively and knowingly allows the app to track certain data or get access to certain functions on the data subject's device, the situation is less clear with relation to the metadata relating to such primary measurements, such as network traffic data, raw data from connected objects, activity logs, search history and location. While such data is sent from the data subject's device, it is observed by the controller, rather than actively provided by the data subject. In many cases the data subject will also not be aware of the fact that he/she is inherently providing the information as well. The position of the Article 29 Working Party is that such 'observed data'[1017] is fully included in the scope of Article 20 GDPR and must be provided at the best possible level of granularity, enabling the full function and reuse of the main data.[1018] Others however, including the European Commission, have questioned this broad interpretation and hold that this is not what the European legislator intended.[1019]

866. Whatever the specific scope of the data, the data subject shall always have the right to receive those data from the controller 'in a structured, commonly used and machine-readable format',[1020] as well as the right to transmit this data to a new controller, without hindrance[1021] of the initial controller. Moreover, Article 20 (2)

1013. Orla Lynskey, 'Article 20. Right to data portability', in Christopher Kuner, Lee A. Bygrave, Christopher Docksey (eds.), *The EU General Data Protection Regulation (GDPR) – A commentary*, 2020, p. 503.

1014. Art. 29 Working Party, Guidelines on the right to data portability (WP242), p. 12, p. 18.

1015. Art. 29 Working Party, Guidelines on the right to data portability (WP242), p. 10.

1016. *See* for a detailed analysis: Paul De Hert, Vagelis Papakonstantinou, Gianclaudio Malgieri, Laurent Beslay, Ignacio Sanchez, 'The right to data portability in the GDPR: Towards user-centric interoperability of digital services', *Computer Law & Security Review* 2018, Vol. 34(2), 193–203.

1017. Art. 29 Working Party, Guidelines on the right to data portability (WP242), p. 10.

1018. Art. 29 Working Party, Guidelines on the right to data portability (WP242), p. 10, p. 18.

1019. *See* for references: Orla Lynskey, 'Article 20. Right to data portability', in Christopher Kuner, Lee A. Bygrave, Christopher Docksey (eds.), *The EU General Data Protection Regulation (GDPR) – A commentary*, 2020, p. 503.

1020. Art. 20(1) GDPR. For more detail on these requirements, please refer to Art. 29 Working Party, Guidelines on the right to data portability (WP242), pp. 17–18; *see* for a critical analysis of this requirement Janis Wong, Tristan Henderson, 'The Right to Data Portability in practice: Exploring the implications of the technologically neutral GDPR', *International Data Privacy Law* 2019, Vol. 9(3), 173–191, p. 186 and following.

1021. Such hindrance can be legal, technical, or financial, aimed at slowing down access, transmission or reuse of the data, such as fees, deliberately added complexity or deliberate obfuscation of the dataset, etc. (Art. 29 Working Party, Guidelines on the right to data portability (WP242), p. 15).

GDPR specifies that, where technically feasible,[1022] the data subject shall have the right to have the personal data transmitted directly from one controller to another.

867. The goal of these provisions, as is also clarified by Recital 68 GDPR, is to create interoperability between formats and controllers' systems, in order to fully enable real portability for the data subject. While Recital 68 GDPR specifies that 'the data subject's right to transmit or receive personal data concerning him or her should not create an obligation for the controllers to adopt or maintain processing systems which are technically compatible', the Article 29 Working Party has clarified that this does not affect the obligation of the controller to strive for interoperability, allowing the direct transmission between two controllers and an effective reuse of information by the receiving controller. Interoperability is more easily reached by providing data in a format that has a high level of abstraction from any internal or proprietary format. Hence, the goal is not for controllers to have compatible systems (which would be impossible), but for their systems to be able to extract and send data that, because of its abstraction from internal or proprietary formats, can easily be reused in another, non-compatible system, namely that of the receiving controller.[1023] The most practical way to achieve greater interoperability and a more effective right to data portability would be to rely on standards.[1024]

D. Relationship with Erasure

868. Article 20(3) GDPR explicitly states that the exercise of the right to data portability is without prejudice to the right of erasure. What Article 20(3) GDPR is trying to clarify, is that the exercise of the right to data portability neither necessarily entails erasure of the data, nor can the right to data portability be used by a controller to delay or refuse erasure. This is logical. Under the GPDR, the exercise of one right generally cannot have the effect of prejudicing another right. All rights can be exercised separately, under their respective conditions, without influencing each other.[1025]

869. Hence, there may be situations in which the data portability also triggers erasure because the controller now no longer needs the data, and no exception under Article 17(3) GDPR applies. However, in other cases, the controller may still need the data to perform the contract or to fulfil the purposes to which the data subject

1022. This is not defined by the GDPR, so controllers have some leeway to argue that direct transfer of data is not technically feasible. For more detail on the technical feasibly, *see*: Art. 29 Working Party, Guidelines on the right to data portability (WP242), pp. 15–16.

1023. Art. 29 Working Party, Guidelines on the right to data portability (WP242), p. 17.

1024. *See* on this Janis Wong, Tristan Henderson, 'The Right to Data Portability in practice: Exploring the implications of the technologically neutral GDPR', *International Data Privacy Law* 2019, Vol. 9(3), 173–191, p. 188; Lucio Scudiero, 'Bringing Your Data Everywhere: A Legal Reading Of The Right To Portability', *European Data Protection Law Review* 2017, Vol. 3(1), 119–127.

1025. *See* Art. 29 Working Party, Guidelines on the right to data portability (WP242), p. 7. Of course, there are indeed connections between the rights. For example, a successful objection under Art. 21 GDPR will be a ground for erasure in Art. 17(1) GDPR. This will however not affect the conditions of Art. 17 GDPR, including the exceptions in Art. 17(3) GDPR.

consented, as Article 20 GDPR does not presuppose that the consent has been withdrawn, the contract terminated or that the relationship with the controller is being permanently terminated. Hence, the original retention period may simply continue to apply. In addition, even where erasure in principle applies, the controller may have an exception under Article 17(3) GDPR.

E. Exceptions

870. Article 20(4) GDPR states that the right to data portability 'shall not adversely affect the rights and freedoms of others'. This introduces a limited scope for the controller to refuse certain portability requests, where these cannot be granted without adversely affecting the rights and freedoms of others. As clarified by Recital 68 this may be relevant in situations where the data set provided by the data subject also contains information on third parties. In its opinion on data portability, the Article 29 Working party included intellectual property and trade secrets as being protected under Article 20(4) GDPR. However, it also clearly indicates that a potential business risk is not a basis for refusal of portability.[1026] It is up to the controller to take the applicable intellectual property into account when designing the process of granting portability. Generally, the exception of Article 20(4) GDPR should be interpreted narrowly. Even where some grounds for limitation may be applicable, the controller should always endeavour the grant data portability, even in a limited form, over refusing the request.[1027]

VIII. Right to Object (Article 21 GDPR)

A. Introduction

871. Article 21 GPDR grants the data subject a right to object to certain types of processing activities, when his or her particular situation justifies such objection. The exception to this rule is when processing is carried out for direct marketing purposes. In that case, the data subject can always object without having to provide justification. The situation envisioned by Article 21 GDPR is a lawful processing activity by a controller, which nonetheless has an unwanted impact on the data subject. Unlawful processing can of course be objected to in the general sense, but specific actions would rather be taken under the right of erasure, where non-compliant processing is a specific ground for erasure, making the right to object superfluous in

1026. Art. 29 Working Party, Guidelines on the right to data portability (WP242), p. 10.
1027. As described above, the controller generally has an obligation to facilitate the exercise of data subject rights (Art. 12(2) GDPR).

situations where the non-compliance is clear to the data subject.[1028] If the data subject is convinced that the unlawful processing is in fact lawful, then the right to object would again be the logical course of action.

B. Scope of Application

1. Only for Processing on Article 6(1), e) and f) GDPR

872. Importantly, the right to object only applies where the controller relies on either legitimate interest as a legal ground (Article 6(1), f) GDPR) or on the legal ground of performance of a task carried out in the public interest or in the exercise of official authority vested in the controller (Article 6(1), e) GDPR). These legal grounds notably involve a lot of discretion for the controller to determine what types of processing is necessary for its goals, without direct involvement of the data subject. The right to object provides some balance by allowing a data subject to oppose a processing activity which, because of his or her particular situation, adversely affects him or her, thereby giving the data subject a measure of control.

2. Objection on the Basis of Particular Situation

873. For the right to object to apply the data subject must base its objections on his or her particular situation, which shows that there is no general right to object to processing for just any reason. The exception to this rule is processing for the purposes of direct marketing, where Article 21(2) and (3) clarify that the data subject may always object to such processing and that such objection must always be accepted by the controller.[1029]

874. Generally however, there must be specific reasons invoked by the data subject to show that he or she in particular is adversely affected by the processing. The language of the GDPR is clearly less restrictive than the DPD, which required the data subject to be able to present 'compelling legitimate grounds relating to his particular situation'. The GDPR no longer requires that the grounds for objection presented by the data subject are 'compelling'. Sadly, the GDPR does not provide much guidance on what threshold the situation of the data subject must meet to be entitled to object to the processing. Clearly, too high a threshold would lead to hollow out the right. Alternately, too low a threshold would mean that a data subject can object simply because he or she does not like the processing, which is not what is meant by the legislator, looking both at the language of Article 21 and the fact

1028. This is because one of the main purposes of the right to object is to be able to subsequently ask for erasure of data. A successful objection is a ground for erasure under Art. 17 GDPR. For personal data that is processed unlawfully, such a ground already exists under Art. 17 GDPR. Hence there is no need to invoke the right to object against unlawful processing, as erasure can already be invoked.

1029. *See also* recital 70 GDPR.

that the right to object to direct marketing at any time without restriction or justification is quite clearly formulated as the exception. What is clear, is that the data subject must be affected in particular, in a way that is specific to him or her and must be able to give details about this to the controller. General statements would not be sufficient. Equally, if the processing generally involves some kind of (potentially negative) effect for the data subjects, this would not be sufficient to invoke the right to object, unless the data subject is for some reason affected more severely than other data subjects.[1030]

875. The Court of Justice has dealt with the right to object in *Nowak*, *Manni* and *Google Spain*, confirming that the right object aims to balance legitimate processing with specific situations where data subjects are adversely affected. In *Nowak*[1031] (relating to exam results being shared outside the examination procedure) and *Google Spain*[1032] (relating to search results causing damage to the data subject being maintained on Google's index, despite having become irrelevant) the right to object was deemed applicable, whereas in *Manni* (relating to personal data showing that the data subject had been the administrator of a bankrupt company more than ten years in the past, being maintained in the public register of companies, to the detriment of the business prospects of the data subject) the Court reaffirmed that the right to object but did not find that it justified the request of the applicant in that case.[1033]

876. Notably, Article 21 GDPR specifically mentions profiling on the basis of Article 6, e) or f) GDPR, as being included in the right to object, thereby expanding the scope of remedies against profiling beyond Article 22 GDPR, which only covers profiling that includes automated decision-making. Under Article 21, any form of profiling can be caught, but there is no general right not to be subjected to profiling. Instead, data subjects can again object if their specific situation justifies this.

1030. The reason for this is that the legal grounds of legitimate interest and processing necessary for public interest or authority, include some balancing of interests prior to the processing activity, weighing the interest of the controller, a third party or the public at large against those of the data subject. For processing based on legitimate interest, this is done by the controller. For processing necessary for the performance of a task carried out in the public interest or in the exercise of official authority vested in the controller, this is largely also done by the legislator providing the framework for the exercise of such tasks or authority, in addition to the controller determining what specific processing is 'necessary'. Hence, if a data subject is only generally affected like any other data subject, this would be covered by the balancing exercise prior to processing. Of course the data subject could still argue that the processing in itself is unlawful, but this would resort more directly under the right to erasure, which specifically foresees erasure of unlawfully processed data.

1031. CJEU, Case C-434/16, Judgment of 20 December 2017, *Nowak*, ECLI:EU:C:2017:994, https://eur-lex.europa.eu/legal-content/en/TXT/?uri=CELEX:62016CJ0434.

1032. CJEU, Case C-131/12, Judgment of 13 May 2014, *Google Spain*, ECLI:EU:C:2014:317, https://eur-lex.europa.eu/legal-content/EN/TXT/?uri=CELEX%3A62012CJ0131.

1033. CJEU, Case C-136/17, Judgment of 24 September 2019, GC and Others v. CNIL, ECLI:EU:C:2019:773, https://eur-lex.europa.eu/legal-content/EN/TXT/?uri=CELEX%3A62017CJ0136.

3. No Overriding Legitimate Interest of the Controller

877. If the data subject objects to the processing on grounds relating to this or her particular situation, the controller must in principle no longer process the personal data, unless the controller can demonstrate compelling legitimate grounds for the processing which:

– override the interests, rights and freedoms of the data subject; or
– relate to the establishment, exercise or defence of legal claims.

878. An exception to this rule is processing for purposes of direct marketing. In such situations, the controller cannot show overriding interests, at least not for continued processing for direct marketing purposes (Article 21(3) GDPR). Continued processing for other purposes is possible, if justification exists.

879. Consequently, if a data subject objects to the processing based on his or her specific situation, the controller has only one option outside the rather limited situation of needing the data for legal proceedings, and that is to show that its interests override the interests, rights and freedoms of the data subject in the specific situation. It is the controller who bears to burden of proof that this is the case,[1034] which effectively means that if the controller cannot prove this, it will have to grant the objection.

880. The fact that the GDPR requires compelling legitimate grounds shows that the threshold for a successful refusal of an objection based on a specific situation is rather high and is certainly higher than the balancing exercise under Article 6(1), f) GPDR.[1035] After all, the purpose of the balancing under Article 21 GDPR is not to confirm that the initial analysis under Article 6(1), f) GPDR was correct, but that the interests of the controller continue to override those of the data subject, even when taking into account the specific circumstances of the data subject, which are now known to the controller.

881. A specific application of this balancing exercise in the context of search engines can be found in the aforementioned *Google Spain* case. In that case, a Spanish citizen was asking Google to delete search results from its index, relating to newspaper articles about the recovery of a social security debt against him. The argument was that the facts were more than ten years old and the proceedings had been fully resolved, so that this information was no longer relevant, while still capable of causing serious prejudice against the data subject. In *Google Spain*, the Court of Justice deals with both the right to erasure, as well as the right to object, and found that:

1034. *See also* recital 69 GDPR.
1035. Art. 29 Working Party, Guidelines on Automated individual decision-making and Profiling for the purposes of Regulation 2016/679 (WP251), p. 19.

> [the rights of the data subject] override, as a rule, not only the economic interest of the operator of the search engine but also the interest of the general public in finding that information upon a search relating to the data subject's name. However, that would not be the case if it appeared, for particular reasons, such as the role played by the data subject in public life, that the interference with his fundamental rights is justified by the preponderant interest of the general public in having, on account of inclusion in the list of results, access to the information in question.[1036]

Hence, in balancing the legitimate interests of Google as a controller with the data subject's to privacy and data protection of the data subject, the outcome would, as a rule, be that Google's economic interests would not suffice to refuse an objection by a data subject.

882. The *Google Spain* case helps to illustrate that in dealing with the right to object, the controller will have to produce more compelling grounds than mere economic interest in order to refuse granting the right to object. Economic interests might be sufficient under Article 6(1), f) GDPR, provided the impact of the processing on the data subject is limited. That is because Article 6(1), f) GDPR deals with impact on the data subject in the abstract. The balancing exercise under Article 21 GDPR, however, deals with impact on the data subject in specific terms and is not as easily set aside. It has been suggested in literature that the compelling legitimate grounds on which the controller relies should be detailed, foreseeable and publicly declared, calling upon the EDPB to issue guidance to that extent.[1037]

4. Modalities of Exercising the Right

883. The general modalities discussed above apply to the exercise of this right. This includes that the exercise of this right must be facilitated by the controller, in principle free of charge and, where data are processed by electronic means the controller should also provide means for the requests to be made electronically. Requests must always be processed without undue delay, within the specified time limits (one month, maximum three).

884. In addition, Article 21(4) GDPR provides for an additional transparency requirement, charging the controller to bring the right to object explicitly to the attention of the data subject, latest at the time of the first communication with the data subject. The controller has to make sure that this information is presented clearly and separately from any other information.

1036. CJEU, Case C-131/12, Judgment of 13 May 2014, *Google Spain*, ECLI:EU:C:2014:317, para. 97, https://eur-lex.europa.eu/legal-content/EN/TXT/?uri=CELEX%3A62012CJ0131.

1037. Jef Ausloos, Réne Mahieu, and Michael Veale, 'Getting Data Subject Rights Right: A submission to the European Data Protection Board from international data rights academics, to inform regulatory guidance,' Journal of Intellectual Property, Information Technology and E-Commerce Law 2019, Vol. 10(3), 283–309, p. 284.

885. In the context of the use of information society services,[1038] Article 21(5) GDPR explicitly mentions that the data subject may exercise the right to object by automated means using technical specifications. While providing automated means to object/opt-out is only obligatory in the context of information society services, it can be considered best practice whenever possible, taking into account the added transparency requirement contained in Article 21 GDPR. This is even more relevant for any processing for direct marketing purposes, since the data subject has an absolute right to object in such cases.

5. Specific Situation: Objection to Processing for Scientific or Historical Research Purposes or Statistical Purposes

886. Article 21(6) GDPR regulates a specific situation, namely where data is being processed for scientific or historical research purposes or statistical purposes in accordance with Article 89 GDPR. In such cases, Article 21(6) GDPR states that the data subjects may again object on grounds relating to his or her particular situation, unless the processing is necessary for the performance of a task carried out for reasons of public interest. Importantly, in this situation, the GPDR does not require from the controller to be able to demonstrate compelling legitimate grounds, in theory lowering the threshold to refuse objections. However, only processing in compliance with Article 89 GDPR is caught by this provision, which means that appropriate safeguards must be in place to protect the rights of data subjects. Note that the restriction of the right to object in Article 21(6) is not applicable to processing for archiving purposes in the public interest, despite this purpose being included in Article 89 GDPR.

C. Consequences of Granting the Right and Relationship with Other Rights

887. The effect of a successful objection is that the controller may no longer process the data in question.[1039] Processing operations performed on the data subject's data prior to the objection, however, remain legitimate. Importantly, the controller has to implement a restriction of processing immediately after the data subject has objected, pending the verification of whether compelling legitimate grounds exist that would justify the continued processing.[1040] If the outcome is that there are indeed no grounds to refuse the right to object, the controller will have to effectively delete the data. This follows from the fact that Article 21(1) GDPR states that the controller in case of successful objection shall no longer process the data. Given

1038. Information society services are defined in Art. 4(25) GDPR, by reference to Directive 2015/1535, which defines information society services as 'services, normally provided for a remuneration, at a distance, by electronic means and at the individual request of a recipient of services'. For instance, Google was held to fall withing this definition in CJEU, Joined Cases C-236/08 to C-238/08, Judgment of 23 March 2010, *Google France and Google*, ECLI:EU:C:2010:159, https://eur-lex.europa.eu/legal-content/en/TXT/?uri=CELEX:62008CJ0236.

1039. Art. 21(1), GDPR.

1040. Art. 18(1), d) GDPR.

that storage is a processing operation, this is no longer allowed after an objection which has not been or could not be refused (direct marketing or no compelling grounds). This is reflected in Article 17(1), c) GDPR, which gives the data subject the right to request erasure in case of a successful objection under Article 21(1) or (2). However, in principle a separate request is not necessary, as a request under the right of objection already includes erasure. Of course, the data subject is free to request erasure if he or she thinks that the controller has not deleted the data.

888. Importantly, the obligation to no longer process the data applies to the data involved in the specific processing on the basis of Article 6(1), e) or f), against which the data subject is objecting. This means that the same data may sometimes still be kept because the controller needs it for other purposes, against which there is no right to object (e.g., processing of the same data for different purposes, based on other legal grounds, e.g., consent or contract), for which the objection is refused, or against which the data subject has not objected. This is reflected in Article 21(3), which relates to direct marketing. An objection to direct marketing must always be accepted, and thus the controller must no longer process the data for those direct marketing purposes. Using the data for other purposes is in principle still allowed if a legal ground exists.

IX. Right Not to Be Subjected to Automated Individual Decision-Making, Including Profiling (Article 22 GDPR)

A. *Scope of the Right*

889. Article 22 GPDR contains a specific right for data subjects not to be subjected to a decision based solely on automated processing, including profiling, which produces legal effects concerning him or her or similarly significantly affects him or her.[1041] The scope of Article 22 GDPR is expressly restricted to decision-making based solely on automated processing, including profiling, which leads to:

- decisions concerning him or her producing *legal effects*;[1042] or
- decision concerning him or her, which *similarly significantly affects him or her.*[1043]

1041. *See* for a general analysis Isak Mendoza, Lee A. Bygrave, 'The right Not to be Subject to Automated Decisions Based on Profiling, in Tatiana-Eleni Synodinou, Philippe Jougleux, Christiana Markou, Thalia Prastitou (eds.), *EU Internet Law*, 2017, 77.

1042. Legal effects means that the data subject's legal rights are affected, such as the cancellation of a contract, the denial of a citizenship application, the denial of a right to vote, etc. For more detail *see* Art. 29 Working Party, Guidelines on Automated individual decision-making and Profiling for the purposes of Regulation 2016/679 (WP251), p. 21.

1043. For a decision that produces no legal effects to reach the threshold of 'similarly significantly' affecting the data subject, the significance must approach that of a legal effect. For more detail on how to determine this, *see* Art. 29 Working Party, Guidelines on Automated individual decision-making and Profiling for the purposes of Regulation 2016/679 (WP251), pp. 21–22. *See also* Lee

890. Importantly, Article 22 GDPR only applies to situations where the decision is made *solely* by automated means, i.e., without human intervention.[1044] Recital 71 GPDR clarifies that profiling refers to 'any form of automated processing of personal data evaluating the personal aspects relating to a natural person, in particular to analyse or predict aspects concerning the data subject's performance at work, economic situation, health, personal preferences or interests, reliability or behaviour, location or movements'. As to what qualifies as a decision, there are no formal requirements in the GDPR, meaning the notion should be interpreted in a broad sense.[1045]

891. Notably, profiling and automated processing activities that do not lead to a decision which produces legal effects or similarly significantly affects the data subject, are not caught by Article 22 GPDR and will be treated under the general rules of the GDPR.[1046] The same is true when the decision does meet this threshold of impact, but was arrived at through human intervention, thus not meeting the criterion of 'solely by automated means'. Despite the fact that such profiling may still determine actions of the controller and therefore have an impact on the data subject, it is not caught under Article 22 GDPR and is in principle allowed, notwithstanding certain data subject rights (e.g., right to withdraw consent, right to object) and assuming all other GDPR requirements are met.[1047]

B. Application of the Right

892. The basic rule of Article 22(1) GDPR is that automated decision-making, including profiling, that leads to a decision which produces legal effects for the data subject or similarly significantly affects him or her, is in principle prohibited. The Article 29 WP has clarified that, despite being worded as a right, which may evoke the idea that the data subject should actively exercise the right through a request, Article 22(1) GDPR is effectively meant as a general prohibition, automatically protecting the data subject without his or her intervention.[1048] Article 22(2) GPDR provides three exceptions to this general prohibition namely when the automated individual decision-making:[1049]

A. Bygrave, 'Article 22. Automated individual decision-making, including profiling', in Christopher Kuner, Lee A. Bygrave, Christopher Docksey (eds.), *The EU General Data Protection Regulation (GDPR) – A commentary*, 2020, pp. 534–536.

1044. *See* Art. 29 Working Party, Guidelines on Automated individual decision-making and Profiling for the purposes of Regulation 2016/679 (WP251), pp. 8–9, p. 20.

1045. *See* on this also: Lee A. Bygrave, 'Article 22. Automated individual decision-making, including profiling', in Christopher Kuner, Lee A. Bygrave, Christopher Docksey (eds.), *The EU General Data Protection Regulation (GDPR) – A commentary*, 2020, p. 532.

1046. This is also expressed in recital 72 GDPR.

1047. *See* on this Art. 29 Working Party, Guidelines on Automated individual decision-making and Profiling for the purposes of Regulation 2016/679 (WP251), part III.

1048. Art. 29 Working Party, Guidelines on Automated individual decision-making and Profiling for the purposes of Regulation 2016/679 (WP251), pp. 19–20. For a more detailed discussion on the question of Art. 22(1) as a right vs. a prohibition, *see* Lee A. Bygrave, 'Article 22. Automated

(1) is necessary for entering into a contract or performing a contract between the controller and the data subject;[1050] or
(2) is authorised by law (EU or Member State) to which the controller is subject, provided that the law provides for suitable safeguards;[1051] or
(3) is based on the data subject's explicit consent.[1052]

893. A controller who invokes the exception of contract or of the data subject's consent must also implement suitable safeguards to protect the data subject's rights and interests, and at least provide for the right to obtain human intervention, so the data subject can express his or her point of view and contest the decision. In the case of automated decision-making authorised by law, the safeguards should be determined by the legal basis in question. Following the principle of accountability, it will be up to the controller to prove that an exception can indeed be relied on, and that the necessary safeguards are in place.

---

individual decision-making, including profiling', in Christopher Kuner, Lee A. Bygrave, Christopher Docksey (eds.), *The EU General Data Protection Regulation (GDPR) – A commentary*, 2020, pp. 530–532; Isak Mendoza, Lee A. Bygrave, 'The right Not to be Subject to Automated Decisions Based on Profiling, in Tatiana-Eleni Synodinou, Philippe Jougleux, Christiana Markou, Thalia Prastitou (eds.), *EU Internet Law*, 2017, p. 87; Maja Brkan, 'Do algorithms rule the world? Algorithmic decision-making and data protection in the framework of the GDPR and beyond', *International Journal of Law and Information Technology* 2019, Vol. 27(2), pp. 98–99.

1049. For more detail on the exceptions, *see* Art. 29 Working Party, Guidelines on Automated individual decision-making and Profiling for the purposes of Regulation 2016/679 (WP251), pp. 22–24.

1050. Necessity here must be interpreted in a different way that the necessity criterion under Art. 6(1), b) GDPR, as it is difficult to imagine that an automated decision without human intervention is indispensable to enter into or perform a contract (*see also* Lee A. Bygrave, 'Article 22. Automated individual decision-making, including profiling', in Christopher Kuner, Lee A. Bygrave, Christopher Docksey (eds.), *The EU General Data Protection Regulation (GDPR) – A commentary*, 2020, p. 536; Maja Brkan, 'Do algorithms rule the world? Algorithmic decision-making and data protection in the framework of the GDPR and beyond', *International Journal of Law and Information Technology* 2019, Vol. 27(2), p 104; Isak Mendoza, Lee A. Bygrave, 'The right Not to be Subject to Automated Decisions Based on Profiling, in Tatiana-Eleni Synodinou, Philippe Jougleux, Christiana Markou, Thalia Prastitou (eds.), *EU Internet Law*, 2017, p. 87). As clarified by the Art. 29 Working Party, the necessity must exist because of practical considerations, e.g., the sheer quantity of requests the controller has to deal with, necessitating the use of automated individual decision-making systems. *See* Art. 29 Working Party, Guidelines on Automated individual decision-making and Profiling for the purposes of Regulation 2016/679 (WP251), p. 23.

1051. With regards to suitable safeguards in national law, *see* Gianclaudio Malgieri, 'Automated decision-making in the EU Member States: The right to explanation and other 'suitable safeguards' in the national legislations', *Computer Law and Security Review* 2019, Vol. 35(5),[105327], p.6.

1052. Consent must as always be freely given, specific, informed and unambiguous (*see* Art. 4(11) GDPR). In this respect it may be relevant whether the automated decision (or at least the process) is in the data subject's interest or not, as this may make it easier to argue the consent was validly given (*see* Lee A. Bygrave, 'Article 22. Automated individual decision-making, including profiling', in Christopher Kuner, Lee A. Bygrave, Christopher Docksey (eds.), *The EU General Data Protection Regulation (GDPR) – A commentary*, 2020, p. 537 *in fine*; Isak Mendoza, Lee A. Bygrave, 'The right Not to be Subject to Automated Decisions Based on Profiling, in Tatiana-Eleni Synodinou, Philippe Jougleux, Christiana Markou, Thalia Prastitou (eds.), *EU Internet Law*, 2017, p.95).

894. Recital 71 GDPR clarifies that children should not be subjected to automated individual decision-making under Article 22 GDPR. Hence, in relation to children, the exceptions of Article 22(2) GDPR should in principle not be applied. However, since Article 22 GDPR itself does not make that distinction, it cannot be considered as an absolute rule and exceptional situations can exist that justify such processing.[1053]

895. Even when allowed under one of the exceptions, automated decisions producing legal or similarly significant effects may in principle not be based (in part) on special categories of data under Article 9 GDPR. Exception to this is when the data subject has explicitly consented to the use of this special categories of data (Article 9(2), a) GDPR) or processing is necessary for reasons of substantial public interest, on the basis of Union or Member State law, which must be proportionate to the aim pursued, respect the essence of the right to data protection and provide for suitable and specific measures to safeguard the fundamental rights and the interests of the data subject. In any case, whenever special categories of data are relied on in the context of Article 22 GDPR, the controller must make sure to implement suitable measures to safeguard the data subject's rights and freedoms and legitimate interests.

C. Link to Other Rights

896. Directly linked to Article 22 GDPR is the right to information of the data subject. Both Articles 13 and 14 GPDPR specify that the data subject must be informed about the existence of automated decision-making, and that at least for the cases referred to in Article 22 GDPR, the data subject must be given meaningful information about the logic involved, as well as the significance and the envisaged consequences they may encounter. The same requirement applies under the right of access of Article 15 GPDR. This is important as it may enable the data subject to also find out which data is being used in the automated decision-making, and to perhaps ask for rectification if the data is in any way inaccurate, because it is e.g., outdated, irrelevant or wrong.

897. Notably, Article 21 GDPR makes explicit mention of profiling as an activity to which the data subject could generally object based on his or her specific situation. This covers both profiling under Article 22 GPDR as other forms of profiling. However, a right to object will exist only when profiling is based on legitimate interest (Article 6(1), f) GDPR) or done for the performance of a task carried out in the public interest or in the exercise of official authority vested in the controller (Article

1053. The Art. 29 WP has confirmed that this is not an absolute prohibition, but that the recital should be followed as a rule. Exceptions may exist, in which case the controller must take into account the specific vulnerable situation of children (Art. 29 Working Party, Guidelines on Automated individual decision-making and Profiling for the purposes of Regulation 2016/679 (WP251), pp. 28–29). This is logical given that recitals do not have authoritative legal value as such.

6(1), e) GDPR). Profiling activities on the basis of other legal grounds, such as consent (Article 6(1), a) GDPR) or contract (Article 6(1), b) GDPR) do not allow the data subject to object, but have their own limitations, namely the right to withdraw in the case of Article 6(1), a) GDPR and the necessity criterion in the case of Article 6(1), b) GDPR.[1054]

X. Restrictions of Data Subject Rights (Article 23 of the GDPR)

A. *Introduction and Scope*

898. The last provision under the GDPR's chapter III, titled 'rights of the data subject', is Article 23 GDPR. Contrary to the other provisions of this chapter, which define ways to protect the data subject, Article 23 GDPR foresees the possibility for EU or Member State law to restrict the data subject's rights, where this is necessary and proportionate to protect specific core values of a democratic society. Article 23 GDPR hence accounts for the fact that the fundamental right to data protection, enshrined in Article 8 of the Charter of fundamental rights of the European Union,[1055] which the GDPR implements into actionable obligations, is not unlimited and must in some circumstances be able to be restricted to protect core values.[1056] Article 23 GDPR already had its counterpart under the Data Protection Directive in relation to restrictions introduced by Member States and builds upon existing case law of the Court of Justice of the European Union, often with reference to existing case law of the European Court of Human Rights, which allows for limited restrictions of the fundamental right to data protection (and privacy).[1057]

899. The situation under Article 23 GDPR should be distinguished from derogations from data subject rights provided for under Article 89 GDPR. While both provisions provide for exceptions to data subject rights, they have a different purpose and a different scope.

1054. Meaning that only data can be processed in as far as this is necessary for the performance of the contract or to enter into the contract. *See* the discussion on this legal ground above.

1055. Charter of Fundamental Rights of the European Union, OJ C 326, 26.10.2012, p. 391–407.

1056. This is recognised by Art. 52 of the Charter which also provides the requirements for restrictions of Charter rights. The CJEU also underlined this specifically for the right to data protection in CJEU, Joined cases C92/09 and C/93-09, Judgment of 9 November 2010, *Schecke*, ECLI: EU:C:2010:662, para. 48 and related case law cited there.

1057. *See* for example: CJEU, Joined Cases C-465/00, C-138/01 and C139-01, Judgment of 20 May 2003, *Österreichischer Rundfunk*, ECLI:EU:C:2003:294, https://eur-lex.europa.eu/legal-content/en/TXT/?uri=CELEX:62000CJ0465; CJEU, Case C-275/06, Judgment of 29 January 2008, *Promusicae*, ECLI:EU:C:2008:54; CJEU, Joined Cases C-293/12 and C-594/12, Judgment of 8 April 2014, *Digital Rights Ireland*, ECLI:EU:C:2014:238, https://eur-lex.europa.eu/legal-content/EN/TXT/?uri=CELEX%3A62012CJ0293; CJEU, Case C-362/14, *Schrems I*, ECLI:EU:C:2015:650, https://eur-lex.europa.eu/legal-content/EN/TXT/?uri=CELEX%3A62014CJ0362; CJEU, Joined Cases C-203/15 and C-698/15, Judgment of 21 December 2016, *Tele 2*, ECLI:EU:C:2016:970, https://eur-lex.europa.eu/legal-content/en/TXT/?uri=CELEX:62015CJ0536.

B. Rights That Can Be Restricted

900. Article 23 GDPR specifies that the following rights can be restricted:

- Article 12 GDPR relating to transparency and modalities of exercising data subject rights;
- Article 13 and 14 GDPR (right to information);
- Article 15 GDPR (right of access);
- Article 16 GDPR (rights to rectification);
- Article 17 GDPR (right to erasure);
- Article 18 GDPR (right to restriction of processing);
- Article 19 GDPR (notification obligations regarding rectification, erasure or restriction);
- Article 20 GDPR (right to data portability);
- Article 21 GDPR (right to object);
- Article 22 GDPR (right not subjected to a decision based solely on automated processing, including profiling, which produces legal effects for the data subject or similarly significantly affects him or her); and
- Article 34 GDPR, which gives the data subject the right to know about a personal data breach when this data breach is likely to result in high risk to the data subject's rights and freedoms.

901. In addition to the above rights, Article 23 GDPR also allows EU or Member State law to restrict the application of the principles relating to the processing of personal data contained in Article 5 GDPR, but only insofar as the provisions of Article 5 GDPR correspond to the above rights. For example, if a restriction is needed on the right to information, this restriction can also restrict the principle of transparency to the extent that this is affected by restricting the data subject's access to information. The accountability principle is not affected by Article 23 GDPR, meaning that the controller will always be accountable for its actions under the GDPR, including how it applies existing restrictions of data subject rights, provided by law.

902. Note that other rights of the data subject, such as the right to lodge a complaint to the supervisory authority (Article 77 GDPR), to an effective judicial remedy (Article 78 and 79 GDPR) or to compensation (Article 82 GDPR) cannot be restricted. The same is true for other obligations of the controller.[1058]

1058. *See* on this also European Data Protection Board, Guidelines 10/2020 on restrictions under Art. 23 GDPR, para. 37, https://edpb.europa.eu/system/files/2021-10/edpb_guidelines202010_on_art23_adopted_after_consultation_en.pdf.

C. Grounds for Restriction of Data Subject Rights

903. Article 23 GDPR states that EU law and Member State law may provide for restrictions when this is a necessary and proportionate measure in a democratic society to safeguard:

(a) national security;
(b) defence;
(c) public security;
(d) the prevention, investigation, detection or prosecution of criminal offences or the execution of criminal penalties, including the safeguarding against and the prevention of threats to public security;
(e) other important objectives of general public interest of the Union or of a Member State, in particular an important economic or financial interest of the Union or of a Member State, including monetary, budgetary and taxation matters, public health and social security;
(f) the protection of judicial independence and judicial proceedings;
(g) the prevention, investigation, detection and prosecution of breaches of ethics for regulated professions;
(h) a monitoring, inspection or regulatory function connected, even occasionally, to the exercise of official authority in the cases referred to in points (a) to (e) and (g);
(i) the protection of the data subject or the rights and freedoms of others;
(j) the enforcement of civil law claims.

The list provided for in Article 23 (1) GDPR is exhaustive, meaning only these objectives can be relied upon as grounds for a restriction by law.

D. Requirements for a Restriction

904. In addition to have a legitimate ground, Article 23 GDPR requires that any restriction of data subject rights in EU or Member State law:

- is introduced only **by way of a legislative measure**, which must be clear and precise and its application should be foreseeable to persons subject to it. A legislative measure does not however necessarily require a legislative act by a parliament;[1059]
- respects **the essence of the fundamental rights** and freedoms of the data subject, and specifically of the right that is being restricted;[1060]

1059. Recital 41 GDPR. *See* for more detail European Data Protection Board, Guidelines 10/2020 on restrictions under Art. 23 GDPR, paras 16–19.

1060. The EDPB explains: 'One of the main objectives of data protection law is to enhance data subjects' control over personal data concerning them. Any restriction shall respect the essence of the right that is being restricted. This means that restrictions that are extensive and intrusive to the extent that they void a fundamental right of its basic content, cannot be justified. In any case, a

– is a **necessary and proportionate measure** in a democratic society, meaning that any restriction must pass a necessity and proportionality test to be compliant with the GDPR. Such a test is based on existing principles in European human rights law, that can be found in Article 52 of the EU Charter, in the European Convention on Human Rights and in case law of the CJEU and the European Court of Human Rights. For restrictions of the right to data protection, the CJEU (and the EDPB accordingly) applies a strict necessity test, meaning that a proposed restriction should be supported by evidence explaining the problem to be addressed by the restriction, how it will be addressed by the restriction, genuinely meeting the proposed objective and why existing or less intrusive measures cannot sufficiently address the issue. In addition, restrictions will need to be strictly limited in scope and time.[1061]

905. In addition to this, Article 23(2) GPDR dictates that any legislative measure introducing a restriction, must contain specific provisions *at least, where relevant*, as to:[1062]

(a) the purposes of the processing or categories of processing;
(b) the categories of personal data;

---

general exclusion of all data subjects' rights with regard to all data processing operations as well as a general limitation of the rights mentioned in Art. 23 GDPR of all data subjects for specific data processing operations or with regard to specific controllers would not respect the essence of the fundamental right to the protection of personal data, as enshrined in the Charter. If the essence of the right is compromised, the restriction shall be considered unlawful, without the need to further assess whether it serves an objective of general interest or satisfies the necessity and proportionality criteria.' (European Data Protection Board, Guidelines 10/2020 on restrictions under Art. 23 GDPR, para. 14). However, what exactly constitutes the essence of the rights to data protection and privacy remains to an extent unclear and is a question of interpreting existing case law of the Court of Justice. *See* on this Dominique Moore, 'Article 23. Restrictions', in Christopher Kuner, Lee A. Bygrave, Christopher Docksey (eds.), *The EU General Data Protection Regulation (GDPR) – A commentary*, 2020, p. 553 and for a detailed discussion Maja Brkan, 'The Concept of Essence of Fundamental Rights in the EU Legal Order: Peeling the Onion to its Core', *European Constitutional Law Review* 2018, Vol. 14(2), 332–368.

1061. *See* on this European Data Protection Board, Guidelines 10/2020 on restrictions under Art. 23 GDPR, paras 38–44 and the following cases mentioned there: CJEU, case C-73/07, Judgment of 16 December 2008, *Satakunnan Markkinapörssi and Satamedia*, ECLI:EU:C:2008:727 (in particular para. 56), https://eur-lex.europa.eu/legal-content/en/TXT/?uri=CELEX:62007CJ0073; CJEU, Joined cases C-511/18, C-512/18 and C-520/18, Judgment of 6 October 2020, *La Quadrature du Net and Others*, ECLI:EU:C:2020:791 (in particular paras 209–210), https://eur-lex.europa.eu/legal-content/en/TXT/?uri=CELEX:62018CJ0511.

1062. For more detail on all these, *see* European Data Protection Board, Guidelines 10/2020 on restrictions under Art. 23 GDPR, paras 45–65. It is also interesting that these requirements apply not only to Member State law, but also to EU law providing for restrictions. That means that, potentially, legislative acts in other fields, which provide for restrictions of the GDPR would need to contain this level of detail. It is unclear what failure to do so would entail, as those acts would in principle be on the same level as the GDPR in the EU legal order in contrast to Member State law, where the principle of supremacy of EU law would bind the legislator to follow the conditions of Art. 23 GDPR and would equally bind other organs of the State, including the judiciary, to interpret potentially or apparently non-compliant provisions in a manner so that they become compliant with the GDPR, or to disapply the legislative measure that cannot be interpreted in compliance with the GDPR.

(c) the scope of the restrictions introduced;
(d) the safeguards to prevent abuse or unlawful access or transfer;
(e) the specification of the controller or categories of controllers;
(f) the storage periods and the applicable safeguards taking into account the nature, scope and purposes of the processing or categories of processing;
(g) the risks to the rights and freedoms of data subjects; and
(h) the right of data subjects to be informed about the restriction, unless that may be prejudicial to the purpose of the restriction.

906. The wording of Article 23(2) GDPR indicates that the list is not exhaustive and that a legislator may decide to provide even more detail. Conversely, Article 23(2) GDPR also leaves room for certain aspects not to be covered where these are not relevant. The EDPB has clarified that despite the wording of Article 23(2) GDPR requiring the above elements only 'where relevant', all elements should be included in the legislative measure as a general rule. Where a legislator considers certain elements not relevant, this needs to be duly justified in the light of the specific circumstances.[1063]

907. A last element of importance is that Article 36(4) requires Member States to consult with the national competent supervisory authority during the preparation of a proposal for a legislative measure to be adopted by the national parliament, or for a regulatory measure based on such a legislative measure, which relates to processing. This only applies to restrictions provided for in Member State law, but is formulated as an obligation and therefore, in those circumstances constitutes an additional requirement.[1064] Member State law may also introduce further additional requirements for the adoption of restrictions, but only if this is in line with the GDPR.

E. Consequences of a Restriction

908. The consequences of a restriction will depend on the scope of the specific restriction measure. Restrictions will often be limited in time and can be limited in scope. In most cases, the data subject will have a right to be informed about the existence of a restriction and when it will be lifted. When the data subject cannot be informed during the restriction they should at least be informed when the restriction is in fact lifted. The controller, in application of its accountability obligation under Article 5(2) GDPR, will in any case be responsible for properly administering the restriction, applying it correctly and only as long as justified, and to provide not restricted data subject rights as usual, as well as for being able to prove this. The controller may need to assess at regular intervals whether a restriction can be (partially) lifted. Controllers should also document their application of restrictions on

1063. European Data Protection Board, Guidelines 10/2020 on restrictions under Art. 23 GDPR, paras 45–46.
1064. For more detail on the potential involvement of the supervisory authority, *see* European Data Protection Board, Guidelines 10/2020 on restrictions under Art. 23 GDPR, paras 68–72.

concrete cases and be able to make this record available on request to the supervisory authority.[1065] In applying restrictions, the controller remains subject to all other GDPR obligations, and supervisory authorities retain all their powers to the extent that the controller does not (correctly) observe a legislative measure in compliance with Article 23 GDPR.[1066]

§9. Duties of Controllers and Processors

909. The GDPR imposes substantially increased data protection obligations on controllers and introduces direct compliance obligations on processors. This section sets out the obligations of controllers and processors contained in Articles 24 to 39 GDPR (Chapter IV. 'Controller and processor').

910. In the first section, the definitions of controller and processor are briefly recalled. The second section sets out the general responsibilities of controllers and processors, including the obligation to cooperate with the supervisory authority. Sections 3 to 8 focus on specific obligations for controllers and processors under the GDPR, namely the obligations following from processing with processors or processing under joint controllership (section 3), the obligation to respect the principles of data protection by design and by default (section 4), the obligation to keep a record of processing activities (section 5), the obligation to take measures to ensure an appropriate level of data security, as well as to appropriately handle data breaches (section 6), the obligation to conduct a data protection impact assessment and prior consultation (section 7), and the requirement to appoint a data protection officer (section 8).

I. Recalling the Concepts of Controller and Processor

911. Article 4(7) and Article 4(8) GDPR define the notions 'controller' and 'processor'. These concepts have already been discussed in detail in Part II, D, Section 1.3.[1067]

1065. European Data Protection Board, Guidelines 10/2020 on restrictions under Art. 23 GDPR, paras 66–67, paras 73–76.
1066. European Data Protection Board, Guidelines 10/2020 on restrictions under Art. 23 GDPR, paras 80–83.
1067. Other concepts that are relevant to this section are the following: 1) 'recipient', meaning '*a natural or legal person, public authority, agency or another body, to which the personal data are disclosed, whether a third party or not*' (Art. 4(9) GDPR). Where public authorities receive personal data in the context of a particular inquiry in accordance with the law, they are not considered as recipients. And, 2) 'Third party', meaning '*a natural or legal person, public authority, agency or body other than the data subject, controller, processor and persons who, under the direct authority of the controller or processor, are authorised to process personal data*' (Art. 4(10) GDPR).

A. Controller

912. A 'controller' is the 'natural or legal person, public authority, agency or other body which, alone or jointly with others, determines the purposes and means of the processing of personal data'.[1068] In order for an organisation to be considered as the controller of a processing operation, the organisation needs to make decisions about the key elements of the processing. This is expressed by the notion 'determines' in the definition, which refers to the controller's influence over the processing, by virtue of an exercise of decision-making power.[1069]

913. The key elements the controller needs to determine are the purposes and means of the processing. A 'purpose' is '*an anticipated outcome that is intended or that guides your planned actions*'[1070]. 'Means' refer to '*how a result is obtained or an end is achieved*'.[1071] The controller thus needs to decide on why the processing is taking place and how this objective shall be reached.[1072] The controller can determine the purposes and means of the processing alone or jointly with others. The situation where more than one controller determines the purposes and means is called joint controllership.[1073]

B. Processor

914. A 'processor' means '*a natural or legal person, public authority, agency or other body which processes personal data on behalf of the controller*'.[1074] There are two basic conditions for qualifying as a processor. First, the processor needs to be a separate entity in relation to the controller. Second, the processor needs to process personal data on behalf of the controller, meaning that the controller delegates processing activities to an external organisation.

915. Where a controller delegates processing activities to a department within its organisation, that department is not to be considered as a processor. Employees and other persons that are acting under the direct authority of the controller, such as temporarily employed staff, etc. cannot be seen as processors since they are part of the controller's organisation.[1075] They are bound by the controller's instructions.

1068. Art. 4(7) GDPR.
1069. EDPB, Guidelines 07/2020 on the concepts of controller and processor in the GDPR, adopted on 7 July 2021, v2, 11.
1070. EDPB, Guidelines 07/2020 on the concepts of controller and processor in the GDPR, adopted on 7 July 2021, v2, 14.
1071. EDPB, Guidelines 07/2020 on the concepts of controller and processor in the GDPR, adopted on 7 July 2021, v2, 14.
1072. *See* CJEU, Case C-210/16, *Wirtschaftsakademie*, Opinion of Advocate General Bot, ECLI-:EU:C:2017:796, para. 46 and CJEU, Case C-25/17, *Jehovah's witnesses*, ECLI:EU:C:2018:551, para. 68, https://eur-lex.europa.eu/legal-content/en/TXT/?uri=CELEX:62017CJ0025.
1073. Art. 26 GDPR.
1074. Art. 4(8) GDPR.
1075. EDPB, Guidelines 07/2020 on the concepts of controller and processor in the GDPR adopted on 7 July 2021, v2, 26.

Article 29 GDPR requires persons acting under the authority of the controller or the processor, who have access to the personal data, to process the data only on instructions from the controller.[1076]

II. General Responsibilities

A. Responsibility of the Controller

916. Article 24 GDPR establishes the responsibility and liability of the controller for any processing of personal data carried out by the controller or on his behalf.[1077] Controllers are required to implement appropriate technical and organisational measures to ensure that processing of personal data is carried out in accordance with the GDPR. Where necessary, those measures need to be reviewed and updated.[1078]

917. Article 24 GDPR only applies to organisations when they are acting in their role as controller. Processors are not formally obliged to comply with Article 24 GDPR, but they have their own GDPR obligations, e.g., under Article 28 GDPR.

918. To determine the appropriate technical and organisational measures the controller should take into account the nature, scope, context and purposes of the processing as well as the risk to the rights and freedoms of natural persons.[1079] Recital 75 GDPR provides a few examples of risks that may result from personal data processing which could lead to physical, material or non-material damage. A risk exists, for example, where the processing may give rise to any significant economic or social disadvantage, such as discrimination or financial loss. A risk also exists where data subjects might be deprived of their rights and freedoms or prevented from exercising controller over their personal data. Any risk must be evaluated by the controller on the basis of an objective assessment of the impact of the controller's processing operations on the data subject.[1080]

919. Controllers need to be able to demonstrate compliance of their processing activities with the GDPR as well as the effectives of the measures that are taken. Article 24(3) GDPR specifies that adherence to approved codes of conduct or approved certification mechanisms may be used as an element to demonstrate such compliance.[1081]

920. The combination of a general responsibility for the controller to comply with the GDPR, together with the obligation to also be able to prove the effective

1076. Unless the person would be legally required to process the personal data.
1077. Art. 24 GDPR; Recital 74 GDPR.
1078. Note that unlike Art. 32 GDPR that requires a regular assessment of the measures, Article 24 GDPR only requires a review and update 'where necessary'.
1079. Art. 24(1) GDPR; Recital 74 GDPR.
1080. Recital 76 GDPR.
1081. *See infra.*

implementation of measures, gives body to the principle of accountability.[1082] As discussed *supra*, the accountability principle is a central principle of the GDPR, meant to strengthen the impact of data protection law and to ensure that data protection becomes part of the shared values and practices of every organisation acting as a controller processing personal data.[1083]

B. Responsibility of the Processor

921. While most data protection obligations are centred around the controller, the GDPR lays down obligations specifically addressing and directly applicable to processors as well. Processors must comply with the requirements directly applicable to them, as well as with requirements imposed by way of contract.[1084]

922. A processor can be held liable or fined in case of failure to comply with such obligations or in case the processor acts outside or contrary to the lawful instructions of the controller.[1085] Where a processor infringes the GDPR by determining the purposes and means of the processing, the processor becomes a controller in respect of that processing.[1086]

C. Cooperation with the Supervisory Authority

923. Article 31 GDPR holds a general requirement for both controllers and processors to cooperate, on request, with the supervisory authority in the performance of its tasks. This means that where information is held by a controller or processor and a competent supervisory authority is requesting this information within the scope of its powers and tasks in accordance with Articles 57 and 58 GDPR, the controller or processor is required to provide the authority with this information. Where a DPO is appointed, the supervisory authority will address its cooperation request to such DPO as single point of contact.[1087]

924. Throughout the GDPR, the general obligation to cooperate with the supervisory authority is specified in certain cases, e.g., in the context of the record of processing activities and for the notification of data breaches.[1088]

1082. Art. 5(2) GDPR.
1083. Art. 29 Working Party, WP168, The Future of Privacy – Joint contribution to the consultation of the European Commission on the legal framework for the fundamental right to the protection of personal data, adopted on 1 December 2009, 3.
1084. Art. 28 GDPR. *See also*: B. Van Alsenoy, Data Protection Law in the EU: Roles, Responsibilities and Liability, Intersentia, Mortsel, 2019, 108.
1085. Art. 82(2) GDPR.
1086. Art. 28(10) GDPR.
1087. Art. 39(2) GDPR.
1088. Art. 30 GDPR; Art. 33 GDPR.

III. Contractual Obligations

A. Joint Controllership Arrangement

925. Where two or more controllers are involved in the processing, they will need to be considered as joint controllers when they jointly determine the purposes and means of processing.[1089]

926. The qualification of joint controllership mainly has consequences in terms of allocation of obligations for data protection compliance. Article 26 of the GDPR requires that joint controllers determine their respective responsibilities, in particular as regards the exercising of the rights of the data subject and their respective duties to inform the data subjects about the processing, in a transparent manner, by means of an arrangement between them.[1090] The GDPR does not require this arrangement to take the form of a contract or other legal act. However, the EDPB recommends that the arrangement is made in the form of a binding document such as a contract, as the arrangement needs to be binding upon each of the joint controllers.[1091]

927. The essence of the joint controllership arrangement needs to be made available to the data subject.[1092] According to the EDPB, the notion 'essence of the arrangement' should at least cover all the elements of the information referred to in Articles 13 and 14 GDPR, and for each of these elements, the arrangement should specify which joint controller is responsible for ensuring compliance with these elements.[1093] It is up to the controllers to decide the most effective way to make the essence of the arrangement available to the data subjects. This could be done together with the information in Article 13 or Article 14 in a data protection notice or upon request, as long as the information is provided in a consistent manner.[1094]

928. The objective of the requirement to have a joint controllership arrangement in place is to ensure that where multiple controllers are involved, especially in complex data processing environments, responsibility for compliance with data protection rules is clearly allocated. This is to avoid that the protection of personal data is reduced or that a negative conflict of competence would lead to loopholes whereby some obligations are not complied with by any of the involved controllers.[1095]

1089. Art. 26 GDPR. The concept of 'joint controllership' has been discussed above in Part II, D, s. 1.3.2.
1090. Joint controllers are not required to have such an arrangement in place when their respective responsibilities are determined by EU or Member State law to which they are subject.
1091. EDPB, Guidelines 07/2020 on the concepts of controller and processor in the GDPR adopted on 7 July 2021, v2, 46.
1092. Art. 26(2) GDPR.
1093. EDPB, Guidelines 07/2020 on the concepts of controller and processor in the GDPR adopted on 7 July 2021, v2, 47.
1094. EDPB, Guidelines 07/2020 on the concepts of controller and processor in the GDPR adopted on 7 July 2021, v2, 47.
1095. EDPB, Guidelines 07/2020 on the concepts of controller and processor in the GDPR adopted on 7 July 2021, v2, 44.

929. The allocation of responsibilities should be in line with the factual circumstances of the processing in order to achieve an operative agreement and is not limited to the topics referred to in Article 26(1) GDPR but extends to the overall joint processing. Next to the obligation to provide information about the processing to the data subjects and the obligation to respond to data subject requests, the joint controllers also need to consider at least the following topics: implementation of general data protection principles (Article 5 GDPR), legal basis of the processing (Article 6 GDPR), security measures (Article 32 GDPR), notification and communication of data breaches (Articles 33 and 34 GDPR), data protection impact assessments (Articles 35 and 36 GDPR), the use of processors (Article 28 GDPR), the transfers of data to third countries (Chapter V GDPR) and the communication with data subjects and supervisory authorities.[1096] Depending on the context of the processing, also other factors need to be included, such as the limitation on the use of personal data for other purposes than one of the joint controllers.

930. It could be pointed out that the obligations of the joint controllers do not need to be equally distributed among them. The existence of joint controllership does not necessarily imply that the various operators have an equal responsibility.[1097] Nonetheless, irrespective of the terms of the arrangement, data subjects may exercise their rights in respect of and against each of the joint controllers – that is, in respect of those operations for which the controllers jointly determine the purposes and means.[1098]

B. Data Processing Agreement

931. Controllers may engage processors to process personal data on their behalf. A processor is defined by the GDPR as 'a natural or legal person, public authority, agency or other body which processes personal data on behalf of the controller'.[1099]

932. To ensure compliance with the GDPR, when entrusting a processor with processing activities, the controller should use only processors that provide sufficient guarantees to implement technical and organisational measures that meet the GDPR requirements.[1100] The adherence of the processor to an approved code of conduct or an approved certification mechanism may be used as one element by which such sufficient guarantees can be demonstrated.[1101]

1096. EDPB, Guidelines 07/2020 on the concepts of controller and processor in the GDPR adopted on 7 July 2021, v2, 44.
1097. CJEU 5 June 2018, C-210/16 (*Wirtschaftsakademie*), ECLI:EU:C:2018:388, para. 43, https://eur-lex.europa.eu/legal-content/EN/TXT/?uri=CELEX%3A62016CJ0210.
1098. Art. 26(3) GDPR. If one entity decides alone the purposes and means of preceding or subsequent processing operations, the entity must be considered as the sole controller of this preceding or subsequent operation (CJEU, Case C-40/17, *Fashion ID*, ECLI:EU:2018:1039, para. 74).
1099. Art. 4(8) GDPR.
1100. Art. 28(1) GDPR; Recital 81 GDPR.
1101. Art. 28(5) GDPR.

933. The carrying-out of processing by a processor needs to be governed by a contract that is binding on the processor.[1102] The controller and processor may choose to use an individual contract or standard contractual clauses in accordance with Article 28(6) GDPR.[1103] The EDPB clarifies that there is no obligation for controllers and processors to enter into a contract based on the standard contractual clauses. The standard contractual clauses are not necessarily preferred over an individual negotiated contract, as long as the contract meets the Article 28(3) GDPR requirements.[1104]

934. Article 28(3) GDPR requires that data processing agreements set out the subject matter and duration of the processing, the nature and purposes of processing, the type of personal data and categories of data subjects, taking into account the specific tasks and responsibilities of the processor in the context of the processing to be carried out and the risk to the rights and freedoms of the data subject.[1105]

935. Moreover, each data processing agreement needs to stipulate that the processor:

(a) Processes the personal data only on documented instructions from the controller, unless the processor is legally required to do so. In the latter case, the processor needs to inform the controller of the legal requirement to process the data, unless the law prohibits such information on important grounds of public interest. Where a processor believes that an instruction from the controller infringes applicable data protection law, the processor must immediately inform the controller thereof.[1106]
(b) Ensures that persons authorised to process the personal data have committed themselves to confidentiality or are under an appropriate statutory obligation of confidentiality.
(c) Takes all security measures required pursuant to Article 32 GDPR.
(d) Respects the conditions for engaging another processor (sub-processor) (Article 28(2) and (4) GDPR). Article 28(2) GDPR requires that the processor does not engage another processor without prior specific or general written authorisation of the controller. In case of general written authorisation, the processor needs to commit to inform the controller of any intended changes of sub-processors to give the controller the opportunity to object to such changes. In addition, Article 28(4) GDPR requires the processor to impose the same contractual obligations

1102. Art. 28(3) GDPR.
1103. The Commission adopted standard contractual clauses for controllers and processors in its Implementing Decision (EU) 2021/915 of 4 June 2021 on standard contractual clauses between controllers and processors under Art. 28(7) of Regulation (EU) 2016/679 of the European Parliament and of the Council and Art. 29(7) of Regulation (EU) 2018/1725 of the European Parliament and of the Council, C/2021/3701, OJ L 199, 7.6.2021, 18–30.
1104. EDPB, Guidelines 07/2020 on the concepts of controller and processor in the GDPR adopted on 7 July 2021, v2, 33.
1105. *See also* EDPB, Guidelines 07/2020 on the concepts of controller and processor in the GDPR adopted on 7 July 2021, v2, 35.
1106. Art. 28(3), second sub-paragraph GDPR.

on his sub-processors as the ones that are imposed on him by the controller. Where a sub-processor fails to fulfil its data protection obligations, the processor remains fully liable to the controller for the performance of that other processor's obligations.

(e) Taking into account the nature of the processing, assists the controller by appropriate technical and organisational measures for the fulfilment of the controller's obligation to respond to data subject requests.
(f) Assists the controller in ensuring compliance with the obligations pursuant to Articles 32 to 36 GDPR taking into account the nature of processing and the information available to the processor.
(g) At the choice of the controller, deletes or returns all the personal data to the controller after the end of the provision of services relating to processing, and deletes existing copies unless storage is required by law.
(h) Makes available to the controller all information necessary to demonstrate compliance with the obligations laid down in Article 28 GDPR and allow for and contribute to audits, including inspections, conducted by the controller or another auditor mandated by the controller.

936. Depending on the context and the risks of the processing and any additional applicable requirement, additional relevant information might need to be included in the data processing agreement.

IV. Data Protection by Design and by Default

937. The protection of the rights and freedoms of data subjects requires that appropriate technical and organisational measures are taken to ensure compliance with the GDPR.[1107] In order to be able to demonstrate such compliance, the controller needs to adopt internal policies and implement measures which meet in particular the principles of data protection by design and data protection by default.[1108]

938. Recital 78 GDPR clarifies that such measures could consist of minimising the processing of personal data, pseudonymising personal data as soon as possible, transparency with regard to the functions and processing of personal data, enabling the data subject to monitor the data processing, and enabling the controller to create and improve security features.

A. Data Protection by Design

1. Appropriate Technical and Organisational Measures

939. Article 25(1) GDPR introduces the requirement for controllers to implement appropriate technical and organisational measures which are designed to

1107. Recital 78 GDPR.
1108. Art. 25 GDPR.

implement data protection principles in an effective manner and to integrate the necessary safeguards into the processing, both at the time of the determination of the means for processing and at the time of the processing itself.[1109] The terms 'technical and organisational measures' and 'necessary safeguards' need to be understood as referring to any method or means that a controller may employ in the processing, from the use of advanced technical solutions to the basic training of personnel.[1110] Being 'appropriate' means that the measures and safeguards need to be suited to achieve the intended purpose, that is to implement the data protection principles effectively.[1111] This implies that the controller needs to determine the measures and safeguards depending on the specific context of the processing and that he is able to demonstrate that the principles have been maintained.[1112]

940. While determining the measures and safeguards of a specific processing operation, the controller needs to take into account the state of the art, the cost of implementation and the nature, scope, context and purposes of the processing as well as the risks varying likelihood and severity for rights and freedoms of natural persons posed by the processing.[1113] The EDPB clarifies the concepts of 'state of the art', 'cost of implementation', 'nature, scope, context and purpose of processing', 'risks of varying likelihood and severity for rights and freedoms of natural persons posed by the processing' in its Article 25 Guidelines. In the context of Article 25 GDPR, the reference to 'state of the art' imposes an obligation on controllers '*to take account of the current progress in technology that is available in the market*'[1114]. This is not only required for determining technological measures, but also applies to organisational ones. The 'cost of implementation' refers to the resources in general, including time and human resources. The EDPB points out, however,

1109. The concept of 'data protection by design' has been intensively discussed in legal literature. *See* e.g., Veale, Michael, et al. 'When Data Protection by Design and Data Subject Rights Clash.' *International Data Privacy Law*, vol. 8, no. 2, 2018, pp. 105–123; Waldman, Ari Ezra. 'Data Protection by Design?: A Critique of Article 25 of the GDPR.' *Cornell International Law Journal*, vol. 53, no. 1, 2020, pp. 147–167; Rubinstein, Ira S, and Nathaniel Good. 'The Trouble with Article 25 (and How to Fix It): the Future of Data Protection by Design and Default.' *International Data Privacy Law*, vol. 10, no. 1, 2020, pp. 37–56; Bygrave, Lee A. 'Data Protection by Design and by Default: Deciphering the EU's Legislative Requirements.' *Oslo Law Review*, vol. 1, no. 2, 2017, pp. 105–120; Hildebrandt, Mireille, and Laura Tielemans. 'Data Protection by Design and Technology Neutral Law.' *The Computer Law and Security Report*, vol. 29, no. 5, 2013, pp. 509–521. Porcedda, Maria Grazia. "Privacy by Design' in EU Law.' *Lecture Notes in Computer Science (Including Subseries Lecture Notes in Artificial Intelligence and Lecture Notes in Bioinformatics)*, vol. 11079, Springer International Publishing, Cham, 2018, pp. 183–204. Lecture Notes in Computer Science.

1110. EDPB, Guidelines 4/2019 on Article 25 Data Protection by Design and by Default v2.0, adopted on 20 October 2020, 6, https://edpb.europa.eu/sites/default/files/files/file1/edpb_guidelines_201904_dataprotection_by_design_and_by_default_v2.0_en.pdf.

1111. EDPB, Guidelines 4/2019 on Article 25 Data Protection by Design and by Default v2.0, adopted on 20 October 2020, 7.

1112. EDPB, Guidelines 4/2019 on Article 25 Data Protection by Design and by Default v2.0, adopted on 20 October 2020, 7.

1113. Article 25(1) GDPR.

1114. EDPB, Guidelines 4/2019 on Article 25 Data Protection by Design and by Default v2.0, adopted on 20 October 2020, 8.

that effective measures need to exist. While the cost element does not require controllers to spend a disproportionate amount of resources on measures, less resource demanding measures are only appropriate where they implement the data protection principles effectively. The concept of 'nature' can be understood as the inherent characteristics of the processing. The 'scope' refers to the size and range of the processing.[1115]

2. Risk-Based Approach

941. The EDPB recalls that the GDPR adopts a coherent risk-based approach with a view to identifying appropriate technical and organisational measures.[1116] Recital 76 GDPR specifies that the likelihood and severity of the risk to the rights and freedoms of the data subject should be determined by reference to the nature, scope, context and purposes of the processing.

942. Risk should be evaluated on the basis of an objective assessment, by which it is established whether data processing operations involve a risk or a high risk. Recital 75 GDPR clarifies that the risk to the rights and freedoms of natural persons, of varying likelihood and severity, may result from different situations. First, the risk could follow from personal data processing which could lead to physical, material or non-material damage, in particular where the processing may give rise to discrimination, identity theft or fraud, financial loss, damage to reputation, loss of confidentiality of personal data protected by professional secrecy, unauthorised reversal of pseudonymisation or any other significant economic or social disadvantage. Second, the risk could follow from a situation where data subjects might be deprived of their rights and freedoms or prevented from exercising control over their personal data. Moreover, the rights and freedoms of natural persons would be in risk where personal data are processed which reveal racial or ethnic origin, political opinions, religion or philosophical beliefs, health information or other special categories of personal data. Other risks could exist where personal aspects of an individual are evaluated in order to create or use personal profiles, where personal data of vulnerable persons are processed (e.g., children), or where processing involved a large amount of personal data and affects a large number of data subjects.

B. Data Protection by Default

943. Article 25(2) GDPR requires controllers to implement appropriate technical and organisational measures for ensuring that, by default, only personal data

1115. EDPB, Guidelines 4/2019 on Article 25 Data Protection by Design and by Default v2.0, adopted on 20 October 2020, 9.
1116. EDPB, Guidelines 4/2019 on Article 25 Data Protection by Design and by Default v2.0, adopted on 20 October 2020, 9 – referring to Arts 24, 25, 32 and 35 GDPR.

which are necessary for each specific purpose of the processing are processed.[1117] This obligation applies throughout the processing lifecycle, to the amount of personal data collected, to the extent of their processing, the period of their storage and their accessibility.[1118] The term 'by default' refers to '*making choices regarding configuration values or processing options that are set or prescribed in a processing system, such as a software application, service or device, or a manual processing procedure that affect the amount of personal data collected, the extent of their processing, the period of their storage and their accessibility*'.[1119]

944. The EDPB clarifies that for the 'amount of personal data collected' both the volume of personal data, as well as the types, categories and level of detail of the processed data need to be considered. The design choices need to take into account the increased risks to the principles of integrity and confidentiality, data minimisation and storage limitation. If certain categories of personal data are unnecessary or if a high level of detail is not needed, then any surplus data should not be collected. In the same line, the data cannot be stored for longer than objectively justifiable as necessary.

C. Implementing Data Protection Principles

945. Article 25 GDPR requires that controllers implement the data protection principles in the processing of personal data using data protection by design and by default.

946. The core data protection principles include: transparency, lawfulness, fairness, purpose limitation, data minimisation, accuracy, storage limitation, integrity and confidentiality and accountability.[1120] In the guidelines on Article 25 GDPR, the EDPB describes several examples of how technical and organisational measures can contribute to implement these principles in different stages of design of processing activities.[1121]

947. The table below provides an overview of these key design and default elements:

1117. About the notion of 'data protection by default' *see* e.g., Bourka, Athena, and Prokopios Drogkaris. *Recommendations on Shaping Technology According to GDPR Provisions: exploring the notion of data protection by default*. ENISA, 2018; Hansen, Marit. 'Data Protection by Design and by Default à La European General Data Protection Regulation.' *IFIP Advances in Information and Communication Technology*, vol. 498, Springer International Publishing, Cham, 2017, pp. 27–38. IFIP Advances in Information and Communication Technology.
1118. Art. 25(2) GDPR.
1119. EDPB, Guidelines 4/2019 on Article 25 Data Protection by Design and by Default v2.0, adopted on 20 October 2020, 11.
1120. Art. 5 GDPR.
1121. EDPB, Guidelines 4/2019 on Article 25 Data Protection by Design and by Default v2.0, adopted on 20 October 2020, 15 e.s.

Transparency	
Clarity	Information shall be in clear and plain language, concise and intelligible.
Semantics	Communication should have a clear meaning to the audience in question.
Accessibility	Information shall be easily accessible for the data subject.
Contextual	Information should be provided at the relevant time and in the appropriate form.
Relevance	Information should be relevant and applicable to the specific data subject.
Universal design	Information shall be accessible to all data subjects, include use of machine-readable languages to facilitate and automate readability and clarity.
Comprehensible	Data subjects should have a fair understanding of what they can expect with regards to the processing of their personal data, particularly when the data subjects are children or other vulnerable groups.
Multichannel	Information should be provided in different channels and media, not only the textual, to increase the probability for the information to effectively reach the data subject.
Layered	The information should be layered in a manner that resolves the tension between completeness and understanding, while accounting for data subjects' reasonable expectations.
Lawfulness	
Relevance	The correct legal basis shall be applied to the processing.
Differentiation	The legal basis used for each processing activity shall be differentiated.
Specified purpose	The appropriate legal basis must be clearly connected to the specific purpose of processing.
Necessity	Processing must be necessary and unconditional for the purpose to be lawful.
Autonomy	The data subject should be granted the highest degree of autonomy as possible with respect to control over personal data within the frames of the legal basis.
Gaining consent	Consent must be freely given, specific, informed and unambiguous. Particular consideration should be given to the capacity of children and young people to provide informed consent.

Consent withdrawal	Where consent is the legal basis, the processing should facilitate withdrawal of consent. Withdrawal shall be as easy as giving consent. If not, then the consent mechanism of the controller does not comply with the GDPR.
Balancing of interests	Where legitimate interest is the legal basis, the controller must carry out a weighted balancing of interest, giving particular consideration to the power imbalance, specifically children under the age of 18 and other vulnerable groups. There shall be measures and safeguards to mitigate the negative impact on the data subjects.
Predetermination	The legal basis shall be established before the processing takes place.
Cessation	If the legal basis ceases to apply, the processing shall cease accordingly.
Adjust	If there is a valid change of legal basis for the processing, the actual processing must be adjusted in accordance with the new legal basis.
Allocation of responsibility	Whenever joint controllership is envisaged, the parties must apportion in a clear and transparent way their respective responsibilities vis-à-vis the data subject, and design the measures of the processing in accordance with this allocation.
Fairness	
Autonomy	Data subjects should be granted the highest degree of autonomy possible to determine the use made of their personal data, as well as over the scope and conditions of that use or processing.
Interaction	Data subjects must be able to communicate and exercise their rights in respect of the personal data processed by the controller.
Expectation	Processing should correspond with data subjects' reasonable expectations.
Non-discrimination	The controller shall not unfairly discriminate against data subjects.
Non-exploitation	The controller should not exploit the needs or vulnerabilities of data subjects.

Consumer choice	The controller should not 'lock-in' their users in an unfair manner. Whenever a service processing personal data is proprietary, it may create a lock-in to the service, which may not be fair, if it impairs the data subjects' possibility to exercise their right of data portability in accordance with Article 20.
Power balance	Power balance should be a key objective of the controller-data subject relationship. Power imbalances should be avoided. When this is not possible, they should be recognised and accounted for with suitable countermeasures.
No risk transfer	Controllers should not transfer the risks of the enterprise to the data subjects.
No deception	Data processing information and options should be provided in an objective and neutral way, avoiding any deceptive or manipulative language or design.
Respect rights	The controller must respect the fundamental rights of data subjects and implement appropriate measures and safeguards and not impinge on those rights unless expressly justified by law.
Ethical	The controller should see the processing's wider impact on individuals' rights and dignity.
Truthful	The controller must make available information about how they process personal data, they should act as they declare they will and not mislead the data subjects.
Human intervention	The controller must incorporate qualified human intervention that is capable of uncovering biases that machines may create in accordance with the right to not be subject to automated individual decision-making in Article 22.
Fair algorithms	Regularly assess whether algorithms are functioning in line with the purposes and adjust the algorithms to mitigate uncovered biases and ensure fairness in the processing. Data subjects should be informed about the functioning of the processing of personal data based on algorithms that analyse or make predictions about them, such as work performance, economic situation, health, personal preferences, reliability or behaviour, location or movements.
Purpose limitation	
Predetermination	The legitimate purposes shall be determined before the design of the processing.

Specificity	The purposes shall be specified and explicit as to why personal data is being processed.
Purpose orientation	The purpose of processing should guide the design of the processing and set processing boundaries.
Necessity	The purpose determines what personal data is necessary for the processing.
Compatibility	Any new purpose must be compatible with the original purpose for which the data was collected and guide relevant changes in design.
Limit further processing	The controller should not connect datasets or perform any further processing for new incompatible purposes.
Limitations of reuse	The controller should use technical measures, including hashing and encryption, to limit the possibility of repurposing personal data. The controller should also have organisational measures, such as policies and contractual obligations, which limit reuse of personal data.
Review	The controller should regularly review whether the processing is necessary for the purposes for which the data was collected and test the design against purpose limitation.
Data minimisation	
Data avoidance	Avoid processing personal data altogether when this is possible for the relevant purpose.
Limitation	Limit the amount of personal data collected to what is necessary for the purpose.
Access limitation	Shape the data processing in a way that a minimal number of people need access to personal data to perform their duties, and limit access accordingly.
Relevance	Personal data should be relevant to the processing in question, and the controller should be able to demonstrate this relevance.
Necessity	Each personal data category shall be necessary for the specified purposes and should only be processed if it is not possible to fulfil the purpose by other means.
Aggregation	Use aggregated data when possible.
Pseudonymisation	Pseudonymise personal data as soon as it is no longer necessary to have directly identifiable personal data, and store identification keys separately.
Anonymisation and deletion	Where personal data is not, or no longer necessary for the purpose, personal data shall be anonymised or deleted.

Data flow	The data flow should be made efficient enough to not create more copies than necessary.
'State of the art'	The controller should apply up-to-date and appropriate technologies for data avoidance and minimisation.
Accuracy	
Data source	Sources of personal data should be reliable in terms of data accuracy.
Degree of accuracy	Each personal data element should be as accurate as necessary for the specified purposes.
Measurably accurate	Reduce the number of false positives/negatives, for example biases in automated decisions and artificial intelligence.
Verification	Depending on the nature of the data, in relation to how often it may change, the controller should verify the correctness of personal data with the data subject before and at different stages of the processing (e.g., to age requirements).
Erasure/ rectification	The controller shall erase or rectify inaccurate data without delay. The controller shall in particular facilitate this where the data subjects are or were children and later want to remove such personal data.
Error propagation avoidance	Controllers should mitigate the effect of an accumulated error in the processing chain.
Access	Data subjects should be given information about and effective access to personal data in accordance with the GDPR Articles 12 to 15 in order to control accuracy and rectify as needed.
Continued accuracy	Personal data should be accurate at all stages of the processing, tests of accuracy should be carried out at critical steps.
Up to date	Personal data shall be updated if necessary for the purpose.
Data design	Use of technological and organisational design features to decrease inaccuracy, for example present concise predetermined choices instead of free text fields.
Storage limitation	
Deletion and anonymisation	The controller should have clear internal procedures and functionalities for deletion and/or anonymisation.
Effectiveness of anonymisation / deletion	The controller shall make sure that it is not possible to reidentify anonymised data or recover deleted data, and should test whether this is possible.

Automation	Deletion of certain personal data should be automated.
Storage criteria	The controller shall determine what data and length of storage is necessary for the purpose.
Justification	The controller shall be able to justify why the period of storage is necessary for the purpose and the personal data in question, and be able to disclose the rationale behind, and legal grounds for the retention period.
Enforcement of retention policies	The controller should enforce internal retention policies and conduct tests of whether the organisation practices its policies.
Backups / logs	Controllers shall determine what personal data and length of storage is necessary for backups and logs.
Data flow	Controllers should beware of the flow of personal data, and the storage of any copies thereof, and seek to limit their 'temporary' storage.
Integrity and confidentiality	
Information security management system	Information security management system (ISMS) – have an operative means of managing policies and procedures for information security.
Risk analysis	Assess the risks against the security of personal data by considering the impact on individuals' rights and counter-identified risks. For use in risk assessment; develop and maintain a comprehensive, systematic and realistic 'threat modelling' and an attack surface analysis of the designed software to reduce attack vectors and opportunities to exploit weak points and vulnerabilities.
Security by design	Consider security requirements as early as possible in the system design and development and continuously integrate and perform relevant tests.
Maintenance	Regular review and test software, hardware, systems and services, etc. to uncover vulnerabilities of the systems supporting the processing.
Access control management	Only the authorised personnel who need to should have access to the personal data necessary for their processing tasks, and the controller should differentiate between access privileges of authorised personnel. – Access limitation (agents) – shape the data processing in a way that a minimal number of people need access to personal data to perform their duties, and limit access accordingly.

	– Access limitation (content) – in the context of each processing operation, limit access to only those attributes per data set that are needed to perform that operation. Moreover, limit access to data pertaining to those data subjects who are in the remit of the respective employee. – Access segregation – shape the data processing in a way that no individual needs comprehensive access to all data collected about a data subject, much less all personal data of a particular category of data subjects.
Secure transfers	Transfers shall be secured against unauthorised and accidental access and changes.
Secure storage	Data storage shall be secure from unauthorised access and changes. There should be procedures to assess the risk of centralised or decentralised storage, and what categories of personal data this applies to. Some data may need additional security measures than others or isolation from others.
Pseudonymisation	Personal data and backups/logs should be pseudonymised as a security measure to minimise risks of potential data breaches, for example using hashing or encryption.
Backups/logs	Keep backups and logs to the extent necessary for information security, use audit trails and event monitoring as a routine security control. These shall be protected from unauthorised and accidental access and change and reviewed regularly and incidents should be handled promptly.
Disaster recovery/ business continuity	Address information system disaster recovery and business continuity requirements to restore the availability of personal data following major incidents.
Protection according to risk	All categories of personal data should be protected with measures adequate with respect to the risk of a security breach. Data presenting special risks should, when possible, be kept separated from the rest of the personal data.
Security incident response management	Have in place routines, procedures and resources to detect, contain, handle, report and learn from data breaches.
Incident management	Controller should have processes in place to handle breaches and incidents, in order to make the processing system more robust. This includes notification procedures, such as management of notification (to the supervisory authority) and information (to data subjects).

D. Processors and Producers

948. Article 25 GDPR is not directly addressed at processors and producers. Nonetheless, Recital 78 GDPR specifies that when developing, designing, selecting and using applications, services and products that are based on the processing of personal data or process personal data to fulfil their task, producers of such products, services and applications should be encouraged to take into account the right to data protection when developing and designing such products, etc., with due regard to the state of the art, to make sure that controllers and processors are able to fulfil their data protection obligations.

949. The EDPB considers processors and producers as key enablers for data protection by design and by default. Hence, they should be aware that controllers are required to process personal data with systems and technologies that have built-in data protection – and they should seek to facilitate the data protection by design and by default implementation in order to support the controller's ability to comply with the Article 25 GDPR obligations. As it is up to the controller to choose producers and processors that offer systems enabling or supporting data protection by design and by default, the EDPB recommends controllers to require that processors and producers demonstrate how their hardware, software, services or systems enable the controller to comply with the requirements to accountability in accordance with Article 25 GDPR. This could be achieved, for example, by using key performance indicators to demonstrate the effectiveness of the measures and safeguards at implementing the principles and rights.[1122]

V. Record of Processing Activities

950. In order to demonstrate compliance with the GDPR, controllers and processors are required to maintain records of processing activities under their responsibility.[1123] A record of processing activities is an internal record that contains information about the processing activities carried out by an organisation. The record needs to be in writing, including in electronic form.[1124] Upon request of the supervisory authority, the controller or processor needs to make the record available to the supervisory authority.[1125]

951. The obligation to keep a record of processing activities is not applicable to organisations employing fewer than 250 persons unless the processing activities are likely to result in a risk to the rights and freedoms of data subject, the processing is not occasional, or the processing includes special categories of data or personal data

1122. EDPB, Guidelines 4/2019 on Article 25 Data Protection by Design and by Default v2.0, adopted on 20 October 2020, 29–30, https://edpb.europa.eu/sites/default/files/files/file1/edpb_guidelines_201904_dataprotection_by_design_and_by_default_v2.0_en.pdf.
1123. Art. 30 GDPR; Recital 82 GDPR.
1124. Art. 30(2) GDPR.
1125. Art. 30(4) GDPR.

relating to criminal convictions and offences.[1126] These three types of processing to which the small organisation derogation does not apply are alternative, meaning that the occurrence of any one of them alone triggers the obligation to maintain the record of processing activities, even though such organisations need only to maintain records for these specific types of processing.[1127] Thus, a company with less than 250 employees, but carrying out processing activities that are likely to result in a risk to the rights of the data subjects, is obliged to maintain a record of processing activities for the types of processing mentioned in Article 30(5) GDPR. This means that even a small organisation that regularly processes personal data regarding its employees, needs to keep a record of processing activities for this type of non-occasional processing.

952. Article 30(1) GDPR sets out the content requirements for the record of processing activities held by the controller. The record must contain the following information:

(a) the name and contact details of the controller and, where applicable, joint controller, the controller's representative and the data protection officer;
(b) the purposes of the processing;
(c) a description of the categories of data subjects and of the categories of personal data;
(d) the categories of recipients to whom the personal data have been or will be disclosed including recipients in third countries or international organisations;
(e) where applicable, transfers of personal data to a third country or an international organisation, including the identification of that third country or international organisation and, in the case of transfers based on derogations for specific situations, the documentation of suitable safeguards;
(f) where possible, the envisaged time limits for erasure of the different categories of data; and
(g) where possible, a general description of the technical and organisational security measures.

953. The record should at all times reflect the reality and must be maintained and updated according to the actual processing activities under the controller's responsibility. The record is a document with inventory and analysis purposes which helps the controller to be compliant with as well as to demonstrate compliance with the GDPR. Creating and updating the record requires the record owner to map the data processing activities, the risks of the processing and so on. Setting up a record can be a time consuming project. Several supervisory authorities have template records available on their websites.

1126. Art. 30(5) GDPR.
1127. Art. 29 Working Party, Position Paper on the derogations from the obligation to maintain records of processing activities pursuant to Art. 30(5) GDPR (endorsed by the European Data Protection Board), 2.

954. A light version of the record is required for processing activities carried out on behalf of a controller. Article 30(2) GDPR requires processors to maintain a record, containing:

(a) the name and contact details of the processor or processors and of each controller on behalf of which the processor is acting, and, where applicable, of the controller's or the processor's representative, and the data protection officer;
(b) the categories of processing carried out on behalf of each controller;
(c) where applicable, transfers of personal data to a third country or an international organisation, including the identification of that third country or international organisation and, in the case of transfers based on derogations for specific situations, the documentation of suitable safeguards; and
(d) where possible, a general description of the technical and organisational security measures.

Also the processor needs to keep the record up to date.

955. The GDPR requires that the record of processing activities is in writing, including in electronic form.[1128] The records need to be made available to the supervisory authority on request.[1129]

VI. Security of Personal Data

A. Security of Processing

956. In order to maintain security and to prevent processing in infringement of the GDPR, controllers and processors must consider the risks that are presented by their processing activities and implement measures to mitigate those risks.[1130] In assessing the appropriate level of security, organisations need to consider the risks that are presented by processing, in particular from accidental or unlawful destruction, loss, alteration, unauthorised disclosure of, or access to personal data transmitted, stored or otherwise processed.[1131]

957. Organisations are required to implement technical and organisational measures to ensure a level of security appropriate to the risk, taking into account the

1128. Art. 30(2) GDPR.
1129. Art. 30(4) GDPR.
1130. Recital 83 GDPR.
1131. Art. 32(2) GDPR ; *see*, for example, Georgiopoulou, Zafeiroula, et al. 'GDPR Compliance: Proposed Technical and Organizational Measures for Cloud Provider.' *Information and Computer Security*, vol. 28, no. 5, 2020, pp. 665–680; Lenhard. *Data Security: Technical and Organizational Protection Measures Against Data Loss and Computer Crime*. Springer Fachmedien Wiesbaden GmbH, 2022.

state of the art, the costs of implementation and the nature, scope, context and purposes of processing as well as the risk of varying likelihood and severity for the rights and freedoms of natural persons.[1132] Such measures include, as appropriate:

- the pseudonymisation and encryption of personal data;
- the ability to ensure the ongoing confidentiality, integrity, availability and resilience of processing systems and services;
- the ability to restore the availability and access to personal data in a timely manner in the event of a physical or technical incident; and
- a process for regularly testing, assessing and evaluating the effectives of technical and organisational measures for ensuring the security of the processing.[1133]

958. Adherence to an approved code of conduct or an approved certification mechanism is considered as one element by which controllers and processors could demonstrate the security of the processing.[1134]

959. As part of the security measures, controllers and processors need to take steps to ensure that any natural person who has access to personal data under their authority, does not process the data except on their instructions, unless the person is legally required to do so.[1135]

B. Notification of Data Breaches

960. Article 33 GDPR requires controllers to notify data breaches that are not unlikely to result in a risk to the rights and freedoms of natural persons to the competent supervisory authority.[1136]

961. Article 4(12) GDPR defines 'personal data breach' as 'a breach of security leading to the accidental or unlawful destruction, loss, alteration, unauthorised disclosure of, or access to, personal data transmitted, stored or otherwise processed'. If not addressed in an appropriate and timely manner, such breaches may result in physical, material or non-material damage to natural persons such as loss of control over their personal data or limitation of their rights, discrimination, identity theft or fraud, financial loss, unauthorised reversal of pseudonymisation, damage to

---

1132. Art. 32(1) GDPR.
1133. Art. 32(1) GDPR.
1134. Art. 32 (3) GDPR.
1135. Art. 32 (4) GDPR.
1136. Nieuwesteeg, Bernold, and Michael Faure. 'An Analysis of the Effectiveness of the EU Data Breach Notification Obligation.' *The Computer Law and Security Report*, vol. 34, no. 6, 2018, pp. 1232–1246; Garrison, Chlotia, and Clovia Hamilton. 'A Comparative Analysis of the EU GDPR to the US's Breach Notifications.' *Information & Communications Technology Law*, vol. 28, no. 1, 2019, pp. 99–114.

reputation, loss of confidentiality of personal data protected by professional secrecy or any other significant economic or social disadvantage to the natural person concerned.[1137]

962. Breaches can be categorised according to the three information security principles.[1138] 'Confidentiality breaches' are breaches that result from unauthorised or accidental disclosure of, or access to, personal data. 'Integrity breaches' follow from the unauthorised or accidental alteration of personal data. Finally, 'availability breaches' are the consequence of accidental or unauthorised loss of access to, or destruction of, personal data.

963. In the event a data breach occurs, the controller needs to consider first, whether the breach needs to be notified to the supervisory authority, and second, whether the breach needs to be communicated to the data subject.[1139] In any case, the controller needs to internally document any data breaches, regardless of whether being reported to the supervisory authority or not. The record of data breaches should comprise the facts relating to the breach, its effects and the remedial action taken.[1140]

964. Notification of the data breach to the supervisory authority is required when the breach is not unlikely to result in a risk to the rights and freedoms of natural persons.[1141] This risk assessment needs to be made at the time that the controller becomes aware of the breach, without awaiting detailed forensic examination and (early) mitigation steps.[1142] The risk that a breach imposes will depend on the prior safety measures taken by the controller. For example, when an unencrypted device without password protection gets stolen from a sales representative personal data of many customers stored on the device may become available to a third party. The lack of basic security measures, such as password protection, enhances the risk level for the affected data subjects because the likelihood that the risk will result increases. According to the EDPB, the supervisory authority needs to be notified where a device storing non-encrypted personal data of a large group of customers gets stolen. Alternately, the theft of a device storing encrypted personal data on, does not trigger the notification requirement.[1143]

965. Where the controller is of the opinion that the breach is likely to result in a risk, the supervisory authority should be notified without undue delay and, where

1137. Recital 85 GDPR.
1138. EDPB, Guidelines 01/2021 on Examples regarding Data Breach Notification, v2.0, adopted on 14 December 2021, 6; WP29, Guidelines on Personal data breach notification under Regulation 2016/679, WP250rev.01, adopted on 3 October 2017, last revised and adopted on 6 February 2018, as endorsed by the EDPB, 7.
1139. *See supra.*
1140. Art. 33(5) GDPR.
1141. Art. 33(1) GDPR.
1142. EDPB, Guidelines 01/2021 on Examples regarding Data Breach Notification, v2.0, adopted on 14 December 2021, 7.
1143. EDPB, Guidelines 01/2021 on Examples regarding Data Breach Notification, v2.0, adopted on 14 December 2021, 25.

feasible, not later than 72 hours after the controller having become aware of it. If not feasible within such 72-hour time frame, notification at a later point should be accompanied with the reasons for the delay.

966. In case a processor becomes aware of a personal data breach, the processor needs to notify the controller without undue delay.[1144]

967. The notification to the supervisory authority first describes the nature of the data breach including where possible, the categories and approximate number of data subjects concerned, and the categories and approximate number of personal data records concerned. Further, the name and contact details of the data protection officer or other contact point where more information can be obtained, needs to be communicated to the supervisory authority. In the notification also the likely consequences of the data breach need to be described, as well as the measures taken or proposed to be taken by the controller to address the reach, including, where appropriate, measures to mitigate its possible adverse effects.[1145] If it is not possible to provide the information at the same time, the information may be provided in phases without undue further delay.

C. Communication of Data Breaches

968. In addition, controllers need to communicate to the data subject a personal data breach, without undue delay, where that breach is likely to result in a high risk to the rights and freedoms of the natural person in order to allow the data subject to take the necessary precautions.[1146] Contrary to the obligation to notify the breach to the supervisory authority, breaches only need to be communicated to the data subject where it is likely that the breach will result in a *high* risk for the affected data subjects.[1147]

969. The data subjects do not need to be informed about the data breach if one of the following conditions are met.[1148] First, where the controller has implemented appropriate security measures to the personal data affected by the breach. In particular, measures that render the personal data unintelligible to any unauthorised person, such as encryption. Second, where the controller has taken subsequent measures which ensure that the high risk to the rights and freedoms of data subjects is no longer likely to materialise. Finally, where the communication of the breach to the data subjects would involve disproportionate effort. In such case, a public communication or similar measure whereby the data subjects are informed in an equally effective manner, would replace the communication.

1144. Art. 33(2) GDPR.
1145. Art. 33(3) GDPR.
1146. Art. 34(1) GDPR.
1147. Alunge, Rogers. 'Breach of Security vs Personal Data Breach: Effect on EU Data Subject Notification Requirements.' *International Data Privacy Law*, vol. 11, no. 2, 2021, pp. 163–181.
1148. Art. 34(3) GDPR.

970. Where communication is required, the data subjects should be informed about the breach as soon as it is reasonably feasible and in close cooperation with the supervisory authority and with respect to the guidance provided by relevant data protection and/or law enforcement authorities.[1149]

971. The communication to the data subject should describe the nature of the data breach as well as recommendations for the data subjects concerned to mitigate potential adverse effects in clear and plain language.[1150]

VII. Data Protection Impact Assessment and Prior Consultation

A. Data Protection Impact Assessment

972. Article 35 GDPR introduces the obligation for data controllers to carry out an assessment of the impact of envisaged processing operations on the protection of personal data, when the type of processing in particular using new technologies, and taking into account the nature, scope, context and purposes of the processing, is likely to result in a high risk to the rights and freedoms of natural persons. This obligation replaces the general obligation to notify processing of personal data to supervisory authorities under Directive 95/46/EC. Instead of having to notify the supervisory authorities about their processing, controllers are now required to assess the particular likelihood and severity of high risk processing activities. In line with the risk-based approach, the data protection impact assessment is only required for high risk processing activities.[1151]

973. The controller is obliged to conduct a data protection impact assessment where processing is likely to result in a high risk for the data subjects, such as for large-scale processing operations which aim to process a considerable amount of personal data at regional, national or supranational level and which could affect a large number of data subjects and which are likely to result in a high risk. The WP29 has specified nine criteria that should be considered in order to determine the need for a data protection impact assessment.[1152]

1149. Recital 86 GDPR.
1150. Art. 34(2) GDPR.
1151. Demetzou, Katerina. 'Data Protection Impact Assessment: A Tool for Accountability and the Unclarified Concept of 'High Risk' in the General Data Protection Regulation.' *The Computer Law and Security Report*, vol. 35, no. 6, 2019, p. 105342; Binns, Reuben. 'Data Protection Impact Assessments: A Meta-Regulatory Approach.' *International Data Privacy Law*, vol. 7, no. 1, 2017, pp. 22–35.
1152. Art. 29 Working Party, Guidelines on Data Protection Impact Assessment (DPIA) and determining whether processing is 'likely to result in a high risk' for the purposes of Regulation 2016/679, WP248 rev.01. adopted on 4 April 2017, as last revised and adopted on 4 October 2017 (endorsed by the EDPB), 9.

1) Evaluation or scoring, including profiling and predicting, especially from 'aspects concerning the data subject's performance at work, economic, situation, health, personal preferences or interests, reliability or behaviour, location or movements' (Recitals 71 and 91 GDPR).
2) Processing aimed at taking decision on data subjects, i.e., automated decision-making, with legal or similar significant effect (Article 35(3)(a) GDPR).
3) Systematic monitoring, where processing is used to observe, monitor or control data subjects, including data collected through networks or '*a systematic monitoring of a publicly accessible area*' (Article 35(3)(c) GDPR).
4) Processing of sensitive data or data of a highly personal nature, including the special categories of personal data defined in Article 9 GDPR and data relating to criminal convictions or offences as defined in Article 10 GDPR.
5) Processing data on a large scale, depending on the number of data subjects concerned (either as a specific number or as a proportion of the relevant population), the volume of data and/or the range of different data items being processed, the duration, or permanence of the data processing activity, and the geographical extent of the processing activity.[1153]
6) Matching or combining datasets in a way that would exceed the reasonable expectations of the data subject, for example, because the different purposes or different controllers involved.
7) Processing data concerning vulnerable data subjects, for example where there is an imbalance between the data subject and the controller (employees) or the processing of children's data.
8) Innovative use or applying new technological or organisational solutions in accordance with the state of technological knowledge (Recital 91 GDPR).
9) Processing that in itself 'prevents data subjects from exercising a right or using a service or a contract' (Article 22 GDPR and Recital 91 GDPR).

In general, a data protection impact assessment will need to be carried out where two out of these criteria are met. The more criteria are met, the more likely a high risk exists. However, a data controller can also find that only one of the criteria requires a data protection impact assessment.

974. In addition to the general high risk criterion, Article 35(3) GDPR specifies three situations that always require a data protection impact assessment. First, the systematic and extensive evaluation of personal aspects relating to natural persons which is based on automated processing, including profiling, and on which decisions are based that produce legal effects concerning the persons or significantly affects them. Second, for processing on a large scale of special categories of personal data or of personal data relating to criminal convictions. And finally, for the systematic monitoring of a publicly accessible area on a large scale.

1153. Art. 29 Working Party, Guidelines on Data Protection Impact Assessment (DPIA) and determining whether processing is 'likely to result in a high risk' for the purposes of Regulation 2016/679, WP248 rev.01. adopted on 4 April 2017, as last revised and adopted on 4 October 2017 (endorsed by the EDPB), 10, https://ec.europa.eu/newsroom/just/document.cfm?doc_id=47711.

975. Supervisory authorities may publish lists of the kind of processing operations which are subject to the requirement for a data protection impact assessment, or on the contrary which processing activities are exempted. For example, the Belgian supervisory authority considers a data protection impact assessment necessary for, among others, the following processing operations: when processing involves the use of biometric data for the unique identification of data subject, when personal data concerning health is collected in an automated way by means of an active implantable medical device, or when special categories of personal data or data with a highly personal nature (such as data about poverty, unemployment, involvement in youth welfare or social work) are systematically exchanged between several controllers.[1154]

976. Whenever necessary, the controller needs to carry out the data protection impact assessment *prior* to the processing.[1155] It is advised to start the DPIA process as early as is practicable feasible in the context of the processing.

977. Controllers may address a set of similar processing activities that present similar high risks in one single assessment. Advice needs to be sought from the data protection officer and where necessary and upon request, the processor should assist the controller in this assessment. Where appropriate, the controller needs to seek the views of the data concerned data subjects or their representatives, without prejudice to the protection of commercial or public interests or the security of processing activities. Data protection impact assessments are not a one-time exercise, but whenever there is a change of the risk represented by the processing operations, the controller will have to carry out a review of the assessment.[1156]

978. Article 35(7) GDPR specifies that the assessment shall contain at least:

(a) a systematic description of the envisaged processing operations and the purposes of the processing, including, where appropriate, the legitimate interest pursued by the controller;
(b) an assessment of the necessity and proportionality of the processing operations in relation to the purposes;
(c) an assessment of the risks to the rights and freedoms of the data subjects; and
(d) the measures envisaged to address the risks, including safeguards, security measures and mechanisms to ensure the protection of personal data and to demonstrate compliance with the GDPR.

1154. Belgian Gegevensbeschermingsauthoriteit / Autorité de protection des données, Decision of the General Secretariat 01/2019, 16 January 2019, 3.
1155. Art. 35(1) GDPR, Art. 35(10) GDPR.
1156. WP29, Guidelines on Data Protection Impact Assessment (DPIA) and determining whether processing is 'likely to result in a high risk' for the purposes of Regulation 2016/679, WP248 rev.01. adopted on 4 April 2017, as last revised and adopted on 4 October 2017 (endorsed by the EDPB), 14.

B. Prior Consultation

979. Where a data protection impact assessment reveals a high residual risk, the controller is required to seek prior consultation for the processing from the supervisory authority.[1157] A residual risk exists when the risks identified for the processing cannot be sufficiently addressed, and thus the risk remains high.[1158]

980. The GDPR requires that where a data protection impact assessment indicates that the processing would, in the absence of safeguards, security measures and mechanisms to mitigate the risk, result in a high risk to the rights and freedoms of natural persons and the controller is of the opinion that the risk cannot be mitigated by reasonable means in terms of available technologies and costs of implementation, the controller needs to consult the supervisory authority prior to the start of the processing activities. A residuary high risk is likely to result from certain types of processing and the extent and the frequency thereof, which may result also in a realisation of damage or interference with the rights and freedoms of data subjects. An unacceptable high residual risk exists, for example, where data subjects would encounter significant, or even irreversible, consequences of the processing, which they may not overcome and which seem to be obvious to occur, e.g., as a well-known vulnerability is not patched.[1159]

981. Where the controller has insufficiently identified or mitigated the risk, the supervisory authority will within period of up to eight weeks of receipt of the request for consultation, provide written advice to the controller and, where applicable to the processor, and the authority may use its powers referred to in Article 58 GDPR (investigative, corrective and advisory powers). Depending on the complexity of the intended processing, this period may be extended by six weeks. The period may be suspended until the authority has obtained all information requested for the purposes of the consultation.

982. Article 36(3) GDPR requires the controller to provide the supervisory authority with: (a) where applicable, the respective responsibilities of the controller, joint controllers and processors involved in the processing, (b) the purposes and means of the intended processing, (c) the measures and safeguards provided to protect the data subjects, (d) where applicable, the contact details of the data protection officer, (e) the data protection impact assessment carried out in compliance with Article 35 GDPR and (f) any other information requested by the supervisory authority.

1157. Art. 36 GDPR.

1158. *See*, WP29, Guidelines on Data Protection Impact Assessment (DPIA) and determining whether processing is 'likely to result in a high risk' for the purposes of Regulation 2016/679, WP248 rev.01. adopted on 4 April 2017, as last revised and adopted on 4 October 2017 (endorsed by the EDPB), 18.

1159. Art. 29 Working Party, Guidelines on Data Protection Impact Assessment (DPIA) and determining whether processing is 'likely to result in a high risk' for the purposes of Regulation 2016/679, WP248 rev.01. adopted on 4 April 2017, as last revised and adopted on 4 October 2017 (endorsed by the EDPB), 19, https://ec.europa.eu/newsroom/just/document.cfm?doc_id=47711.

983. Several supervisory authorities have standard forms available in order to ease the prior consultation process. For example, the Belgian supervisory authority has a standard form available in Dutch and French.

VIII. Data Protection Officer

984. Another obligation, for both controllers as processors, introduced by the GDPR is the designation of a data protection officer (DPO).

985. Article 37 GDPR requires that controllers and processor appoint a DPO in any case where a) processing is carried out by a public authority or body, except for courts acting in their judicial capacity, b) the core activities of the controller or processor consist of processing operations which, by virtue of their nature, their scope and/or their purposes, require regular and systematic monitoring of data subjects on a large scale, or c) the core activities of the controller or processor consist of processing on a large scale of special categories of personal data or personal data relating to criminal convictions and offences.

986. As 'core activities' should be considered '*the key operations necessary to achieve the controller's or processor's goals*'.[1160] The term refers to the organisation's primary activities as opposed to data processing as ancillary activities.[1161] However, where processing of data forms an inextricable part of the organisation's activity, this factor should be considered as well. The WP29 provides the example of a hospital. The core activity of a hospital is to provide healthcare, but no hospital could provide healthcare safely and effectively without health data, such as patients' health records. Therefore, processing these data needs to be considered as one of any hospital's core activities and thus designate DPOs.

987. Article 37 GDPR does not define what constitutes 'large-scale' processing. The WP29 recommends to consider the following criteria for determining whether the processing is carried out on a large scale: the number of data subjects concerned (either as a specific number or as a proportion of the relevant population), the volume of data and/or the range of different data items being processed, the duration or permanence of the data processing activity and the geographical extent of the processing activity.[1162] Taking these criteria into account, the processing of personal data for behavioural advertising purposes by a search engine is an example of a large-scale processing operation. The processing of patient data by an individual physician, on the contrary, is not.

1160. WP29 Guidelines on Data Protection Officers, WP243 rev.01, adopted on 13 December 2016, as last revised and adopted on 5 April 2017, and endorsed by the EDPB during its first plenary meeting, 7.
1161. Recital 97 GDPR.
1162. Art. 29 Working Party, Guidelines on Data Protection Officers, WP243 rev.01, adopted on 13 December 2016, as last revised and adopted on 5 April 2017, and endorsed by the EDPB during its first plenary meeting, 8.

988. Article 37 GDPR does not specify what is meant with 'regular and systematic monitoring', but the notion '*monitoring of the behaviour of data subjects*' is mentioned in Recital 24 GDPR, referring to all forms of tracking and profiling on the Internet. However, the WP29 points out that 'monitoring' is not restricted to an online environment and online tracking is only one example of monitoring the behaviour of data subjects. The WP29 interprets 'regular' as '*ongoing or occurring at particular intervals for a particular period*', '*recurring or repeated at fixed times*', or '*constantly or periodically taking place*'. And 'systematic' as '*occurring according to a system*', '*prearranged, organised or methodical*', '*taking place as part of a general plan for data collection*', or '*carried out as part of a strategy*'.[1163]

989. An organisation may decide that there is no need for them to appoint a DPO. Unless it is obvious that the organisation is not required to do so, the EDPB recommends to document the internal analysis leading to this decision, in order to be able to demonstrate that the relevant factors have been taken into account properly.[1164]

990. On the contrary, even when it is not mandatory, an organisation may appoint a DPO on a voluntary basis. If so, the requirements under Articles 37 to 39 GDPR apply as if the designation had been mandatory. Where an organisation for which the designation of a DPO is not required decides to employ staff or outside consultants with tasks relating to data protection, it is important to ensure that there is no confusion regarding their title, status, position and tasks. It should be made clear, in any communications within the organisation, as well as with supervisory authorities, data subjects and the public at large, that the title of the privacy professional (e.g., privacy manager) is not a DPO.[1165]

991. The DPO is designated for all the processing operations carried out by the controller or processor. However, it is the organisation that is required to ensure compliance in accordance with Article 24 GDPR. The DPO is not personally responsible in case of non-compliance.

992. Each DPO must be designated on the basis of professional qualities and, in particular, expert knowledge of data protection law and practices and the ability to fulfil the DPO tasks as set out in Article 39 GDPR.[1166] The necessary level of expert knowledge should be determined in particular according to the data processing activities carried out and the protection required for the personal data processed by

1163. Art. 29 Working Party, Guidelines on Data Protection Officers, WP243 rev.01, adopted on 13 December 2016, as last revised and adopted on 5 April 2017, and endorsed by the EDPB during its first plenary meeting, 8.
1164. Art. 29 Working Party, Guidelines on Data Protection Officers, WP243 rev.01, adopted on 13 December 2016, as last revised and adopted on 5 April 2017, and endorsed by the EDPB during its first plenary meeting, 5.
1165. WP29 Guidelines on Data Protection Officers, WP243 rev.01, adopted on 13 December 2016, as last revised and adopted on 5 April 2017, and endorsed by the EDPB during its first plenary meeting, 6.
1166. Art. 37(5) GDPR.

the organisation.[1167] The required level of expertise is hence determined considering the sensitivity, complexity and amount of data processed by the organisation.[1168] According to the WP29, relevant skills and expertise include expertise in national and European data protection laws and practices, an understanding of the processing operations carried out, an understanding of information technologies and data security, knowledge of the organisation's business sector and the ability to promote a data protection culture within the organisation.[1169]

993. Provided that the data protection officer is easily accessible, a group of undertakings may appoint one single data protection officer.[1170] The DPO needs to be accessible as a contact point for data subjects, the supervisory authority and also internally, within the organisation.[1171] Public authorities may also designate one single data protection taking into account their organisational structure and size.

994. The contact details of the DPO must be published and communicated to the supervisory authority.[1172] The contact details of the DPO should include information allowing data subjects and supervisory authorities to reach the DPO in an easy way, without having to contact another part of the organisation.[1173]

995. The DPO may be either internal to the organisation, being a staff member of the controller or processor, or external to the organisation, fulfilling his/her tasks on the basis of a service contract.[1174] However, the controller and processor must ensure that the DPO is involved, properly and in a timely manner, in all issues which relate to the protection of personal data.[1175] The DPO must be supported in performing their tasks by providing resources necessary to carry out those tasks and access to personal data and processing operations, and to maintain his or her expert knowledge.[1176] The DPO cannot receive any instructions regarding the exercise of those tasks and shall directly report to the highest management level of the controller or processor.[1177]

996. The DPO must be given sufficient autonomy and resources to carry out their tasks effectively.[1178] The WP29 lists a number of resources that need to be

1167. Recital 97 GDPR.
1168. Guidelines DPO, 11.
1169. WP29 Guidelines on Data Protection Officers, WP243 rev.01, adopted on 13 December 2016, as last revised and adopted on 5 April 2017, and endorsed by the EDPB during its first plenary meeting, 23.
1170. Art. 37(2) GDPR.
1171. Art. 38(4) GDPR ; Art. 39(1)(e) GDPR; Art. 39(1)(a) GDPR.
1172. Art. 37(7) GDPR.
1173. WP29 Guidelines on Data Protection Officers, WP243 rev.01, adopted on 13 December 2016, as last revised and adopted on 5 April 2017, and endorsed by the EDPB during its first plenary meeting, 12.
1174. Art. 37(6) GDPR.
1175. Art. 38(1) GDPR.
1176. Art. 38(2) GDPR.
1177. Art. 38(3) GDPR.
1178. Art. 38(2) GDPR.

provided to the DPO, depending on the nature of the processing operations and the activities and size of the organisation. These include active support of the DPO's function by the senior management of the organisation, sufficient time for DPOs to fulfil their tasks, adequate support in terms of financial resources, infrastructure and staff, official communication of the designation of the DPO to all staff, access to other services within the organisation so the DPOs can receive essential support, input or information from those other services, and continuous training.[1179]

997. The DPO can fulfil other tasks and duties, but the controller or processor needs to ensure that any such tasks and duties do not result in a conflict of interests.[1180] Several safeguards exist to enable the DPO to act in an independent manner. For example, not giving instructions regarding the exercise of the DPO's tasks and no dismissal or penalty for the performance of the DPO's tasks.[1181]

998. **Tasks**. Article 39 GDPR sets out the minimum tasks of the DPO. First, the DPO needs to inform and advise the organisation and staff who carries out processing about their data protection obligations. Second, the DPO needs to monitor compliance with data protection law and with the data protection policies of the organisation, including the assignment of responsibilities, awareness-training and training of staff involved in processing activities, and the related audits. Third, the DPO needs to provide advice where requested as regards the data protection impact assessment. It is not the responsibility of the DPO to carry out the impact assessment, but the DPO can play a very important and useful role in assisting the controller.[1182] Fourth, the DPO needs to cooperate with the supervisory authority. Finally, the DPO needs to act as the contact point for the supervisory authority on issues relating to processing, including the prior consultation, and to consult, where appropriate, with regard to any other matter.

999. Article 39(2) GDPR requires the DPO to have due regard to the risk associated with processing, taking into account the nature, scope, context and purposes of processing. According to the WP29 this requires the DPO to prioritise activities and focus efforts on issues that present higher data protection risks (risk-based approach).[1183]

1179. WP29 Guidelines on Data Protection Officers, WP243 rev.01, adopted on 13 December 2016, as last revised and adopted on 5 April 2017, and endorsed by the EDPB during its first plenary meeting, 23.
1180. Art. 38(6) GDPR.
1181. WP29 Guidelines on Data Protection Officers, WP243 rev.01, adopted on 13 December 2016, as last revised and adopted on 5 April 2017, and endorsed by the EDPB during its first plenary meeting, 24.
1182. WP29 Guidelines on Data Protection Officers, WP243 rev.01, adopted on 13 December 2016, as last revised and adopted on 5 April 2017, and endorsed by the EDPB during its first plenary meeting, 17.
1183. WP29 Guidelines on Data Protection Officers, WP243 rev.01, adopted on 13 December 2016, as last revised and adopted on 5 April 2017, and endorsed by the EDPB during its first plenary meeting, 18.

§10. Codes of Conduct and Certification

1000. The principle of accountability requires that controllers are able to demonstrate compliance with the GDPR.[1184] Codes of conduct, as set out in Articles 40 and 41 GDPR, as well as certification mechanisms, as set out in Articles 42 and 43 GDPR, can act as a mechanism to demonstrate such compliance.

I. Codes of Conduct

A. *GDPR Codes of Conduct*

1001. In the context of the GDPR, codes of conduct are 'voluntary accountability tools' which set out specific data protection rules for categories of controllers and processors. They can be a useful and effective accountability tool, providing a detailed description of what is the most appropriate, legal and ethical set of behaviours of a sector. From a data protection viewpoint, codes can therefore operate as a rulebook for controllers and processors who design and implement GDPR compliant data processing activities which give operational meaning to the principles of data protection set out in European and National law.'[1185]. They represent a practical, potentially cost effective and meaningful method to achieve more consistent data protection and they can act as a mechanism to demonstrate compliance with the GDPR.[1186]

1002. The GDPR aims to encourage trade organisations or bodies representing a sector to draw up codes of conduct so as to facilitate the effective application of the GDPR taking into account the specific characteristics of the processing carried out in certain sectors and the specific needs of micro, small and medium enterprises.[1187] With such codes, those associations and other bodies could help their sector to comply with the GDPR in an efficient and potentially cost-effective way, by calibrating the obligations of controllers and processors in their sector.[1188] An example of an approved code of conduct is the EU Cloud COC, which is intended to address all service types of the cloud market and creates a '*baseline for implementation of GDPR*' for these services.[1189]

1184. Art. 5(2) GDPR.
1185. Guidelines 1/2019 on Codes of Conduct and Monitoring Bodies under Regulation 2016/679 – version adopted after public consultation v2.0, adopted on 4 June 2019, 7.
1186. Guidelines 1/2019 on Codes of Conduct and Monitoring Bodies under Regulation 2016/679 – version adopted after public consultation v2.0, adopted on 4 June 2019, 5.
1187. Recital 98 GDPR.
1188. Recital 98 GDPR; Guidelines 1/2019 on Codes of Conduct and Monitoring Bodies under Regulation 2016/679 – version adopted after public consultation v2.0, adopted on 4 June 2019, 7.
1189. Belgian supervisory authority (Gegevensbeschermingsautoriteit/Autorité de protection des données), General Secretariat, Decision n° 05/2021 of 20 May 2021, https://www.dataprotectionauthority.be/publications/decision-n05-2021-of-20-may-2021.pdf.

1003. Codes could be prepared for the purpose of specifying the application of the GDPR on several topics. Article 40(2) GDPR refers in a non-exhaustive way to topics such as:

- fair and transparent processing;
- the legitimate interests pursued by controllers in specific contexts;
- the collection of personal data;
- the pseudonymisation of personal data;
- the information provided to the public and to data subjects;
- the exercise of the rights of data subjects;
- the information provided to, and the protection of, children;
- the measures and procedures relating to the responsibility of the controller, data protection by design and by default and security measures;
- the notification and communication of personal data breaches;
- the transfer of personal data; and
- out-of-court proceedings and other dispute resolution procedures for resolving disputes between controllers and data subjects.[1190]

B. Approval Procedure

1004. Codes of conduct need to be approved. A draft code, amendment or extension needs to be submitted to the competent supervisory authority. In case of a national code, meaning that the code does not relate to processing activities in several Member States, the competent supervisory authority approves the draft code, amendment or extension if it finds that it complies with the GDPR.[1191] The competent supervisory authority also registers and publishes the code.[1192] If, on the contrary, the code covers processing activities in multiple Member States, the supervisory authority needs to submit the draft code (transnational code), amendment or extension to the European Data Protection Board after which the Board may provide an opinion on whether the draft complies with the GDPR.[1193] Where this opinion confirms such compliance, the Board submits this opinion to the Commission.[1194]

1190. Art. 40(2) GDPR.
1191. Art. 40(5) GDPR. *See* for this procedure, Guidelines 1/2019 on Codes of Conduct and Monitoring Bodies under Regulation 2016/679 – version adopted after public consultation v2.0, adopted on 4 June 2019, 17.
1192. Art. 40(6) GDPR.
1193. Art. 40(7) GDPR. *See* for this procedure, Guidelines 1/2019 on Codes of Conduct and Monitoring Bodies under Regulation 2016/679 – version adopted after public consultation v2.0, adopted on 4 June 2019, 18; EDPB, Document on the procedure for the development of informal 'Codes of Conduct sessions', adopted on 10 November 2020, https://edpb.europa.eu/sites/default/files/files/file1/edpb_documentprocedurecodesconductsessions_en.pdf.
1194. Art. 40(8) GDPR ; *see* ander Maelen, C. 'European Union First of Many? First GDPR Transnational Code of Conduct Officially Approved After EDPB Opinions 16/2021 and 17/2021.' *European Data Protection Law Review (Internet)*, vol. 7, no. 2, 2021, pp. 228–231.

1005. The Commission may declare the codes of conduct that are recommended by the Board to have general validity within the Union, by way of implementing acts.[1195] In such case, the Commission needs to ensure appropriate publicity for the approved code.[1196] The Board collates all approved codes of conduct, amendments and extensions in a register and makes them publicly available by way of appropriate means.[1197]

1006. The EDPB Guidelines on Codes of Conduct and Monitoring Bodies provide a detailed overview of the approval procedure and guidelines on the submission of a draft code.[1198] An important choice relates to the identification of the competent supervisory authority for the purposes of seeking approval of a transnational draft code.[1199] While the GDPR does not itself specify the rules for identifying the competent authority, there are some factors that could be taken into account, for example, the location of the largest density of the processing activity or sector; the location of the largest density of data subjects affected by the processing activity or sector; the location of the code owner's headquarters; the location of the proposed monitoring body's headquarters; or the initiatives developed by a supervisory authority in a specific field. The choice of competent authority should be prudently considered, as this authority will take up the role of single point of contact with the code owners during the approval process, manage the application procedure in its cooperation phase, accredit the monitoring body (if relevant) and act as the supervisory lead in ensuring that an approved code is being monitored effectively.

1007. The EDPB provides the following checklist for submitting a draft code to the competent supervisory authority:[1200]

1) Have you provided an explanatory statement and all relevant supporting documentation? – The draft code must contain a clear and concise explanatory statement which provides details as to the purpose and scope of the code and to the envisioned effective application of the GDPR. The submission also needs to include any supporting documentation to underpin the draft code and statement.

1195. Art. 40(9) GDPR.
1196. Art. 40(10) GDPR.
1197. Art. 40(11) GDPR. The EDPB keeps a register for codes of conduct, amendments and extensions on its website: https://edpb.europa.eu/our-work-tools/accountability-tools/register-codes-conduct-amendments-and-extensions-art-4011_en.
1198. EDPB, Guidelines 1/2019 on Codes of Conduct and Monitoring Bodies under Regulation 2016/679 – version adopted after public consultation v2.0, adopted on 4 June 2019.
1199. Art. 55 in conjunction with Recital 122 GDPR; Guidelines 1/2019 on Codes of Conduct and Monitoring Bodies under Regulation 2016/679 – version adopted after public consultation v2.0, adopted on 4 June 2019, 28.
1200. EDPB, Guidelines 1/2019 on Codes of Conduct and Monitoring Bodies under Regulation 2016/679 – version adopted after public consultation v2.0, adopted on 4 June 2019, Appendix 3 – Checklist for submission, 29. Next to the general checklist provided by the EDPB, some supervisory authorities published additional checklists.

2) Are you an association or other body representing categories of controllers or processors? – The draft code needs to be submitted by an association/ consortium of associations or other bodies representing categories of controllers or processors (code owners). Code owners could be, for example, trade and representative associations, sectoral organisations and interest groups.
3) Have your provided details in your submission to substantiate that you are an effective representative body that is capable of understanding the need of your members? – The code owner needs to demonstrate that they are an effective representative body with the capability of understanding the needs of their members.
4) Have you clearly defined the processing activity or sector and the processing problems to which the code is intended to address? – The draft code needs to have a defined scope that clearly and precisely determines the processing operations as well as the categories of controllers or processors it governs.
5) Have you identified the territorial scope of your code and included a list of all concerned supervisory authorities (where relevant)? – The draft code must specify whether it is a national or a transnational code. It needs to provide details relating to the territorial scope, including the identification of all relevant jurisdictions to which it intends to apply.
6) Have you provided details to justify the identification of the competent supervisory authority? – The code owners need to ensure that their choice of competent supervisory authority is in accordance with Article 55 GDPR.
7) Have you included mechanisms that allow for the effective monitoring of compliance of the code? – The draft code must propose mechanisms that allow for the monitoring of compliance with its provisions in accordance with Article 40(4) GDPR.
8) Have you identified a monitoring body and explained how it will fulfil the code monitoring requirements? – A draft code that involves processing activities of private, non-public authorities and bodies needs to identify a monitoring body in accordance with Article 41 GDPR.
9) Have you included information as to the extent of consultation carried out in developing the code? – The code owners need to confirm and demonstrate that an appropriate level of consultation has taken place with the relevant stakeholders.
10) Have you provided confirmation that the draft code is compliant with Member State law(s) (where relevant)? – The code owners need to provide confirmation that the draft code is in compliance with relevant legislation, including sector-specific national law.
11) Have you met the language requirements? – The code owners need to comply with the language requirements of the competent supervisory authority to whom they submit the draft code. National codes should be submitted in the language of the competent supervisory authority. Transnational codes should be submitted in the language of the competent supervisory authority and also in English.
12) Does you submission include sufficient details to demonstrate the proper application of the GDPR? – The code owners need to be able to demonstrate

that their draft code meets a particular need of the sector or processing activity; facilitates the application of the GDPR; specifies the application of the GDPR; provides sufficient guarantees; and provides effective mechanisms for monitoring compliance with a code.

C. Monitoring of Approved Codes of Conduct

1008. Codes of conduct need to contain mechanisms which enable mandatory monitoring of compliance.[1201]

1009. Compliance with codes of conduct is monitored by bodies accredited for that purpose by the competent supervisory authority in accordance with Article 41 GDPR.

1010. In order to become accredited to monitor compliance with codes of conduct, the body needs to demonstrate an appropriate level of expertise in relation to the subject matter of the code and has:

(a) demonstrated its independence and expertise to the satisfaction of the competent supervisory authority;
(b) established procedures which allow it to assess the eligibility of controllers and processors concerned to apply the code, to monitor their compliance with its provisions and to periodically review its operation;
(c) established procedures and structures to handle complaints about infringements of the code or the manner in which the code has been, or is being, implemented by a controller or processor, and to make those procedures and structures transparent to the data subjects and the public; and
(d) demonstrated to the satisfaction of the competent supervisory authority that its tasks and duties do not result in a conflict of interests.

If after accreditation, the condition for accreditation are not or are no longer met or where the actions taken by the body infringe the GDPR, the competent supervisory authority revokes the accreditation of the body.

1011. If an accredited body establishes an infringement of the code by a controller or a processor, it takes appropriate action, including suspension or exclusion of the controller or processor concerned from the code. In such case, the accredited body informs the supervisory authority of such actions and the reasons for taking them.

1201. Art. 40(4) GDPR.

D. Codes of Conduct as an Appropriate Safeguard for Data Transfers

1012. Approved codes of conduct could be adhered to by controllers or processors that are not subject to the GDPR in order to provide appropriate safeguards within the framework of personal data transfers to third countries or international organisations.[1202] In such case, those controllers and processors make binding and enforceable commitments, via contractual or other legally binding instruments, to apply those appropriate safeguards including with regard to the rights of the data subjects.[1203]

1013. In order to get approval in a transfer-context, the supervisory authority, Board or Commission reviews submitted draft codes, amendments or extensions on whether they provide sufficient appropriate safeguards.

II. Certification

A. GDPR Certification

1014. Next to codes of conduct, certification, seals and marks are another form of self- or co-regulation under the GDPR.[1204] Certification can play an important role in the accountability framework for data protection because they enhance transparency and compliance with the GDPR and allow data subjects to quickly assess the level of data protection of relevant products and services.[1205] The establishment of certification mechanisms and data protection seals and marks needs therefore to be encouraged.

1015. However, certification does not prove compliance in and of itself but rather forms an element that can be used to demonstrate compliance. Therefore it should be produced in a transparent manner.[1206] In order for certification to provide reliable evidence of data protection compliance, Article 42 GDPR clearly sets out the rules for the provision of certification mechanisms. The EDPB emphasises that '*Demonstration of compliance requires supporting documentation, specifically written reports which not only repeat but describe how the criteria are met and if not*

1202. Art. 40(3) GDPR and Art. 46-2(e) GDPR.
1203. Art. 40(3) GDPR.
1204. Lachaud, Eric. 'What GDPR Tells about Certification.' *The Computer Law and Security Report*, vol. 38, 2020, p. 105457.
1205. Recital 100 GDPR. Art. 42(2) GDPR provides that certification can provide the existence of appropriate safeguards for the transfer of personal data to a third country, where the importing controller-processor adheres to the certification mechanism, seal or mark, together with binding and enforceable commitments to apply those appropriate safeguards.
1206. *See*, for example, Art. 25(3) GDPR on the use of certification mechanisms as one element to demonstrate compliance with the data protection by design and data protection by default requirements; EDPB, Guidelines 1/2018 on certification and identifying certification criteria in accordance with Arts 42 and 43 of the Regulation, v3, adopted on 4 June 2019, 7.

initially met, describe the corrections and corrective actions and their appropriateness, thus providing the reasons for granting and maintaining the certification. This includes the outline of the individual decision for granting, renewing, or withdrawing of a certificate. It should provide the reasons, arguments, and proofs resulting from the application of criteria and the conclusions, judgments, or inferences from facts or premises collected during certification.'[1207]

1016. The GDPR does not define 'certification', and other definitions of the notion could thus be used. The GDPR does not define the notion 'certification mechanisms, seals or marks' either, while collectively using the terms. The EDPB clarifies that a 'certificate' is a statement of conformity, while a 'seal' or 'mark' can be used to signify the successful completion of a certification procedure. Certification schemes consist of two key elements. First, the criteria outlining the specific requirements – the 'standard' against which conformity is assessed, and second, the audit methodology and testing methods that are used to carry out the assessment.[1208] The EDPB refers to the universal definition of 'certification' as '*the provision by an independent body of written assurance (a certificate) that the product, service or system in question meets specific requirements*' of the International Standards Organisation (ISO).[1209] In the context of certification under Articles 42 and 43 GDPR, certification refers to third-party attestation related to processing operations by controllers and processors.[1210]

1017. GDPR certification should be distinguished from other types of certification. For example, the Cybersecurity Act defines 'cybersecurity certification scheme' as '*a comprehensive set of rules, technical requirements, standards and procedures that […] apply to the certification or conformity assessment of specific ICT products, ICT services or ICT processes*'.[1211] Recital 74 of the Cybersecurity Act clarifies that its provisions regarding the establishment of certification mechanisms are without prejudice to the provisions of the GDPR on the establishment of certification mechanisms for the purpose of demonstrating compliance of processing operations by controllers and processors with the GDPR, including when such operations are embedded in ICT products, ICT services and ICT processes. Certification under the GDPR concerns the certification of processing activities and not products or systems. GDPR certification is different from many data protection certification products as the focus is less on the governance and management around

1207. EDPB, Guidelines 1/2018 on certification and identifying certification criteria in accordance with Arts 42 and 43 of the Regulation, v3, adopted on 4 June 2019, 7.
1208. https://ico.org.uk/for-organisations/guide-to-data-protection/guide-to-the-general-data-protection-regulation-gdpr/certification-schemes-detailed-guidance/how-do-we-develop-a-certification-scheme/#1.
1209. For example defined here: https://www.iso.org/conformity-assessment.html.
1210. EDPB, Guidelines 1/2018 on certification and identifying certification criteria in accordance with Arts 42 and 43 of the Regulation, v3, adopted on 4 June 2019, 8.
1211. Art. 2(9) EU Cybersecurity Act.

the processing and more about an in-depth assessment of how personal data are processed in a specific processing operation.[1212]

1018. Certification under the GDPR is voluntary, meaning that controllers and processors are free to decide themselves whether or not to submit to a certification procedure.[1213] Controllers and processors are thus not obliged to submit processing to a certification mechanism.

B. Certification Procedure

1019. Certification is issued for a maximum period of three years and can be renewed, under the same conditions, if the relevant requirements continue to be met.[1214] Once an organisation no longer complies with the requirements, the certification or seal needs to be withdrawn by the certification bodies or by the competent supervisory authority.[1215]

1020. Certification can be issued and renewed by a competent supervisory authority or by an accredited certification body.[1216] The EDPB may also issue certification. Where the certification criteria are approved by the EDPB, this may result in a common certification, the European Data Protection Seal.[1217]

1021. Certification bodies can be accredited for a renewable maximum period of five years,[1218] by either the competent supervisory authority or by the competent national accreditation body named in accordance with Regulation (EC) No 765/2008 in accordance with EN-ISO/IEC 17065/2012 and with additional national requirements, if applicable.[1219]

1022. In order to be accredited, the certification body needs to have:

1212. https://ico.org.uk/for-organisations/guide-to-data-protection/guide-to-the-general-data-protection-regulation-gdpr/certification-schemes-detailed-guidance/how-do-we-develop-a-certification-scheme/#1.
1213. Art. 42(3) GDPR. An example of mandatory certification is the CE marking, which is actually self-declaration of conformity.
1214. Art. 42(7) GDPR.
1215. *Ibid.*
1216. *See*, EDPB, Guidelines 4/2018 on the accreditation of certification bodies under Art. 43 of the General Data Protection Regulation (2016/679), v3, adopted on 4 June 2019.
1217. Art. 42(5) GDPR. *See also*, EDPB, Document on the procedure for the approval of certification criteria by the EDPB resulting in a common certification, the European Data Protection Seal, adopted on 28 January 2020, https://edpb.europa.eu/sites/default/files/files/file1/edpbprocedureforeudataprotectionseal_postplencheck_en.pdf.
1218. Art. 43(4) GDPR.
1219. Art. 43(1) GDPR. Regulation (EC) No 765/2008 of the European Parliament and of the Council of 9 July 2008 setting out the requirements for accreditation and market surveillance relating to the marketing of products and repealing Regulation (EEC) No 339/93, OJ L 218, 13.8.2008, 30.

(a) demonstrated its independence and expertise in relation to the subject matter of the certification to the satisfaction of the competent supervisory authority;
(b) undertaken to respect the certification criteria approved by the competent supervisory authority or by the Board,
(c) established procedures for the issuing, periodic review and withdrawal of data protection certification, seals and marks;
(d) established procedures and structures to handle complaints about infringements of the certification or the manner in which the certification has been, or is being, implemented by the controller or processor, and to make those procedures and structures transparent to the data subjects and the public; and
(e) demonstrated to the satisfaction of the competent supervisory authority, that their tasks and duties do not result in a conflict of interests.[1220]

1023. The EDPB has a designated page on its website to publish the list of all certification mechanisms and data protection seals and marks in accordance with Article 42(8) GDPR. This register is currently still empty.[1221]

§11. International Data Transfers

I. General Principle for Data Transfers

1024. Chapter V 'Transfers of personal data to third countries or international organisations' of the GDPR provides for specific requirements for the transfer (and onward transfer) of personal data to third countries or to an international organisation, in addition to the general requirements for processing which are also applicable to the transfer of personal data.[1222]

1025. The specific transfer requirements are intended to ensure that the level of protection of natural persons guaranteed under the GDPR is not undermined as a consequence of the transfer to a controller, processor or other recipient outside the EU.[1223]

1026. The concept of 'data transfer' is not explicitly defined by the GDPR, but in line with Article 44 GDPR and Recital 101 GDPR a 'transfer' can be described as the flow of personal data from a controller or processor established in the EEA to a controller, processor or recipient in a third country or to an international organisation. The EDPB has identified the three following cumulative criteria that qualify a processing as a transfer: 1) a controller or a processor is subject to the GDPR for

1220. Art. 43(2) GDPR.
1221. For the register of certification mechanisms, seals and marks: https://edpb.europa.eu/our-work-tools/accountability-tools/certification-mechanisms-seals-and-marks_en (last visited 11 August 2021).
1222. Art. 44 GDPR ; *see also* Recital 101 GDPR.
1223. Yakovleva, Svetlana. 'Personal Data Transfers in International Trade and EU Law: A Tale of Two 'Necessities'.' *The Journal of World Investment & Trade*, vol. 21, no. 6, 2020, pp. 881–919.

the given processing; 2) this controller or processor ('exporter') discloses by transmission or otherwise makes personal data, subject to this processing, available to another controller, joint controller or processor ('importer'); 3) the importer is in a third country or is an international organisation, irrespective of whether or not this importer is subject to the GDPR in respect of the given processing in accordance with Article 3.[1224]

1027. The first criterion requires that the processing at stake meets the requirements of Article 3 GDPR, i.e., a controller or processor is subject to the GDPR for the given processing.[1225] Consequently, not only controllers and processors established in the European Union but also those which are not established in the EU, may be subject to the GDPR pursuant to Article 3 for a given processing and, thus, will have to comply with Chapter V when transferring personal data to a third country or to an international organisation.

1028. The second criterion requires that there is a controller or processor disclosing by transmission or otherwise making data available to another controller or processor. This requirement cannot be considered as fulfilled where the data are disclosed directly and on his/her own initiative by the data subject to the recipient. In such case, there is no controller or processor sending or making the data available ('exporter'). The EDPB mentions the example of a data subject (Maria) living in Italy, who inserts her personal data by filling a form on an online clothing website in order to complete her order and receive the dress she bought online at her residence in Rome. The online clothing website is operated by a company established in Singapore with no presence in the EU. In this case, the data subject (Maria) passes her personal data to the Singaporean company, but this does not constitute a transfer of personal data since the data are not passed by an exporter (controller or processor), since they are passed directly and on her own initiative by the data subject herself.[1226]

1029. It is further noteworthy that Article 44 of the GDPR clearly envisages that a transfer may not only be carried out by a controller but also by a processor. Therefore, there may be a transfer situation where a processor sends data to another processor. The EDPB gives the example of Company A established in Germany, acting as controller, which has engaged B, a French company, as a processor on its behalf. B wishes to further delegate a part of the processing activities that it is carrying out on behalf of A to sub-processor C, a company established in India, and hence to

1224. EDPB, Guidelines 05/2021 on the Interplay between the application of Art. 3 and the provisions on international transfers as per Chapter V of the GDPR, version adopted for public consultation on 18 November 2021, 4, https://edpb.europa.eu/system/files/2021-11/edpb_guidelinesinterplaychapterv_article3_adopted_en.pdf.

1225. This has been further elaborated on in the EDPB Guidelines 3/2018 on the territorial scope of the GDPR (Art. 3). Version 1.2, 12 November 2019, https://edpb.europa.eu/sites/default/files/files/file1/edpb_guidelines_3_2018_territorial_scope_after_public_consultation_en_1.pdf.

1226. EDPB, Guidelines 05/2021 on the Interplay between the application of Art. 3 and the provisions on international transfers as per Chapter V of the GDPR, 5, https://edpb.europa.eu/system/files/2021-11/edpb_guidelinesinterplaychapterv_article3_adopted_en.pdf.

send the data for this purpose to C. The processing performed by both A and its processor B is carried out in the context of their establishments in the EU and is therefore subject to the GDPR pursuant to its Article 3(1), while the processing by C is carried out in a third country. Hence, the passing of data from processor B to sub-processor C is a transfer to a third country, and Chapter V of the GDPR applies.[1227]

1030. The second criterion also implies that the concept of 'transfer of personal data to a third country or to an international organisation' only applies to disclosures of personal data where two different (separate) parties (each of them a controller, joint controller or processor) are involved. In order to qualify as a transfer, there must be a controller or processor disclosing the data (the exporter) and a different controller or processor receiving or being given access to the data (the importer). Consequently, Chapter V of the GDPR will not apply when an employee travels with personal data stored on her/his laptop computer to a third country outside Europe or when a company sends data to this employee while the latter is traveling abroad. Alternately, the provisions of Chapter V are applicable to data transfers between companies or organisations belonging to the same group, for example between subsidiaries of a multinational company.

1031. Finally, the third criterion that qualifies a processing as a transfer to which Chapter V of the GDPR applies, requires that the importer is geographically in a third country or is an international organisation, but regardless of whether the processing at hand falls under the scope of the GDPR. This means that a mother company established outside the European Union which collects personal data from its subsidiaries located in the EU, is submitted to the provisions of Chapter V, notwithstanding the fact that the mother company is already processing the personal data under the scope of the GDPR pursuant to Article 3(1). The mother company is, in other words, in a transfer situation and is requested to frame the transfer by using the instruments which aim at protecting personal data after they have been transferred to a third country or an international organisation.[1228]

1032. The notion 'onward transfer' refers to the situation where a controller, processor or recipient in a third country or an international organisation further transfers the personal data to another controller, processor or recipient in either the same or another third country or another international organisation.

1033. The lawfulness of a transfer can be based on an adequacy decision adopted by the European Commission,[1229] appropriate safeguards as set out in Article 46 of the GDPR or any of the derogations as set out in Article 49 of the GDPR. In the absence of an adequacy decision, EU or Member State law could set

1227. *Ibid.*, p. 6.
1228. *Ibid.*, p. 8 ; The position of the EDPB on this point has been criticised in Kuner, Christopher, Territorial Scope and Data Transfer Rules in the GDPR: Realising the EU's Ambition of Borderless Data Protection (April 16, 2021). University of Cambridge Faculty of Law Research Paper No. 20/2021, Available at SSRN: https://ssrn.com/abstract=3827850 or http://dx.doi.org/10.2139/ssrn.3827850.
1229. Art. 45 GDPR.

limits to the transfer of specific categories of personal data to a third country or an international organisation for important reasons of public interest.[1230]

II. Adequacy Decision

1034. A transfer of personal data to a third country or an international organisation may take place without any specific authorisation, where the European Commission has decided that a third country, a territory or one or more specified sectors within that third country, or the international organisation in question ensures an adequate level of protection.[1231] The effect of such decision is that personal data can flow from the EEA to that third country or region, without any further safeguard being necessary.[1232]

1035. It is the European Commission that has the power to determine whether a country or a region outside of the EEA offers an adequate level of protection. Adequate level of protection means that the level of protection is essentially equivalent by virtue to that guaranteed in the EEA, without being identical.[1233]

1036. When the Commission assesses the level of protection afforded in a third country, it takes the following elements particularly into account:[1234]

(a) the data protection regime of the country or international organisation concerned, more specifically, the rule of law, respect for human rights and fundamental freedoms, relevant legislation (general and sectoral), including concerning public security, defence, national security and criminal law and the access of public authorities to personal data, as well as the implementation of such legislation, data protection rules, professional rules and security measures, including rules for onward transfers, case law, as well as effective and enforceable data subject rights and effective administrative and judicial redress for the data subjects whose personal data are being transferred;
(b) the existence and effective functioning of one or more independent supervisory authorities in the third country or to which an international organisation is subject, with responsibility for ensuring and enforcing compliance with data protection rules, including adequate enforcement powers, for assisting and advising

1230. Art. 49(5) GDPR.
1231. Art. 45(1) GDPR.
1232. Gonzalo Domenech, Juan José 'Las Decisiones De Adecuación En El Derecho Europeo Relativas a Las Transferencias Internacionales De Datos y Los Mecanismos De Control Aplicados Por Los Estados Miembros = Adequacy Decisions in European Law Related to International Data Transfers and Control Mechanisms Applied by the Member States.' *Cuadernos De Derecho Transnacional*, vol. 11, no. 1, 2019, p. 350.
1233. CJEU, Case C-362/14, *Schrems I*, ECLI:EU:C:2015:650, para. 73, https://eur-lex.europa.eu/legal-content/EN/TXT/?uri=CELEX%3A62014CJ0362; CJEU, Case C-311/18, *Schrems II*, ECLI:EU:C:2020:559, para. 94, https://eur-lex.europa.eu/legal-content/EN/TXT/?uri=CELEX%3A62018CJ0311.
1234. Art. 45(2) GDPR.

the data subjects in exercising their rights and for cooperation with the supervisory authorities of the Member States; and

(c) the international commitments the third country or international organisation has entered into, or other obligations arising from legally binding conventions or instruments as well as from its participation in multilateral or regional systems, in particular in relation to the protection of personal data. In particular, the third country's accession to the Council of Europe Convention of 28 January 1981 for the protection of individuals with regard to the automatic processing of personal data and its additional protocols are taken into account.[1235]

1037. In order to be considered as essentially equivalent, the third country's or international organisation's system must contain the following basic content and procedural/enforcement data protection principles and mechanisms:[1236]

Content Principles	
Concepts	Basic data protection concepts and/or principles should exist and be consistent with the European concepts.
Grounds for lawful and fair processing for legitimate purposes	Data must be processed in a lawful, fair and legitimate manner.
Purpose limitation principle	Data should be processed for a specific purpose and subsequently used only insofar as this is not incompatible with the purpose of the processing.
Data quality and proportionality principle	Data should be accurate and, where necessary, kept up to date. The data should be adequate, relevant and not excessive in relation to the purposes for which they are processed.
Data retention principle	Data should, as a general rule, be kept for no longer than is necessary for the purposes for which the personal data is processed.
Security and confidentiality principle	Any entity processing personal data should ensure that the data are processed in a manner that ensures security of the personal data, including protection against unauthorised or unlawful processing and against accidental loss, destruction or damage, using appropriate technical or organisational measures. The level of the security should take into consideration the state-of-the-art and the related costs.

1235. Recital 105 GDPR.

1236. WP29, Adequacy referential, as last revised and adopted on 6 February 2018 and as endorsed by the EDPB, WP254 rev. 01, 5.

Transparency principle	Each individual should be informed of all the main elements of the processing of his/her personal data in a clear, easily accessible, concise, transparent and intelligible form.
Data subject rights	Data subjects should have the right of access, rectification, erasure and objection. The exercise of those rights should not be excessively cumbersome for the data subject.
Restrictions on onward transfers	Further transfers of the personal data by the initial recipient of the original data transfer should be permitted only where the further recipient (i.e., the recipient of the onward transfer) is also subject to rules (including contractual rules) affording an adequate level of protection and following the relevant instructions when processing data on behalf of the data controller. The level of protection of natural persons whose data is transferred must not be undermined by the onward transfer.
Additional content principles (to be applied to specific types of processing)	
Special categories of data	Specific safeguards should exist where 'special categories of data are involved. These categories should reflect those enshrined in Articles 9 and 10 of the GDPR.
Direct marketing	Where data are processed for the purposes of direct marketing, the data subject should be able to object without any charge from having his/her data processed for such purposes at any time.
Automated decision-making and profiling	Decisions based solely on automated processing (automated individual decision-making), including profiling, which produce legal effects or significantly affect the data subject, can take place only under certain conditions established in the third-country legal framework.
Procedural and enforcement mechanisms	
Competent independent supervisory authority	One or more independent supervisory authorities, tasked with monitoring, ensuring and enforcing compliance with data protection and privacy provisions in the third country should exist. The supervisory authority shall act with complete independence and impartiality in performing its duties and exercising its powers and in doing so shall neither seek nor accept instructions. In that

	context, the supervisory authority should have all the necessary and available powers and missions to ensure compliance with data protection rights and promote awareness. Consideration should also be given to the staff and budget of the supervisory authority. The supervisory authority shall also be able, on its own initiative, to conduct investigations.
The data protection system must ensure a good level of compliance	A third-country system should ensure a high degree of accountability and of awareness among data controllers and those processing personal data on their behalf of their obligations, tasks and responsibilities, and among data subjects of their rights and the means of exercising them. The existence of effective and dissuasive sanctions can play an important role in ensuring respect for rules, as of course can systems of direct verification by authorities, auditors, or independent data protection officials.
Accountability	A third-country data protection framework should oblige data controllers and/or those processing personal data on their behalf to comply with it and to be able to demonstrate such compliance in particular to the competent supervisory authority.
The data protection system must provide support and help to individual data subjects in the exercise of their rights and appropriate redress mechanisms	The individual should be able to pursue legal remedies to enforce his/her rights rapidly and effectively, and without prohibitive cost, as well as to ensure compliance. To do so there must be in place supervision mechanisms allowing for independent investigation of complaints and enabling any infringements of the right to data protection and respect for private life to be identified and punished in practice. Where rules are not complied with, the data subject should be provided as well with effective administrative and judicial redress, including for compensation for damages as a result of the unlawful processing of his/her personal data. This is a key element which must involve a system of independent adjudication or arbitration which allows compensation to be paid and sanctions imposed where appropriate.

1038. 1038 The European Commission adopts adequacy decisions by means of implementing acts in the meaning of Article 291 TFEU[1237] and in accordance with the examination procedure referred to in Article 93(2) GDPR. The Commission has so far recognised Andorra,[1238] Argentina,[1239] Canada[1240] (commercial organisations), Faroe Islands,[1241] Guernsey,[1242] Israel,[1243] Isle of Man,[1244] Japan,[1245] Jersey,[1246] New Zealand,[1247] Switzerland,[1248] South Korea[1249] and Uruguay[1250] as providing an adequate level of protection for personal data.[1251] However, these adequacy decisions do not cover data exchanges in the law enforcement sector. The first adequacy decision covering the law enforcement sector, was adopted in June

1237. Art. 291 Treaty on the Functioning of the European Union, OJ C 326, 26.10.2012, 47-390.
1238. Commission Decision 2010/625/EU of 19 October 2010 pursuant to Directive 95/46/EC of the European Parliament and of the Council on the adequate protection of personal data in Andorra, C(2010) 7084, OJ L 277, 21.10.2010, 27–29.
1239. Commission Decision 2003/490/EC of 30 June 2003 pursuant to Directive 95/46/EC of the European Parliament and of the Council on the adequate protection of personal data in Argentina, OJ L 168, 5.7.2003, 19–22.
1240. Commission Decision 2002/2/EC of 20 December 2001 pursuant to Directive 95/46/EC of the European Parliament and of the Council on the adequate protection of personal data provided by the Canadian Personal Information Protection and Electronic Documents Act, C(2001) 4539, OJ L 2, 4.1.2002, 13–16.
1241. Commission Decision 2010/146/EU of 5 March 2010 pursuant to Directive 95/46/EC of the European Parliament and of the Council on the adequate protection provided by the Faeroese Act on processing of personal data, C(2010) 1130, OJ L 58, 9.3.2010, 17–19.
1242. Commission Decision 2003/821/EC of 21 November 2003 on the adequate protection of personal data in Guernsey, C(2003) 4309, OJ L 308, 25/11/2003, 27–28.
1243. Commission Decision 2011/61/EU of 31 January 2011 pursuant to Directive 95/46/EC of the European Parliament and of the Council on the adequate protection of personal data by the State of Israel with regard to automated processing of personal data, C(2011) 332, OJ L 27, 1.2.2011, 39–42.
1244. Commission Decision 2004/411/EC of 28 April 2004 on the adequate protection of personal data in the Isle of Man, OJ L 151, 30.4.2004, 48–51.
1245. Commission Implementing Decision (EU) 2019/419 of 23 January 2019 pursuant to Regulation (EU) 2016/679 of the European Parliament and of the Council on the adequate protection of personal data by Japan under the Act on the Protection of Personal Information, C(2019) 304, OJ L 76, 19.3.2019, 1–58.
1246. Commission Decision 2008/393/EC of 8 May 2008 pursuant to Directive 95/46/EC of the European Parliament and of the Council on the adequate protection of personal data in Jersey, C(2008) 1746, OJ L 138, 28.5.2008, 21–23.
1247. Commission Implementing Decision 2013/65/EU of 19 December 2012 pursuant to Directive 95/46/EC of the European Parliament and of the Council on the adequate protection of personal data by New Zealand, C(2012) 9557, OJ L 28, 30.1.2013, 12–14.
1248. Commission Decision 2000/518/EC of 26 July 2000 pursuant to Directive 95/46/EC of the European Parliament and of the Council on the adequate protection of personal data provided in Switzerland, C(2000) 2304, OJ L 215, 25.8.2000, 1–3.
1249. Commission Implementing Decision of 17 December 2021 pursuant to Regulation (EU) 2016/679 of the European Parliament and of the Council on the adequate protection of personal data by the Republic of Korea under the Personal Information Protection Act, C(2021) 9316 final.
1250. Commission Implementing Decision 2012/484/EU of 21 August 2012 pursuant to Directive 95/46/EC of the European Parliament and of the Council on the adequate protection of personal data by the Eastern Republic of Uruguay with regard to automated processing of personal data, C(2012) 5704, OJ L 227, 23.8.2012, 11–14.
1251. The European Commission publishes the list of its adequacy decisions on its website, *see*: https://ec.europa.eu/info/law/law-topic/data-protection/international-dimension-data-protection/adequacy-decisions_en.

2021, when the Commission adopted two adequacy decisions for transfers of personal data to the United Kingdom, under the GDPR and the Law Enforcement Directive respectively.[1252]

1039. Article 45 GDPR specifies the requirements of the implementing act by which adequacy decisions are adopted in accordance with the examination procedure referred to in Article 93(2) GDPR. First, the implementing act needs to provide for a mechanism for a periodic review, at least every four years, which takes into account all relevant developments in the third country or international organisation. The maximum review cycle of four years can be adjusted (shortened) depending on the particular circumstances of each adequacy decision. Second, the implementing act needs to specify the territorial and sectoral application of the adequacy decision and identify the supervisory authority or authorities in the third country or to which the international organisation is subject.[1253]

1040. The Commission has the task to monitor developments in third countries and international organisations that could affect the functioning of the adequacy decisions adopted, also between scheduled periodic reviews.[1254] Where available information reveals that a third country, a territory or an international organisation no longer ensures an adequate level of protection, the Commission will repeal, amend or suspend the decision to the extent necessary without retroactive effect and without prejudice to transfers subject to appropriate safeguards or based on derogations for specific situations. Such decision is also adopted by means of implementing act in accordance with the examination procedure referred to in Article 93(2) GDPR.[1255] In such case, the Commission will enter into consultations with the third country or international organisation concerned with a view to remedying the situation giving rise to this decision.[1256] The Commission publishes the list of the third countries, territories and specified sectors within a third country and international organisations for which it has decided that an adequate level of protection is or is no longer ensured.[1257]

1041. Adequacy decisions are adopted for the entire EEA. Therefore, they provide a high level of legal certainty and uniformity throughout the EEA as regards the third country or international organisation to provide such level of protection.

1252. Commission Implementing Decision of 28 June 2021 pursuant to Regulation (EU) 2016/679 of the European Parliament and of the Council on the adequate protection of personal data by the United Kingdom, C(2021) 4800 final; Commission Implementing Decision of 28 June 2021 pursuant to Directive (EU) 2016/680 of the European Parliament and of the Council on the adequate protection of personal data by the United Kingdom, C(2021) 4801 final.
1253. Art. 45(3) GDPR.
1254. Art. 45(4) GDPR.
1255. Art. 45(5) GDPR.
1256. Art. 45(6) GDPR.
1257. More information can be found here: https://ec.europa.eu/info/law/law-topic/data-protection/international-dimension-data-protection/adequacy-decisions_en. The European Commission has so far recognised Andorra, Argentina, Canada (commercial organisations), Faroe Islands, Guernsey, Israel, Isle of Man, Japan, Jersey, New Zealand, Switzerland, Uruguay and the United States of America (limited to the Privacy Shield Framework) as providing adequate protection.

However, data exporters need to stay alert and they need to ensure themselves that the adequacy decisions relevant to their transfers are not revoked or invalidated.[1258] Moreover, adequacy decisions cannot prevent data subjects from filing a complaint or prevent supervisory authorities from starting a legal procedure to challenge the validity of the decision.[1259]

III. Appropriate Safeguards

A. Transfers Subject to Appropriate Safeguards

1042. In the absence of an adequacy decision, the controller or processor needs to take measures to compensate for the lack of data protection in the third country.[1260] Data transfers to a third country or an international organisation may take place only if the controller or processor has provided appropriate safeguards, and on condition that enforceable data subject rights and effective legal remedies for data subjects are available.[1261]

1043. Article 46 GDPR lists the appropriate safeguards by which a data transfer can be legitimised. There are appropriate safeguards which require additional authorisation from a supervisory authority for a specific transfer and safeguards that do not require such authorisation. The following appropriate safeguards do not require additional authorisation:[1262]

- a legally binding and enforceable instrument between public authorities or bodies;[1263]
- binding corporate rules;
- standard data protection clauses adopted by the Commission;
- standard data protection clauses adopted by a supervisory authority and approved by the Commission;
- an approved code of conduct together with binding and enforceable commitments of the controller or processor in the third country to apply the appropriate safeguards; and

1258. Art. 45(5) GDPR. *See*, for example, CJEU, Case C-362/14, *Schrems I*, ECLI:EU:C:2015:650 (invalidity Safe Harbour), https://eur-lex.europa.eu/legal-content/EN/TXT/?uri=CELEX%3A62014CJ0362; CJEU, Case C-311/18, *Schrems II*, ECLI:EU:C:2020:559 (invalidity Privacy Shield), https://eur-lex.europa.eu/legal-content/EN/TXT/?uri=CELEX%3A62018CJ0311.

1259. *See*, for example, CJEU, Case C-362/14, *Schrems I*, ECLI:EU:C:2015:650, https://eur-lex.europa.eu/legal-content/EN/TXT/?uri=CELEX%3A62014CJ0362 and CJEU, Case C-311/18, *Schrems II*, ECLI:EU:C:2020:559, https://eur-lex.europa.eu/legal-content/EN/TXT/?uri=CELEX%3A62018CJ0311,

1260. Recital 108 GDPR.

1261. Art. 46(1) GDPR.

1262. Art. 46(2) GDPR.

1263. *See also*, EDPB, Guidelines 2/2020 on Arts 46(2) and 46(3) of Regulation 2016/679 for transfers of personal data between EEA and non-EEA public authorities and bodies, v2, adopted on 15 December 2020.

– an approved certification mechanism together with binding and enforceable commitments of the controller or processor in the third country to apply the appropriate safeguards.

1044. Article 46(3) GDPR provides for two additional appropriate safeguards that require authorisation from the competent supervisory authority. These are:

(1) contractual clauses between the controller or processor and the controller, processor or recipient of the personal data in the third country or international organisation; and
(2) provisions to be inserted into administrative arrangements between public authorities or bodies which include enforceable and effective data subject rights.[1264]

1045. As discussed above, the Court of Justice of the European Union upheld the validity of the standard contractual clauses as a transfer tool to ensure contractually an essentially equivalent level of protection for the transfer of personal data to third countries.[1265] However, it is emphasised that the transfer tools mentioned in Article 46 GDPR do not operate in a vacuum. Controllers and processors, acting as exporters, are responsible for verifying, on a case-by-case basis and, where appropriate, in collaboration with the importer in the third country, if the effectiveness of the appropriate safeguards is not impinged by the law or practice of the third country.[1266] If so, exporters need to assess whether supplementary measures could fill the gaps in the protection.[1267]

1046. The EDPB issued 'Recommendations 01/2010 on measures that supplement transfer tools to ensure compliance with the EU level of protection of personal data' to help exporters with this complex transfer assessment.[1268] The recommendations provide exporters with a series of steps to follow, potential sources of information, and some examples of supplementary measures.

1047. As a first step, exporters need to know their transfers. Exporters need to map the data transfers to be aware of where the personal data goes. Exporters also need to verify that the data transferred is adequate, relevant and limited to what is necessary in relation to the purposes for which it is processed.

1264. *See also* EDPB, Guidelines 2/2020 on Arts 46(2)(a) and 46(3)(b) of Regulation 2016/679 for transfers of personal data between EEA and non-EEA public authorities and bodies, v2, adopted on 15 December 2020. https://edpb.europa.eu/sites/default/files/consultation/edpb_guidelines_202002_art46guidelines_internationaltransferspublicbodies_v1.pdf.
1265. CJEU, Case C-311/18, *Schrems II*, ECLI:EU:C:2020:559, https://eur-lex.europa.eu/legal-content/EN/TXT/?uri=CELEX%3A62018CJ0311.
1266. *Ibid.*, para. 142.
1267. *Ibid.*, para. 133.
1268. EDPB, Recommendations 01/2010 on measures that supplement transfer tools to ensure compliance with the EU level of protection of personal data, v2, adopted on 18 June 2021.

1048. As a second step, the exporters need to verify the transfer tool on which they rely on. Exporters should only rely on an Article 46 transfer tool in the absence of an adequacy decision. The derogations provided in Article 49 GDPR (see *infra*) cannot become 'the rule' in practice and need to be restricted to specific situations.

1049. As a third step, it needs to be assessed if there is anything in the law and/or practices in force in the third country that may impinge on the effectiveness of the appropriate safeguards of the transfer tool in the context of the specific transfer.[1269] Focus should go first to the applicable legislation in the third country relevant in light of all circumstances of the transfer. Moreover, the practices of the third country's public authorities should be considered as well, as this allows the exporter to verify whether the safeguards provided by the transfer tool can ensure, in practice, the effective protection of the personal data transferred. Where it is found that the legislation in the third country is manifestly not applied/complied with in practice, or where there are practices incompatible with the commitments of the transfer tool, the transfer should be suspended or adequate supplementary measures need to be implemented. Where the exporter remains uncertain after the transfer assessment as to whether the transferred data and/or importer falls within the scope of problematic legislation the transfer should either be suspended, appropriate supplementary measures implemented, or, if the exporter decides and is able to demonstrate and document that there are no reasons to believe that the relevant and problematic legislation will be interpreted and/or applied in practice in the context of the transfer, the exporter may decide to proceed with the transfer.

1050. The fourth step is to identify and adopt supplementary measures that are necessary to bring the level of protection of the data transferred up to the EU Standard of essential equivalence.[1270] This step is of course only required when the third-country legislation and/or practices impinge on the effectiveness of the transfer tool. The exporter needs to assess the potential effectiveness of supplementary measures on a case-by-case basis, taking into account the gaps of the protection and the required level of protection. Supplementary measures could have a contractual, technical or organisational nature. The combination of these measures may enhance the level of protection and contribute to reaching EU standards. The EDPB lists a non-exhaustive list of examples of supplementary measures with some of the conditions they would require to be effective.[1271] It is important to note that not every imbalance can be balanced with supplementary measures. There are certain scenarios for which the EDPB cannot envision any (set of) effective measures. This is the case, for example, where data are transferred for business purposes including by way of remote access and this data is not pseudonymised or encrypted, because the

1269. EDPB, Recommendations 01/2010 on measures that supplement transfer tools to ensure compliance with the EU level of protection of personal data, v2, adopted on 18 June 2021, 14.
1270. EDPB, Recommendations 01/2010 on measures that supplement transfer tools to ensure compliance with the EU level of protection of personal data, v2, adopted on 18 June 2021, 21.
1271. EDPB, Recommendations 01/2010 on measures that supplement transfer tools to ensure compliance with the EU level of protection of personal data, v2, adopted on 18 June 2021, 28.

processing requires accessing data in the clear.[1272] This has severe consequences for groups of undertakings as this means that personal data cannot travel within the group freely, if the data are processed in the clear by another group entity in a third country that does not provide an adequate level of protection.

1051. The EDPB reminds exporters, as a fifth step, to take any formal procedural steps that the adoption of supplementary measures may require, depending on the choice of Article 46 GDPR transfer tool.[1273]

1052. The sixth and final step is to re-evaluate at appropriate intervals the level of protection afforded to the data transferred where there are developments that may affect it. This obligation follows from the accountability principle in Article 5(2) GDPR and requires the exporters, where appropriate in collaboration with the importers, to monitor, on an ongoing basis, any developments in the third country which may have an impact on the initial transfer assessment. If the importer is no longer able to honour his commitments or the supplementary measures implemented are no longer effective, the transfer should be suspended or ended.[1274]

B. Standard Contractual Clauses

1053. One of the most commonly used transfer mechanisms are the standard data protection clauses (standard contractual clauses).[1275]

1054. Standard contractual clauses are standardised and pre-approved model data protection clauses for the transfer of personal data to a third country. These clauses can be incorporated into contractual arrangements on a voluntary basis. While the clauses themselves cannot be modified by the parties, the clauses can be supplemented by other clauses or additional safeguards as long as they do not contradict the standard contractual clauses.[1276]

1055. Standard contractual clauses can be adopted by the Commission or by a supervisory authority with approval by the Commission.[1277] The Commission recently adopted new standard contractual clauses on the basis of Article 46(1)(c) GDPR.[1278]

1272. Use case 7 described in EDPB, Recommendations 01/2010 on measures that supplement transfer tools to ensure compliance with the EU level of protection of personal data, v2, adopted on 18 June 2021, 35.
1273. EDPB, Recommendations 01/2010 on measures that supplement transfer tools to ensure compliance with the EU level of protection of personal data, v2, adopted on 18 June 2021, 23.
1274. EDPB, Recommendations 01/2010 on measures that supplement transfer tools to ensure compliance with the EU level of protection of personal data, v2, adopted on 18 June 2021, 25.
1275. Art. 46(2)(c)-(d) GDPR.
1276. Recital 109 GDPR.
1277. Art. 46(2)(c)-(d) GDPR.
1278. Commission Implementing Decision (EU) 2021/914 of 4 June 2021 on standard contractual clauses for the transfer of personal data to third countries pursuant to Regulation (EU) 2016/679 of the European Parliament and of the Council (notified under document C(2021)3972 final), OJ L 199, 7.6.2021, 31–61.

1056. The new clauses are based on a multifunctional, modular approach to increase contract effectiveness, and replace the old standard contractual clauses adopted on the basis of Article 26(4) Directive 95/46/EC.[1279] Standard contractual clauses still require an effort from the exporter and importer. The parties need to provide detailed information about the transfer in up to three annexes, depending on the relationship between the exporter and importer.

C. Binding Corporate Rules

1057. Organisations that are part of the same group or a group of enterprises engaged in a joint economic activity may make use of binding corporate rules as appropriate safeguards for the transfer of personal data within the group.[1280]

1058. Binding corporate rules need to include all essential principles and enforceable rights to ensure appropriate safeguards for the data transfers and need to be legally binding to every member of the group. Binding corporate rules need to be approved by the supervisory authority in accordance with the consistency mechanism.[1281]

1059. Article 47(2) GDPR requires that at least the following elements are specified in the corporate rules:

a) the structure and contact details of the group and each of the members;
b) the context of the data transfer, including the categories of personal data, the type of processing, the purposes of the processing, the type of data subjects affected and the third country or countries involved;
c) the legally binding nature of the corporate rules, both internally and externally;
d) the application of the general data protection principles and the requirements in respect of onward transfers to bodies not bound by the binding corporate rules;

1279. For controller-to-controller transfers: Commission Decision 2001/497/EC of 15 June 2001 on standard contractual clauses for the transfer of personal data to third countries under Directive 95/46/EC (notified under document number C(2001) 1539), OJ L 181, 4.7.2001, 19–31; Commission Decision 2004/915/EC of 27 December 2004 amending Decision 2001/497/EC as regards the introduction of an alternative set of standard contractual clauses for the transfer of personal data to third countries (notified under document number C(2004) 5271), OJ L 385, 29.12.2004, 74–84. The latter containing more flexible auditing requirements, a liability regime based on due diligence obligations and optional clauses, e.g., on dispute resolution mechanisms.
    For controller-to-processor transfers: Commission Decision 2010/87 of 5 February 2010 on standard contractual clauses for the transfer of personal data to processors established in third countries under Directive 95/46/EC of the European Parliament and of the Council (notified under document C(2010)593), OJ L 39, 12.2.2010, 5–18.

1280. Art. 46(2)-(b) GDPR; Moerel, Lokke. *Binding Corporate Rules: Corporate Self-Regulation of Global Data Transfers.* 1st ed., Oxford University Press, 2012.

1281. Art. 47(1) GDPR.

e) the rights of the data subjects in regard to processing and the means to exercise those rights;
f) the acceptance by the exporters of liability for any breaches of the binding corporate rules by any importing group member;
g) how the information on the binding corporate rules is provided to the data subjects in addition to the general transparency requirements in Articles 13 and 14 GDPR;
h) the tasks of any data protection officer or any other person or entity in charge of the monitoring compliance with the binding corporate rules within the group, as well as monitoring training and complaint-handling;
i) the complaint procedures;
j) the mechanisms within the group for ensuring the verification of compliance with the corporate rules. These mechanisms need to include data protection audit methods for ensuring corrective actions to protect the rights of the data subject. Results should be available upon request to the competent supervisory authority;
k) the mechanisms for reporting and recording changes to the rules and reporting those changes to the supervisory authority;
l) the cooperation mechanism with the supervisory authority to ensure compliance by any member of the group;
m) the mechanisms for reporting to the competent supervisory authority any legal requirements to which a member of the group is subject in a third country which are likely to have a substantial adverse effect on the guarantees provided by the corporate rules; and
n) the appropriate data protection training to personnel having permanent or regular access to personal data.

1060. The Article 29 Working Party adopted several documents, which have been endorsed by the EDPB, that describe the procedure of approval of binding corporate rules and provide guidance on the structure and requirements of the rules.[1282]

D. Codes of Conduct

1061. Importers of personal data who are based outside of the EEA and who are not subject to the GDPR can adhere to approved codes of conduct with general validity within the EEA in order to provide appropriate safeguards for the transfer of personal data.[1283] The controller or processor can then transfer personal data on

1282. WP29, Working Document on the approval procedure of the Binding Corporate Rules for controllers and processors, WP263 rev.1, as endorsed by the EDPB; WP29, Recommendation on the approval of the Controller Binding Corporate Rules form, WP264, as endorsed by the EDPB; WP29, Recommendation on the approval of the Processor Binding Corporate Rules form, WP265, as endorsed by the EDPB; WP29, Working Document on Binding Corporate Rules for Controllers, WP265 rev.01, as endorsed by the EDPB; WP29, Working Document on Binding Corporate Rules for Processors, WP257 rev. 01, as endorsed by the EDPB.
1283. Art. 40(3) GDPR. *See supra.*

the basis of the code of conduct together with binding and enforceable commitments – via contractual or other legally binding instruments – of the controller or processor in the third country to apply the appropriate safeguards.[1284] It is not required that the controller-processor, data exporter, also adheres to the code of conduct in order to rely on the code for complying with their data transfer obligations.[1285] Codes of conduct can be used as a transfer tool by organisations performing particular processing activities, e.g., within a specific sector or for processing activities which share the same processing characteristics and needs. Unlike BCRs, it is not required that the organisations belong to the same group of companies.

1062. The object of a code of conduct intended for data transfers needs to set out the rules that will need to be complied with by the data importer to ensure that personal data are adequately protected in accordance with Chapter V GDPR when being processed by the data importer.[1286] In particular, the transfer codes need to address first, the essential principles, rights and obligations arising under the GDPR for controllers/processors, and second, guarantees that are specific to the context of transfers, e.g., with respect to onward transfers or conflict of laws in a third country.

E. Certification

1063. As is the case for approved codes of conduct, approved certification mechanisms, seals or marks, may also provide for appropriate safeguards to transfer personal data to a third country or an international organisation, if there are binding and enforceable commitments of the controller or processor in the third country to apply the appropriate safeguards.[1287]

F. Individual Authorisation of Contractual Clauses

1064. A last option to provide appropriate safeguard for private actors to transfer personal data based on appropriate safeguards are contractual clauses that are authorised by the supervisory authority.[1288] Those clauses need to ensure compliance with data protection requirements and the rights of the data subjects, including the availability of enforceable data subject rights and of effective legal remedies, including to obtain effective administrative or judicial redress and to claim compensation in the EEA or in a third country. The clauses should relate in particular to

1284. Art. 46(2)(e) GDPR.
1285. EDPB, Guidelines 04/2021 on codes of conduct as tools for transfers, v2.0, adopted on 22 February 2022, 3, https://edpb.europa.eu/system/files/2022-03/edpb_guidelines_codes_conduct_transfers_after_public_consultation_en_1.pdf.
1286. EDPB, Guidelines 04/2021 on codes of conduct as tools for transfers, v2.0, adopted on 22 February 2022, 7.
1287. Art. 46(2)(f) GDPR; Art. 42(2) GDPR.
1288. Art. 46(3)(a) GDPR.

compliance with the general principles relating to data processing, the principles of data protection by design and by default.[1289]

IV. Derogations for Specific Situations

1065. In the absence of an adequacy decision or of appropriate safeguards, a transfer or a set of transfers can take place on one of the bases set out in Article 49(1) GDPR. These bases are derogations for specific situations which need to be interpreted restrictively so that the exception does not become the rule in practice.[1290]

1066. Since derogations do not provide adequate protection or appropriate safeguards for the transferred personal data, transfers on the bases of these derogations leads to increased risks for the rights and freedoms of the data subjects concerned. Exporters need to be aware of that and expressly limit those transfers.[1291]

1067. Article 49(1) GDPR considers the following derogations:[1292]

(a) the informed explicit consent of the data subject for the particular data transfer or set of transfers;
(b) the necessity of the transfer for the performance of a contract between the data subject and the controller or the implementation of pre-contractual measures taken at the data subject's request;
(c) the necessity of the transfer for the conclusion or performance of a contract concluded in the interest of the data subject between the controller and another natural or legal person;
(d) the necessity of the transfer for important reasons of public interest that are recognised in Union law or in the law of the Member State to which the controller is subject;[1293]
(e) the necessity of the transfer for the establishment, exercise or defence of legal claims;
(f) the necessity of the transfer for the protection of the vital interests including physical integrity or life, of the data subject or of other persons, where the data subject is physically or legally incapable of giving consent;

1289. Recital 108 GDPR.
1290. EDPB, Guidelines 2/2018 on derogations of Art. 49 under Regulation 2016/679, adopted on 25 May 2018, 4; WP29, Working Document on a common interpretation of Art. 26(1) of Directive 95/46/EC of 24 October 1995, adopted on 25 November 2005, WP114, 7, https://edpb.europa.eu/sites/default/files/files/file1/edpb_guidelines_2_2018_derogations_en.pdf.
1291. EDPB, Guidelines 2/2018 on derogations of Art. 49 under Regulation 2016/679, adopted on 25 May 2018, 4, https://edpb.europa.eu/sites/default/files/files/file1/edpb_guidelines_2_2018_derogations_en.pdf.
1292. Art. 49(1) GDPR.
1293. Art. 49(1)(d) GDPR and Art. 49(5) GDPR.

(g) the necessity of the transfer from a register that is established by Union or Member State law that is intended for consultation by the public or persons who demonstrate a legitimate interest to the extent that the conditions laid down for consultation are fulfilled in the particular case and limited to the personal data necessary.

1068. In the second sub-paragraph of Article 49(1) GDPR, a final exception is made for transfers that can neither be based on an adequacy decision, nor on appropriate safeguards or derogations for specific situations. In such case, the transfer of personal data to a third country or an international organisation may take place only if the transfer is not repetitive, concerns only a limited number of data subjects, is necessary for the purposes of compelling legitimate interests pursued by the controller which are not overridden by the interests or rights and freedoms of the data subject. If so, the controller needs to assess all the circumstances surrounding the data transfer and provide suitable safeguards with regard to the protection of the personal data on the basis of that assessment, and in addition, the controller needs to inform the supervisory authority and the data subjects of the transfer and of the compelling legitimate interests pursued.[1294]

V. Transfers or Disclosures Not Authorised by Union Law

1069. Article 48 GDPR specifies that decisions from third-country authorities, courts or tribunals do not by themselves provide a legitimate basis for the transfer of personal data to third countries. Transfers should only be allowed where the conditions of Chapter V GDPR are met, for example, where disclosure is necessary for an important ground of public interest recognised by the EU or Member State law to which the controller is subject.[1295]

1070. Any third-country judgment or administrative decision can only be recognised or enforced if based on an international agreement that is in force between the requesting third country and the EU or relevant Member State. In situations where there is an international agreement, such as a mutual legal assistance treaty, European companies should generally refuse direct requests to the personal data, and refer the requesting third-country authority to the existing agreement.[1296]

VI. International Cooperation

1071. An important concern regarding data transfers is that data transfers put at increased risk the ability of data subjects to exercise their data subject rights in

1294. Art. 49(1), second sub-paragraph GDPR.
1295. Recital 115 GDPR.
1296. EDPB, Guidelines 2/2018 on derogations of Art. 49 under Regulation 2016/679, adopted on 25 May 2018, 5, https://edpb.europa.eu/sites/default/files/files/file1/edpb_guidelines_2_2018_derogations_en.pdf.

particular to protect themselves from the unlawful use or disclosure of their personal data. Moreover, supervisory authorities may find themselves unable to pursue complaints or conduct investigations relating to the activities outside their borders or their efforts to work together in a cross-border context may be hampered by insufficient preventative or remedial powers, inconsistent legal regimes, and practical obstacles like resource constraints.[1297]

1072. In order to address these concerns, Article 50 GDPR promotes international cooperation for the protection of personal data in relation to international data transfers. It requires the Commission and supervisory authorities to take appropriate steps to:

(a) 'develop international cooperation mechanisms to facilitate the effective enforcement of legislation for the protection of personal data;
(b) provide international mutual assistance in the enforcement of legislation for the protection of personal data, including through notification, complaint referral, investigative assistance and information exchange, subject to appropriate safeguards for the protection of personal data and other fundamental rights and freedoms;
(c) engage relevant stakeholders in discussion and activities aimed at furthering international cooperation in the enforcement of legislation for the protection of personal data;
(d) promote the exchange and documentation of personal data protection legislation and practice, including jurisdictional conflicts with third countries'.

1073. The EDPB considers it one of its key action points to facilitate the engagement between the EDPB members and the supervisory authorities of third countries with a focus on cooperation in enforcement cases involving controllers and processors located outside the EEA. This commitment to ensure effective protection of personal data beyond the EU borders is part of Pillar IV – 'The global dimension' of the EDPB Work Programme 2021/2022 and the EDPB Strategy 2021–2023.[1298]

§12. Oversight and Enforcement

I. Introduction

1074. Article 16 TFEU enshrines the right to the protection of personal data, a right which has also obtained the status of *fundamental* right with its integration in Article 8 of the Charter of Fundamental Rights of the European Union ('Charter'). Both Article 16, 2nd para. TFEU as well as Article 8, 3rd para. of the Charter foresee

1297. Recital 116 GDPR.
1298. EDPB, EDPB Strategy 2021–2023, adopted on 15 December 2020, 6, https://edpb.europa.eu/sites/default/files/files/file1/edpb_strategy2021-2023_en.pdf; EDPB, EDPB Work Programme 2021/2022, 6, https://edpb.europa.eu/system/files/2021-03/edpb_workprogramme_2021-2022_en.pdf.

an oversight mechanism whereby independent supervisory authorities must monitor compliance with the rules laid down in Union and Member State law which ensure the protection of this fundamental right.

1075. Such an oversight mechanism relying on independent supervisory authorities (hereinafter referred to as 'data protection authorities' or 'DPAs') already existed under the GDPR's predecessor, i.e., Directive 95/46/EC. The tasks, competences and powers of enforcement of these independent supervisory authorities have been expanded upon significantly, however, with the introduction of the GDPR and specifically its Chapter VI. The GDPR in its Chapter VII furthermore places a lot of additional emphasis on cooperation between these independent supervisory authorities in the performance of their tasks and the exercise of their competences. This idea of cooperation is again not new but has become more outspoken and far more compelling than it has been in the past.

II. Independent Supervisory Authorities

A. *Independence*

1. Independence in General

1076. It follows directly from the aforementioned provisions in the TFEU and the Charter that authorities, who are assigned the task to monitor the application of the data protection rules, must be independent. This independence requirement must be interpreted broadly, in the sense that supervisory authorities must be free from undue influence from the private as well as the public sphere. Supervisory authorities are indeed not only required to supervise compliance of personal data processing by citizens, civil society and the private sector with data protection rules but should supervise the compliance of personal data processing by public sector entities with such rules as well.[1299]

1077. While all Member States must provide for an independent data protection authority, Article 51 GDPR makes it very clear that there can be more than one DPA per Member State. The Federal Republic of Germany, for instance, has DPAs in all of its States, while Belgium has one supervisory authority at the federal level and then a separate supervisory authority that is competent for the institutions of the Flemish government. When a Member State has more than one supervisory authority, it must designate one authority who shall represent the others at the European Data Protection Board. The European Data Protection Board, often abbreviated as the 'Board' or 'EDBP', is the successor of the Working Party Article 29 under Directive 95/46/EC.

1299. Schütz P. 2012) Comparing formal independence of data protection authorities in selected EU Member States. Paper for the 4th Biennial ECPR Standing Group for Regulatory Governance Conference.

1078. The requirement for a supervisory authority to remain independent, is crucial to the effective protection of personal data considering its status as a fundamental right. And yet, as ample case law of the European Court of Justice demonstrates, Member States often struggled to give full effect to this requirement, especially with regard to independence vis-à-vis governmental authorities.[1300]

1079. A supervisory authority can only be effective and do its work independently, when that authority has the necessary resources to fulfil its supervisory tasks. The GDPR explicitly provides that each Member State must ensure that the supervisory authorities receive the human, technical and financial resources as well as the infrastructure required to perform those tasks.[1301] Financial resources can come from the public budget, but that budget must be separate. The requirement that the budget must be separate, is new when compared with what applied under Directive 95/46/EC. Under the previous Directive the budget of the authority could be placed under a ministerial department, as confirmed by the European Court of Justice.[1302]

1080. The independence requirement does not mean that the supervisory authority is free from any sort of control or oversight. The GDPR explicitly provides that the supervisory authority shall be subject to financial control, but that such control should not affect its independence.[1303] As the European Court of Justice confirmed, subjecting the supervisory authority to control exercised by parliament does not, in and of itself impede the independence of the authority.[1304] Furthermore, the decisions of the supervisory authority can be challenged before the courts and tribunals.

1081. Finally, the independence requirement is also ensured vis-à-vis the staff of the supervisory authority. Under Directive 95/46/EC there had been case law on circumstances where the staff of the supervisory authority in fact belonged to the executive branch of the government. The European Court of Justice ruled that such an arrangement, where the staff of the authority were in fact staff members on the payroll of a department of the executive government, led to problems of independence.[1305] Indeed, the staff would not be inclined to go against their hierarchical

1300. CJEU Case C-518/07, Judgment of 9 March 2010, Commission v. Germany, ECLI:EU:C:2010:125, https://eur-lex.europa.eu/legal-content/EN/TXT/?uri=CELEX%3A62007CJ0518; CJEU, Case C-614/10, Judgment of 16 October 2012, Commission v. Austria, ECLI:EU:C:2012:63, https://eur-lex.europa.eu/legal-content/en/TXT/?uri=CELEX:62010CJ0614; CJEU, Case C-288/12, Judgment of, 8 April 2014, Commission v. Hungary, ECLI:EU:C:2014:237, https://eur-lex.europa.eu/legal-content/EN/TXT/?uri=CELEX%3A62012CJ0288; CJEU, Case C-210/16, Judgment of 5 June 2018, Wirtschaftsakademie Schleswig-Holstein, ECLI:EU:C:2018:388, https://eur-lex.europa.eu/legal-content/EN/TXT/?uri=CELEX%3A62016CJ0210.
1301. Art. 52.4 GDPR.
1302. CJEU, Case C-614/10, Judgment of 16 October 2012, Commission v. Austria, ECLI:EU:C:2012:63, para. 58, https://eur-lex.europa.eu/legal-content/en/TXT/?uri=CELEX:62010CJ0614.
1303. Art. 52.6 GDPR.
1304. CJEU Case C-518/07, Judgment of 9 March 2010, Commission v. Germany, ECLI:EU:C:2010:125, https://eur-lex.europa.eu/legal-content/EN/TXT/?uri=CELEX%3A62007CJ0518.
1305. Case C-614/10, Judgment of 16 October 2012, Commission v. Austria, ECLI:EU:C:2012:63, para. 59, https://eur-lex.europa.eu/legal-content/en/TXT/?uri=CELEX:62010CJ0614.

superior on whose payroll they are. The European legislator therefore included an explicit obligation for the Member States in the GDPR to ensure that the staff of the supervisory authority are truly the supervisory authority's own, in terms of selection and control.[1306]

2. Independence of the Members of the Supervisory Authority

1082. The independence requirement for a supervisory authority evidently does not only encompass the authority as an institution but extends to its members as well. The GDPR provides that the members of the supervisory authority must be free from external influence, whether that influence is direct or indirect, and these members should also refrain from seeking or taking instructions from anybody.[1307] It is useful to highlight that the GDPR creates a distinction between members and staff of a supervisory authority.[1308] The member or members are the ones who, within the supervisory authority, take the decisions about the performance of tasks and the execution of powers and bear the responsibility for the supervisory authority's functioning. The staff of the supervisory authority support the member(s) of the supervisory authority in the performance of its tasks and the exercise of its powers.

1083. Free from influence means that the members should not receive instructions from anyone regarding the exercise of their tasks or competences or with regard to their interpretation of the GDPR. It also means that the members should be credibly perceived as being objective and impartial and free from indirect influence such as possible sanctions or interesting career opportunities which may be respectively imposed or offered by other branches of government.

1084. Only the parliament, the government, the head of state or an independent body made competent by national law should be allowed to appoint the members and then only on the basis of a transparent procedure.[1309] The members should be sufficiently qualified and skilled for their tasks and their appointment shall end only when:[1310]

- their term in office expires; or
- they resign; or
- they are made to retire; or
- they are dismissed on the basis of serious misconduct or the non-fulfilment of the aforementioned requirements.

Each member shall be held to a duty of professional secrecy with regard to the confidential information to which they gain access in the performance of their

1306. Art. 52.5 GDPR.
1307. Art. 52.2 GDPR.
1308. *See*, for instance, Art. 54.2 and 62.1 GDPR.
1309. Art. 53.1 GDPR.
1310. Art. 53.2, 53.3 and 53.4 GDPR.

tasks.[1311] The rules on the establishment of the supervisory authority, the qualifications and eligibility of its members, the appointment procedure, their term in office and their obligations and prohibitions are all to be arranged for in Member State law, in accordance with the provisions of the GDPR.[1312]

B. A Dual Role

1085. The supervisory authority must work towards two key objectives under the GDPR: it must protect the fundamental rights and freedoms of natural persons in relation to processing and it must facilitate the free flow of personal data within the European Union.[1313] Both these objectives concern the core subject matter of the GDPR itself, as evidenced by its Article 1.

1086. To achieve the first objective, i.e., the protection of fundamental rights and freedoms of natural persons in relation to processing, the supervisory authority must monitor the application of the provisions of the GDPR within its territory. The first main task of the supervisory authority is therefore, quite simply put, to check within its territory that anyone who falls within the personal scope of the GDPR complies with its obligations under the GDPR. The European legislator has broken down this first main task of monitoring the application of the provisions of the GDPR in several, more specific tasks.[1314] Subsequently, the supervisory authority is endowed with certain competences and powers to fulfil these tasks.[1315] Both the tasks of the supervisory authority as well as its competences and powers are analysed in more detail later on in this chapter.

1087. To achieve the second objective, i.e., to facilitate the free flow of personal data within the European Union, the supervisory authority must, to the extent that it falls within its competences, ensure that there are no barriers within its territory that would prevent personal data from flowing.

Such barriers could stem from national law, when national legislators draft laws which impose data localisation requirements or impose stringent protection measures upon processing activities in their territory and where such requirements or measures are not explicitly allowed by the GDPR.[1316] Yet supervisory authorities' powers to influence national legislation are limited, since they are typically only allowed to advice on new legislative initiatives related to personal data protection.[1317]

Such barriers could however stem from inconsistent application of the GDPR by supervisory authorities across the different Member States as well. It would indeed make it very difficult for controllers and processors to process personal data across

1311. Art. 54.2 GDPR.
1312. Art. 54.1 GDPR.
1313. Art. 51.1 GDPR.
1314. Art. 57 GDPR.
1315. Art. 55, 56 and 58 GDPR.
1316. Recital 9 GDPR.
1317. Art. 57.1 (c) GDPR.

Member State borders when each supervisory authority would be allowed to interpret the obligations of those same controllers and processors under the GDPR differently. This would lead to a patchwork of different national flavours of the GDPR and was one of the problems that arose under the GDPR's predecessor.[1318]

To prevent such inconsistent application and ensure legal certainty for controllers and processors, the GDPR reiterates the obligation for supervisory authorities to cooperate with one another as it existed before,[1319] but then complements that obligation with an elaborate cooperation and consistency mechanism.[1320] By requiring supervisory authorities to cooperate and creating a mandatory mechanism that fosters consistency, the European legislator has taken steps to ensure that the provisions of the GDPR are interpreted and applied in the same way in all of the different Member States.

C. Competences, Tasks and Powers

1. Competences

a. Territorially Delineated Competences

1088. The GDPR adheres to the basic principle that the competence of a supervisory authority is tied directly to the territory of a Member State.[1321] This same principle existed under Directive 95/46/EC as well.[1322] Supervisory authorities are competent to supervise (and take actions against) not only private individuals and organisations, but also the bodies and entities of national governments. Their competence therefore ties in directly with the sovereignty of the Member States. The link between territorially delineated competence and sovereignty is most tangible in Article 55.2 GDPR. This provision emphasizes that only the supervisory authority of the Member State in question is competent to supervise that Member State's public authorities. Any other mechanism in the GDPR that would make another Member State's authority potentially competent, does not apply.

1089. As explained above, Member States can have more than one supervisory authority within their territory. It is then up to those Member States to determine how the competences are divided between the different supervisory authorities within that Member State's territory. The division can be based on a territorial delineation within the Member State, or it can be based on other parameters as well.[1323]

1318. Explanatory Memorandum to the Proposal of the European Commission for a Regulation of the European Parliament and of the Council on the protection of individuals with regard to the processing of personal data and on the free movement of such data (General Data Protection Regulation) of 25 January 2012, COM(2012) 11 final, 4.
1319. Art. 28.6, 2nd para. Directive 95/46/EC.
1320. Chapter VII GDPR.
1321. Art. 55.1 GDPR.
1322. Art. 28.1 Directive 95/46/EC.
1323. An example can be an authority competent for a specific sector or for specific public sector bodies.

b. A Novel Approach for Cross-Border Processing Activities: Introducing the 'One Stop Shop'

1090. The principle of territorial delineation of competence is not absolute, however. In response to calls from companies and organisations to have a more homogeneous system of enforcement for cross-border processing activities, the European legislator introduced the so-called one stop shop (OSS) mechanism in the GDPR to replace Directive 95/46/EC's more heterogenous enforcement system.[1324] The previous Directive solely relied on a vaguely described obligation for supervisory authorities to cooperate.[1325] With the OSS mechanism the GDPR introduces a more concrete and effective system for *mandatory* cooperation between supervisory authorities.[1326]

1091. The idea behind the OSS mechanism is that controllers and processors engaging in cross-border processing activities in two or more Member States should have one supervisory authority that acts as the single interlocutor for the controller or processor with regard to these processing activities.[1327] A processing activity is to be considered cross-border when it concerns:[1328]

– a processing activity taking place in the context of the activities of establishments in more than one Member State of a controller or processor;[1329] or
– a processing activity taking place in the context of the activities of a single establishment of a controller or processor, but which substantially affects or is likely to substantially affect data subjects in more than one Member State.[1330]

1092. This supervisory authority acting as single interlocutor is called the *lead* supervisory authority, the authority that coordinates the enforcement actions towards the controller or processor.[1331] Article 56.1 GDPR clarifies that a controller's or processor's lead supervisory authority for cross-border processing of personal data is the authority of the main establishment or single establishment of that controller or processor in the Union. Identifying the main establishment is different for controllers and processors:[1332]

– for a controller the main establishment is the place of the controller's central administration in the EU, unless the decisions on purposes and means for the

1324. *Supra* note 20, 5.
1325. Art. 28.6, 2nd para. Directive 95/46/EC.
1326. Art. 56.1 and 60.1 GDPR.
1327. Art. 56.6 GDPR.
1328. Art. 4.23 GDPR.
1329. With regard to determining whether a processing of personal data takes place in the context of the activities of an establishment, as clarified by the case law of the European Court of Justice, we refer to the section on territorial application of the GDPR elsewhere in this contribution.
1330. The Working Party Art. 29 ('WP29'), the predecessor to the European Data Protection Board ('EDPB'), has provided guidance on when a processing of personal data substantially affects data subjects in more than one Member State. *See* WP29, Guidelines for identifying a controller or processor's lead supervisory authority, 13 December 2016 (rev. 5 April 2017), WP 244 rev.01, 3–4.
1331. Art. 60.1 GDPR.
1332. Art. 4.16 GDPR.

cross-border processing activities are taken in another establishment in the EU and this establishment has the power to have these decisions implemented;
- for a processor the main establishment is the place of its central administration in the EU, unless the processor does not have a place of central administration in the EU, in which case it is the establishment where the main processing activities in the context of the activities of an establishment of the processor take place.

1093. In groups of undertakings, i.e., a controlling undertaking and its controlled undertakings,[1333] the establishment of the group in the EU with overall control is presumed the decision-making centre unless, again, the decisions about purposes and means of the processing activity are taken elsewhere.

When there are two or more joint controllers, the joint controllers should determine which establishment among them shall have the power to implement decisions about the processing in order to benefit from the OSS mechanism.[1334]

When there is a cross-border processing activity involving a controller and a processor, the supervisory authority of the controller shall be the lead supervisory authority and the supervisory authority of the processor shall be a supervisory authority concerned.[1335]

1094. When exercising its competence, the lead supervisory authority must follow a strict procedure, which has been set forth in Article 60 GDPR and which will be explained later on.[1336] It is important to stress that the lead supervisory authority is not solely competent with regard to these cross-border processing activities but acts as a coordinator for the cooperation between different supervisory authorities *concerned.*

1095. The GDPR discerns three circumstances in which a supervisory authority becomes a supervisory authority concerned:[1337]

(1) the controller or processor is established in the territory of the Member State of that supervisory authority;
(2) data subjects residing in the Member State of that supervisory authority are substantially affected or likely to be substantially affected by the processing; or
(3) a complaint has been lodged with that supervisory authority.

These supervisory authorities concerned remain competent on their territory but the exercise of powers towards the controller or processor is now funnelled through the lead supervisory authority. The European legislator feared that, if all competences were to reside exclusively with the lead supervisory authority, as was the case in the European Commission's first proposal for the GDPR, that this would

1333. Art. 4.19 GDPR.
1334. *Ibid.*, 7–8.
1335. *Ibid.*, 9.
1336. Art. 56.1 GDPR.
1337. Art. 4.22 GDPR.

adversely impact the supervisory authorities' independence.[1338] Hence, the final version GDPR introduced this system of one coordinator cooperating with other concerned supervisory authorities.

1096. The OSS mechanism in principle only applies to cross-border processing activities involving more than one Member State. This necessarily means that for processing activities involving only *one* local establishment or substantially affects data subjects in just *one* Member State, the supervisory authority for that establishment or that Member State remains competent.[1339] In such a case the local supervisory authority informs the lead supervisory authority, who must then decide within three weeks whether to handle the case or not.[1340] If the lead supervisory authority decides to handle the case, the local supervisory authority is entitled to submit a draft decision which the lead supervisory authority must take into account.[1341] If the lead supervisory authority decides not to handle the case, the local supervisory authority can handle the case on its own but it can ask assistance and support from other supervisory authorities.[1342]

1097. The OSS mechanism thus avoids that controllers and processors have to engage with multiple supervisory authorities whenever a processing activity takes place or affects data subjects in multiple Member States, as was often the case under Directive 95/46/EC. It simultaneously avoids that they are confronted with conflicting opinions and enforcement actions regarding the same subject matter. Finally, the mechanism ensures sufficient proximity between the competent supervisory authority, the controller or processor and the data subject by keeping supervisory authorities concerned closely involved with the enforcement actions undertaken by the lead.

c. Processing Operations of Courts

1098. Article 55(3) of the GDPR states that 'supervisory authorities shall not be competent to supervise processing operations of courts acting in their judicial capacity'. Recital 20 of the GDPR explains that it should be possible to entrust supervision of processing operations carried out by the courts 'acting in their judicial capacity' to specific bodies within the judicial system of the Member State concerned rather than to the supervisory authority under the authority of that Member State, in order to 'safeguard the independence of the judiciary in the performance of its judicial tasks, including decision-making'.

1338. European Parliament, Report on the proposal for a regulation of the European Parliament and of the Council on the protection of individuals with regard to the processing of personal data and on the free movement of such data (General Data Protection Regulation) (COM(2012)0011 – C7-0025/2012 – 2012/0011(COD)), 21 November 2013, A7-0402/2013, 202.
1339. Art. 56.2 GDPR.
1340. Art. 56.3 GDPR.
1341. Art. 56.4 GDPR.
1342. Art. 56.5 GDPR.

1099. The objective of Article 55(3) is to guarantee the independence of the judiciary. According to the Court of Justice, 'safeguarding the independence of the judiciary presupposes, in general, that judicial functions are exercised wholly autonomously, without the courts being subject to any hierarchical constraint or subordinate relationship and without taking orders or instructions from any source whatsoever, thus being protected from any external intervention or pressure liable to jeopardise the independent judgment of their members and to influence their decisions. Observance of the guarantees of independence and impartiality necessary under EU law requires rules in order to dispel any reasonable doubt in the minds of individuals as to the imperviousness of the body in question to external factors and its neutrality with respect to the interests concerned'.[1343]

1100. In its judgment in Case C-245/20, the Court of Justice was asked to determine the scope of the concept of processing operations carried out by courts acting in their judicial capacity, within the meaning of Article 55(3). Must this provision be interpreted as meaning that the fact that a Court makes temporarily available to journalists, documents from Court proceedings containing personal data falls within the exercise, by that court, of its 'judicial capacity'? The Court answered positively to this question. The fact that a Court makes temporarily available to journalists documents from Court proceedings containing personal data in order to enable them better to report on the course of those proceedings falls within the exercise, by that court, of its 'judicial capacity', within the meaning of that provision.[1344]

2. Tasks

1101. Supervisory authorities are not only competent to supervise and enforce data protection law, they are *required* to monitor and enforce data protection law.[1345] The GDPR sets forth a, virtually open-ended, list of tasks that the supervisory authorities should be entrusted with. These tasks include, apart from the general task to supervise and enforce the application of the GDPR:[1346]

1343. CJEU, Case C-245/20, Judgment of 24 March 2022, X and Z v Autoriteit Persoonsgegevens, ECLI:EU:C:2022:216, para. 33, https://eur-lex.europa.eu/legal-content/en/TXT/?uri=CELEX:62020CJ0245.

1344. *Ibid.*, para. 39.

1345. The obligation for a supervisory authority to carry out and fulfil its tasks under the GDPR has already been confirmed by the European Court of Justice in paras 108 and 109 of its Schrems II Judgment: '*It follows from those provisions that the supervisory authorities' primary responsibility is to monitor the application of the GDPR and to ensure its enforcement. The exercise of that responsibility is of particular importance where personal data is transferred to a third country since, as is clear from recital 116 of that regulation, 'when personal data moves across borders outside the Union it may put at increased risk the ability of natural persons to exercise data protection rights in particular to protect themselves from the unlawful use or disclosure of that information'. In such cases, as is stated in that recital, 'supervisory authorities may find that they are unable to pursue complaints or conduct investigations relating to the activities outside their borders'. In addition, under Article 57(1)(f) of the GDPR, each supervisory authority is required on its territory to handle complaints which, in accordance with Article 77(1) of that regulation, any data subject is entitled to lodge where that data subject considers that the processing of his or her*

- promote public awareness and understanding of the obligations under, and application of, the GDPR;
- advise national legislators and governments on legislative and administrative initiatives related to data protection;
- promote awareness under controllers and processors with regard to their obligations under GDPR;
- inform data subjects about the exercise of their rights;
- handle complaints lodged by data subjects or by entities competent to act on behalf of data subjects, investigate complaints in a timely manner and keep data subjects abreast of the progress made;
- cooperate with other supervisory authorities;
- conduct investigations;
- monitor relevant developments, among others with regard to IT and commercial practices;
- adopt standard contractual clauses for data processing agreements and data transfers (without prejudice to the competence of the European Commission in this area, of course);
- establish a list of circumstances when data protection impact assessments are required;
- give controllers advice when they seek prior consultation after data protection impact assessments;
- encourage the drawing up of codes of conduct and approve them when adequate;
- encourage data protection certification mechanisms and approve the criteria for certification;
- carry out periodic reviews of certifications issued;
- draft and publish the accreditation criteria for bodies monitoring codes of conduct;
- conduct the accreditation of the bodies monitoring the codes of conducts and of certification bodies;
- authorise contractual clauses and provisions agreed between public or private parties for providing safeguards when transferring personal data to a third country;
- approve binding corporate rules;
- contribute to the activities of the EDPB;
- keep internal records of infringements of the GDPR and the measures taken to remedy them;
- fulfil any other tasks related to the protection of personal data.

---

personal data infringes the regulation, and is required to examine the nature of that complaint as necessary. The supervisory authority must handle such a complaint with all due diligence (see, by analogy, as regards Article 25(6) of Directive 95/46, CJEU (Grand Chamber), Case C-362/14, Judgement of 6 October 2015, Maximillian Schrems v. Data Protection Commissioner (Request for a preliminary ruling from the High Court, Ireland), ECLI:EU:C:2015:650, para. 63), https://eur-lex.europa.eu/legal-content/EN/TXT/?uri=CELEX%3A62014CJ0362; CJEU, Case C-311/18, Judgment of 16 July 2020, Data Protection Commissioner v. Facebook Ireland and Maximillian Schrems. (Request for a preliminary ruling from the High Court, Ireland), ECLI:EU:C:2020:559, paras 108–109, https://eur-lex.europa.eu/legal-content/EN/TXT/?uri=CELEX%3A62018CJ0311.

1346. Art. 57.1 GDPR.

With respect to the task of handling complaints of data subjects, the supervisory authorities must make it easy for data subjects to submit such complaints, among others by accommodating an electronic complaint submission process.[1347]

1102. The supervisory authority is not allowed to charge data subjects and data protection officers for the performance of its tasks.[1348] That said, if a supervisory authority receives requests which are unfounded or excessive, it is allowed to charge a reasonable fee.[1349] The GDPR is silent on whether supervisory authorities are allowed to charge controllers and processors for the performance of its tasks.[1350]

1103. Supervisory authorities are required to be transparent about their activities and the measures they have taken when exercising their corrective powers (see later). Article 59 GDPR requires them to draw up annual reports which are sent to the relevant governmental institutions as prescribed by Member State law, the European Commission, but also made available to the public.

3. Powers

1104. Many of the tasks listed in Article 57.1 GDPR require the supervisory authorities to have specific powers. Indeed, monitoring the application of the GDPR or handling complaints presupposes that the supervisory authority is able to investigate infringements or complaints, request input from controllers and processors and take corrective actions against those of them who do not comply with their data protection obligations.

1105. Under Directive 95/46/EC it was largely left to the Member States to endow their supervisory authorities with the powers required to fulfil their tasks, which were not everywhere as numerous as they are today under the GDPR. This led to a big discrepancy between Member States in terms of the investigative and corrective actions that their supervisory authorities could take. In some Member States the supervisory authority could issue fines, whereas in others its power was limited to issuing non-compliance findings with no real consequences tied to them or engage in lengthy legal proceedings.[1351] The European legislator has now created a level playing field across the European Union in terms of the powers with which supervisory authorities are endowed.

1347. Art. 57.2 GDPR.
1348. Art. 57.3 GDPR.
1349. Art. 57.4 GDPR.
1350. Prior to Brexit the United Kingdom was a Member State where the supervisory authority charged controllers and processors a data protection fee.
1351. The French supervisory authority already had the power to issue fines under the previous regime of Directive 95/46/EC, while the Belgian supervisory authority could only issue negative findings.

1106. The GDPR makes a distinction between different categories of powers:

- investigative powers;[1352]
- corrective powers;[1353]
- authorisation and advisory powers;[1354]
- powers to inform judicial authorities and engage in legal proceedings;[1355]
- additional powers granted by Member State law.[1356]

The last category highlights that even under the GDPR there may still be differences between Member States in terms of the powers with which supervisory authorities are endowed. However, even if there are certain differences, all supervisory authorities will have the powers required to fulfil the tasks imposed upon them by the GDPR.

1107. Notwithstanding the independence of supervisory authorities when exercising these powers, such exercise should still be subject to effective judicial remedy, due process and should be subject to appropriate safeguards as set forth in EU and Member State law.[1357] In practice this means for instance that when a supervisory authority issues an enforcement decision, the party to whom the decision pertains and who believes to have been wronged, should be able to seek legal remedy from an appellate body.

a. Investigative Powers

1108. The investigative powers of a supervisory authority allow the authority to collect all information required to assess compliance with the requirements of the GDPR:

- to order the controller or processor (or their representatives) to provide information;
- to carry out data protection audits;
- to carry out certification reviews;
- to notify controllers and processors about alleged infringements;
- to obtain access to information and personal data from the controller or processor;
- to obtain access to the premises of a controller or processor.

As can be seen from this list, the investigative powers are quite far-reaching. They not only encompass the power to order controllers and processors to provide information, but the power to perform data protection audits and on-premises searches as well. The power to search a controller's or processor's premises mimics

1352. Art. 58.1 GDPR.
1353. Art. 58.2 GDPR.
1354. Art. 58.3 GDPR.
1355. Art. 58.5 GDPR.
1356. Art. 58.6 GDPR.
1357. Art. 58.4 GDPR.

to an extent the power that judicial authorities typically have when performing on-premises searches in criminal investigations. As with criminal investigations by the judicial authorities, the procedural aspects of a search by a supervisory authority should be further specified in Member State law.

b. Corrective Powers

1109. With its corrective powers the supervisory authority is able to act against, and where possible put a stop to, infringements of the provisions of the GDPR and effectively safeguard the rights of data subjects. These corrective powers are mainly aimed at operational measures that the supervisory authority can impose (e.g., ordering a controller or processor to do or not do something) but they encompass punitive powers as well. Under Article 58.2 GDPR the supervisory authorities shall have the following corrective powers:

- to issue warnings to controllers and processors;
- to issue reprimands to controllers and processors;
- to order a controller or processor to comply with a data subject request for exercising a right;
- to order a controller or processor to bring processing operations into compliance;
- to order a controller to communicate a personal data breach to the data subject;
- to impose a temporary or definitive limitation (including a ban) on a processing activity;
- to order rectification, erasure or restriction of processing and notification of such actions to recipients;
- to withdraw a certification or order a certification body to do so or not to grant one;
- to impose administrative fines;
- to order suspension of data flows which include a data transfer.

1110. The Article 29 Working Party emphasised already in 2017 that the exercise of corrective powers should adhere to the principle of equivalence, as set forth in recital 11 GDPR.[1358,1359] This principle of equivalence helps to ensure a consistently high level of protection for natural persons across the EU while simultaneously safeguarding the free flow of personal data in the EU.[1360] In more concrete terms, it means that supervisory authorities should choose similar corrective measures in similar cases, even though they remain independent in exercising their enforcement powers.

1358. Art. 29 Working Party, Guidelines on the application and setting of administrative fines for the purposes of the Regulation 2016/679, 3 October 2017, WP 253, 5.
1359. Recital 11 GDPR: '*Effective protection of personal data throughout the Union requires the strengthening and setting out in detail of the rights of data subjects and the obligations of those who process and determine the processing of personal data, as well as equivalent powers for monitoring and ensuring compliance with the rules for the protection of personal data and equivalent sanctions for infringements in the Member States.*'
1360. Recital 10 GDPR.

1111. The Article 29 Working Party also stressed that the corrective measures taken by supervisory authorities should be effective, proportionate and dissuasive and they should be assessed for each individual case (no 'automatic' application of a corrective measure).

c. Authorisation and Advisory Powers

1112. The supervisory authorities not only have reactionary powers related to discovering infringements and enforcing data protection rules but are also able to act in a more preventive manner. They can, among others, authorise processing activities, advise national legislators, approve codes of conducts and certification mechanisms, approve standard contracts and binding corporate rules. Article 58.3 sets forth the following authorisation and advisory powers:

- to advise the controller in the context of a prior consultation procedure (see earlier in this contribution);
- to issue opinions to governments, other public bodies and the public regarding data protection topics;
- to authorise processing activities undertaken for the performance of a task carried out in the public interest;
- to issue opinions on, and approve, codes of conduct;
- to accredit certification bodies;
- to issue certifications and approve certification criteria;
- to adopt standard contractual clauses for controller-processor relationships and data transfers;
- to authorise standard contractual clauses for data transfers between specific parties;
- to authorise administrative arrangements for data transfers between public sector entities;
- to approve binding corporate rules.

d. Powers to Inform Judicial Authorities and Engage in Legal Proceedings

1113. All of the powers listed under §§1–3 are powers that the supervisory authority can exercise on its own, with respect of course for the cooperation and consistency requirements set forth in Chapter VII GDPR and in accordance with appropriate safeguards and due process rules set forth in EU and national law. However, supervisory authorities may have their reasons why they would rather have judicial authorities take action or why they would bring a certain case before the national courts. Directive 95/46/EC already foresaw that supervisory authorities could bring matters to the attention of judicial authorities or commence or engage in legal proceedings.[1361] The European legislator has reprised this power in Article 58.5 GDPR.

1361. Art. 28.3 Directive 95/46/EC.

1114. However, in contrast with Directive 95/46/EC, the GDPR now has the elaborate OSS mechanism that centralizes enforcement to an extent with the lead supervisory authority This then brings the question whether the power to bring cases to the attention of judicial authorities or to commence or engage in legal proceedings falls under the OSS mechanism as well. While it is quite clear that the powers listed in Articles 58.1, 58.2 and 58.3 GDPR are all to be exercised in accordance with the OSS mechanism in the context of cross-border processing activities, the matter is less straightforward in the context of Article 58.5 GDPR.

Consider, for instance, the circumstance where a supervisory authority obtains knowledge of an infringement of the GDPR which is also a crime under national law. It concerns a cross-border processing activity, but the controller has its main establishment in another Member State. If the OSS mechanism were applicable to the power set forth in Article 58.5 GDPR, everyone else would be able to bring the matter to the attention of the national judicial authorities (it is a crime, after all) but the supervisory authority would not be allowed to do so. This would seem a bit odd, to say the least.

This particular question was brought before the European Court of Justice.[1362] The Court of Justice decided that allowing a supervisory authority to exercise the power laid down in Article 58.5 GDPR indiscriminately without being the lead supervisory authority, would threaten the objective of consistent and homogenous application of the GDPR as laid down in its Recital 10.[1363] Nonetheless, the European Court of Justice emphasised that that power can be exercised by a supervisory authority that is not the lead authority to the extent that that supervisory authority is allowed to act in accordance with the OSS mechanism, and the requirements of Chapter VII GDPR are observed.[1364] This is for instance the case when the lead supervisory authority decides not to handle the case in application of Article 56.5 GDPR. This means that for cross-border processing activities the competence of the lead supervisory authority is the rule, and the possibility that a non-lead supervisory authority can act is the exception.[1365]

c. Additional Powers Granted by Member State Law

1115. In addition to the powers discussed above, the GDPR allows Member States to endow their supervisory authorities by law with other powers. When granting these additional powers, however, Member States must ensure that the effective operation of Chapter VII GDPR, i.e., of the cooperation and consistency mechanism is not impaired.[1366]

1362. CJEU Case C-645/19, Judgment of 15 June 2021, Facebook v. Belgian Data Protection Authority, ECLI:EU:C:2021:483, https://eur-lex.europa.eu/legal-content/EN/TXT/?uri=CELEX%3A62019CJ0645.
1363. *Ibid.*, paras 64–65.
1364. *Ibid.*, para. 75.
1365. *Ibid.*, para. 63.
1366. Art. 58.6 GDPR.

That means, among others, that even when a supervisory authority has specific national power on its territory and the OSS mechanism applies for a particular cross-border processing activity, that national power can only be exercised to the extent that:

- the supervisory authority is the *lead* supervisory authority; or
- one of the exceptions by which a non-lead supervisory authority is allowed to act, applies.

§13. Cooperation and Consistency

1116. As explained earlier (see section 2.3.1), with the introduction of the GDPR the European legislator has substantially strengthened the obligation of the supervisory authorities to cooperate and has taken steps to ensure that the GDPR is applied in a consistent and homogenous manner. Chapter VII sets forth:

- a cooperation mechanism that is based on consensus building and active participation of all the supervisory authorities concerned;
- a consistency mechanism that allows matters to be escalated to the EDPB to allow homogenous interpretation and timely application of the provisions of the GDPR and to resolve disputes between supervisory authorities.

The consistency mechanism should be seen as a fall back for situations where the cooperation mechanism fails to provide an adequate solution.[1367]

I. Cooperation

1117. The cooperation mechanism essentially consists of three components:

(1) the OSS mechanism, whereby the lead supervisory authority coordinates the supervision and enforcement actions with regard to cross-border processing activities of controllers and processors which have their main establishment on the lead supervisory authority's territory;[1368]
(2) the mutual assistance mechanism, whereby supervisory authorities must assist one another, specifically with regard to obtaining information and taking supervisory measures;[1369]
(3) the joint operations mechanism, whereby supervisory authorities can jointly conduct investigations and take enforcement measures.[1370]

1367. Recital 138 GDPR.
1368. Art. 60 GDPR.
1369. Art. 61 GDPR.
1370. Art. 62 GDPR.

The mutual assistance mechanism and the joint operations mechanism are of course available in the context of the OSS mechanism but can operate in circumstances outside the OSS as well.

A. Operating the OSS Mechanism

1118. As indicated above, the OSS mechanism is essentially a system based on coordinated supervision and enforcement as well as decision-making through consensus. The lead supervisory authority, as the single interlocutor for the controller or processor, exchanges information with the supervisory authorities concerned and vice versa. These supervisory authorities then collaborate to reach consensus on the actions, measures and decisions to take vis-à-vis the controller's or processor's cross-border processing activities under consideration. Article 60 GDPR sets forth the procedure which the lead supervisory authority and the supervisory authorities concerned must follow under the OSS.

1119. The OSS mechanism can be activated in different ways, much the same as local supervision and enforcement actions can be launched in different ways. Some common ways in which the OSS mechanism can be triggered, are:

- a lead supervisory authority may decide on its own initiative to investigate, and potentially take corrective actions against, a controller or processor engaging in cross-border processing activities;
- a controller or processor may seek an authorisation or advice concerning a cross-border processing activity for which the controller or processor proactively contacts the lead supervisory authority;
- the lead supervisory authority may receive a complaint, from a data subject directly or organisation competent to file a complaint, about a cross-border processing activity of a controller or processor having its main establishment on its territory;
- a supervisory authority concerned may decide on its own initiative to investigate a cross-border processing activity. It may then subsequently conclude that another supervisory authority is the lead supervisory authority and then contact that lead supervisory authority with the request to investigate;
- a supervisory authority concerned may receive a complaint, in the same way as the lead supervisory authority would. It may then, after a *prima facie* investigation again reach the decision that it is not the lead supervisory authority and may contact the lead supervisory authority to handle the complaint.

These last two examples show that, even if a supervisory authority is *not* the lead supervisory authority, it still has certain powers to contact the controller or processor and make a preliminary investigation. Indeed, if the supervisory authority would not be able to do this, it would have no means to identify the lead supervisory authority. When a procedure is started, the roles of the different supervisory authorities involved are registered through the EDPB's IMI system.[1371]

1120. Once the OSS mechanism has been activated, the lead supervisory authority will commence its investigations and/or monitoring activities. It may very well be that parts of the investigation or monitoring activities need to take place in another territory than the lead supervisory authority's. While the GDPR appoints the lead supervisory authority as a single interlocutor, it does not grant that lead supervisory authority the power to operate unilaterally on another Member State's territory. To ensure that the lead supervisory authority is nonetheless able to make a complete and thorough investigation or successful monitoring activity, the GDPR foresees that the lead supervisory authority can invoke the mutual assistance and joint operations mechanisms.[1372] How these two mechanisms work, is explained further below.

1121. During its supervision and monitoring activities the lead supervisory authority must keep the supervisory authorities concerned informed. It is important that the supervisory authorities concerned are kept abreast of the progress made by the lead supervisory authority and are provided with the information required to form their own opinions.[1373] The lead supervisory authority must without delay submit a draft decision to the other supervisory authorities concerned.[1374] The latter authorities can then give their opinion which the lead supervisory authority must duly consider.[1375] They can do so within four weeks after having been consulted.[1376]

If a supervisory authority concerned formulates objections, the lead supervisory authority can either disagree with the objection (or consider it not relevant and reasoned) or can follow the objection. In the former instance, the matter must be escalated to the EDPB using the GDPR's consistency mechanism.[1377] The decision will then be taken at the level of the EDPB. In the latter instance, the lead supervisory authority will draft a revised decision, which the supervisory authorities concerned can then review within two weeks.[1378] After those two weeks, if no relevant and reasoned objections have been formulated, the decision then becomes final, and the lead supervisory authority and the supervisory authorities concerned are bound by it.[1379]

1371. The IMI is the 'Internal Market Information System' used by the European Commission. The legal basis is Regulation (EU) 1024/2012 of the European Parliament and of the Council of 25 October 2012 on Administrative cooperation through the Internal Market Information System and repealing Commission Decision 2008/49/EC.
1372. Art. 60.2 GDPR.
1373. Art. 60.3 GDPR.
1374. *Ibid.*.
1375. *Ibid.*.
1376. Art. 60.4 GDPR.
1377. The consistency mechanism set forth in Art. 63 GDPR.
1378. Art. 60.5 GDPR.
1379. Art. 60.6 GDPR.

1122. Advocate General Bobek stated, as confirmed by the European Court of Justice, that the lead supervisory authority must never ignore the views of the other supervisory authorities concerned.[1380] On the contrary, the Advocate General noted that any formal objection expressed by a supervisory authority concerned even has the power to block the adoption of the lead supervisory authority's draft decision. It makes sense that the opinions of the supervisory authorities concerned are given due regard, since all of these authorities are ultimately bound by the decision that is adopted.

1123. Once the decision has become final, the lead supervisory authority must formally adopt it and inform the controller or processor through the main (or single) establishment of that decision.[1381] The lead supervisory authority must equally inform the EDPB and the other supervisory authorities concerned.[1382] The supervisory authority with which a complaint, which gave rise to the activation of the OSS mechanism, was lodged, must inform the complainant of that decision.[1383] It may also happen, of course, that a complaint is dismissed or rejected. In such case, it is the supervisory authority with which the complaint was lodged, which is not necessarily the lead supervisory authority, that adopts the decision and informs the complainant.[1384] If a complaint is partially accepted and partially rejected or dismissed, which the lead supervisory authority must agree on with the supervisory authorities concerned, then separate decisions are adopted for all parts:[1385]

- decisions involving actions in relation to the controller or processor are adopted by the lead supervisory authority;
- decisions involving dismissals or rejections are adopted by the supervisory authority which received the complaint.

It is highly relevant to know which supervisory authority adopted the decision, because it will determine in which Member State judicial remedy mechanisms are to be activated against a decision. That applies both for controllers or processors which are ordered to take actions as well as for complainants who see their complaints partially or wholly rejected or dismissed. Both categories of stakeholders enjoy an explicit right to judicial remedy against legally binding decisions taken by supervisory authorities concerning them.[1386]

1124. Without prejudice to the right to seek judicial remedy, the controller or processor which is confronted with a decision, must proceed to take the actions

1380. Opinion Advocate General Bobek, *Facebook v. Belgian Data Protection Authority*, C-645/19, 13 January 2021, para. 111, https://eur-lex.europa.eu/legal-content/EN/TXT/?uri=CELEX%3A62019CC0645.
1381. Art. 60.7 GDPR.
1382. *Ibid.*.
1383. *Ibid.*.
1384. Art. 60.8 GDPR.
1385. Art. 60.9 GDPR.
1386. Art. 78 GDPR.

required to be in compliance with that decision.[1387] The controller or processor must inform the lead supervisory authority of the actions taken and the lead supervisory authority shall in turn inform the supervisory authorities concerned. It should be noted that in some Member States the controller or processor must already proceed with taking the actions required by the decision, notwithstanding that controller's or processor's right to judicial redress.[1388]

1125. As explained above, a supervisory authority not only has the powers to supervise and enforce, it has the legal obligation to use these powers and actively supervise and enforce. In the context of the OSS mechanism this principle includes the obligation for the lead supervisory authority to be diligent in handling the matters brought to its attention by supervisory authorities concerned and avoid falling prey to what Advocate General Bobek calls 'administrative inertia'.[1389] If the lead supervisory authority nonetheless refrains from acting diligently, the GDPR foresees procedures that would allow to bypass such an 'inert' lead supervisory authority. The supervisory authority concerned which brought the matter to the attention of the lead supervisory authority could then, among others, take provisional measures on its own territory in application of Article 60.8 GDPR using the urgency procedure of Article 66 GDPR.

The supervisory authority concerned could use this urgency procedure in exceptional circumstances as well, when it considers that the interests of data subjects warrant urgent intervention on their behalf which cannot wait for the OSS mechanism to have led to a certain outcome.[1390] In such an event, the supervisory authority concerned must demonstrate that there is indeed such an urgent need to act, whereas the urgent need is presumed to exist when a lead supervisory authority remains inert.

B. Providing Mutual Assistance

1126. Under the mutual assistance mechanism supervisory authorities are required to provide mutual assistance to one another and put mechanisms in place for effective cooperation.[1391] Mutual assistance is to be understood as providing information but also assistance on prior consultations, inspections and investigations.[1392] It is up to the requesting supervisory authority to provide the purpose and reasons for the request, and it cannot use the information it receives for any other

1387. Art. 60.10 GDPR.
1388. In Belgium, for instance, the national law on the creation of the supervisory authority stipulates that all decisions taken by the litigation chamber of the data protection authority are provisionally enforceable. It is then up to the controller or processor to immediately file an appeal against the decision and ask the Court of Appeal to declare the provisional enforceability inapplicable due to it risking irreparably damaging that controller's or processor's right to effective judicial remedy. *See* Art. 108 of the Act of 3 December 2017 on the creation of the Data Protection Authority, *Official Gazette* 10 January 2018, 989.
1389. Opinion of Advocate General Bobek, para. 114.
1390. Art. 60.11 GDPR.
1391. Art. 61 GDPR.
1392. Art. 61.1 GDPR.

purposes than those which have been communicated to the supervisory authority which received the request.[1393] Hence, by setting the purpose, the requesting supervisory authority immediately determines the usefulness of the information obtained through the request.

1127. The supervisory authority which receives the request then has a month to respond.[1394] That does not mean that the request must be fulfilled within that month, since the duration may depend on the type of assistance requested, but the supervisory authority should at least keep the requesting supervisory authority abreast of the steps that it is taking to fulfil the request.[1395] There are only two circumstances in which the supervisory authority can refuse to fulfil the request:[1396]

(1) when the supervisory authority does not have the required competence;
(2) when fulfilling the request would violate EU or Member State law.

1128. As BLUME notes, one impediment to effective cooperation through mutual assistance may arise from obligations to professional secrecy imposed by national law on the members of data protection authorities.[1397] The author looks to pragmatic solutions to the problem, but in general one could ask the broader question whether national law should not be interpreted in such a way that it does not impede the proper application of Article 61 GDPR.

C. Engaging in Joint Operations

1. A Legally Challenging Concept

1129. Supervisory authorities are not only required to provide assistance by exercising their own investigative powers on their own territory, but they are also required to support each other operationally in joint operations.[1398] These operations include investigations as well as taking enforcement measures against a controller or operator. Joint operations are legally more challenging than providing mutual assistance, because the former pertain to taking actions on the territory of another (sovereign) Member State, whereas the latter only pertains to actions taken on a supervisory authority's own territory. Moreover, while the GDPR largely harmonises the powers of supervisory authorities, there may still be discrepancies between Member States in what powers they have under national law as well as in the way in which they should exercise their powers.[1399]

1393. Art. 61.3 GDPR.
1394. Art. 61.2 GDPR.
1395. *Ibid.*
1396. Art. 61.4 GDPR.
1397. P. BLUME, 'Article 61. Mutual assistance' in C. KUNER, L.A. BYGRAVE and C. DOCKSEY, *The EU General Data Protection Regulation (GDPR) A commentary*, Oxford, Oxford University Press, 2020, p. 982.
1398. Art. 62 GDPR.
1399. *See* specifically Art. 58.6 GDPR.

1130. To mitigate to an extent these problems of sovereignty and discrepancies in powers, the GDPR introduces a system that puts the law of the host Member State first. The idea is that a supervisory authority acting as the host can confer its powers granted under national law to members or staff of a participating (or, in the terminology of the GDPR, 'seconding') supervisory authority in accordance with, and to the extent allowed by, the laws of the host supervisory authority's Member State. The powers are thus not conferred to the participating supervisory authority in its entirety, but only to the members or staff of that authority involved in the joint operation who will at that moment be subject to the law of the host Member State.[1400] It is therefore the law of the host Member State which will determine if, and to what extent, joint operations on its territory are possible.

1131. As BLUME observes, it may very well be the case that a Member State's law does not allow for members or staff of foreign supervisory authorities to operate on its territory.[1401] While Article 62 makes it clear that Member States can still largely shape the manner in, and the extent to, which joint operations can be undertaken on their territory, the question could nonetheless be raised whether Member States' law can be considered to be in violation of the GDPR when its national law prevents joint operations entirely.

2. The Participants to Joint Operations

1132. Joint operations are possible in those circumstances where they are 'appropriate'.[1402] Read in conjunction with Article 60.2 GDPR it means that joint operations are possible in- and outside the OSS mechanism.[1403] Article 62.2 GDPR provides two criteria to determine whether a supervisory authority is *entitled* to participate to a joint operation:

(1) the controller or processor, having establishments in multiple Member States, has an establishment on the territory of the participating supervisory authority;
(2) a significant number of data subjects in different Member States, including the Member State of the participating supervisory authority, are likely to be affected by the processing activity.

To the extent that the OSS mechanism applies, it is up to the lead supervisory authority or, if the lead supervisory authority has indicated that the local supervisory authority concerned can handle the matter, that local supervisory authority concerned to invite the other supervisory authorities to participate in the joint

1400. Art. 62.3 GDPR.
1401. P. BLUME, 'Article 62. Joint operations of supervisory authorities' in C. KUNER, L.A. BYGRAVE and C. DOCKSEY, *The EU General Data Protection Regulation (GDPR) A commentary*, Oxford, Oxford University Press, 2020, 991–992.
1402. Art. 62.1 GDPR.
1403. Such an interpretation is also supported by recital 138 GDPR.

operations. If they refrain from doing so within one month, provisional measures can be taken by the supervisory authority that has not been invited for the joint operations under the conditions set forth in Article 66 GDPR.[1404]

1133. The question could be raised whether supervisory authorities are allowed to participate in joint operations even if the aforementioned criteria were not met. One could, for instance, imagine that a data subject in a supervisory authority's territory files a complaint against a processing activity concerning him with that supervisory authority. There is neither an establishment of the controller or processor, however, in that territory nor does the processing activity concern other data subjects in that territory. It would then make sense, considering the limited influence that this supervisory authority could exercise over the controller or processor, that the joint operations mechanism could be used to involve this supervisory authority in any investigations undertaken against the controller or processor.

3. Performing Joint Operations

1134. When performing joint operations there are two possibilities for members and/or staff of the seconding supervisory authority to exercise investigative powers.[1405] On the one hand they can, with the permission of their own (seconding) supervisory authority, exercise investigative powers conferred by the host supervisory authority. On the other hand, the law of the host Member State could also stipulate that those members and/or staff can exercise the investigative powers conferred by their *own* national law on the territory of the host Member State. No matter, however, which possibility applies, a member or staff of the host supervisory authority must be present whenever these investigative powers are exercised. Moreover, when exercising these investigative powers, the members and/or staff of the seconding supervisory authority will be subject to the law of the host Member State, even when they exercise powers conferred by their own national law.

1135. The responsibility and liability of joint operations will always lie with the host Member State. Any damage will have to be fixed by the host Member State.[1406] If it were any of the members and/or staff of the seconding supervisory authority who caused the damage, the Member State of the seconding supervisory authority will have to reimburse the host Member State.[1407] Other Member States cannot be asked to reimburse the host Member State.[1408]

1404. Art. 62.7 GDPR.
1405. Art. 62.3 GDPR.
1406. Art. 62.4 GDPR.
1407. Art. 62.5 GDPR.
1408. Art. 62.6 GDPR.

II. Consistency

A. In General

1136. Although the GDPR puts a lot of emphasis on cooperation between supervisory authorities and strengthens that cooperation through mandatory mechanisms, supervisory authorities may not always agree with one another or may not be as diligent as required in complying with these cooperation mechanisms. Moreover, supervisory authorities have ample opportunities to take decisions on their own within their own territory, which nonetheless may be relevant for controllers and processors located elsewhere or may have broader impact than just their own territory. The consistency mechanism set forth in Articles 63 to 67 GDPR intends to provide a solution for these potential difficulties. It grants the EDPB the powers necessary to safeguard consistent application of the provisions of the GDPR by way of issuing opinions and taking decisions. It also allows supervisory authorities to take provisional measures unilaterally in urgent cases and allows the EDPB to make such provisional measures final and binding.

1137. For a correct understanding of what follows, it is important to stress that EDPB opinions and EDPB decisions are not the same. They do not have the same legal effect and the timings and majorities required for rendering them are different.

Opinions are rendered outside of an official dispute resolution procedure and are, although authoritative, not binding. This means that supervisory authorities are still allowed to take decisions which diverge from the opinion of the EDPB.

Decisions, on the contrary, are the outcome of an official dispute resolution procedure before the EDPB and are binding on the supervisory authorities. When a decision has been rendered by the EDPB, the supervisory authorities can no longer take any decisions themselves which would contradict or diverge from the decision of the EDPB with the same subject matter.

B. Opinions of the EDPB

1. Circumstances in Which the EDPB Can Issue Opinions

1138. There are two specific circumstances, set forth in Articles 64.1 and 64.2 GDPR respectively, in which the EDPB must issue an opinion:[1409]

(1) a supervisory authority intends to take one of the measures listed in Article 64.1 GDPR;

1409. When the conditions of Arts 64.1 or 64.2 GDPR are fulfilled, the EDPB is required to issue an opinion unless it has already rendered an opinion on the same matter (*see* Art. 64.3 GDPR). This means that the EDPB does not have a choice whether or not it wants to render an opinion, it has a hard obligation to do so.

(2) a supervisory authority, the Chair of the EDPB or the Commission requests that the EDPB issues an opinion on matters of general application or producing effects in more than one Member State.

1139. In the first circumstance listed above, it is up to the specific supervisory authority that aims to take the measure to proactively inform the EDPB. The measures which require such proactive consultation of the EDPB are:

- the adoption of lists of processing activities which require a DPIA;[1410]
- the approval, amendment or extension of a code of conduct which concerns processing activities in several Member States;[1411]
- the determination of standard contractual clauses for data transfers or for controller-to-processor relationships;[1412]
- the authorisation of ad-hoc contractual clauses for data transfers;[1413]
- the approval of binding corporate rules.[1414]

The supervisory authority is required to seek the opinion of the EDPB whenever it intends to take one of these measures, even when the supervisory authority is of the opinion that there can be no doubt regarding the application of the GDPR on the specific matter. Even more so, the supervisory authority is explicitly prohibited from adopting its draft decision.[1415] But one could raise the question what the consequence would be if the supervisory authority were to proceed anyway. Would then only the other supervisory authorities (through the dispute resolution procedure) or the EDPB be allowed to act against it, but would the decision remain valid vis-à-vis the controller or processor at which it is directed. Or is the decision substantially invalid because the EDPB's opinion has not been sought? Put differently, can a controller or processor rely on a decision taken by a supervisory authority which has not sought a prior opinion from the EDBP?

The answer would have to be that they cannot, and that the decision of the supervisory authority is indeed substantially invalid. This follows from Recital 138 GDPR, the first sentence of which reads: '*The application of such mechanism* [referring to the consistency mechanism] *should be a condition for the lawfulness of a measure intended to produce legal effects by a supervisory authority in those cases where its application is mandatory.*'

Considering that the application of the consistency mechanism *is* mandatory for all measures listed in Article 64.1 GDPR, any decision which is not preceded by an

1410. *See* Art. 35.4 GDPR.
1411. *See* Art. 40.7 GDPR.
1412. *See* Art. 46.2.d GDPR and Art. 28.8 GDPR.
1413. *See* Art. 46.3.a GDPR.
1414. *See* Art. 47 GDPR.
1415. Art. 64.6 GDPR.

opinion should be considered unlawful and therefore invalid. Hence, the consistency mechanism essentially and effectively suspends the national procedure by which the decision can be adopted by the supervisory authority.[1416,1417]

1140. In the second circumstance listed above, it is not necessarily the supervisory authority which intends to take a measure that asks the EDPB to issue an opinion. It may not even be a supervisory authority, but it can even be the European Commission or the Chair of the EDPB that requests the EDPB to issue an opinion. In contrast to Article 64.1, Article 64.2 GDPR is also not limited to an enumerated set of measures for which an opinion can be asked. Rather, *any* matter can be the subject of a request for an opinion, as long as it concerns a matter of general interest or producing effects in more than one Member State. It may concern matters relevant to a particular sector or when interpretations of a particular matter by supervisory authorities diverge.[1418] The scope of Article 64.2 GDPR is therefore quite wide. The European legislator has nonetheless stressed that is should in any case be possible to request an opinion where a supervisory authority does not comply with its obligations under the mutual assistance and joint operations mechanisms.[1419]

2. Timing and Procedure for Issuing Opinions

1141. The supervisory authority which is required to ask for an opinion under Article 64.1 GDPR or the supervisory authority or the European Commission requesting an opinion under Article 64.2 GDPR must provide the EDPB with relevant information to allow the EDPB to come to a reasoned and factually correct opinion. They should particularly provide the EDPB with a summary of the facts and, where relevant, the draft decision, the reasons why a particular measure is taken, and the views of the other supervisory authorities concerned.[1420] All that information must be provided electronically and in a standardised format.

1142. Upon receipt of the information from the supervisory authority or the European Commission, it is the task of the Chair of the EDPB to communicate through electronic means all relevant input to the members of the EDPB allowing them to participate to the opinion-adoption process in an informed manner.[1421] Any translations are to be made by the secretariat of the EDPB.

1416. P. Van Eecke and A. Simkus, 'Article 64. Opinion of the Board' in C. Kuner, L.A. Bygrave and C. Docksey, *The EU General Data Protection Regulation (GDPR) A commentary*, Oxford, Oxford University Press, 2020, p. 1011.
1417. R. Robert, 'Titre 12 Le Comité européen de la protection des données: le garant d'un nouvel ordre?' in C. de Terwangne and K. Rosier, *Le Règlement Général sur la Protection des Données*, Brussels, Larcier, 2018, 628.
1418. *Ibid.*, 627.
1419. Art. 64.2 GDPR.
1420. Art. 64.4 GDPR.
1421. Art. 64.5 GDPR.

1143. Especially considering that for opinions requested in application of Article 64.1 GDPR the decision of a supervisory authority is suspended until the EDPB issues an opinion, it is only fair to assume that the EDPB would be required to issue its opinion within a reasonably short time frame. And indeed, Article 64.3 determines that the EDPB has an initial period of eight weeks to adopt its opinion, which can be extended by another six weeks if the matter under consideration is complex. With regard to opinions concerning draft decisions in the sense of Article 64.1 GDPR, members vote in favour by not objecting within a reasonable time frame. In practice it is the secretariat of the EDPB (see further) that prepares a draft opinion, and this draft is then brought before the EDPB for adoption. Opinions are adopted when approved by simple majority.

1144. Upon approval of the opinion, the Chair of the EDPB must communicate the adopted opinion to the supervisory authority and the European Commission and must make that opinion public. All opinions of the EDPB are published on its website.[1422] The supervisory authority at which an opinion is directed, must take the utmost account of it. Note that the supervisory authority is not legally obliged to follow it but is still required to consider it very thoroughly. In practice, supervisory authorities will acknowledge the highly authoritative nature of these EDPB opinions, especially considering that if they decide not to follow it, they may be subject to the dispute resolution procedure.[1423]

A supervisory authority therefore has two possible choices: it can either choose to maintain or to amend its draft decision.[1424] Whatever the supervisory authority chooses, it is required notify the Chair of the EDPB of its decision within two weeks after having received the opinion. When the supervisory authority decides to amend, the amended draft decision must be sent to the Chair of the EDPB.

C. Decisions of the EDPB

1. Triggering the Dispute Resolution Mechanism

1145. The dispute resolution mechanism is a key component in ensuring consistency in the application of the GDPR in those circumstances where national supervisory authorities do not agree among themselves. It offers a system where disputes can be escalated to a higher level, but final decisions are made by a majority of peers which helps safeguarding the independence of supervisory authorities.

1146. As explained above, the dispute resolution mechanism gives the EDPB the power to take binding decisions: the EDPB settles the dispute between supervisory authorities once and for all, notwithstanding the possibility to appeal the decision (see further). Then again, that immediately sets the limits of such EDPB decisions: they are directly binding upon the supervisory authorities, but not necessarily upon

1422. https://edpb.europa.eu/our-work-tools/consistency-findings/opinions_en.
1423. Art. 64.8 and 65 GDPR. *Supra* note 122, 1012.
1424. Art. 64.7 GDPR.

the controllers, processors and data subjects involved in individual cases. In each case it will be the competent supervisory authority to take a final decision vis-à-vis a controller, processor and/or data subject.

1147. The GDPR makes a distinction between different scenarios in which the dispute resolution mechanism can be activated. The list of scenarios is exhaustive and includes the following circumstances:

- a supervisory authority concerned does not agree with the draft decision of the lead supervisory authority and raises a relevant and reasoned objection;
- the lead supervisory authority considers the objection raised by a supervisory authority concerned as not relevant and reasoned and disregards it;
- there are conflicting views between supervisory authorities on which authority is the lead supervisory authority;
- a supervisory authority does not comply with its obligation to seek an opinion of the EDPB;[1425]
- a supervisory authority does not follow the opinion of the EDPB and takes a different final decision.

1148. The dispute resolution mechanism is typically meant to settle disputes between supervisory authorities. The possibility to commence proceedings before the EDPB is not, however, limited to supervisory authorities or the EDPB itself, but is also available to the European Commission. HIJMANS points out that this reference to the European Commission is not logical when considering Recital 136 GDPR, which clearly refers to the dispute resolution mechanism as a system to resolve disputes between supervisory authorities.[1426] The author is justified in raising the concern whether the possibility for the European Commission to start proceedings before the EDPB does not adversely impact the complete independence of DPAs.[1427]

2. Proceedings Before the EDPB

1149. The proceedings before the EDPB, in particular the application of the relevant provisions of the GDPR and Rules of Procedure, the main stages of the procedure and the competence of the EDPB when adopting a legally binding decision on the basis of Article 65(1)(a) GDPR are extensively clarified in the EDPB Guidelines 03/2021 on the application of Article 65(1)(a, adopted on 13 April 2021.[1428]

1425. Art. 64 GDPR.
1426. H. HIJMANS, 'Article 65. Dispute resolution by the Board' in C. KUNER, L.A. BYGRAVE and C. DOCKSEY, *The EU General Data Protection Regulation (GDPR) A commentary*, Oxford, Oxford University Press, 2020, p. 1022.
1427. *Ibid.*
1428. EDPB Guidelines 03/2021 on the application of Art. 65(1)(a) GDPR, adopted on 13 April 2021 for public consultation (https://edpb.europa.eu/our-work-tools/documents/public-consultations/2021/guidelines-032021-application-article-651a-gdpr_en).

The guidelines also include a description of the applicable procedural safeguards and remedies. They do not concern dispute resolution by the EDPB in cases where:

- there are conflicting views on which of the supervisory authorities concerned is competent for the main establishment (Article 65(1)(b) GDPR);
- a competent supervisory authority does not request the opinion of the Board in the cases referred to in Article 64(1), or does not follow the opinion of the Board issued under Article 64.

1150. Similarly as with the opinions of the EDPB, the supervisory authority which is confronted with a dispute resolution proceeding cannot proceed to take a decision on the matter until the EDPB has reached its own decision.[1429] Hence, national proceedings are suspended as soon as the matter has been brought before the EDPB.

1151. When a matter is brought before the EDPB, a final decision must be adopted with a two-thirds majority within one month after the referral of the matter.[1430] The one-month period can be extended by another month if the subject matter is complex. If the EPDB is still not able to reach a decision, the period can be extended by another two weeks and the decision can be adopted with a simple majority.[1431] In case the votes are split, the Chair has the deciding vote.

1152. The decision of the EDPB must be reasoned and is explicitly addressed to the lead supervisory authority and/or all supervisory authorities concerned.[1432] This again demonstrates clearly that the dispute resolution mechanism is limited to the supervisory authorities (and the European Commission) only, and that controllers, processors and data subjects are not parties in matters referred to the EDPB. The Chair of the EDPB must then communicate the decision without undue delay to the supervisory authorities concerned and to the European Commission.[1433]

1153. The supervisory authority concerned or the lead supervisory authority, depending on the case, must then take a final decision within one month which follows the decision taken by the EDPB.[1434] The final decision of the supervisory authority must refer to the decision of the EDPB, attach that the decision as an appendix thereto, and shall specify that the decision of the EDPB will be published on the EDPB's website. The supervisory authority must then inform the controller, processor and/or data subject of its final decision. The supervisory authority will then notify the EDPB that its decision has been communicated to the parties concerned. Upon such notification, the secretariat of the EDPB will publish the EDPB's decision, not the final decision of the supervisory authority, on its website.[1435]

1429. Art. 65.4 GDPR.
1430. Art. 65.2 GDPR.
1431. Art. 65.3 GDPR.
1432. Art. 65.2 GDPR.
1433. Art. 65.5 GDPR.
1434. Art. 65.6 GDPR.
1435. Art. 65.5 GDPR.

3. Appealing Decisions of the EDPB

1154. The substantive provisions of the GDPR do not refer to a possibility to appeal the decisions of the EDPB. Recital 143 GDPR, however, refers explicitly to such a possibility in application of Article 263 TFEU. While only supervisory authorities and the European Commission are allowed to bring matters before the EDPB, anyone who is directly and individually impacted by an EDPB decision has the possibility to appeal such a decision with a request for annulment before the European Union Court of Justice. Supervisory authorities concerned themselves are also entitled to appeal decisions of the EDPB with which they do not agree.

1155. It should be noted that anyone who is directly and individually impacted by an EDPB decision (i.e., the controller, the processor or the complainant; both natural and legal persons) has the opportunity to appeal the final decision of the national supervisory authority as well under the national judicial remedy mechanisms.[1436] However, considering that the decisions of the EDPB are binding upon the national supervisory authorities, it makes sense that the controller, processor or complainant affected by them can appeal them as well. Indeed, it may not make much sense to act against a decision of the national supervisory authority if that supervisory authority only follows what the EDPB has decided. That then raises the question whether the national courts are bound by the decisions of the EDPB when a final decision of a supervisory authority is brought before them. HIJMANS explains that, while national courts are not bound by the decisions of the EDPB, it is not up to them to declare them invalid either. If a national Court has doubts with regard to the validity of an EDPB decision, it must ask for preliminary ruling by the European Union Court of Justice.[1437]

1156. Supervisory authorities concerned, as addressees of the EDPB decision, have until two months after having been notified of the decision to appeal them before the CJEU.[1438] Anyone else who is directly and individually impacted by the decision has two months to file such an appeal starting from the moment when the decision was published on the EDPB's website.

One could imagine that a controller, processor or complainant who has not filed an appeal against the decision of the EDPB within the allotted two-month period tries to make up for it by filing an appeal against the final decision of the supervisory authority before the national courts and asking the national Court to request a preliminary ruling on the EDPB's decision. Recital 143 GDPR explicitly considers this eventuality and states that in those circumstances the national courts cannot revert to the CJEU with a request for a preliminary ruling on the validity of the EDPB's decision. It is doubtful whether this last statement is correct. Moreover, it is relatively simple to circumvent that prohibition, considering that the national

1436. *Infra*, Art. 78 GDPR.
1437. Recital 143, 2nd para. GDPR, with reference to Art. 267 TFEU.
1438. Recital 143 GDPR.

Court can always ask the CJEU for a preliminary ruling on matters of general application in the GDPR, whether or not they have been dealt with in an EDPB's decision. It would then not be challenging the decision as such but would be asking the CJEU for an interpretation of the substantive provisions of the GDPR.

D. Urgency Proceedings

1157. The cooperation and consistency mechanisms all have mandatory time frames, as explained above. Notwithstanding these time frames, supervision and enforcement through these mechanisms takes a significant amount of time. Cases may take months, if not longer, when supervisory authorities need to cooperate or the EDPB needs to issue an opinion or take a decision. In urgent cases it may not be possible to wait that long. Hence, the European legislator introduced an urgency procedure that can be invoked in exceptional cases, and which allows a supervisory authority to act unilaterally even if in principle the cooperation and consistency mechanisms should have been used.[1439]

1158. The first step in the urgency procedure is that a supervisory authority must establish that:[1440]

(1) there are exceptional circumstances;
(2) that bring about an urgent need to act;
(3) '*in order to protect the rights and freedoms of data subjects*'.

All three of these conditions must be satisfied for a supervisory authority to use the urgency procedure and essentially bypass the mandatory cooperation and/or consistency mechanisms. These three conditions make it unambiguously clear that the urgency procedure is only meant to be able to act quickly in the interest of data subjects, not in the interest of controllers or processors.[1441]

When these conditions are fulfilled, the supervisory authority can take provisional measures which are restricted in time and space. The measures should only have legal effect on the supervisory authority's own territory and should be valid for only three months. Once they are taken, the supervisory authority must without delay inform the other supervisory authorities concerned, the EDPB and the European Commission of the measures and the reasons for adopting them.

1159. Considering that the (effect of) measures taken should be limited in time and space, the urgency procedure restricts in principle the measures that a supervisory authority can take. It would for instance not be possible to order a controller or processor to permanently and irrevocably delete personal data that this controller or processor has been processing. Such a measure would not be limited in time and, depending on the processing activity, quite possibly not limited in space either.

1439. Art. 66 GDPR.
1440. Art. 66.1 GDPR.
1441. This interpretation is supported by Recital 137 GDPR as well.

The circumstances may warrant, however, that such a measure with permanent effect is adopted urgently as well, e.g., when the personal data are processed illegally, and the processing activity has significant negative effects for a data subject on a supervisory authority's territory. A supervisory authority is not allowed to take such permanent measures unilaterally, however, when that supervisory authority should have followed the OSS, mutual assistance, joint operations or consistency mechanisms. It would indeed be all too simple for a supervisory authority to avoid those mechanisms by claiming that urgent circumstances have arisen, because the supervisory authority for instance considers that the lead supervisory authority does not act as fast that supervisory authority concerned would want.

Hence, if measures of a permanent nature need to be taken, the supervisory authority must involve the EDPB and may request an urgent opinion or decision.[1442] The supervisory authority must motivate its request for urgent opinion or decision. If the request is warranted, the EDPB will issue an opinion or take a decision within two weeks by simple majority.[1443]

1160. The urgency procedure not only serves as a mechanism to allow supervisory authorities to act more quickly, it also serves as a system for monitoring the activities of peers. Article 66.3 GDPR allows any supervisory authority to request an urgent opinion or decision of the EDPB when that authority believes that the competent supervisory authority has not taken an appropriate measure in a situation where there is an urgent need to act to protect the rights and freedoms of data subjects. Supervisory authorities have therefore a certain degree of leverage over peers which they consider that are failing in their monitoring and supervision obligations.

III. The European Data Protection Board

A. *Successor to the WP29: An Independent EU Body*

1161. From the explanations of the cooperation and consistency mechanisms above it becomes clear that the European Data Protection Board has a key role to play in the consistent and effective application of the GDPR in the European Union. In that role the EDPB has real decision-making power, which is a rather significant difference when compared with the EDPB's predecessor, the WP29.

The Article 29 Working Party under Directive 95/46/EC essentially acted in an advisory capacity. It could issue opinions and recommendations to the European Commission, it could advise on national measures and give opinions on codes of conduct at EU level.[1444] It could not take binding opinions and decisions, however, and as such intervene in concrete enforcement cases. The Article 29 Working Party was not a separate body of the EU either, and relied for its secretariat and administrative functions on the European Commission.

1442. Art. 66.2 GDPR.
1443. Art. 66.4 GDPR.
1444. Art. 30 Directive 95/46/EC.

1162. With the introduction of the GDPR, The Article 29 Working Party was replaced by the EDPB as a separate body of the EU which has legal personality.[1445] The EDPB derives its power directly from the EU legislator and is not dependent on powers delegated from the European Commission.[1446] The EDPB can therefore act on its own, albeit within the strict limits of its competences as set forth in the GDPR.

1163. Although the EDPB is a body on its own, it is dependent on the European Data Protection Supervisor ('EDPS') for providing the premises and staff for its secretariat.[1447] Considering that the EDPB must fulfil its tasks independently,[1448] similar to what was explained above regarding the independence of supervisory authorities, the European legislator saw it necessary to ensure that the secretariat of the EDPB can only follow the instructions of the Chair of the EDPB.[1449] There are separate reporting lines for the staff of the EDPS working for the secretariat of the EDPB and the staff working for the EDPS itself.[1450]

1164. Article 69 and Recital 139 GDPR stress that the EDPB must act independently when performing its tasks and exercising its powers. This independence is among others ensured by letting the EDPB be accountable to the European Parliament, not to the European Commission. The European Commission cannot give instructions to the EDPB but can only formulate requests. The way in which these requests are answered, including regarding the substantive interpretation and application of the provisions of the GDPR, are the EDPB's sole prerogative. There is one exception, however, and that is the European Commission's right to fix a time limit for urgent matters in which advice needs to be rendered by the EDPB as per Article 70.2 GDPR.

B. Composition of the EDPB

1165. Comparable with the Article 29 Working Party under Directive 95/46/EC, the EDPB is mainly composed of the heads (or their representatives) of the national supervisory authorities.[1451] In Member States where there is more than one supervisory authority, a joint representative for that Member State must be appointed.[1452] Supervisory authorities of non-EU EFTA EEA Member States shall also designate

---

1445. Art. 68.1 GDPR.
1446. C. Docksey, 'Article 68. European Data Protection Board' in C. Kuner, L.A. Bygrave and C. Docksey, *The EU General Data Protection Regulation (GDPR) A commentary*, Oxford, Oxford University Press, 2020, p. 1045.
1447. Art. 75.1 GDPR.
1448. Art. 69 GDPR.
1449. Art. 75.2 GDPR.
1450. Art. 75.3 GDPR.
1451. Art. 68.3 GDPR.
1452. Art. 68.4 GDPR.

representatives, but those representatives in principle do not have voting rights.[1453] The European Commission and the EDPS shall also designate a representative.[1454] The representative of the European Commission can participate in activities and meetings but does not have any voting rights.[1455] The representative of the EDPS has voting rights, but only on decisions which concern principles and rules which are the same in substance as those in the Regulation 2018/1725 ('EUIDPR').[1456,1457] Members of the EDPB *with* voting rights take decisions by simple majority, unless the GDPR itself requires a different majority (e.g., in Article 65 GDPR and when adopting the EDPB's own rules of procedure, which must happen with a two-thirds majority).[1458] The heads or their representatives and the joint representatives may bring staff members to the meetings, but only so many as minimally required to deal with the matter at hand.[1459]

1166. The EDPB, as separate body of the European Union, is represented by its Chair. The Chair and two deputy Chairs are elected by the members of the EDPB by simple majority for a five-year period which is renewable once. The representatives of Non-EU EFTA EEA Member States and of the European Commission are not eligible to become Chair or Deputy Chair.[1460]

Whether the representative of the EDPS is eligible to become Chair or Deputy Chair is not entirely clear. Certain authors are of the opinion that the EDPS representative can be elected Chair or Deputy Chair.[1461] However, if that were true, this may cause problems considering the limited voting rights attributed to the representative of the EDPS according to Article 68.6 GDPR. If the EDPB is split on a decision, the Chair has the deciding vote according to Article 65.3 GDPR. However, the EDPS representative does not have, as explained in the previous paragraph, voting rights on *all* decisions taken. There are then two possible outcomes: either the EDPS representative, then Chair, suddenly obtains voting rights on any type of decision by the mere fact of being the Chair, or the EDPS representative is simply not eligible to become Chair or Deputy Chair. It remains to be seen which outcome is the correct one.

1453. Art. 4.1 of the European Data Protection Board Rules of Procedure, 25 May 2018 and amended 8 October 2020, https://edpb.europa.eu/sites/default/files/files/file1/edpb_rop_version_7_adopted_20201008_en.pdf ('Rules of Procedure').
1454. Art. 68.3 and 68.5 GDPR.
1455. Art. 68.5 GDPR.
1456. Regulation (EU) 2018/1725 of the European Parliament and of the Council of 23 October 2018 on the protection of natural persons with regard to the processing of personal data by the Union institutions, bodies, offices and agencies and on the free movement of such data, and repealing Regulation (EC) No 45/2001 and Decision No 1247/2002/EC, *OJ.L.* 295, 21 November 2018, 39–98, https://eur-lex.europa.eu/legal-content/EN/TXT/?uri=CELEX%3A32018R1725.
1457. Art. 68.6 GDPR.
1458. Art. 72.
1459. Art. 4.5 Rules of Procedure.
1460. Art. 4.1 and 4.2 Rules of Procedure.
1461. C. Docksey, 'Article 73. Chair' in C. Kuner, L.A. Bygrave and C. Docksey, *The EU General Data Protection Regulation (GDPR) A commentary*, Oxford, Oxford University Press, 2020, p. 1099.

1167. The Chair and the Deputy Chairs remain heads of their national supervisory authority and do not become full-time Chair and Deputy Chairs. It is up to the Chair and the Deputy Chair to inform the Secretariat of the EDPB of the impending end of their five-year mandate or of their wish to resign two months in advance.[1462] If a sitting Chair or Deputy Chair stops being the head of a national supervisory authority unexpectedly during the five-year term, the Secretariat must be informed immediately.[1463] Chairs and Deputy Chairs can be dismissed by simple majority, if at least a third of the members submit a reasoned proposal for dismissal.[1464]

1168. The tasks of the Chair and the Deputy Chairs are set forth in Article 74 GDPR and Article 7 of the Rules of Procedure. These tasks include:

- convene the meetings of the EDPB and prepare the agenda;
- notify the decision of the EDPB as explained above;
- ensure timely performance of tasks of the EDPB as set forth in Article 70 GDPR.

C. *Tasks of the EDPB*

1169. Article 70 GDPR describes the overarching mission of the EDPB, which is the consistent application of the GDPR. Against the backdrop of this overarching mission, it contains an extensive list of tasks which the EDPB must perform on its own initiative or, where relevant, upon request of the European Commission. These tasks can be divided in 6 main categories:

(1) issuing opinions and taking decisions;
(2) advising the European Commission;
(3) issuing guidelines, recommendations and best practices and reviewing their practical application;
(4) promoting cooperation and knowledge sharing;
(5) tasks related to codes of conduct and certification mechanisms, seals and marks;
(6) maintaining a publicly accessible register of decisions of supervisory authorities and courts on issues handled in the consistency mechanism.

1170. When exercising its tasks, the EDPB should consult interested parties and allow them to comment.[1465] The outcome of such a consultation procedure should be made public, unless there are pressing reasons for confidentiality, as set forth in Article 76 GDPR.[1466] On the website of the EDPB, anyone can easily follow which

1462. Art. 6.1 Rules of Procedure.
1463. *Ibid.*.
1464. Art. 7.2 Rules of Procedure.
1465. Art. 70.4 GDPR.
1466. Art. 33 Rules of Procedure sets forth the circumstances where discussions of the EDPB are confidential (e.g., when they concern a particular individual or the consistency mechanism).

EDPB guidelines, recommendations, etc. are currently open for public consultation.[1467] Anyone can respond, and reactions can be published on that same website. Final opinions, recommendations, guidelines and best practices, must also be made public. This also happens through the EDPB's website.[1468] The EDPB must communicate these final opinions, recommendations, guidelines and best practices to the European Commission and the committee referred to in Article 93 GDPR.[1469]

1171. The EDPB must draw up yearly reports on the protection of personal data in the EU and internationally.[1470] That is different when compared with the national supervisory authorities, who also have to draw up yearly reports, but those concern their own activities. The EDPB is tasked, however, with drafting reports that provide a more overarching perspective on the status of data protection everywhere and to review the practical applications of its own guidelines, recommendations and best practices, as well as its binding decisions.

1. Issuing Opinions and Taking Decision

1172. The first category of tasks of the EDPB entails issuing opinions and taking decision. Decisions are taken in the context of the dispute resolution mechanism set forth in Article 65 GDPR, as explained above. The list of circumstances where the EDPB can issue opinions set forth in Article 70 GDPR is more granular, however, than the circumstances set forth in Article 64 GDPR. An opinion shall specifically be provided:

- to the European Commission on certification requirements;[1471]
- to the European Commission on icons which can be used by controllers to inform data subjects of the processing of their personal data;[1472]
- to the European Commission on the assessment of adequacy of the level of protection in a third country or international organisation;
- on draft decisions of supervisory authorities pursuant to Article 64.1 GDPR and on matters submitted pursuant to Article 64.2 GDPR;
- on codes of conduct.[1473]

2. Advising the European Commission

1173. A second category of tasks of the European Data Protection Board is to advise the European Commission on a range of matters of EU policy and law related to data protection. This includes advice on:

1467. https://edpb.europa.eu/our-work-tools/general-guidance/public-consultations-our-guidance_en.
1468. https://edpb.europa.eu/our-work-tools_en.
1469. Art. 70.3 GDPR.
1470. Art. 71 GDPR.
1471. Art. 43.8 GDPR.
1472. Art. 12.7 GDPR.
1473. Art. 40.9 GDPR.

– any issue related to the protection of personal data in the European Union;
– the format and procedures for the exchange of information between controllers, processors and supervisory authorities for binding corporate rules.

The European Commission can set time limits within which the EDPB has to provide its advice, taking into account the urgency of the matter.[1474] This prevents that the EDPB (deliberately or accidentally) stalls urgent tasks and activities of the European Commission itself.

3. Issuing Guidelines, Recommendations and Best Practices

1174. A third category of tasks of the European Data Protection Board, which in practice has a very profound impact on how data protection law is applied across the European Union, is issuing guidelines, recommendations and best practices on matters concerning data protection. While these guidelines, recommendations and best practices are not legally binding on anyone, they are authoritative and used by national courts and supervisory authorities to help interpret the GDPR in specific cases. The EDPB must not only issue such recommendations, guidelines and best practices, but must also review what the practical application is of the recommendations, guidelines and best practices that it issues.

1175. The EDPB can issue such recommendations, guidelines or best practices on the following topics:

– procedures for erasure of personal data from publicly available communication services;
– any question concerning the application of the GDPR;
– criteria and conditions for decisions based on profiling;
– establishing personal data breaches, interpreting undue delay, the particular circumstances in which a personal data breach must be notified and the particular circumstances in which a personal data breach is likely to result in a high risk for the rights and freedoms of natural persons;
– the criteria and requirements for personal data transfers based on binding corporate rules;
– the criteria and requirements for personal data transfers based on the derogations in Article 49.1 GDPR;
– the application of investigative, corrective and authorisation and advisory powers by supervisory authorities and the setting of fines;
– establishing common procedures for letting natural persons report infringements of the GDPR.

1474. Art. 70.2 GDPR.

4. Promoting Cooperation and Knowledge Sharing

1176. A fourth category of tasks relates to the promotion of certain activities, which are in essence activities geared towards improving the cooperation between supervisory authorities. The EDPB is required to promote:

- cooperation and information and best practices exchange between supervisory authorities;
- common training programmes and facilitate personnel exchanges (also with supervisory authorities of third countries and international organisations);
- the exchange of documentation and knowledge on data protection law and practice (again, also with supervisory authorities outside the European Economic Area).

5. Tasks Related to Codes of Conduct and Certification Mechanisms, Seals and Marks

1177. A fifth category of tasks relates to the GDPR's particular focus on codes of conduct, certification mechanisms, seals and marks, which are explained elsewhere in this book. The EDPB has a rather operational role to play in this domain, particularly in relation to certification mechanisms. The tasks of the EDPB in this category are:

- encouraging codes of conduct, certification mechanisms, data protection seals and marks;
- accrediting certification bodies and period reviews thereof and setting up a public register of accredited bodies;
- specifying the requirements for the accreditation of certification bodies.

6. Maintaining a Publicly Accessible Register of Decisions of Supervisory Authorities and Courts on Issues Handled in the Consistency Mechanism

1178. The sixth category consists of only one task, which is maintaining a public register of decisions related to the matters handled in the consistency mechanism. The EDPB is essentially tasked with creating a central repository of national decisions, whether taken by a supervisory authority or a court, which is publicly accessible. It creates pan-European transparency on matters which are of cross-border relevance. This register is directly accessible from the EDPB's website.[1475]

1475. https://edpb.europa.eu/our-work-tools/consistency-findings/register-for-decisions_en.

§14. Remedies, Liability and Penalties

1179. The previous chapter in this contribution explained the supervision and enforcement mechanisms of the GDPR from the perspective of the independent supervisory authorities. This chapter takes a different perspective and looks at opportunities for redress for data subjects, controllers and processors.

1180. Data subjects are not condemned to a passive approach when it comes to protecting their rights under the GDPR. On the contrary, the European legislator has given data subjects several distinct possibilities to proactively seek protection of their rights, both via the national supervisory authorities as well as via the 'traditional' judicial system. At the same time, there is the clear objective of keeping the bar for data subjects seeking enforcement of rights as low as possible, providing them with real and effective access to the redress mechanisms that are created.

1181. At the other side of the same coin, the European legislator had to come up with a way to allocate liabilities between controllers and processors infringing the provisions of the GDPR, while giving them the opportunity to defend themselves against any allegations of infringements made against them. Controllers and processors should have opportunities for judicial redress as well when faced with enforcement decisions by supervisory authorities.

1182. Consistent application of the GDPR across the EU requires a coordinated approach between supervisory authorities but ideally such a consistent application of the GDPR is also ensured by judicial authorities when deciding in cases with the same parties and the same subject matter. Considering the redress opportunities for data subjects, controllers and processors and the borderless nature of many processing activities, it cannot be avoided that data subjects commence judicial proceedings against the same controller or processor for the same processing activities in more than one Member State simultaneously. The judicial authorities of Member States are not bound by the decisions of courts in another Member State and act autonomously in accordance with national procedural law. To ensure nonetheless a minimal level of consistent interpretation of EU law, national courts can ask the European Union Court of Justice for a preliminary ruling on matters of general scope.[1476] From a litigation economics standpoint it would not be very efficient, however, if multiple judicial proceedings against the same controller or processor and the same subject matter would remain ongoing, even when such a system of preliminary rulings exists. Hence, the GDPR has introduced a system whereby judicial proceedings in one Member State can be suspended whilst essentially the same case is being dealt with by the courts of another Member State. It avoids contradictory interpretations of the GDPR, as shall be explained in more detail further on in this chapter.

1183. A last topic covered in this chapter relates to one of the bigger issues perceived under the previous Directive 95/46/EC, which was the lack of a convincing

1476. Art. 267 TFEU.

sanction mechanism that worked as a real deterrent for controllers and processors who did not take data protection legislation seriously.[1477] Some national legislators had introduced a sanction mechanism in national data protection laws, but the severity of the sanctions that could be imposed as well as the frequency with which sanctions were applied, differed greatly.[1478] To create a pan-European level playing field, the European legislator introduced a harmonised sanction mechanism that is intended to give supervisory authorities across the EU real teeth when enforcing data protection obligations and obligate them to use these teeth. At the heart of this mechanism is the possibility for supervisory authorities to impose administrative fines.

I. Remedies for Data Subjects

A. *Lodging Complaints and Effective Judicial Remedy*

1184. Data subjects are given several choices to seek protection of their rights. They can, among others, go through the supervisory authority or through the national courts.[1479] The text of the GDPR does not create a hierarchy between both these possibilities: the data subject can freely decide whether to seek redress through the supervisory authority or through the national courts. The data subject is not required to first file a complaint with a supervisory authority and only when the latter does not act appropriately, revert to the national courts.[1480]

KOTSCHY notes, however, that the case law of the European Union Court of Justice does not prevent Member States from requiring data subjects to first seek recourse to an administrative body before being able to seize the court.[1481] Put differently, Member States can determine that the data subject should first file a complaint before judicial proceedings are brought against the controller or processor.

1. Enforcing Rights Through the Supervisory Authority

1185. The handling of complaints is one of the tasks assigned to the national supervisory authority.[1482] That means that the supervisory authority must allow data

1477. S. J. GOLLA, 'Is Data Protection Law Growing Teeth? The Current Lack of Sanctions in Data Protection Law and Administrative Fines under the GDPR', JIPITEC 2017, 8, 70.
1478. P. NEMITZ, 'Fines under the GDPR' in R. LEENES et al., *Data Protection and Privacy: The Internet of Bodies*, Oxford, Hart Publishing, 2019, 231–248.
1479. Art. 77 and 79 GDPR.
1480. Recital 141 GDPR: '*Every data subject should have* the right to lodge a complaint with a single supervisory authority, *in particular in the Member State of his or her habitual residence*, and the right to an effective judicial remedy *in accordance with Article 47 of the Charter if the data subject considers that his or her rights under this Regulation are infringed* ***or*** *where the supervisory authority does not act on a complaint, partially or wholly rejects or dismisses a complaint or does not act where such action is necessary to protect the rights of the data subject.*' (emphasis added)
1481. W. KOTSCHY, 'Article 79. Right to an effective judicial remedy against a controller or processor' in C. KUNER, L.A. BYGRAVE and C. DOCKSEY, *The EU General Data Protection Regulation (GDPR) A commentary*, Oxford, Oxford University Press, 2020, pp. 1138–1139.
1482. Art. 57.1.f GDPR.

subjects to file complaints, but Member States can still set procedural and formal requirements to which the complaint must adhere. If a complaint does not comply with the formal requirements, the supervisory authority can dismiss the complaint and inform the data subject of the outcome. Of course, the national procedural and formal requirements should not prevent data subjects from exercising a real and effective right to complain.[1483] Moreover, the supervisory authority cannot dawdle and should handle complaints with all due diligence.[1484]

1186. In terms of territory the distinction must be made between complaints filed against public sector bodies and complaints filed against private sector entities.

In the former case, Article 55.2 GDPR makes it clear that complaints against public sector bodies can only be filed with the supervisory authority of that Member State.

In the latter case, data subjects can file a complaint with the supervisory authority of the Member State where they have their habitual residence, where they work or where the alleged infringement took place.[1485] For complaints against private entities, with the exception of complaints pertaining to processing activities on the basis of Article 6.1.c and 6.1.e GDPR, the OSS mechanism must be taken into account. That means that to the extent that the complaint pertains to a cross-border processing, the supervisory authority which receives the complaint will either be the lead supervisory authority or a supervisory authority concerned, depending on where the controller's or processor's main establishment is.

1187. The supervisory authority with which the complaint is lodged is required to keep the complainant informed of the progress made with regard to the complaint, the outcome and the possibility to seek judicial remedy against the decision of the supervisory authority.[1486] In the context of the OSS mechanism, the lead supervisory authority will inform the supervisory authority concerned with which the complaint was filed and the latter will in turn inform the complainant. It provides the data subject with the information required to assess whether the supervisory authority is indeed pursuing the complaint with all due diligence.

2. Proceedings Before National Courts

1188. Instead of filing a complaint or relying on other administrative or non-judicial remedies provided for by Member State law, data subjects can always opt to bring legal proceedings against the controller or processor infringing their

---

1483. W. Kotschy, 'Article 77. Right to lodge a complaint with a supervisory authority' in C. Kuner, L.A. Bygrave and C. Docksey, *The EU General Data Protection Regulation (GDPR) A commentary*, Oxford, Oxford University Press, 2020

1484. CJEU, *Schrems v. Data Protection Commissioner*, C-362/14, 6 October 2015, 63.

1485. Art. 77.1 GDPR.

1486. Art. 77.2 GDPR.

rights.[1487] Such proceedings will follow the normal procedural rules applicable to the courts of the Member State where the proceedings are brought, i.e., the Member State:[1488]

– where the controller or processor has an establishment;
– where the data subject has his or her habitual residence;
– of the public authority against which the proceedings are brought.

Recital 147 GDPR clarifies that the allocation of territorial competence of the national courts for cases concerning judicial remedies sought by data subjects against controllers or processors as set forth in Article 79 GDPR prevails over other legal instruments allocating territorial competence such as Regulation (EU) 1215/2012, which is commonly known as the Recast Brussels Regulation.[1489]

3. Comparison Between Administrative and Judicial Redress Possibilities

1189. Filing a complaint with a supervisory authority instead of commencing proceedings before a national Court has some distinct advantages.

First, the supervisory authority is a body which is dedicated to the monitoring of the proper application of the GDPR.[1490] Its members should be skilled and experienced in data protection law.[1491] Hence, filing a complaint with a supervisory authority ensures that it is handled by experts, which may not always be the case when bringing a case before a national court..

Second, a supervisory authority has investigative powers which it can use on its own initiative for fact-finding purposes. The supervisory authority is indeed not a Court or tribunal, but an administrative body, which means that it is not required to base its decision in a particular case exclusively on the evidence presented by the parties or perhaps an appointed expert. This greatly alleviates the burden of proof upon the data subject, considering that most of the investigative work can be done by the authority itself. This in turn reduces the expenses for the individual, who may otherwise have to pay for potentially expensive experts and investigators to uncover evidence of any infringements.

Third, involving the supervisory authority would arguably carry more weight, considering that the alternative would be that the individual has to go up against an often larger and more powerful counterparty.

Fourth, and although this will be different in each Member State, proceedings before supervisory authorities may move faster than they do before the normal courts. As noted above, supervisory authorities cannot dawdle and must proceed

1487. Art. 79.1 GDPR.
1488. Art. 79.2 GDPR.
1489. Regulation (EU) 1215/2012 of the European Parliament and of the Council of 12 December 2012 on jurisdiction and the recognition and enforcement of judgments in civil and commercial matters, *OJ.L.* 351, 20 December 2012, 1–32, https://eur-lex.europa.eu/legal-content/EN/ALL/?uri=celex%3A32012R1215.
1490. Art. 57.1.a GDPR.
1491. Art. 53.2 GDPR.

with all due diligence, whereas the pace of proceedings before national courts are solely dependent on Member States' national procedural laws.

1190. There are also a few downsides to filing complaints with supervisory authorities instead of starting proceedings before the national courts.

First, when filing a complaint, most control over the ensuing proceedings is transferred to the supervisory authority. The supervisory authority can decide:

- not to handle a complaint;
- to conduct its own investigation and come up with very different evidence than the complainant had;
- to reorient the complaint to an extent;
- to continue an investigation even if a data subject has indicated the wish to stop proceedings against a controller or processor;
- etc.

Second, the supervisory authority must comply with the OSS mechanism, whereas the national courts are not bound by the OSS mechanism. For data subjects it may be interesting to engage in proceedings in their own Member State. They retain control over the proceedings instead of having to file a complaint with the national supervisory authority, which must then transfer the case to a lead supervisory authority in a Member State. If the cooperation and consistency mechanisms need to be activated, it will take a substantial amount of time to resolve them.

Third, a data subject may have suffered damages due to an infringement of rights under data protection law and may seek to be compensated. Not all supervisory authorities are competent to award damages, which often remains the prerogative of the national courts. Hence, if a data subject believes that compensation is due, the national courts may be the only way to go.

Fourth, LUNDSTEDT notes that under the Brussels Ia Regulation[1492] and Lugano Convention[1493] Court judgments before Member States' national courts must be recognised and enforced in other Member States.[1494] Whereas Member States may be hesitant to enforce measures taken by public authorities from another Member State, which would include the measures taken by a supervisory authority under the GDPR, they would not have the same reluctance to enforce judgments from another Member State's courts.[1495]

1492. Regulation (EU) No 1215/2012 of the European Parliament and of the Council of 12 December 2012 on jurisdiction and the recognition and enforcement of judgments in civil and commercial matters, *OJ.L.* 351, 20 December 2012, 1–32, https://eur-lex.europa.eu/legal-content/EN/ALL/?uri=celex%3A32012R1215.

1493. Convention on jurisdiction and the recognition and enforcement of judgments in civil and commercial matters, *O.J. L.* 339, 21 December 2007, 3–41, https://eur-lex.europa.eu/legal-content/EN/ALL/?uri=CELEX%3A22007A1221%2803%29.

1494. L. LUNDSTEDT, 'International Jurisdiction over Cross-border Private Enforcement Actions under the GDPR', Stockholm Faculty of Law Research Paper Series 57, 2017, 218–219.

1495. *Ibid.*.

B. The Right to Compensation

1191. Article 82.1 GDPR provides data subjects with the right to claim compensation for material or non-material damages suffered as a consequence of an infringement of the GDPR by a controller or processor. The claim on the basis of Article 82.1 GDPR can only be brought before the national courts of a Member State where the controller or processor has an establishment or where the data subject has his or her habitual residence, but cannot be brought before a supervisory authority as part of a complaint.[1496] KNETSCH clarifies that Article 82.1 GDPR can be relied upon directly by data subjects as a basis for a claim to compensation and that no specific provision in Member State law is required to make such a claim possible under national law.[1497]

1192. The data subject can rely on 82.1 GDPR to receive *full* compensation, which means that both pecuniary as well as non-pecuniary loss must be compensated.[1498] In practice, infringements on the right to the protection of personal data will only in a minority of cases lead directly to pecuniary damages. Most often those damages are of a non-material nature, making it rather difficult to ascertain the height of what would constitute a full compensation.

1193. As is normal in civil non-contractual liability claims, the data subject will have to show that there is a causal link between the damages suffered and the alleged infringement of the GDPR. In contrast with civil non-contractual liability claims in some Member States, however, the data subject is not required to demonstrate a fault on the part of the controller or processor. It suffices that any controller or processor is party to an unlawful processing of personal data, irrespective of whether the unlawful nature is that controller's or processor's fault, to allow a data subject to bring a claim for compensation against that controller or processor.[1499]

C. Possibilities for Representation

1194. Whereas data subjects have several possibilities to take action against infringing controllers or processors, it requires specialised knowledge and sufficient financial resources to take such actions. Data protection is a complex and rapidly evolving field of law which has become the domain of many highly specialised professionals providing services mainly to controllers and processors which have the resources to procure such services. Private individuals often do not have easy access

1496. Art. 82.6 *jo.* Art. 58.2 GDPR.
1497. J. KNETSCH, 'The compensation of non-pecuniary loss in GDPR infringement cases', *European Journal of Privacy Law & Technologies* September 2020, 66.
1498. *Ibid.*.
1499. G. ZANFIR-FORTUNA, 'Article 82. Right to compensation and liability' in C. KUNER, L.A. BYGRAVE and C. DOCKSEY, *The EU General Data Protection Regulation (GDPR) A commentary*, Oxford, Oxford University Press, 2020, 1176.

to such services, which may hamper individuals in successfully exercising their right to an effective remedy as enshrined in Article 47 of the Charter.[1500]

1195. Article 80 GDPR endeavours to bridge this knowledge- and resources-gap between controllers and processors on the one hand and individual data subjects on the other hand.[1501] The European legislator has made it possible for non-profit organisations to act on behalf of individuals. In every Member State it will be possible for non-profit organisations to act upon the mandate of a single data subject.[1502] Member States can, but are not required to, allow non-profit organisations to act in the collective interest, meaning that they can file a complaint with a supervisory authority or bring judicial action against a controller or processor on their own initiative whenever they perceive infringements on data subjects' rights in general.[1503]

1196. A non-profit organisation that wants to represent data subjects in complaints before the supervisory authorities, or in proceedings against supervisory authorities, controllers or processors before the national courts, must fulfil five requirements:

(1) it must be a body, organisation or association, which means that natural persons cannot act as representatives;
(2) it must be a not-for-profit, which excludes the possibility to represent for financial gain;[1504]
(3) the not-for-profit must be properly constituted in accordance with the law of the Member State, which excludes voluntary ad-hoc initiatives which have no formal structure of some sort;
(4) it must have statutory objectives which are in the public interest;
(5) it must be active in the field of the protection of data subjects' rights and freedoms with regard to the protection of their personal data.

1197. Whereas Member States must allow a data subject to mandate a non-profit organisation to represent him or her to lodge a complaint with a supervisory authority or in a claim against a controller, processor or supervisory authority before the courts, Member States can decide *not* to allow a non-profit organisation to exercise the right to receive compensation.[1505] The competence of non-profit organisations to exercise the right to receive compensation was contested during the GDPR's

1500. G.G. Fuster, 'Article 80. Representation of data subjects' in C. Kuner, L.A. Bygrave and C. Docksey, *The EU General Data Protection Regulation (GDPR) A commentary*, Oxford, Oxford University Press, 2020, 1143–1144.
1501. F. Casarosa, 'Transnational collective actions for cross-border data protection violations', *Internet Policy Review* 16 September 2020, 9, 3.
1502. Art. 80.1 GDPR.
1503. Art. 80.2 GDPR.
1504. *Supra* note 205, 1147.
1505. *Supra* note 206, 5.

legislative process.[1506] Several Member States have chosen not to allow non-profit organisations to exercise this right to receive compensation.[1507]

1198. The ability for a non-profit organisation to combat infringements of the rights of data subjects under the GDPR without a specific mandate is limited to lodging complaints or seeking judicial redress, with the explicit exclusion of claims for compensation.[1508] This ability can therefore not be used, as one typically sees in Anglo-Saxon class action suits, to claim very high damages for alleged infringements. The non-profit organisation that uses the possibility to lodge a complaint or start judicial proceedings without a mandate cannot target abstract violations of the GDPR. Much the same as any data subject who files a complaint or start judicial proceedings must be able to show an interest (i.e., demonstrating that the data subject's own rights have been infringed and he or she is therefore directly impacted), the non-profit organisation must demonstrate that there is a specific processing activity that infringes data subjects' rights in a concrete manner.[1509] The data subjects themselves may very well be unidentified as of yet, but the alleged infringement itself must be specific.

II. The Position of Controllers and Processors

1199. As shown in the previous sections, supervisory authorities have far-reaching powers under the GDPR to enforce the data protection obligations upon controllers and processors. At the same time, data subjects have multiple instruments at their disposal to have their rights enforced against controllers and processors. All these elements put controllers and processors in a less favourable position than one would typically expect under general civil law.

The European legislator clearly believes that effective judicial redress for data subjects requires additional tools that further alter the procedural position of controllers and processors in judicial proceedings:

- Article 82.2 GDPR introduces a low threshold for establishing the liability of a controller or a processor whenever a processing activity violates the provisions of the GDPR;
- Article 82.4 GDPR introduces the joint liability of controllers and/or processors involved in an infringing processing activity; and,
- Article 82.3 GDPR, read in conjunction with Article 24.1 GDPR (the principle of accountability), to an extent reverses the burden of proof, placing the onus on the controller or processor.

1506. F. Sorace, 'Collective redress in the General Data Protection Regulation. An opportunity to improve access to justice in the European Union?', Working Papers Jean Monnet Chair 7/2018, 15.
1507. *Ibid.*, 16–18.
1508. *Supra* note 206, 6.
1509. *Supra* note 205, 1149.

A. The Low Threshold for Establishing a Controller's and Processor's Liability

1200. According to Article 82.2, first sentence GDPR a controller is liable for the damage caused by processing which infringes the GDPR. At first sight, that would seem like a somewhat superfluous statement: obviously someone should be liable for damages caused by that person's non-compliance with the law. Its intent, however, is to clarify that the controller's liability arises even without the presence of 'fault'. STRUGAŁA argues that the same interpretation already existed under Article 23 Directive 95/46/EC, read in conjunction with Recital 55 Directive 95/46/EC.[1510] According to the author, the intent is to lower the bar for triggering the controller's liability, because having to prove a controller's intent or negligence would in practice make it exceedingly difficult for data subjects to actually obtain full and effective compensation, as required by Recital 146 GDPR.[1511]

Processors are, according to the second sentence of Article 82.2 GDPR, similarly liable on a no-fault basis. It suffices that a claimant shows that the processor has not complied with obligations under the GDPR which are directed specifically at processors or where it violates, or acts outside, lawful instructions of the controller. The circumstances in which a processor is liable are delineated more sharply in Article 82.2 GDPR, than those in which a controller is liable. By clearly delineating the liability of processors, but retaining a broad description of the liability of the controller, Article 82.2 GDPR effectively establishes a regime in which controllers may be liable for the damages caused by a processor, without the controller himself having breached any provision.[1512] That said, in the event damages were caused by a processor that violates the obligations in Article 28 GDPR, the controller which has paid compensation to the data subject, can seek compensation from that processor. Again, there would be no need for the controller to prove any negligence or intent on the part of the processor.

1201. To avoid liability entirely, a controller or processor would have to show that it is not in any way responsible for the event giving rise to the damage.[1513] Read together with the liability regime established in Article 82.2 GDPR, this would mean that the controller or processor must show that it has not violated any obligation under the GDPR, or that such violation is completely attributable to another controller or processor which was also involved in the processing and which violated its obligations under the GDPR. However, for a controller it would not be possible to escape liability vis-à-vis the data subject for an infringement committed by the processor, even when the processor has acted outside its mandate or has violated the GDPR.[1514] The controller can only seek restitution from the processor by relying on the processor's own liability set forth in Article 82.2 GDPR. Not all authors seem to support, however, this very broad notion of controller liability for

1510. R. STRUGAŁA, 'Art. 82: Strict Liability or Liability Based on Fault?', *European Journal of Privacy Law & Technologies* 2020, Special Issue, pp. 74–76.
1511. *Ibid.*, p. 74.
1512. *Ibid.*, p. 76.
1513. Art. 82.3 GDPR.
1514. *Supra* note 219, p. 77.

the damages caused by their processors. Some defend the position that a controller can escape liability if it proves that the processor was solely responsible for causing the damage.[1515]

B. Joint Liability Between Controllers and Processors

1202. Under Directive 95/46/EC the notion of joint liability between controllers and/or processors was not explicitly foreseen. Indeed, Article 23.2 Directive 95/46/EC allowed for partial exemption from liability for the controller that showed not to be responsible for the event giving rise to the damage, which cannot be reconciled with the existence of a joint liability regime under Directive 95/46/EC.[1516]

1203. With the introduction of the GDPR the European legislator opted explicitly for a joint liability regime. This joint liability regime makes it easier for data subjects to obtain compensation for damages, considering that they now have to start proceedings against only one of the parties responsible for the damages. Recital 147 GDPR nonetheless clarifies that partial attribution (and therefore exemption from) liability is still possible, albeit only when all relevant controllers and/or processors are joined in the same proceeding, Member State law allows such partial attribution and the data subject receives full and complete compensation.

When more than one controller and/or processor are responsible for the damage caused by their non-compliance with the GDPR in the sense of Articles 82.2 and 82.3 GDPR, they can be held jointly and severally liable for the entirety of the damage. This means that in case of joint controllership a data subject could act against just one of the joint controllers to receive full compensation for the damages suffered due to these controllers' non-compliance with their obligations under the GDPR. The same applies for a controller which is jointly liable for the damages caused by its processor: the data subject could claim all damages from the controller, which must then seek compensation from the processor. The processor, however, can only be held responsible to the extent that it is liable under Article 82.2 GDPR. If such liability is established, then the processor can also be held to pay the entirety of the compensation for damages and shall subsequently have to seek compensation from the controller.

1515. G. Zanfir-Fortuna, 'Article 82. Right to compensation and liability' in C. Kuner, L.A. Bygrave and C. Docksey, *The EU General Data Protection Regulation (GDPR) A commentary*, Oxford, Oxford University Press, 2020, p. 1176.

1516. E. Truli, 'The General Data Protection Regulation and Civil Liability' in M. Bakhoum, B. Conde Gallego, M.-O. Mackenrod and G. Surblytė-Namavičienė, *Personal Data in Competition, Consumer Protection and Intellectual Property Law. Towards a Holistic Approach?*, Berlin, Springer-Verlag GmbH Germany, 2018, p. 321.

C. Reversal of the Burden of Proof

1204. Traditionally under tort law it would be up to the claimant to prove that he suffered damages due to an act or omission on the part of the defendant. It would require the claimant to prove essentially three things:

(1) the existence of damages;
(2) the act or omission on the part of the defendant;
(3) a causal link between said act or omission and the occurrence of the event which led to the damages.

In European data protection law, however, the burden of proof is reversed to an extent. The claimant, i.e., the data subject, still must prove that he has suffered damages and that those damages were caused by an event for which the controller or processor is responsible. However, at that point, the controller or processor is *presumed* to be responsible for the event, unless it can show to be in no way responsible for the event. Hence, non-compliance is presumed unless evidence is provided to the contrary. The reversal of the burden of proof is therefore only partial yet substantial in nature.

1205. Such reversal of the burden of proof existed already under Article 23.2 Directive 95/46/EC, at least where it concerns controllers. Article 82.3 GDPR has now expanded the reversal of the burden of proof to processors as well. According to KAHLER, the reversal of the burden of proof to the detriment of the controller should be understood against the backdrop of the strengthened accountability principle in Articles 5.2 and 24.1 GDPR.[1517] The accountability principle requires the controller to be able to demonstrate that its processing activities comply in their entirety with the GDPR. Hence, by relying on its internal documentation, the controller should be able to provide the evidence required under Article 82.3 GDPR. If the controller does not succeed in providing the evidence, the infringement of the GDPR is presumed. Not all authors agree with this interpretation of Article 82.3 GDPR in light of the accountability principle and argue that the accountability principle only applies vis-à-vis supervisory authorities.[1518]

III. Ensuring Consistent Application by National Courts

1206. As explained earlier in this contribution, the GDPR has introduced elaborate mechanisms which are meant to ensure consistent application and interpretation of the GDPR by supervisory authorities. The European legislator thought it

---

1517. T. KAHLER, 'Accountability – the gravity centre of GDPR' in T. KAHLER, *Turning Point in Data Protection Law*, Baden-Baden, Nomos, 2020, p. 27.

1518. E. TRULI, 'The General Data Protection Regulation and Civil Liability' in M. BAKHOUM, B. CONDE GALLEGO, M.-O. MACKENRODT and G. SURBLYTĖ-NAMAVIČIENĖ, *Personal Data in Competition, Consumer Protection and Intellectual Property Law. Towards a Holistic Approach?*, Berlin, Springer-Verlag GmbH Germany, 2018, pp. 323–324.

necessary to include a far less elaborate mechanism to ensure consistent application and interpretation of the GDPR by national courts as well.

1207. It should be noted that for the national courts a mechanism already existed to ensure consistent interpretation. Article 267 TFEU allows the national Court to request a preliminary ruling from the European Union Court of Justice on the interpretation and validity of EU law, including the GDPR. That does not prevent, however, that a case can be brought before the courts of two distinct Member States against the same controller for the same processing activity. Even with the possibility to ask for a preliminary ruling, each of these national courts may interpret the factual circumstances of the case differently which in turn may lead to very different or even contradictory judgments for essentially the same factual circumstances. Indeed, the CJEU will in principle only look at the correct interpretation of EU law, but it will still be up to the national courts to apply EU law, following the interpretation given by the CJEU, to the specific case at hand.

1208. Article 81 GDPR introduces a system whereby a national Court can watch over the consistent application of the GDPR in a case with the same subject matter against the same controller or processor that is already pending before the Court of another Member State. This system consists of three distinct actions that a national Court can (or must) take:

(1) contacting the other national Court to confirm the existence of proceedings with the same subject matter against the same controller or processor;
(2) suspending its own proceedings if it is not the first Court seized;
(3) upon application of one of the parties, declining jurisdiction as long as the case is at first instance, the other Court has jurisdiction and its national law allows consolidation of the actions brought in both Member States.

The first action is mandatory: the national Court must contact its peer in the other Member State to confirm that there truly is another case with the same subject matter and against the same controller or processor. The other two actions are voluntary, meaning that the national Court is not required to suspend its own proceedings or decline jurisdiction.

The GDPR does not clarify what should happen after a Court has suspended its proceedings. It stands to reason, however, that after the Court first seized has rendered its judgment, the Court that has suspended its proceedings, must resume them. Suspension does indeed not mean that the proceedings have been dropped, they have only temporarily been stayed. The Court that resumes its proceedings is by no means bound by the decision of the Court first seized.

IV. Penalties for Data Protection Law Infringements

A. A Two-Pronged Sanction Mechanism

1209. Effective enforcement of data protection rules requires sufficiently dissuasive penalties.[1519] Article 24 Directive 95/46/EC required Member States only to lay down sanctions to be imposed in case of infringements but did not stipulate explicitly that supervisory authorities should have the power to impose fines. Article 84 GDPR repeats this rather open-ended obligation for Member States to impose sanctions when controllers or processors violate their obligations under data protection law. This open-ended obligation to impose sanctions under national law is complemented, however, with an explicit power for supervisory authorities to impose administrative fines.[1520] The GDPR thus relies on a two-pronged approach for sanctioning infringements of its provisions: administrative fines imposed by the national supervisory authorities and other sanctions imposed by national law which Member States must notify to the European Commission.[1521]

The Member States decide themselves whether national public authorities or bodies acting as controllers or processors can be subjected to this regime of administrative fines as well.[1522] As can be expected, there should be adequate judicial remedy and due process with regard to the power of supervisory authorities to impose administrative fines.[1523]

Not all Member States' legal systems allow supervisory authorities to impose fines. In Denmark and Estonia, for instance, the supervisory authorities are not allowed to impose such fines directly. Hence, Article 83.9 GDPR foresees that in those countries the supervisory authority will 'initiate' the fine, but the fine is ultimately imposed by the competent national courts.

B. Administrative Fines Imposed by Supervisory Authorities

1210. The corrective power of supervisory authorities to impose administrative sanctions must be seen as complementary to the other corrective powers granted under Article 58.2 GDPR.[1524] A controller or processor can thus be faced with a decision requiring it to bring a processing activity in line with the GDPR while simultaneously be required to pay a fine. Article 83.2 lists eleven criteria which supervisory authorities should take into account when determining whether an administrative fine is appropriate and if so, how high that fine should be. When

1519. S.J. Golla, 'Is Data Protection Law Growing Teeth? The Current Lack of Sanctions in Data Protection Law and Administrative Fines under the GDPR', *J. Intell. Prop. Info. Tech. & Elec. Com. L.* 2017, 8, 70.
1520. Art. 58.2.i GDPR.
1521. Art. 84.2 GDPR.
1522. Art. 83.7 GDPR.
1523. Art. 83.8 GDPR.
1524. Art. 83.2 GDPR.

applying these criteria, the supervisory authority must always ensure that the fine is effective, proportionate and dissuasive.[1525] The eleven criteria are:

(1) the nature, gravity and duration of the infringement, which in turn is determined by nature, scope or purpose of the processing activity as well as the number of affected data subjects and the level of damages suffered by them;
(2) whether the infringement was caused by negligence or even intent;
(3) whether the controller or processor did anything to mitigate the damage for data subjects;
(4) the degree of responsibility of the controller or processor;
(5) any prior infringements of the controller or processor;
(6) the degree of cooperation with the supervisory authority
(7) the categories of personal data affected;
(8) how the supervisory authority found out about the infringement (particularly whether the controller or processor was forthcoming);
(9) whether the controller or processor has complied with previously ordered measures when the supervisory authority exercised its corrective powers;
(10) adherence to approved codes of conduct;
(11) any other factor (financial gains, losses avoided, etc.).

The EDPB has already clarified that the aforementioned list of criteria is non-exhaustive.[1526] This interpretation is supported by point (k) of the aforementioned list, which clearly indicates its open-ended nature. Moreover, the EDPB has explained that applying this list does not, in and of itself, ensure that the fine is effective, proportionate and dissuasive. Even when it has applied these criteria, the supervisory authority should still, among others, pay due regard to the turnover of the controller or processor to determine the height of the fine and ensure that it is sufficiently effective, proportionate and dissuasive.[1527] The dissuasive effect of a fine refers both to its capacity to deter the controller or processor from committing the same infringement again as well as to its capacity to deter others from committing that infringement.

When there are multiple infringements, the total amount of the fine shall not exceed the amount specified for the gravest infringement.[1528] The EDPB takes the view that the gravest infringement only determines which fining tier as set forth in Articles 83.4 and 83.5 GDPR is to be applied, but the supervisory authority should still take all infringements into account when determining the height of the fine and not only the most serious one.[1529]

1525. Art. 83.1 GDPR.
1526. European Data Protection Board, Binding decision 1/2021 on the dispute arisen on the draft decision of the Irish Supervisory Authority regarding WhatsApp Ireland under Art. 65(1)(a) GDPR, 28 July 2021, p. 83, https://edpb.europa.eu/system/files/2021-09/edpb_bindingdecision_202101_ie_sa_whatsapp_redacted_en.pdf.
1527. *Ibid.*.
1528. Art. 83.3 GDPR.
1529. European Data Protection Board, Binding decision 1/2021 on the dispute arisen on the draft decision of the Irish Supervisory Authority regarding WhatsApp Ireland under Art. 65(1)(a) GDPR, 28 July 2021, p. 66, https://edpb.europa.eu/system/files/2021-09/edpb_bindingdecision_202101_ie_sa_whatsapp_redacted_en.pdf.

1211. The GDPR maintains a two-tier system for the administrative fines imposed under its Article 83. The lower tier sets fines up to 10 million euros or up to 2% of the total worldwide annual turnover of the controller or processor in the preceding financial year, whichever is the highest. The higher tier sets fines up to 20 million euros or up to 4% of the total worldwide annual turnover of the controller or processor in the preceding financial year, which is the highest. The higher tier applies for infringements of the core provisions of the GDPR:

- the core principles for processing personal data (Article 5);
- the lawfulness of processing (Article 6);
- the conditions for consent (Article 7);
- the processing of special categories of personal data (Article 9);
- the rights of the data subject (Articles 12 to 22);
- the rules on transfers of personal data (Articles 44 to 49);
- any obligations imposed under Member State law pursuant to Chapter IX (Articles 85 to 91);
- non-compliance with an order of a supervisory authority pursuant to Article 58.1 or 58.2 GDPR.

All other violations by a controller or processor fall in the lower tier.

Selected Bibliography

Alessandro, M. 'The EU Proposal for a General Data Protection Regulation and the Roots of the "Right to Be Forgotten"'. *Computer Law & Security Review* vol. 29, no. 3 (2013): 229–235.

Andrew, C. 'Is the Subject Access Right Now Too Great a Threat to Privacy?'. *European Data Protection Law Review* (2016), 15–27.

Arianna, R. & M. Palmirani. 'What's in an Icon? Promises and Pitfalls of Data Protection Iconography'. In *Data Protection and Privacy: Data Protection and Democracy*, edited by R. Leenes, D. Hallinan, S. Gutwirth & P. de Hert, 2020, 59–92.

Asscher, L.F. & Hoogcarspel, S.A., *Regulating Spam: A European Perspective after the Adoption of the E-Privacy Directive*. Information Technology & Law Series. The Hague: TMC Asser Press, 2006.

Ausloos, J., R. Mahieu & M. Veale. 'Getting Data Subject Rights Right: A Submission to the European Data Protection Board from International Data Rights Academics, to Inform Regulatory Guidance'. *Journal of Intellectual Property, Information Technology and E-Commerce Law* vol. 10, no. 3 (2019): 283–309.

Bağlayan, B. & J.H. Fahner. '"One Can Always Do Better": The Referral Procedure before the Grand Chamber of the European Court of Human Rights'. *Human Rights Law Review* vol. 17, no. 2 (2017-06).

Barcelo, R. & P. Traung. 'The Emerging European Union Security Breach Legal Framework: The 2002/58 e-Privacy Directive and Beyond'. In *Data Protection in a Profiled World*, edited by S. Gutwirth, Y. Poullet & P. De Hert. Dordrecht: Springer, 2010.

Bates, E. *The Evolution of the European Convention of Human Rights: From Its Inception to the Creation of a European Court of Human Rights*. Oxford: Oxford University Press, 2010.

Bettinson, V. 'Deportation of Migrant Following Criminal Conviction: European Convention on Human Rights, Article 8'. *Journal of Criminal Law (Hertford)* vol. 74, no. 2 (2010): 113–117

Binns, R. 'Data Protection Impact Assessments: A Meta-Regulatory Approach'. *International Data Privacy Law* vol. 7, no. 1 (2017): 22–35.

Bourka, A. & P. Drogkaris. *Recommendations on Shaping Technology According to GDPR Provisions: Exploring the Notion of Data Protection by Default*. ENISA, 2018.

Selected Bibliography

Brems, E. & J.H. Gerards. *Shaping Rights in the ECHR: the Role of the European Court of Human Rights in Determining the Scope of Human Rights*. Cambridge: Cambridge University Press, 2013.

Brkan, M. 'The Concept of Essence of Fundamental Rights in the EU Legal Order: Peeling the Onion to its Core'. *European Constitutional Law Review* vol. 14, no. 2 (2018): 332–368.

Bygrave, L., 'Information Concepts in Law: Generic Dreams and Definitional Daylight'. *Oxford Journal of Legal Studies* vol. 35, no. 1 (2015): 91–120.

Bygrave, L.A. 'Data Protection by Design and by Default: Deciphering the EU's Legislative Requirements'. *Oslo Law Review*, vol. 1, no. 2 (2017): 105–120.

Bygrave, L.A. 'The Body as Data – Biobank Regulation via the Back Door of Data Protection Law'. *Law, Innovation and Technology* vol. 2 (2010): 1–26.

Casarosa, F. 'Transnational Collective Actions for Cross-Border Data Protection Violations'. *Internet Policy Review* (16 September 2020), 9, 3.

Chen, J. 'The Dangers of Accuracy: Exploring the Other Side of the Data Quality Principle'. *European Data Protection Law Review* vol. 4, no. 1 (2018): 36–52.

Chen, J., et al. 'Who Is Responsible for Data Processing in Smart Homes? Reconsidering Joint Controllership and the Household Exemption'. *International Data Privacy Law*, vol. 10, no. 4 (2020): 279–293.

Cimina, V. 'The Data Protection Concepts of "Controller", "Processor" and "Joint Controllership" under Regulation (EU) 2018/1725.' ERA Forum vol. 21 (2021): 639–654.

Cinar, O.H. 'The Current Case Law of the European Court of Human Rights on Privacy: Challenges in the Digital Age' . *The International Journal of Human Rights* vol. 25, no. 1 (2021): 26–51.

Claessens, J., et al. 'Revocable Anonymous Access to the Internet'. *Journal of Internet Research* vol. 13, no. 4 (2003): 242–258.

Corte, L.D. 'A Right to a Rule: On the Substance and Essence of the Fundamental Right to Personal Data Protection'. In *Data Protection and Privacy: Data Protection and Democracy*, edited by Dara Hallinan, Ronald Leenes, Serge Gutwirth &and Paul De Hert. Oxford: Hart Publishing, 2020.

Daniel, S. & P. Schwartz. *Information Privacy Law*. 3rd edn. Aspen, Wolters Kluwer, 2008, 1128 pp.

de Hert, P. and M. Czerniawski. 'Expanding the European Data Protection Scope Beyond Territory: Art. 3 of the General Data Protection Regulation in Its Wider Context'. IDPL 6 (2016): 230, 237.

de Hert, P., et al. 'The Right to Data Portability in the GDPR: Towards User-Centric Interoperability of Digital Services'. *Computer Law & Security Review* vol. 34, no. 2 (2018): 193–203

De Terwagne, C. 'Council of Europe Convention 108+: A Modernised International Treaty for the Protection of Personal Data'. *The Computer Law and Security Report* vol. 40 (2021).

de Vries, S. 'The EU Single Market as "Normative Corridor" for the Protection of Fundamental Rights: The Example of Data Protection'. In *The EU Charter of Fundamental Rights as a Binding Instrument: Five Years Old and Growing*, edited by S. de Vries, U. Bernitz & S. Weatherill. Studies of the Oxford Institute of European and Comparative Law. Oxford: Hart Publishing, 2015, 235–260.

Debusseré, F. 'The EU E-Privacy Directive: A Monstrous Attempt to Starve the Cookie Monster?'. *International Journal of Law and Information Technology* vol. 13 (2005): 84–85.

Demetzou, K. 'Data Protection Impact Assessment: A Tool for Accountability and the Unclarified Concept of "High Risk" in the General Data Protection Regulation'. *The Computer Law and Security Report* vol. 35, no. 6 (2019): 105342.

Donovan, C. 'Implementation of the e-Privacy Directive in the UK. Understanding the New Rules'. *Computer Law and Security Report* vol. 20, no. 6 (2004): 128.

Drzemczewski, A. *The Right to Respect for Private and Family Life, Home and Correspondence as Guaranteed by Article 8 of the European Convention on Human Rights*. Strasbourg: Council of Europe, 1984.

Dumortier, J. & C. De Preter. 'The European Regulatory Framework for Security and Privacy Protection in Electronic Communications'. *Annales des Télécommunications* vol. 61, no. 3 (2006): 443–457.

Dumortier, J. & C. Geuens.. 'Mandatory Implementation for In-Vehicle eCall: Privacy Compatible?'. *Computer Law and Security Report* vol. 26, no. 4 (2010): 385–390.

Dumortier, J. & C. Goemans. 'Online Data Privacy and Standardization: Towards e More Effective Protection?'. In *A Decade of Research @ the Crossroads of Law and ICT*. Gent: Larcier, 53–70.

Dumortier, J. (ed.) *Recent Developments in Data Privacy Law: Belgium's Data Protection Bill and the European Draft Directive*. (ICRI, 2). Leuven: Leuven University Press, 1992.

Dumortier, J. 'Confidentiality and Privacy: Complementary or Conflicting Values?'. *Revue Européenne de Droit de la Consommation* (3) (2011): 477–494.

Dumortier, J. 'Directive 98/48/EC of the European Parliament and of the Council'. In *Concise European IT Law*, edited by A. Büllesbach, Y. Poullet & C. Prins. Alphen aan den Rijn: Kluwer Law International, 2006, 481–524.

Dumortier, J. 'The Protection of Personal Data in the Schengen Convention'. *International Review of Law, Computers & Technology* vol. 11, no. 1 (1997): 93–106.

Eckhardt, J. 'Zehnter Teil. Telekommunikationsgesetz (TKG)'. *Recht der elektronischen Medien*, in edited by Gerald Spindler & Fabian Schuster. München: Verlag C.H. Beck, 2008.

Efroni, Z.J.M., et al. 'Privacy Icons: A Risk-Based Approach to Visualisation of Data Processing'. *European Data Protection Law Review* vol. 5, no. 3 (2019): 352–366.

Erdos, D. 'From the Scylla of Restriction to the Charybdis of Licence? Exploring the Scope of the "Special Purposes" Freedom of Expression Shield in European Data Protection'. *Common Market Law Review* vol. 52, no. 1 (2015): 119–153.

Esayas, S. 'Breach Notification Requirements under the European Union Legal Framework: Convergence, Conflicts, and Complexity in Compliance'. J. *Marshall J. Info. Tech. & Privacy L.* vol. 31 [i] (2014–2015).

Eva, L. & V. Verdoodt. 'Looking for Needles in a Haystack: Key Issues Affecting Children's Rights in the General Data Protection Regulation'. *Computer Law & Security Review* vol. 34, no. 2 (2018): 269–278.

Gadzheva, M. 'Privacy Concerns Pertaining to Location-Based Services'. *International Journal of Intercultural Information Management* (IJIIM) (2007): 53.

Garrison, C. & C. Hamilton. 'A Comparative Analysis of the EU GDPR to the US's Breach Notifications'. *Information & Communications Technology Law* vol. 28, no. 1 (2019): 99–114.

Gas-Aixendri, M. 'Protection of Personal Data and Apostasy: Comparative Law Considerations'. *A Journal of Church and State* vol. 57, no. 1 (2015): 72–89.

Gellert, R. & S. Gutwirth. 'The Legal Construction of Privacy and Data Protection'. *Computer Law and Security Report* vol. 29 (2013): 522–530.

Georg, R. 'The Effect of Decisions and Judgments of the European Court of Human Rights in the Domestic Legal Order'. *Texas International Law Journal* 40 (2004–2005): 359, at 359–385.

Georgiopoulou, Z., et al. 'GDPR Compliance: Proposed Technical and Organizational Measures for Cloud Provider'. *Information and Computer Security* vol. 28, no. 5 (2020): 665–680.

Gianclaudio, M. & G. Comandé. 'Why a Right to Legibility of Automated Decision-Making Exists in the General Data Protection Regulation'. *International Data Privacy Law* vol. 7, no. 4 (2017): 243–265.

Gloria, G.F. *The Emergence of Personal Data Protection as a Fundamental Right of the EU.* Springer Law, Governance and Technology Series, 2014

Golla, S.J. 'Is Data Protection Law Growing Teeth? The Current Lack of Sanctions in Data Protection Law and Administrative Fines under the GDPR', *Journal of. Intellectual. Property. Information Technology & Electronic Communications Law* (2017): 8.

Greze, B. The extraterritorial enforcement of the GDPR: A genuine issue and the quest for alternatives. *International Data Privacy Law* vol. 9, no. 2 (2019): 109–128.

Hannum, H. 'The Status of the Universal Declaration of Human Rights in National and International Law'. *Georgia Journal of International and Comparative Law* vol. 25 (1995): 287–397.

Hansen, M. 'Data Protection by Design and by Default à La European General Data Protection Regulation'. *IFIP Advances in Information and Communication Technology*, vol. 498. Cham: Springer International Publishing, 2017.

Hildebrandt, M. & L. Tielemans. 'Data Protection by Design and Technology Neutral Law'. *The Computer Law and Security Report* vol. 29, no. 5 (2013): 509–521.

Hladik, J. 'Location Based Services: European Data Protection Rules for Mobile Commerce'. *Privacy and Security Law Report* vol. 8 (2009): 24.

Hudobnik, M.M. 'Data Protection and the Law Enforcement Directive: A Procrustean Bed Across Europe?'. *ERA Forum* vol. 21 (2020): 485–500.

Hughes, K. 'The Child's Right to Privacy and Article 8 European Convention on Human Rights'. In *Law and Childhood Studies: Current Legal Issues*, vol. 14. Oxford: Oxford University Press, 2012.

Irene, K. and P. de Hert. 'Understanding the Balancing Act Behind the Legitimate Interest of the Controller Ground: A Pragmatic Approach'. In *Cambridge Handbook of Consumer Privacy*, edited by E. Selinger, J. Polonetsky & O. Tene. 2018, 321–352.

Isak, M. L.A. Bygrave. 'The Right Not to Be Subject to Automated Decisions Based on Profiling'. In *EU Internet Law*, edited by T.-E. Synodinou, P. Jougleux, C. Markou & T. Prastitou. Springer, 2017, 77–98.

Janis, W. & T. Henderson. 'The Right to Data Portability in Practice: Exploring the Implications of the Technologically Neutral GDPR'. *International Data Privacy Law* vol. 9, no. 3 (2019): 173–191

Janneke, G. 'Margin of Appreciation and Incrementalism in the Case Law of the European Court of Human Rights'. *Human Rights Law Review* vol. 18, no. 3 (September 2018): 495–515.

Jozwiak, M. 'Balancing the Rights to Data Protection and Freedom of Expression and Information by the Court of Justice of the European Union'. *Maastricht Journal of European and Comparative Law* vol. 23, no. 3 (2016): 404–420.

Juliane, K. & C. Sobotta. 'The Distinction Between Privacy and Data Protection in the Jurisprudence of the CJEU and the ECtHR'. *International Data Privacy Law* vol. 3, no. 4 (November 2013).

Kahler, T. 'Accountability – The Gravity Centre of GDPR'. In *Turning Point in Data Protection Law*, edited by T. Kahler. Nomos: Baden-Baden, 2020, 27.

Kajcsa, A. 'Access to Official Document in the Light of the General Data Protection Regulation'. *Perspectives of Law and Public Administration* vol. 7, no. 2 (2018): 193–198.

Kaltsounis, A.T. 'Re-examining the GDPR's Territorial Scope'. *Computer and Internet Lawyer* vol. 37, no. 5 (2020): 10–11.

Ken, G. 'One Hundred Years of Privacy'. *Wisconsin Law Review* vol. 1992, no. 5 (1992): 1335–1442.

Kiestra, L.R. *Introduction to the European Convention on Human Rights. In: The Impact of the European Convention on Human Rights on Private International Law*. The Hague: T.M.C. Asser Press, 2014.

Kindt, E. *Privacy and Data Protection Issues of Biometric Applications: A Comparative Legal Analysis*. 1st ed. Springer Netherlands: Imprint: Springer, 2013.

Knetsch, J. 'The Compensation of Non-pecuniary Loss in GDPR Infringement Cases'. *European Journal of Privacy Law & Technologies* (September 2020): 66.

Kosta, E. & J. Dumortier. 'Searching the Man Behind the Tag: Privacy Implications of RFID Technology'. *International Journal of Intellectual Property Management* vol. 2, no. 3 (2008): 276–288. doi: 10.1504/IJIPM.2008.021141

Kosta, E., et al. 'Privacy Issues in Location Based Services - Legal Considerations on Privacy-Enhancing Location Based Services Using PRIME Technology. *Computer Law and Security Report* vol. 24, no. 2 (2008).

Kosta, E., F. Coudert & J. Dumortier. 'Data Protection in the Third Pillar: In the Aftermath of the ECJ Decision on PNR Data and the Data Retention Directive'. *International Review of Law, Computers & Technology* vol. 21, no. 3 (2007): 343–358

Kranenborg, H. 'Access to Documents and Data Protection in the European Union: On the Public Nature of Personal Data'. *Common Market Law Review* vol. 45, no. 4 (2008): 1079–1114.

Kuner C., L.A. Bygrave & C. Docksey (eds). *The EU General Data Protection Regulation (GDPR): A Commentary*. Oxford: Oxford University Press, 2020.

Kuner, C. 'International Organizations and the EU General Data Protection Regulation'. *Int'l Orgs. L. Rev.* 19 (2019): 158.

Kuner, C. 'The GDPR and International Organizations' . *AJIL Unbound* vol. 114 (2020): 15–19.

Selected Bibliography

Laura, D. 'Comparing LED and GDPR Adequacy: One Standard Two Systems', *Global Privacy Law Review* vol. 1, no. 2 (2020): 93–103.

Lee, B. 'Privacy and Data Protection in an International Perspective'. *Scandinavian Studies in Law* vol. 56: 168.

Leiser, M. & B. Custers. 'The Law Enforcement Directive'. *European Data Protection Law Review* vol. 5, no. 3 (2019): 367–378.

Lenaerts, K. 'The Role of the EU Charter in the Member States'. In *The EU Charter of Fundamental Rights in the Member States*, edited by Michal Bobek & Jeremias Adams-Prassl. Oxford: Hart Publishing, 2020, 19–36.

Lenhard. *Data Security: Technical and Organizational Protection Measures Against Data Loss and Computer Crime*. Springer Fachmedien Wiesbaden GmbH, 2022.

Louis, H. 'Privacy and Autonomy'. *Columbia Law Review* VOL. 74 (1974): 1410, 1425.

Lucio, S. 'Bringing Your Data Everywhere: A Legal Reading of the Right To Portability'. *European Data Protection Law Review* vol. 3, no. 1 (2017): 119–127.

Lundstedt, L. 'International Jurisdiction over Cross-Border Private Enforcement Actions under the GDPR'. Stockholm Faculty of Law Research Paper Series 57, 2017, 218.

Magee, J. 'The Law Regulating Unsolicited Commercial E-mail: An International Perspective. *Santa Clara Computer & High Technology Law Journal* vol. 19 (2003): 372.

Mark, C. 'Privacy and Electronic Communications'. *Computer Law & Security Review* vol. 19, no. 4 (July 2003): 299–303.

Marquenie, T. 'The Police and Criminal Justice Authorities Directive: Data Protection Standards and Impact on the Legal Framework'. *Computer Law & Security Review* vol. 33, no. 3 (2017): 324–340.

Marshall, J. 'S.A.S. v France: Burqa Bans and the Control or Empowerment of Identities'. *Human Rights Law Review* vol. 15, no. 2 (2015): 377–389.

Martyn, B. *The Council of Europe and Human Rights: An Introduction to the European Convention of Human Rights*. Strasbourg: Council of Europe Publishing, 2010, 86 p.

Merlin, G. 'The New Territorial Scope of EU Data Protection Law: Deconstructing a Revolutionary Achievement'. *Common Market Law Review* vol. 54 (2017): 567, 575.

Miadzvetskaya, Y. & G. Van Calster. 'Google at the Kirchberg Dock. On Delisting Requests, and on the Territorial Reach of the EU's GDPR'. *European Data Protection Law Review (Internet)* vol. 6, no. 1 (2020), pp. 143–151

Milenković, J. 'The Right to Privacy under Article 8 of the European Convention of Human Rights and Legality of Epidemiological Monitoring Measures to Combat the Covid-19 Virus Pandemic'. *Zbornik Radova Pravnog Fakulteta u Nišu* vol. 59, no. 89 (2020): 303–320.

Mondschein, C. 'Some Iconoclastic Thoughts on the Effectiveness of Simplified Notices and Icons for Informing Individuals as Proposed in Article 12 (1) and (7) GDPR'. *European Data Protection Law Review* vol. 2, no. 4 (2016): 507–520.

Mowbray, A.R. *The Development of Positive Obligations under the European Convention on Human Rights by the European Court of Human Rights*. Hart Publishing, 2004.

Nemitz, P. 'Fines under the GDPR'. In *Data Protection and Privacy: The Internet of Bodies*, edited by R. Leenes et al. Oxford: Hart Publishing, 2019, 231–248.

Nieuwesteeg, B. & M. Faure. 'An Analysis of the Effectiveness of the EU Data Breach Notification Obligation'. *The Computer Law and Security Report* vol. 34, no. 6 (2018): 1232–1246.

Ohlenburg, A. 'Der neue Telekommunikationsdatenschutz – Eine Darstellung von Teil 7 Abschnitt 2 TKG'. *Multimedia und Recht* (MMR) (2004), p. 436.

Oliver, D. & M.N. Cleis. 'How the Right to Privacy Became a Human Right'. *Human Rights Law Re*view vol. 14 (2014): 441–458.

Olsen, T. & T. Mahler. 'Identity Management and Data Protection Law: Risk, Responsibility and Compliance in "Circles of Trust" – Part II'. *Computer, Law & Security Review* (2007): 419.

Oskar, G. 'The Cascade of Decaying Information: Putting the "Right to Be Forgotten" in Perspective'. *Computer and Telecommunications Law Review* vol. 21, no. 2 (2015): 40–48.

Pablo, S. 'The Right to a Private and Family Life (Notably Extended Right to Privacy) (Art. 8 ECHR)'. In *Europe of Rights: A Compendium on the European Convention of Human Rights*, edited by J.G. Roca & P. Santolaya. Leiden, The Netherlands: Brill | Nijhoff, 2012, 337–351.

Papapavlou, G. 'Latest Developments Concerning the EC Draft Data Protection Directive'. In *Recent Developments in Data Privacy Law*, edited by J. Dumortier. Leuven University Press, 1992, 29–42.

Paul, S. & D. Solove. 'Reconciling Personal Information in the United States and European Union'. *California Law Review* 102 (2014): 877.

Peter, B. 'Data Protection and Privacy'. *Scandinavian Studies in Law* vol. 56 (2010): 154, https://www.scandinavianlaw.se/pdf/56-7.pdf.

Porcedda, M.G. '"Privacy by Design" in EU Law'. *Lecture Notes in Computer Science (Including Subseries Lecture Notes in Artificial Intelligence and Lecture Notes in Bioinformatics)*, vol. 11079. Cham: Springer International Publishing, 2018, 183–204.

Purtova, N. 'The Law of Everything: Broad Concept of Personal Data and Future of EU Data Protection Law'. *Law, Innovation and Technology* vol. 10, no. 1 (2018): 40–81.

Reventlow, N.J. 'Can the GDPR and Freedom of Expression Coexist?', AJIL 114 (6 January 2020): 32.

Robbers, G. 'Church Autonomy in the European Court of Human Rights—Recent Developments in Germany'. *The Journal of Law and Religion* vol. 26, no. 1 (2010): 281–320.

Robert, R. 'Titre 12 Le Comité européen de la protection des données: le garant d'un nouvel ordre?'. In *Le Réglement Général sur la Protection des Données*, edited by C. de Terwangne & K. Rosier. Brussels: Larcier, 2018, 628.

Roberts, A. 'Covert Video Identification: European Convention on Human Rights, Article 8'. *Journal of Criminal Law (Hertford)* vol. 67, no. 6 (2003): 480–485.

Rogers, A. 'Breach of Security vs Personal Data Breach: Effect on EU Data Subject Notification Requirements'. *International Data Privacy Law* vol. 11, no. 2 (2021): 163–181.

Roscoe, P. 'Interests in Personality'. *Harvard Law Review* vol. 28 (1915): 343.

Rubinstein, I.S. & N. Good. 'The Trouble with Article 25 (and How to Fix It): The Future of Data Protection by Design and Default'. *International Data Privacy Law* vol. 10, no. 1 (2020): 37–56.

Ryngaert, C. & M. Taylor. 'The GDPR as Global Data Protection Regulation?'. *AJIL Unbound* vol. 114 (2020): 5–9.

Sandra, W., B. Mittelstadt & L. Floridi, 'Why a Right to Explanation of Automated Decision-Making Does Not Exist in the General Data Protection Regulation'. *International Data Privacy Law* vol. 7, no. 2 (2017): 76–99.

Selbst, Andrew D. & J. Powles. 'Meaningful Information and the Right to Explanation'. *International Data Privacy Law* vol. 7, no. 4 (2017): 233–242.

Sorace, F. 'Collective Redress in the General Data Protection Regulation. An Opportunity to Improve Access to Justice in the European Union?'. *Working Papers Jean Monnet Chair* 7/2018, 15.

Strugała, R. 'Art. 82: Strict Liability or Liability Based on Fault?'. *European Journal of Privacy Law & Technologies* Special Issue (2020): 74–76.

Sylvia, K., et al. '30 Years On. The Review of the Council of Europe Convention 108'. *The Computer Law and Security Report*, vol. 27, no. 3 (2011): 223–231.

Temme Merle, 'Algorithms and Transparency in View of the New General Data Protection Regulation, *European Data Protection Law Review* 2017, 473–485

Truli, E. 'The General Data Protection Regulation and Civil Liability'. In *Personal Data in Competition, Consumer Protection and Intellectual Property Law. Towards a Holistic Approach?*, edited by M. Bakhoum, B. Conde Gallego, M. O. Mackenrodt & G. Surblytė-Namavičienė. Berlin: Springer-Verlag GmbH Germany, 2018, 323.

Urgessa, W.G. 'The Feasibility of Applying EU Data Protection Law to Biological Materials: Challenging "Data" as Exclusively Informational'. *JIPITEC* vol. 7 (2016): 96.

Van Alsenoy, B. 'Allocating Responsibility among Controllers, Processors, and "Everything in Between": The Definition of Actors and Roles in Directive 95/46/EC'. *The Computer Law and Security Report* vol. 28, no. 1 (2012): 25–43.

Van Alsenoy, B. 'Reconciling the (Extra)Territorial Reach of the GDPR with Public International Law'. *Data Protection and Privacy Under Pressure. Transatlantic Tensions, EU Surveillance and Big Data*, Maklu, 2017, 77–100.

Van Alsenoy, B. *Data Protection Law in the EU: Roles, Responsibilities, Liability.* Mortsel: Intersentia, 2019, 679 p.

Van Alsenoy, B., E. Kosta & J. Dumortier. 'Privacy Notices Versus Informational Self-Determination: Minding the Gap'. *International Review of Law, Computers & Technology*, 2013). Art.No. 10.1080/13600869.2013.812594. doi: 10.1080/13600869.2013.812594.

Van Alsenoy, B., et al. 'Social Networks and Web 2.0: Are Users Also Bound by Data Protection Regulations?'. *Identity in the Information Society* vol. 2, no. 1 (2009): 65–79.

Van Alsenoy, B., et al. Social Networks and Web 2.0: Are Users Also Bound by Data Protection Regulations?'. *Identity in the Information Society* vol. 2, no. 1 (2009), https://link.springer.com/article/10.1007/s12394-009-0017-3.

van Drunen, M. N. Helberger & M. Bastian. 'Know Your Algorithm: What Media Organisations Need to Explain to Their Users about News Personalisation'. *International Data Privacy Law* vol. 9, no. 4 (2019): 220–235.

Vandezande, N. & J. Dumortier. 'Law Enforcement Use of Drones to Enforce COVID-19 Measures'. *European Data Protection Law Review* vol. 7, no. 3 (2021): 400–412.

Veale, M., et al. 'When Data Protection by Design and Data Subject Rights Clash'. *International Data Privacy Law*, vol. 8, no. 2 (2018): 105–123.

Vogiatzoglou, P., et al. 'From Theory to Practice: Exercising the Right of Access under the Law Enforcement and PNR Directives' *Journal of Intellectual Property, Information Technology and E-Commerce Law* vol. 11, no. 3 (2020): 274–302.

Voigt, P. & A. Von dem Bussche. 'Scope of Application of the GDPR.' *The EU General Data Protection Regulation (GDPR)*. Cham: Springer International Publishing, 2017, 9–30.

Volker, B.-N. Privacy: A Matter of Democracy: Why Democracy Needs Privacy and Data Protection. *International Data Privacy Law* vol. 6, no. 3 (2016): 222–229.

Waldman, A.E. 'Data Protection by Design?: A Critique of Article 25 of the GDPR.' *Cornell International Law Journal* vol. 53, no. 1 (2020): 147–167.

Warren Samuel D. & Louis D. Brandeis, The Right to Privacy, 4 *Harvard Law Review* 193 (1890

Witzleb, Normann. *Emerging Challenges in Privacy Law: Comparative Perspectives.* Cambridge University Press, 2014

Yakovleva, S. 'Personal Data Transfers in International Trade and EU Law: A Tale of Two "Necessities"'. *The Journal of World Investment & Trade* vol. 21, no. 6 (2020): 881–919.

Yvonne, K. 'Protocol No. 11 to the European Convention for Human Rights: A Drastic Revision of the Supervisory Mechanism under the ECHR'. *Netherlands Quarterly of Human Rights* vol. 14, no. 1 (1996)

Zuiderveen Borgesius, F.J. & D. Hallinan. 'Opinions Can Be Incorrect (in Our Opinion)! On Data Protection Law's Accuracy Principle'. *International Data Privacy Law* vol. 10, no. 1 (2020): 1–10.

Zuiderveen Borgesius, F.J. 'Breyer Case of the Court of Justice of the European Union: IP Addresses and the Personal Data Definition'. *European Data Protection Law Review* vol. 3, no. 1 (2017): 130Ib.

Selected Bibliography

Table of CJEU Case Law (by Date of Judgement)

CJEU, Joined cases C-465/00, C-138/01 and C-139/01, Judgment of 20 May 2003, Österreichischer Rundfunk, ECLI:EU:C:2003:294, https://eur-lex.europa.eu/legal-content/en/TXT/?uri=CELEX:62000CJ0465.

CJEU, Case C-101/01, Judgment of 6 November 2003, Bodil Lindqvist, ECLI:EU:C:2003:596, https://eur-lex.europa.eu/legal-content/EN/TXT/?uri=CELEX%3A62001CJ0101.

CJEU, Case C-73/07, Judgment of 16 Dec 2008, Satakunnan Markkinapörssi and Satamedia, ECLI:EU:C:2008:727, https://eur-lex.europa.eu/legal-content/en/TXT/?uri=CELEX:62007CJ0073.

CJEU, Case C-553/07, Judgment of 7 May 2009, Rijkeboer, ECLI:EU:C:2009:293, https://curia.europa.eu/juris/liste.jsf?num=C-553/07&language=en.

CJEU Case C-518/07, Judgment of 9 March 2010, Commission v. Germany, ECLI:EU:C:2010:125, https://eur-lex.europa.eu/legal-content/EN/TXT/?uri=CELEX%3A62007CJ0518.

CJEU, Joined Cases C-236/08 to C-238/08, Judgment of 23 March 2010, Google France and Google, ECLI:EU:C:2010:159, https://curia.europa.eu/juris/liste.jsf?num=C-236/08.

CJEU, Case C-614/10, Judgment of 16 October 2012, Commission v. Austria, ECLI:EU:C:2012:63, https://eur-lex.europa.eu/legal-content/en/TXT/?uri=CELEX:62010CJ0614.

CJEU, Case C-119/12, Judgment of 22 November 2012, Josef Probst, ECLI:EU:C:2012:748, https://eur-lex.europa.eu/legal-content/en/TXT/?uri=CELEX:62012CJ0119.

CJEU, Case C-342/12, Judgment of 30 May 2013, Worten, ECLI:EU:C:2013:355, https://eur-lex.europa.eu/legal-content/en/TXT/?uri=CELEX:62012CJ0342.

CJEU, Case C-288/12, Judgment of, 8 April 2014, Commission v. Hungary, ECLI:EU:C:2014:237, https://eur-lex.europa.eu/legal-content/EN/TXT/?uri=CELEX%3A62012CJ0288.

CJEU, Case C-293/12, Judgment of 8 April 2014, Digital Rights Ireland, ECLI:EU:C:2014:238, https://eur-lex.europa.eu/legal-content/EN/TXT/?uri=CELEX%3A62012CJ0293.

CJEU, Case C-131/12, Judgment of 13 May 2014, Google Spain SL v Agencia Espanola de Proteccion de Datos (AEPD)), ECLI:EU:C:2014:317, https://eur-lex.europa.eu/legal-content/EN/TXT/?uri=CELEX%3A62012CJ0131.

Table of CJEU Case Law (by Date of Judgement)

CJEU, Case C-141/12, Judgment of 17 Jul 2014, YS and Others, ECLI:EU:C:2014:2081, https://eur-lex.europa.eu/legal-content/en/TXT/?uri=CELEX:62012CJ0141.

CJEU, Case C-212/13, Judgment of 11 December 2014, Ryneš, ECLI:EU:C:2014:2428, https://eur-lex.europa.eu/legal-content/EN/TXT/?uri=CELEX%3A62013CJ0212.

CJEU, Joined Cases C-446/12 to C-449/12, Judgment of 16 April 2015, Willems and Others, ECLI:EU:C:2015:238, https://eur-lex.europa.eu/legal-content/EN/TXT/?uri=CELEX%3A62012CJ0446.

CJEU, Case C-230/14, Judgment of 1 October 2015, Weltimmo, ECLI:EU:C:2015:639, https://eur-lex.europa.eu/legal-content/EN/TXT/?uri=CELEX%3A62014CJ0230.

CJEU, Case C-201/14, Judgment of 1 October 2015, Smaranda Bara & Others, ECLI:EU:C:2015:638, https://eur-lex.europa.eu/legal-content/EN/TXT/?uri=CELEX%3A62014CJ0201.

CJEU, Case C-362/14, Judgement of 6 October 2015, Maximillian Schrems v Data Protection Commissioner (Schrems 1), ECLI:EU:C:2015:650, https://eur-lex.europa.eu/legal-content/EN/TXT/?uri=CELEX%3A62014CJ0362.

CJEU, Case C-191/15, Judgment of 28 July 2016, Verein für Konsumenteninformation, ECLI:EU:C:2016:612, https://eur-lex.europa.eu/legal-content/EN/TXT/?uri=CELEX%3A62015CJ0191.

CJEU, Case C-582/14, Judgment of 19 Oct 2016, Breyer, ECLI:EU:C:2016:779, https://eur-lex.europa.eu/legal-content/en/TXT/?uri=CELEX:62014CJ0582.

CJEU, Joined Cases C203/15 and C698/15, Judgment of 21 December 2016, Tele2 Sverige AB, ECLI:EU:C:2016:970, https://eur-lex.europa.eu/legal-content/en/ALL/?uri=CELEX:62015CJ0203.

CJEU, Case C-536/15, Judgment of 15 March 2017, Tele2 (Netherlands), ECLI:EU:C:2017:214, https://eur-lex.europa.eu/legal-content/en/TXT/?uri=CELEX:62015CJ0536.

CJEU, Case C-398/15, Judgment of 9 March 2017, Manni, ECLI:EU:C:2017:197, https://curia.europa.eu/juris/liste.jsf?language=en&num=C-398/15.

CJEU, Case C-13/16, Judgment of 4 May 2017, Rīgas satiksme, ECLI:EU:C:2017:336, https://curia.europa.eu/juris/liste.jsf?num=C-13/16.

CJEU, Case C-73/16, Judgment of 27 September 2017, Peter Puškár, ECLI-:EU:C:2017:
725, https://eur-lex.europa.eu/legal-content/en/TXT/?uri=CELEX:62016CJ0073.

CJEU, Case C-434/16, Judgement of 20 December 2017, Peter Nowak v Data Protection Commissioner, ECLI:EU:C:2017:994, https://eur-lex.europa.eu/legal-content/en/TXT/?uri=CELEX:62016CJ0434.

CJEU, Case C-210/16, Judgment of 5 June 2018, Wirtschaftsakademie Schleswig-Holstein, ECLI:EU:C:2018:388, https://eur-lex.europa.eu/legal-content/EN/TXT/?uri=CELEX%3A62016CJ0210.

CJEU, Case C-25/17, Judgment of 10 July 2018, Jehovan todistajat, ECLI:EU:C:2018:551, https://eur-lex.europa.eu/legal-content/en/TXT/?uri=CELEX:62017CJ0025.

CJEU, Case C-207/16, Judgment of 2 Oct 2018, Ministerio Fiscal, ECLI:EU:C:2018:788, https://eur-lex.europa.eu/legal-content/EN/TXT/?uri=CELEX%3A62016CJ0207.

CJEU, Case C-345/17, Judgment of 14 February 2019, Buivids, ECLI:EU:C:2019:122, https://eur-lex.europa.eu/legal-content/EN/TXT/?uri=CELEX%3A62017CJ0345.

CJEU, Case C-40/17, Judgment of 29 Jul 2019, Fashion ID, ECLI:EU:C:2019:629, https://eur-lex.europa.eu/legal-content/en/TXT/?uri=CELEX:62017CJ0040.

CJEU, Case C-136/17, Judgment of 24 September 2019, GC and Others v. CNIL, ECLI:EU:C:2019:773, https://eur-lex.europa.eu/legal-content/EN/TXT/?uri=CELEX%3A62017CJ0136.

CJEU, Case C-507/17, Judgment of 24 September 2019, Google v. CNIL, ECLI-:EU:C:2019:772, https://eur-lex.europa.eu/legal-content/en/TXT/?uri=CELEX:62017CJ0507.

CJEU, Case C-673/17, Judgment of 1 October 2019, Planet49 GmbH, ECLI:EU:C:2019:801, https://eur-lex.europa.eu/legal-content/EN/TXT/?uri=CELEX%3A62017CJ0673.

CJEU, Case C-708/18, Judgment of 11 December 2019, Asociatia de Proprietari bloc M5A-ScaraA, ECLI:EU:C:2019:1064, https://eur-lex.europa.eu/legal-content/GA/TXT/?uri=CELEX:62018CJ0708.

CJEU, Case C-272/19, Judgment of 9 July 2020, Land Hessen, ECLI:EU:C:2020:535, https://eur-lex.europa.eu/legal-content/EN/TXT/?uri=CELEX%3A62019CJ0272.

CJEU, Case C-311/18, Judgement of 16 July 2020, Data Protection Commissioner v Facebook Ireland and Maximillian Schrems (Schrems 2), ECLI:EU:C:2020:559, https://eur-lex.europa.eu/legal-content/EN/TXT/?uri=CELEX%3A62018CJ0311.

CJEU, Joined Cases C-511/18, C-512/18 and C-520/18, Judgment of 6 October 2020, La Quadrature du Net and Others, ECLI:EU:C:2020:791, https://eur-lex.europa.eu/legal-content/en/TXT/?uri=CELEX:62018CJ0511.

CJEU, Case C-623/17, Judgment of 6 October 2020, Privacy International, ECLI:EU:C:2020:790, https://eur-lex.europa.eu/legal-content/en/TXT/?uri=CELEX:62017CJ0623.

CJEU, Case C-61/19, Judgment of 11 November 2020, Orange Romania, ECLI:EU:C:2020:901, https://eur-lex.europa.eu/legal-content/en/TXT/?uri=CELEX:62019CJ0061.

CJEU, Case C-746/18, Judgment of 2 March 2021, Prokuratuur, ECLI:EU:C:2021:152, https://eur-lex.europa.eu/legal-content/en/TXT/?uri=CELEX:62018CJ0746.

CJEU, Case C-645/19, Judgment of 15 June 2021, Facebook v. Belgian Data Protection Authority, ECLI:EU:C:2021:483, https://eur-lex.europa.eu/legal-content/EN/TXT/?uri=CELEX%3A62019CJ0645.

CJEU, Case-C-439/19, Judgment of 22 June 2021, Latvijas Republikas Saeima, ECLI:EU:C:2021:504, https://eur-lex.europa.eu/legal-content/en/TXT/?uri=CELEX:62019CJ0439.

Table of CJEU Case Law (by Date of Judgement)

CJEU, Case C-102/20, Judgment of 25 November 2021, StWL Städtische Werke Lauf, ECLI:EU:C:2021:954, https://eur-lex.europa.eu/legal-content/EN/TXT/?uri=CELEX%3A62020CJ0102.

CJEU, Case C-175/20, Judgment of 24 February 2022, „SS' SIA v. Valsts ieņēmumu dienests, ECLI:EU:C:2022:124, https://eur-lex.europa.eu/legal-content/EN/TXT/?uri=CELEX:62020CJ0175.

CJEU, Case C-245/20, Judgement of 24 March 2022, X and Z v Autoriteit Persoonsgegevens, ECLI:EU:C:2022:216, https://eur-lex.europa.eu/legal-content/en/TXT/?uri=CELEX:62020CJ0245.

CJEU, Case C140/20, Judgment of 5 April 2022, Commissioner of the Garda Síochána and Others, ECLI:EU:C:2022:258, https://eur-lex.europa.eu/legal-content/EN/TXT/?uri=CELEX%3A62020CJ0140.

www.ingramcontent.com/pod-product-compliance
Ingram Content Group UK Ltd.
Pitfield, Milton Keynes, MK11 3LW, UK
UKHW020131290926
15471UKWH00003B/406

9 789403 507064